MELANCHOLIA AND DEPRESSION

Melancholia and Depression

*From Hippocratic Times
to
Modern Times*

STANLEY W. JACKSON

Yale University Press
New Haven and London

Designed by James J. Johnson
and set in Janson Roman type.
Printed in the United States of America by
Edwards Brothers, Ann Arbor, Michigan.

Library of Congress Cataloging-in-Publication Data

Jackson, Stanley W., 1920–
    Melancholia and depression.

    Bibliography: p.
    Includes index.
    1. Depression, Mental—History.   I. Title.
[DNLM: 1. Depressive Disorder.   2. Depressive
Disorder—history.   WM 171 J14m]
RC537.J28 1986   616.85′27′009   86-5541
ISBN 0-300-03700-7

The paper in this book meets the guidelines for permanence
and durability of the Committee on Production Guidelines
for Book Longevity of the Council on Library Resources.

10   9   8   7   6   5   4   3   2   1

To Joan
My love, my friend, my colleague

The author gratefully acknowledges permission to reprint from the following sources:

Michael MacDonald, *Mystical Bedlam: Madness, Anxiety, and Healing in Seventeenth-Century England* (Cambridge: Cambridge University Press, 1981). Copyright © 1981 by Cambridge University Press. Reprinted by permission.
Oskar Diethelm and Thomas F. Heffernan, "Felix Platter and Psychiatry," *Journal of the History of the Behavioral Sciences*, 1965, *1*, 10–23. Copyright © 1965 by Psychology Press, Inc.

And the author gratefully acknowledges the following for permission to reprint previously published material:

Bulletin of the History of Medicine, for "Acedia the Sin and Its Relationship to Sorrow and Melancholia in Medieval Times," 1981, *55*, 172–185. Copyright © 1981 by The Johns Hopkins University Press.
Journal of the History of Medicine and Allied Sciences, for "Unusual Mental States in Medieval Europe. I. Medical Syndromes of Mental Disorder: 400–1100 A.D.," 1972, *27*, 262–297; "Melancholia and the Waning of the Humoral Theory," 1978, *33*, 367–376; "Melancholia and Mechanical Explanation in Eighteenth-Century Medicine," 1983, *38*, 298–319. All copyright © by the Journal of the History of Medicine and Allied Sciences, Inc.
Psychiatric Forum, for "Two Sufferers' Perspectives on Melancholia: 1690s to 1790s," Tenth Anniversary Supplementary Volume, *Essays in the History of Psychiatry*, ed. Edwin R. Wallace, IV, and Lucius C. Pressley, 1980. Copyright © by Wm. S. Hall Psychiatric Institute.

Contents

Preface

This is the history of a clinical syndrome, or perhaps I should say a group of closely related clinical syndromes. The tracking of any such condition over time is bound to be a difficult undertaking, although a fascinating one. One cannot be guided merely by the name, though that provides some guidance and is often of considerable interest. It is the clinical description that is essential—the symptoms and the signs, the observations that could be attested to by the sufferer or noted by another person. Accounts of this clinical description have been traced in approximately two and a half millennia of medical writings, and these accounts have been intermittently supplemented from other sources over this lengthy stretch of time. While there have certainly been variations in the content of this clinical disorder, there have been both a remarkable consistency and a remarkable coherence in the basic cluster of symptoms. This consistency has been at least the equal of that with any other mental disorder over these many centuries. And melancholia as one of the three cardinal forms of madness in earlier times is clearly a close kin to the depressions grouped as affective disorders today, one of the modern cardinal forms of mental disorder.

At the same time, this historical undertaking has allowed, perhaps necessitated, a survey of the theories that have come and gone in Western man's efforts to understand and explain the etiology and pathogenesis of melancholia and depression. As these theories have commonly been the same ones that have been used to explain other mental disorders, and often other diseases in general medicine, one gains a sense of explanatory practices in medicine at large over these same centuries.

Further still, this study has involved a survey of the therapeutics of melancholia and depression over the same two and a half thousand years. And this has provided a perspective on the history of treatment practices beyond the limits of these particular conditions.

A professional lifetime of interest in and efforts to ameliorate the distress of various sufferers, many of them depressed, gradually became joined with an associated professional lifetime of attention to the history of medicine in general and the history of psychiatry in particular. The degree of consistency and coherence in the clusters of symptoms and signs referred to as melancholia and depression attracted my attention early on. As long as fifteen years ago, I began drafting outlines of this present work. Ten years ago, I began the first of several articles that focused on selected problems within the larger enterprise. A sabbatical leave in 1982 provided the opportunity to write about half the book, and I then remained in its grip until completing it in the early autumn of 1985.

I could hardly have written a work such as this without incurring many a significant debt along the tortuous paths that eventually led to its completion. The many notes and references throughout this book reflect an almost limitless array of such debts. Beyond these, though, I would like to take special note of a few more personal debts. Dr. Lloyd G. Stevenson provided an opportunity, taught and counseled, and helped as both formal and informal editor on earlier projects; and so, these years later, I am able to write this book. To this man to whom so many owe so much from their experiences as students and as authors, I say thank you. To a series of leaders in the Department of Psychiatry at Yale University's School of Medicine—Dr. Fredrick C. Redlich, Dr. Theodore Lidz, Dr. Stephen Fleck, Dr. Morton F. Reiser, and Dr. Boris M. Astrachan—I wish to express my appreciation for their support of and benevolence toward this psychiatrist and psychoanalyst who also worked as a historian. To a valued colleague of many years, Professor Frederic L. Holmes, chairman, Section of the History of Medicine, at Yale University's School of Medicine, I wish to express my thanks for his support of and benevolence toward this historian who also worked as a psychiatrist and psychoanalyst. For unstinting and helpful assistance, I thank Ferenc A. Gyorgyey, Historical Librarian, and his colleagues, Thomas G. Falco and Susan Alon, of the Historical Library of the Yale Medical Library. For her patience, guidance, and many helpful contributions, I thank my editor at the Yale University Press, Gladys Topkis. For his rigorous and constructive contributions, I thank Alexander Metro of Yale University Press, who copyedited the manuscript. To Joan K. Jackson, there is no way of properly conveying my appreciation in words. She has been a helpful and supportive spouse, indeed. She has typed the manuscript of this work; she has been an informal editor and critic to my considerable benefit; and she has helped this book along in other invaluable ways beyond number.

I

Introduction

CHAPTER ONE

Introduction

In the terms *melancholia* and *depression* and their cognates, we have well over two millennia of the Western world's ways of referring to a goodly number of different dejected states. At any particular time during these many centuries the term that was in common use might have denoted a disease, a troublesome condition of sufficient severity and duration to be conceived of as a clinical entity; or it might have referred to one of a cluster of symptoms that were thought to constitute a disease; or it might have been used to indicate a mood or an emotional state of some duration, perhaps troublesome, certainly unusual, and yet not pathological, not a disease; or it might have referred to a tempera- ment or type of character involving a certain emotional tone and disposition and yet not pathological; or it might have meant merely a feeling state of relatively short duration, unhappy in tone but hardly a disease. Clearly the various conditions so denoted were unusual mental states, but they ranged over a far wider spectrum than that covered by the term *disease*.

As a mood, affect, or emotion, the experience of being melancholy or depressed has probably been as well known to our species as any of the many other human feeling states. The wide range of terms, and the emotional variations to which they refer, have reflected matters at the very heart of being human: feeling down or blue or unhappy, being dispirited, discouraged, disappointed, dejected, despondent, melancholy, sad, depressed, or despair- ing—states that surely touch something in the experience of just about every- one. From discouragement or dejection over material and interpersonal disap- pointments to sadness or despondency over separation and loss, to be human is to know about such emotions. We recognize many aspects of such affective experiences as being within the normal range, however unusual or unhappy.

3

To be melancholic or depressed is not necessarily to be mentally ill or in a pathological state. It is only with greater degrees of severity or longer durations that such affective states come to be viewed as pathological, and even then the affective state is usually accompanied by other symptoms before being so judged.

These latter conditions—the pathological states—constitute the focus of this study. Its essential roots are grounded in the history of medicine. I have approached it as a history of clinical conditions over the centuries. But the charting of some sort of reasonable boundaries for melancholia and depression as clinical entities has necessitated giving some attention to sadness, sorrow, acedia, despair, and other troubled, dejected states.

On choosing to focus on melancholia and depression as clinical conditions, I was immediately faced with the issue of whether they are diseases or some other sort of assemblage of signs and symptoms. Thus it became necessary to address the evolving history of the concept of disease, to consider the question of disease versus clinical syndrome, and to weigh the issues involved in disease versus illness. And, whether disease or syndrome, it was crucial to trace the changes in clinical content. Then, what relationship did these conditions have to symptoms, temperaments, sustained feeling states, and passing frames of mind by the same names? Here the history of the passions and the emotions became relevant.

The next set of issues consisted of the evolving conceptual schemes used to explain melancholia and depression. The history of physiology and the history of explanations of disease were important here. And some attention to belief-action systems other than medicine was relevant—for example, the Christian system of thought in explaining and dealing with those dejected states conceived of as acedia. Taking the medical-historical perspective to its logical next step, I have surveyed the measures taken to help or otherwise deal with the sufferers from these disorders. This is the study of therapeutics, and yet it is more than the study of therapeutics.

TERMINOLOGICAL ISSUES

Melancholia was the Latin transliteration of the Greek μελαγχολία, which in ancient Greece usually meant a mental disorder involving prolonged fear and depression. It sometimes merely meant "biliousness" and, along with its cognates, was sometimes used in popular speech "to denote crazy or nervous conduct."[1] This term, in turn, was derived from μέλαινα χολη (*melaina chole*), translated into Latin as *atra bilis* and into English as *black bile*. As one of the four humors in the humoral theory, the black bile was thought to be the crucial etiological factor in melancholia. Various other disorders were thought to be caused by the black bile, and these came to be referred to as melancholic diseases. The black bile was known as the melancholic humor. The temperament or character type thought to be due to the black bile, and given special status in the Aristotelian writings, was named the melancholic temperament.

The various forms of melancholia and its cognates, taken with relatively little change from the Latin, began to appear in English writings in the fourteenth century. Terms such as *malencolye, melancoli, malencolie, melancholie, melancholy*, and others with only slight variations in spelling emerged as synonyms for *melancholia*, the basic term in medical thought. *Melancholie* in the sixteenth century and *melancholy* by the beginning of the seventeenth century became common in English as equivalent terms to *melancholia* for naming the disease, as did nearly identical terms in other vernacular languages; and these terms were also frequently used to mean the black bile itself. With the Renaissance rehabilitation of Aristotelian melancholia as a character correlate of genius or being gifted rather than strictly as an illness, *melancholia, melancholie*, and *melancholy* came to be popular terms as well. In addition to denoting the illness, they were often used for almost any state of sorrow, dejection, or despair, not to mention respected somberness and fashionable sadness. During the seventeenth and eighteenth centuries *melancholia* seems gradually to have become restricted once again to the disease, while *melancholy* remained both a synonym for melancholia and a popular term used with a breadth and diffuseness not unlike our use of the term *depression* today. And remarkably similar trends occurred in many of the other vernacular languages of Western Europe.

Depression is a relative latecomer to the terminology for dejected states. Devised originally from the Latin *de* (down from) and *premere* (to press), and *deprimere* (to press down), and carrying the meanings from these Latin terms of pressing down, being pressed down, and being brought down in status or fortune, this term and its cognates came into use in English during the seventeenth century. And in that same century there were occasional instances of the term's being used to mean "depression of spirits" or "dejection." But it was during the eighteenth century that *depression* really began to find a place in discussions of melancholia, with Samuel Johnson having a prominent role in this emerging trend (see chap. 7). In contexts more closely associated with medicine, Richard Blackmore in 1725 mentioned the possibility of "being depressed into deep Sadness and Melancholy, or elevated into Lunacy and Distraction."[2] Robert Whytt in 1764 associated "depression of mind" with low spirits, hypochondriasis, and melancholy.[3] David Daniel Davis in 1806 translated, from the French of 1801, Philippe Pinel's *Treatise on Insanity*, rendering *"l'abattement"* as "depression of spirits" and *"habitude d'abattement et de consternation"* as "habitual depression and anxiety."[4] John Haslam in 1808 referred to "those under the influence of the depressing passions."[5] And Samuel Tuke in 1813 included under melancholia "all cases . . . in which the disorder is chiefly marked by depression of mind."[6]

The nineteenth century saw an increasingly frequent use of *depression* and its cognates in literary contexts to mean depression of spirits, melancholia, and melancholy. The use of the same terms in medical contexts gradually increased, usually in descriptive accounts of melancholic disorders to denote affect or mood; the terms had not yet acquired formal status as diagnostic categories. But Wilhelm Griesinger around the middle of the century introduced the term *states of mental depression (Die psychischen Depressionzustände)* as a synonym for *melancholia (Melancholie)*, while using *depression* and its kin mainly to indicate affect or mood in the manner just mentioned.[7] During the latter half of the nineteenth century the descriptive uses of *depression* to indicate affect became increasingly common, but the basic diagnostic term was still usually *melancholia* or *melancholy*. Much like Griesinger, Daniel Hack Tuke, in his *Dictionary of Psychological Medicine* in 1892, listed *mental depression* as a synonym for *melancholia* and defined *nervous depression* as "a term applied sometimes to a morbid fancy or melancholy of temporary duration";[8] but he dealt with clinical states of dejection under *melancholia*.[9] In the 1880s in the psychoses section of his *Lehrbuch*, Emil Kraepelin began using *depressive insanity (depressive Wahnsinn)* to name one of the categories of insanity, and he included a *depressive form (depressive Form)* as one of the categories of paranoia *(Verrücktheit)*; but he continued to employ *melancholia*, and subtypes thereof, in a manner quite in keeping with his times and to use *depression* mainly to describe affect. Parenthetically, he considered the melancholias to be forms of mental depression *(psychische Depression)*, Griesinger's term.[10] And then in 1899 he introduced *manic-depressive insanity* as a diagnostic term.[11] Since that time some form or variant of the term *depression* has had a prominent place in most nosological schemes for mental disorders. The trend away from the use of the term *melancholia* and toward *depression* may have been specially furthered by Adolf Meyer. The report of a discussion in 1904 indicates that he was "desirous of eliminating the term melancholia, which implied a knowledge of something that we did not possess. . . . If, instead of melancholia, we applied the term depression to the whole class, it would designate in an unassuming way exactly what was meant by the common use of the term melancholia."[12]

As just indicated, *depression* and its cognates were increasingly to be found in psychiatric classifications toward the end of the century, and yet the basic diagnostic term for dejected states still tended to be *melancholia*. Then, with the emergence of the category of manic-depressive disease, the term *melancholia* became much less prominent, although it continued to be used in the form of *involutional melancholia*. The latter diagnostic term has since disappeared as a distinct disorder, reappeared, and then disappeared again.

But the term *melancholia* has recently emerged once again, this time as a subtype of the *major depressive episode* in the newest classificatory system. This *depression with melancholia* has the implication of a severer form of depression and is characterized by symptoms much like those of the earlier category of *endogenous depression*.

THE BLACK BILE AND THE HUMORAL THEORY

As just noted, the term *melancholia* had its origins in terms that meant black bile and itself was used to mean the black bile as well as to name a disease. The black bile was a concept embedded in the context of the humoral theory, which for approximately two thousand years was the central explanatory scheme for dealing with diseases. The black bile was considered to be the essential element in the pathogenesis of melancholia.

The notion of bodily humors as crucial elements in health and disease was a familiar one by the time of Hippocrates in the latter part of the fifth century B.C.[13] But the bringing together of the four humors—blood, yellow bile, phlegm, and black bile—in the theory that was to be known as humoralism probably did not occur until they were so presented in the Hippocratic work *Nature of Man*.

> The notion of the humours as such comes from empirical medicine. The notion of the tetrad, the definition of health as the equilibrium of the different parts, and of sickness as the disturbance of this equilibrium, are Pythagorean contributions (which were taken up by Empedocles). The notion that in the course of the seasons each of the four substances in turn gains the ascendancy seems to be purely Empedoclean. But the credit for combining all these notions in one system, and thereby creating the doctrine of humoralism which was to dominate the future, is no doubt due to the powerful writer who composed the first part of . . . [*Nature of Man*]. This system included . . . also the doctrine of the qualities that Philistion handed down to us—first, in groups of two, forming a link between the humours and the seasons, later also appearing singly and connecting the humours with the Empedoclean primary elements. From this the author of . . . [*Nature of Man*] evolved the following schema, which was to remain in force for more than two thousand years.

Humour	Season	Qualities
Blood	Spring	Warm and Moist
Yellow Bile	Summer	Warm and Dry
Black Bile	Autumn	Cold and Dry
Phlegm	Winter	Cold and Moist

Probably as early as with the Pythagoreans, the four seasons had been matched with the Four Ages of Man, the latter being counted either as boyhood, youth, manhood and old age; or, alternatively, as youth till twenty, prime till about forty, decline till about sixty, and after that old age. A connexion could therefore be established without more ado between the Four Humours (and later the Four Temperaments) and the Four Ages of Man—a connexion which held good for all time and which was to be of fundamental significance in the future development of both speculation and imagery.[14]

While the black bile was apparently not established as one of the four natural humors until its appearance as such in the *Nature of Man*,[15] it was "considered a noxious degeneration of the yellow bile, or, alternatively, of the blood," perhaps even in pre-Hippocratic times.[16] In Hippocratic works thought to be earlier than *Nature of Man*, there were at times two or three, at times four humors, but the black bile was not among them. Sometimes blood, but more commonly bile and phlegm, were mentioned, with the usually clear implication that this bile was the yellow bile.[17] With the emergence of the balanced quartet of humors in *Nature of Man*, the black bile seems to have graduated from the status of toxic product to join the yellow bile, blood, and phlegm as another basic natural ingredient in the body. And then various environmental influences and foodstuffs came to be connected with its formation, and with normal and abnormal proportions or amounts in the body.

In its status as merely a pathogenic agent, and not yet a cardinal humor with both normal and pathological roles, in the fifth century B.C. the black bile "was held responsible for a great variety of diseases ranging from headache, vertigo, paralysis, spasms, epilepsy, and other mental disturbances, to quartan fever and diseases of the kidney, liver, and spleen."[18] Although, in contrast to yellow bile, phlegm, and blood, it is difficult to reconcile the black bile with any known substance today, Sigerist suggested that

> in this as in other cases the Greeks based their theories on observations. We know that the stool of patients suffering from bleeding gastric ulcers is black, as sometimes are the substances vomited by patients with carcinoma of the stomach. A form of malaria is still known as "blackwater fever" because the urine as a result of acute intravascular hemolysis suddenly becomes very dark, if not black at least mahogany-colored. Similar observations may have led to the assumption that ordinary yellow bile through corruption could become black and that this black bile caused diseases, notably the "black bile disease," named melancholy.*

Plato (428–347 B.C.), a younger contemporary of Hippocrates and someone who knew his views, employed a version of the humoral theory in *Timaeus.*[19] He apparently conceived of a form of black bile among the causes of disease, as being the outcome of flesh decomposing and sending material back into the blood; he noted that this waste grew black from "long burning" and

---

*The diagram included here is taken from *A History of Medicine*, by Henry E. Sigerist, and usefully illustrates what came to be the accepted relationships of the four humors to the four elements, the four seasons, and the four qualities.

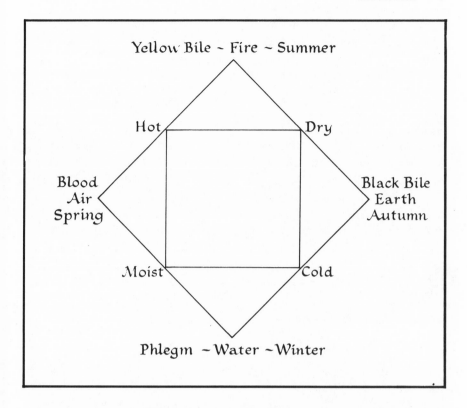

The Humors and Their Relationships (from Henry E. Sigerist, A History of Medicine, *2 vols.* *[New York: Oxford University Press, 1961], 2:323).*

became bitter, and that sometimes the "bitter element was refined away" and "the black part assumes an acidity which takes the place of the bitterness." He stated that the blood was composed of two parts, "the watery part," which "is innocent," and the part that is "a secretion of black and acid bile," which is potentially malignant. He also noted that the pathogenic forms of the humors have the potential to wander around the body and, finding "no exit or escape," become "pent up within and mingle their own vapours with the motions of the soul" and so cause a variety of diseases. "Being carried to the three places of the soul," they "create infinite varieties" of emotional distress and mental disorder, including "melancholy."

Also important to the humoral theory and to the pathogenesis of melancholia was the spleen, which had a particularly significant connection with the black bile. In the Hippocratic writings, it was identified as "spongy and of loose texture" and thus having the capacity to "easily absorb fluid from the nearby parts of the body."[20] From there, despite the assertion by Erasistratus that it was an organ of no consequence, it eventually acquired the crucial status in Galen's writings of a spongy organ that served to filter out "the thick, earthy, atrabilious humors that formed in the liver."[21]

ADUST MELANCHOLY (UNNATURAL BLACK BILE)

At times variant forms of black bile were said to exist, and, in light of the frequent references to it in the medical literature of the Middle Ages and the Renaissance, one of these variants merits some consideration here. In addition to the *natural* black bile, which had its place in health and caused melancholic diseases when in excess, there was a second type known as *unnatural melancholy, adust melancholy, melancholia adusta, burnt choler*, and *burnt black bile*. Although he did not know it by any of these names, it was taken note of by Galen, who seems to have derived his ideas about it from Rufus of Ephesus.

Galen mentioned "the other atrabilious humor which is [generated] by combustion of yellow bile and provokes violent delirium in the presence or absence of fever, because it occupies the substance of the brain itself."[22] Then, in discussing melancholia, he noted that some cases may be caused by a black bile "produced by intense local heat which burns the yellow bile or the thicker and darker blood."[23] Also, in *On the Natural Faculties*, he referred to natural and unnatural forms of black bile, the latter being the result of "combustion caused by abnormal heat."[24]

Earlier, Rufus had said that black bile could be formed either by the chilling of the blood or by the overheating of other bodily humors.[25] Following Rufus's lead, some later physicians thought of natural black bile as one of the four basic humors, sometimes derived from foodstuffs and merely present, and sometimes as a thick and cold residue derived from the blood by a process of chilling; and of unnatural black bile, or melancholia adusta, as formed by the corruption, overheating, or burning of yellow bile.[26] As Klibansky and his colleagues have pointed out, these two forms of black bile with roots in processes of chilling and overheating are vaguely reminiscent of the cold and hot qualities in the black bile mentioned by the Aristotelian author of the *Problemata*. These authors suggest that Rufus drew on Aristotelian notions, but, "rather than attribute two different symptoms and effects to one and the same substance, he preferred to recognise two different substances."[27]

Gradually the idea of an unnatural black bile, or adust melancholy, was developed to the point where a process of burning or combustion could affect any one of the four natural humors and so lead to the formation of burnt or adust black bile. It became common to think of there being potentially four types of this adust black bile, each corresponding to one of the natural humors. Among the causes suggested for such a process were improper diet, physiological disorders, and immoderate passions. The burning process would lead to a hot adust melancholy; cooling would eventually result in cold adust melancholy, which resembled natural black bile in its appearance and effects.

THE SIX NON-NATURALS

In ancient medicine the term *non-naturals* (not innate) was used to refer to a group of acquired environmental factors, usually six in number, the careful management of which was thought to be crucial to health in the sense later referred to as *hygiene*, and any of which could cause disease if imbalance or disproportion was the case. These were distinguished from the seven *naturals* (innate), which were the factors of normal function and constituted the basic science of ancient medicine: the elements, the temperaments, the humors, the parts of the body, the faculties, the functions, and the spirits. These naturals were innate constitutional factors that might be disturbed in disease, or the disturbance of which (particularly the humors) might be crucial in the pathogenesis of a disease. The non-naturals were also distinguished from the *contranaturals*, which were the causes of disease in the usual sense of the term *pathology*.

The six non-naturals, or the six things non-natural, were usually air, exercise and rest, sleep and wakefulness, food and drink, excretion and retention of superfluities, and the passions or perturbations of the soul. As Rather put it, the doctrine of the non-naturals "may be stated briefly as follows: *there are six categories of factors that operatively determine health or disease, depending on the circumstances of their use or abuse, to which human beings are unavoidably exposed in the course of daily life.* Management of the regimen of the patient, that is, of his involvement with these six sets of factors, was for centuries the physician's most important task."[28]

Probably having its origins in a set of factors listed by Galen in his *Ars medica*, this scheme became a standard and significant part of later versions of Galenic medicine. The term *non-natural* came into common use only in the wake of Latin translations of Arabic works largely based on Galen,[29] but *non-natural* was used in works on the pulse by Galen,[30] who seemed to imply that both the term and the classification of six non-natural factors antedated him.[31]

The non-naturals continued to receive significant attention in medical works well into the eighteenth century, and eventually concerns about such matters became the physical and moral (psychological) hygiene of more recent times. The doctrine ranked alongside the humoral theory as a significant system of thought for the explanation of both health and disease, but it remained in active use well beyond the demise of the humoral theory. The non-naturals were frequently given careful attention in considering the pathogenesis of melancholia and in outlining therapeutic plans for melancholic patients. And the doctrine, within its category of the passions or perturbations of the soul or mind, provided a way to take account of the role of the emotions, including grief and sorrow, in the etiology of disease.

THE CONCEPT OF DISEASE

Just what is disease? What do we mean by the term *disease?* King has summed it up in the following thoughtful statement:

> Disease is the aggregate of those conditions which, judged by the prevailing culture, are deemed painful, or disabling, and which, at the same time, deviate from either the statistical norm or from some idealized status. Health, the opposite, is the state of well-being conforming to the ideals of the prevailing culture, or to the statistical norm. The ideal itself is derived in part from the statistical norm, and in part from the ab-normal which seems particularly desirable. Environmental states (both external and internal) which are intimately connected with the ideals and norms, are part of health, even though the general public is unaware of them, while environmental states intimately connected with disease are similarly parts of disease.[32]

But then what do we mean by "a disease," a particular disease? King stated: "In this more limited sense, the term refers to a pattern of factors which somehow hang together and recur, more or less the same, in successive individuals. . . . Each [disease] . . . is a congeries of factors, and no single factor, by itself, identifies the disease. It is only the recurrence of a pattern of events, a number of elements combined in a definite relationship, which we can label a disease."[33] Several symptoms occur together with sufficient frequency and regularity that they come to be viewed as a symptom cluster or clinical syndrome. The efforts to determine etiology and explain pathogenesis may give further stability to the notion of a particular disease, although they also have the potential to bring facts to light that would challenge the usefulness of viewing a particular symptom cluster as a disease entity. And, of course, the ongoing accumulation of clinical observations may lead to adding symptoms to or subtracting symptoms from a clinical syndrome.

Although there has been a useful trend in modern times toward giving different meanings to *illness* and *disease*, it should be noted that historically these terms were essentially synonyms. It was only in the nineteenth century that the growing strength of pathology and the emergence of bacteriology and laboratory medicine began to provide the basis for the modern differentiation of *illness* as the combination of the *symptoms* testified to by the sick person and the *signs* observed by others, and *disease* as a combination of anatomical, physiological, biochemical, and even psychological deviations from the norm that could be the basis for a complex of symptoms and signs. Feinstein would add the "host" to illness and disease as a third category of data. [34] Engelhardt would differentiate *disease state* (essentially the same as *disease* above) from *disease* as "those pathophysiological or psychopathological generalizations used to correlate the elements of a disease state in order to allow" explanation of its course and character, prognosis, and planful treatment. [35] In this study, disease and illness will be used synonymously, reflecting both the usage of many centuries and the symptom-cluster nature that still characterizes the diagnosis of depression. Explanations of disease will be differentiated from disease without the introduction of a term such as *disease state*.

In addition to the meaning of *disease* as elucidated by King, however, we need to give some thought to the inherent implications of the very concept of disease. Over the centuries there have been two main notions as to the basic meaning of this concept. [36] Either a disease was a distinct entity, something that had been added to a healthy person to make him ill, or it was a deviation from the normal, where one or more factors had changed a person from his usual state and caused him to suffer. Those of the first group have been commonly referred to as ontological theories of disease, implying "the independent self-sufficiency of diseases running a regular course and with a natural history of their own." [37] Those of the second group have often been referred to as physiological theories of disease, sometimes as reactive theories, implying bodily reactions and deviations from the norm in response to a pathogenic agent.

Ontological theories have varied from demonic possession, in which a demon had entered the person and attacked him in such a way as to produce symptoms of the disease, to the hostile entities of Paracelsus and Van Helmont, [38] to Sydenham's various disease species that were distinct, body-alien entities, to some of the nineteenth century bacteriological theories in which the organism was thought of as the disease. But as Temkin pointed out, the disease entity brought about its symptom complex or syndrome through its damaging effects on parts or organs of the body or by otherwise interfering with their normal functions. [39]

Physiological theories of disease have a history dating back to the humoral theory of the Hippocratic writers and Galen, continuing down through the years with the generations of humoralists that followed in Galen's footsteps. Although these various medical authorities recognized diseases as patterned symptom clusters with a certain nature of their own, they also conceived of disease as a process in time with a pathogenesis leading to a pathophysiological state. Diseases were rooted in the general nature of man and were conceived of as deviations from the normal balance of his bodily humors that was associated with health. These physicians usually advocated attention to the nature of the individual as well as the nature of the disease. Other physiological theories of disease came and went as other theories of normal physiology came and went. Then, as the laboratory medicine and medical technology of the nineteenth and twentieth centuries emerged and developed, measurable physiological variables were gradually identified, norms were established, and the measurement of deviations from them became common practice. Newer physiological theories of disease took root in modern scientific medicine, but, still, the basic question was what degree of deviation from the normal meant disease.

Still another issue in the consideration of disease was alluded to by King in the passage quoted at the beginning of this section and is reflected in the modern viewpoint that the concept of disease is a highly relative one. That is, it varies in meaning and implication from culture to culture, and often from one subculture to another, according to conceptual schemes and other standards favored in a particular culture. More recently many well-argued views have been developed to the effect that all notions of disease are relative in the sense that they are all rooted in values; in other words, all norms for "measuring" health and disease are value-laden.

In matters psychiatric or psychological, most, if not all, cultures and historical eras recognize some mental states as distinctly unusual. However atypical, by no means all unusual mental states have been conceived of as diseases or as symptoms of disease. Many persons who have been affected by such states neither have thought of themselves as ill or mentally disordered nor were so thought of by others. Some have been considered sinners, with their unusual mental states as merely reflections of their sins (as distinct from those instances where recognized diseases have been thought to have occurred as a result of sin), and were thought to be in need of religious corrective measures. Others have been considered ascetics, prophets, holy men, or mystics and have been honored rather than treated. That is, unusual mental states may or may not be considered unfortunate, and, if thought of as unfortunate, they may or may not be conceived of and treated in terms of the medical system of their time and place. Thus, in our study of melancholia and depression over the centuries as clinical conditions, it will at times be useful, if not necessary, to consider similar conditions that may have been distinctly kindred to melancholia and depression and yet were not thought of as illness or disease.

THE PASSIONS, AFFECTIONS, AND EMOTIONS

Emotion, the more usual English term in recent times, has commonly been defined as an experience characterized by a distinctive feeling-tone, such as love, hate, fear, disgust, anger, joy, or sadness, and some disposition to motor expression. Until relatively recently *affection* and *passion* were the more common English terms, with *passion* and *perturbation of the soul* the terms of longest standing. Key Latin roots for some of these terms were *affectiones, affectus* for "affections" and later "affects," *passiones* for "passions," *motus animorum* for "the soul's motions" and eventually "emotions," and *perturbationes animorum* for "perturbations of the soul."

In the clinical descriptions of melancholia over the centuries, fear and sadness were usually central features. Thus these emotional states, or passions or perturbations of the soul as they were called in earlier times, had the status of symptoms in a disease. But they also had the status of affects, and this led to their having a place in various theories of the passions or emotions over the centuries. In those contexts, they were usually aspects of someone's philosophical views on the nature of man or, later, someone's philosophical psychology. And in some of these contexts the passions themselves were thought of as "diseases of the soul." They did not tend to turn up in medical writings among other diseases, but their appearance in philosophical contexts often entailed the use of a medical metaphor with the implication that something was seriously amiss and that corrective measures were called for. Also, some affects or passions were taken up in religious systems of thought and given the status of sins, and here again it was not uncommon for a medical metaphor to be used.

In all these various contexts we find terms and emotional states that are kindred to melancholia. Sadness has commonly been a cardinal symptom of melancholia; it was frequently one of the basic passions in various theories of the emotions; and tristitia (sadness, sorrow) was for a long while one of the cardinal sins of the Christian church. Similarly, one comes across sorrow, dejection, grief, despair, etc., and eventually depression. Thus a brief history of theories of the emotions or passions is in order here.

According to Gardiner et al., for Plato excesses of pain or pleasure amounted to diseases of the soul in the sense that great distress or joy diminished a person's capacity to reason.[40] The irrational aspects of the soul that were the wellsprings of appetite and feeling were located in the abdominal region and in the chest, respectively, and were potential threats to or antagonists of the smooth functioning of the rational soul, located in the brain. The passions that derived from these irrational aspects of the soul were given meanings in terms of the bodily conditions associated with them and so were related to physiology and medical thought. And these same passions were given ethical meanings, thus placing them in philosophers' theories of emotions and providing the grounds for their place in schemes of religious explanation. From the lowest part of the soul (below the midriff) stemmed the various desires and appetites; from the spirited part of the soul (in the chest) came the affections or passions. Here we see the roots of the medieval classification of the concupiscible affections (the desires and appetites) and the irascible affections (the passions). Plato regarded the various passions in part as modifications of pleasure and pain, and in part as distinct. Joy and hope were categorized as species of pleasure, and grief and fear as species of pain, a scheme which suggests the fourfold classification of the passions that was to emerge later. It is of special interest to note that Plato viewed "the intemperance of the passion of love" as "a disease of the soul" and conceived of love as one of the four cardinal forms of madness, for we will intermittently find love madness or love melancholy among the categories or forms of melancholia.

Aristotle enumerated various passions which he conceived of as a category partway between faculties, or predisposing susceptibilities to such affective states, and formed habits, the results of the repeated exercise of said affects (Gardiner et al., pp. 26–57). Habits were capacities for behavior that had become fixed as features of character; in a sense, chronic affective tendencies had become established. While not proceeding to the Stoic conclusion that passions should be suppressed, Aristotle did think that they ought to be brought under conscious control. In general, they were states accompanied by pleasure or pain, even thought of as species of pleasure or pain; but they differed from pleasure and pain in that they were more complex, were "motions of the soul" and not mere complements of a function. He conceived of "somatic passions," which seemed to be the pains of want and the pleasures of replenishment of the appetites, and of other passions, other pleasures and pains, which were of the soul. That some passions were defined as pains or perturbations of the soul did not imply that they were not rooted in bodily processes. Some were described as having origins in both a psychological process and the person's physiological processes. For example, anger was defined as a propensity toward retaliation and as an ebullition of the blood about the heart. The passions were ways in which the soul was affected and were akin to what we call emotions.

After Aristotle the emphasis in the studies of the passions was primarily in the direction of ethical concerns, including religious concerns. Although Epicurus is associated with a doctrine of pleasure, his views were a far cry from any sort of hedonistic orientation (pp. 59–62). He explicitly dissociated himself from hedonistic ways, indicating that by pleasure he meant the absence of pain in the body and trouble in the soul. With the Epicurean ideal being freedom from pain, intemperate desire, and all disturbing affections of the soul, imperturbability became the basic good. Thus many of the passions, and particularly extreme forms of the passions, were frowned upon. One was to avoid whatever might lead to the greater tumults in the soul.

In contrast to the Aristotelian orientation that the passions should be controlled, the Stoics thought that they should be done away with (pp. 64–68). Except in the case of the wise man, they viewed them as perverted judgments. They sought inner peace as the basic good and thought of the passions as disorders of the soul, disturbing to reason and contrary to nature. The passions were now defined as "diseases of the soul analogous to those of the body" and thought to be distinguishable from one another in both predisposing temperament and the nature of the disease itself. Nevertheless, the Stoics allowed a class of "good affections," grouped under cheerfulness, discreetness, and a virtuous habit of will; these were "species of quiet emotion befitting the wise" in contrast to the turbulent passions. They also recognized two other categories of emotions: "the natural affections arising from kinship, companionship, etc.," which were viewed favorably; and "the physical pleasures and pains as distinguished from the elation or depression of mind attending them," which were pleasures and pains viewed "as at least necessary." For the Stoics, in addition to the *feeling state*, the passion involved an *impulse* toward or away from an object and a *judgment* about that object. In their scheme of things there were four basic passions: (1) appetite or desire, an irrational inclination toward, implying an opinion of good to come; (2) fear, an irrational recoil from, implying an opinion of impending evil that seems intolerable; (3) pleasure or delight or joy, an irrational expansion or elation of mind, implying a recent opinion of a present good; and (4) pain or grief or sadness, an irrational contraction or depression of mind, implying a recent opinion of a present evil. Then, under these four fundamental passions, various Stoics grouped lists of individual affections and emotional dispositions. From those times to the end of the seventeenth century writers tended to follow the Stoics in "seeking to reduce, classify, and logically define the passions" (p. 75). The Stoic tradition served to establish sorrow, sadness, or grief as one of the basic passions. And, of special significance for the study of melancholia, it contributed to the emerging recognition of the fundamental antithesis of elation and melancholy.

Like Plato and the Aristotelian writers, the Stoics gave more or less explicit recognition to the physiological roots of the affections. Whereas those earlier authors had thought in terms of the humors and their qualities when considering the bodily conditions associated with the passions, the Stoics tended to think in terms of an enervated pneuma* as the bodily concomitant of

*In ancient thought, pneuma or spirit, usually considered a most subtle material substance, was a life-giving principle in the body that was replenished from the air through the lungs and pores of the skin and from the digestion of food. The vital spirit was associated with the heart and mediated the vital functions. The animal spirit, or psychic pneuma, was associated with the brain and nerves and mediated the activities of the nervous system. Later, the natural spirit was added, associated with the liver and mediating nutrition and growth.

the troubled states of the soul that were the passions; but some of them employed notions of dispositions of temperament expressed in terms of the humoralists' qualities. And, for the most part, the Stoics followed the tradition that held that the passions had their seat in the heart.

For Plotinus in the third century, all the ordinary passions were nothing but the soul's consciousness of the affections of its body (pp. 81–86). Like Plato, he thought that the liver was the seat of the bodily appetites and the heart of the nobler impulses. He took the view that there were certain blindly working activities of the soul that led to a complex of bodily changes; the soul immediately became aware of these perturbations of the body and associated them with the idea of impending evil; and this awareness and experience of the soul was the passion. Temperaments and states of illness, conceived of in humoral terms, were thought to dispose a person to particular passions. In his further notions that those who were little inclined to indulge their bodily appetites were less disposed to the various passions and that there were sources of good feelings independent of the body, Plotinus subscribed to views that were taken up by the Church Fathers, supported the endeavors of many mystics, and became integral elements of Christian doctrine.

As was the case with the somatic factors associated with mental disorders in the medical conceptions of ancient Greece and Rome, the bodily commotions associated with the passions were conceived of as integral parts of the passions. Similarly, the humors, the qualities, the temperaments, and the pneuma served the ancient theories of the passions much as they did the ancient theories of diseases. And these orientations continued to prevail throughout the Middle Ages and the Renaissance and in the writings of many later authors.

Nemesius in the late fourth century was the most significant of the Patristic writers on the affections (pp. 90–94). He conceived of the soul as being divided into two parts, the rational and the irrational, a view shared by most Patristic and Scholastic authors. The irrational part had two divisions: a vegetative faculty that regulated physiological processes such as waste and repair and was not subject to reason; and a part that was subject to reason and subdivided into the concupiscible faculty of appetite or desire and the irascible faculty of anger, resentment, or resistance to evil. The passions were associated with the concupiscible and irascible faculties and thus with the irrational part of the soul; yet they were subject to reason. Nemesius viewed them as essential elements of a living person; he thought that they were not naturally evil but became so only in combination with reason and will. He distinguished the affections of the body from those of the soul; the former were accompanied by pleasure or pain, while the psychic affections entailed a movement of the appetitive faculty or the irascible faculty sensed as an apprehension of good or evil. He also distinguished between passions that were contrary to nature and induced by alien influences and passions that were associated with a normal fulfillment of function. While employing far fewer subtypes in each category than the Stoics, he essentially used a version of their system of four basic species of passion. Of special interest to this study is his view that the seat of grief was in the stomach.*

In the fourth century Gregory of Nyssa elaborated a physiological theory to the effect that in joy and other positive affections the vessels conveying the bodily fluids were dilated, and in painful affections such as grief the vessels were contracted (p. 95). Sadness, despair, and fear were long thought to be caused by the constriction of the heart and the blood vessels caused, in turn, by the black bile, with its cold and dry qualities.

In the fifth century Augustine conceived of the affections as the soul's motions and identified the passions as a subgroup of the affections, as "those perturbing motions of the soul which are contrary to nature" (pp. 96–99). Against the background of a triadic system of faculties (memory, intelligence, and will), he thought that the root of all affections, including the passions, lay in the will, and he did not refer them to a bodily source.

For many centuries some form or other of Plato's scheme of a tripartite soul with concupiscible, irascible, and rational aspects continued to predominate. The former two parts of the soul usually had the affections or passions associated with them and were thought to be actually or potentially in conflict with the rational part. The list of basic affections varied in length, though the most common number was four, most often desire and joy, associated with the concupiscible soul, and fear and sorrow, associated with the irascible soul.

Medieval ideas on the passions reached their most complex and probably most influential form in the thirteenth century with the theories of Thomas Aquinas, in which Aristotelian thought was very effectively integrated with the developing intellectual trends of the Latin West.[41] Aquinas conceived of three levels of the soul—vegetative, sensitive, rational—each with its own powers or capacities. The vegetative level of the soul entailed the powers of nutrition, growth, and reproduction. The sensitive level and the rational level were each subdivided into cognitive powers and appetitive powers. The cognitive powers were associated with the apprehension of knowledge, and the appetitive powers were the basis for each individual's tendency to fulfill himself or actualize his potential. For the sensitive level of the soul, the cognitive powers meant five exterior senses (touch, taste, smell, hearing, sight) and four interior senses (common sense, imagination, memory, the estimative

---

*Against the background of the Galenic notion that there was a splenic secretion of black bile into the stomach, apparently Nemesius conceived of grief, like melancholia, as resulting from an excess of black bile.

power), and the appetitive powers meant the concupiscible and the irascible passions. For the rational level of the soul, the cognitive powers were active and passive reason, and the appetitive power referred to the function of the will.

In the conception of the concupiscible and irascible powers as the appetitive powers associated with the sensitive level of the soul, Aquinas was using notions akin to Plato's concupiscible and irascible aspects of the soul. In each case these terms referred to concepts that were key features in the author's theory of the passions. For Aquinas the concupiscible and irascible powers were tendencies toward objects apprehended intuitively by the exterior and interior senses as either good or evil, and the intensity of such tendencies was the source of the passions. As concupiscible passions he grouped together love, desire, joy, hate, aversion, and sorrow; as the irascible passions he grouped together hope, despair, courage, fear, and anger. Regarding the relationship of the passions to bodily processes, Aquinas saw the physical changes as essential accompaniments of the affective states but not as causes of these states.

Along with these various theological and philosophical perspectives on the passions, the medical thought of the medieval era involved two important viewpoints on these states. On the one hand there was the doctrine of the six non-naturals—air, sleep and wakefulness, food and drink, exercise and rest, evacuation and retention, and the passions—which had long provided a framework in which the passions could be viewed as the causes of various somatic effects; and so grief and sorrow could cause bodily ailments. On the other hand, during those same centuries the humoral theory allowed the view that the humors—that is, somatic factors—were causes which could produce affective states as results; and so the black bile could cause the sadness and fear that were key symptoms in melancholia.

During the Renaissance there was a significant increase in the amount of writing about the passions, and gradually the affective life came to be viewed in ways somewhat less dependent on theological considerations (Gardiner et al., pp. 119–148). The term *affect* and its equivalents were increasingly used, while some began to reserve the terms *passions* and *perturbations* for the more violent affects or the severer troublings of the soul. Physiological explanations of affective states were increasingly employed once again, with the most common being some notion of the spirits drawn from the traditional doctrine of the pneuma, although the humors and qualities of the humoral theory were still prominent. In conjunction with the humors, the affects brought about alterations in the body; and in conjunction with the spirits, they affected the imagination and reason. The distinction between concupiscible and irascible was gradually dropped as the central categorizing principle for affects. Instead, in the various classifications there were often two main groupings, those associated with striving for or attaining the good and those associated with avoiding or resisting evil; this system reflected organizing principles reminiscent of Aquinas's views. Good in the present was associated with pleasure or joy, and evil in the present with pain or sadness; an anticipation of good in the future was associated with desire, and an anticipation of evil with fear. A common scheme was a set of primary passions, each of which had associated with it a number of secondary affective states. Some classificatory systems were organized around pleasure and pain as the two primary passions, some were organized around joy and sadness, and still others were constructed around a set of four primary passions. Quadripartite systems were particularly common, with the terminology varying somewhat—*joy* (or delight, or pleasure), *sadness* (or grief, or pain), *desire*, and *fear*. Thus sadness, sorrow, or grief was usually one of the basic passions.

The sixteenth century also saw the first hints of a change in the long-standing view that the heart was the principal seat of the affects, a trend that was to eventuate in the neurocentric suggestions of the seventeenth and eighteenth centuries. In perhaps the best known of these neurocentric theories, Descartes reaffirmed the tradition of physiological explanation for the passions, using the animal spirits of the nervous system as a key factor and introducing mechanical explanations in place of the long familiar humoral notions (ibid., 149–170). The passions were conceived of as perceptions of affective states by the soul and as caused by movements of the animal spirits that agitated the brain and sustained the impression. With Descartes's dualistic view of soul and body, it was these animal spirits of the nervous system that mediated the interaction between the soul and body, particularly through the pineal gland. While the passions were caused by physiological factors, they were *of the soul*, experienced by the soul. As for what we might term the somatic aspects of an affect, he thought of them merely as accompaniments or effects rather than essential elements. With his concept of neural causation, both the bodily aspects and the felt emotion were effects derived from the same basic somatic cause. He thought of joy and sorrow as the first passions in a person's experience, and he developed a system of six primary passions: admiratio (astonishment or surprise), love, hate, desire, joy, and sorrow.

In addition to Descartes's important role in the trend toward a neurocentric explanation, his views on the passions were significant in other ways. Although it was by no means new to conceive of the passions as caused by somatic processes, prior to Descartes the Christian church's ideology had influenced many to think of the affective experience as caused by or stemming from the soul or mind, with its bodily features thus secondary to the passion as felt. He became a principal influence in favor of somatic factors as the root causes of the passions. Further, prior to Descartes the predominant trend in theories of affects had favored the Stoic view that the passions should be subdued rather than expressed, that tranquillity was the preferred state. On balance, this view had been favored over the Aristotelian perspective that the passions could be useful spurs toward action. Descartes's *Les passions de l'âme* contributed to a shift away from the Stoic orientation.

Another significant seventeenth-century thinker on the passions was Hobbes, who gave them a central place in his considerations of human nature, viewing them as the guide to thought and the wellspring of action, a constituent of the will, and a determinant of both intellectual and moral tendencies (pp. 183–192). As to their seat, he held more to the traditional cardiocentric notion, thinking of the spirits in the region of the heart as the key somatic factors. From basic roots in either appetite or aversion, he developed his set of simple or primary passions: appetite, desire, love, aversion, joy, and grief.

Although it was far from new to think of the passions as appetitive, as reflecting strivings or desires, Spinoza in the seventeenth century simplified this orientation to the single basic striving of self-preservation (pp. 192–205). As derivatives of this basic conative tendency, he conceived of three primary passions—desire, pleasure, and pain. "This simplification plausibly combines the classical representation of them in all systems which operate mainly with logical definitions, where they invariably appear either as forms of conation or as forms of pleasure and pain" (pp. 197–198).

In the eighteenth century *affections* and *passions* continued to be frequently used as synonyms (pp. 210–247). Where they were differentiated, the latter usually referred to the more violent or turbulent states. The terms commonly meant the actions or modifications of the mind that followed on the perception of an object or an event usually conceived of as good or evil. Following the Lockean tradition, various sensationalist systems conceived of the passions as being gradually built up from sensations with associationist principles determining the complex of ideas that went to make up a particular passion. Sets of basic passions were postulated. Frequently good and evil, sometimes pleasure and pain, were conceived of as tended toward or avoided, respectively; and, along with factors of certainty or uncertainty, these determined the groupings of both the primary passions and the secondary or compound passions. Some viewed the more violent passions as temporary or, if they persisted, chronic forms of madness.

During the latter part of the eighteenth century, affects were increasingly given a central and fundamental place in considerations of mental life. This gradually led to assigning the affects an importance that approximated that of the intellect. Viewed less in terms of "traditional rationalism and conventional morality, the passions came to be extolled as the great impelling forces of human nature" (pp. 247–248). Particularly through the influence of a series of

German authors in the late eighteenth and early nineteenth centuries, the status of the affects gradually shifted so that a distinct faculty of feeling or affect joined understanding (or knowing, or cognition) and will (or striving, or appetition) in a new tripartite system of faculties (pp. 255–263). In contrast to the medieval tendency to connect the passions with appetition or desire and to post-Cartesian views that often connected them more with cognition, they came to be thought of as being "as distinct and unique an aspect of mental life as knowing or striving" (p. 255). In summary, during the eighteenth century

> the study [of the affects] is still made by philosophers and the subject matter is treated largely from a logical viewpoint. The psychological aspects of feeling, due to a more conscientious use of introspection, have more frequently been singled out and emphasized. The added knowledge of the nervous system has challenged the theories of dualism and parallelism. But the interest in the feelings has remained keenly alive and a desire to consider them for their own sake foreshadows the coming outgrowth of psychology from philosophy (pp. 274–275).

In surveying the nineteenth-century trends in theories of affects, Beebe-Center divided them into peripheral and central theories (pp. 276–355). By *peripheral* he meant those views that grew out of the sensationalism of the eighteenth century and that emphasized the place of sense organs and physiological processes. By *central* he meant those views that emphasized higher mental processes and sought to explain affects in terms of mental entities. In either case, the theory commonly began with the conscious affective state and then looked in one of these two directions for the factors that were thought to have brought it about.

Regarding the peripheral theories, some developed their views almost exclusively in terms of physiological processes, with little attention to mental factors. Such was the case with Cabanis, who thought of affects as arising from the peripheral excitation of nerves which were stimulated either by external objects or by internal conditions that caused visceral movements. Affects were cerebrospinal events in some of these theories, as with Cabanis, and visceral events in others, as with Bichat. It continued to be common to organize a system of affects around pleasantness and unpleasantness (or pleasure and pain), with desire and aversion being derived from them or being ideas associated with pleasant and unpleasant sensations. With the dichotomy of past and future, along with the notions of certainty and uncertainty in the case of the future, schemes of a small number of basic affects were developed, with other affective states being either modifications or combinations of the primary affects.

To the peripheral physiological factors some theories added central notions, but with a somatic emphasis. Sometimes these notions involved the cerebrum, other times other intracranial structures. And still other theories of somatic explanation were primarily associated with the central nervous system. Some of the various physiological theories viewed the subjective states as conscious perceptions of the somatic processes; others thought of them as the end result of these processes; and still others considered them to be merely epiphenomenal.

These various reflections of a physiological explanatory tradition eventually led to the well-known challenge to mental explanations provided by the James–Lange theory of emotions. Noting that there had been a tendency for many to think that "the mental perception of some fact excites the mental affection called the emotion, and that this latter state of mind gives rise to the bodily expression," James went on to say that, on the contrary, *"the bodily changes follow directly the* perception *of the exciting fact, and that our feeling of the same changes as they occur* is *the emotion"* (p. 296).

Given that melancholia and depression are basic to this study, it is of interest to note that Lange concluded that essential bodily features for both sorrow and fear were "weakening of voluntary innervation" and "vasoconstriction," and that joy and elation were associated with an "increase of voluntary innervation" and "vasodilation" (p. 327). We have here distinctly familiar themes, as sadness, fear, and melancholy had recurrently been associated with ideas such as contraction of the mind, constriction of the heart and blood vessels, weakness of the nerves, low nerve energy, low nervous pressure, and constriction of the nerves; and joy and elation had recurrently been associated with ideas such as expansion of the mind, dilation of the heart and blood vessels, excessive nervous excitation, excessive nerve energy, high nervous pressure, and dilation of the nerves.

In contrast to the various peripheral theories with their emphasis on somatic explanations, the nineteenth century also had its share of central theories, theories of affects in which mental entities of one sort or another were thought to be the basic factors or causal elements. Whether it was some type of intellectual factor or the will or some aspect of a faculty psychology, the mental entity was conceived of as the starting point in a process that resulted in the affective state and its bodily changes. Sometimes physiological factors were hardly considered; in other instances they were merely assigned a secondary place in the explanations. But the century saw a steady decrease in such essentially mental theories of affects or emotions. Physiological explanations became increasingly important, and gradually the focus of such explanations shifted from peripheral organic structures such as the sense organs to central structures of the nervous system. Affects or emotions came to be commonly viewed as attitudes toward objects that involved bodily changes and only secondarily entailed subjective states.

During the early years of the twentieth century the James–Lange theory continued to hold a major place among theories of emotions. Behaviorism emerged, with its rejection of consciousness and its attention to emotions as correlations of forms of behavior with physiological processes. In reaction to James–Lange and to the behaviorists there came those who emphasized the whole organism, some conceiving of the emotions in mental terms within this organism (such as Freud and McDougall) and some in physiological terms (such as Cannon and Dumas) (pp. 336–386). Although the uncertainties and arguments about what an emotion is and how it should best be explained are far from resolved, there are several themes that have characterized subsequent twentieth-century views. Some have emphasized the notion of a subjective feeling state usually accompanied by some form of motor expression; some have stressed the conscious state with a tone of either pleasantness or unpleasantness; some have characterized emotions as the reflections of motivational stirrings; and some have emphasized a total complex of conscious feeling state, motor expression, physiological process, and orientation to external factors.

II

Tracing the Variations in a
Remarkable Consistency

CHAPTER TWO

Melancholia in
Ancient Greece and Rome

Although in Greek literature it was not uncommon for abnormal behavior and disease to be explained in terms of supernatural agency,[1] the earliest of the surviving Greek medical texts completely rejected supernatural factors as satisfactory explanations of disease.[2] In nonmedical contexts one or another supernatural force or entity might be thought to be the cause of a mental aberration or a disease, sometimes from an influence exerted from outside the person's body and sometimes as a result of entering the person's body and exerting an influence from that vantage point.[3] The afflicted person might be caused to suffer capriciously or because of some form of wickedness or sinfulness. The affliction might be visited on him by one of the gods, by some demon or evil spirit, or in later times by the God of the Christian church as a punishment or a test of the faithful, by the Devil, or by various demons suggested by the Christian system of thought. Although such views came and went in explanations of disease during the ancient and medieval centuries, such was not the case in the Greek theory of medicine, which held that mental aberrations either constituted a disease or were symptoms of a disease, and, like other diseases and symptoms, should be explained in naturalistic terms. Further, ancient Greek medicine affirmed that mental disorders were psychological reflections of physiological disturbances. The Hippocratic writers insisted that the locus of such disorders was in the brain, and, in spite of the cardiocentric notions of Aristotle and others, this view gradually became the predominant one.[4]

There were various speculations and arguments as to whether there was one or several psychic faculties, whether psychic activity might be appropriately divided into imagination, perception, reason, memory, and other functions, and whether such functions were localized in different parts of the brain or in other organs. There were various experimental efforts from Alcmaeon's study of the brain to the discoveries of Herophilus, Erasistratus, and Galen on the structure and function of the brain and the nervous system.[5] There were many instances, in both the medical and nonmedical literatures, of psychological and emotional factors leading to bodily changes, and of somatic factors having psychological and emotional effects; in short, what modern thought would term "psychosomatic" and "somatopsychic" orientations were not uncommon, although neatly dualistic notions were not the case.

The extant medical writings from Ancient Greece and Rome, when they deal with the subject of mental disorders, tend to refer to three types of madness with sufficient regularity to suggest that they were well-established as nosological categories. It is within such a context that one usually finds melancholia in these medical writings. Despite variations from author to author, these three traditional forms of madness—phrenitis, melancholia, and mania—had a certain descriptive consistency, and certain themes tended to recur in the medical theories employed to explain them. Further, they were frequently compared to and contrasted with one another. It was usual to think of phrenitis as an acute disease, and of melancholia and mania as chronic diseases. Phrenitis characteristically meant delirium and fever, while melancholia and mania were differentiated from it by a lack of fever. Descriptions of phrenitis are sometimes reminiscent of the modern category of delirious states in acute organic diseases, sometimes of meningitis or encephalitis; and descriptions of melancholia and mania often suggest the present-day functional psychoses, sometimes the conditions of the same name. And phrenitis was usually said to be caused by yellow bile, and melancholia by black bile.

THE HIPPOCRATIC WRITINGS

Melancholia as a distinct disease is taken note of at least as early as the fifth and fourth centuries B.C. in the Hippocratic writings. Although these authors did not leave a systematic discussion of this condition, their scattered comments allow us to assemble the following clinical picture. Melancholia was associated with "aversion to food, despondency, sleeplessness, irritability, restlessness," and they stated that "fear or depression that is prolonged means melancholia."[6]

When it came to explaining diseases, the Hippocratic writers drew upon an early version of the humoral theory (*Works*, IV, 3–41), somewhat less systematized than it was to become in the hands of Galen and later authors. The four humors—blood, yellow bile, black bile, and phlegm—were each thought to be in the ascendancy in a particular one of the four seasons—spring, summer, autumn, and winter, respectively; and each humor and its correlated season were associated with a paired combination of primary opposites or qualities—blood with warm and moist, yellow bile with warm and dry, black bile with cold and dry, and phlegm with cold and moist. In this scheme an optimal mixture (eucrasia) of the humors constituted a state of health; there was a balance or equilibrium. Disease was a disturbance of this equilibrium (dyscrasia) of the humors; there was an imbalance in the form of an excess, a deficit, or an inadequate mixture of one or more of the humors. Although there is no such systematic statement in the Hippocratic writings, scattered references suggest that melancholia was one condition among several termed melancholic diseases, that the black bile was the key factor in causing such diseases, that autumn was the season when a person was at particular risk from the effects of this humor, that the black bile was viscous in nature and associated with the qualities of coldness and dryness, and that such a syndrome with its mental disturbances was surely the result of the brain being affected (II, 175; IV, 3–41, 183, 193). Further, one passage maintained: "Most melancholics usually also become epileptics, and epileptics melancholics. One or the other [condition] prevails according to where the disease leans: if towards the body, they become epileptics, if towards reason, melancholics."[7]

As to treatment, again one can draw only on scattered passages. That purging was prescribed is clearly implied, and the reputed character of the black bile indicates that vigorous effects were sought. An allusion to the benefits of hemorrhoidal blood flow suggests the role of the removal of blood in allowing the evacuation of impurities and excesses (IV, 19, 41, 137, 183).

ARISTOTLE

Although not strictly part of the medicine of their time, the Aristotelian views on melancholia both had their own importance and were gradually absorbed into the medical views of the classical world; and, although thought to have been written by Theophrastus or some other follower of Aristotle (384–322 B.C.) rather than by Aristotle himself, they seem to be of a piece with much in the Aristotelian corpus. Further, the rehabilitation of Aristotelian "melancholy" in the Renaissance was to give them a later, renewed influence in the history of melancholia.

The question raised in the Aristotelian *Problemata* was "Why is it that all those who have become eminent in philosophy or politics or poetry or the arts are clearly of an atrabilious temperament, and some of them to such an extent as to be affected by diseases caused by black bile?"[8] With the framework of the humoral theory implied, the author outlined a scheme in which there were the ordinary persons in whom there was some black bile but nothing disproportionate and a minority in whom there was a distinct excess of black bile in a relatively stable balance. The latter were designated as having a melancholic temperament and were thought to be disposed to being gifted persons as a result. Everyone shared the potential for "the despondency which occurs in everyday life (for we are often in the condition of feeling grief without being able to ascribe any cause for it, while at other times we feel cheerful without knowing why)" as they all had some black bile in them; but those of a melancholic temperament were "thoroughly penetrated" by such feelings and had "them as a permanent part of their nature." They shared with others the risk of a pathological excess of black bile that could result in various melancholic diseases, but they were also at risk for having severer illnesses of this nature. On the other hand, ordinary persons did not have this temperamental disposition to outstanding accomplishment.

In contrast to the qualities of coldness and dryness that were to become firmly associated with the black bile (and had been in the Hippocratic writings), the author conceived of this humor as "a mixture of heat and cold" with the potential to become very hot or very cold. He then referred to the black bile as being naturally cold, and, "if it abounds in the body, produces apoplexy or torpor or despondency or fear"; but it may also become overheated, and, if it did, "it produces cheerfulness accompanied by song, and frenzy, and the breaking forth of sores, and the like. . . . Many too, if this heat approaches the region of the intellect, are affected by diseases of frenzy and possession; and this is the origin of Sibyls and soothsayers and all inspired persons, when they are affected not by disease but by natural temperament."

Toward the end of this essay the author noted that, if the temperament "be cold beyond due measure, it produces groundless despondency" and the person would be at risk for suicide. Then, after noting that "heat in the region in which we think and form hopes makes us cheerful" and that this was why men "drink until they become intoxicated," he discussed the danger of suicide in the state of coldness and despondency that often followed drinking. He added that, as a result of the hot and cold effects of the black bile, "the young are more cheerful, the old more despondent, the former being hot and the latter cold; for old age is a process of cooling." And he noted that "also after sexual intercourse most people tend to be despondent . . . for by so doing they become cooled."

As Klibansky et al. have suggested, we may have here an integration of the medical notions about melancholia with the divine madness of Plato, perhaps a secularization of the supernatural origins of his inspired madness.[9] As they go on to say, in problem XXX, "The mythical notion of frenzy was replaced by the scientific notion of melancholy, a task made the easier as "melancholic" and "mad"—in the purely pathological sense—had long been synonymous, and as the peculiar gift of true dreams and prophecies belonging to the diseased melancholic corresponded to the Platonic equation of "mantic" and "mania."[10] Thereafter, ideas about melancholia often included something of this theme of specialness; references to prophecy occurred sometimes as suggestions that a melancholic disposition had allowed such an accomplishment, sometimes as an implication that prophesying was a reflection of delusional trends in someone suffering from melancholia; and a melancholic disposition became one of the four cardinal temperaments (also sanguine, choleric, and phlegmatic) associated with the humoral theory, a scheme that was the forerunner of the many systems of character types offered over the centuries. With this "eucrasia within an anomaly" or "normal abnormality," with this status of someone special with great potential and yet someone at high risk, we have an important example of the often fine line between melancholic or depressive nature and melancholic or depressive disease.

CELSUS

The next surviving medical account of melancholia is found in the *De Medicina* of Celsus (ca. 30), the Roman encyclopedist. Much as the Hippocratic author had done, he stated that "the black bile disease supervenes upon prolonged despondency with prolonged fear and sleeplessness."[11] He extended his clinical description further when he referred to this condition as "another sort of insanity, of longer duration because it generally begins without fever, but later excites a slight feverishness. It consists in depression which seems caused by black bile" (p. 299). Here he was contrasting melancholia with phrenitis—the chronic, subdued condition without fever to the acute, excited condition with fever—in a way that was to be customary for many centuries to come.

Although Celsus was significantly influenced by the Hippocratic writers, he did not make a systematic use of humoralism or of any other theoretical scheme. Nevertheless, in suggesting that melancholia was caused by the black bile, he seemed to imply a use of the humoral theory.

When considering treatment he noted that "bloodletting is here of service; but if anything prohibit this, then comes firstly abstinence, secondly a clearance by white hellebore and a vomit. After either, rubbing twice a day is to be adopted; if the patient is strong, frequent exercise as well: vomiting on an empty stomach." He recommended "food of the middle class [that is, of medium strength] . . . without wine." He then added that

> the motions are to be kept very soft, causes of fright excluded, good hope rather put forward; entertainment sought by story-telling, and by games, especially by those with which the patient was wont to be attracted when sane; work of his, if there is any, should be praised, and set out before his eyes; his depression should be gently reproved as being without cause; he should have it pointed out to him

now and again how in the very things which trouble him there may be cause of rejoicing rather than of solicitude. (pp. 299–301)

SORANUS OF EPHESUS

The next medical author to leave us any significant material on mental diseases was Soranus of Ephesus, who worked first in Alexandria and later in Rome during the reigns of the emperors Trajan (98–117) and Hadrian (117–138) and who is the best known physician of the Methodist school. This work has come down to us through the Latin translation by Caelius Aurelianus at the end of the fourth or the beginning of the fifth century.[12] Soranus described melancholia and mania as chronic diseases without fever and contrasted them to phrenitis on both counts. As further points of differentiation, he mentioned that, in both these diseases, there was usually no pain and the patient did not pluck at bits of wool and straw as the phrenitic patient did. But they were similar to phrenitis "in respect to loss of reason"; that is, all three were forms of madness. He detailed "the signs of melancholy" as

> mental anguish and distress, dejection, silence, animosity toward members of the household, sometimes a desire to live and at other times a longing for death, suspicion on the part of the patient that a plot is being hatched against him, weeping without reason, meaningless muttering, and, again, occasional joviality; precordial distention, especially after eating, coldness of the limbs, mild sweat, a sharp pain in the esophagus or cardia . . . , heaviness of the head, complexion greenish-black or somewhat blue, body attenuated, weakness, indigestion with belching that has a foul . . . odor; intestinal cramps; vomiting, sometimes ineffectual and at other times bringing up yellowish, rusty, or black matter; similar discharges through the anus. (p. 19)

He also noted that "the disease is more frequent among men, especially in middle age; it rarely occurs in women, and is also uncommon in other ages."

The Methodist theory that governed Soranus' explanations held that "the basic types of disease are (1) an excessively dry, tense, and stringent state; (2) an excessively fluid, relaxed, atonic state; and (3) a condition which involves both types of abnormality" (p. xvii). Against this background he stated that "melancholy is a serious disease, involving essentially a state of stricture; and sometimes a state of looseness is also involved, as the copious evacuations indicate." He disagreed with those who considered melancholia "a form of the disease of mania"; and, in contrast to mania, he argued that not the head but "the esophagus is chiefly affected" (p. 563). Rejecting the humoral theory, Soranus maintained that, although the term *melancholia* was derived from the Greek words for black bile, "the name is not derived, as many believe, from the notion that black bile is the cause or origin of the disease." Rather, it stemmed "from the fact that the patient often vomits black bile" (p. 561). Then, as antecedent causes, he cited "indigestion, habitual vomiting after eating, the drinking of drugs, acrid food, grief, fear" (p. 563).

Soranus advocated a program of treatment similar to that for mania, and the reader was directed to that section of his work (pp. 543–553). He was primarily concerned with relaxing a state of stricture. Although he discussed at length physical measures designed to relieve a physical state that resulted in mental symptoms, he also emphasized psychological measures, enunciating a principle that he considered applicable to the treatment of mental disorders in general. He stated that "the particular characteristic of a case of mental disturbance must be corrected by emphasizing the opposite quality, so that the mental condition, too, may attain the balanced state of health" (pp. 547–549). He provided extensive advice on the general management of the patient and his immediate environment, and thoughtful psychological considerations are threaded through this part of his discussion.

As to physical remedies, in considerable detail Soranus described a complex regime of fasting, bloodletting, anointings, fomentations, and a limited, light diet; cupping with scarification, clysters, poultices, and leeches were each used at times. For wakefulness he prescribed "passive exercise, first in a hammock and then in a sedan chair"; and the sound of dripping water was mentioned as inducing sleep (p. 547). Specifically for melancholia he recommended the application of external local remedies of a soothing nature, "particularly to the region over the cardia and between the shoulder blades," and advised against bloodletting or purging with hellebore while the disease was active. Considering the possibility of an admixture of symptoms of looseness, such as "excessive vomiting or discharges from the bowels," in such instances he advised astringent measures and binding foods (p. 563).

When the disease declined, his regime changed in character. This phase of treatment included a carefully chosen diet, local and general applications of soothing oils, ointments, and plasters, passive exercise, walking, various types of mental exercise, various entertainments, massage, and baths. If the patient was willing, he recommended listening to the discussions of philosophers, "for by their words philosophers help to banish fear, sorrow, and wrath, and in so doing make no small contribution to the health of the body" (p. 551).

RUFUS OF EPHESUS

A leading eclectic and often ranked next to Galen among the Greek physicians of the Roman Empire, Rufus of Ephesus flourished during the time of Trajan (98–117). References are frequently made to his work on melancholia, but, like most of his numerous medical writings, it is available to us only in the form of a few fragments.

As Klibansky et al. have argued, Rufus's views on melancholia seem to have crucially influenced medical thought on the subject up to the threshold of modern times. Not only did Galen mention this work with respect and draw upon it, but it was used as authoritative by the great ninth-century Arabic writers. In particular Ishaq ibn Imran based his work on melancholia on Rufus, and in turn his work seems to have been the direct source of Constantinus Africanus's *De Melancholia*. Along with Constantinus's significant influence on medieval medicine in general, his views were crucial to late medieval and renaissance thought on melancholia. Thus, through his influence on Galen and through Constantinus's *De Melancholia*, Rufus may be said to have "led the way with regard to the medical conception of melancholy for more than fifteen hundred years."[13]

Rufus noted that those suffering from melancholia were gloomy, sad, and fearful;[14] and he stated that the chief signs were fear and doubting, with a single delusional idea and yet quite sane on all other matters.* He said that "some are anxious about loud noises, and some wish they were dead, and some delight in washing, and some had an aversion to any food or drink, or detested some kind of animal; and some believed that they had swallowed snakes and the like" ([Rufus], *Oeuvres*, p. 455). Some melancholics saw dangers where there were none; some saw advantages in objects in which there were none; some feared their friends and others the whole of mankind (p. 354). And melancholics tended to turn from the company of others and to seek solitude (p. 456). Rufus cited various delusions that were to become characteristic in later accounts of melancholia, such as the person who believed himself to be an earthenware pot, the person who thought that his skin had dried up and become like parchment, and the person who thought that he did not have a head (p. 355). It is of special note, however, that he mentioned that some melancholics manifested the gift of prophecy rather than conceiving of this as delusional (p. 456). He referred to chronic dyspepsia as an important symptom, mentioned flatulence, and alluded to a tendency to commit suicide (pp. 355–356). He mentioned a longing for coitus in melancholia and attributed it to melancholic flatulence (p. 457). He noted blinking and protruding eyes, thickened lips, darkening of the complexion, development of hairiness, and speech difficulties (p. 356). He commented that melancholia was more common in men than women but that it was more serious in women when it did occur. It did not occur in adolescents, but it occasionally occurred in infants and in young boys; and it was sufficiently common in the elderly as to seem to be an intrinsic feature of growing old (p. 455).

*[Rufus], *Oeuvres*, p. 455. This may be the earliest recorded instance of this view that melancholia entailed a limited degree of insanity.

Rufus stated that "much thinking and sadness caused melancholia" (p. 455). In this regard, Klibansky et al. pointed out that, in contrast to the Aristotelian notion that the black bile and a melancholic temperament led to either intellectual preeminence or a predisposition to melancholia the disease, Rufus here was saying that "activity of the mind became the direct cause" of melancholia, and so "the tragic destiny of the man of genius became merely the 'spleen' of an overworked scholar."[15] And, in fact, this more modest relationship of intellectual activity to melancholia was to turn up again and again in later accounts of this disease. On the other hand, this particular theme is far from all there is to Rufus's views on the etiology and pathogenesis of melancholia. Albeit he is fairly classified among the eclectics, he made considerable use of the humoral theory in explaining melancholia. The black bile was the crucial factor, and its qualities of coldness and dryness and the "thickened superfluities" that it caused were used by him to explain many of the symptoms (*Oeuvres*, pp. 355–356). And he emphasized the role of the black bile again and again in his references to the various discharges and evacuations that were associated with the disease and with its successful treatment (pp. 456–457). Also, in addition to the place that he gave to excessive intellectual activity, Rufus thought that other factors that contributed to melancholia were too much thick and dark wines, the heavy meats of cows and goats, too much of any food and wine, and insufficient exercise (p. 455).

Rufus addressed the question of types of melancholia in two quite different ways. In one context, he made the point that there were two types: (1) "some melancholics are that way by nature, by virtue of their congenital temperament"; (2) "others . . . become that way as a consequence of a bad diet" (p. 357). In thus distinguishing the innate form in someone with a disposition to melancholia from a strictly acquired form, Rufus might have been drawing on the somewhat similar distinction made by Aristotle.[16]

He also categorized melancholia into three types according to the basic site of the disease: (1) a form in which "the whole body is full of a melancholy blood"; (2) a form in which "only the brain has been invaded"; and (3) a form in which "the hypochondria" are "primarily affected" (*Oeuvres*, pp. 358–359, 457). In this regard he seems to have been the originator of this triadic classification that was taken up by Galen and that became a crucial feature of texts on melancholia for many centuries thereafter.*

*Klibansky et al. see Rufus as having "established" this classification: *Saturn and Melancholy*, p. 53. But Ishaq ibn Imran (ca. 900) maintained that Rufus dealt only with the hypochondriacal type, and Ullmann seems to agree with this: Manfred Ullman, *Islamic Medicine* (Edinburgh: Edinburgh University Press, 1978), pp. 37, 76. And yet Rhazes (865–923), in using Rufus's work, interposed the comment that Galen did not say that Rufus dealt only with the hypochondriacal type: [Rufus], *Oeuvres*, p. 457.

Rufus took some pains to emphasize that the longer the symptoms of melancholia continued, the more fixed they became and the more difficult it was to treat them. Therefore, it was important to recognize the disease early in its course and to begin treatment promptly (pp. 455–456). He noted first that "where the whole body is full of a melancholy blood, the treatment should begin with blood-letting; but, when only the brain has been invaded, the patient does not need to be bled, unless either he has a surfeit of blood or we remove some as a precaution (p. 358). In both the hypochondriacal type and the type in which the brain was primarily affected, he advocated measures "aimed at relaxing the stomach." Care must be taken "to obtain a good digestion" and then "to purge with dodder of thyme and aloe, because these two substances, taken daily in a small dose, bring about a moderate and soothing opening of the bowels" (p. 359).

Following the purging, wormwood should be given, perhaps for its reputation as both a cathartic and a diuretic that eliminated bilious humors. Colocynth and black hellebore were also suggested as purgatives. Wholesome foods were stressed. Walking about was urged as the best type of exercise. Bathing before eating was recommended for those with difficulty digesting their food, and easily digested food was emphasized. He suggested white wine, perhaps diluted with water, probably to relax the person and to promote digestion; and he advised a drink of vinegar before going to sleep, preferably flavored with squills, probably for its capacity to thin and dissipate a thick humor. For those whose stomachs were weak, vomiting was to be avoided, and wholesome and tasty foods were to be given. Travel was suggested as a means to change the patient's physical constitution and improve his digestion, and to distract him from his preoccupations and raise his spirits. He emphasized the importance of a careful determination of the primary cause and then the implementation of a treatment program based on the principle of contraries. Such patients should be warmed by the application of heat to the hypochondriac regions, and their digestion should be strengthened and their flatulence dispelled. Afterward, a mustard plaster to the area of the stomach would eradicate the internal pains (pp. 457–459). Rufus also mentioned several other purgatives for melancholia, and he advised the use of various remedies for their sudorific and diuretic properties (pp. 387–388). Also of note was "the sacred remedy of Rufus against attacks of melancholia," which was to be referred to frequently down through the ages (pp. 323–324). This was composed of colocynth, yellow bugle, germander, cassia, agaric, asafetida, wild parsley, aristolochia, white pepper, cinnamon, spikenard, saffron, and myrrh, mixed with honey and given in four-dram doses in hydromel and salt water. According to the ancient views on its various ingredients, this remarkable bit of polypharmacy promoted digestion, eliminated flatulence, had purgative and diuretic effects, was warming, was good for the liver and spleen, cut thick humors, and cleared away obstructions, among other alleged effects.

ARETAEUS

Not very much later Aretaeus of Cappadocia (ca. 150), probably a contemporary of Galen, included a chapter on melancholia in his *On the Causes and Symptoms of Chronic Diseases.* His clinical observations are fairly extensive, and, although apparently not influential until long after his own time, they stand as points of reference for much that was said about melancholia many centuries later. He described this chronic condition as

> a lowness of spirits from a single phantasy, without fever; . . . the understanding is turned . . . in the melancholics to sorrow and despondency only. . . . Those affected with melancholy are not every one of them affected according to one particular form; but they are either suspicious of poisoning, or flee to the desert from misanthropy, or turn superstitious, or contract a hatred of life.[17]

He was perhaps the earliest to suggest an intimate connection between melancholia and mania when he stated, "It appears to me that melancholy is the commencement and a part of mania" (*Extant Works*, p. 299). He added that

> the patients are dull or stern, dejected or unreasonably torpid, without any manifest cause: such is the commencement of melancholy. And they also become peevish, dispirited, sleepless, and start up from a disturbed sleep.
> Unreasonable fear also seizes them, if the disease tend to increase, when their dreams are true, terrifying, and clear: for whatever, when awake, they have an aversion to, as being an evil, rushes upon their visions in sleep. They are prone to change their mind readily; to become base, mean-spirited, illiberal, and in a little time, perhaps, simple, extravagant, munificent, not from any virtue of the soul, but from the changeableness of the disease. But if the illness become more urgent, hatred, avoidance of the haunts of men, vain lamentations; they complain of life, and desire to die. In many, the understanding so leads to insensibility and fatuousness, that they become ignorant of all things, or forgetful of themselves, and live the life of the inferior animals. . . . They are voracious, indeed, yet emaciated; for in them sleep does not brace their limbs either by what they have eaten or drunk, but watchfulness diffuses and determines them outwardly. (pp. 299–300)

He described various other physical signs that indicated gastrointestinal difficulties, associating some of them with "the hypochondriac region" and several times using the term "bile"; and he noted, "Pulse for the most part small, torpid, feeble, dense, like that from cold" (ibid.).

He then concluded this chapter with an account of a state of severe dejection that he differentiated from melancholia and yet acknowledged that it would appear as such to the average person.

A story is told, that a certain person, incurably affected, fell in love with a girl; and when the physicians could bring him no relief, love cured him. But I think that he was originally in love, and that he was dejected and spiritless from being unsuccessful with the girl, and appeared to the common people to be melancholic. He then did not know that it was love; but when he imparted the love to the girl, he ceased from his dejection, and dispelled his passion and sorrow; and with joy he awoke from his lowness of spirits, and he became restored to understanding, love being his physician. (p. 300)

Although he is thought to have been a follower of Archigenes and thus of the Pneumatic school, Aretaeus's writings reveal a sound clinical observer who made less use of theory and preconceived ideas than was characteristic for his era. In view of this approach and of his various unacknowledged quotations from the Hippocratic writings, it seems fair to say, as many have, that his general orientation was predominantly Hippocratic.[18] Although not a devotee of the humoral theory, Aretaeus accepted a role for the black bile in melancholia, noting that "if it be determined upwards to the stomach and diaphragm, it forms melancholy; for it produces flatulence and eructations of a fetid and fishy nature, and it sends rumbling wind downwards, and disturbs the understanding. On this account, in former days, these were called melancholics and flatulent persons." He then added, however, that "in certain of these cases, there is neither flatulence nor black bile, but mere anger and grief, and sad dejection of mind; and these were called melancholics, because the terms *bile* and *anger* are synonymous in import, and likewise *black* with *much* and *furious*." ([Aretaeus], p. 298). That is, black bile might mean no more than that much anger was the cause of some instances of melancholia. Here we may have a suggestion that, in some cases, the crucial etiological factors were psychological, in contrast to the prevailing somatogenic theories of the time. Discussing the pathogenesis further, he stated that "if the cause remain in the hypochondriac regions, it collects about the diaphragm, and the bile passes upwards, or downwards in cases of melancholy." He emphasized that dryness was a basic cause. He commented that adult men were particularly prone to this disorder. And he stated that "the seasons of summer and of autumn engender, and spring brings it to a crisis" (p. 299).

As to treatment, addressed in his *On the Cure of Chronic Diseases*, the central themes for Aretaeus were the presence of black bile and evacuative remedies in order to remove it (pp. 473–478); and he viewed the disorder as a humoral dyscrasia in much the same spirit as a more confirmed humoralist would have. He recommended bloodletting, with cautions that the amount be keyed to the weakness (deficient blood) or strength (much blood) of the patient. He was particularly concerned that this evacuation allow a flow from the liver, "for this viscus is the fountain of the blood, and the source of the formation of the bile, both of which are the pabulum of melancholy" (p. 473). He advised "a fuller diet than usual" to strengthen the patient for the evacuations and to "assist the stomach, it being in a state of disease, and distress from the black bile lodging there." He prescribed black hellebore and "the capillary leaves of Attic thyme" as purgatives with a reputation for evacuating the black bile (p. 474). After a bath, a little wine, and food for their tonic effects following the weakening effects of purgation, he recommended cupping in the area of the liver and stomach for more evacuation. After further strengthening measures, he advocated shaving the head and "applying the cupping instrument to it, for the primary and greatest cause of the disease is in the nerves. But neither are the senses free from injury, for hence are their departure and commencement. Wherefore these also are changed, by participating in the affection. Some, likewise, from alienation of the senses have perverted feelings" (pp. 474–475). He then emphasized the need "to cure the stomach as being disordered of itself, and from black bile being lodged in it"; and substances were recommended to prevent the formation of bile and to bring "down the bile into the lower gut." After noting that this disease might "appear after suppression of the catamenial discharge in women, or the hemorrhoidal flux in men," he urged that, in such cases, measures be taken so that those "parts" would "throw off their accustomed evacuation" (p. 475). If there were signs of relapse, he advocated even more vigorous versions of the same evacuative remedies. Then, for when the disease had subsided, he outlined an extensive strengthening regime. But he also acknowledged a tendency to recurrence, and it was in this context that he put forward the following, often-quoted statement: "It is impossible, indeed, to make all the sick well, for a physician would thus be superior to a god; but the physician can produce respite from pain, intervals in diseases, and render them latent" (p. 476).

GALEN

In Galen's (131–201) *On the Affected Parts,* book III deals with the function and diseases of the brain and spinal cord, and within that he devoted a chapter to melancholia.[19] He considered that there was a group of illnesses known as melancholic diseases, among which was melancholia proper, and that an excess of black bile was the cause of these diseases.[20] In that context he suggested that the Hippocratic description was something to be taken for granted, that "the most essential symptoms" were contained in the Hippocratic statement that "fear or a depressive mood which last for a long time render [patients] melancholic [that is, atrabilious]" (Galen, p. 92). He noted that "all persons call this affection *melancholia,* indicating by this term the humor responsible for it." Then he elaborated his description as follows:

Fear generally befalls the melancholic patients, but the same type of abnormal sensory images do not always present themselves. As for instance, one patient believes that he has been turned into a kind of snail and therefore runs away from everyone he meets lest [its shell] should get crushed; or when another patient sees some crowing cocks flapping their wings to their song, he beats his own arms against his ribs and imitates the voice of the animals. Again, another patient is afraid that Atlas who supports the world will become tired and throw it away and he and all of us will be crushed and pushed together. And there are a thousand other imaginary ideas.

Although each melancholic patient acts quite differently than the others, all of them exhibit fear or despondency. They find fault with life and hate people; but not all want to die. For some the fear of death is of principal concern during melancholy. Others again will appear to you quite bizarre because they dread death and desire to die at the same time.

Therefore, it seems correct that *Hippocrates* classified all their symptoms into two groups: fear and despondency. Because of this despondency patients hate everyone whom they see, are constantly sullen and appear terrified, like children or uneducated adults in deepest darkness. As external darkness renders almost all persons fearful, with the exception of a few naturally audacious ones or those who were specially trained, thus the color of the black humor induces fear when its darkness throws a shadow over the area of thought [in the brain]. (p. 93)

Before I proceed any further it is important to outline here Galen's relevant physiological and pathological views so as to provide a context for his explanations of melancholia; and, perhaps just as important, these views were to continue as the basis for most explanations of disease for nearly another fifteen hundred years, albeit often systematized further and at times varied somewhat.[21] Central to his thinking was the humoral theory. To the long-established cosmic theory of the four elements had already been added the notion that each of these elements possessed a certain quality—to fire belonged heat, to air cold, to water the moist, to earth the dry. From empirical medicine had emerged the idea of humors which, in the Hippocratic writings, became four in number—blood, yellow bile, black bile, and phlegm—each of which was thought to be in the ascendancy in one of the four seasons—spring, summer, autumn, and winter, respectively. Then, perhaps under the influence of Galen himself, paired combinations of qualities became associated with each humor and its correlated season: blood was warm and moist, yellow bile warm and dry, black bile cold and dry, and phlegm cold and moist.

Galen thought that three of the humors—yellow bile, black bile, phlegm—existed in normal and abnormal forms. In optimal amounts the normal forms were useful in the body; but the abnormal forms, or an excess of the normal forms, led to disease. Acute diseases tended to be the result of anomalies of blood or yellow bile, and chronic diseases the result of anomalies of phlegm or black bile.

Although he conceived of the humors as being formed in the body rather than ingested as such, he believed that different foods had different proclivities for being acted upon within the body to produce the different humors (for example, warm foods tended to produce yellow bile). And, similarly, seasons of the year, periods of life, geographic regions, and occupations influenced the nature of the humors formed, by virtue of their predominant qualities. Then, in turn, the qualities of the humors determined the natures of the diseases they might cause (for example, yellow bile caused warm diseases).

The humors in Galen's theoretical system were not quite the basic units that they had been in the humoralism that was by then traditional. Rather, the four qualities—warm, cold, dry, moist—were the more fundamental notions for him. The way in which the four qualities were compounded determined how each part functioned and how the organism as a whole functioned, and damage to the qualities led to dysfunction and disease. From these qualities Galen developed his theory of temperaments, in which there were nine possible types. The ideal temperament meant a balanced mixture of the four qualities. Then there were four in which one of the qualities predominated, and there were four more derived from the humoral theory's system of paired qualities. It was the latter four that were to be known as the sanguine, choleric, melancholic, and phlegmatic temperaments. Although the term *temperament* later came to refer to characteristic psychological dispositions, Galen used it in the sense of bodily dispositions, characteristic individual physical tendencies. On the one hand, in themselves they were not diseases but, rather, were excesses milder than those that caused pathology, and were relatively stable imbalances. On the other hand, these various temperaments, or constitutions as we might say, were thought of as determining the diseases to which a person would be susceptible, as well as the behaviors and emotions to which he would be inclined.

In this scheme of things the place of the black bile was crucial. Ordinarily a certain amount of separation out of black bile from the blood occurred in the liver. The resultant thick, earthy humor was thought to have a heightened pathogenic potential. But, again under ordinary circumstances, this material was transmitted to the spleen, which, with its allegedly sponge-like character, attracted or absorbed this atrabiliary material.[22] Indicating that Plato and Hippocrates among other ancient authorities were of the same opinion, he conceived of the spleen as the organ that cleansed the blood of black bile (*Natural Faculties*, p. 205). This black bile was then "elaborated, broken up, altered, and transformed" in the spleen. Some of this became "nutriment for the spleen," and the portion that could not be "changed into the nature of thin, useful blood" was discharged into the stomach (*Usefulness of the Parts*, p. 233). Again ordinarily, this material stimulated the stomach to contract and thus hold the food there to allow the process of digestion (p. 255).

Galen thought that there were three types of melancholia (*Affected Parts*, pp. 89–94), in each of which he believed that the black bile was the essential etiological factor and that it had affected the substance of the brain. One of these was a primary disease of the brain, with only a local excess of black bile. In the other two types the brain was affected only secondarily. In one of the secondary forms the entire mass of the blood was affected, and it caused a darkening of the skin. Galen apparently thought that "the attractive power of the spleen" for the black bile had failed, thus allowing the black bile to "prevail all over the body."[23] In the other secondary type, melancholia hypochondriaca, the primary disease was in the upper abdominal area with resultant flatulence and digestive disturbances. Galen stated that "it seems that there is an inflammation in the stomach and that the blood contained in the inflamed part is thicker and more atrabilious," with the result that "an atrabilious evaporation produces melancholic symptoms of the mind by ascending to the brain like a sooty substance or a smoky vapor" (*Affected Parts*, pp. 92–93). He also explained it in terms of the patient's suffering from an affection of the spleen that led to a "noxious serum" flowing "from this organ into the stomach" and resulted in this "gassy or hypochondriac disease" which rendered "people despondent, hopeless and sad" due to the "evaporations of toxic humors" that ascended to the brain (p. 153).

Galen dealt at some length with the types of meat and vegetables that predisposed to an excess of black bile in the blood and thus left the person vulnerable to melancholia; and in the same way he briefly mentioned "heavy and dark wine" and "aged cheeses" (pp.90–91). But if the person had "kept a well-balanced diet," he might still be disposed to this disorder as a result of worries or sleeplessness and anxiety (p. 91). In another context he had noted that such predisposing atrabiliary excesses were more likely to occur "in the fall of the year" and "after the prime of life" due to the cold and dry qualities of that season and that time of life; and he then implied that "cold and dry modes of life, regions, constitutions" might have similar effects (*Natural Faculties*, p. 203).

As to treatment in those cases where the entire blood was affected, Galen advised bloodletting but, where only the brain was affected, he thought that it was usually unnecessary. He also urged that the initial blood drawn be examined to prove or disprove that it reflected an atrabilious condition, and that the phlebotomy be continued only if the diagnosis was confirmed (*Affected Parts*, pp. 90–91). Where "the damaging humor did not resist evacuation for any length of time," he recommended "frequent bathing; a well-balanced and fluid regimen, without other remedies"; but, if "the illness had become chronic, it required stronger methods of treatment" (p. 94). He advocated a diet of ingredients that would have warming and moistening effects in this cold and dry disease. The reestablishment of the menstrual flow or the hemorrhoidal flow was thought to facilitate the evacuation of the pathogenic humor. Various purgative remedies were recommended in order to eliminate the black bile. And he advised "exercise, massage and all kinds of active motion" for their evacuative effects.[24]

CHAPTER THREE

Melancholia in Medieval Times

As with so many other matters, what constituted melancholia and how it was explained did not suddenly change with the advent of those centuries now termed medieval. In fact, there is every indication of a substantial continuity in these areas of study. To appreciate this continuity it is important to examine briefly the outlines of the medieval medicine that was the context for considerations of melancholia the disease.

Although after Galen there was a profound change in the nature of medical writings, medieval medical thought possessed a coherent core that resembled its Greek origins to a remarkable degree. As Temkin expressed it, "What follows is on the one hand, encyclopedias and shorter treatises serving practical purposes, and on the other, commentaries explaining the classical authors, which means Hippocrates and Galen, for the use of the schools. In this encyclopedic and scholastic form, Greek medicine is bequeathed to the peoples of the East."[1] "The medieval works of late antiquity as well as historical accounts of Arabic physicians make it clear that this type of medicine developed between about A.D. 200 and 700, and that Alexandria was the chief center of this development, though probably not the only one."[2] This is usually referred to as Byzantine medicine, and the writings of three medical compilers—Oribasius of Pergamon (325–403), Alexander of Tralles (525–605), and Paul of Aegina (625–690)—are representative of it. Although other authorities were used, particularly Dioscorides in materia medica, this tradition of compilation drew primarily upon the works of Galen, with attention to the Hippocratic writings in addition to the Hippocratic influence through Galen.

Matters were somewhat different in the Latin West. With the various invasions of the Germanic tribes, Western Europe was to a significant extent cut off from Greek medicine; and the disruptions in the Western Empire were associated with deterioration in the training and practice of medicine. Nevertheless, much that was Roman culture continued, and something of Greek medicine was transmitted through the developing Latin literature of the West. Some works of Hippocrates and Galen found their way into Latin translations in the early medieval centuries. A valuable portion of the writings of Soranus was presented in Latin by Caelius Aurelianus at the end of the fourth or the beginning of the fifth century. The materia medica of Dioscorides was translated. And parts of the works of the Byzantine medical compilers—Oribasius, Alexander of Tralles, and Paul of Aegina—appeared in Latin versions.[3]

A number of early Church Fathers, from St. Jerome to Isidore, took note of classical medicine; and, as educated laymen where medicine was concerned, they endeavored to familiarize themselves with it and to conserve it as useful information.[4] Although this patristic medical literature was essentially compilation, some valuable translation was done; and it constituted an important mode of transmission of knowledge by contributing significantly to the foundation of monastic medicine.[5] At the same time, the patristic writers showed considerable tendency to summarize, particularly by eliminating theoretical discussions "in favor of portions of more practical applicability"; and they tended to reconsider the views of the classical authorities "in the light of Christian faith and morals."[6] Ultimately, it was in the monasteries and cathedral schools that the Latin world carried on a tradition of systematic medical knowledge, with the few representatives of classical tradition mentioned above constituting the bulk of their sources and with patristic medical writings contributing both content and orientation.

Using these materials, the developing monasteries included a knowledge of medicine in their general educational activities,[7] conserved a medical literature, and provided the sources for manuscript copies for which their monks were often the scribes. Then, at Chartres in the tenth century and at Rheims and others later, the cathedral schools emerged as centers of medical learning in the Latin West, joining and to some extent succeeding the monasteries as conservers and transmitters of a medical heritage.[8] These centers were priestly rather than monastic, and, being more "in" the lay world around them and more responsive to it, their medicine seems somewhat more advanced than that of the monasteries.[9]

While information is specially limited concerning lay medicine in the early medieval Latin West, it appears that lay physicians gradually came to play a less significant role than they had previously.[10] Although the profession may have deteriorated with the disintegration of the Roman Empire, other contributing factors may have been the Church's emphasis on various forms of spiritual healing and the emergence of the monasteries and cathedral schools as centers of medical knowledge. Nevertheless, lay medicine continued to play a role of some consequence, as indicated by the frequent references to physicians who failed to cure, with the result that patients resorted to spiritual healing.[11] And the school at Salerno has frequently been put forward as evidence of a lay medical tradition of some importance.[12]

The medical perspectives outlined above did not change all that much in the later medieval centuries. In the East, the Byzantine compilers mentioned above were representative of the Hippocratic-Galenic traditions that continued to prevail. The Arabic medical authorities—who included Rhazes, Haly Abbas, and Avicenna—built on this tradition and continued it. And these Eastern sources became influences in the Latin West through translations from their works by Constantinus Africanus in the eleventh century and by others who followed him. These influences joined those from Greek medicine that had been transmitted directly through the developing Latin literature of the West.

The Arabic medicine alluded to above is an important part of the history of medieval medicine, although it should be noted that the medicine was Arabic primarily in the sense of the language used.[13] Many of the authors were not Arabs. Some were Syrians, some leading figures were Persians, and some later authors of importance were Spaniards. Also, despite the fact that the Islamic world was the context for this medicine, they were not all of the Islamic faith. There was a significant number of Christians and Jews among these Arabic medical authorities.

To a significant extent this Arabic medicine was built on translations of Greek medicine, with both important commentaries and original observations added later by Arabic authors. Various Christian groups who were driven out of the Byzantine empire are thought to have had a key role as translators of the Greek medical authors into Syriac and Arabic. And foremost among the Greek medical authorities who thus determined the nature of Arabic medicine was Galen. The bulk of his writings had been translated into Arabic by the end of the ninth century. But the influence of Galen's medicine also stemmed from the translation of the works of the Byzantine compilers with their Galenic orientation, and it was probably their influence that accounted for Arabic medicine's systematized versions of Galen's views being associated more with Galenism than strictly with Galen himself. Hippocratic views, too, found their way into Arabic medicine. Although this was to some extent directly via translations, it was much more from Galen's commentaries, the work of other commentators, and the writings of the various compilers. Also important was the place of Dioscorides in Arabic pharmacology. Less prominent perhaps, yet still very significant, were the works of Rufus of Ephesus and of the Byzantine compilers (Oribasius of Pergamon, Alexander of Tralles, and Paul of Aegina). And some Indian medical works found their way into Arabic via Persian translations. Ultimately, Arabic medicine of this era was derived from Greek, Syrian, Persian, and Indian sources, but the Greek sources were predominant, and the Galenic medical scheme was central in those Greek sources.

Leading figures in the golden age of Arabic medicine, the tenth and eleventh centuries, were Al-Razi, or Rhazes (865–923), Ali ibn Abbas, or Haly Abbas (d. 994), and Ibn Sina, or Avicenna (980–1037), all of the Eastern Caliphate and of Persian origins. Of significance for the history of melancholia in particular is Ishaq ibn Imran (fl. early tenth century). Important medical figures of a slightly later era were Ibn Rushd, or Averroes (1126–1198), and Musa ibn Maymun, or Maimonides (1135–1204), both of the Western Caliphate and of Spanish origin. Although these are only a few of the many medical authors of the Islamic Middle Ages, they were outstanding contributors; and their works constituted a significant proportion of the materials that both continued to constitute Islamic medicine for a good many centuries thereafter and were drawn on by Constantinus Africanus and Gerard of Cremona in the numerous translations of Greco-Arabic medicine that they contributed to the Latin West.

In the eleventh century Constantinus Africanus (1020?–1087), a well-traveled and learned Muslim, settled in Salerno, eventually converting to Christianity, joining the Benedictine community at nearby Monte Cassino, and embarking on an extensive task of translation that brought a crucial portion of Greco-Arabic medical literature from Arabic into Latin for Western Europe. Then "in Toledo in the twelfth century Gerard of Cremona and his students translated a large number of Greek and Arabic medical . . . writers from Arabic into Latin. In the early thirteenth century the western world possessed the Greek medical tradition as the Arabs had done three hundred years before, and possessed in addition the experience of many Arabic scholars."[14]

In part influenced by Constantine's translations, the center of medical learning at Salerno grew and flourished; and the Toledo translations made their contributions as medieval universities began to emerge and became centers of medical learning. In the West this translated Greco-Arabic medicine joined the existing Hippocratic-Galenic influences in determining the nature of medical thought into the Renaissance era and beyond. In the Arabic world this Greco-Arabic medicine was the prevailing scheme of things for an even longer period.

ORIBASIUS OF PERGAMON

The earliest of the well-known Byzantine compilers and encyclopedists, Oribasius of Pergamon (325–403), was the personal physician of Emperor Julian the Apostate. He was a carrier of the emerging Galenic tradition, and his works found their way into Latin in the West and into Syriac and Arabic in the East.

In the materials left to us, Oribasius's views on melancholia bear a clear relationship to those of Galen. He cited the familiar sadness and fear as cardinal symptoms. Otherwise he only referred to "symptoms related to the stomach," which he indicated were characteristic of that form of melancholia known as the hypochondriac or flatulent illness.[15] These clinical references were made in the context of noting the by then traditional three types of melancholia. In addition to the hypochondriac type, he mentioned the type in which "the body is pervaded with blood containing black bile" and the type in which "only the brain contains such blood" or "the brain is primarily affected" (*Oeuvres*, 5:409–410). And he made it clear that the crucial causative factor was an excess of black bile.

The larger portion of his extant writings on melancholia is devoted to treatment recommendations. In cases where only the brain was affected, he followed Galen in advocating early treatment, as then such patients could be completely cured merely by frequent baths and a moist, nourishing diet; but, if the condition had become chronic and the noxious humor had thus become difficult to evacuate, more powerful remedies were required (pp. 410–411). Then he would recommend a mild purgative, such as aloe, and, after purgation, some wormwood, possibly in its role as a stomachic to counteract the unfortunate side effects of purgatives; and he suggested several further medicaments that were purported to cut thick humors or to serve as evacuants. He also mentioned stronger purgatives, clysters, diuretic drugs, and evacuations through perspiration (pp. 411–412). In cases where the whole body was affected by atrabilious blood, he again followed Galen in recommending that treatment begin with bloodletting; but, where only the brain was affected, bloodletting was thought to be useless (p. 409).

For the hypochondriacal type, Oribasius advised fomentations and poultices with a decoction of various medicaments reputed to soothe intestinal pains and diminish flatulence. He also recommended dry-cupping against flatulence and cupping with scarification against the pains. He implied that one should promote "bowel movements, vomiting, good digestion, and belching"; and, where the illness was alleviated by achieving such effects, such a diagnosis was confirmed (p. 410).

Elsewhere than in his discussion of melancholia, Oribasius drew on

Rufus of Ephesus for the opinion that coitus was the most helpful remedy of all against melancholia because it dissipated fixed ideas of the soul and calmed ungovernable passions (1:541). He also suggested that being afflicted with phrenitis would cure melancholia, and vice versa (4:97).

ALEXANDER OF TRALLES

Alexander of Tralles (525–605) traveled widely and is said to have taught and practiced in Rome. Like Oribasius, he made extensive use of Galen's views in his compilations, although he is thought to have added more from his own experience than was characteristic of the other great Byzantine compilers. His views on mental disorders were known in the early medieval Latin West and in the world of Arabic medicine, and they found their way into later medieval and Renaissance thought by both these routes.

Alexander began his descriptive comments on melancholia by emphasizing the symptoms, strange behaviors, and mental disturbances that might occur. As he referred to a range of deranged states that included the euphoric, the rageful, the sluggish and withdrawn, the fearful, the suicidal, and the homicidal, it is clear that he included under the rubric of melancholia a much more extensive group of types of madness than did most medical writers on this subject, although many authors included some instances of excited forms of madness along with a majority of sad and fearful cases. He also made the point that some were continually deranged, whereas others had periods of rationality in which they were able to take up their usual occupations. After stressing this diversity, he indicated that therefore it behooved physicians to study each case separately and investigate its origins in order to care for and treat the individual properly.[16]

To further indicate the complexity of melancholia, Alexander referred to the variety of organs that might be diseased, but this turns out to refer to the, by then, traditional three types of melancholia: "In some, the brain alone is diseased; in others, it is the whole body; in others, it is only the stomach and the hypochondria" (*Oeuvres*, 2:223). He primarily reasoned within the framework of the humoral theory, but he emphasized that the humoral etiology varied considerably. In this regard, he discussed cases due to (1) a plethora of blood, which caused vapors to rise to the brain; (2) a stoppage of blood, which seems to have involved an obstruction in the brain; and (3) an excess of black bile, with the bile resulting from a transformation of the blood and giving off vapors that moved toward the brain.

In those cases where a plethora of blood was the cause, Alexander stated that "hairy men, of dark skin and frail constitution" were "more easily attacked by this disease than those who were robust and of a white body" (p. 224).

Similarly predisposed were those in their youth and in the prime of life, those who ate too lightly, and those who were inclined to anger, were filled with anxieties, and had passed a lengthy period in regrets and sadness. The arrest of a customary drainage of blood—hemorrhoids in men, menstrual flow in women—was also thought to be a precipitant of this form of melancholia. The physician was urged to be alert to the possibility that the patient might feel as though his entire body was borne down by a sensation of heaviness, and he was advised to check the face for evidence of increased redness and of the veins being more turgid and tense; such signs were suggestive of the plethora of blood that could cause the vapors to rise to the head and harm the brain. He indicated that the humor was merely excessive in amount, rather than particularly corrupted or biting, in those cases in which the patients laughed without reason and seemed to have cheerful delusions.

Except for his treatment advice, Alexander said relatively little about those cases that involved a stoppage of blood. But he discoursed at length about those cases that were caused by an excess of black bile that, in turn, gave off vapors that rose to the head and had deleterious effects on the brain. And he suggested that the excess of black bile might stem from the transformation of the blood due to "many privations," "great anxieties," or an unsuitable diet, seeming to imply a process akin to the formation of adust black bile. Such patients were irritable and agitated, and he conceived of these symptoms as the outcome of the bitter nature of the black bile (p. 226). His description included many of the more familiar symptoms of melancholia noted by earlier authors: sadness without reason, being dispirited and a prey to terrors, desiring death, being hostile to his friends, and suspecting that someone is seeking to kill him (p. 230). He then mentioned that there was a wide variety of "fantastic" and "strange" delusions that might be present, such as the person believing that he was made of earthenware or of leather, that he was a cock and trying to imitate its cry, that he was a nightingale and mourning the death of Itys, or that he was supporting the heavens like Atlas and they might fall and crush him and the whole world with him (pp. 230–231). And by noting that some believed that they could foretell the future, he implied the delusion that they were prophets rather than crediting them with true prophesies (p. 223). Drawing somewhat on Rufus of Ephesus and Galen in developing this list of delusions, Alexander added some new ones and joined these two earlier authors as an authority whose list was made use of again and again by later authors on melancholia.

Alexander's therapeutic recommendations tended to revolve around his three types of etiology rather than the three traditional types of melancholia based on the primary sites of the disease. In the case of a plethora of blood, a phlebotomy was indicated early and above all else, and the diet was to be nutritious, mild, and minimally blood-forming (p. 225). In the case of a stoppage of the blood and obstruction in the brain, he again emphasized early treatment, which included bloodletting, evacuation of wastes, and local treatment to the head (pp. 225–226).

When melancholia was due to black bile, the main therapeutic theme was that of evacuating the black bile by one means or another, with secondary themes of attenuating the black bile so as to facilitate its elimination and following a diet that was minimally inclined to form black bile. He recommended a mild moist diet for several days and then a purgative, the thick and noxious humor already being somewhat thinned and liquefied and thus readier to be purged. As the purgative, he favored the storied hiera picra, or holy bitter, with some juice of scammony added.* He advised against drugs that were too hot for fear of driving the patient into a state of raving, and reminded his readers that they had all known of such patients being cured by diet alone.[17] His detailed advice on diet included cautions against bitter foods, those with a drying effect, and those that increased black bile (*Oeuvres*, 2:228–229). He specially recommended baths for eliminating black bile and for tempering it with their moistening power; he emphasized that they were to be of only moderate warmth (pp. 229–230). After acknowledging that "the ancients" had used cupping to the head and leeching in such cases, he advised against these measures, except "when the noxious matter proceeds violently to the brain, accumulates there very thickly and no longer has any tendency to yield to different medications" (p. 230). After purging and baths, the patient was to be allowed to sleep; and, after renewing his strength with sleep, he was to be allowed conversation with intimate friends. He noted that many patients had been cured by hearing or seeing something that was specially reassuring to them, and so he advised a careful attention to the mode and expression of the derangement, with an eye to understanding its psychological origins and providing a basis for psychological treatment measures (p. 231). Of the cases he cited, one was disabused of the delusion that he had been beheaded for

---

*2: 227. Hiera picra, or holy bitter, was a compound medicine containing several purgatives. Its formula varied from one authority to another, but the predominant active components were aloes and cinnamon, with aromatics added along with other purgatives; sometimes colocynth took the place of aloes as a leading component, and sometimes both were present; and black hellebore, germander, and scammony were often included. Tradition would have it that the first variant of this remedy dated back to Asclepian temple medicine, and reference to the "sacred medicine" usually meant one of the hierae. The hierae of Rufus of Ephesus and of Galen acquired a lasting fame, including being well-known in Alexander's time; and Alexander's own hiera came to be highly regarded. In various forms hiera picra has been known and used since, even into the twentieth century. Influenced by transitions from one language to another and by colloquial usages, there have been innumerable variations in its name, from "hygry pigry" and "gira pigra" to "hickery pickery." See [Paul of Aegina], The Seven Books of paulus Aeginata, 3 vols., trans. and ed. Francis Adams (London: Sydenham Society, 1844–1847), 3:500–502, and C. J. S. Thompson, *The Mystery and Art of the Apothecary* (London: John Lane, Bodley Head, 1929), pp. 35–43.

having been a tyrant by having a lead cap suddenly placed on his head; a second was reassured in the framework of her delusion that she had swallowed a snake by being made to vomit and having a snake surreptitiously placed in the vomitus; and a third, an angry, melancholic woman distressed by the long absence of her husband, was cured by his sudden return. Accordingly, he recommended that, except in chronic cases, all manner of contrivances should be tried in an endeavor to cure the various fantastic ideas, especially when there seemed to be an established cause for them (pp. 231–232). But, where the condition had become chronic and the symptoms fixed, he stated that one must turn to phlebotomy and then to the use of purgatives, followed by a mild, nutritious diet and baths of soft water to reestablish the patient's strength. For purgation, he recommended epithyme with a little whey, and the hiera picra, or holy bitter. If this combination was not successful, he advised more energetic treatment, particularly with the hiera picra of Galen. For monitoring the patient's progress, he specially advised attention to whether the patient's "fears and groundless sadnesses" were being eased (p. 233). But, if "the phantasms of the atrabiliary state" still showed no signs of subsiding, he recommended the Armenian stone as a stronger evacuant; he preferred this remedy to the white hellebore that "the ancient physicians" would have favored at this juncture, as the former was without the often drastic side effects of the latter (pp. 233–235).

PAUL OF AEGINA

Like Oribasius and Alexander, Paul of Aegina (625–690) belonged to the Byzantine world, was a prominent medical author in his own time, and left posterity an extensive compilation of medical thought derived largely from Galen. These writings were an important part of what was taken up from the Greco-Roman medical tradition by Arabic authors in the era of Islamic ascendancy, and, as part of Arabic medicine, they found their way into Latin in the later medieval centuries. Of his famous *Epitome Medica*, only the third book appeared in Latin in the earlier medieval era, but this was the book that included the diseases of the head, with melancholia among them.

In his chapter that dealt with melancholia, he stated:

> Melancholy is a disorder of the intellect without fever. . . . The common symptoms of them all [that is, all three types] are fear, despondency, and misanthropy; and that they fancy themselves to be, some, brute animals, and imitate their cries; and others, earthen-vessels, and are frightened lest they be broken. Some desire death, and others are afraid of dying; some laugh constantly, and others weep; and some believe themselves impelled by higher powers, and foretell what is to come, as if under divine influence; and these are, therefore, properly called demoniacs, or possessed persons.[18]

His further descriptive comments were organized in terms of the three traditional types of melancholia and were interwoven with notions on the condition's pathogenesis; and the whole was based on the humoral theory. The
disease was

> . . . occasioned mostly by a melancholic humour seizing the understanding;
> sometimes the brain being primarily affected, and sometimes it being altered by
> sympathy with the rest of the body. And there is a third species called the
> flatulent and hypochondriac, occasioned by inflammation of the parts in the
> hypochondria adjoining to the stomach, by which sometimes noxious vapors or
> aurae are transmitted to the brain, and sometimes part of the substance of the
> humour. . . . The peculiar symptoms of melancholy, from sympathy with the
> general system, are leanness, darkness, and shagginess; the whole appearance
> melancholic, either by nature, or acquired by anxiety, want of sleep, the
> administration of noxious food, or stoppage of the hemorrhoidal, or menstrual
> discharge. Melancholy, from affection of the hypochondria, is indicated by
> indigestion, acid eructations, heat and heaviness of them, retraction of the
> hypochondria, and sometimes inflammation, especially in the beginning; and
> then, when they increase, melancholic symptoms supervene. These are relieved
> by digestion, or copious discharges, or flatus, or vomiting, or eructations. When
> none of these symptoms, or very few of them, are present, melancholic symp-
> toms appearing indicate that the brain is primarily affected, and for the most part
> from a melancholic humour. (*Seven Books*, 1:383)

As to treatment, Paul said that those in whom the melancholia was a
primary disease of the brain "are to be treated with frequent baths, and a
wholesome and humid diet, together with suitable exhilaration of mind,
without any other remedy, unless when, from its long continuance, the
offending humour is difficult to evacuate, in which case we must have recourse
to more powerful and complicated plans of treatment" (pp. 383–384). In that
case, one should turn to purgings, first with dodder of thyme or with aloes, a
small amount daily sufficing for an effective and gentle opening of the bowels.
After purging, give wormwood frequently, probably for its evacuative ca-
pability. He also recommended a drink of vinegar before sleep and dipping
food in it, perhaps for its reputation for thinning and dissipating thick humors.
In an incipient case "from sympathy with the general system," if "the body is
firm," he advised beginning with a phlebotomy, and then, "when the strength
is recruited, purge downwards, with the wild cucumber, and the composition
from the black hellebore, and promote the hemorrhoidal and menstrual discharges, if the affection be occasioned by retention of them. Diuretic remedies
are likewise proper, as also evacuations by perspiration." In those cases where
the hypochondria were affected, he recommended applying poultices with a
decoction designed to "soothe the pains and diminish flatulence, . . . dry
cupping for flatulence, and cupping with scarifications for pains and inflamma-

tions" (p. 384). For chronic cases, the most powerful remedy is evacuation, by vomiting with hellebore" (p. 384). He concluded by stating that "the diet for all melancholics should be wholesome, and moderately moistening," and they should abstain "from whatever things engender black bile" (p. 385). In another context, after extolling the benefits to be derived from "sexual enjoyments," Paul (from Rufus via Oribasius) stated that "the best possible remedy for melancholy is coition" (p. 44).

Paul also dealt with some related matters that call for two addenda of some significance. First he referred to mania as being caused by black bile, but in such cases "yellow bile . . . by too much heat, has been turned into black" (p. 383). It is clear that he was using the notion of adust black bile here, implying a contrast with the natural black bile that caused melancholia.

Second, he referred to "demoniacs, or possessed persons" (p. 383), but the translator's (Adams's) choice of the term *demoniacs* here is open to some question. The words used in the Greek text,[19] the Greek word used in a number of Latin texts,[20] and the transliterated Greek words of some Latin texts[21] are all from the Greek term, ἔνθεος (entheos); this suggests that the translation might better have read "filled with a god," "possessed by a god," or "divinely inspired." From Dodds and others it is clear that divine possession and demonic possession were competing supernatural explanations in antiquity, the choice depending on whether the utterances were viewed as truly prophetic or not.[22] In this instance Paul used the terminology of divine possession rather than demonic possession, and yet his context and his comments suggest that he did not believe in the prophetic nature of such utterances. He seems to have been implying that such persons were suffering from delusions and to have been seeking a natural explanation for them, apparently suggesting that they were an aspect of the mental disturbances of some melancholics. Perhaps he was following Alexander of Tralles, who mentioned foretelling the future as a symptom in some melancholics with the implication that it was a delusion (*Oeuvres*, 2:223). He was certainly a long way from the Aristotelian view that true prophecy might be a gift in someone of a melancholic disposition.

ARABIC MEDICINE

As already indicated, Arabic medicine was an important part of the history of medieval medical thought, and melancholia the disease had its place among the mental disorders dealt with in the writings of Arabic medical authorities. Although there were variations from author to author, a schematized Galenism in the tradition of the Byzantine compilers served as the frame of reference for the Arabic physicians in considering disease in general, and melancholia in particular.

A particularly significant figure among Arabic medical writers on melancholia was Ishaq ibn Imran (fl. early tenth century), an Islamic physician from Baghdad. Among a number of other medical works, he wrote an important treatise on melancholia. After pointing out that the term *melancholy* denoted not the condition itself but rather the black bile that was its immediate cause, Ishaq defined this illness as "a certain feeling of dejection and isolation which forms in the soul because of something which the patients think is real but which is in fact unreal" (Ullman, *Islamic Medicine*, p. 72). He employed the traditional three types of melancholia in presenting his views: (1) the form that originated in the brain itself; (2) the form in which the black bile affected the whole body, spreading from the legs and eventually affecting the brain secondarily; and (3) the hypochondriacal form in which the brain was again affected secondarily (pp. 74–75).

As to clinical description, the following symptoms were characteristic of all three forms of melancholia. The patients were

> sunk in an irrational, constant sadness and dejection, in anxiety or brooding. For many, horrible pictures and forms pass before their eyes. For example, Diocles, when he was ill, saw negroes who wanted to kill him, as well as trumpeters and cymbal players who played in the corners of his room. One patient imagined that he had no head. Another's ears were ringing but this was his senses deceiving him. Yet another believed he was made of clay. A fourth disliked walking under the open sky because he thought that God, who holds the heavens, might get tired and let it fall to the ground. A characteristic symptom is for patients to demand to see a doctor urgently and to offer him all their money, and then when he comes, not to follow his advice. (p. 75)

In addition to these various psychological symptoms there were the somatic symptoms of "loss of weight and sleeplessness. Skin eruptions can also appear" (p. 75).

Ishaq extended his clinical outline to include additional, special symptoms associated with one of the three types. In "the sort that only occurs in the brain, are sleeplessness, headache, flickering eyes, burning hunger or, on the other hand, loss of appetite." In the second type, where the whole body was involved, there were "the same symptoms as the first, but in addition there may also be depressions, anxiety-feelings and terror." Then, in the hypochondriacal type, "there appears in particular a distended body and flatulence or a feeling of heaviness in the head. Many vomit an acid, black-bilious juice; others love solitude. Some have to weep a lot, because vapour pierces the brain. But sometimes it happens that the patients laugh a lot; in their case, the black bile is not so bad, rather their bodies possess plenty of good blood" (p. 75).

In explaining this disorder Ishaq reasoned in terms of the humoral theory, with the black bile as the basic cause and the disease as a somatic illness in which "a vapour rises from the black bile, and this presses forward to the seat of reason, dimming its light and confusing it, thus destroying the power of apprehension" (pp. 72–73). Melancholia could be innate or acquired. A person was "predisposed to melancholy if his temperament has already been injured prenatally as the result of the father's sperm having been damaged or if the mother's uterus was in a bad condition." Postnatal causes could be "immoderate eating and drinking," "neglect of the internal cleanliness of the body," or "disruption of the correct rhythms or measures of the six necessary basic presuppositions of living, namely, movement and rest, sleeping and waking, bowel evacuation and retention, eating and drinking, inhalation and exhalation and the soul's moods." As examples, "too much rest and sleep lead to an accumulation of waste matter in the body, which rots and turns into black bile"; or, "too much movement" could cause an increased heat with the result that "the moisture in the body is used up, producing vapours which become black bile." Further postnatal causes were "love of heavy foods which engender blood that is too hot or too dry and which quickly turns into black bile"; "living in places that are very hot and dry or cold and dry" or "a stay in marshy country and sultry regions"; "interruption of a habit, for example, of physical exercise or of regular cupping"; "drunkenness"; "asceticism, as, for example, that practised by philosophers who fast and remain awake all night." In these various cases "the blood is reduced; it becomes thick and turns into black bile." He added, however, that by itself "the excess of black bile produced by such errors does not produce melancholy. It becomes an illness only when the brain is weakened. But the weakness of the organ can come about as the result of too much heat or hypersensitivity. If both occur together, the organ attracts illness as the cupping-glass the blood" (p. 73).

Ishaq also stated that "melancholy may have purely psychical causes. Fears, annoyance, or anger, which appear in the 'animal soul,' can encourage melancholy. So the loss of a beloved child or of an irreplaceable library can release such sadness and dejection that melancholy is the result. In the 'rational soul' too, a similar process can occur; if doctors, mathematicians, or astronomers meditate, brood, memorize and investigate too much, they can fall prey to melancholy" (pp. 73–74). In fact, Ishaq brought psychical factors into a position of unusual prominence as causes of melancholia.

> The activities of the rational soul are strenuous thinking, remembering, studying, investigating, imagining, seeking the meaning of things, and fantasies and judgements, whether apt [founded on fact] or mere suspicions. And all these

conditions—which are partly permanent forces [mental faculties], partly accidental symptoms [passions]—can turn the soul within a short time to melancholy if it immerses itself too deeply in them. There are very many holy and
pious men who become melancholy owing to their great piety and from fear of
God's anger or owing to their great longing for God until this longing masters
and overpowers the soul; their whole feeling and thoughts are only of God, the
contemplation of God, His greatness and the example of His perfection. They
fall into melancholy as do lovers and voluptuaries, whereby the abilities of both
soul and body are harmed, since the one depends on the other. And all those will
fall into melancholy who overexert themselves in reading philosophical books, or
books on medicine and logic, or books which permit a view [theory] of all things;
as well as books on the origin of numbers, on the science which the Greeks call
arithmetic; on the origin of the heavenly spheres and the stars, that is, the science
of the stars, which the Greeks call astronomy; on geometry, which bears the
name "science of lines" among the Arabians, but which the Greeks call geometry; and finally the science of composition, namely of songs and notes, which
means the same as the Greek word "music." These sciences are products of the
soul, for the soul isolates and explores them; knowledge [recognition] of them is
innate to the soul, as Galen says, in recalling the philosopher Plato. . . . Such
men—Allah knows—assimilate melancholy . . . in the consciousness of their
intellectual weakness, and in their distress thereat they fall into melancholy. The
reason why their soul falls sick [disorders of the understanding and the memory,
and other disorders which affect the soul] lies in fatigue and overexertion, as
Hippocrates says in Book VI of the *Epidemics:* "Fatigue of the soul comes from
the soul's thinking." Just as bodily overexertion leads to severe illnesses of which
fatigue is the least, so does mental overexertion lead to severe illnesses of which
the worst is melancholy.[23]

Ishaq also mentioned "the possibility that the melancholic may become
an epileptic, an idea which appears in the *Epidemics* of Hippocrates (6:8, 31) and
which was accepted by all ancient doctors."[24]

Regarding treatment, the excess of black bile was to be dealt with by
various evacuants, with purgatives the most prominent. Moistening effects
against the dry nature of the black bile were sought through a careful choice of
food and drink. Massages with warm and moist ointments were prescribed for
this cold and dry disease. Moderate exercise was recommended. And much
thoughtful attention was given to psychological interventions, such as reassuring and gratifying measures to combat their suspicions, and pleasant and
diverting conversation to lift their spiritis. Music was also to be used to lift
their spirits, and mental exertion was to be avoided.[25]

In most of what he had to say about melancholia Ishaq seems to have
been following Galen to a significant extent. He referred with considerable
respect to Rufus's treatise on melancholia, and he was clearly drawing on
Rufus's views in many ways, although he mistakenly stated that Rufus dealt
only with the hypochondriacal type.[26] It is perhaps best to say that he followed
both Rufus and Galen fairly closely.

Ullmann has traced very similar views on melancholia in the work of Haly Abbas two generations later, noting some variations here and there that are clearly akin to one or another of the Byzantine compilers (pp. 77–78). Avicenna, in turn, followed Haly Abbas very closely in his presentation of melancholia. In summing up, Ullmann stated, "In this way, nearly all the ideas produced by Arab authors about melancholy go back to ancient sources" (p. 78).

LATER MEDIEVAL MEDICINE

As previously noted, Constantinus Africanus (1020?–1087) was a learned and well-traveled Muslim convert to Christianity who, originally from North Africa, eventually settled in Salerno and Monte Cassino and was a key figure in the translation of Greco-Arabic medical writings from Arabic into Latin. Among his translations was *De Melancholia*, taken from the Arabic of Ishaq ibn Imran, which was to be a significant influence on later medieval and Renaissance views of melancholia in the Latin West. Galen's thought on the subject was important for these later centuries, but the role of Rufus of Ephesus was perhaps the more crucial one—through his direct influence on Galen, through his general influence on various Arabic authors whose writings were part of the Greco-Arabic medical thought that gradually made its way into Latin, and through this just-cited transmission of his views via Ishaq and Constantinus. As with many of the works that appeared under his name, Constantinus's *De Melancholia* has a history of being thought of as his own work, of this coming to be doubted, and of having eventually been established as essentially a translation from an Arabic author.

As had long been customary, Constantinus emphasized the symptoms of fear and sadness. He stated that melancholia was an illness that produced gloomy ideas and caused the patient to fear imaginary things that he believed were quite real; and he noted that there were various suspicions which might affect the sufferer's soul and lead to fear and anguish.[27] In this latter regard, he followed Ishaq closely and cited Rufus in the process of mentioning a number of the familiar melancholic delusions (*Opera*, 1:287). He recognized the three traditional types of melancholia (that in which the whole body was affected, that in which the stomach and hypochondriacal region were affected primarily and the brain secondarily, and that in which the brain was affected primarily), but he attended mainly to the latter two (pp. 280, 284–286). He emphasized the significant connections between the mouth of the stomach and the brain and thus accounted for the ready effects of the hypochondriacal form on the brain. In each of these types it was ultimately the black bile that led to the various pathological effects, reaching the brain, affecting the seat of the intellect whose light it darkened, and thus corrupting the understanding to the point of preventing it from functioning as it ordinarily would (pp. 284–286). He also mentioned the vapors from the black bile that served to darken the mind and interfere with its functions (pp. 280–281). Other symptoms included sleeplessness, a tendency to favor solitude and dark places, and an inclination to avoid other people; and yet Constantinus noted that some melancholics showed opposite tendencies (pp. 287–288). His reference to "fear of things that were not frightening" seems remarkably akin to our modern notion of anxiety (p. 287). And, among the various serious possibilities that might befall someone suffering from melancholia, he stated that some cases changed into epilepsy—an observation dating back to the Hippocratic writings, as Constantinus observed (p. 289).

He indicated that there were a variety of causes which might lead to these pathogenic processes and symptoms. He mentioned that the temperament might be congenitally harmed, and so be predisposed to melancholia, by the corrupted nature of either the male sperm or the maternal menses. He then commented that the temperament might later, postnatally, be corrupted by a disturbed balance of any of the six non-naturals (p. 281). For example, insufficient exercise might lead to such a condition, as might the excessive ingestion of those foods and drinks that served to manufacture the melancholic humor and thicken the blood. Such persons were prone to fluctuating emotional states. Considerable attention to the activities of the mind tended to precipitate such illnesses; and those who excessively exerted themselves in philosophical and scientific studies were specially inclined to melancholia. Very religious persons were also particularly at risk due to their excessive desires toward God and their fear of God's anger (p. 283). Another source of the sadness of melancholia was often the loss of a loved one or of specially beloved possessions, such as a scholar's loss of his books (p. 284).

In his section on the treatment of melancholia, Constantinus emphasized the careful management of the six non-naturals in the direction of reestablishing a balanced state (pp. 290–298). The introduction of materials and activities associated with warm and moist characteristics was important in correcting this cold and dry disorder. Medications and diets were recommended in order to digest or dissolve the black bile. Various evacuative remedies were prescribed to relieve the patient of the corrupt material: specially purgatives, also sternutatives. Coitus was recommended as both evacuative and calming. Psychological measures were advocated to counter the patient's suspicions, to grant him satisfactions that were familiar to him, to soothe and calm him, and to divert and entertain him in the interest of lightening his mood.

AVICENNA

Another significant set of views on melancholia in the Latin West was provided by Avicenna (980–1037) in his *Canon of Medicine*. Originally translated from Arabic into Latin by Gerard of Cremona (1114–1187) in Toledo, with the translation later improved by Andrea Alpago (d. 1522), the *Canon* was a singularly influential medical work during the rest of the medieval era, through the Renaissance, and well into the seventeenth century. The *Canon's* chapters on melancholia were derived from Haly Abbas, who in turn had been strongly influenced by Ishaq ibn Imran on melancholia. Thus, as was the case with Constantinus Africanus, Avicenna's presentation of melancholia was ultimately derived from Rufus and Galen.

Avicenna defined melancholia as a deviation from the natural state accompanied by fear and a malignancy of the black bile, in which vapors from within rose to the brain and frightened the person with their gloominess, just as external darkness was frightening, and which was determined by a cold and dry temperament.* He observed that, when melancholia was associated with a tendency to anger, restlessness, and violence, it changed its character and was called *mania;* and he emphasized that melancholia designated only the condition that was caused by the non-adust black bile.

In outlining the signs of melancholia, Avicenna mentioned fear without cause, sadness, anguish, being prone to anger, and having a preference for solitude; palpitations, dizziness, ringing in the ears, discomfort in the hypochondria, and loss of appetite with much flatus; being firmly convinced of various frightening notions, putting the worst interpretation on things, and absurd talk. Various dreaded fancies or illusions occur, some with apparent causes but most such as would not be customarily feared, and these were endless in their varieties. Some believed that they had been turned into animals; some entertained delusional beliefs of a grandiose nature, such as being made a king; and some held notions such as being turned into demons or worms. Some would laugh, and others would weep, the latter being those affected by an unadulterated black bile. Some sought death, and others feared it.

In addition to the natural black bile, Avicenna postulated three different types of unnatural black bile derived from mixtures with the other three basic humors. Whereas the pure black bile led to much thoughtfulness and little agitation, except when provoked or given to a lasting hatred, the black bile mixed with blood led to gladness, laughter, and less sadness; mixed with

---

*Avicennae, *Liber Canonis De Medicinis* . . . , trans. Andreas Alpagus (Venetiis [Venice]: Junta, 1582), pp. 204–205 (translation from the Latin by Joan K. Jackson). Although Avicenna wrote earlier than Constantinus, his work was later than and derived from that of Ishaq ibn Imran, and his work appeared in Latin about a century after Constantinus had brought Ishaq's work into Latin. Accordingly, his views are being presented after the *De Melancholia* of Constantinus.

phlegm it led to sluggishness and listlessness; and mixed with yellow bile it led to turmoil and violence and was similar to mania.

Avicenna recognized the three traditional types of melancholia—that in which the primary site was in the brain, that in which the whole body was affected, and that which originated in the hypochondriacal region. He thought of it as a disorder basically caused by the black bile, with its effect being derived from its cold and dry nature. When the brain was the primary site, he commented that the black bile had the effect of darkening the brain and impairing the lucidity of the spirits. In the hypochondriacal type of melancholia, a disturbed process in one or other of the hypochondriacal organs led to smoky vapors that rose to the brain and caused a clouded and darkened atmosphere there. He thought that dietary excesses or food that produced black bile were often crucial causative factors. He acknowledged that some thought that demons sometimes caused melancholia, but he was not inclined to this explanation. Men were more frequently afflicted; women were more seriously affected when they were afflicted; and the condition was common with aged persons. Dark complexioned and hairy people were predisposed to this disorder.

Regarding treatment Avicenna favored the traditional pattern of evacuative remedies—purgatives, bloodletting, and emetics—with an eye to eliminating the excessive or the noxious humor.[28] Dietary considerations were stressed, with emphasis on nourishing foods and the avoidance of foods that produced black bile. Warm baths were recommended. Efforts were to be made to lighten the patient's mood and to divert and distract him with entertainment and occupation.

It was primarily on these two sources, Constantinus Africanus and Avicenna, that late medieval authors drew for their writings on melancholia. Thus the views of that era in the Latin West were significantly indebted, through these two important intermediaries, to the work of Ishaq ibn Imran on melancholia; and, as this latter was essentially presenting the thought of Rufus of Ephesus, those views were ultimately derived from Rufus. The most important leavening additions to Rufus's views came, through the contributions of the Byzantine compilers, from Galen; and Galen was respectful of and influenced by Rufus on the subject of melancholia. A fair summary statement would be that the medieval authors on melancholia ultimately left for their successors a heritage derived from Rufus and Galen.

Indicative of how widely these influences were diffused is the section on melancholia in *De Proprietatibus Rerum* by Bartholomaeus Anglicus. Two centuries after the flow of translations from the Arabic had begun with Constantinus Africanus, about the middle of the thirteenth century, Bartholomaeus completed this encyclopedia, which was representative of the views of his time and was widely used in several languages during the next three centuries. Citing Constantinus, he stated:

> Melancholy is the infection of the middle cell of the head, with privation of reason, as *Constant.* saith in *Libro de Melancolia. Melancholia* (saith he) is an infection that hath mastry of the soule, the which cometh of dread and of sorrow. And these passions be diverse after the diversity of the hurt of their workings: . . . reson is hurted. And these passions come sometime of melancholy meats, & sometime of drinke, of strong wine, that burneth the humours, & turneth them into ashes, sometime of passions of the soule, as of businesse and great thoughts, of sorrow, & of too great studie, & of dread: . . . sometime of the malice of a corrupt humour, that hath the mastry in the bodie of a man prepared to such sicknesse: and as the causes be diverse, the tokens and signes be divers. For some cry & leape, & hurt & wound themselves & other men, & darken & hide themselves in privy & secret places: . . . The medicine of them is, that they be bound, that they hurt not themselves and other men. And namely, such shall be refreshed & comforted, & withdrawn from cause & matter of dread & busie thoughts. And they must be gladded with instruments of musick, & some deale be occupied. And at the last, if purgations & electuaries suffice not, they shal be holpe with craft of Surgery.[29]

Physicians who addressed the subject of melancholia during these remaining medieval centuries and into the early Renaissance did so in much this same vein, but with somewhat more detail. Their accounts readily reflect their indebtedness to Rufus, Galen, Constantinus, and Avicenna, whether explicitly or implicitly, whether directly or through intermediaries.[30]

CHAPTER FOUR

Acedia the Sin and Its Relationship to Sorrow and Melancholia in Medieval Times

By the late fourth century A.D. the Christian church had come to use the term *acedia* to designate a constellation of feelings and behaviors that were considered unusual, undesirable, and indicative of a need for remedial attention.* In the words of John Cassian (ca. A.D. 360–435) it was a "weariness or distress of heart," "akin to dejection," and "especially trying to solitaries."[1]

The gradual development of acedia as a distinct condition and the beginnings of a systematic concern about it had their roots in the experiences of the Egyptian desert monks near Alexandria in the fourth century. The symptoms of this condition were intimately associated with the struggles of the anchorites against the hazards of isolation and the temptations of their own fleshly inclinations while they strove for spiritual perfection and oneness with God. Important among these early ascetics and a person of prime significance in the development of the notion of acedia was Evagrius Ponticus (A.D. 345–399). He was a direct influence on Cassian, whose description of acedia was diffused throughout the medieval Christian world and remained the main point of reference for many later considerations of the subject. Although somewhat transformed in its applications to the cenobitic life and eventually employed beyond the walls of the monasteries, acedia continued as a familiar notion throughout the medieval era.

---

*The Latin *acedia* was the transliteration of the Greek ἀχηδια meaning heedlessness, sluggishness, torpor, literally non-caring-state. *Accidia* became the accepted term in the later Middle Ages. *Accedia* and *acidia* also occurred. In English, spelling has ranged from the *accidie* and *accydye* of Chaucer to the later *acedy*, still recognized but obsolete, and the *acedia* of modern historical writings on the subject.

Some modern authors have viewed acedia as little more than a medieval term for what we would call depressive states or as a synonym for melancholia in its own time. Others have thought of it as merely a term for sloth or laziness. These are clearly misleading simplifications. This troublesome state was not merely dejection or sorrow. Nevertheless, from its beginnings it was associated with *tristitia* (dejection, sadness, sorrow), and this connection continued; there were frequent references to *desperatio* (despair) in writings about acedia; and it was intermittently brought into association with *melancholia* in the late Middle Ages. Similarly, despite having come to be referred to as "the sin of sloth" in the later medieval period and subsequently, acedia was not merely sloth. Nevertheless, lassitude, weariness, inaction, carelessness, and neglect were all aspects of acedia to varying degrees in various instances.

Viewed another way, this unusual mental state and its associated behaviors were both troublesome and common enough to receive considerable attention in medieval times. As in other times and places, there were a number of ways to deal with unusual mental states and their associated behaviors.* In the case of acedia it was mainly religious beliefs and, to a lesser extent, medicine that a society used in attempting to explain and ameliorate the condition. Thus the history of acedia was intimately connected with changes in Christianity and medicine.

The scattered uses of the term *acedia* in extant writings from before the time of Evagrius indicate the following meanings: carelessness, weariness, exhaustion, apathy, anguish, sadness, low spirits, and sloth or negligence from excessive attention to worldly matters.[2] Evagrius used as his frame of reference the eight main temptations or evil thoughts against which the monk had to fight; these were akin to the sometimes eight, sometimes seven, cardinal sins of later Christendom. In this scheme his description of acedia was much more comprehensive and systematic than those of his predecessors. The condition was characterized by exhaustion, listlessness, sadness or dejection, restlessness, aversion to the cell and the ascetic life, and yearning for family and former life.[3]

With the work and writings of Cassian, directly influenced by Evagrius, the concept of acedia was effectively transmitted to the West in a context of the eight chief vices. In Cassian's *Institutes of the Coenobia*, book X is entitled "Of the Spirit of Accidie," and there he describes the condition as follows:

---

*Acedia is thought of here as an "unusual mental state," a generic term for a variety of conditions. In medieval times some of the commoner unusual mental states were conceived of as syndromes of mental disorder within the medical system. Others were conceived of within the Christian framework as atypical "states of the soul." Of those conceived of in the Church's terms, some—e.g., ecstatic states and mystical states—were often thought to be blessings rather than afflictions and were often honored rather than treated; others—e.g., acedia and tristitia—were considered sinful afflictions and in need of corrective measures.

Our sixth combat is with . . . [acedia], which we may term weariness or distress of heart. This is akin to dejection, and is especially trying to solitaries, and a dangerous and frequent foe to dwellers in the desert; and especially disturbing to a monk about the sixth hour, like some fever which seizes him at stated times, bringing the burning heat of its attacks on the sick man at usual and regular hours. Lastly, there are some of the elders who declare that this is "the midday demon" spoken of in the ninetieth Psalm. . . . It produces dislike of the place, disgust with the cell, and disdain and contempt of the brethren. . . . It also makes the man lazy and sluggish about all manner of work which has to be done within the enclosure of his dormitory.[4]

The afflicted monk became restless; he complained that his situation was no longer spiritually fruitful and that he was useless in it; and he thought that he would never be well unless he left the place. In his continuing restlessness, time seemed to pass very slowly; he yearned for company; and he considered seeking solace in sleep. In short, he tended either to remain idle in his cell or to wander from it in restless pursuit of diversionary activities, in either case to no spiritual end (Cassian, *Twelve Books*, 11:267–268).

In keeping with some previous references to "this disease" (ibid.), when he took up the question of a remedy Cassian approached it in terms of a sustained medical metaphor. He referred to St. Paul as being "like a skillful and excellent physician," and his advice as "the healing medicines of his directions" for the treatment of "this disease, which springs from the spirit of accidie" (p. 268). Cassian consistently urged manual labor as a remedial measure, again using St. Paul as his authority. While at first describing a gentle, soothing approach, when he discussed afflicted persons who were unresponsive or rebellious, he urged a much sterner approach, including such measures as brethren of the afflicted withdrawing from him and avoiding him. Throughout these passages there are injunctions against idleness and an emphasis on work (pp. 268–275).

Another significant feature of early accounts of acedia is related to the use of demons in the Christian system of explanation. For the desert fathers, the struggle with their own inclinations had frequently come to be viewed as a struggle with demons that came from outside to tempt them. Following a tradition with Stoic origins, they strove for an inner peace against their own inclinations toward passions. With the stirring of the passions, disturbing thoughts might arise and interfere with this inner peace. So these ascetics frequently turned to the notion of demons playing upon their passions to stir up evil or disturbing thoughts. Such thoughts became the demons' tools or weapons for tempting the person to consent to sin. In the writings of Evagrius the language of demons and evil spirits came into more systematic use with regard to the various temptations to sin, among which he included acedia. Acedia was an evil spirit; the demon of acedia, or "noonday demon," attacked the ascetic or tempted him. Sometimes acedia meant the demon, and sometimes it meant the evil thought that the demon provoked the ascetic to entertain. In these terms, as demon *and* evil thought, acedia was one of the eight main temptations.[5]

Cassian left acedia established as a troublesome condition within the context of the Christian scheme of eight principal faults or chief vices. For many centuries thereafter the chief vices or cardinal sins, eight or seven in number, constituted the basic frame of reference for the continuing history of acedia. Cassian had recognized eight chief vices—gluttony, fornication, covetousness, anger, dejection, accidie, vainglory, and pride. Gregory the Great (ca. A.D. 540–604), however, altered the composition of the list of cardinal sins and reduced the number to seven—vainglory, anger, envy, dejection, covetousness, gluttony, fornication. Although he dropped pride from the list, in a sense he retained it by setting it apart as the root of all the other sins. He added envy and he dropped acedia, although apparently for him dejection had come to subsume both conditions. Certainly his descriptions of the latter included several elements that were commonly associated with acedia; and these vices shared a good many symptoms with the Evagrian and Cassianic descriptions. "Such effects as dejection and sorrow, absence of the wonted elation in spiritual exercises, impatience in work and devotion, wrath against the brethren, and despair of ever reaching one's spiritual goals, are all common to both *tristitia* and *acedia*.[6]

During the next several centuries, both the Gregorian list and the Cassianic list were in frequent use, but with the former tending to predominate. Whether a list included tristitia or acedia, the sin listed was often described in a way that could subsume both. Gradually Gregory's total of seven became the accepted number, and pride and vainglory were merged, with pride as the surviving term. Further, by the twelfth century, Gregory's tristitia had been replaced by Cassian's acedia, at times cited as "acedia or tristitia."[7]

Another important point to note in the relationship of acedia to tristitia stemmed from the distinction made by Saint Paul and by various ascetic authors between a positive and a negative kind of tristitia, the former leading to penance and salvation, the latter to death.[8] Cassian had characterized the "wholesome sorrow" as stemming from "penitence for sin" or "desire for perfection," whereas the more objectionable sorrow resulted from worldly frustration and distress.[9] Over the centuries, this positive sorrow appeared in the lists of cardinal sins within the notion of tristitia, but gradually it disappeared along with the term *tristitia* itself. On the other hand, the negative sorrow, the dejection about worldly matters, continued to be associated with the sin of acedia.

Through the eleventh century, writers on acedia tended to emphasize the physical phenomena of idleness and somnolence, whereas, in the twelfth century, they "laid greater stress on its inner phenomena of . . . spiritual slackness, weariness and boredom with religious exercises, lack of fervor, and a state of depression in the ups and downs of spiritual life."[10] That is, there had been a shift in emphasis from mode of behavior to state of mind, a shift more in keeping with the original perspective of the desert monks and Cassian. Also of note is the more benevolent view of acedia manifested by some medieval writers who recognized how natural it was for someone's attention to slacken and for him to have difficulty in continuing at the same activity for a prolonged period of time.[11]

Although from the time of Cassian to the spiritual treatises of the twelfth century acedia was largely an affliction of monks and contemplatives, in conjunction with the whole system of cardinal sins the concept gradually became part of the moral life of all Christians. Various lists of sins, commonly the cardinal sins, were used by priests as guidelines for the ritual of confession. Such lists became the basis for numerous penitentials, or handbooks of penance, that served confessors as systematic keys to the questions to ask the penitent and to the various penances to impose. When confession was made obligatory by the Fourth Lateran Council (1215–1216) and the requirement was instituted that clergy should preach regularly to their parishioners, there was an extensive production of penitential literature, manuals for preachers, and catechetical handbooks in the period 1200 to 1450. This meant that knowledge of the cardinal sins spread among the general population, and the notion of acedia was a crucial part of this knowledge.[12]

Acedia's designation as a cardinal sin meant that there were moral injunctions against it. However, the penitentials clearly reveal an additional perspective of a more benevolent nature on this sin. While they often chastised different aspects of acedia, the handbooks frequently implied that confession was a form of healing and the sins of the penitent were afflictions for which he was to be treated and cured. This theme can be traced back through the various penitential writings, and it probably reflects some influence from the sustained use of a medical metaphor by Cassian, whose works were so influential in other ways.[13] This literature frequently involved "the conception of penance as medicine for the soul," with the medical principle of contraries curing contraries as the commonest governing notion.[14] The processes of penance were conceived of

> as constituting a treatment in itself effective toward the recovery of the health that has been lost through sin. . . . The authors of these handbooks . . . had a sympathetic knowledge of human nature and a desire to deliver men and women from the mental obsessions and social maladjustments caused by their mis-

deeds. . . . "Not all are to be weighed in the same balance, although they be associated in one fault" but there must be discrimination according to cases. The physician of souls must . . . identify himself as far as possible with the patient. . . . [Despite a severity of prescription at times] the penitentials often reveal the considerateness of the experienced adviser of souls, wise in the lore of human nature and desiring to "minister to the mind diseased."[15]

The tradition of the pastor/confessor as "physician of souls" can be traced back further still[16] and probably has roots in the idea of Christ as healer and in the notion of philosophers as "physicians of the soul."[17] Perhaps too the medical knowledge of the early Church Fathers and their commitment to ministering to the sick might have been a factor.[18]

With the flowering of Scholasticism, the sustained efforts at a systematic analysis of matters of faith included a considerably greater attention to acedia in the strictly theological literature (Wenzel, *Sin of Sloth*, pp. 47–67). In the process, acedia, while continuing to be conceived of as a sin, became integrated into theories of the passions and emerged as a disorder in man's emotional life. At times, it came to be thought of in medical terms.

For Saint Thomas Aquinas (1225?–1274), the traditional seven vices derived from the interaction of the will with the world of its objects. That is, "objects move the appetite, the appetite responds in a certain way, certain kinds of responses are capable of leading to moral evil, or sin, if consented to" by the will (Wenzel, p. 45). In this framework, acedia arose out of the will's shrinking from some good because the concupiscible desires were perverted, either by an inappetence for or an aversion to the spiritual good.

In a usage not to be confused with its place in any system of sins, the term *tristitia* also referred to one of a small number of basic passions within a system of passions that took shape as part of Scholastic psychology. Tristitia and gaudium (sorrow and joy: compare pain and pleasure) were paired as opposites to which many other feelings could be reduced. Tristitia was the basic reaction of man's sensitive nature in withdrawing from an evil, whether present or anticipated, real or imagined. Within this generic use of *tristitia*, Thomas's fundamental definition of *acedia* as species was "*tristitia de spirituali bono:* the sorrow about, or the aversion man feels against, his spiritual good. 'Sorrow' is here understood as the negative reaction of man's sensitive appetite to an object which is either truly evil, or evil only in appearance but good in reality. The latter reaction constitutes *acedia* properly speaking" (p. 48). From the early twelfth century on, accounts of acedia increasingly emphasized some form of sadness or grief. Eventually acedia conceived as a severe or "depressing sorrow" became a significant use of this term, and one shared by Thomas. Finally, it came to be viewed as a species of tristitia the passion *and* as the sin that subsumed dejection or sorrow in the scheme of cardinal sins.

In acquiring this connection with the passions, acedia began to be described occasionally in physiological terms. The passions were conceived of as varying in strength and in combination with the various temperaments or constitutions of individuals, so some persons were thought to be more disposed to acedia than others. Many Scholastic writers considered some instances of acedia to be derived from an imbalance of the humors, thus making it a disease or the outcome of a disease. At times, this involved the notion of a temperamental disposition to the condition. Scattered passages in their writings indicate that it was sometimes associated with "the cold and moist disposition" (the humor, phlegm, and the phlegmatic temperament) and sometimes with "the melancholy humor" (the black bile and the melancholic temperament) (Wenzel, pp. 59, 191–194). The presence of such a natural cause tended to lessen the sinfulness of the vice in the eyes of these authors; it resulted more from disease than moral failing. This view could lead to some modification of the usual rigorous remedial advice in favor of suggesting relaxation in the sufferer's way of life. Some suggested that the afflicted could be helped by listening to music, although this led to the qualification that such matters should be left to physicians.

The spiritual authors of the twelfth century and the Scholastics of the thirteenth century had tended to emphasize the state of mind in acedia (weariness, disgust, lack of fervor, sorrow), but, influenced by the increased activity of confessors and preachers, the common man's image of acedia came to center on spiritual idleness or neglect in the performance of spiritual duties. During this period the standard English term for the sin became *sloth* (or similar terms from the adjective *slow*), and similar changes occurred in other vernacular languages (Wenzel, p. 89). With this shift of emphasis to idleness and negligence, *busyness* emerged as a significant antidotal virtue in addition to the traditional pair of fortitude and spiritual joy. Also, by the late Middle Ages, this sin sometimes came to include many rather worldly faults of neglect or dereliction. There were indications that it sometimes meant "neglect of the obligations of one's *status* or profession," and it became intimately associated with the notion that the obligation to work was an essential element of man's nature, with the result for many that the sin included the simple failure to work that might lead to poverty (p. 91). Nevertheless the predominant popular view of the sin of sloth still remained that of sloth in one's service to God.

In the numerous literary works that portrayed acedia in the late medieval period, the condition took one of the various forms already outlined. Many have cited Chaucer's views in *The Parson's Tale*, where the condition was presented as stemming from bitterness, being associated with heaviness, moodiness, and anger, and involving neglect of spiritual and worldly duties, idleness, tardiness, sorrow, and despair.[19] Also well-known is Petrarch's view of acedia, in which the emphasis was on grief, sorrow, and dejection. While his account may be said to deal with a somewhat secularized version of the condition, it clearly represents one aspect of acedia's traditional meanings. He placed it in a historical tradition dating back to the *aegritudo* (grief, sorrow) of classical times.[20]

As we have seen, acedia clearly did not mean merely sloth or merely sorrow and dejection, although some have tried to portray it as such. Both sorrow-dejection-despair and neglect-idleness-indolence were important themes in the earliest accounts of this condition, and each recurred in varying combinations with the others in descriptions of acedia throughout the Middle Ages. Rather than which description was truly characteristic of acedia, the question is more one of how these apparently disparate features might be integrated. One solution to this problem is to view them as different types of acedia, as David of Augsburg did in the thirteenth century.

> The vice of *accidia* has three kinds. The first is a certain bitterness of the mind which cannot be pleased by anything cheerful or wholesome. It feeds upon disgust and loathes human intercourse. This is what the Apostle calls the sorrow of the world that worketh death. It inclines to despair, diffidence, and suspicions, and sometimes drives its victim to suicide when he is oppressed by unreasonable grief. Such sorrow arises sometimes from previous impatience, sometimes from the fact that one's desire for some object has been delayed or frustrated, and sometimes from the abundance of melancholic humors, in which case it behooves the physician rather than the priest to prescribe a remedy.
>
> The second kind is a certain indolent torpor which loves sleep and all comforts of the body, abhors hardships, flees from whatever is hard, droops in the presence of work, and takes its delight in idleness. This is laziness *(pigritia)* proper.
>
> The third kind is a weariness in such things only as belong to God, while in other occupations its victim is active and in high spirits. The person who suffers from it prays without devotion. He shuns the praise of God whenever he can do so with caution and dares to; he hastens to rush through the prayers he is obliged to say and thinks of other things so that he may not be too much bored by prayer.[21]

Another way of reconciling the two main themes would be to think of them as both present as potentially observable parts of a whole condition, but with different observers emphasizing one part or the other. Thus sorrow or dejection could be viewed as the state of mind and the slothful behavior as the external manifestation. Whereas traditionally acedia had implied just such a combination of inner state and mode of behavior, through the eleventh century there had been a trend toward more emphasis on the physical phenomenon of idleness and drowsiness. During the following century, however, spiritual authors laid more stress on the inner phenomenon of spiritual slackness, weariness and boredom with religious exercises, and a dejected state of mind.[22] The Scholastic contributions of the thirteenth century tended to confirm this "interiorization," and acedia came to be viewed as a severe or depressing sorrow. In contrast, the popular views of the later Middle Ages often focused more on external behavior and cited the person's idleness or sloth. It has been suggested that this shift in emphasis toward external behavior was related to the "practical" concerns of both the clergy and their flocks, that is, their preoccupation with sinfulness in general, its assessment in confession, and penance. In short, acedia may well have been a single, although complex, condition that was vulnerable to a distorting emphasis on one or another of its facets, depending on the social context and the purposes of the observer.

At first acedia was one of several unusual mental states and associated behaviors that tended to occur in the lives of the early desert monks. Then, through the earlier medieval centuries, these conditions came to affect those in both the anchoritic and the cenobitic life. So, in these early phases, acedia was the term for a condition experienced by some members of a restricted group, the Christian ascetics. Whereas today we might wonder about the impact of isolation on the anchorites and about the effects of the loss of customary human relationships and usual social comforts on both anchorites and cenobites, at the time the affected persons were judged as suffering from a troublesome state of the soul as the result of sin or as committing a sin by allowing their soul to be in such a state. In those early centuries there seems to have been little or no tendency to approach the afflicted in any terms other than religious ones. In the later medieval period, the use of the notion of acedia was extended to Christians in general. It seems to have been only then that medical ideas came to be of some significance for this condition.

By the late Middle Ages, it was accepted that a broad range of both members of the clergy and lay persons might experience dejected states and be thought of and dealt with as suffering from acedia the sin. To say this, however, only begins to address the complexities of the relationship of acedia to states of sorrow and dejection. While dejection was an element of acedia from its beginnings, it was also the central feature of tristitia, another of the chief vices or, later, cardinal sins. Thus, for a religious in the earlier medieval period, a state of sadness might be conceived of as a sin in either of two different forms—as tristitia or, if there were significant elements of neglect or physical inaction, as acedia. As already remarked, these two notions were gradually merged, first under the rubric of tristitia and then of acedia. This development seems to have further accentuated the place of sorrow-dejection-despair in the complex condition referred to as acedia in the later medieval era.

Further, as tristitia faded from the list of sins, so too did the positive sorrow that arose from remorse for one's sins and that led to penance and salvation. But the negative sorrow, or dejection about worldly matters, continued to be viewed as a sin and to evolve within the notion of acedia. Tristitia, as this positive sorrow, became more identified with the Christian tradition of the sufferer as an object for care, concern, and cure; and the negative sorrow was associated with the idea of the afflicted person as an object to be moralized against.

Another important issue to consider is the relationship of acedia to the medical explanation of the illness known as melancholia. Throughout the medieval era the term *melancholia* referred to the traditional Galenic picture of a condition in which the sufferer was fearful, sad, misanthropic, suspicious, tired of life, and often, but not always, afflicted with one of a number of circumscribed delusions. Thus the sorrow-dejection-despair aspect of acedia the sin shared some common ground with melancholia the disease. Nevertheless, cases of acedia did not tend to include delusions, in contrast to what was often the case in conditions diagnosed as melancholia; and therefore it was usually fairly clear whether a dejected state might be diagnosed as melancholia or conceived of as acedia. Yet there was some tendency for the more seriously dejected, but not deranged, states of that era to be included under melancholia, while at the same time acedia clearly included instances of severe dejection to the point of despair, and even suicide, without reference being made to melancholia. Therefore, some dejected states may have posed somewhat of a problem in "differential diagnosis" between the two explanatory systems.*

At least in later medieval times, some religious authors assessed some conditions as cases of acedia *and* brought them into frank connection with the system of mental disorders in a medical framework, so there was a tendency to consider their treatment as the province of physicians. In such contexts, the associations of acedia with being phlegmatic certainly suggest the condition's traditional idleness;† and its associations with being melancholic similarly suggest its commonly noted inner state of dejection.

Also of interest are the indications that the medical frame of reference

---

*A further separate, and yet difficult to distinguish, theme was that of despair: Susan Snyder, "The left hand of God: Despair in medieval and renaissance tradition," *Stud. Renaissance*, 1965, *12:* 18–59. Deriving from *tristitia saeculi*, the negative sorrow of Saint Paul that works death, despair was often the translation of *tristitia*, but also it was often the translation of *desperatio* found at times in accounts of tristitia and at other times in accounts of acedia.

†One author has argued that acedia was strictly a phlegmatic condition. See Noel L. Brann, "Is acedia melancholy? A re-examination of this question in the light of Fra Battista da Crema's Della cognitione et vittoria di se stesso (1531)," *J. Hist. Med.*, 1979, *34:* 180–199. I find Brann's argument unconvincing. He seems to be speaking from the context of a sixteenth-century argument that had little application to the medieval period, a controversy from a period when some could argue that acedia was merely melancholia and others would argue that melancholia was too fine a thing to be equated with acedia the sin. To my already stated view that acedia was not merely melancholy, I would add only that acedia was not merely lethargy.

implied a lesser degree of sinfulness and reduced responsibility, thus at times allowing the person suffering from acedia to be judged less harshly. During the medieval era a dejected person dealt with in medical terms was likely to have met with concern for his distress and to have been ministered to in a relatively compassionate way, but, if such a person was dealt with in religious terms as being afflicted with acedia, the tendency was toward a harsher approach. Yet one cannot attribute this solely to a religious approach as it was religious authorities who, in the later medieval period, introduced the medical perspective for some instances of acedia and thereby found the afflicted less culpable. Furthermore, earlier Christian functionaries had sometimes approached the sinner in religious terms with an emphasis on concern for the person's distress and on the introduction of measures to make him feel better. McNeill has brought this out in his studies of the penitential literature, though the extent to which a medical metaphor was used for expressing this attitude and its accompanying "prescriptions" is significant.[23] Thus, while a more benevolent approach was by no means restricted to a particular set of social functionaries, it does seem that it was more readily integrated with a healing outlook. To place all this in perspective, one needs to take note of the fact that over the centuries there have been many troublesome mental conditions for which the afflicted person might be moralized against with an outcome of judgment and punishment or might meet an empathic concern with an outcome of care or cure. Ultimately, a focus on outward manifestations was more likely to have been associated with moralizing against, while a focus on the unusual mental state of the distressed person was more likely to have been associated with empathic concern. So, rather than one's social role or one's frame of reference determining whether one approached the sufferer with judgmental harshness or healing concern, the aspect of the troubled person's condition to which one was most sensitive may have been more critical.

With the Renaissance there were to be further important changes in acedia and in its relationship to melancholia. This era saw a weakening of the powerful central position held by the Christian church and an associated loss of its integrative influence in the explanation of human behavior. The increased interest in classical authorities, the trends toward more secularized thought, and the splintering effects of emerging Protestantism were all factors in this gradual change. In the process the cardinal sins became less significant, and the notion of acedia gradually lost the prominent place it had held in the scheme of sins; the neglect-idleness-indolence aspect became more and more the focus; and the trend toward the use of sloth and related terms became more predominant. Although the surviving notion of the sin of sloth never totally lost its association with some element of sadness, to a significant degree the sorrow-dejection-despair aspect became associated with other terms.

Gradually this latter aspect of acedia seems to have become interwoven with trends in both terminology and meaning associated with melancholia. The Latin *melancholia* was often translated as melancholia in English, but increasingly it was also translated as melancholy or other, nearly identical terms in other vernacular languages. During the sixteenth century melancholia/melancholy continued to refer to the mental disorder in a medical context, but the terms were also used to mean the black bile or to denote the person of melancholic temperament, *and*, more loosely, they were often used to refer to almost any state of sorrow, sadness, grief, dejection, or despair. To complicate matters further, tristitia in particular, but also other related Latin terms, came to be frequently translated as melancholia/melancholy.* Over time the tendency seems to have been for melancholia to come once again to be restricted to denoting the illness, while melancholy remained both a synonym for melancholia and a popular term used with a breadth and diffuseness not unlike our use of the term depression today. Many states of dejection that might have been conceived of as acedia during the medieval centuries came to be viewed as melancholy, occasionally in the sense of a medical condition but more frequently in the sense of an unhappy, sad, or grief-stricken condition without significant clinical implications.

A further indication of the continuity between the sorrow-dejection-despair aspect of acedia and the melancholy of the sixteenth century is to be found in the world of pictorial representation. In the shift from the religious to a more secular outlook, the conventional illustrations of the cardinal sins were gradually appropriated to depict the four temperaments or characters as derived from humoral theory. As part of this process in the sixteenth century, images that had traditionally portrayed acedia came to be used to portray melancholy.[24]

In subsequent centuries acedia received much less attention in the Western world as a distinct condition, and sloth became the usual denotation of the sin when it was mentioned.† Further, sloth acquired a certain life of its

---

*Twentieth-century translators have further complicated the modern perspective on relevant late medieval literature by their use of "melancholy" when it was frequently "tristitia" in the original, but rarely, if ever, "melancholia." See, e.g., Caesarius of Heisterbach (1220–1235), *The Dialogue of Miracles*, trans. H. von E. Scott and C. C. Swinton Bland with intro. by G. G. Coulton, 2 vols. (London: George Routledge & Sons, 1929), and [Petrarch], *Petrarch's Secret*.

†The condition was occasionally taken serious note of in more recent centuries under its original name, as Paget indicated in his interesting essay "Concerning Accidie," in which he did the same. See Francis Paget, *The Spirit of Discipline* (London: Longmans, Green, 1902), pp. 1–50. Tuke gave it the status of a syndrome in psychological medicine as "acedia" in D. Hack Tuke, *A Dictionary of Psychological Medicine*, 2 vols. (Philadelphia: P. Blakiston, 1892), 1:51. In the twentieth century Connell termed it "accidie" in his unpublished Ph.D. dissertation: M. A. Connell, "A Study of Accidie and Some of Its Literary Phases" (Cornell University, 1932). But *sloth* has been the common term in the goodly number of volumes entitled "The Seven Deadly Sins."

own in postmedieval religious and secular writings. The emerging Protestant concerns about the importance of work meant that idleness became a danger to be guarded against.[25] Also, urban leaders faced with the problem of growing masses of able-bodied poor made strenuous efforts to contain idle persons who were conceived of as culpable by their inactivity.[26] Sloth came more and more to mean a reprehensible idleness that was preached against by lay and religious leaders alike, usually with no indication of attention to the presence or absence of dejection in the persons under criticism. The neglect-idleness-indolence aspect of acedia seemed to have acquired a history of its own.

The sorrow-dejection-despair aspect of acedia seems to have merged into the sometimes mild, sometimes severe forms of dejected distress that were short of madness. Such troublesome conditions often had as much to do with popular notions of melancholy—from efflorescences such as that in the Elizabethan drama to the Romantic melancholy, ennui, and Weltschmerz of the early nineteenth century—as with the traditional picture of melancholia the disease. But, at other times, such conditions would be thought of as instances of melancholia the disease, although they may not seem to be instances of madness to us. Finally, there was the age-old tradition of sorrow and grief to which the dejected aspects of acedia long seemed to have some relation and into which at times they tended to merge. More than a few instances of what would have been acedia in medieval times would be conceived of in this continuing tradition in more recent centuries.

CHAPTER FIVE

Melancholia in the Renaissance

The use of *renaissance* here does not reflect any particular position on just what time period is covered by this term or on just what its meaning should be. Although variously used in general history to cover a range of periods from 1300–1600 to 1475–1610, in the history of medicine the term has been associated more with the sixteenth century and the early decades of the seventeenth century. Various authorities have suggested important influences on the medicine of the era stemming from the spread of Greek scholars and the knowledge of original Greek medical texts across Europe following the fall of Constantinople to the Turks in 1453, from the diffusion of medical information and opinion in the wake of the developments in printing around the middle of the fifteenth century, from a zeitgeist associated with Lutheran protestations, and from the outpouring of "humanistic" contributions in art, literature, and philosophy usually associated with the Renaissance. Whatever may have been the case in these regards, the sixteenth century and the early decades of the seventeenth century constitute the era of such significant contributions to the physical sciences as those of Copernicus, Galileo, and Gilbert. And in medicine this was the era of the crucial additions to anatomical knowledge provided by Vesalius and his successors, along with their implicit and explicit challenges to Galen's authority in anatomy; of the crucial contributions to physiological knowledge provided by Harvey and his predecessors, along with the undermining of Galen's authority in physiology; of the challenges of Paracelsus and his successors to Galenic medicine and therapeutics; of the beginnings of medical chemistry; of Paré's contributions to surgery; and of the emergence of bedside teaching in medicine.

The transition from the Middle Ages to the Renaissance, however one

conceives of it and whatever dates one assigns to it, did not bring any significant change in how melancholia was described, explained, or treated. Common knowledge of this disease was well represented by the account of it in *De
Proprietatibus Rerum* by Bartholomaeus Anglicus, and this continued to be the
case well into the sixteenth century. Medical writings on the subject were
essentially more elaborated versions of the same, reflecting their ultimate
indebtedness to Rufus of Ephesus and Galen of Pergamon and their more
immediate sources such as Avicenna and Constantinus Africanus.

The sixteenth century began with medicine essentially Galenic in its
basic theories and its practical applications. Although the sixteenth and seventeenth centuries involved a series of challenges to Galenic medicine that did
harm to much of its structure, from Vesalius's *Fabrica* in 1543 to Harvey's *De
Motu Cordis* in 1628, the Galenic edifice gave way only slowly. Despite
challenges to Galenic theory and therapeutics such as those provided by
Paracelsus, the Galenic orientation prevailed through the sixteenth century
and, for many, through much of the seventeenth century. Iatrochemical
notions were offered to the medical world by Paracelsus in the first half of the
sixteenth century, but they had little effect on how melancholia was conceived
until the last half of the seventeenth century. Mechanical notions were shown
by Harvey in 1628 to be crucial to the understanding of physiology, but it was
close to the end of the century before they had any significant effect on
conceptions of melancholia. In spite of all the changes occurring in medicine
during this renaissance era, it remained remarkably Galenic until well into the
seventeenth century. Although there is rich meaning in the idea of the Renaissance for medicine and although the metaphor of revolution (as in Scientific
Revolution) is meaningful for the medicine of the sixteenth and seventeenth
centuries, one might say with equal confidence that those centuries saw the
slow decline and fall of Galenic medicine.

PARACELSUS

Theophrastus Bombastus von Hohenheim (1493–1541), called Paracelsus,
took note of melancholia in "The Diseases that Deprive Man of his Reason," a
volume apparently written in the 1520s, although not published until 1567.
But he gave this disorder only passing attention. Noting that *Melancholici* were
one of the "four kinds of insane people," he stated that they were "those who
by their nature lose their reason and turn insane."[1] Indicating that details
about the melancholic type of insanity would "remain unmentioned as there
exists a great body of philosophy and contemplation" on its nature, he observed that there were four kinds of melancholy persons and added that, "if
such complexions deprive man of his reason, it is due to their driving the

spiritus vitae up toward the brain so that there is too much of it there" ("Diseases," p. 157). In discussing the treatment of such disorders, he commented that "the *melancholici* . . . are disturbed by their own nature—there is no apparent defect of reason; their complexes are affected and they suppress reason, ruling it as they wish" (p. 179). He then went on to say:

> There are two questions to be considered in the cure of melancholy. First, from what complex it originated, and second, how it can be expelled. They can be understood as follows: if it is melancholy, then one should apply *contraria*. If the melancholic patient is despondent, make him well again by a gay medicine. If he laughs too much, make him well by a sad medicine. There are some medicines which make people laugh and make their minds happy, removing all diseases which have their origin in sadness. This is not incidental, not just laughter in sadness: the entire sadness is removed. There are also medicines which induce sadness, in such a way that they soothe unseemly laughter and exaggerated, unsuitable pleasure by changing it. Thus, the reason is set free and the memory is completely normal. In this treatment it must be remembered that this medicine can be made from quintessence alone, which has such tempering qualities that it leads nature back to the right course. The following medicines should be known, as they serve against melancholic disease and expel all sadness, or free reason from sadness: *aurum potabile, croci magisterium, arbor maris, ambra acuata, letitia veneris.* (pp. 179–180)

He noted that "there are four kinds of melancholy, originating from the four complexions" but that "there is no need to mention specific medicines for each separate complexion." Despite their differences, "*sanguis* and *cholera*" were much alike, each being "accompanied by joy," and so the same remedies could be used for both. Similarly, "the other two complexions, phlegm and melancholy, behave the same way" and so could be treated with the same remedies (p. 180).

In another context, Paracelsus had written of the four traditional temperaments or complexions: choleric, sanguine, melancholic, and phlegmatic; and he had associated them with four basic tastes: bitterness, saltiness, sourness, and sweetness, respectively. He rejected the humoral theory and associated the melancholic temperament with acidity and sourness: "sourness makes a melancholic"; but he retained the traditional association of the melancholic nature with the qualities of "cold and dry" that he correlated with sourness.[2]

Although, as Mora has effectively outlined, there is much in Paracelsus's writings that bears on the topic of mental disorders and their treatment, it is not clear that he had any significant impact on the care of the mentally ill in his time.[3] Nevertheless, it is noteworthy that, in his preface to *The Diseases That Deprive Man of His Reason*, Paracelsus reflected the inclination of the clergy of his day to attribute such diseases to supernatural causes, and he made a point of disagreeing with them.[4] His references to melancholia were few and limited in

their nature, but his challenges to Galenic medicine were to have later reper-
cussions for this disease. His rejection of humoral theory was the beginning of
a trend that would greatly affect explanations of melancholia in the following
century, and his influence on the iatrochemists of the seventeenth century
would eventually affect therapeutic styles.

THOMAS ELYOT

An interesting perspective on common knowledge about melancholy matters
in the sixteenth century can be obtained from Thomas Elyot's (1490–1546) *The
Castel of Helthe*, a domestic guide to medicine that was first published in the
1530s and was reprinted many times during the course of the century. Although not a physician, Elyot had studied medicine with Thomas Linacre,
and this work fairly reflects the medical thought of the day, albeit in a
somewhat simplified form. As a close follower of the Galenic tradition, he used
the familiar humoral theory, with the "melancoly" humor or "black choler"
among the four humors, the "melancolyke" temperament among the four
temperaments, and the two forms of melancholy humor, "naturall, whyche is
the dregges of pure bloud," and "unnaturalle, whyche procedeth of the
adustion."[5]

In the process of discussing the six "thynges not naturall," Elyot devoted
a chapter to the "affectes of the mynde" as one category of those non-naturals.

> If they be immoderate, they do not onely annoye the body, & shorten the lyfe,
> but also they do appaire, and sometimes lose utterly a mans estimation. And that
> moche more is, they bringe a man from the use of reason, and sometyme in the
> displeasure of almighty god. Wherfore they do not only require the helpe of
> phisyke corporall, but also the counsell of a man wyse and well lerned in morall
> philosophye. . . . Affectes of the mynde, whereby the body is annoyed, and do
> bring in siknes, be these, yre or wrath, hevyness or sorow, gladnes, or re-
> joycynge. (*Castel of Helthe*, fol. 62)

He then went on to devote a separate chapter to "dolour or hevynesse of
minde," in which this affect/disorder was the sorrow or sadness then commonly considered one of the "passions of the mind" and, at the same time,
closely akin to the melancholia of that era.

> There is nothynge more ennemye to lyfe, than sorowe, callyd also hevynes, for it
> exhausteth bothe naturall heate and moysture of the bodye, and dothe extenuate
> or make the body leane, dulleth the wytte, and darkeneth the spirites, letteth the
> use and judgement of reason, and oppresseth memorye . . . Sorowe drieth up
> the bones . . . Hevynesse annoye the harte of a manne. . . . Also by hevynesse
> deth is hastened, it hydeth vertue or strengthe, and hevynesse of harte boweth
> downe the necke. This is so puissant an ennemye to nature and bodily helth, that

> to resiste the malyce and violence thereof, are required remedies, as well of the holsome counsayles founde in holy scripture, and in the bokes of morall doctrine, as also of certayne herbes, fruites, and spyces, havynge the propretie to expelle melancolyke humours, and to comfort and kepe lyvely the spirites, whyche have their proper habytation in the harte of man, and moderate nourishynge of the naturall heate and humour callyd radicall." (fol. 64)

Elyot provided extensive counsel, or "remedies of morall philosophie," against sorrow and distress in reaction to "ingratitude," "deathe of chylderen," "losse of goodes or authoritie," "lacke of promotion or advauncement," and "chaunces of fortune" (fols. 64–67). He then turned to

> the counsayle of phisycke, as in relievynge the body, whiche eyther by the sayde occasions, or by the humoure of melancolye is brought out of temper.
>
> The fyrste counsayle is, that durynge the tyme of that passion, eschewe to be angry, studyous, or solytarie, and rejoyse the with melody, or els be alway in suche company, as beste may contente the.
>
> Avoyde all thynges that be noyous in syghte, smellyng, and heryng, and imbrace al thinge that is dilectable.
>
> Flee darknes, moche watche, and busynesse of mynde, moch companieng with women, the use of thinges very hote and drie: often purgations, immoderate exercise, thirst, moche abstinence, dry wyndes and colde.

He recommended that the sufferer "absteyne from" a variety of foods, essentially those thought to engender the melancholy humor; and he recommended various light, fresh, and moist foods that would be relatively easy to digest (fol. 67).

ANDREW BOORDE

In the mid-sixteenth century, Andrew Boorde (1490–1549), an English monk and physician, wrote about "a certen kynde of madnes named melancholia" whose name was "derived out of ii wordes of greke" for "blacke" and "humour."

> This sicknes is named the melancoly madnes whiche is a sicknes full of fantasies, thynkyng to here or to se that thynge that is nat harde nor sene, and a man havynge this madnes shall thynke in him selfe that thynge that can never be for some be so fantasticall that they wyll thynke them selfe good or as god, or suche lyke thynges pertaynynge to presumpcion or to desperacion to be dampned the one havynge this sicknes doth nat go so farre the one way but the other doth dispayre as muche the other way.[6]

He stated that "the cause of this impediment" was "an evyl melancoly humour" and "a stubburne hert and runnynge to farre in fantasies or musynge or studienge upon thynges that his reason can nat comprehende." As to treatment, Boorde recommended that such sufferers should "beware of melancoly meates" and "let them use company and not to be alone nor to muse of this thynge nor of the matter, but to occupy him selfe in some manual operacion or some honest pastyme, & let them purge melancoly & use to eat cassia fistula, and use myrth sport, play, and musical instrumentes, for there is nothynge doth hurt this impediment so much as doth musynge and solicitudnes" (*Breviary*, bk. 1, chap. 228). He then devoted his next chapter to the "humour named melancoly," which was derived from the same two Greek words as the disease melancholia. It was also known as "blacke color" and "one of the iiii complexions or humours" and "is colde & drye and there be ii kyndes of melancoly, the one is natural & the other is unnatural. Natural melancoly is lyke the dregges of blode whiche is somewhat blackyshe, unnatural melancoly is ingendred of coler adusted, and of the dregges of fleume and of the dregges of blode." He concluded this chapter with several recommendations of materials "to purge coler and melancoly if it be superfluous or unnatural" (chap. 229).

In the second book of this same work, Boorde took note of "melancholia" as one of the "iiii. kindes of madnesse," along with "Mania, . . . Frenisis, and Demoniacus." "They the which be infested with this madnesse be ever in feare and drede, and doth thynke they shall never do well, but ever be in parell either of soule or body or both, wherefore they do fle from one place to another, and can nat tel where to be except they be kept in safegarde" (bk. 2, chap. 43).

TIMOTHIE BRIGHT

In 1586 Timothie Bright (1550?–1615), a physician and later a clergyman, brought out *A Treatise of Melancholie* in which he provided a detailed account of contemporary thought on "the nature of melancholie, what causeth it, what effectes it worketh, how cured."[7] Although known to and cited by Burton, this work was not the orienting influence for Burton that Du Laurens's study was, and it did not become as widely known as the studies by Du Laurens and Burton. Nevertheless, it was influential for English readers and was probably a significant source of information for Shakespeare. Using the device of addressing the work to a hypothetical friend, he wrote of "that parte" of the "practise of phisick . . . which not only releeveth the bodily infirmity, but after a sort even also correcteth the infirmities of the mind" (*Treatise*, p. i); and he stated that he had "layd open how the bodie, and corporall things affect the soule, & how the body is affected of it againe." He then carefully distinguished "betwixt natural melancholie [that is, the disease], and that heavy hande of God upon the afflicted conscience, tormented with remorse of sinne, & feare of his judgment" (p. iv).

Bright took note of the "diverse maners of takinge the name of melancholie": (a) melancholia the disease, "a certayne fearefull disposition of the mind altered from reason," and (b) the melancholy humor, "an humour of the body" which was the cause of the reason being "depraved" (p. 1). This humor in turn was of two types: (i) "naturall melancholie" and (ii) "unnaturall melancholie." One of the four humors ususaly in equilibrium in the body, this *natural melancholy humor* could lead to disease in two ways: as "the grosser part of the bloud ordained for nourishment," by either "abundance or immoderate hotenesse," it "yeeldeth up to the braine certaine vapors, whereby the understanding is obscured"; *or*, as "an excrement" or dregs left at the end of natural bodily processes, this humor might become "corrupt and degenerate" and, by seriously disturbing the passions, "so outragiously oppresse and trouble the quiet seate of the mind, that all organicall actions thereof are mixed with melancholie madness" (pp. 1–2). The *unnatural melancholy humor*, known to many as adust melancholy, arose from the effects of "an unkindly heate" on natural melancholy humor, on blood, or on choler [yellow bile], and its "substance and vapor" caused "strange alterations in our actions" (pp. 2–3). He reserved the name "black choller" [black bile] for the "putrified" form of the natural melancholy humor. Melancholia the disease, then, was "a doting of reason through vaine feare procured by fault of the melancholie humour." Using the word *natural* in a different way, he again referred to this disease as "this naturall kinde" of melancholia and indicated that it had significant similarities to and differences from "the conscience oppressed with sence of sinne" (p. 3). Of particular note is the fact that he did not make use of the three traditional types of melancholia that were so commonly mentioned by both his contemporaries and his predecessors.

As to clinical description, Bright noted "feare, sadnes, desperation, teares, weeping, sobbing, sighing" and then devoted detailed chapters to the pathogenesis of these various symptoms. Interestingly, he also observed that "unbrideled laughter" occurred at times but that it did not rise "from any comforte of the heart, or gladnes of spirit." Rather, it was a "gesture . . . in a counterfet maner" which masked "that disagreeing passion" (p. xiii). In the following passage, he eloquently illustrated the common phrases, "without cause" and "without apparent cause," that were so often added to the main symptoms of "fear and sadness":

> We do see by experience certaine persons which enjoy all the comfortes of this life whatsoever wealth can procure, and whatsoever friendship offereth of kindnes, and whatsoever security may assure them: yet to be overwhelmed with heavines, and dismaide with such feare, as they can neither receive consolation, nor hope of assurance, notwithstanding ther be neither matter of feare, or discontentment, nor yet cause of danger, but contrarily of great comfort, and gratulation. (p. 90)

From this, he went on to outline his theory of pathogenesis, a standard one among explanations of melancholia, and sought to support it with deductions drawn from what was therapeutically successful.

> This passion being not moved by any adversity present or imminent, is attributed to melancholie the grossest part of all the blood, either while it is yet contained in the vaines: or aboundeth in the splene, (ordained to purge the blood of that drosse and setling of the humours) surcharged therwith for want of free vent, by reason of obstruction, or any wayes else the passage being let of cleare avoydance. The rather it seemeth to be no lesse, because purgation, opening of a vayne, diet, and other order of cure and medicine, as phisick prescribeth, have bene meanes of chaunging this disposition, and mitigation of those sorowes, and quieting of such feares, as melancholie persons have fancied to themselves, & have as it seemeth restored both wit and courage. (ibid.)

He took further note as follows of the main symptoms, with a complex admixture of theoretical views that were representative of his times:

> The perturbations of melancholy are for the most parte, sadde and feare-full, and such as rise of them: as distrust, doubt, diffidence, or dispaire, some-times furious, and sometimes merry in apparaunce, through a kinde of Sardo-nian, and false laughter, as the humour, is disposed that procureth these diversities. Those which are sad and pensive, rise of that melancholick humour, which is the grossest part of the blood, whether it be juice or excrement, not passing the naturall temper in heat whereof it partaketh, and is called cold in comparison onely. This for the most part is setled in the spleane, and with his vapours anoyeth the harte and passing up to the brayne, counterfetteth terible objectes to the fantasie, and polluting both the substance, and spirits of the brayne, causeth it without externall occasion, to forge monstrous fictions, and terrible to the conceite [that is, faculty of conceiving, reason], which the judge-ment taking as they are presented by the disordered instrument, deliver over to the hart, which hath no judgement of discretion in it self, but giving credite to the mistaken report of the braine, breaketh out into that inordinate passion, against reason. (p. 102)

He then made extensive use of the metaphor of darkness and cloudiness obscuring the functions of the mind, with "melancholie vapours rising from that pudle of the splene" to obscure the normal "clearenes, which our spirites are endued with" (pp. 102ff.). And he also described at length the "monstrous terrors of feare and heavinesse without cause" that came from the effects of "the unnaturall melancholie rising by adustion" and that led to various excited, agitated, and frightened states, which states he indicated were "of another nature far disagreeing from the other, & by an unproper speech called melan-choly" (pp. 110–116).

In several later chapters Bright turned his attention to "the affliction of soule through conscience of sinne," arguing at length that this condition, however similar superficially, was "quite another thing then melancholy" (p.

187). The former was "a sorrow and feare upon cause, & that the greatest cause that worketh misery unto man," that is, the sufferer had committed a sin and lived in fear of God's avenging wrath against his guilty soul; the body was in good health, with the "complexion" or humoral balance normal; the outward and inward senses were usually functioning normally; and usual medical care was of no avail. The latter was "a meere fancy & hath no ground of true and just object"; the body was in ill-health due to the disordered "complexion" or humoral imbalance; the outward and inward senses were enfeebled; and medical remedies were indicated and useful (pp. 187–190). As Hunter and Macalpine have suggested, the careful differentiation of these two forms of dejected disorder does remind one of twentieth-century dichotomies such as reactive versus endogenous depressions and psychological versus somatic depressions.[8] Further, after studying these chapters on the sorely guilty conscience, one is not surprised to learn that this physician gradually gave more and more attention to theological matters and became a practicing clergyman.

Bright approached the treatment of melancholia by first emphasizing the importance of removing the causes and of countering the troublesome factors with contrary factors. Then he noted the importance of the non-naturals in undertaking a therapeutic regimen: sound choice in diet and drink, exercise, attention to living quarters and apparel, careful attention to sleep and rest, avoidance of unduly burdensome study and intellectual labors, seeking of peaceful surroundings and activities in the interest of tranquillity, soothing music, and careful management of the affections of passions (*Treatise*, pp. 242–265). As to medical remedies (as distinct from regimen), he advised evacuation of the melancholic humor, first through cleansing with a clyster, then by phlebotomy with some prior exercise to facilitate the flow of blood, by facilitating the bleeding of hemorrhoids, and finally by purgings. He also noted that, in some cases, evacuation by vomit might be in order. He recommended warm, soothing baths. And he mentioned the need for strengthening measures between evacuations (pp. 269–283). Although the "phisicke cure" was essential for natural melancholia, for the guilty conscience he laid primary emphasis on spiritual consolation.

ANDRÉ DU LAURENS

In the late sixteenth century André Du Laurens (1560?–1609) wrote *A Discourse . . . of Melancholike Diseases*, which stood as authoritative in its day, which was representative of Renaissance medical thought on melancholia, which provided a review of much of the medical thought on melancholia from Galen up to its own time, and which was a respected and even a principal source for

Burton in the following century. He defined melancholia as a "delirium" or "a kinde of dotage without any fever, having for his ordinarie companions, feare and sadness, without any apparent occasion"; and then he added, "We call that dotage, when some one of the principall faculties of the minde, as imagination or reason is corrupted."⁹ He emphasized that melancholia was one of the three "diseases which doe most sharply assaile our mindes," thus following a traditional practice in so grouping "frensie, madnes, and melancholie" as the three cardinal forms of madness (*Discourse*, p. 81). He then outlined the clinical picture of melancholia as follows:

> The melancholike man properly so called (I meane him which hath the disease in the braine) is ordinarilie out of heart, alwaies fearefull and trembling, in such sort as that he is afraid of every thing, yea and maketh himselfe a terrour unto himselfe, as the beast which looketh himselfe in a glasse; he would runne away and cannot goe, he goeth alwaies sighing, troubled with the hicket, and with an unseparable sadnes, which often times turneth into dispayre; he is alwaies disquieted both in bodie and spirit, he is subject to watchfulnes, which doth consume him on the one side, and unto sleepe, which tormenteth him on the other side: for if he think to make truce with his passions by taking some rest, behold so soone as hee would shut his eyelids, hee is assayled with a thousand vaine visions, and hideous buggards, with fantasticall inventions, and dreadfull dreames; if he would call any to helpe him, his speech is cut off before it be halfe ended, and what he speaketh commeth out in fasting and stammering sort, he can not live with companie. To conclude, hee is become a savadge creature, haunting the shadowed places, suspicious, solitarie, enemie to the Sunne, and one whom nothing can please, but onely discontentment, which forgeth unto it selfe a thousand false and vaine imaginations (p. 82).

In a separate chapter on "hypochondriake or flatuouse" melancholia, in addition to the fear and sadness, Du Laurens mentioned flatuousness, a variety of other gastrointestinal symptoms, weakness and tiredness, and other aches and pains (pp. 128–131). After reporting that "all melancholike persons have their imagination troubled," he devoted two chapters to their delusions. He began by stating, "The imagination of melancholike men bringeth forthe such diversitie of effects, according to the difference of the matters whereabouts it is occupied, as that a man shall scarse find five or sixe among ten thousand, which dote after one and the same maner" (p. 96). Drawing upon "the Greeke, Arabian, and Latine writers" who had gone before him and adding some examples from his own experience, he developed a long list of noteworthy melancholic delusions (pp. 101–104). There were familiar fancies such as being a pitcher and fearing being broken, being a cock and crowing, fearing that Atlas might drop the world, having been beheaded, and having swallowed a serpent. There were two variations on the delusion of being made of glass and fearing being broken; there was the conviction that an arm and a leg had been lost to a crocodile; there was the young scholar who imagined that his nose had become unusually long and that it would be seriously damaged if he dared to move; there was the baker who thought he was made of butter and feared going near his oven; there was the man who feared to urinate lest he drown the whole town; and there were delusions of being dead, of being nothing, of being made of brick, and numerous versions of being someone of exalted status. Then there were two cases in which the person seemed to be quite rational on topics other than that of his delusion. In one of these, the man "had not his imagination troubled, otherwise then in this one only thing, for he could speak mervailouslie well of any other thing"; and in the other, "in other points hee is able to talke very sensible" (pp. 102–103).[10]

Subscribing to the three traditional types, Du Laurens discussed "the differences and divers sorts" of melancholia as follows:

> There are three kindes of melancholie: the one commeth of the onely and sole fault of the braine, the other sympatheticallie proceedeth from the whole bodie, when as the whole temperature and constitution of the bodie is melancholike; the third ariseth from amongst the bowels, but especially from the spleene, liver and the membrane called mesenterium. The first is called simplie and absolutelie by the name of melancholie, the latter is called the windie melancholie with an addition. The first is the most tedious of all the rest, it vexeth the patient continuallie, affoording little or no breathing whiles unto him: that which riseth from amongst the bowels, doth handle the grieved nothing so roughlie, it hath his periods, oftentimes making truce with the diseased. The first hath many degrees of afflicting: if it have nothing in it extraordinarie, it shall not alter his name, but and if it fall out to affect the partie altogether with savage conditions, it shall be called Wolves melancholie; if with raging and violent passion of love, Knights melancholie. The flatuous or windie melancholie hath also his degrees, for there is some sorts of it but easie and light, and there are other some that are very fierce and violent. (pp. 88–89)

Du Laurens also subscribed to the Hippocratic opinion, shared by most medical authors from ancient times until his own, that those who "have the falling sickness" tended to "become melancholike" and "such as are melancholike" tended to "fall into the falling sicknes" (p. 88).

Du Laurens noted that, in addition to melancholia the disease, the term *melancholie* was also used for one of the four humors and for one of the temperaments. After outlining the humoral theory, he indicated that each individual had a preponderance of one of the humors over the other three, and thus that most persons showed the characteristics of one of these four complexions or temperaments but "within the bounds of health." Although there were such "melancholike constitutions, which keep within the bounds and limits of health," he emphasized that he would be writing "onely of the sicke, and such as are pained with the griefe which men call melancholie" (pp. 84–86). But he took note of the Aristotelian tradition to the effect that those of a melancholic temperament were often particularly capable or even gifted. He differentiated the usual melancholic humor that was "grosse and earthie, cold and drie" from the "hot and adust" type of melancholic humor. And he briefly referred to the melancholic humor sometimes growing hot and causing "a kinde of divine ravishment, commonly called *Enthousiasma*, which stirreth men up to plaie the Philosophers, Poets, and also to prophesie: in such maner, as that it may seeme to containe in it some divine parts" (pp. 85–86).

In his etiologic considerations Du Laurens thought in terms of "a cold and drie distemperature of the braine" as a result of the pathogenic influence of the cold and dry melancholic humor, or black bile (p. 88). The coldness of this humor affected the heart so that the patient became fearful (p. 91); and, in a less clear manner, the coldness and dryness were directly the cause of the sadness (p. 93). The humor's coldness and blackness also affected the animal spirits, which in turn affected the faculties of the mind, "principally the imagination, presenting unto it continually black formes and strange visions" (p. 91). As these explanations suggest, he conceived of some of the melancholic delusions as stemming from the effect of various bodily states on the imagination (p. 97), but he added two other categories. "Other imaginations in melancholike folkes, that proceede not of the disposition of the bodie," he attributed to "their maner of living, and of such studies as they bee most addicted unto" (p. 98). And a third group of "strange imaginations" he thought derived from neither cause, their cause being unknown or perhaps "above nature" (pp. 98–99).

In stating that "all melancholike persons have their imagination troubled" and adding that they often have "their reason corrupted" as well (p. 87), Du Laurens was employing the system of faculties (imagination, reason, and memory) associated with the medieval cell doctrine.* He carefully outlined this system of faculties and their purported localization in the ventricles of the

*In its simplest form this theory involved three faculties of the mind—imagination, reason, and memory—and localized them within the ventricles of the brain. The lateral ventricles considered as one cavity constituted the first or anterior cell and contained *imagination*. The third ventricle was the second, or middle, cell and contained *reason*. And the fourth ventricle was the third, or posterior, cell and contained *memory*. The first cell received sensations from the special senses and the rest of the body and so was also considered the site of the *common sense*, sometimes as an additional faculty. Imagination integrated the sensations into images, held them for consideration, passed them on to the reason, and could recall them later from the memory. Reason compared, judged, laid the basis for action, filed images in the memory, and later had access to these stored memories. To say the least, there were numerous variations on this model. See Walter Pagel, "Medieval and Renaissance Contributions to Knowledge of the Brain and Its Functions," in *The History and Philosophy of Knowledge of the Brain and Its Functions*, ed. F. N. L. Poynter (Oxford: Blackwell, 1958), pp. 95–114; Edwin Clarke and C. D. O'Malley, *The Human Brain and Spinal Cord: A Historical Study Illustrated by Writings from Antiquity to the Twentieth Century* (Berkeley and Los Angeles: University of California Press, 1968), pp. 461–469; and Edwin Clarke and Kenneth Dewhurst, *An Illustrated History of Brain Function* (Oxford: Sandford, 1972), pp. 10–48.

brain; he acknowledged the usefulness of the cell doctrine while indicating that he personally was inclined toward Galen's view that these faculties were located in the brain substance rather than in the ventricles (pp. 72–80). As to just what was affected in melancholia, until this time the preponderance of opinion had favored the view held by Du Laurens: that imagination was the faculty primarily affected, with reason frequently affected secondarily depending on the extent or duration of the melancholic disorder.

Regarding the treatment, Du Laurens dealt with recommendations that would serve for both "that melancholie which chiefly affecteth the braine" and that which affected the whole body; and then he dealt separately with "the windie melancholie" or "hypochondriake disease." He first considered a general regimen in an essentially traditional way, keying his comments to disequilibria in one of the six non-naturals. In fact, he thought that "the maner of living" might be more important than "whatsoever can be drawne out of the most precious boxes of the Apothecaries" (p. 104). The air should be temperate and moist. The diet was to be carefully chosen: meat and fish chosen to avoid those that engendered the melancholy humor; bread for its purity; "pottage and brothes" for their moistening effects in this dry disease, while avoiding bitter vegetables; materials that would "send up pleasant vapours unto the braine"; certain fruits; and light wine (pp. 104–06). With "watching" such a problem, sleep was to be promoted. He gave detailed instructions on various preparations to be taken inwardly but cautioned against an excessive use of "all these stupefactive medicines"; and he then outlined a number of "outward remedies" for sleep that were "not altogether so dangerous" (pp. 106, 114–116). There should be moderate exercise in pleasant surroundings. Such persons should not be left alone but should have company that was pleasant, soothing, and encouraging. "To be short, wee must turne backe, and drive away as much as wee can from their understanding, al maner of passions overthrowing the mind, especially choler, feare and sadnes: for as *Plato* saith in his Dialogue called *Charmides*, the greatest part of the mischiefes that fall upon the bodie, doe come from the minde" (p. 107). Soothing music was recommended.

Noting that "all melancholike diseases are rebellious, long and very hard to cure" and "the very scourge and torment of Phisitions" (pp. 107–108), he turned from matters of regimen to the three traditional "kindes of remedies, that is to say, diminutives, alteratives, and comfortatives." Regarding the *diminutives*, that is, bloodletting and purgation, he picked his way carefully through the various recommendations of his predecessors as to mode and site for bloodletting but cautioned against these efforts "in the beginning of this disease" (p. 108). Instead, he advised that one begin with purging. Then he mentioned materials to "attenuate, soften, and dissolve" the melancholic humor and thus prepare it for further purgings (pp. 109–111). He then addressed the use of *alteratives*, that is, remedies to moisten the dryness and warm the coldness of this disease; he indicated that this was a milder approach, preferred by him as a first measure in many cases, as it had been by Galen and Alexander of Tralles (pp. 111–112). Broths and syrups were recommended to moisten inwardly, and baths to moisten outwardly. Finally, he discussed *comfortatives*, or "comforting medicines" to "strengthen and cheere up the spirits": "Syrupes, Opiates, Lozenges and pouders" to be taken inwardly, and "Epithemes, bags and ointments" to be applied outwardly to the brain and heart (p. 112).

For the hypochondriacal form of melancholia, he recommended blood-letting and gentle purgings. As he had with "brain melancholy," he advised various "inward and outward" alterative remedies in order to moisten and warm in this dry and cold disease (pp. 134–137). Rather than the "comforta-tives" used for "brain melancholy," he recommended "corroboratives," that is, various strengthening remedies to counter the weakness associated with hypo-chondriacal melancholia, particularly of the heart, the stomach, and the brain (pp. 137–139).

FELIX PLATTER

Another influential medical authority toward the end of the sixteenth century was Felix Platter (1536–1614), professor, dean of the medical school at the University of Basle, and outstanding clinical teacher. His textbook *Praxeos Medicae* was first published in 1602, had several further editions in the seven-teenth century, appeared again as late as 1736, and was "quoted by teachers as well as by students in their theses and their textbooks during the 17th and early 18th centuries."[11] And he joined Du Laurens as one of the Renaissance authorities most frequently cited by Burton. The following is his clinical description of melancholia:

> Melancholy, which is named from black bile is a kind of mental alienation [*mentis alienatio*] in which imagination and judgment are so perverted that without any cause the victims become very sad and fearful. For they cannot adduce any certain cause of grief or fear except a trivial one or a false opinion which they have conceived as a result of disturbed apprehension.
>
> This is the case when they persuade themselves that they are damned, abandoned by God, and are not predestined, even though they had been religious and faithful all the while and when they fear the last judgment and eternal punishment. This frightful melancholy, which often drives men to despair, is the most common form of melancholy. In curing it I have been frequently very much impeded. They have often confessed to me with many tears and deep sighs, with the greatest anguish of heart and with their whole

body trembling that, when seized by this, they have felt themselves driven toward blaspheming God and committing many horrible things, toward laying violent hands on themselves, killing their husbands or wives or children or neighbors or rulers, not out of motives of jealousy and not out of envy toward them, whom rather they fondly love, but out of an involuntary compulsion. They say that such thoughts creep up on them against their will and that they continually and urgently call upon God to deign to free them from such impious thoughts.

Others are troubled by terror at the thought of death and especially by fear of it at a time when they falsely imagine that they are in bad grace with princes and magistrates and that they have done something wrong and are being summoned to punishment, or when they otherwise become terribly frightened of a death which they fancy had been threatening them for a long time.

Others deceive themselves with someother nonsense conceived in and impressed on their minds, like the man who thought he had become an earthenware vessel and gave way to everyone and everything he met, fearing that he would collide with them. Thus, some believe that they are turned into brute animals. Likewise, someone who thought he had a long nose did not rid himself of that opinion until a surgeon by pretending to cut and then showing him some flesh deceived him into believing that he had amputated part of the nose. Likewise, there was a woman who was remarkably upset over being obliged to put her clothes on every day and take them off again. Another woman suffered these symptoms whenever she thought that her husband would take another wife after her death. Others talk foolishly that they have devoured serpents or frogs and are bearing them alive in their bodies, or have other delusions; they talk foolishly of many such marvelous things. With great pity and amazement, and sometimes not without laughter, I have listened to their disturbed and painful narrations of these things. In all of these cases they show the marks of sadness and fear with an abundance of continual tears, while they complain, cry out, and get their bodies and minds marvellously disturbed.

At other times they are indolent and quiet. When questioned they do not answer; when shoved forward they proceed feebly. They have solitude and flee the company of men. This variety is called misanthropy, from hatred of men. And if out of hatred of light they seek the darkness and the forests and hide in coverts and caves (as the sacred writings testify about Nabuchodonosor) it is called lycanthropy after the behavior of wolves, or, according to others, lupine melancholy. They are afflicted by these perverse imaginings, by pains and dire sufferings not only for many months but years and are finally overcome unless they come to themselves again and are helped by advice and the healing art, or they waste away to their death (or they inflict on themselves by hanging or drowning or some other violence the death that they formerly feared. It has been our sorrow to know many examples of this kind.)

Just as these disorders just described, of grief and fear do not produce the same effects in all, but pervert the mind less in some and more in others, so it happens that even though they keep a continual hold on those whom they have invaded, still they have in turn their periods of aggravation and remission, as we showed happens in continual fevers on account of a cause contained in a like manner in the veins. We have observed some people to be thus troubled only at certain times: at some season, or changes of the moon, and especially in the case of women who are pregnant or who are being purged by menstruation. . . .

There is another kind of this (melancholy) which they call hypochondriacal after the place affected. In this kind the symptoms described are very often intermittent, often recurring the same day. Those who suffer from it, as often as they come to themselves know that they are really sick. (Herein they differ from others who, unless some further symptom has acceded, complain only of headaches or heaviness of the head.) Although they hardly ever lie down, and can nonetheless perform their other duties, still they complain of a continual pain especially on their left side (which they call heart pain [*cordis dolor*]) of sweating, of pulse, rumbling in the bowels, belching vomiting, expectorations, headache, vertigo, ringing in their ears, throbbing arteries, and other innumerable disorders which they feel and which they imagine. They importune their doctors, beg for cures, try various remedies, and, unless they are soon relieved, they change their doctors and their drugs.[12]

Most of this detailed clinical description is familiar from earlier authors on melancholia. The central themes of sadness and fear were emphasized by almost all his predecessors and many scores of successors. And, among other familiar features, the list of melancholic delusions included many cited in earlier accounts. But Platter's account is more comprehensive in many ways. As Diethelm and Heffernan suggest, this picture reminds one of "our present clinical entity of endogenous depression," but, as they also suggest, the fullness of this account seems to bring out the likelihood that some such cases would be today diagnosed as "schizophrenia, with or without depressive features."[13]

Platter approached a discussion of causes by first stating that "the Cause of every Alienation of Mind" might be "Preternatural proceeding from an evil Spirit," or might be "Natural, a certain affect so affecting the Brain the seat of Reason." In the latter instances, the cause might be in the brain itself, or it might be elsewhere with the brain affected "by consent"; he stated that, in the primary condition, "the Functions of the Mind" were "impaired," whereas in the secondary condition they were merely "depraved."[14] He noted that "a grievous Melancholy" was among the types of alienation which might be caused by "An Evil Spirit the Devil." He stopped short of further consideration as to how this occurred but mentioned that Matthiolus referred each of the several types of madness "to black Choler"; his view was that "the *Cacodaemons* do this by Mediation of that Humor, in which he saith they have their residence" (Platter et al., *Golden Practice*, p. 29). He observed that "*A Fright* or *grievous Fear* especially happening of a sudden" might induce "a true Melancholy." He stated that "*Sadness* or *vehement Grief* lasting long doth also beget a *Melancholick Peturbation of the Mind*, which also may degenerate into the true one if it take deeper roote and disturb the Spirits, and change the

Temperament of the Body"; and he added that " this *Sadness of Mind* proceeds from grief or mourning most commonly for some things lost of Money, Honour, or any other thing, as the Death of Children, Parents, Friends, with which the Mind oftentimes is wonderfully tormented and afflicted for a long time" (p. 31).

Considering "true melancholly," Platter said that "*A perturbation of the Spirits of the Brain*" induced "*Melancholly* and *Madness* [mania] also, if it Act more vehemently," and that this resulted from the fact that "*some matter mixt with the Spirits* doth cloud obscure, darken the animal Spirits which ought to be bright clear lucid and most pure" (pp. 31–32). This matter was "either a Melancholick vapor or humor"; and this humor was "called a *melanchollick blood* such as they think to be either black choler it self or that which is faeculent." He thought, however, that this matter was not wanting for "malignity" in itself, not necessarily needing to become "faeculent." He noted that this matter was called "Melancholick because they think it is black, and they contend that it doth alter the Mind not only by troubling the Spirits, but also by cooling the Brain; seeing that they hold this humor is cold and dry"; but he maintained that "this *Melancholick matter* which we also call *Turbulent impure and filthy*" did not have its effects "by cooling, but because tis mixt with the spirits disturbs them, and the Brain in whose substance the Spirits are every where connate," and by virtue of its inherent malignity (p. 32).

In an essentially traditional discussion of "Hypochondriacal Melancholy," he stated that "*A Melancholick filthy Vapor troubling the Spirits and affecting the Head* breeds that Species of *Melancholy* which they call *Hypochondriacal*" and that this vapor arose from "*melancholy blood*" lying in the hypochondriacal region. He favored "the mesarick Veins" as the specific site but mentioned also the spleen, stomach, liver, bowels, and mesentery. As "*the cause* and *original* of this *melancholly blood* collected in the mesaraick veins," he thought that "*an ill course of Diet* long continued" was primarily responsible but that the closing down of ordinary avenues of evacuation might be a contributory cause (ibid.).

Although he made it clear that melancholia the disease might result from these various causes alone, he took note of "a *melancholly constitution*, which they have contracted to themselves by *nature* or by an *ill course of living*" as a predisposing factor, in which case there would be "*a double cause*" (p. 33).

When the cause of melancholia was a "*preternatural Cause* proceeding from *the Divel*," the "Cure" did "no waies belong to the Physitian" as "*the Divel* is forcibly expel'd by the Prayers of Divines and godly people in the Name of Jesus" (p. 34 [35]). In "a Melancholly Humor troubling the Spirits," he recommended evacuations, including phlebotomy, "Purgations made by stool and by vomiting," provocation of menstrual or hemorrhoidal flow, and scarification with or without cupping-glasses (pp. 39–40). Then "we will correct with things altering or changing that distemper or Melancholick constitution in the Blood . . . by giving of Medicines and applying outward helps to the Head, Heart, Liver, Spleen, and certain other parts of the Body," using materials whose moisture and modest warmth were thought to counter the pathological effects of the malignant humor (p. 39). "The Course of Living or Diet, must be so ordered, that both laudable humors may be generated, and the Malignant distemper of others and evil constitution of the Body may be amended and contemperated, and the strength refreshed" (p. 43). This entailed attention to the non-naturals: careful arrangement of air and environment, a diet designed to moisten and to avoid foods that produced the melancholic humor, careful selection of drink, the induction of sleep where insomnia was the case, disturbing passions or perturbations of the mind modified by arguments and by ruses to correct delusions (pp. 43–44). He also mentioned baths, "actual operation by gelding" in intractable cases, and the wearing of amulets (pp. 39, 43).

ROBERT BURTON

A survey of Renaissance thought on melancholia is reasonably brought to a close by a consideration of Robert Burton (1557–1640) and his *The Anatomy of Melancholy*, first published in 1621 and containing a detailed account of Renaissance views on melancholia. This work is a comprehensive presentation of medical-psychological thought on melancholia up to and into the second quarter of the seventeenth century, but it surveys melancholia/melancholy well beyond those already extensive limits. As Fox has nicely put it,

> Robert Burton forged the *Anatomy* out of his Renaissance scholar's familiarity with the literature of Western civilization, working centuries of authors into a compendium of science, philosophy, poetry, history, and divinity which contains examples of numerous literary genres yet remains *sui generis*, the singular expression of its author's humane knowledge. Unlike other Renaissance "anatomies" generally accounted to be primarily artistic creations . . . the *Anatomy of Melancholy* contains a scientific discourse treating a medical subject by means of traditional methodology in a traditional schema.[15]

For Burton *melancholy* was used primarily to signify the disease known as "melancholia" to many, whether they wrote in Latin or in one of the vernacular languages. But he also made periodic use of the term to refer to the melancholy humor (black choler, black bile) and occasionally to the melancholy temperament. In defining melancholy/melancholia the disease, he duly acknowledged the wide array of variations among his predecessors and essentially accepted the definition subscribed to by the majority: *"a kind of dotage without a fever, having for his ordinary companions fear and sadness, without any apparent occasion."* Dotage, following Du Laurens, meant that *"some one principal faculty of the mind, as imagination, or reason, is corrupted, as all melancholy persons have"*; our closest equivalent would be *delusional.* He took note of the tendency to consider the mental disturbance as less pervasive than in madness (mania) and commented that *"Fear* and *Sorrow* make it different from *madness* [mania]." And *"without any apparent occasion"* or *"without a cause* is lastly inserted, to specify it from all other ordinary passions of *Fear* and *Sorrow."* Acknowledging that there were some cases associated with laughter or with boldness, he emphasized again that *"Fear & Sorrow* are the true characters and inseparable companions, of most melancholy."[16] He went on in some detail to indicate that such sufferers were frequently discontent, restless, and tired of life; and often they were suspicious and jealous, given to solitariness (*Anatomy*, pp. 332–338). In many cases they were also troubled by a particular, circumscribed fear or delusion, and Burton elaborated a traditional list of such possible fears and delusions, perhaps the most extensive and certainly the most colorful of such accounts (pp. 327–331). But, regarding these fears and delusions, he added: "Yet for all this, . . . *in all other things they are wise, staid, discreet, & do nothing unbeseeming their dignity, person, or place."** In all these various descriptive details Burton's views reflected the main themes of the past, and they fairly represented the medical views of the Renaissance. Moreover, it should be noted that, under the generic heading of "Love-Melancholy," he gave unusual and lengthy attention to three species: *love-melancholy* or *heroical melancholy, jealousy,* and *religious melancholy* (pp. 611–971; see chaps. 13 and 15 below).

As to the theories that were favored in attempts to explain the pathogenesis of melancholy, Burton's survey indicated that the Galenic tradition was still active and the humoral theory central. The disease continued to be considered one in which the substance of the brain was affected, and it was thought to be the result of an excess of black bile, thus being a cold and dry condition (pp. 120, 148–149). The familiar three types of melancholia were detailed—a primary condition of the brain, a generalized condition in which the brain was involved secondarily, and a primary condition of the hypochondriacal regions with the brain secondarily involved (pp. 153–154). Regarding the third of these, he took note of, in addition to the familiar fear and sorrow, the many and varied symptoms of gastrointestinal distress that commonly

*Burton, *Anatomy*, p. 331. In this passage Burton was drawing on the work of Leonartus Jacchinus, a sixteenth-century physician, translator of Galen, and commentator on Rhazes.

went along with the "windiness" or "flatuousness" that so often gave it its name (pp. 350–352). In addition to these types that resulted from an excess of natural black bile, Burton faithfully reported on an extensive, complex, and sometimes confusing, literature that dealt with unnatural forms of black bile (pp. 151–152, 320–322). As a result of a burning or scorching process, any of the various natural humors might be transformed into an unnatural form of black bile, "adust melancholy," and cause "adventitious" types of melancholia that were hot in nature and associated with excitement and madness.

Beyond his basic view that melancholy was caused by the melancholy humor, Burton addressed the subject of cause in this disease in exhaustive detail (pp. 155–325), but he provided his reader with the accompanying very useful table of these various possible causes.*

Burton's attention to the treatment of melancholy was no less detailed (pp. 381–606). Although he acknowledged that melancholy was a difficult disease to cure, he counseled: "Never despair. It may be hard to cure, but not impossible, for him that is most grievously affected, if he be but willing to be helped." He rejected the "unlawful cures" of "Sorcerers, Witches, Magicians, etc." (p. 381). Rather, "lawful cures," or those "which God has appointed," were to be sought from physicians, "God's intermediate Ministers"; but sufferers were cautioned not to "rely too much, or wholly upon" the physicians. They should "first begin with prayer, and then use physick; not one without the other, but both together" (p. 384). He was distinctly dubious about seeking aid from saints (pp. 386–389). He then emphasized the importance of and gave detailed attention to the careful rectifying of any disturbances or imbalances in the realm of the "six non-natural things": diet, retention and evacuation, air, exercise of both body and mind, sleeping and waking, and passions or perturbations of the mind (pp. 395–487). In the last of these, much that we might call psychological treatment was recommended: personal efforts to resist his own distress; confessing his grief to a friend; counsel, comfort, and entertaining distractions from friends or physician; soothing music; mirth, merry company, and other entertainments (pp. 467–487). He then delivered a lengthy "Consolatory Digression" that provided comfort and reasoned counsel for the managing of "all manner of Discontents" (pp. 491–557). Turning to "Physick which cureth with Medicines" or "Pharmaceutics," he cited various "purging medicines" for "purging upwards or downwards"; and "alterative medicines" that served to strengthen, to correct

---

*Burton, *Anatomy*, pp. 110–111. One sees here that there is nothing new about the elaborate, multifactorial schemes put forward by some twentieth-century authors in efforts to reconcile many conflicting etiological views of a particular mental disorder.

A. Sect. 2. Causes of Melancholy are either

General, as *Memb.* 1.

Supernatural
- As from God immediately, or by second causes, *Sub.* 1.
- Or from the devil immediately, with a digression of the nature of spirits and devils, *Sub.* 2.
- Or mediately by Magicians, Witches, *Sub.* 3.
- Primary as stars, proved by Aphorisms, signs from Physiognomy, Metoposcopy, Chiromancy, *Subs.* 4.

Or Natural
- Congenite, inward from
  - Old age, temperament, *Sub.* 5.
  - Parents, it being an hereditary disease, *Sub.* 6.
- Or, Outward, or adventitious, which are
  - Evident, outward, remote, adventitious, as,
    - Necessary, see 8.
    - Not necessary, as *M. 4. S. 2.*
      - Nurses, *Sub.* 1.
      - Education, *Sub.* 2.
      - Terrors, affrights, *Sub.* 3.
      - Scoffs, calumnies, bitter jests, *Sub.* 4.
      - Loss of liberty, servitude, imprisonment, *Sub.* 5.
      - Poverty and want, *Sub.* 6.
      - An heap of other accidents, death of friends, loss, &c. *Sub.* 7.
  - Or, Contingent inward, antecedent, nearest. *Memb.* 5. *Sect.* 2.
    - In which the body works on the mind, and this malady is caused by precedent diseases; as agues, pox, &c. or temperature innate, *Sub.* 1.
    - Or by particular parts distempered, as brain, heart, spleen, liver, Mesentery, Pylorus, stomack, &c. *Sub.* 2.

Secondary, as Particular to the three Species. See Ⅱ.

Ⅱ Particular causes. *Sect.* 2. *Memb.* 5.

Of head Melancholy are. *Sub.* 3.
- Inward Or
  - Innate humour, or from distemperature adust.
  - A hot brain, corrupted blood in the brain.
  - Excess of Venery, or defect.
  - Agues, or some precedent disease.
  - Fumes arising from the stomach, &c.
- Outward
  - Heat of the Sun immoderate.
  - A blow on the head.
  - Overmuch use of hot wines, spices, garlick, onions, hot baths, overmuch waking, &c.
  - Idleness, solitariness, or overmuch study, vehement labour, &c.
  - Passions, perturbations, &c.

Of hypochondriacal, or windy Melancholy are,
- Inward Or
  - Default of spleen, belly, bowels, stomack, mesentery, meseraick veins, liver, &c.
  - Months, or hemrods stopt, or any other ordinary evacuation.
- Outward
  - Those six non-natural things abused.

Over all the body are, *Subs.* 5.
- Inward Or
  - Liver distempered, stopped, over-hot, apt to ingender melancholy, temperature innate.
- Outward
  - Bad diet, suppression of hemrods, &c. and such evacuations, passions, cares, &c. those six non-natural things abused.

---

8 Necessary causes, as those six non-natural things, which are, *Sect.* 2. *Mem.* 2.

Diet offending in *Sub.* 3.
- Substance
  - Bread; coarse and black, &c.
  - Drink; thick, thin, sour, &c.
  - Water unclean, milk, oil, vinegar, wine, spices, &c.
  - Flesh
    - Parts; heads, feet, entrails, fat, bacon, blood, &c.
    - Kinds { Beef, Pork, Venison, Hares, Goats, Pigeons, Peacocks, Fen fowl, &c.
  - Fish, Herbs, &c.
    - Of fish; all shell-fish, hard and slimy fish, &c.
    - Of herbs; pulse, cabbage, melons, garlick, onions, &c.
    - All roots, raw fruits, hard and windy meats.
- Quality, as in
  - Preparing, dressing, sharp sauces, salt meats, indurate, soused, fried, broiled, or made dishes, &c.
- Quantity
  - Disorder in eating, immoderate eating, or at unseasonable times, & *Subsect.* 2.
  - Custom; delight, appetite, altered, &c. *Subs.* 3.

Retention and evacuation, *Subs.* 4. { Costiveness, hot baths, sweating, issues stopped, Venus in excess, or in defect, phlebotomy, purging, &c.

Air; hot, cold, tempestuous, dark, thick, foggy, moorish, &c. *Subs.* 5.

Exercise, *Sub.* 6. { Unseasonable, excessive or defective, of body and mind, solitariness, idleness, a life out of action, &c.

Sleep and waking, unseasonable, inordinate, overmuch, overlittle, &c. *Subs.* 7.

Memb. 3. *Sect.* 2. Passions and perturbations of the mind, *Subsect.* 2. With a digression of the force of imagination. *Sub.* 2. & division of passions into *Sub.* 3.
- Irascible or concupiscible
  - Sorrow, cause and symptom, *Sub.* 4. Fear, cause & symptom, *Sub.* 5. Shame, repulse, disgrace, &c. *Sub.* 6. Envy and malice, *Sub.* 7. Emulation, hatred, faction, desire of revenge, *Sub.* 8. Anger a cause, *Sub.* 9. Discontents, cares, miseries, &c. *Sub.* 10.
  - Vehement desires, ambition, *Sub.* 11. Covetousness, φιλαργυρία, *Sub.* 12. Love of pleasures, gaming in excess, &c. *Sub.* 13. Desire of praise, pride, vainglory, &c. *Sub.* 14. Love of learning, study in excess, with a digression of the misery of Scholars, and why the Muses are melancholy, *Sub.* 15.

or alter imbalances, or to in "any way hinder or resist the disease" (pp. 558–582). Under the heading "Chirurgical Remedies" he mentioned bloodletting, "cupping-glasses, with or without scarification," leeches, cauteries, lancings, blistering plasters, and other measures aimed at evacuating the offending humors (pp. 582–583). But Burton saved his ultimate piece of advice against melancholia until the very end of his book, where he urged: "Be not solitary, be not idle" (p. 970).

THE MELANCHOLY TEMPERAMENT

Although the authorities drawn upon above have provided a valid perspective on melancholia the disease during the Renaissance, there is another side to melancholia/melancholy during that era. Whether it was the Latin *melancholia*, the English *melancholia* or *melancholy*, or one of the very similar terms in another of the vernacular tongues, the term used could mean the disease with all or most of the implications of the various descriptions and explanations detailed above. But, as we have seen, these same terms were often employed to refer to the melancholy humor (black bile, black choler, atra bilis, atra bilia), an element in the humoral theory that was understood to be an aspect of normal physiology and to be a key aspect of the pathophysiology of melancholia the disease. And, third, melancholy and these kindred terms were also used to signify one of the four main temperaments (constitutions, complexions, characters, or dispositions) based on the humoral theory; this temperament might be a predisposing factor toward melancholia the disease or merely a reasonably stable way of being for the particular person.

It was out of this third use of melancholia/melancholy that there developed a universe of meaning and discourse that, while based on the humoral theory and often discussed in relation to melancholia the disease, had its own standing, a life of its own. Further, it shaded into common language practices, so that it is sometimes difficult to discern whether a colloquial usage grew out of the common person's understanding of melancholia the disease or whether it was a reflection of this Renaissance philosophy and characterology. In somewhat simplified terms, this melancholy disposition was thought to be the basis for intellectual and imaginative accomplishments, to be the wellspring from which came great wit, poetic creations, deep religious insights, meaningful prophecies, and profound philosophic considerations; and yet, at the same time, those so disposed lived at a certain risk that their melancholic temperament might lead them into melancholia the disease. Thus, for all the apparent

---

Causes of Melancholia (from Robert Burton, The Anatomy of Melancholy, *ed. Floyd Dell and Paul Jordan-Smith [New York: Tudor, 1948], pp. 110–111).*

discrepancy between the slowed, dulled, fear-ridden, sorrowful melancholic who was ill and the intelligent, profound, witty, often inspired melancholic who was blessed with a superior temperament, "Great wits" were "sure to madness near allied."[17] Clearly connected with the views of pseudo-Aristotle in *Problem XXX* (see chap. 2), which were not forgotten in the intervening centuries, this orientation was revitalized by Marsilio Ficino (1433–1499) with far-reaching effects on his own and later times. Philosopher, physician, and priest, this Florentine humanist brought Platonic thought into the Christian world of the Renaissance, and, in this particular case, he seems to have fused the Platonic divine inspiration with the Aristotelian superior melancholic disposition.[18] Knowing himself to be born under Saturn and viewing himself as being of a melancholy temperament, sometimes bitterly bemoaning this nature as a burdensome curse and sometimes appreciating it as a source of probing intelligence and creativity, Ficino thought that studious and intellectual persons were inclined to melancholy states of mind and were at risk for melancholia the disease. If they were not so predestined by having been born under Saturn, their studious habits and intellectual pursuits would eventually bring them under the influence of Saturn. It was the natural melancholy humor that was involved, *not* the adust or unnatural melancholy humor. The black bile inclined one in the direction of scholarly activities, and the scholar's way of life and intellectual efforts bred black bile in turn, with a considerable risk. Yet the black bile's association with the earth, even the center of the earth, accounted for the penetrating thought of the intellectual; and its association with Saturn, the highest of the planets, raised the intellectual's thought to an understanding of the higher problems. Ficino delineated "the dangerous bipolarity of Saturn" and undertook "to show the Saturnine man some possibility of escaping the baneful influence of his temperament (and its celestial patron) and of enjoying its benefits" (Klibansky et al., p. 261). He outlined a system of remedies, divided into "dietetic, pharmaceutic and iatromathematical methods" in keeping with "the three kinds of cause which predisposed the highly gifted to melancholy" (pp. 266–268). In the first, he addressed questions of a healthy regimen in the tradition of the non-naturals: "avoidance of intemperance, reasonable division of the day, suitable dwelling-place and nourishment, walking, proper digestion, massage of head and body, and, above all, music." Then he discussed "medicaments, principally prepared from plants of all kinds, to which may be added fragrant inhalations. Finally, the astral magic of talismans, which evoked the influence of the stars and ensured their most concentrated effect" (p. 267). Ultimately, however, Ficino took the view that "the highly gifted melancholic—who suffered under Saturn, in so far as the latter tormented the body and the lower faculties with grief, fear and depression—might save himself by the very act of turning voluntarily towards that very same Saturn," to a life of creative contemplation (p. 271).

In one form or another, these views of the melancholy temperament became aspects of Renaissance medical thought. Furthermore, the main elements joined the common symptoms of melancholia the disease as part of general Renaissance thought.

LITERARY AND POPULAR FORMS OF MELANCHOLY

Out of the medical literature on melancholia the disease, with admixtures from the literature on the melancholy temperament, were developed popular ideas about melancholy that contributed terms and notions to the common language and that repeatedly found a place in the drama and poetry of the late sixteenth and seventeenth centuries. Considering Elizabethan literature in particular, Babb has said: "As I read the literary evidence, there is no clear distinction in the layman's mind between the melancholy temperament and the melancholic disease. There is no clear knowledge of the differentia which mark the various melancholic disorders. Yet the layman has heard enough about the odd varieties of melancholy to be prepared for any sort of eccentricity or extravagance from a melancholy man" (*Elizabethan Malady*, p. 71). Babb went on to indicate that the main clinical features of melancholia had become common knowledge for the layman, along with the rudiments of its therapeutics and scattered fragments of its theory (pp. 71–72). Out of this were developed the melancholy characters of Elizabethan literature, which were derived from medical lore, yet "definitely literary, not scientific, types" (p. 72). With the Florentine humanists as the crucial influence, the study of melancholy had continued to receive serious philosophical attention but also had served as the source for much popular thought on melancholy, with Italian scholars and artists finding both prestigious support for existing melancholic inclinations and a model for the affectation of allegedly superior traits. Babb traced the probable role of English travelers in bringing back this popular melancholy to England, with the resultant efflorescence of such attitudes and behaviors in the life of Elizabethan London and in the English drama of the late sixteenth and early seventeenth centuries (pp. 72–74). Prominent among the literary types that emerged was *the malcontent*, "the primary malcontent type, which comprises the melancholy travelers and their imitators," and three "derivative malcontent types appearing principally in the drama: the melancholy villain, the melancholy cynic, and the melancholy scholar." However, it should be noted that the association of scholars with melancholia was much older than either this literary type or the Continental popular melancholy. Babb also mentioned that *the melancholy lover* was sometimes referred to as another type of malcontent or "discontented" person, but this notion too had much older roots, both in ancient and medieval medical thought and in romantic literature (p. 76).[19] And he gave careful attention to pathological grief and its reflections in the grief-distracted characters of the drama, noting how medical authorities conceived of immoderate sorrow as depriving the body of its natural heat and moisture, with resultant coldness and dryness that might well lead to severe melancholy (pp. 102–127). Toward the end of his valuable monograph, Babb summed up as follows:

> In its Elizabethan usage *melancholy* suggests so many and such diverse mental phenomena that generalization might seem impossible. Yet two rather definite and very different conceptions of melancholy emerge from the diversity. According to one, melancholy is a degrading mental abnormality associated with fear and sorrow. It may be a morose, brooding morbidity of mind, it may be a sottish lethargy, or it may be an insanity accompanied by sorrowful and fearful delusions, often ridiculous. This conception appears especially in the dramatists' representations of sorrow. Its source is the medical literature in the tradition of Galen. According to the second conception, melancholy is a condition which endows one with intellectual acumen and profundity, with artistic ability, sometimes with divine inspiration. This idea shows its influence especially in the malcontent types. Its source is the Aristotelian problem and its popularity is largely due to Marsilio Ficino. . . .
>
> The strangely persistent vogue of melancholy among English intellectuals was a complex phenomenon with various contributing causes. . . . Among them was the general diffusion of psychological information (especially information about melancholy), which suggested introspection and supplied the terms for thinking of one's own mental states and processes. Another cause was the adversity which many educated men suffered because of England's inability to provide dignified employment for all its cultivated citizens. Several of the men of letters mentioned above attributed their melancholy to frustrated ambition. Another cause was the general currency of the idea that intellectual labor bred melancholy. The Elizabethan Englishman believed that in exerting his brain he was sacrificing the heat and moisture of his body. If he engaged in mental toil, he would expect to become at least a little melancholy. The principal reason for the popularity of melancholy, however, was the general acceptance of the idea that it was an attribute of superior minds, of genius. The Aristotelian concept had invested the melancholy character with something of somber philosophic dignity, something of Byronic grandeur.
>
> There was undoubtedly some connection, furthermore, between the vogue of intellectual melancholy and the temper of the age. The late English Renaissance was a period of progressively deepening despondency. God, says Donne, "hath reserved us to such times, as being the later times, give us even the dregs and lees of misery to drinke. . . . God hath accompanied, and complicated almost all our bodily diseases of these times, with an extraordinary sadnesse, a predominant melancholy, a faintnesse of heart, a chearlesnesse, a joylesnesse of spirit." Many explanations for this joylessness have been offered: social, political, and religious turmoil, reaction after the surging enthusiasm of the earlier

Renaissance, intellectual satiety and confusion, loss of faith in man's freedom and pre-eminence, bewilderment and uncertainty due to the discoveries of the new science, belief in the senility of nature and the degeneration of man. All of these explanations are doubtless partly right, and taken together they represent something like the truth. It is not strange that melancholy should have appealed so strongly to intelligent men in such an era. It offered—or seemed to offer—an avenue of retreat from a disheartening world. The melancholy man might retire within himself and find compensation for the ills of the world in sober con- templative pleasures. It is evident, however, that many thoughtful Englishmen found no escape from despondency. In that case the concept of melancholy gave them a name for their state of mind, a satisfying explanation of what was going on within them, and a dignified pattern of conduct. (pp. 175, 184–185)

As the French *merencolie* was used for both the fashionable *tristesse* and melan- cholia the disease, and as the Italian *malinconia* could mean either the popu- larized version of Aristotelian melancholy or the distressing melancholic ill- ness, so the English *melancholy* came to mean either the fashionable melancholy character, whether affected or actual, or the despondent sufferer in need of medical attention.

Melancholia in the Seventeenth Century: From Humoral Theory to Chemical Explanation

By the mid-seventeenth century melancholia had been an established clinical syndrome with an intimate, even inseparable, association with the humoral theory for approximately two thousand years. From the fragmentary passages in the Hippocratic writings to the important contributions of Rufus to the influential presentation of Galen, the developing accounts of melancholia the disease were clearly connected with one another; and the many Galenists of the succeeding centuries handed down a tradition with a significant degree of clinical coherence and with explanatory and therapeutic features that were held together by the humoral theory. As was indicated in the previous chapter, in 1621 Burton had produced a comprehensive review of these matters that was representative of medical-psychological thought on melancholia up to and into the second quarter of the seventeenth century.[1] But the second half of the century brought important conceptual changes regarding melancholia that were associated with the waning of the humoral theory.

RICHARD NAPIER

Before turning to these changes, we will take advantage of an unusual opportunity. From a contemporary of Burton have been passed down materials for a different perspective on melancholic disturbances in the early seventeenth century. Richard Napier (1559–1634), a physician and clergyman in rural England, left more than sixty manuscript volumes of notes on his years of medical practice, from 1597 to 1634, which included the records of his work with more than two thousand mentally disturbed patients. Among the psychological symptoms that were reasonably common in

Napier's mentally troubled patients, the following were both significantly frequent and particularly relevant to the study of melancholia: "melancholy," "took grief," and "grieving," "simply sad" and "all sadness symptoms," "suicidal" and "despair."[2] In his fine study of Napier's medical notebooks, MacDonald has identified several "broad types of mental disorder" that were also to be found "in drama and poetry, legal records and medical treatises composed before 1640" (*Mystical Bedlam*, p. 120). The severer forms, with tendencies to raving or violence—madness, mania, lunacy, distraction— seem to have been relatively uncommon; but other, less extreme mental afflictions were common, perhaps even more prevalent than they had been prior to the late sixteenth century, and most of them were emotional distur- bances. The commoner forms among the latter were melancholy/melan- cholia, mopishness, anxiety and fear, sadness, and suicidal gloom; and it was these disorders that tended to entail the symptoms just noted (pp. 148–149). Also, in contrast to the more extreme disorders, where the disturbed state was usually brought to the physician's attention by the complaint of others, in the latter conditions the "sufferers *themselves* frequently judged that their emotions were abnormal" (p. 149).

"Contemporaries believed that the feelings experienced by melancholy and troubled people were exaggerations of normal states of mind. The sheer intensity of their moods was abnormal" (ibid.). As Burton noted about melan- choly people, "the symptoms of the mind are superfluous and continual cognitations . . . grievous passions, and immoderate perturbations of the mind" (*Anatomy*, p. 349). The Stoic notion that any emotion in significant excess constituted a disorder of the mind had continued over the centuries. It constituted an aspect of common wisdom, was reflected in the general litera- ture of the era, and was part of Napier's orientation in considering his mentally troubled patients. For Napier this could lead to the assessment that someone was "troubled in mind," and, with the addition of delusions or false percep- tions, the patient was usually diagnosed as suffering from melancholy (*Mystical Bedlam*, p. 150).

As was remarked in the previous chapter, melancholy was much in the popular mind in Western Europe by this time, and its less severe forms were considered by many to be a mark of distinction—a sign of intellectual and moral superiority, if not genius. Some of the moderately melancholic found comfort in the label, and many merely added the label to enhance themselves. Approximately twenty percent of Napier's mentally disturbed patients were recorded as suffering from melancholy, but the percentage was dispropor- tionately high among those of the higher social ranks and disproportionately low among the common folk. Those diagnosed as "troubled in mind" and "mopish" included a disproportionately high number of the ordinary folk and a disproportionately low number of the higher social ranks (ibid., pp. 151–152). Napier seems to have been sensitive to the social propriety of using the diagnosis of melancholy for certain social classes, and, further, "persons of rank and learning frequently judged themselves to be melancholy rather than merely sad, troubled, or fearful" (p. 152). Also, some of them showed a significant familiarity with standard medical ideas on melancholy in their letters to Napier, for example, (1) "Desirous to have something to avoid the fumes arising from the spleen"; (2) "Deep melancholy fearfulness, almost of every object. Fumes ascending from the stomach, distempering the brain. . . . He feareth that it will turn into mania" (pp. 152–153).

In addition to experiencing the traditional sadness and fear, Napier's melancholic patients frequently manifested another customary symptom, namely, delusional belief or hallucination, but it was rare for this to be as remarkable as the traditionally cited examples (pp. 153–155). As bizarre as any of the delusions he encountered in his melancholic patients was the following obsessive-compulsive preoccupation of delusional proportions:

> Extreme melancholy, possessing her for a long time, with fear; and sorely tempted not to touch anything for fear that then she shall be tempted to wash her clothes, even upon her back. Is tortured until that she be forced to wash her clothes, be them never so good and new. Will not suffer her husband, child, nor any of the household to have any new clothes until they wash them for fear the dust of them will fall upon her. Dareth not to go to the church for treading on the ground, fearing lest any dust should fall upon them. (p. 154)

Further regarding the delusions in melancholia, MacDonald has pointed out:

> The knowledge that exotic fancies were symptoms of melancholy rather than of madness or lunacy was spread beyond the expanding circle of readers familiar with the niceties of psychological medicine by two controversies. Skeptics argued that the confessions of accused witches were melancholy delusion, and the early opponents of religious enthusiasm declared that the inspirations of the enthusiasts were also melancholy fancies. (p. 155)

Belief in the Devil was still well enough established that Napier would consider two significant alternatives in his assessment of those sufferers who claimed to have seen "the Tempter" or otherwise associated their distress with Satan:

> These, then, were the alternatives: Flat claims that one was in league with the Devil or had been tempted by him might be evidence that one was suffering from melancholy, suicidal gloom, or (rarely) another mental disorder; or they might be true. As long as men continued to believe that Satan could appear to rational people, encounters with him could not be dismissed simply as symptoms of madness. (p. 156)

Similarly, claims of prophecy might be delusions indicative of a melancholy disorder, but they might well be regarded as valid (pp. 156–157). "Because Elizabethans believed that the world was vibrant with supernatural forces and invisible beings, it was understandable that they were reluctant to presume that fantastic visions and disembodied voices were experienced only by the most insane madmen" (p. 157).

The fears and the sorrows of Napier's melancholic patients were emotions known to the least troubled among their contemporaries, but they were either disproportionate in their intensity or they were "aroused by false apprehensions and amplified by delusion." To an observer, these were the fears and sorrows "without cause" or "without apparent cause," to use the phrases so often found in medical accounts. Instances of grieving or sadness occasioned by the loss of loved ones (sadness "with cause") were often considered akin to melancholy without being thought to be indicative of that disease, but, if they acquired an "unusual intensity or duration," they might well be considered examples of melancholy the disease (p. 159). Still other trends reported in traditional accounts of melancholia, and found with frequency in Napier's melancholic patients, were summed up by MacDonald as follows:

> Whether melancholy crept unprovoked upon the sufferer's affections or stormed into the void created by the death of a child, a spouse or a parent, its effect was to draw him away from normal involvement in the emotional and social world around him. Melancholy men and women lost the capacity to take pleasure from activities they had previously delighted in or to enjoy the social relations that gave happiness to others. . . . The alienation of melancholy men and women from the pleasures of everyday life was symbolized in literature and in descriptions of actual sufferers by their love of solitude. . . . Melancholy made men and women inner exiles (p. 160).

Parenthetically, it is significant to note that Napier recognized another disorder, *mopishness*, that was akin to melancholia. "Mopish men and women often suffered from the characteristic symptoms of melancholy, especially gloom and solitude . . . 'despairing, heavy-hearted, exceeding sad' . . . 'solitary and will do nothing.' . . . Indeed, one connotation of the word *mopish* current during the seventeenth century was a pale kind of melancholy (p. 161). In contrast to melancholy there was a "socially pejorative aura" to mopishness. "The dumpish moods of idle gentlefolk frequently earned the classical appellation [of melancholy]; the sullen inactivity of husbandmen and artisans merited more often the rude and common word *mopish*" (pp. 161–162). But there was a category of symptoms often associated with mopishness and usually not associated with melancholy, namely, disturbances of the senses. Mopish patients were noted to be "sottish," "foolish," "not well in his wits," "troubled in his senses," or "senseless" (p. 162). Such a diagnosis was quite uncommon in medical writings, but the nature of the condition was often similar to *lethargy*, which was often mentioned in medical works. On the other hand, mopishness was commonly mentioned in the popular literature of the day.

Early in his years of medical practice Napier made ready and traditional use of the humoral theory in his efforts to explain melancholy, but his notebooks suggest that he fell away from this tendency after a while, only to return to it after his reading of Burton's *Anatomy of Melancholy* in 1624 (pp. 152, 189). In general, Napier rarely thought that a mental disturbance was due to a single cause. Usually he held the view that astrological factors had predisposed a patient to suffer a mental disorder peculiar to his particular temperament, but such factors were not sufficient to explain the illness. "There was almost always a more immediate cause as well" (p. 173). And these immediate causes were as many and varied as Burton suggested (see chap. 5). Although a variety of supernatural causes, either divine or diabolical, were commonly held responsible for mental disturbances in Napier's time, he seldom attributed such disorders to God; but he accepted the view that Satan might well be responsible in some cases (p. 174). Napier also seems to have thought that

> disturbing events affected the physical health and social relationships of their victims as well as their psychological condition. Like popular medical writers and philosophers, Napier and his patients assumed a powerful sympathy between mind and body. Emotional stress could cause physical illnesses as well as mental disturbances, and almost any sort of bodily sickness could deprive a person of his reason. The many different events in the natural world that were deemed potential causes of insanity disturbed the entire lives of the people they affected, not merely their mental tranquility. (pp. 173–174)

As to treatment, like so many of his contemporaries Napier drew on a variety of healing traditions in ministering to his mentally disturbed patients, including the melancholics.

> [He] practiced at a time when it was still possible for learned men to reconcile all of the main types of causal explanations for insanity and to offer all of the remedies appropriate to them. The traditional medieval and Renaissance model of the universe postulated the existence of both natural and supernatural forces at work in a hierarchical order of powers and beings. Man existed at the point of convergence between the natural and the supernatural orders, and he was subject to both kinds of powers. This model permitted contemporaries to explain mental disorder as the consequence of events that occurred on any of the several planes of existence, acting singly or in concert. Most people in early seventeenth-century England saw no theoretical incompatibility among the different kinds of explanation for mental disorders, and many practitioners combined therapies justified by medical, magical, and religious beliefs. Napier was one of these eclectics. (pp. 177–178)
>
> Regardless of their symptoms, almost every one of Napier's mentally disturbed patients was purged with emetics and laxatives and bled with leeches

or by cupping. . . . The drugs that Napier and his fellow physicians used to purge their patients were a medley of native and exotic plants, traditional recipes, and new inorganic compounds. (p. 187)

Napier supplemented his arsenal of traditional organic medicaments with [Paracelsian] metallic compounds and distillations; he even collected bizarre folk remedies and occasionally resorted to them. . . . He became an avid medical alchemist, preparing his own chemical medicines. . . . Although Napier was fascinated by the mystical aspirations of medieval alchemy and probably knew something about the substance of Paracelsus's medical thought, he nevertheless remained chiefly interested in the practical side of alchemy and regarded chemical medicines as a novel and effective complement to traditional therapies. . . . Nothing in his notes indicated that he explained any illness in Paracelsian terms. . . . He employed Paracelsian preparations, such as compounds of antimony, as substitutes for organic remedies that acted as vomits and purges, and he often combined modern chemical medicines with traditional substances. The notes he made about the best treatments for the mentally disturbed illustrate his eclecticism: A prescription for "all melancholy and mopish people," for example, recommends *hiera logadii*, lapis lazuli, hellebore, cloves, licorice powder, *diambra*, and *pulvis sancti*, all of which were to be infused in a solution of white wine and borage. This olio of plants and chemicals would act as a violent purge. Napier collected many other recipes for medicines to cure melancholy, the majority of which were steadfastly traditional. (pp. 189–190).

Napier used opiates to calm and to induce sleep in melancholic patients, but much less frequently than with the more severely distracted patients (p. 190). In addition to purgatives and emetics, he made modest use of phlebotomy to evacuate noxious humors and restore the humoral balance (pp. 191–192). He used astrological determinations in choosing the herbs and the metals with the appropriate qualities that would fit them for dealing with the humor, black bile, and the disease, melancholy; and he similarly determined the propitious times for the use of medicaments and the drawing of blood (p. 194). Where he thought that supernatural factors were at work in a melancholic illness, he might well, guided by astrological principles, have an amulet made for the sufferer to wear as protection against such forces (pp. 213–214). Among the many persons who suffered from anguish or despair about their status in the eyes of God or other spiritual concerns, and sought Napier's help, some were distinctly melancholic. Such persons, and those grieving from loss, were considered candidates for "spiritual physic"—"religious worry" called for "religious counseling." In this counseling Napier

favored formal prayer to searching self-examination as a means to restore his patients' confidence in God's mercy. He often prayed together with his troubled clients, and he sometimes composed prayers for them to repeat to themselves. . . . He urged his patients to pray and perform regular religious exercises, for he felt that they would foster piety and happiness. . . . Napier's preference for a style of religious counsel that emphasized ministerial guidance, set prayers, and participation in the rituals and sacraments of the church was a consequence of his theological conservatism. He preferred to stress the traditional authority of the church and the value of formal piety rather than to expound upon the mysteries of the scriptures and the threat of damnation. (pp. 221–222).

In addition, he occasionally had "astrological amulets" made to bolster the religious faith of melancholic patients (p. 222).

Regarding most of the various symptoms noted by Napier, the syndromic patterns of mental disturbance that guided him, and the details of his views on melancholy in particular, there was little that was unique to early seventeenth-century England. Renaissance medical literature and seventeenth-century medical writings in other European countries constituted a whole fabric, of which Napier's materials were a recognizable and essentially representative part.

THOMAS WILLIS

Against a background of views fairly represented by Burton, with practical applications akin to those in Napier's notebooks, in the second half of the century Thomas Willis (1621–1675) approached the subject of melancholia, among other diseases that affected "The Brain and Nervous Stock," in the second part of *Two Discourses Concerning the Soul of Brutes* . . . , which was first published in 1672.[3] Willis described melancholia in familiar terms, stating "*Melancholy* is commonly defined to be, a raving without a Feavour or fury, joined with fear and sadness." On the traditional theme of melancholic delusions, he stated that "it would be a prodigious work, and almost an endless task to rehearse the diverse manner of ravings of *Melancholy* persons; and there are great Volumes already of Histories and examples of this sort; and more new and admirable observations and examples daily happen," and then he briefly noted a few of the familiar instances (*Soul of Brutes*, p. 188). He also differentiated melancholia into two types: a *universal* type in which "the distemper'd are *Delirious* as to all things, or at least as to most; so that they judge truly almost of no subject"; and a *particular* type in which "they imagine amiss in one or two particular cases, but for the most part in other things, they have their notions not very incongruous."*

When one turns to his theoretical considerations on melancholia, how-

---

*Willis, *Two Discourses*, p. 188. Willis seems to have played a role of some consequence in the history of the concept of *particular insanity* or *partial insanity*. Matthew Hale probably appropriated the notion from him for legal use; Willis's student, John Locke, took it up; and various eighteenth-century medical authorities made it part of the very essence of melancholia. See Stanley W. Jackson, Melancholia and Partial Insanity, *J. Hist. Behav. Sci.*, 1983, *19*, 173–184.

ever, one finds a distinct shift away from traditional views. Briefly, and notably, he stated, "But we cannot here yield to what some *Physicians* affirm, that *Melancholy* doth arise from a *Melancholick* humor" (p. 192). Instead Willis put forth his notions of pathogenesis in terms of his own version of the newer iatrochemical theories. In a casebook in the early 1650s he clearly indicated skepticism of the humoral theory and began to introduce iatrochemical explanations, but humoral considerations were still prominent in his views.[4] And these trends were developed further in his *Lectures* in the early 1660s.[5] In his treatise on fermentation (1659) he had argued against the traditional four elements and the theory of qualities derived from them,[6] and in his treatise on fevers (1659) he had argued against the traditional humoral theory that had rested on these notions (*Practice of Physick*, p. 48). He also declined to espouse the emerging corpuscularian notions (p. 2). He favored instead the five "Principles of Chymists" (pp. 3–8), which meant "affirming all Bodies to consist of Spirit, Sulphur, Salt, Water, and Earth, and from the diverse motion, and proportion of these, in mixt things, the beginnings and endings of things, and chiefly the reasons, and varieties of fermentation, are to be sought" (p. 2).

Referring back to his definition cited above, Willis said that it "follows, that it is a complicated Distemper of the Brain and Heart: for as *Melancholick* people talk idly, it proceeds from the vice or fault of the Brain, and the inordination of the Animal Spirits dwelling in it; but as they become very sad and fearful, this is deservedly attributed to the Passion of the Heart" (*Soul of Brutes*, p. 188). Taking up the first part of this statement, he commented that, while the animal spirits would ordinarily have been "transparent, subtle, and lucid," they "become in *Melancholy* obscure, thick, and dark, so that they represent the Images of things, as it were in a shadow, or covered with darkness." He then suggested that the animal spirits, "with the Vehicle to which they cleave" (namely, the blood), were analogous "to some *Chymical* Liquors, drawn forth by distillation from natural mixtures" (ibid., p. 189).

After discussing various chemical notions as bases by analogy for the formation of the animal spirits and for their pathological alterations in various mental disorders (ibid.), he continued his explanation of those aspects of the condition that he viewed as a "Distemper of the Brain." He stated:

> That we may deliver the formal reason and causes of *Melancholy*, let us suppose, that the liquor instilled into the Brain from the Blood (which filling all the Pores and passages of the Head, and its nervous Appendix, and watring them, is the Vehicle and bond of the Animal Spirits) hath degenerated from its mild, benign, and subtil nature, into an Acetous, and Corrosive, like to those liquors drawn out of Vinegar, Box, and *Vitriol;* and that the Animal Spirits, which from the middle part of the Brain, irradiating both its globous substance, as also the nervous *System*, and do produce all the Functions of the Senses and Motions, both interior and exterior, have such like Effluvia's, as fall away from those Acetous *Chymical*

Liquors. Concerning which there may be observed these three things, 1. Their being in perpetual motion: 2. Not long able to flow forth: 3. not only to be carried in open ways, but to cut new Porosities in the neighboring bodies, and to insinuate themselves into them. From the *Analogy* of these conditions, concerning the Animal Spirits, it comes to pass, that *Melancholick* persons are ever thoughtful, that they only comprehend a few things, and that they falsely raise, or institute their notions of them. (pp. 189–190)

He took up each of these three clinical observations in turn and, on analogy to his chemical notions, elaborated a physiological psychology to explain them (pp. 190–191). In summing up, he commented that, in addition to the functioning of the brain being so affected by "the Acetous disposition of the Spirits," eventually "the conformation of the Brain itself" may be affected and become "a part of the cause" (p. 191).

Turning to the "fear and sadness" aspects of the condition, Willis indicated that

> *Melancholy* is not only a Distemper of the Brain and Spirits dwelling in it, but also of the *Praecordia*, and of the Blood therein inkindled, from thence sent into the whole Body: and as it produces there a *Delirium* or idle talking, so here fear and sadness.
>
> First, in Sadness, the flamy or vital part of the Soul is straitned, as to its compass; and driven into a more narrow compass; then consequently, the animal or lucid part contracts its sphere, and is less vigorous; but in Fear both are suddenly repressed and compelled as it were to shake, and contain themselves within a very small spaces; in either passion, the Blood is not circulated, and burns not forth lively, and with a full burning, but being apt to be heaped up and to stagnate about the *Praecordia*, stirs up there a weight or a fainting; and in the mean time, the Head and Members being destitute of its more plentiful flux, languishes.

Then he elaborated these matters further in terms of his chemical theories (ibid.).

At this point he commented that, in some instances, the melancholic condition began with the acetous disturbance of the animal spirits and then later caused "the *Melancholick* disposition of the Blood," and "No less often doth it come to pass, that the seeds of *Melancholy*, being at first laid in the Blood, do at length impart their evil to the Spirits," in which instances he conceived of the blood as having become "*Salino-sulphureous*" in nature (p. 192). He then mentioned the three traditional types of melancholia—that which arose from an original disorder in the brain, that which arose from the hypochondriac area (he specified the spleen), and that which involved the whole body—and he added a fourth type which arose from the womb (pp. 192–193). In discussing them he showed some tendency to consider the blood as the primary locus for all.

Regarding hypochondriacal melancholy, Willis referred the reader to his "Tract of Convulsive Diseases," and he suggested that it originated in the blood, which deposited "*Melancholick* foulnesses" in the spleen, which in turn "exalted" these materials "into the nature of an evil Ferment" and returned this result to the blood, whose condition was then such that it tended to cause this form of melancholia (ibid.). In this treatise, he included the "hypochondriack distempers," along with hysterical disorders, among the convulsive diseases (*Practice of Physick*, pp. 81–92). He acknowledged as a common view that this condition was thought to stem from the spleen, from which "vapours" arose to cause the various symptoms (ibid., p. 81).

As the physiological background to the spleen's role in hypochondriacal conditions, he referred to the blood as depositing there certain "dregs" that were "composed of a fixed Salt, and an earthly matter;" these materials were then transformed into "a juice very fermentive" in the spleen, and this was returned to the blood to give it "a certain austerity and sharpness, with vigour of motion." But, in addition to thus influencing "the Brain and nervous stock" indirectly via the blood, the spleen more directly had an invigorating effect on the brain and the animal spirits via its intimate nervous connections. To sum it up, the spleen exercised a "fermenting virtue" that, when things went normally, had an enlivening effect on "the Blood and nervous Liquor" (p. 84).

Against this background Willis indicated that, if the spleen was not functioning normally, both the blood and the nervous juice may be either sharper or duller than usual, with resultant disorders. This may occur either when the spleen "doth not strain forth the melancholy Recrements of the Blood" or when it failed to "Cook them into a fermentative matter" once they were in the spleen (p. 85). Then, elaborating on these basic notions, he outlined how the various mental and physical symptoms might come about in the hypochondriacal disorders (pp. 85–86). In view of the blood's direct effect on the brain, he thought that such disorders may have been "chiefly derived from the Head" in many instances, and yet the basic fault in those cases would still lie with the spleen for its failure to "strain forth the atrabilarie dregs from the blood" (pp. 86–87).

As Burton had so clearly outlined, by the second quarter of the seventeenth century explanations of pathogenesis in melancholia were still couched in terms of disturbances of the traditional humors, usually as an excess of black bile, the melancholy humor. By the 1630s Galenic views had long ago been effectively challenged in anatomy and more recently in cardiovascular physiology. Paracelsian arguments against humoral physiology had been extant for over a century. Yet the newer views had made very limited inroads into the explanations of disease. By mid-century the writings of Jean-Baptiste van Helmont had come to constitute both a new and more persuasive criticism of

Galenic humoral theory and a more influential advocacy for chemical explanations.[7] Then Franciscus Sylvius (de le Boë), a contemporary of Willis, emerged as another significant proponent of iatrochemical views (King, *Road*, [n. 7], pp. 93–112). Yet an influential medical author like Riverius (Lazare Rivière) continued with a consistently Galenic explanatory scheme, and his writings were printed and reprinted from just before the mid-century on into the eighteenth century (ibid., pp. 15–36). He was both a continuing influence for the persistence of humoral explanations and, in the seventeenth century, representative of a strong tendency for those explanations to persist. Another contemporary of Willis who was very influential in the latter half of that century was Thomas Sydenham (pp. 113–133). Reputedly independent of the fetters of traditional explanations, as one might think to be the case from his discussion of hysteria,[8] he nevertheless explained most diseases in terms of the humoral theory.[9]

Thus, although his views seem to reflect his own synthesis of iatrochemical themes rather than being easily identifiable as Paracelsian, Helmontian, or whatever,[10] Willis was not new in introducing chemical explanations of disease. And corpuscularian notions were also emerging as contenders in the struggle for explanatory preeminence in the realm of pathogenesis (King, pp. 62–86). But traditional humoral theory was still predominant when, in the 1650s, he began to develop a system of chemical explanations. Then, as he began to replace the four humors with the "Principles of Chymists" as the cardinal factors in the pathogenesis of nervous disorders, the black bile began to lose its place in explanations of melancholia. This humor never regained its previous status in the various theories that were later put forward to explain the pathogenesis of this disorder.

Parenthetically, it should be noted that neither the term *humor* nor the four familiar humors disappeared from Willis's writings. The term *humor* was still frequently used by him, and by many after him, to refer to bodily fluids in general or to this or that body fluid in particular. And blood, yellow bile, phlegm, and black bile continued in his system and in those of other authors after him. Perhaps reflecting his assessment of the new status of blood following Harvey's work (*Practice of Physick*, p. 45) blood became *the* humor, and it was joined by the "Nervous Liquor," the "Chyme or nourishing Juice, continually coming to the Mass of Blood, and the serous Latex, perpetually departing from the same" as natural humors or body fluids (ibid., p. 47). Yellow bile, black bile, and phlegm were relegated to the status of waste products to be separated from the blood by the liver, the spleen, and the solid parts, respectively; they became "only the recrements of the Blood, which ought continually to be separated from it." The "common acception of humors" was "laid aside," and Willis developed this new view in which these "excrementitious" substances were stored in the parts or organs that separated them from the blood and that then had the task of their gradual elimination (p. 48).

Although Willis developed a different theory of melancholia in keeping with the chemical notions to which he subscribed, he took familiar therapeutic paths in recommending venesection in moderate quantity, gentle cathartics, and emetics, with the aim of relieving the body of its burden of pathological materials. He also wrote about stimulating and strengthening the animal spirits, which was to be achieved by applying his evacuative remedies and by diverting the soul from its troubling passions and cheering up the person. Among other measures he mentioned gentle hypnotics for sleeplessness, and spa waters that contained iron and various remedies containing steel for the purpose of strengthening the nervous juice (*Soul of Brutes*, pp. 193–199). Otherwise employing traditional remedies, Willis was innovative in advising these metals for the treatment of melancholia, perhaps reflecting the Paracelsian trend toward the use of metals in therapeutics.

During the last quarter of the century the humoral theory continued to lose ground in favor of other theoretical systems. As noted above, iatrochemical ideas were prominent in this process, but the new chemical explanations were short-lived in theories of melancholia. By the 1690s mechanical notions were already displacing them and serving to complete the displacement of humoral explanations.

CHAPTER SEVEN

Melancholia in the Eighteenth Century: Mechanical Explanation and Beyond

THE RISE AND FALL OF MECHANICAL EXPLANATION

As we have seen, by the late seventeenth century the humoral theory was losing its preeminent place in medical explanations in general, and theoretical considerations of melancholia were no exception. As the humoral theory came under challenge, Willis's scheme of chemical explanations was first used to develop new etiological and pathogenetic formulations for melancholia. Although medical chemistry developed and grew in influence, and Willis was again and again cited as an authority on nervous and mental diseases in the eighteenth century, the new chemical explanations were short-lived in theories of melancholia. Mechanical explanations soon began to displace them.

The mechanical philosophy had gradually become a significant feature of seventeenth-century science. The fundamental explanations of physical phenomena had come to involve the motion and interaction of the various particles of matter. As an aspect of this trend, through influences from Descartes, Gassendi, Borelli, and Bellini, among others, and, particularly in England, from Boyle and Newton, mechanical principles, corpuscular notions, and hydrodynamic theories had crucially changed the nature and language of physiology during the latter half of the century. The far-reaching impact of Harvey's establishment of the circulation of the blood had given special encouragement to the use of hydrodynamic ideas. As a result of these trends, by the last decade of the seventeenth century iatromechanical ideas had come to inform much of the medical explanation of the day, and such ideas were part of the knowledge of many educated persons. Pitcairn and Hoffmann were among the earliest exponents of mechanical theories who adapted them to the explanation of melancholia. Each of them first put forth his ideas close to the end of the seventeenth century and then continued to be a significant influence in the early eighteenth century.

With meaningful influence from the works of Bellini and Newton, Archibald Pitcairn (1652–1713) systematically espoused a mechanical viewpoint in his medical theories, disowning the theories of the ancients and arguing against the iatrochemists' doctrine of fermentation.[1] For him, the living body was composed of "Canals of divers kinds" (the containing parts) "conveying different sorts of Fluids" (the contained parts) (*Elements of Physick*, p. 338); and, on mechanical principles, these fluids moved in their various canals with the circulation of the blood as the central factor in the motions of the parts of the system (pp. 35–71). Against this background, he stated that "Disease is an unusual Circulation of Blood, or the circular Motion of the Blood augmented or diminished, either throughout the whole Body, or in some Part of the Body" (p. 72). Pitcairn defined melancholia in familiar terms as a delirium (disordered thought) without a fever and accompanied by fear and sadness, and then introduced his mechanical views when he indicated that this disease "proceeded" from a "Defect" of the normal "vivid Motions" (pp. 192–193). He conceived of a thicker than usual condition of the blood, its excessive accumulation in the brain, and a sluggish circulation: "If then the Blood that is less comminuted begins to accumulate in the Brain, and to move more slowly, the Parts secerned from it will have a lesser Impetus, and will excite Vibrations less vivid, and less frequent; and will thereby produce the Disease of Melancholy" (p. 288). The implication is that this disorder in the hydrodynamics of the blood, in turn, affected the flow of the animal spirits in the nerves to bring about the disordered thought or delirium associated with the disease (pp. 56–60, 186, 192).

Like Pitcairn, Friedrich Hoffmann (1660–1742) was critical of the traditional medical theories. He too was dubious about the views of the iatrochemists, but he did use a notion of fermentation in combination with his mechanical views. Conceiving of the human body as being "like a machine which is composed of solid and fluid particles, disposed and arranged in varying order and position,"[2] he systematically employed the principles of motion in his physiology (*Fundamenta Medicinae*, pp. 6–10). Of central significance was the "twofold motion" of the blood: "One, internal, is of the smallest particles reciprocally with each other; and the other is circulatory or progressive, by means of which the blood is carried through the vessels" (ibid., p. 17). In addition to the blood, the chief fluids were considered to be the lymph and the animal spirits, which circulated in the lymphatic vessels and in the tubular nerves, respectively (p. 11); Hoffmann tended to emphasize the fluids over the solid parts in both his physiology and his pathology. The body fluids were composed of particles of various sizes and shapes, which were of two main types—"volatile, fluid, and spirituous" and "fixed, earthy, and mucilaginous" (p. 40). Normal functioning was associated with an "equilibrium" and "due proportion" of these two types of particles; and disease stemmed from "the motion of the blood and of the fluid parts" being "either diminished or increased"; there were two main categories of disorder according to which type of particles predominated. The volatile and spirituous particles were associated with salinity and sulfurousness, and an excess of them led to excessive warmth, sharpness, and motion that was "more rapid and increased"; the fixed, earthy, and mucilaginous particles were associated with viscidity and acidity, and an excess of them led to excessive coldness along with "both the internal and circulatory movements" being "diminished and slow" (pp. 40–41). Obstructions in the solid parts might also be crucial in interfering with the equilibrium of motion (p. 41).

Hoffmann described melancholia in familiar terms as a delirium without fever and "associated with sadness and fear not having any manifest cause." He defined delirium as "reason perverted in thought and words," with the added comment that "deliria are the dreams of the waking" (p. 71). He also included among its signs "mental anxiety, thoughts strongly fixed on some particular thing, and scantly restless sleep" (p. 94). As others had done before him, he observed that "mania can easily pass over into melancholy, and conversely, melancholy into mania" (p. 72). Having in mind the nervous system and the flow therein of the animal spirits, he added, "In melancholics the spirits are indistinct and fixed, and approach a sort of acid nature. They not only leave enduring fixed ideas in the brain pores, but promptly uncover similar traces, of ideas of sadness, terror, fear, and so on" (pp. 71–72). With this body fluid turning acidic and fixed, its motions became sluggish, and the person became slow, timid, and sad (pp. 12, 70).

From these beginnings in the 1690s Hoffmann's influence increased during the next several decades, with only Boerhaave matching him in his impact on medical theories during the first half of the eighteenth century. In this process Hoffmann remained a consistent advocate of mechanical explanations in physiological and pathological matters. He later elaborated on his clinical comments, stating that "in the melancholy, the mind is strongly fixed on some particular object, with great anxiety, dejection, groundless fears, and grief, peevishness, love of solitude, and a disposition to receive quick displeasure from the slightest cause." He continued to view melancholia and mania as intimately related forms of madness, but he modified somewhat his view of that relationship. "Though usually reckoned different disorders, [they] appear to be rather different stages of one; the mania being properly an exacerbation of melancholy, and leaving the patient melancholic in the calmer intervals."[3] While he conceived of hypochondriasis as a separate condition and not as a form of madness, he stated that the "hypochondriacal and hysterical indispositions" might lead to a "symptomatic melancholia" as distinct from the primary melancholia under consideration here (*Practice of Medicine*, p. 301). After noting that "the mental functions are disordered by a preternatural quality or quantity of blood and juices in the vessels of the brain" and that "an obstruction . . . of the circulation there" led to "a retardation of the circulation" as the "proximate cause of melancholy," he added that in turn "the causes of these irregular motions" were "a debility of the brain, from long grief or fear, love, immoderate venery, diseases, the abuse of spiritous liquors, narcotic medicines; a preternatural afflux of blood to the brain, from vehement anger, external cold, suppressions of evacuations of blood, hypochondriacal and hysterical affections; or a siziness of the blood itself, from gross foods, a sedentary life, or other causes" (p. 300).

Herman Boerhaave (1668–1738) emerged as a significant figure in the early 1700s and widely influenced Western medicine throughout much of the eighteenth century. Although he made important contributions to chemistry, he was critical of the medical chemistry that was prevalent at the turn of the century, and he systematically argued that mechanistic reasoning should have a central place in medical explanation. Strongly influenced by Newton's mechanical principles and employing the hydrodynamics of circulatory physiology, Boerhaave outlined his physiology in his famous *Institutes* and his pathology in his equally well-known *Aphorisms*.[4] Viewing the human body as a machine, he developed a system of *containing* solid parts that served as framework and vessels and of *contained* circulating fluids that were composed of microparticles and were directed, changed, separated, and excreted by mechanical forces.

In writing about melancholia Boerhaave put forward the classical descriptive statement that it was "that Disease . . . in which the Patient is long and obstinately delirious without a Fever, and always intent upon one and the same thought." His three categories of melancholia are familiar, but he discussed them more as though they were three degrees of severity within a single illness rather than three types of melancholia affecting different sites; and he explained them, and connected them to one another, in terms of mechanical principles. While he stated that "this Disease arises from that Malignancy of the Blood and Humors, which the Antients have called *Black Choler*," he was not employing the traditional humoral theory and implying that there was an excess of black bile.[5] Instead, while retaining the term *black bile*, he was conceiving of it as a pathogenic material that developed from certain mechanical or hydrodynamic actions. When "the most moveable Parts of all the Blood be dissipated and have left the less moveable united, then will the Blood become thick, black, fat and earthy. And this Defect will be call'd by the name of an *Atrabiliar Humor*, or *Melancholy Juice*."* Thus, for Boerhaave, the causes of melancholia were those factors that eliminated or reduced the "most moveable" parts of the blood, and fixed or slowed the movement of the rest of the blood (*Aphorisms*, p. 313).

Boerhaave described the first degree of melancholic illness as being much like the traditional type that affected the entire mass of blood, with the added statement that it "doth yet infect equally all the circulating Mass of Humors"; and he thought of it in terms of a thickening and slowing of these fluids (pp. 313–314). He also noticed "a lessen'd Appetite; a Leanness; Sorrowfulness; Love of Solitude; all the Affections of the Mind violent and lasting; an Indifference to all other Matters; a Laziness as to Motion; and yet a very great and earnest Application to any sort of Study or Labour" (p. 314).

For the second degree of this condition, Boerhaave used the terms "an *Hypochondriac Disease*" and "*The Spleen*." He saw it as being the result of the pathogenic material growing "thicker, tougher, and [even] less moveable" and so being driven "into the Hypochondriac Vessels; . . . Here it will gradually stop, be accumulated and stagnate" (p. 315). In addition to a worsening of the symptoms already mentioned, there was "a Sense of a constant Weight, Anguish, Fulness, chiefly after eating and drinking; a difficult Breathing from the Bowels of the Abdomen being burthened," along with other symptoms associated with the hypochondriacal region (pp. 315–316).

The third form or stage of melancholia was the outcome of still further worsening, and it was only then that Boerhaave cited disturbances in mental functioning. If the pathogenic matter associated with the hypochondriacal form

> already fixed, and drove in close, has been detained there long; the same begins already to grow sharp and gnawing by its Stagnation, the Motion of the Bowels and the Heat of the surrounding Parts; new Matter is continually laid on, because the Obstruction is made already, and the same causes do subsist; hence it extends, gnaws, and corrupts the Vessels by its increased Bulk, its present Acrimony and continual Motion. (p. 317)

As a result, chiefly disturbed were "all the Functions, and above all, those of the Brain, by the constant Steam of the putrefied Matter received into the Veins. And then may it be called by the true Name of *Atra Bilis*" (ibid.).

---

*Aphorisms, pp. 312–313. As with others before him, Boerhaave had abandoned the traditional humoral theory, but he used the term *humor* to refer to the various bodily fluids and secretions. Black bile was no longer a normal component in a physiological theory that, in excess, might have pathological results. It was now a darkened substance that separated out from the blood on standing or on slowing, a thickening mass with an obstructive potential rather than a traditional humor with the qualities of coldness and dryness. Boerhaave was introducing a then modern meaning for a notion that had gradually lost its traditional conceptual matrix.

Although the notion of putrefaction added an element of chemical explanation, mechanical explanation still predominated.

In summarizing the pathogenetic sequence already outlined, Boerhaave stated "that from a long continued preceding Sorrowfulness, the Vessels of the abdominal Bowels create a Stagnation, Alteration, and Accumulation of black Choler Which insensibly increaseth, though the Body was very healthful but a little before: And also that the same black Choler, when bred from bodily Causes, doth produce that Delirium" mentioned in his original definition of melancholia (p. 320).

While the influence of the mechanical philosophy on medical explanation, and the influence of Boerhaave's mechanical theories in particular, continued into the second half of the eighteenth century, important changes were under way. By the 1740s mechanistic explanation was being doubted and challenged in natural philosophy and in physiology.[6] Corpuscular dynamics and hydraulics were gradually losing their central place in physiological and medical explanations. Electrical experimentation was becoming a significant area of scientific endeavor, and questions were emerging as to the nature of electricity and as to its possible role in organic processes.[7] Electricity increasingly had a place in physiological and medical explanation and in medical therapeutics.

Some were questioning the tenets of the mechanical philosophy while favoring less theorizing and a more empirical approach. Others were arguing that these tenets were inadequate for the task of explaining activity in living organisms. Of central importance in eighteenth-century physiology, Albrecht von Haller (1708–1777) illustrates much that was important in this era.[8] Opposing the tendency to rationalistic schemes and leaning toward a positivistic position, he argued against the mechanical philosophy while retaining a place for mechanistic notions in the realm of efficient causes. He favored an experimental approach as the basis for a more modest theorizing. While he was an effective critic of Stahlian animism,* his careful analysis of the contributions of others and of his own experiments brought him to define two crucial vital properties, sensibility and irritability.[9] Although then and later many viewed him as a mechanist on the basis of his explanations for these and other factors, still others found his work crucial for their development of systematically vitalistic views. Because Haller was safely grounded in his experimentalism, it is difficult to conceive of him as a vitalist. It is also of note that he did not take up aetherial views but retained the idea of a nerve fluid flowing in hollow nerves and argued against its being electrical in nature.[10]

---

*George Stahl (1659–1734) argued against mechanical medicine and for the *anima* as an immaterial force with motive and directional influences on the passive mechanisms of the living organism.

Among the notions that came to the fore as the mechanical philosophy was being questioned, derivatives of the aetherial hypothesis were of considerable significance. The aether, although not weightless for all natural philosophers, came to be commonly conceived of as an ever-so-subtle fluid—imperceptible and weightless, yet elastic and vibratory—that pervaded space. This subtle matter variously served as a medium through which gravitational force was transmitted and light, heat, electricity, and magnetism passed from one perceptible body to another. Usually it was thought to be composed of subtle, indivisible particles that moved or vibrated in the process of transmitting these various influences. It was as concepts akin to this subtle, elastic fluid that the various imponderable fluids of the eighteenth century emerged to explain electricity and magnetism, as well as other phenomena in the physical sciences.[11]

Particularly significant for physiology and medicine, including medical psychology, were the aetherial notions suggested by Isaac Newton (1642–1727) that briefly, but explicitly, addressed sensation, motion, and nervous transmission. Although he put forward such ideas as early as 1675,[12] the first of his influential statements on these matters was the following paragraph from the *General Scholium*, which he added to the second edition of his *Principia* in 1713.

> And now we might add something concerning a certain most subtle spirit which pervades and lies hid in all gross bodies; by the force and action of which spirit the particles of bodies attract one another at near distances, and cohere, if contiguous; and electric bodies operate to greater distances, as well repelling as attracting the neighboring corpuscles; and light is emitted, reflected, refracted, inflected, and heats bodies; and all sensation is excited, and the members of animal bodies move at the command of the will, namely, by the vibrations of this spirit, mutually propagated along the solid filaments of the nerves, from the outward organs of sense to the brain, and from the brain into the muscles. But these are things that cannot be explained in few words, nor are we furnished with that sufficiency of experiments which is required to an accurate determination and demonstration of the laws by which this electric and elastic spirit operates.[13]

Then, in 1717 in the second English edition of his *Opticks*, he added his *Queries*, which included references to sensation and motion as resulting from vibrations of the aetherial medium being propagated along solid nerves.[14]

In the wake of the growing dissatisfaction with a systematic mechanical approach in physiological and medical explanation, the Newton of mechanics and mathematics seems to have waned as a source of influence; but the Newton of aetherial notions emerged as an active influence in physiology and pathology. Whereas the earlier Newton had directly influenced Pitcairn and Boerhaave, this newer Newtonian influence can be seen in medical explanations of melancholia around mid-century.

Richard Mead (1673–1754), perhaps the most eminent English medical man of his time and well-known abroad, fittingly illustrates some of these transitions. A student of Pitcairn and a friend of Newton, he had long been a staunch advocate of Newtonian thought and of the application of mechanistic notions in physiological and medical explanations. In the original version of his *A Mechanical Account of Poisons* in 1702 he undertook the study of "the Animal Machine" so as to "Discover the Footsteps of Mechanism in those surprising Phaenomena which are commonly ascribed to some Occult or unknown Principle."[15] Employing corpuscularian notions and using a hydrodynamic scheme drawn from Bellini and Pitcairn, he wrote in submacroscopic terms about foreign particles disrupting the forces of attraction of the particles of the blood with damaging effects on blood flow and, in turn, on the flow of nerve fluid in the nerves (pp. 9–21).

In revising his early works in the 1740s, Mead retained a mechanical orientation in the form of a hydrodynamic scheme; he stated that the human body "ought to be considered as a hydraulick machine . . . in which there are numberless tubes properly adjusted and disposed for the conveyance of fluids of different kinds,"[16] but he dropped his detailed corpuscularian discussions. By this time influenced by the views expressed in Newton's *Opticks* and the associated *Queries* and *Suggestions* and impressed by the recent findings of the electrical investigators, he introduced comments about nerve juice and nerve function cast in terms of Newton's aether.[17] A form of this subtle fluid was brought to the brain in the blood; the brain, functioning as "a large gland," separated it from the blood; the nerves served as excretory ducts for this "thin volatile liquor, of great force and elasticity," and, "lodged in the fibres of the nerve," this nerve fluid or animal spirits became "the instrument of muscular motion and sensation" (*Medical Works*, p. xxi). He was equivocal as to whether the nerves were solid or hollow. His ardent espousal of Newton's views suggests that he conceived of them as solid, but occasional hints seem to imply a flow of nerve fluid in hollow nerves. Also, citing both recent electrical studies and Newton's speculations, he wondered whether this fluid might be electrical in nature (pp. iv, xxiii). A significant aspect of this introduction of an aetherial nerve fluid was the extent to which it involved a shift from a vasocentric to a neurocentric view as a basic feature of his reasoning on pathogenesis. From his earlier views, in which the blood was primarily affected in the beginnings of a disease process and other bodily fluids only indirectly via the effects on the blood, he shifted to allow that the nerve fluid might be directly affected and might be the vehicle for secondary effects in other parts of the body.[18]

In the course of these same revisions Mead commented that "the surprising appearances" in "melancholy disorders" must surely be brought about by "alterations . . . made in that active liquor [animal spirits], by which the mind governs the body" (p. xxv), but he did not give systematic attention to melancholia in his writings until *Medical Precepts and Cautions* in 1751. In this work he prefaced his consideration of diseases by asserting that "health consists in regular motions of the fluids, together with a proper state of the solids; and diseases are their aberrations," and that it was "time to pass to the defects of this machine, which disturb and destroy its motions."[19]

When he came to "the diseases of the head," he described melancholia as a "kind of Madness" involving "a constant disorder of the mind without any considerable fever" and associated with "sadness and fear" (*Medical Precepts*, p. 79). To suffer from melancholia was "to be sad and dejected, to be daily terrified with vain imaginations; to fancy hobgoblins haunting him; and after a life spent in continual anxiety, to be persuaded that his death will be the commencement of eternal punishment" (p. 74). "A frequent cause" was "an excessive intention of the mind, and the thoughts long fixed on any one subject," and he added that "such intention of the mind, such fixed thought, is capable of perverting the natural faculties, as we sometimes observe in studious persons." When such a state was "blended" with disturbing passions, melancholia might ensue (p. 75). Madness might be of a melancholic or a furious type, "according to the nature of the cause, and chiefly according to the natural propensity of mind in the patient to this or that passion"; and then, after noting that nothing disordered the mind as much as love and false religion or superstition, he asserted that "the Madness of persons in love is more generally of the maniacal, and that of superstitious people of the melancholic kind" (pp. 75–76). On the pathogenesis of these illnesses, he first noted that "images present themselves to the mind" and that "they necessarily excite certain affections or passions in the soul, which are instantly followed by suitable motions in the body"; these passions caused "alterations in the body, by raising commotions in the blood and humours" (p. 77). Then he added that "the instrument of all these motions, both of the mind and body, is that extremely subtile fluid of the nerves, commonly called *animal spirits*" (p. 78).

During the latter part of the eighteenth century William Cullen (1710–1790) gradually displaced Boerhaave as the preeminent authority on the explanation of disease. Although acknowledging the continuing usefulness of mechanical ideas in some areas of physiology, he stated that "it would be easy to show" that they "neither could, nor ever can be, applied to any great extent in explaining the animal oeconomy."[20] He saw himself as crucially revising many ideas of Boerhaave, the mechanist, and yet he objected to the animism of Stahl, the antimechanist; and he expressed reservations about Hoffmann's mechanical orientation, but he saw merit in and acknowledged being influenced by Hoffmann's view that the nervous system had a significant role in disease.[21] He shifted from the heart and the vascular system to the brain and the nervous system as the basic elements in his physiology; and with this shift he abandoned the hydraulics and the hydrodynamic principles of the Boerhaavian system both for the immediate functions of the nervous system and for its new functions as a source of primary causes for physiological activities in general.

Central to Cullen's neural explanations in physiology and pathology were a system of forces and a nerve fluid reflecting elements of both Haller's physiology and Newton's speculative mechanics for the nervous system.[22] He rejected any notions of the brain as a secretory organ and of hollow nerves with a circulatory nerve fluid. He cautiously put forward the idea of "nervous power" but ultimately chose to refer to it as a nerve fluid. This fluid was inherent in the nerves and mediated the transmission of oscillatory or vibratory motions; and he conceived of it as one of a group of imperceptible and imponderable fluids that were modifications of Newton's aether.[23] On these foundations Cullen constructed a theory of disease in which the ideas of "excitement" and "collapse" were used extensively in the discussion of both normal and abnormal states. Excitement referred to conditions ranging from the normal state of waking to a pathological extreme such as mania, and collapse referred to conditions ranging from the normal state of sleeping to pathological extremes such as syncope and death. He conceived of excitement and collapse as states of increased and decreased mobility of the nervous power or nervous fluid in the brain whose effects were felt throughout the nervous system.[24]

The terms *motion* and *force*, although employed vaguely at times, were used again and again throughout his *Physiology* and his *First Lines of the Practice of Physic*. Cullen consistently referred to "motions" being "communicated" to and from the brain, and these phenomena were termed "mechanical communications" (*Institutions*, pp. 27, 78, 80). He conceived of the normal and abnormal instances of excitement and collapse as being due to variations in the "mobility and force" of the nervous power (ibid., pp. 96–101). Then he concluded a similar passage in the *First Lines* by cautiously denying any intention "by these terms, to explain the circumstance or condition, mechanical or physical, of the nervous power or fluid in these different states" (4:126).

Was Cullen continuing the tradition of mechanical explanation or was he not? Hall has classified him as a "medical vitalist,"[25] and others have referred to him as vitalistic in orientation. In an earlier study I have expressed reservations about this assessment of him,[26] and since then Bowman has struggled with the question in some detail, apparently concluding that to a considerable degree Cullen had continued in a mechanical tradition.[27]

Cullen did employ a category of vital solids that were to be found only in living bodies, and contrasted them to simple solids that were to be found in both animate and inanimate bodies. The crucial medullary substance of the brain, the spinal cord, the nerves, and the muscle fibers (conceived of as extensions of the nerves by Cullen) was composed of such vital solids. Then there was his notion of nervous power or nervous fluid as an energizing factor which was responsible for the excitement that identified a person as being alive rather than dead. One might suggest that there was a vitalistic view at work here, and Cullen occasionally equated his "Nervous Power" with "the vital Principle of Animals."[28] Yet he seems to have stopped short of a clearly vitalistic position—begging ignorance at some relevant juncture points, declining to speculate further at other points, actively opposing vitalistic notions in their Stahlian form, explicitly associating the nerve fluid with the aetherial fluids derived from Newton at some moments,[29] and indicating that the nerve fluid was either analogous to or identical with the electrical fluid at still other moments.[30] Furthermore, as we have seen, he regularly used mechanical notions in his explanations, and he frequently indicated that there were crucial mechanical factors at work whose nature was not understood.

Because one can search Cullen's works and come up with passages to support either side of the argument as to whether he was a vitalist or a mechanist, it may be less than accurate to consider him as either one. Somewhat like Haller, he was actively critical of the mechanical philosophy, and yet he frequently retained mechanical explanations in the realm of efficient causes. Again like Haller, he was critical of Stahl's animism, his attention to vital activities led others to allege that he was a vitalist, and yet it is difficult to see him as truly a vitalist. He might be better seen as reflecting the dilemmas of an era when systematic mechanical schemes had been found wanting in physiology and unique properties in living systems had to be taken into account.

As to melancholia, first there is its position in Cullen's extensive nosological system, which earned him a place as a noted systematizer alongside Boissier de Sauvages and Linné in the eighteenth-century proliferation of nosologies. In his *Nosology* he organized his system of diseases into four *Classes*—Febrile Disorders, Nervous Disorders, Cachexies, and Local Disorders. The Nervous Disorders, frequently termed "Neuroses" by him, were characterized as follows: "Sense and motion injured, without an idiopathic pyrexy, and without a local disorder."[31] The Nervous Disorders, in turn, were divided into four *Orders:* Comata (deprivations of voluntary motion), Adynamia (deprivations of involuntary motions, whether vital or natural), Spasms (irregular motions of the muscles), and Vesania (disorders of the intellectual functions). He characterized the Vesania as having "the functions of judgment injured; without pyrexy or coma" (*Nosology*, p. 119), and he grouped them into four categories: Amentia, Melancholia, Mania, and Onierodynia.

Cullen defined melancholia as "partial insanity, without dyspepsia" (p. 120), the latter point differentiating it from the kindred condition, hypochondriasis. But in the *First Lines*, while stating that it was "very often a partial insanity only," he was distinctly uncertain as to how strictly the insanity was limited to a single subject, and he noted that it might at least "produce much inconsistency in the other intellectual functions" (4:168–170, 174–175). At the beginning "without pyrexy or coma" is named as a characteristic among the Vesania and is assumed thereafter. Then he stated that "it must be chiefly distinguished by its occurring in persons of a melancholic temperament, and by its being always attended with some seemingly groundless, but very anxious, fear" (ibid., p. 175). He added that "costiveness" was a frequent symptom (pp. 184–185).

In outlining the nature of the melancholic temperament, he noted that such persons

> are for the most part of a serious thoughtful disposition, and disposed to fear and caution . . . are less moveable than others by any impressions; and are therefore capable of a closer or more continued attention to one particular object, or train of thinking. They are even ready to be engaged in a constant application to one subject; and are remarkably tenacious of whatever emotions they happen to be affected with. (pp. 175–176)

In physiological terms, "this melancholic temperament especially consists" of "a degree of torpor in the motion of the nervous power, both with respect to sensation and volition; . . . a general rigidity of the simple solids" (p. 181). While putting forward his ideas somewhat tentatively, he further stated:

> It is probable the melancholic temperament of mind depends upon a drier and firmer texture in the medullary substance of the brain; and . . . this perhaps proceeds from a certain want of fluid in that substance, which appears from its being of a lesser specific gravity than usual. That this state of the brain in melancholia does actually exist, I conclude, *first*, from the general rigidity of the whole habit; and, *secondly*, from dissections, showing such a state of the brain to have taken place in mania, which is often no other than a higher degree of melancholia. It does not appear to me anywise difficult to suppose, that the same state of the brain may in a moderate degree give melancholia; and in a higher, that mania which melancholia so often passes into; especially if I shall be allowed further to suppose, that either a greater degree of firmness in the substance of the brain may render it susceptible of a higher degree of excitement, or that one portion of the brain may be liable to acquire a greater firmness than others, and consequently give occasion to that inequality of excitement upon which mania so much depends. (pp. 182–183)

In considering delirium and mania, Cullen had postulated inequalities in the degree of excitement in different parts of the brain, "the force of the animal [that is, mental] functions" being increased while that of other functions remained unchanged (pp. 130–138). As disordered judgment or delirium was a crucial feature of melancholia, it was implied that the latter also involved inequalities of excitement in the brain, with the further implication of increased excitement associated with the subject on which the person was particularly disordered.

Considerations of Cullen on the subject of melancholia would be incomplete if one did not address its relationship to hypochondriasis. He categorized hypochondriasis, like melancholia, in the Class Nervous Disorders, but in contrast to melancholia he assigned it to the Order Adynamia, with the implication that it was a condition in which involuntary motions, whether vital or natural, were lessened.

After emphasizing that this condition, "like every other state of mind," was "connected with a certain state of the body" (3:251), Cullen stated that the disease was "the effect of that same rigidity of the solids, torpor of the nervous power, and peculiar balance between the arterial and venous systems which occur in advanced life, and which at all times takes place more or less in melancholic temperaments" (p. 256). Thus hypochondriasis tended to occur in persons of the same basic temperament as those who came to suffer from melancholia, and so the two conditions shared the same alleged physiological deviations from the normal. But he explicitly differentiated these two disorders by the usual absence in melancholia of the dyspepsia that was so commonly present in hypochondriasis, and he implicitly differentiated them by the absence in hypochondriasis of the delirium or mental derangement that was regularly present in melancholia (4:177–180). Although Cullen did not say as much, his view of the relationship between the two diseases was not unlike Boerhaave's arrangement of them along a continuum of severity.

During the earlier part of this era mechanical ideas became nearly irresistible for most who sought to explain physiological and medical phenomena. But as the mechanical philosophy lost its preeminent position, an important support for mechanical medicine was eroded. Moreover, the hopes that the laws of mechanics might directly provide the essential explanations of physiological processes had not been realized; in contrast to the situation in natural philosophy, it proved much more difficult to identify physiological variables that could be satisfactorily measured. Some who were concerned with vital activities and processes successfully challenged primarily mechanistic schemes as insufficient. Others proposed electrical explanations. Nevertheless, the relevance of hydrodynamic explanations for the circulation of the blood and of traditional mechanics for some aspects of the work of the muscles made it difficult for medicine to drop mechanical explanations altogether. More generally, the retention of mechanical notions frequently seemed useful and reasonable in addressing proximate causes and explaining local bodily conditions. Even the vitalists thought of their vital forces as having mechanical effects.

The earlier efforts to explain melancholia in mechanical terms (Pitcairn, Hoffmann, and Boerhaave) were parts of systematic mechanical schemes in physiology and pathology. Each of these three men developed medical theories based on hydrodynamic principles, dynamic microparticles, and forces of attraction. They each rooted their notions of pathogenesis in various forms of disordered flow in their system of circulations (blood, lymph, nerve fluid). Pitcairn's and Boerhaave's views were essentially vasocentric, with the basic disorder in fluid flow being in the blood. While Hoffmann gave a great deal of attention to disordered blood flow in his explanations of disease, he veered toward a neurocentric view when he addressed mental disorders. For Pitcairn and Hoffmann the central theme in melancholia was a sluggishness or slowing of the circulation of the blood in the brain, resulting in a less lively nerve fluid and in the person's becoming slow and sad. Boerhaave, too, thought in terms of a slowing of the circulation of the blood, but he managed to retain a version of the black bile by reinterpreting its nature in mechanical terms.

Mead provides us with a reflection of some of the mid-century changes in physiological and medical explanation. He shifted from his earlier corpuscularian notions and a vasocentric orientation to a neurocentric system with an aetherial nerve fluid in which irregular motions could lead to melancholia. Influenced by Newton's suggestions, as well as by recent electrical investigations, he thought that the nerve fluid might be electrical in nature. Although he seems to have been equivocal as to whether this nerve fluid flowed or not, the general trend was away from fluid flow notions and in favor of an aetherial nerve fluid that did not flow but, instead, served as a medium for the transmission of "motions." Cullen, too, abandoned corpuscularian ideas and espoused a neurocentric orientation with an aetherial nerve fluid that clearly did not flow and through which oscillatory or vibratory motions were transmitted. He replaced the theme of a slowing of flow in melancholia with that of a depleted amount of excitement, although this was also described as a torpor or a decreased mobility in a nerve fluid that did not flow. Although he expressed grave reservations about mechanical explanations and speculated as to whether the nerve fluid might be electrical in nature, he continued to use mechanical notions at the level of efficient causes.

To what extent did the descriptive outline of the syndrome of melancholia remain constant or change during the eighteenth century, and how might the explanatory developments traced above have influenced any such changes? The traditional notion of three types of melancholia was gradually abandoned. The differentiation of hypochondriasis from melancholia continued until the former became established as a loose category of nonpsychotic nervous and mental troubles. But the basic clinical description of melancholia remained fairly stable. This condition continued to be described as a form of madness and as a chronic illness without fever. It still usually involved a state of dejection and fearfulness without an apparent cause, and some particular circumscribed delusion was still a common feature. Sleeplessness, irritability, restlessness, and constipation continued to be usual elements. Gradually the idea of melancholia as a partial insanity shifted from being a not uncommon feature to being considered an essential element, but this point was in doubt again by the end of the century.* Some mania-like syndromes and some monodelusional states that would be termed paranoid today were brought under the technical rubric of melancholia defined as partial insanity, but these were distinctly a minority.

It is difficult to link satisfactorily these relatively limited changes in the clinical picture to the shifts in explanatory schemes. It is of note that, during the long heyday of the humoral theory, notions of black bile and smoky vapors were commonly associated with references to the patient as dark and gloomy in his melancholic state. Then, with the emergence of mechanical explanations, such references faded from clinical accounts, and the idea of the slowing of the patient's circulation became associated with a slow and dejected state. With Cullen's scheme of too much and too little energy in the brain and mobility in the nervous fluid, the notion of a depleted state became associated with the anergic behavior of the melancholic person; and his excited and depleted states are reminiscent of the charged and discharged electrical states of an emerging explanatory fashion. Having in mind these observations and their larger theories, one can say that the shifts in explanatory style certainly influenced how the disease of melancholia was discussed. Yet they do not appear to have had any significant effect on the basic clinical outline. Rather, it seems that a relatively stable clinical description provided a sufficient array of characteristics that each explanatory scheme found features that could be reconciled with its concepts.

Concerning the gradual separation of hypochondriasis from melancholia until the former was usually a syndrome of physical complaints and a non-psychotic depressed state, it seems likely that the logic of separating nonmad dejected states from mad dejected states was more compelling to clinical observers than any effect of mechanical explanations. Partial insanity had long been thought to be an accurate description of some cases of melancholia. During this century the assertion that it characterized all cases became common without any apparent influence from the mechanical philosophy; and the

---

*This term implied that the derangement was limited to the sphere of a particular fixed delusion with sound mental functioning on other topics. See Stanley W. Jackson, "Melancholia and Partial Insanity," *J. Hist. Behav. Sci.*, 1983, *19*, 173–184.

later challenging of this view very likely came from the court of clinical evidence rather than from any change in explanatory fashion.

Although it would have been risky without a careful examination of the facts to have assumed that a change in the prevailing explanatory mode might have little effect on clinical description, it is not surprising when the clinical constellation has some coherence and abiding connections between its parts. The increasing rate of change in modes of explanation from the late seventeenth century onward could be conceived of as a challenge to the stability of a clinical syndrome, and it could be said that this challenge served to demonstrate a reasonable validity to the continuing association of these various symptoms as a syndrome. Further, what changes did occur very likely stemmed more from clinical observation.

In the still Galenic medicine of the seventeenth century, common treatment measures were bloodletting, cathartics, and emetics, which were aimed at evacuating the melancholic humor. Diet was to be light and easily digested, with due attention to warm and moist foods in this cold and dry disease. Also emphasized were cheerful company and diverting activities, warm bathing, and moderate exercise. Usually it seems as though the prescriber had run down a checklist of the six nonnaturals (air, food and drink, rest and motion, retention and evacuation, sleep and waking, perturbations of the mind). In spite of his different theory of melancholia, Willis had changed very little in the way of therapeutic practices. Along with the familiar emphasis on evacuative remedies, he wrote of diverting the soul from its troubling passions, cheering up the patient, employing gentle hypnotics for sleeplessness, and using spa waters that contained iron and various remedies containing steel for the purpose of strengthening the nervous juice.[32]

From Pitcairn to Cullen, we find a remarkable consistency of therapeutic themes.[33] Bloodletting was usually advocated, but caution was urged in view of the melancholic patient's weakened state. Some authors thought that menstrual or hemorrhoidal flow should be promoted if they had been suppressed. Purgatives were consistently mentioned but always with the caveat that they should be mild. Some mentioned emetics, again with warnings that they not be too strong. There was the occasional mention of materials containing steel or iron for their tonic effect. Hypnotics were only rarely suggested. Dietary advice was frequently given, with the emphasis on a light yet nourishing diet for a weakened person in need of strengthening. Exercise was frequently recommended, and sometimes riding or travel, or both, with the goal of energizing a debilitated patient. Providing cheerful conversation, diverting the melancholic from his fixed line of thought, and stimulating other emotions were each commonly mentioned. The principle of contraries was often cited as the basis for a therapeutic regimen. Other central themes that supported treatment recommendations, sometimes made explicit but often implicit, were the evacuating of pathological materials, the dissolving or thinning of a thickening in the blood so that a slowed circulation might return to normal, the enlivening of a weakened nerve fluid, and the strengthening and bestirring of a weakened and slowed-down person.

Thus, although mechanical explanations for melancholia emerged and then flourished, they apparently did little to change the therapeutic practices usually recommended. Later, as mechanical explanations lost much of the preeminent position, patterns of treatment still changed relatively little. As Risse has noted in surveying records of Cullen's consultation practice, his "neural pathogenesis played only a minor role in his therapeutical efforts. Thus, like Boerhaave, Cullen was a physician attempting to systematize new explanations of physiology and pathogenesis without abandoning his conservative and eclectic methods of treatment."[34] And so it is not surprising that, at the end of the century, Bichat would comment, "The same medicaments have been used successively by humoralists and solidists. Theories changed, but the medicaments remained the same."[35]

The increasing attention to "management" and psychological interventions in these accounts of therapeutic advice is of interest. Melancholia had long been approached in terms of a physiological psychology and thought to be rooted in a disordered physiology. Perhaps the emphasis on psychological factors in the contributions of Stahl and Gaub to the emerging psychosomatic orientation[36] influenced medical authorities to think that psychological measures might crucially change this condition. On the other hand, some of this advice seems to have derived from the older tradition of attention to the passions (as one of the nonnaturals) on the basis of the principle of contraries.

In summing up, we find that mechanical explanations had little in the way of either substantive or lasting effect on melancholia. For all their influence on terminology and theoretical formulations, they left the clinical syndrome essentially unchanged. While mechanical ideas sometimes colored the theoretical rationale for a treatment endeavor, the therapeutics of melancholia continued much the same, or at least relatively unchanged by any influence from such ideas. As much as anything else, under the influence of a series of leading medical authors and teachers, melancholia was kept terminologically and conceptually in fashionable dress. And each explanatory scheme offered its own metaphors for referring to the signs and symptoms of melancholia.

TWO SUFFERERS' PERSPECTIVES ON MELANCHOLIA

In this same era—from the 1690s to the 1790s—thanks to two British authors who wrote about their experiences as victims of melancholia, we are able to obtain interesting and useful answers to some important questions about this disorder. What was melancholia the disease to those who were afflicted with it? How did they describe their experiences? And how did they attempt to formulate their views of these experiences and explain them to themselves and to others?

The first of these accounts, which appeared in 1691, was *A Discourse Concerning Trouble of Mind, and the Disease of Melancholly* by Timothy Rogers (1658–1728), "who was long afflicted with both" as he noted on the title page.* After "near two years in great pain of Body, and greater pain of Soul," he recovered in 1690.[37] This volume was the direct outcome of that lengthy illness and was "Written for the Use of such as are, or have been Exercised" by melancholia (*Discourse*, title page).

Although Rogers only infrequently referred to having been melancholic in the first person, he repeatedly made it clear that the basis for his knowledge and his advice was his own experience as a victim of this disorder; and he stated in his preface that "where ever I speak of inward distress, as by a third person I there speak what I myself have felt" (p. xxxii). He spoke of himself as having been "overwhelmed with the deepest sorrows, for many doleful Months" (pp. A2–A3). He felt that he had to be cautious in describing his "inward Troubles" as a safeguard against once again being overwhelmed by them and for fear that he might "sink some poor souls, who are already low enough" (pp. A1–A5). His own case involved "the sense of Tormenting, Racking Pain, the immediate prospect of Death, and together with this, an apprehension of God's Displeasure, and the fear of being cast out of his Glorious Presence for ever," and he alluded to "that Anguish and Tribulation, which such apprehensions cause in a desolate and a mourning Soul!" (p. A4). He referred to "Anxieties of Soul" and emphasized that melancholia "is the worst of all Distempers; and those sinking and guilty Fears which it brings along with it, are inexpressibly dreadful" (p. A3). Then, in a lengthy section "from the Author's own Experience," he portrayed himself as having wept bitterly, having bemoaned his lot, having castigated himself, and having lived in fear of punishment for his sins from a wrathful God (pp. 352–369). Themes of anguish, terror, guilt, bitterness, sadness, desolation, and suffering are interwoven throughout this chapter. At first he had prayed and had poured out his troubles to God, but eventually he became so discouraged that he could no longer pray. A recurrent theme in this and subsequent chapters, and an occasional one earlier in this volume, is a sense of loss expressed in terms of a

---

*Rogers, a nonconformist minister, was born at Barnard Castle, Yorkshire, and educated at Glasgow University. After recovery from the illness that occasioned this book, he served in the London area for many years, but his melancholia returned and in 1707 he left the ministry, retiring to Wantage, Berkshire, where he died in 1728.

soul "that is under desertion,"* with the implication that God had withdrawn or departed from the deserted soul, which was then alone, sorrowing, and desolate.

Nowhere did Rogers provide the neat descriptive outline of melancholia typical of the medical authors. But that the traditional fear and sadness were central features is repeatedly made clear (pp. A2–A3, iii, 223). He emphasized that it was a chronic condition (title page, pp. A2, iii), and he implied that it was without fever (p. ii). He indicated that sleeplessness was characteristic (pp. ii–iii), and delirium or disordered thought was noted to be part of the condition (pp. ii, xi, 104–105). Nearly omnipresent is evidence that, for Rogers, guilt was an additional central affect; but here he was being less traditional, guilt having emerged as a common descriptive element only in the seventeenth century.† On the subject of guilt, he took some pains to differentiate those who suffered from "a deep, and a rooted Melancholly" from those who were "only under trouble of Conscience."‡ He saw himself as one of the former group, his treatise as relevant to that group, and his deeply troubling guilt as an element in a larger condition in which "Bodies are greatly diseased at the same time" (p. i).

As Rogers conceived of "Melancholly" as a disease, what were his medical notions? He emphasized that "it does generally indeed first begin at the Body, and then conveys its venom to the Mind"; and he stressed the importance of the ministrations of physicians and attending to *physical* factors, as well as the significance of the clergy and attending to spiritual factors (pp.

---

*Discourse, p. 352. Using either *dereliction* or *abandonment*, Christian writings have related this concept to Christ's cry on the Cross: "My God, my God, why hast thou forsaken me?" [New Testament, Mark, 15:34, and Matthew, 27:46; see also Old Testament, Psalms, 22:1]. *Spiritual abandonment* emerged to mean "dereliction of man by God," a state of "desolation" when "God leaves the sinner in punishment for his sin." And *desolation* implied "a perception of the absence of God as he is real," in contrast to *despair* meaning "a loss of God as though he were nothingness." Or, in other words, desolation meant a sense of being forsaken, while despair meant hopelessness. See Paul Kevin Meagher, Thomas C. O'Brien, and Consuelo Maria Aherne (eds.), *Encyclopedic Dictionary of Religion*, 2 vols. (Washington: The Sisters of St. Joseph of Philadelphia, & Corpus Publications, 1979), 1:2. This tradition of meanings found particular fresh roots in the literature of mysticism, especially in *The Dark Night of the Soul* by St. John of the Cross, with the implication of the sufferer's sense of identification with Christ often easily discerned. Eventually *desertion* came to be used as a synonym for dereliction in English, and the Latin word for each of them was *derelictio*.

†An interesting study of this theme has been made by H. B. M. Murphy, "The Advent of Guilt Feelings as a Common Depressive Symptom: A Historical Comparison on Two Continents," *Psychiatry*, 1978, *41*, 229–242. Despite Murphy's suggestion to the contrary, the theme of a guilty conscience was an element in Burton's thorough study of religious melancholia and had begun to appear even earlier. Robert Burton, *The Anatomy of Melancholy*, ed. Floyd Dell and Paul Jordan-Smith (New York: Tudor, 1948), pp. 866–971.

‡*Discourse*, p. i. This distinction between melancholia the disease and a guilty conscience was carefully emphasized by Timothy Bright, *A Treatise of Melancholie* (London: Thomas Vautrollier, 1586), pp. 184–198, and by others after him.

iii–iv). Rogers did not consistently adhere to a particular medical theory in his efforts to explain melancholia. He showed no inclination toward the chemical notions of his time, but he did employ elements of the new mechanical theories. He indicated that whatever "might keep the Blood and Spirits in their due temper and motion" would oppose the tendency to this disease (p. iii); "a disordered motion of the natural Spirits" was a common cause of the disease, and a depleted force of the spirits was associated with being sick (p. 105); despair was related to the dulling of a person's "motions" (pp. 125–126); "Sorrow of heart contracts the natural spirits, makes all their motions slow and feeble" (p. 374); "great and unusual stagnation or fixing of the Spirits" was characteristic of melancholia (p. 149); and melancholia was associated with stagnation of the blood and loss of the usual "brisk and cheerful motion of the Spirits" (p. 323).

At the same time, though, Rogers intermittently used residues of the traditional humoral theory in a way that suggested its continuing meaningfulness for him and his readers. He seemed to be alluding to the black bile when he referred to "this ugly Humour" and "its Malignant Influence" in melancholia (p. ii). And he explicitly referred to it in stating that the melancholic's troubled thoughts were not merely fancy or imagination, but rather that his "disordered Fancy" was "one of the sad affects that are produced by that black Humour that has vitiated all the natural spirits" (p. xi).

Rogers also considered the notion that "the Devil" might be the cause of melancholia; but, while indicating an acceptance of "the Devil" as a cause of disease at times "by God's permission," he dismissed this as a satisfactory explanation of melancholia (pp. xiv–xvii). On the other hand, Rogers readily assigned God a significant role in this disease (pp. 1–82, 352–392). The sufferer was conceived of as a sinner, like most of his fellowmen. The illness was then a punishment for sins; however, in some instances it might have been more a test of a Christian's steadfastness in the face of suffering, with parallels drawn to the suffering of Christ. A central notion was that of a soul deserted by God, which then supplied the rationale for heartrending descriptions of the person as alone, left, deserted, desolate, and otherwise forlorn. Although the sufferer might well have been undeserving of God's consideration, there were still grounds for hope because, most often via the mediation of Jesus Christ, God was disposed to forgive the sinner and relieve him of his melancholic burdens. In short, although Rogers emphasized strongly that melancholia was a disease with natural causes, he saw supernatural factors as significant in the form of God as the ultimate cause making use of the natural factors as immediate causes to punish or test the troubled person with the symptoms of the illness. Furthermore, these religious themes were very compelling ones for our author. Often enough he began a passage close to the clinical data of being melancholic, only to drift inexorably to the unfortunate plight of the sufferer in bemoaning terms with a steadily mounting accumulation of religious language and a steadily developing complexity of religious concept. Sometimes such a passage was almost an ode to gloom, but frequently a hopeful note crept in, and occasionally he approached the rhapsodical in his hope and encouraging mood.

Rogers's preoccupation with religious factors suggests that many in his era might have termed his condition religious melancholia. In his extensive section on this condition, Burton had conceived of it as one of the two categories of "Love-Melancholy," this one being related to God as the love object.[38] Its differentiating characteristics were religious delusions or aberrant religious convictions from superstition, heresy, and schism. Burton himself might well have included Rogers's case and general presentation under the rubric of *religious melancholy*, but what might have been religious delusions or indications of religious melancholia to him may have largely been elements of a painful reality in Rogers's eyes. On the other hand, Rogers did conceive of the condition as a delirium, that is, a form of madness.

As already noted, the theme of loss was a frequent one in the form of references to the sufferer's soul being under desertion by God. The soul had suffered the loss of God or separation from God; God had withdrawn from the soul, or forsaken the soul, or departed from the soul. Rogers also assessed the possible role of loss in melancholia in more naturalistic terms. He stated: "Many that are far from being naturally inclined to Melancholly, have been accidentally overwhelmed with it, by the loss of Children, by some sudden and unlooked for disappointment that ruines all their former Projects and Designs" (*Discourse*, p. v). But he did not attribute his own melancholia to such causes, and, in his dedication to Lady Mary Lane, he clearly implied that important losses did not necessarily lead to melancholia. As an example he differentiated his own disorder from her grief and sorrow in response to the deaths of her father, mother, and several children (pp. A3–A4).

Other than what has already been said, what was this book about? It was clearly a book of comfort and instruction for those suffering from melancholia and for their families and friends (title page, i–xxxiii). In spite of being explicitly autobiographical at times and obliquely autobiographical at other times, it was not truly an autobiography. On the other hand, as with many of the true autobiographies of that era, Rogers was using his own experience as an exemplum.[39] Much of his message seems to have been: "Do not despair. Have faith. Keep up your hope. However distressed or despairing you may feel, see, you too can recover with God's help, and perhaps Christ's intervention." Also, he made it clear that this volume was a thanksgiving to God for his own recovery. And it often sounds as if, in the process of writing, he was somehow trying to work out his own salvation.

Another victim of melancholia was William Cowper (1731–1800),* who left both brief and lengthy references to his illnesses in forty-five years' worth of letters and in his *Memoir of the Early Life of William Cowper, Esq.*[40] In 1753 he was "struck . . . with such a dejection of spirits, as none but they who have felt the same, can have the least conception of. Day and night I was upon the rack, lying down in horror, and rising up in despair" (*Memoir*, p. 26); and that disorder lasted nearly a year.

In 1763 he experienced an even more disruptive illness. He was apprehensive when faced with the prospect of a government appointment and its attendant responsibilities. The problem was compounded by having wished for the death of the previous officeholder that he might succeed him, only to have his wish realized and to feel profoundly guilty as a result (pp. 31–32). And this shy man was further disturbed when his sponsor's authority to appoint him was challenged and he found himself faced with an examination in the House of Lords (pp. 35–36). He became deeply distressed, and "an air of deep melancholy" characterized all he said or did (p. 33). His "continual misery at length brought on a nervous fever"—apparently a state of severe anxiety—and he came to wish for madness as a way out of his dilemma (pp. 36, 41). He became sullen and socially withdrawn (pp. 41–42). He was plagued by ideas of reference, at first in relation to a letter in a newspaper and later in relation to the expressions on people's faces and the writings of various authors (pp. 45–46, 61–62). He ruminated at length about the possibility of suicide; and several suicidal plans were approached with considerable ambivalence, each in turn being aborted or failing (pp. 42–56). This only added to his sense of sinfulness and guilt, and he developed a strong "sense of God's wrath, and a deep despair of escaping it" (p. 58). He was restless, agitated, "overwhelmed with despair," and convinced that he was guilty of an unpardonable sin (p. 63). He suffered from gloomy thoughts by day and dreadful visions by night (p. 64). He felt that he was damned, and "gave myself up to despair" (p. 66). Soon afterward he became flagrantly deranged and was taken to a private asylum kept by Dr. Nathaniel Cotton at St. Alban's and known as the Collegium Insanorum (pp. 70–71). He was afflicted with "a sense of self-loathing and abhorrence"; and "all that passed" in the next eight months "may be classed under two heads: conviction of sin, and despair of mercy" (pp. 71–72). Then his despair shifted to joy in a manner that quite encouraged him but rather alarmed his physician lest it "should terminate in a fatal frenzy" (p. 79). After nearly another year he left the asylum, experienced some melancholic mo-

*Cowper, the English poet, was born at Berkhampsted, Hertfordshire. He studied law in London, but never practiced his profession. Following his stay at St. Alban's (1763–1765), he settled in Huntingdon, soon taking up residence with the Unwin family. After Mr. Unwin's death he moved with the Unwins to Olney in 1767, moved from there to Weston Underwood in 1786, and left there, in turn, in 1795 to spend his final years in Norfolk.

ments on settling in a strange place and being surrounded by strangers, but found comfort and antidote in a sense of God's being with him (pp. 84–85). He made special mention of a brief period of finding himself "in a state of desertion"—an interrupted sense of communion with God, a feeling of distressing aloneness once again—that seems to have ended with the establishment of new friendships (p. 88).

In 1773 Cowper "plunged into a melancholy that made me almost an infant" (Wright, *Correspondence*, 3:9). He likened it to the experience ten years earlier, "only covered with a still deeper shade of melancholy, and ordained to be of much longer duration" (ibid., 2:442). It was following this episode that, after various efforts at what we might call occupational therapy, he turned to his writing in a significantly more earnest fashion (2:443). As he put it, "dejection of spirits, which, I suppose, may have prevented many a man from becoming an author, made me one" (2:364). And it was during this episode that he had a frightening dream in which he was told, "It is all over with thee, thou hast perished." After this he felt that he was a doomed man, that God had permanently forsaken him, and he continued with that disturbing conviction most of the rest of his life (1:132). He also intimated that he was never again free of melancholy (4:280, 321).

In 1786, when looking back over thirteen years of chronic, but not disabling, melancholy, Cowper referred to himself as having been under desertion by God all that while (3:40–41). Then in 1787 his melancholy worsened once again to the point of frank derangement, which lasted about six months. And, after his close companion's first paralytic stroke in 1791, he seems to have been more seriously melancholy through much of the 1790s.

Although Cowper clearly thought of himself as suffering from a disease, and a grave one indeed, and although at times he received medications and was otherwise ministered to by physicians, neither his letters nor his *Memoir* reveals any inclination to introduce medical theories, old or new, into his efforts to describe or explain his condition. On the other hand, like Rogers, he was preoccupied with God in his efforts to understand and explain his illness. Like Rogers, he conceived of himself as sinful and guilty, and he thought of his illness as punishment from God, albeit extreme and perhaps even unfair in its duration and severity. Like Rogers, he considered himself to have been in a state of desertion by God. While in our terms he suffered from chronic depression with intermittent anxiety, and his periods of derangement would be thought of as psychotic episodes of agitated depression, in his own time some would have thought him to have been suffering from religious melancholy, as they would have with Rogers.

In contrast to Rogers's work, Cowper's *Memoir* was more truly an autobiography. Unlike Rogers he did not publish it, and he guarded its circulation carefully.[41] But he did think of it as an exemplum. As he stated in one of his letters, it was intended to teach "the Sovereignty of God's free grace in the deliverance of a Sinful Soul from the nethermost Hell."[42] Again unlike Rogers's *Discourse*, the *Memoir* was the story of a religious conversion, a spiritual autobiography serving as a testimony. Noteworthy is the tone of joy to the point of elation on his recovery, an emotional tone that lasted for several years. For Cowper this joy was associated with a sense of communion with God, in contrast to his sense of being in a state of desertion previously and for most of the remainder of his life.

These works by Rogers and Cowper belong to an era in Britain that seems to have been particularly sensitized to and interested in melancholic matters, what with the melancholic themes in so much of the literature of the day and the allegedly high incidence of milder melancholic states that were the basis for much complaining and were at times even fashionable.[43] But these two cases are readily distinguished from those commoner maladies. When one studies them, it soon becomes evident that, in each instance, the sufferer had been severely disturbed—anxious, depressed, and delusional. That is, they both suffered from melancholia the disease in its classical sense as one of the three traditional forms of madness. As, additionally, each was severely guilt-ridden and preoccupied with religious concerns, the diagnosis of religious melancholia might have been made in their own time. The much more prevalent contemporary diagnosis of hypochondriasis, at times referred to as melancholy, would not have subsumed these two psychotic experiences, although Cowper's melancholy-tinged years when he was not insane might have been so categorized by some. And neither Rogers nor Cowper used the term *hypochondriasis*, or any of its popular equivalents, to refer to his own condition.

To pursue this matter a bit further, it is useful to review briefly the implications of the term *hypochondriasis* in those times. In the seventeenth century both Willis and Sydenham had separated hypochondriasis out from the other types of melancholia, grouping it with hysteria instead, describing the two conditions as syndromes that included a broad range of physical and psychological complaints but not madness, citing them as accounting for a significant percentage of the problems seen by physicians, and identifying hysteria as the aspect of this conglomerate that generally afflicted women and hypochondriasis as the aspect that generally afflicted men.[44] From there, often in tandem with hysteria, hypochondriasis more or less went its own way. Frequently referred to as "the Hyp," "the Vapours," or "the Spleen," but also often as melancholy, this condition continued to subsume a loose-knit collection of physical complaints, anxiety, and depression. It seems to have included conditions that we might term "psychoneurotic" and "psychosomatic" today,[45] but it usually did not include instances of madness or insanity.* The term *melancholy* in the eighteenth century often referred to this condition, often to vaguer forms of malaise, often to just plain unhappiness, but, unfortunately and sometimes confusingly, it was also still used to refer to the traditional disease of melancholia, a form of madness.

The literature of Britain during this period is replete with uses of the term *melancholy* in the ill-defined ways just outlined. Whereas Rogers and Cowper were unusual as victims of traditional melancholia who wrote about it, autobiographical references to these other troublesome conditions were moderately common. James Boswell (1740–1795) referred to his own melancholy again and again in his letters, in the many volumes of his journals, and in his essays as *The Hypochondriack.*[46] And George Cheyne (1671–1743), in his *The English Malady*, intermittently used the term *melancholy* in his lengthy section entitled "The CASE of the Author."† But these authors, and most others who made such references to their own melancholy, hypochondriasis, or spleen, were referring to very different states and experiences from those of Rogers and Cowper. They were not referring to psychotic states, however freely they threw around the word *melancholy* or even the word *madness*.

While our two authors left us with moving accounts of their troubles, they have provided us with only a very limited perspective on the medical theories used in the explanation of melancholia. Rogers gives us clear indications of the shift toward the mechanical explanations that were to develop further and hold the field for a number of decades. The absence of any tendency to chemical explanations is perhaps indicative of the fact that this system did not last for very long in the explaining of melancholia. And his uses of the older humoral theory suggest that it died hard, even while the mechanical theory was taking over. But these medical theories were not prominent elements in his account. As to Cowper, there is nothing to tell us what medical theories, if any, he may have entertained in thinking about his own disorder, or even what relevant medical views might have been familiar in his immediate circle. Clearly, both our authors were far more given to religious notions in endeavoring to cope with and explain their illnesses.

In summary, we have two eloquent accounts of severely distressing

*Robinson endeavored to reconcile these various conditions by conceiving of "the Spleen" and "the Vapours" as milder disorders, of "the Hip" as a more serious disorder, and of "Melancholy" as madness and the severest disorder, all deriving from basically similar causes: *New System* [n. 43], pp. 196–201. For a detailed study of hypochondriasis, including its roots in hypochondriacal melancholia and its eighteenth-century status, see chap. 11.

†Cheyne, *English Malady* [n. 43], pp. 325–364. Despite often being cited as the prototypical study of melancholy for this era, Cheyne's work might better be referred to as a representative account of hypochondriasis in its eighteenth-century meanings, as his syndrome was only minimally related to traditional melancholia.

experiences of being deranged, profoundly anxious and depressed, guilt-ridden, and preoccupied with religious concerns. Each instance fits well the patterns long associated with the traditional disease of melancholia, one of the classical forms of madness; each was referred to as melancholy in its time; each might have been termed religious melancholia in its own era; and each would today be thought of as a psychotic depression with severe anxiety, guilt, and religious delusions. They had more in common with one another across a span of nearly seventy-five years than either of them had with most of the minor melancholies of their own times, notwithstanding the sharing of depressive features with the latter. And their contrast to those other melancholies strongly suggests the psychotic versus nonpsychotic distinction that is often used in considering depressive states today.

LITERARY AND POPULAR MELANCHOLY

As just noted, in ways not unlike those of the late sixteenth and early seventeenth centuries, the eighteenth century was an era of much mention of melancholy, particularly in the British Isles. As a complex of character traits, a set of manners, or a coloration to a personality, melancholy was well regarded by many and thus often taken on as an affectation. For many, it was an indication of a superior mind, or at least of refinement and superior social status. Others suffered, however, and yet found comfort, whether small or great, in associating themselves with melancholic traditions. Many literary persons wrote of it in periodical essays, popular works on health and manners, novels, and, above all, poetry.

As briefly remarked above and as will be detailed in a later chapter (11), the transformation of hypochondriacal melancholia into *hypochondriasis, the hyp,* or *the spleen* had produced a spate of medical writings on the subject of milder dejected or gloomy states accompanied by varying mixtures of physical complaints. Against this backdrop, literary figures complained of their gloominess, moaned about their fate, found solace in their "superiority," took pride in their melancholic cast of mind, and often enough transmuted these personal trends into literary works of some consequence. Twentieth-century literary scholars have carefully mined these materials to bring us some interesting and valuable studies, such as those by Reed, Doughty, Sickels, Moore, Sena, and Ingram (see n. 43). They tell of the "night thoughts" and other gloomy ruminations of the "graveyard poets," the satirical essays of Addison and Steele, the recurrent use of "the spleen" in novels, the "splenetic travellers," the entertaining poem *The Spleen,* by Matthew Green, the "white melancholy" of Thomas Gray, the repeated recurrence of dejected themes in Cowper's letters and poems, and Boswell *the Hypochondriack's* many references to his melancholic disposition. And they comment on the thread of dejection and melancholy connecting these productions to the *Weltschmerz* of the turn of the century and the melancholic odes and other examples in the "Romantics" of the early nineteenth century.

SAMUEL JOHNSON'S MELANCHOLY

Meriting some separate mention is the less typical case of Samuel Johnson (1709–1784), who recurrently feared a melancholy insanity, who made reference to his "vile melancholy," and who suffered through two lengthy periods of serious dejection. In his early twenties and again in his fifties, he experienced several years of melancholy distress.[47] After leaving Oxford University in his early twenties, Johnson went through a long spell of considerable anxiety, lassitude, and discouragement, at times fearing that he was becoming insane.[48] He "felt himself overwhelmed with an horrible melancholia, with perpetual irritation, fretfulness, and impatience; and with a dejection, gloom, and despair, which made existence misery."[49] Over the next approximately thirty years, productive though they were, he lived with nearly constant self-criticism, exacting self-demands and an inner protest against them, a severe sense of guilt with associated anxiety, various compulsive movements and tics, and numerous physical complaints. As he was to tell Joshua Reynolds in later years, "the great business of his life . . . was to escape from himself; this disposition he considered as the disease of his mind, which nothing cured but company."[50] Again in later life, in the course of arguing for the significant role of nurture in a person's development, he also "owned . . . that we inherit dispositions from our parents," and added, "I inherited a vile melancholy from my father, which has made me mad all my life, at least not sober."[51] From the extensive eighteenth-century evidence and from modern scholarly work on these materials, it seems that both recurrent distress and hyperbole contributed to this latter remark.

His friend Arthur Murphy has left us a particularly perceptive observation regarding Johnson's struggles with indolence and mental distress, along with a selection of Johnson's own comments on his lifelong tendencies.

> Indolence was the time of danger: it was then that his spirits, not employed abroad, turned with inward hostility against himself. His reflections on his own life and conduct were always severe; and, wishing to be immaculate, he destroyed his own peace by unnecessary scruples. He tells us, that, when he surveyed his past life, he discovered nothing but a barren waste of time, with some disorders of body, and disturbances of mind, very near to madness. His

life, he says, from his earliest youth, was wasted in a morning bed; and his reigning sin was a general sluggishness, to which he was always inclined, and, in part of his life, almost compelled, by morbid melancholy and weariness of mind. This was his constitutional malady, derived, perhaps, from his father, who was, at times, overcast with a gloom that bordered on insanity.[52]

Inordinate attention to "vain scruples" was to be with him most of his life, and, during his second serious disturbance in his fifties, he referred again and again to "scruples" in taking note of his distress.[53]

In an early stage of this second breakdown in his fifties he commented in his diary on Easter Eve 1761 as follows: "Since the Communion of last Easter I have led a life so dissipated and useless, and my terrours and perplexities have so much increased, that I am under great depression and discouragement."[54] The next several years involved "the distresses of vain terrour," being "disturbed with doubts and harassed with vain terrours," being severely low in "spirits," lassitude and a bemoaning of his lack of accomplishment, and much misery and melancholy; and they occasioned comments from friends, for example: "such a torpor had seized his faculties, as not all the remonstrances of his friends were able to cure."[55]

Many people in the twentieth century might look back and conclude that Johnson was burdened with an obsessive-compulsive character and frequent obsessive-compulsive symptoms, that he was of a depressive disposition, and that he suffered two lengthy breakdowns with severe depression and anxiety. One such person, Balderston, a literary scholar of note, drew on fragmentary references by Johnson and others to padlocks and chains, and concluded that his "vile melancholy" was some form of erotic and masochistic disorder in which he desired domination and pain.[56] Although some modern scholars with a rather indifferent concern for the evidence have gone along with Balderston's conclusions, Bate, after examining the evidence carefully, was highly dubious about such conclusions. He thought rather that such allusions were aspects of Johnson's recurrent metaphorical use of chains and shackles to refer to his burdens, worries, sins, guilt, and so forth, with the likelihood that the concrete evidence ("the padlock") was related to being confined when most deeply disturbed and frightened (*Johnson*, pp. 384–388). Bate was of the opinion that Johnson's terrible secret was, instead, that of actually having been insane for a while and thus was intimately connected with his recurrent fear of becoming insane (pp. 388–389). In an eighteenth-century frame of reference, however, he appears to have been chronically plagued with a distress that many conceived of as *hypochondriasis* or *the spleen* and for which *melancholy* was often used synonymously with those terms. On the other hand, his two protracted breakdowns seem to merit the severer eighteenth-century diagnosis of *melancholia*, for which *melancholy* was again used as a synonym.* As in the case of Cowper, the eighteenth-century view that hypochondriasis and melancholia were closely related as the lesser and the greater on a continuum of severity seems to have been supported by Johnson's history. Johnson's own alarms and concerns about his own state—including his fear of insanity—may have been symptomatic worries only, may reflect the view that he suffered from melancholia as a form of madness by his era's standards, may represent informed worries that his disorder might worsen and become *mania*, or may be indicative of "secret" knowledge that he had been more deranged than anyone else knew. Boswell was frequently concerned to dispute the severer of these conclusions (*Life of Johnson*, 1:35, 65–66; 3:175), at times indicating that he thought the first of these possibilities to be the case. At other times, he argued that Johnson suffered merely from melancholy, sometimes reflecting the view that melancholy was a less severe form of derangement than madness (as mania) and sometimes that it was hypochondriasis and not a form of derangement at all. Boswell also maintained that Johnson was often misleadingly sloppy about these distinctions. Regarding Johnson's own concerns as to the nature of his condition, for all the fact that he "was a great dabbler in physic" (3:152) and "had studied medicine diligently in all its branches" with "particular attention to the diseases of the imagination,"[57] he showed almost no inclination to discuss or even refer to his melancholy in the medical jargon of his time or to pursue his frequent worries about it in medical terms.

Further perspective on both Johnson's troubled mind and his depth of understanding of mental life can be gained from some passages from his novel *Rasselas*. There one finds his chronic fear of insanity, his preoccupation with his own guilt, his recurrent attention to his own mental functions, and further concerns with melancholy turned to account as aspects of a literary work.

> Of the uncertainties of our present state, the most dreadful and alarming is the uncertain continuance of reason. . . .
>   Disorders of intellect . . . happen much more often than superficial observers will easily believe. Perhaps, if we speak with rigorous exactness, no human mind is in its right state. There is no man whose imagination does not

---

*Johnson himself, as the author of the *Dictionary*, provided us with the following samples of eighteenth-century meanings. *Melancholia* was not listed. *Melancholy* was defined as "a kind of madness, in which the mind is always fixed on one object," and "a disease, supposed to proceed from a redundance of black bile; but it is better known to arise from too heavy and too viscid blood: its cure is in evacuation, nervous medicines, and powerful stimuli." He also attested to the continuing use of *melancholy* to refer to one of the temperaments: "a gloomy, pensive, discontented temper." *Hypochondriasis* was not listed. Only the adjectival forms, *hypochondriacal* and *hypochondriack*, were mentioned, and they were defined as "melancholy; disordered in the imagination." See Samuel Johnson, *A Dictionary of the English Language* . . . , 2 vols. (London: J. and P. Knapton; T. and T. Longman; C. Hitch and L. Hawes; A. Millar; and R. and J. Dodsley, 1755).

sometimes predominate over his reason, who can regulate his attention wholly by his will, and whose ideas will come and go at his command. No man will be found in whose mind airy notions do not sometimes tyrranise, and force him to hope or fear beyond the limits of sober probability. All power of fancy over reason is a degree of insanity; but while this power is such as we can control and repress, it is not visible to others, nor considered as any deprivation of the mental faculties: it is not pronounced madness but when it becomes ungovernable and apparently influences speech or action.

To indulge the power of fiction, and send imagination out upon the wing, is often the sport of those who delight too much in silent speculation. When we are alone we are not always busy; the labour of excogitation is too violent to last long; the ardour of inquiry will sometimes give way to idleness or satiety. He who has nothing external that can divert him, must find pleasure in his own thoughts, and must conceive himself what he is not; for who is pleased with what he is? He then expatiates in boundless futurity, and culls from all imaginable conditions that which for the present moment he should most desire, amuses his desires with impossible enjoyments, and confers upon his pride unattainable dominion. The mind dances from scene to scene, unites all pleasures in all combinations, and riots in delights, which nature and fortune, with all their bounty, cannot bestow.

In time some particular train of ideas fixes the attention; all other intellectual gratifications are rejected; the mind, in weariness or leisure, recurs constantly to the favorite conception, and feasts on the luscious falsehood whenever she is offended with the bitterness of truth. By degrees the reign of fancy is confirmed; she grows first imperious, and in time despotic. Then fictions begin to operate as realities, false opinions fasten upon the mind, and life passes in dreams of rapture or of anguish.

This . . . is one of the dangers of solitude. . . .

No disease of the imagination . . . is so difficult of cure as that which is complicated with the dread of guilt; fancy and conscience then act interchangeably upon us, and so often shift their places, that the illusions of one are not distinguished from the dictates of the other. If fancy presents images not moral or religious, the mind drives them away when they give it pain; but when melancholic notions take the form of duty, they lay hold on the faculties without opposition, because we are afraid to exclude or banish them. For this reason the superstitious are often melancholy, and the melancholy almost always superstitious.[58]

Finally, Johnson's use of the term *depression* is of some special interest. While there was an occasional seventeenth-century reference to "depression of spirits" and Burton referred to "such as are depressed (*Anatomy*, p. 476), it was during the eighteenth century that "depression" really began to find a place in discussions of melancholia and dejection, and Johnson was prominent in this emerging trend. In 1752 in *The Rambler* he used the phrase "observed their depression";[59] in 1761 in his diary he wrote of being "under great depression";[60] and in 1763 in writing about William Collins he stated that "he languished some years under that depression of mind which enchains the faculties without destroying them, and leaves reason the knowledge of right without the power of pursuing it."[61] And Boswell followed his lead, noting that, at the time of completing the preface to his *Dictionary* in 1755, "Johnson's mind appears to have been in such a state of depression . . ." (*Life,* 1:297). Although Johnson made these various uses of the noun *depression* that seem to foreshadow the language of late nineteenth- and twentieth-century psychiatry, he did not offer any such definitions in his *Dictionary.* On the other hand, in his *Dictionary's* entry for the verb *to depress,* he made it clear that one meaning involved "to deject" or "to depress the mind," and he included supporting examples from Locke, Addison, and Prior (no p.). Apparently, though, he was a significant influence in the emerging trend that would eventually lead to *depression* largely displacing *melancholy* and *melancholia* in the literature of dejected states.

CHAPTER EIGHT

Melancholia in the Nineteenth Century

PHILIPPE PINEL

An outline of the views of Philippe Pinel (1745–1826) is a particularly appropriate way to approach the subject of melancholia during the nineteenth century. He was central among the late eighteenth-century figures who brought increased and sharpened attention to the mentally ill, and his turn-of-the-century writings on mental disorders were much attended to in their time. Reacting against the systems of De Sauvages and Cullen and leaving behind the overly elaborate classification of his own *Nosographie Philosophique* of the 1790s, Pinel presented in 1801 a much simplified scheme of mental disorders composed of *mania, melancholia, dementia,* and *idiotism* in his *Traité Médico-philosophique sur l'Aliénation Mentale.* He entitled his section on melancholia "Melancholia, or Delirium upon One Subject Exclusively," thus reaffirming support for the idea that it was a partial insanity, in contrast to the doubts expressed on that point by Cullen twenty years earlier.[1] He introduced this section with the statement that "the symptoms generally comprehended by the term melancholia are taciturnity, a thoughtful pensive air, gloomy suspicions, and a love of solitude" (*Treatise*, p. 136). Expanding on his title, he noted that "melancholics are frequently absorbed by one exclusive idea, to which they perpetually recur in their conversation, and which appears to engage their whole attention" (p. 141). He recognized "two opposite forms of melancholia with delirium," commenting that "sometimes it is distinguished by an exalted sentiment of self-importance, associated with chimerical pretensions to unbounded power or inexhaustible riches. At other times, it is characterized by great depression of spirits, pusillanimous apprehensions and even absolute despair" (p. 143). He mentioned that occasionally cases of melancholia degenerated into mania and that some melancholics manifested suicidal inclinations (pp. 145–149). And he summed it up in the following way:

> Delirium exclusively upon one subject; no propensity to acts of violence, independent of such as may be impressed by a predominant and chimerical idea; free exercise in other respects of all the faculties of the understanding: in some cases, equanimity of disposition, or a state of unruffled satisfaction: in others, habitual depression and anxiety, and frequently a moroseness of character amounting even to the most decided misanthropy, and sometimes to an invincible disgust with life. (p. 149)

Pinel did not offer any sort of systematic theory to explain how cases of melancholia had come about. And he decried any view that suggested that particular causes brought about particular species of insanity. As he put it, "my experience authorizes me to affirm, that there is no necessary connection between the specific character of insanity, and the nature of its exciting cause" (pp. 14–15). Instead he conceived of instances of insanity as individual outcomes determined by the effect of particular exciting causes on unique premorbid dispositions. He noted that "numerous results of dissection . . . have shewn no organic lesion of the head" (pp. 110–111); and, in general, his experience suggested that moral causes were the essential ones. He observed that "the exciting causes" had usually been "very vivid affections of the mind, such as ungovernable or disappointed ambition, religious fanaticism, profound chagrin, and unfortunate love." In one study he identified "domestic misfortunes . . . obstacles to matrimonial connections which they had ardently desired to form . . . events connected with the revolution, and . . . religious fanaticism" as the four basic exciting causes (p. 113).

He expressed serious reservations about treating melancholic patients "in the usual way, by copious and repeated bloodletting, water and shower baths, low diet, and a rigorous system of coercion" and advocated instead a program of moral treatment (pp. 101–102). With such patients he emphasized the importance "of forcibly agitating the system; of interrupting the chain of their gloomy ideas, and of engaging their interest by powerful and continuous impressions on their external senses" (p. 180). Then he used the example of "temples dedicated to Saturn" in ancient Egypt to illustrate the importance of pleasant surroundings, and entertaining and diverting activities in the treatment of melancholics (pp. 180–182). He was prepared to resort to "energetic measures of coercion" in the case of serious suicidal threat (pp. 183–184). Pinel had grave reservations about medications in general, and evacuants in particular, but considered tonic remedies appropriate (pp. 223–224). He advocated "the art of counteracting" debilitating passions "by others of equal or superior force" (pp. 228–231).

BENJAMIN RUSH

Benjamin Rush (1745–1813), "the father of American psychiatry," dealt with melancholia in his *Diseases of the Mind* but in a somewhat unusual way. Cullen's student and considerably influenced by his theories, he moved away from them in significant ways. Pinel's contemporary, he was very different indeed in his approach to mental disorders. On mental diseases, he was not particularly influential beyond his own shores, but his views related to melancholia were received with great respect by Esquirol. Regarding melancholia, Rush recognized the notion of "partial insanity" or "partial derangement," which many had previously mentioned in defining and describing this disorder. After stating that "partial derangement consists in error in opinion and conduct, upon some one subject only, with soundness of mind upon all, or nearly all other subjects," he added that the nosologists of the day had identified two forms of partial derangement as follows:

> When it relates to the persons, affairs, or conditions of the patient only, and is attended with distress, it has been called hypochondriasis. When it extends to objects external to the patient, and is attended with pleasure, or the absence of distress, it has been called melancholia. They are different grades only of the same morbid actions in the brain, and they now and then blend their symptoms with each other.[2]

He was dissatisfied with these names for these two disorders, and he coined the terms *tristimania* for the former and *amenomania* for the latter (*Diseases*, pp. 73–74).

To avoid confusion, it should be noted here that Rush was *not* following the eighteenth-century custom in his use of the term *hypochondriasis*. Although it continued to involve dyspepsia, a variety of other bodily complaints, and usually the traditional fear and sadness, it was no longer customary for hypochondriasis to imply a delirium, that is, to be a form of madness. It had come to be usually viewed as a milder disorder than melancholia, sometimes categorized separately from melancholia and sometimes conceived of as a separate but related condition on a continuum of severity from hypochondriasis to melancholia to mania. Thus Rush, in speaking of hypochondriasis as a partial insanity, may have been reverting to the older meaning of hypochondriacal melancholia, a form of madness. However, in light of the clinical picture that he then proceeded to describe, he might be said to have fused eighteenth-century hypochondriasis and the form of madness known to the eighteenth century as melancholia. When he turned to what he alleged was considered melancholia by others, he was dealing with a condition that would have sometimes been so named during the eighteenth century as a reflection of a tendency to use the term to refer to more than merely those whom we might diagnose as suffering from psychotic depression; and yet he ignored the fact that melancholia still usually implied fear and sadness. Thus, in his brief description of what he maintained was melancholia, he was not accurately reflecting the use of the term in that era, although he was selecting out a minority group of those insane persons who were so diagnosed. When we consider his clinical description of tristimania, it would seem that later authors who referred to Rush's tristimania as equivalent to his predecessors' melancholia were more or less correct, but Rush himself did not hold this view.

As to the clinical picture of tristimania, he noted the bodily "symptoms of this form of derangement" to include dyspepsia, either costiveness or diarrhea, flatulency, various other gastrointestinal symptoms, either strong sexual desires or an absence of sexual desires, and disturbed sleep (ibid., pp. 76–77). "The characteristic symptom . . . , as it appears in the mind, is *distress*, the causes of which are numerous, and of a personal nature" (pp. 77–78). He then detailed examples of these "causes," which turned out to be delusional beliefs about bodily afflictions and various delusions akin to the traditional lists so often cited in earlier accounts of melancholia (pp. 78–80). He commented that, although such a patient started from one of these basic delusional beliefs, he thereafter reasoned correctly from the erroneous starting point; and he observed that "all the erroneous opinions, persons affected with this form of derangement entertain of themselves, are of a degrading nature" (p. 80). He concluded his descriptive account by stating that more extreme symptoms might occur, such as despair, the wish to die, and even suicide (pp. 93–95).

When it came to efforts to explain tristimania, or any other disease of the mind, Rush's views were rooted in a complex pathogenetic theory. Concluding that all diseases were essentially fevers and thus were variants of one basic condition, by the 1790s he had developed his own unitary theory of disease.[3] Shifting away from Cullen's notions of a nervous power and neurally determined levels of excitement in explaining much of physiology and pathology, Rush gradually developed a theory in which the vascular system was central and disordered excitement therein was the crucial explanatory factor. He grounded his theory in the notion of life as a forced state, that is, life as a state of motion or excitement that resulted from stimuli acting upon some quality or substance in animal matter. In this regard, he disclaimed any influence from the theories of John Brown and indicated that he had derived this notion from Cullen, although the latter had subsequently abandoned it. He thought in terms of a state of "general debility" that resulted from the reduction to pathological levels of "the excitement of the system" (*Medical Inquiries*, 3:4–7). With the system so predisposed, the continued action of stimuli led to a "re-action" that was the disease or fever. This "re-action" occurred "primarily in the blood-vessels, and particularly in the arteries," and consisted of "irregular" or "convulsive" motions, also termed "morbid excitement." This activity was "mechanical" in nature and was a result of the "elastic and muscular texture" of the blood vessels (ibid., 3:9–10).

Against this background Rush developed his ideas about the disorders of the mind as one more set of illnesses with basically the same pathogenesis as other illnesses. Early on in his *Medical Inquiries and Observations upon the Diseases of the Mind* he outlined his credo as a physiological psychologist: "All the operations in the mind are the effects of motions previously excited in the brain, and every idea and thought appears to depend upon a motion peculiar to itself. In a sound state of mind these motions are regular, and succeed impressions upon the brain with the same certainty and uniformity that perceptions succeed impressions upon the senses in their sound state" (*Diseases of the Mind*, p. 9). Having rejected various other sites "as the primary seats of madness" or "derangement," he then went on to state that "the cause of madness is seated primarily in the blood-vessels of the brain, and that it depends upon the same kind of morbid and irregular actions that constitutes other arterial diseases. There is nothing specific in these actions. They are a part of the unity of disease, particularly of fever; of which madness is a chronic form, affecting that part of the brain which is the seat of the mind" (pp. 15–16).

As to treatment, Rush began with a program of depleting measures: bloodletting, purges, emetics, and a reduced diet (pp. 97–99). After thus "reducing the action of the blood-vessels to a par of debility with the nervous system" (p. 99), he turned to a stimulating program of diet, drinks, and medicines, making special mention in this last category of "preparations of iron" and opium (pp. 99–101). He also mentioned warm baths followed by cold baths, "frictions to the trunk of the body and limbs," exercise, "the excitement of pain," salivation, and "blisters and issues" (pp. 101–103). He then gave considerable attention to "remedies for the body, which are intended to act through the mind" (pp. 103ff.). He advocated "a change of company, pursuits, and climate" and stated that "the errors which predominate in the mind should be soothed, diverted, or opposed by reasoning or ridicule, according to their force" (p. 137).

JEAN-ETIENNE-DOMINIQUE ESQUIROL

Although he had been Pinel's student and was strongly influenced by him in many ways, Jean-Etienne-Dominique Esquirol's (1772–1840) writings were based to a significant degree on his own experience and were much more influential than those of his teacher in many areas, including the subject of melancholia.[4] In considering melancholia he took note of the long association of the term with "that form of delirium which is characterized by moroseness, fear, and prolonged sadness" and with the black bile as the cause of the disease; and he then referred to the newer tradition that had "called melancholic, every form of *partial* delirium, when chronic, and unattended by fever" (*Mental Maladies*, pp. 199–200). He objected to the name "melancholy" on the basis of its association with the black bile and its loose use in the common language to denote various states of sadness. Observing that "the ancients . . . were obliged to rank among melancholics certain cases of partial delirium, which were maintained by an extreme exaltation of the imagination, or by passions of a gay and sprightly character" (p. 202), and, apparently troubled by this lumping together of "manialike" cases and the traditional fearful and sad cases as both being instances of melancholia, he introduced the term *monomania* to denote "that form of insanity, in which the delirium is partial, permanent, gay *or* sad" (p. 200; emphasis added). He then subdivided monomania into two types: (1) "monomania properly so called, which is indicated by a partial delirium, and a gay or exciting passion" and which "corresponds with maniacal melancholy, maniacal fury, or with melancholy complicated with mania; in fine, with *amenomania*"; and (2) the monomania that "corresponds with the melancholy of the ancients, the *tristimania* of Rush, and the melancholy with delirium of Pinel." Although conceiving of monomania as the generic term, he proposed to reserve its usual use for the first of these two species, and he introduced the term *lypemania* for the second species, indicating that he would use *lypemania* and *melancholy* as synonyms (p. 202).

Esquirol defined melancholia (or lypemania) as "a cerebral malady, characterized by partial, chronic delirium, without fever, and sustained by a passion of a sad, debilitating or oppressive character" (p. 203). Turning to clinical description, he stated:

> In person, the lypemaniac is lean and slender, his hair is black, and the hue of his countenance pale and sallow. . . . The physiognomy is fixed and changeless; but the muscles of the face are in a state of convulsive tension, and express sadness, fear or terror; the eyes are motionless, and directed either towards the earth or to some distant point, and the look is askance, uneasy and suspicious. . . . (ibid.)
>
> Lypemaniacs sleep little; inquietude and fear, terror, jealousy and hallucinations, keep them awake. If they grow drowsy, no sooner do their eyes close, than they see a thousand phantoms which terrify them. If they sleep, their rest is interrupted, and agitated by dreams of an inauspicious character. . . . They dread obscurity, solitude, insomnia, the terrors of sleep, etc. The secretions also, present remarkable disorders among lypemaniacs. In some cases, the urine is abundant, clear, and limpid; in others, scanty, thick and turbid. (p. 205)

He then detailed the picture of an apprehensive and depressed person who readily found grounds in the slightest thing for further fear or further despair. Such persons tended to be preoccupied with their delusional concerns. "External objects, no longer sustaining their natural relations, grieve, astonish, and frighten them. They have illusions of the senses, and hallucinations. They associate ideas the most strange and unlike; from all which spring convictions more or less opposed to common sense, unjust prejudices, fear, fright, dread, awe and terror" (pp. 205–206). His view was that "the depressing passions produce also a partial lesion of the understanding," and so it followed that delusional thinking would occur; and "fear, with all its shadows, whether the cause of it be real or imaginary, exercises the most general influence over melancholics" (p. 206). He also emphasized the frequency of fear without any object at all, what we would today term "anxiety" (p. 207). Such patients tended to be preoccupied with the narrow range of their worries and delusional concerns. "Some . . . possess a knowledge of their condition, have a consciousness of its falsity, and of the absurdity of the fears in which they are tormented. They perceive clearly that they are irrational, and often confess it, with grief and even despair" (p. 208). While "the monomaniac [excited partial insanity] lives *without* himself, and diffuses among others the excess of his emotions," the melancholic "fastens upon himself all his thoughts, all his affections; is egotistical, and lives *within* himself" (p. 320). In addition to viewing such persons as insane only in the sphere of their particular delusion, he added that "lypemaniacs are never unreasonable, not even in that sphere of thought which characterizes their delirium. They proceed upon a false idea, as well as wrong principles; but all their reasonings and deductions are conformable to the severest logic" (p. 209).

Esquirol indicated that "the causes of melancholy are numerous and are common to other forms of insanity" (ibid.). He proceeded to enumerate some factors "which have a more immediate influence on the frequency and character of melancholy"—a conflicting variety of seasonal and climatic influences; a tendency to reach its peak in the prime of life and slowly diminish in incidence thereafter; an uncertainty as to whether women were more or less prone than men; the melancholic temperament as a predisposing factor; physically active modes of life less prone, idleness predisposed, and scholarly and intellectual vocations more prone; the depressing passions (pp. 209–215). He then provided a "table of causes" of melancholia that had "hereditary predisposition" as decidedly the most frequent, with the following as high on the list—domestic troubles, reverses of fortune and consequent misery, disappointed affection, critical periods of life, childbirth, suppression of menses, and libertinism (p. 214). Among the various pathological lesions that might be found in melancholics on postmortem examination, "organic lesions of the lungs" were by far the most common, with "colon displaced" as the only other finding with any frequency (p. 225).

Esquirol stated that treatment "ought not to be limited to the administration of certain medicines. . . . Moral medicine, which seeks in the heart for the cause of the evil, which sympathizes and weeps, which consoles, and divides with the unfortunate their sufferings, and which revives hope in their breast, is often preferable to all other." He advocated "a dry and temperate climate, a clear sky, a pleasant temperature, an agreeable situation with varied scenery" as being "well adapted to melancholics" (p. 226). He recommended warm clothing, careful attention to diet, exercise, travel if feasible, horseback riding, useful labors—all reminiscent of the traditional therapeutic attention to the non-naturals (p. 227). He noted that solitude often served to reestablish "the moral forces that have been exhausted by the passions." He emphasized the value of tepid baths and the need to relieve constipation, suggesting for this dietary approaches, baths, and enemata. He said that coitus may be helpful, adding that "it is not easy to establish the degree of influence which, in this act, belongs, respectively, to the physical and moral impression" (p. 228). He strongly advocated moral treatment in the interests of bringing the patient's passions back into balance; and he emphasized that "each melancholic should be treated on principles resulting from a thorough acquaintance with the tendency of his mind, his character and habits, in order to subjugate the passion which, controlling his thoughts, maintains his delirium" (pp. 228–230). He mentioned various physical symptoms that might require appropriate medications: agents to reestablish suppressed menstrual or hemorrhoidal flow; gentle laxatives or mild purgatives for constipation; various other evacuants as indicated; and occasionally "local sanguine evacuations" for suppressed menstrual or hemorrhoidal flow, or signs of "cerebral congestion" (pp. 230–231). In "melancholy not depending upon a physical agency"—the "nervous" disorders of the eighteenth century—he advised against evacuants and in favor of soothing drinks, narcotics, opium, tepid baths, and calming hygienic measures (p. 231).

Esquirol had removed from the syndrome of melancholia a minority group of monodelusional states with exalted mood. He had thus reduced the clinical content of melancholia somewhat and had sharpened its outlines. He differed from his teacher Pinel in removing the "manialike" partial insanities from melancholia, but he followed him closely in continuing to view melancholia as a partial insanity. He carefully differentiated melancholia from mania, the latter involving a general rather than a partial delirium as well as an exalted mood. And he equally carefully differentiated melancholia from hypochondria, noting that in the latter "there is no delirium, but the patient exaggerates his sufferings" and, as Cullen had emphasized, that dyspepsia was present (p. 203). He made the traditional observation that melancholia "sometimes passes into mania" and added that this might well have been what "caused melancholy to be confounded with mania" (p. 217). The various syndromes that some predecessors had conceived of as distinct diseases yet

akin to melancholia and others had conceived of as subtypes of melancholia—
such as lovesickness, nostalgia, and religious melancholia—were referred to
explicitly or implicitly at scattered points in his account of melancholia. With
melancholia as one of his two types of monomania, the syndromes fitted in
nicely as instances of particular topics that could become the foci for partial
insanity. Parenthetically, it is relevant here to remark that, in the hands of
James Cowles Prichard (1786–1848), Esquirol's monomania just about eliminated melancholia from a nosological system. Prichard used the term *monomania* in Esquirol's generic sense to mean all the partial insanities; he did not
use *lypemania* or *melancholia*.[5] In spite of Prichard's significant influence on
other psychiatric topics, a category of melancholia very soon reentered most
psychiatric nosologies with its descriptive outline for the most part restricted
to severe depressive disturbances, and monomania gradually disappeared as
the century continued.

JOHANN CHRISTIAN HEINROTH

In a difficult, yet significant, textbook on "disturbances of the soul" or "mental
disturbances," Johann Christian Heinroth (1773–1843) dealt with melancholia
in ways that were both familiar and interestingly novel. In an ingenious, but
labored, nosological scheme, his "highest or class concept" was "disturbances
of the soul (vesaniae)."[6] Within this class, he had three Orders: (1) Exaltations
(vesaniae hypersthenicae), (2) Depressions (vesaniae asthenicae), and (3) Mixtures of Exaltation with Weakness (vesaniae mixta). And within each Order he
had three Genera: (i) disturbances of the disposition, (ii) disturbances of the
spirit, and (iii) disturbances of the will. In this system, with hints of John
Brown's sthenic and asthenic conditions, and with genera derived from faculty
psychology, Heinroth established melancholia as the first Genus (disturbances
of the disposition) in the second Order (Depressions, or vesaniae asthenicae).
Among the several species within this genus, one finds much that is familiar in
earlier clinical descriptions of melancholia; but, in addition, the other genera in
the Order Depressions have depressive features as associated symptoms.
Further still, several of the mixed conditions in the third Order also have
depressive features, and some of these conditions had been subtypes of melancholia in the systems of earlier nosologists.

In thus approaching mental disorders as *disturbances of the soul*, Heinroth's notion of the *soul* included the *disposition*, the *spirit*, and the *will* as
faculties. The disposition was the *temperament*, the *animus*, or the *heart* in the
figurative sense of the capacity for desire. He thought of this disposition or
temperament as the receptivity to joy and sorrow, as the "site" where emotions
were experienced.

Within the genus denominated *melancholia* his first species was *pure*

melancholia, or *melancholia simplex.* He described it as "Paralysis of the disposition, that is, loss of freedom of the disposition accompanied by depression,
withdrawal into oneself, and brooding over some loss, death, pain, or despair.
Restless, anxious, rapid movements, or a fixed stare. The patient is insensitive
to everything except the interests of the fettered disposition; he sighs, weeps,
and laments" (*Disturbances,* 1:189). He then outlined the premorbid picture
that tended to lead to melancholia.

> If the temperament of a person is melancholic, from which the name of the
> disease is taken, or if it is sanguine or phlegmatic, joy is missing from the former
> state and excitement from the latter; then in general, if there is no resistance in
> the disposition, or if there is depression due to a serious loss or the fear of a loss,
> with the resultant grief, the person gradually becomes quiet, withdrawn, secre-
> tive. He loses appetite and sleep, loses weight, becomes shy and fearful or
> suspicious, withdraws from the company of his friends and acquaintances, is
> reluctant to go about his usual business, and gradually sinks deeper into his
> gloomy broodings; and thus the disease overtakes him. (ibid., pp. 189–190)

From a beginning state that might be subdued or overactive in character, the
disorder progressed to where the person was severely depressed and relatively
uncommunicative, and eventually to where he was still depressed but more
communicative. "What ails him now becomes clearer, for he now loudly
bewails the object of his loss or his sorrow; but this object soon becomes the
only point around which all his thoughts and speech revolve" (p. 190). Heinroth then addressed the topic of the "idée fixe," the traditional fixed preoccupation of melancholic patients that so often developed to become the delusional
focus of their concerns. He disagreed with the traditional view that the origin
of this fixed idea was in the intellect and that this reflected a primary harm to
the intellect or understanding. From there he argued that "it is the disposition
which is seized by some depressing passion, and then has to follow it, and since
this passion then becomes the dominating element, the intellect is forced by
the disposition to retain certain ideas and concepts" (pp. 190–191). Rather
than the emotional state being determined by primary damage to the intellect,
the primary damage was to the disposition or temperament with the intellect
affected only as "a mere servant of the sick disposition." "The idée fixe may or
may not be present, or at least may not be apparent, but melancholia still
remains what it is: depression of the disposition, withdrawal into oneself,
detachment from the external world, without interest in anything better than
this world" (p. 191). In twentieth-century terms, we might say that he was
describing a primary affective disorder. He concluded with comments about
the patient as slowed down, preoccupied, and deeply depressed, along with
sleeplessness and either a subdued silence or "sighing and lamentation" (pp.
191–192).

The three other species in the genus Melancholia involved more extreme disturbances of behavior and general functioning, along with severe depression (pp. 192–194). The outline of this continuum of worsening conditions is reminiscent of twentieth-century descriptions of the course of some schizophrenic patients; and the immobile apathy of the third genus that he termed *melancholia attonita* is very suggestive of the *catatonia* of Kahlbaum later in the century and of the *catatonic schizophrenia* of the twentieth century. He concluded his discussion of the genus Melancholia with brief references to *homesickness* and *religious melancholia* as "subspecies . . . of melancholia" (p. 195). He also characterized melancholia in another way that was novel and that bears some consideration.

> If we now consider the main forms of disturbances of the disposition, insanity and melancholia, we find that they are distinguished by altogether different characters; in melancholia the disposition has lost its world, and becomes an empty, hollow Ego which gnaws at itself, while the insane disposition is torn and removed from itself and flutters among the dream images and airy figures of the imagination. We find here signs of two opposite physical principles: the centripetal or contractive force, that is, a tendency to lose oneself in one central point and thus gradually fade out into nothing; and the centrifugal, or expansive force, that is, a tendency to expand without limit and thus also fade out into nothing. (pp. 221–222)

Heinroth's views on the causes and the pathogenesis of melancholia are extremely difficult to decipher and to present briefly. He emphasized hereditary influences (pp. 101–141), but he also considered psychological factors as causal; and he introduced a psychological perspective that, although soon overshadowed by the biological convictions of Griesinger, was part of a psychological explanatory tradition that came and went throughout the century.

On treatment, Heinroth advised that, in this condition's earlier stages,

> the "quiet, reserved, withdrawn behavior" must be overcome by friendly sympathy and persuasion, by searching for the sources of the disease, such as a great loss or the fear of such a loss; and then, if possible, by deflection of these sources, not all at once and not through one medicament, but by persistence and by repeated efforts. If the patient cannot be compensated for his loss by some substitute, and if the fear which is dominating his disposition cannot be dispelled by any reasonable argument or by any encouraging prospect, the patient must be forcibly withdrawn from his situation, his disposition must be violently stimulated, some new interest must be awakened, and he must be removed from his situation and his environment, if possible by a journey to a far distant place, which involves much excitement, much discomfort, and much activity. For such patients, traveling is a universal medicine. This is also the best means of giving back to the patient "the lost appetite and the lost sleep," of chasing away his "fearfulness and timidity, and his gloomy brooding," and of leading him back to

the "society and business activities from which he has escaped." If this purpose cannot be obtained by traveling, since this is precluded by the situation and means of the patient, the lack of this powerful remedy must be compensated for as much as possible by distractions of all kinds taken near home, physical exertion, general activity, and occupations imposed on the patient, through which he is torn out of his preoccupation with himself. (2:358)

If the disease was not dealt with successfully in these earlier stages, any excitement must be calmed, and he mentioned the elimination of disturbing noises and, "if necessary, restraint by a straitjacket" (ibid.). If apathy or rigidity was present, "powerful means of excitement" might be in order, as "the patient's tendency to withdraw into himself" must be countered by reawakening his "receptivity" (2:358–359). He referred here to "the swing machine" and "pharmaceutical and dietetic stimulation," followed by "bodily and spiritual occupation and distraction, with due regard to his individuality." The severest cases called for various evacuative remedies, the ancients' "warm baths, fomentations, and frictions," and wine and nourishing, restorative foods (2:359). Once there was some improvement, "all species of means of encouragement" were in order (2:359–360). He stated that "loneliness, inactivity, or a closed room are poison" to the melancholic patient; that "anything that can stimulate his body and keep him in action should be tried"; and that he needed to be "awakened from his withdrawal into himself" and "torn away from the monotonous ideas which are gnawing at him" (2:249).

ERNST VON FEUCHTERSLEBEN

Ernst von Feuchtersleben (1806–1849) did not employ a category of melancholia but, instead, wrote about a type of disorder termed *fixed delusion*. "It begins with a caprice, and represents a sensation or an impulse, which has absorbed the entire personality of the man; it is characterised by the predominance of one idea, or of a series of ideas constantly recurring. Whether this idea or series of ideas be sorrowful or joyous, is not essential," although it was more frequently the former.[7] He was continuing the idea of *partial insanity* that was already so familiar,[8] and he briefly noted that another author's use of *partial fixed insanity* was a synonym for his own term. He related it to melancholia by indicating that it included conditions so named whether the term was used in the more traditional sense of a depressive partial insanity or in the more recent sense that included both sorrowful and joyous partial insanities. He thought that *melancholia* was a "too restricted term" to use for the whole group (*Medical Psychology*, pp. 276–277). He saw this nosological category as synonymous with Esquirol's *monomania* in the latter's generic use of this term. He thought of these fixed delusional states as evolving "by means of fixation" out of general bodily sensations, out of hypochondriasis conceived of as the transition state in which such sensations were most frequent, out of hallucinations, and out of the passions (ibid., p. 276). He emphasized that any one of a wide range of possible ideas might serve as the governing *idée fixe*, and that it was fallacious to base a classification on the nature of the object of the delusion.

When it came to clinical description, Feuchtersleben made separate observations about those afflicted with sorrowful delusions: "The patient . . . no longer pays attention to the world beyond his own idea; hence he is glad to flee society in order to indulge, in undisturbed solitude, the ungenial, irresistible impulse of his delusion." Considering more generally the person with a fixed delusion, he then added, "Beyond its influence he is often capable of acting sanely, and with acuteness and energy. Such patients are frequently capable of accounting for and defending their delusions with a rationality which confounds even the most sensible" (p. 277). He later devoted a brief section to "the fixed delusion that life, either by compulsion or necessity, must be quitted, which, sometimes as fear of death (*Thanatophobia*), sometimes as weariness of life (spleen), apparently proceeds from directly opposite causes." He commented that this was the condition "properly represented by melancholy . . . in the more restricted acceptation of the word," and that Esquirol's term *lypemania* applied here. He mentioned the danger of suicide. He stated: "That turn of melancholy which is caused by home-sickness likewise often leads to suicide. Melancholy has been distinguished as restless (*errabunda*) and dull (*attonita*), yet these are not distinct forms, but only individually varied manifestations of the same form" (p. 281). In discussing various emotional states, he addressed "melancholy" as an emotion in a way that provided further clinical description. He asserted that "in melancholy, especially in its highest degree, hopelessness," one found that "the senses, memory, and reactive give way, the nervous vitality languishes at its root, and the vitality of the blood, deprived of this stimulant, is languid in all its functions. Hence the slow and often difficult respiration, and proneness to sighing, the slow weak pulse, diminished warmth, pale, dry, shrivelled skin, the impediment to peristaltic motion, and to all secretions and excretions, which phenomena indicate stases and their consequences" (p. 135).

Feuchtersleben did not offer a systematic explanation as to how sorrowful fixed delusional states came about, but he mentioned that "hyperaemia of the substance and of the membranes of the brain" was frequently found at autopsy in "melancholy patients"; that "the organic focus" from which such disorders stemmed was "the vegetative nervous sphere"; that those were predisposed to melancholy who were "debilitated, and particularly if debilitated by sexual excesses, and those parts supplied by the *nervus vagus* are in general the seat of their bodily sufferings"; and that the remote causes were more commonly physical in nature, such as the bodily sensations leading to "phantasms" and the senses leading to "hallucinations" (pp. 284–285).

As to treatment, "the cure by diversion" was specially applicable "in melancholy," but "with caution and strict regard to the state of the individual."

> If it assume the character of spleen, sense of honour, duty, and religion, are perhaps the only interests which can rouse the deadened vitality of the mind. If it assume the character of thanatophobia, let the cure, by means of occupation, gymnastics, riding, etc., be declared to be a cure for the disorder of which the patient is afraid he shall die. Emotions, sometimes of the sthenic kind, but often asthenic, e.g. fear which furnishes a negative excitement, are likewise useful in every kind of melancholy.
>
> Somatically the fixed delusion, especially the metamorphotic and melancholic, is often referable to an abdominal disorder, as a concurrent cause, to which the treatment, as far as the body is concerned, must be directed. (p. 348)

WILHELM GRIESINGER

Toward mid-century, Wilhelm Griesinger (1817–1868) brought out his *Mental Pathology and Therapeutics*, a work that had a tremendous influence on his contemporaries and on their nineteenth-century successors. He included in it an exhaustive and significant presentation of ideas on melancholia, accompanied by extensive clinical accounts, in a chapter entitled "States of Mental Depression—Melancholia." In his approach to mental disorders in general, and melancholia in particular, he was crucially influenced by the emerging nineteenth-century concept of a unitary psychosis (*Einheitspsychose*), for which he cited his teacher, Ernst A. Zeller (1804–1877), who in turn had taken up the idea from Joseph Guislain (1797–1860), the famous Belgian alienist. His basic thesis was that the various forms of mental illness were essentially stages in a single disease process: "a certain definite *succession* of the various forms of emotional states, whence there results a method of viewing insanity which recognizes in the different *forms*, different *stages* of one morbid process."*

*W. Griesinger, *Mental Pathology and Therapeutics*, 2d ed., trans. C. Lockhart Robertson and James Rutherford (London: New Sydenham Society, 1867), p. 207. Guislain postulated that the various mental disorders were not separate diseases but rather stages in a single disease process. Each syndrome was an outward manifestation of an inner effort to deal with the basic psychic distress. At the onset this psychic distress was usually manifested by sadness or melancholia. Such depressive feelings might well be a part of any subsequent syndrome (or phase); one such syndrome might be melancholia itself, either simple melancholia (mélancolie sans délire) or melancholia with delusions (mélancolie avec délire); and it was not uncommon for depressive feelings to be a residual at the end of a clinical episode. See J. Guislain, *Traité sur les Phrénopathies* . . . , (Bruxelles: Etablissement Encyclographique, 1833), pp. 12–14, 186–190, 335–339. Following Griesinger, Neumann in Germany and Sankey in Great Britain were other prominent subscribers to this idea of a unitary psychosis.

Under "States of Mental Depression" he identified "a state of profound emotional perversion, of a depressing and sorrowful character" that he termed the *"stadium melancholicum"* or initial melancholic stage that he considered "the initiatory period" in "the immense majority of mental diseases." This "melancholia which precedes insanity" commonly was "the direct continuation of some painful emotion dependent upon some objective cause (moral causes of insanity), *e.g.*, grief, jealousy; and it is distinguished from the mental pain experienced by healthy persons by its excessive degree, by its more than ordinary protraction, by its becoming more and more independent of external influences" (*Mental Pathology*, p. 210).

He then went on to discuss hypochondriasis as the next stage in his sequence of "States of Mental Depression" ranged along a continuum of gradually increasing severity. He said:

> The hypochondriacal states represent the mildest, most moderate form of insanity, and have many peculiarities which essentially distinguish them from the other forms of melancholia. While they, of course, share with the others the generic character of dejection, sadness, depression of mind, diminution of the activity of the will, and of a delirium which corresponds to this mental disposition, they yet differ from them in this characteristic manner—that in these states the emotional depression proceeds from a strong *feeling* of BODILY *illness* which constantly keeps the attention of the patient concentrated upon itself; that, consequently, the false opinions relate almost exclusively to the *state* of *health* of the subject, and the delirium turns constantly upon apprehensions of some grave malady—upon unfounded and curious ideas regarding the nature, the form, and the danger of this his disease. This feeling of bodily illness is sometimes general and vague, sometimes it resolves itself into particular anomalous and disconnected sensations.

He noted that such conditions were essentially emotional disorders with the intellect unaffected, stating:

> In spite of this emotional disorder and of the false conceptions, the association of ideas is usually unimpaired; the abnormal sensations and ideas are logically connected throughout, and justified by reasons which are still within the bounds of possibility. And just because of this absence of actual derangement of the understanding, hypochondria appears to be essentially a *folie raisonnante* mélancholique. (p. 211)

He added that hypochondriasis had "exactly the same origin—the same objective groundlessness and subjective foundation of the delirious conceptions as in the other forms of melancholia and more advanced insanity" (p. 213). The bodily sensations were real but somatically unfounded; the intellect functioned soundly but started from false premises; and the derangement was limited to the sphere of the false premises. Although the condition might well remain circumscribed or be reversed, it was not uncommon for it gradually to worsen. In such instances the patient frequently became more dejected, more preoccupied with his various bodily sensations, and more indecisive, and so eventually a disorder of the will was added to the basic emotional disorder. Then "the higher degrees of hypochondria" might "gradually pass, partly through increase of the feeling of anxiety, partly through the fixing of certain attempts at explanation, not only into true melancholia, but even complicated with delusions" (p. 215).

From there Griesinger proceeded to describe melancholia proper, which he introduced as follows:

> In many cases, after a period of longer or shorter duration, a state of vague mental and bodily discomfort, often with hypochondriacal perversion, depression and restlessness, sometimes with the dread of becoming insane, passes off, a state of mental pain becomes always more dominant and persistent, but is increased by every external mental impression. This is the essential mental disorder in melancholia, and, so far as the patient himself is concerned, the mental pain consists in a profound feeling of *ill-being*, of inability to do anything, of suppression of the physical powers, of depression and sadness, and of total abasement of self-consciousness. (p. 223)

He went on to describe a tendency toward increased unhappiness and dejection, irritability, either discontent or withdrawal from others, preoccupation with self, sometimes hatred of others, and sometimes contrariness. And a tendency toward indecisiveness and inactivity was thought to reflect a worsening of the disorder of the will (pp. 223–226). Eventually a variety of "melancholic insane ideas" would appear, false ideas and judgments "corresponding to the actual disposition of the patient" (p. 227). Physical activity lessened and slowed (p. 230). "Usually . . . the course of melancholia is chronic, with remissions; more rarely with complete intermissions, of variable duration" (p. 234).

In keeping with his concept of a single disease process with the familiar symptom patterns as stages along a continuum of severity, he described how some cases might gradually worsen and be transformed from melancholia into cases of mania.* He commented on a variety of "sub-forms" of melancholia that might occur; and, as he described types that involved violence and "excitement of the will," he stated that "the more vague and permanent the excitement, the less are we inclined to regard this condition as one of melancholia, and the nearer does it approach to the form of mania"; he then added

---

*See pp. 264–267 (chap. 10) for more detail on how Griesinger related melancholia and mania. See that chapter also regarding the events of the 1850s, when Baillarger (folie à double forme) and Falret (folie circulaire) brought cases of melancholia-mania together to establish a discrete disease separate from both melancholia and mania. This development was eventually to have profound effects on the status of melancholia as a factor in the transformations wrought by Kraepelin at the end of the century.

that there were a variety of "intermediate forms through which this transition from melancholia passes into maniacal excitement" (*Mental Pathology*, p. 271). He followed this by dealing with mania at length in the next chapter. He there referred back to the depressed activity and incapacity for exertion characteristic of so many melancholics, and alluded to the increasing inclinations to activity in the forms that began to approximate mania. In beginning his discussion of mania Griesinger referred to such cases as "morbid states in which the patients are *out of themselves*," in contrast to the turned-inward, self-preoccupied tendencies of melancholic patients (p. 273). Although he cited Jessen as his source for this notion, it is remarkably akin to the earlier ideas of Heinroth's regarding centrifugally determined, out-of-themselves states in mania and centripetally determined, into-themselves states in melancholia. Then, in the last of his three chapters on the various states of mental disease, Griesinger outlined the transition from "States of Mental Exaltation" to "States of Mental Weakness" and dealt with the latter in some detail. In the spirit of his continuum of severity within the idea of a unitary psychosis, he stated that these conditions "do not constitute primary, but consecutive forms of insanity," and that "they continue as remnants and residues of the forms which we have already been considering when these are not cured" (p. 319). The emphasis had shifted from disordered emotions to disorders of the intelligence. These introductory comments were followed by detailed sections on chronic mania, agitated dementia, and apathetic dementia; and he noted that these conditions constituted the vast majority of chronic cases in psychiatric institutions.

Griesinger's essential views on etiology and pathogenesis are rather well-known and yet not really very well understood. In the first chapter of his textbook he enunciated his basic hypothesis, which has been variously paraphrased and which was to become the credo of both the "brain psychiatry" of the late nineteenth century and the biological psychiatry of the twentieth century; and he reaffirmed his conviction about this hypothesis again and again throughout his work. Yet he was singularly careful and sophisticated in his use of this assertion, in contrast to the simplistic perspective so often attributed to him by twentieth-century authors. He stated:

> Insanity itself, an anomalous condition of the faculties of knowledge and of will, is only a symptom. . . . Physiological and pathological facts show us that this organ [that is, the one affected in mental diseases] can only be the brain; we therefore primarily, and in every case of mental disease, recognise a morbid action of that organ. . . . Pathology proves as clearly as physiology, that the brain alone can be the seat of normal and abnormal mental action; that the normal state of the mental process depends upon the integrity of this organ; and that both together are influenced by the state of the other organs in disease. The invariable and essential symptoms of cerebral diseases may arise from internal

causes or external lesions; may proceed from anomalies of sensation and move-ment, and, in serious diseases, even from mental disturbance (exaltation or depression of the ideality, loss of self-consciousness, delirium, etc.). . . . We must not speak of diseases of the soul alone . . . but of disease of the brain. . . . Although, however, every mental disease proceeds from an affection of the brain, every disease of the brain does not, on that account, belong to the class of mental diseases. . . . Insanity being a disease, and that disease being an affection of the brain. (pp. 1, 3, 7, 9)

But Griesinger did not develop any sort of systematic pathogenetic theory but took the view that the evidence was far too uncertain. Instead, he discussed predisposing factors and then immediate or precipitating factors, and left it at that. In keeping with already apparent German trends, he emphasized the need for a highly individual assessment of each patient when it came to any attempt to determine etiology or plan treatment. And he thought that there were usually multiple causal factors involved.

Among predisposing factors, he emphasized that the most potent was hereditary predisposition (p. 150), and in this context he gave respectful consideration to Morel's theory of degeneration. He also gave prominence to influences in the person's upbringing (pp. 156–157). Although he thought that they were essentially reflections of hereditary influences, he made special mention of "mental dispositions" such as a "nervous constitution" and "irrit-able weakness"; and he noted that such dispositions might also be acquired secondary to physical illness (pp. 158–161).

Turning to precipitating causes, he first mentioned several general factors that might be involved: frank cerebral pathology; subtle, as yet uniden-tified, cerebral pathology; subtle functional (that is, physiological) changes, perhaps from simple nervous irritation or perhaps from slight changes in nutrition that cannot yet be defined; inflammatory processes in the brain; and either anemia or hyperemia of the brain, with the latter being associated with cerebral congestion, stagnation, and slowness of the circulation (pp. 162–164). He cited "the depressing emotions when long continued, grief or anxiety" among the factors that might cause such stagnation and slowing of the circula-tion (p. 163). He then considered precipitating factors under three headings: psychical, mixed, and physical. The *psychical causes* were the most frequent, and foremost among these were "passionate and emotional states," particularly "disagreeable, adverse, or depressive states" (p. 165).

In individual cases these painful emotional states may vary very much in their nature and in their causes: sometimes it is sudden anger—shock or grief excited by injury, loss of fortune, a rude interference with the modesty, a sudden death, etc.; sometimes it is the result of the slow gnawings of disappointed ambition on the mind, regret on account of certain unjust actions, domestic affliction, unfortunate love, jealousy, error, forced sojourn in inadequate circumstances, or any other injured sentiment. In every case there are influences which, through intense disturbance of the mass of ideas of the *ego*, cause a mournful division in consciousness, and we always see the most powerful effects where the wishes and hopes have been for a long time concentrated upon a certain object. Where the individual has made certain things indispensable to his life, and when these are forcibly withdrawn, the passage of the ideas into efforts is cut off, and accordingly a gap in the *ego* and a violent internal strife results. (pp. 165–166)

These emotions have their deleterious effects by producing "a state of intense irritation of the brain." Often, too, the emotions disturbed "the functions of the organs of circulation, respiration, digestion, and of blood formation," and "the cerebral disease proceeds as a secondary result" (p. 167). An important mediating factor here was often "continued *sleeplessness*, which often accompanies the depressing emotions, which overexcites the brain, and lowers the nutrition" (p. 168). In the case of important losses, such as

the loss of a loved relative, . . . the boundary betwixt the physiological state of emotion and insanity is often difficult to trace. At least, it may demand profound consideration; the latter may appear as the immediate continuation of a physiological state of the established emotion.

The essential difference between the two, therefore—between melancholia and a gloomy disposition—consists in this, that in the former the patient cannot withdraw himself from his ill-humour, because it has become fixed through the mediation of abnormal organic phenomena. (pp. 168–169)

Under *mixed causes* he particularly mentioned drunkenness (pp. 169–173) and sexual excesses, including onanism (pp. 173–174), although in another context he noted that the occasional case was caused by sexual deprivation (p. 198). Finally, under *physical causes* he cited various other nervous diseases, including injuries to the head, acute febrile diseases, chronic constitutional diseases, local disorders of various organs, pregnancy, childbirth, and lactation (pp. 174–205).

Griesinger addressed the treatment of melancholia only within the context of a lengthy discourse on the treatment of insanity more generally (pp. 459–505). He emphasized the importance of prompt and early intervention, if at all possible. He thought that treatment needed to be individualized for each patient. He argued that "both the psychical and somatic methods of treatment" were crucial, irrespective of whether the basic pathology might lie in organic lesions or not; and he went on to say that treatment should be "simultaneously directed to the physical and mental nature of the individual" (pp. 460–461). He advised at least temporary removal from the patient's usual surroundings, and particularly from any noxious influences (pp. 463–464, 466); but he added that melancholia called for hospitalization only where the condition was at least of moderate severity and had continued unchanged for some months (p. 469). He commented on the benefits of rest and quiet (pp. 464–465). He considered bloodletting to be usually contraindicated (p. 472). He specially recommended opium (p. 477). He would prescribe hydrocyanic acid as a preferred sedative; purgatives, but of a mild nature; emetics; and often "dietetic means and mild clysters" rather than the ingestion of medications (pp. 478–480). He urged careful regulation of diet, rest and activity, fresh air, and exercise (pp. 481–482). He particularly favored the humane approach of moral treatment, and he was inclined toward a nonrestraint orientation (pp. 483–495). He advised distracting the patient from his preoccupations, "mild, cheering external influences," encouragement, and occupational activity, although he thought that both the patient's previous occupation and mental exertion should be avoided (p. 496). He recommended "a regulated diet, exclusion of all alcoholics, abundant out-door exercise, refreshing sleep, and a healthy maintenance of all the secretions," along with careful attention to any concomitant "disease in other parts" (p. 497). He urged that the topics of melancholics' preoccupations and delusions be avoided and commented that often a moderately severe manner was more helpful than consolation (p. 498).

D. HACK TUKE AND JOHN CHARLES BUCKNILL

D. Hack Tuke (1827–1895), in Bucknill and Tuke's *A Manual of Psychological Medicine* in 1858, presented melancholia as one of the main "forms of mental disease," along with idiocy, dementia, delusional insanity, emotional insanity, mania, and puerperal insanity. He stated that "it corresponds to the tristimania of Rush; the *melancolie, phrenalgia, luperophrenie*, of Guislain; and the *sadness*, and *melancholy* of English writers."[9] Although he categorized "melancholia, without delusion" as a type of *emotional insanity* and considered one of the types of *delusional insanity* to be "of a melancholy character" (*Manual*, p. 100), he dealt with these two types of melancholic disorder together under the heading of *melancholia*, while recognizing their distinctness from one another. He approached the definition of melancholia circuitously but eventually settled on a modification of Esquirol's definition, to the effect that it was "a cerebral malady . . . without fever, and sustained by a passion of a sad, debilitating, or oppressive character" (p. 152). He objected to Esquirol's view of it as a "chronic delirium" on the basis that a "disorder of the intellect," or delusion, was not "an essential part of the disorder." He then proceeded to classify the melancholias as (1) *simple melancholia*, "no disorder of the intellect . . . no delusion or hallucination. It is the *mélancolie sans délire* of Etmuller and Guislain; the *lypemanie raisonnante* of Esquirol; and the *melancholia simplex* of Heinroth"; (2) *complicated melancholia*, "melancholy with decided disturbance of the intellectual faculties. (*Mélancolie avec délire, la mélancolie délirante* of the

French writers.)" (pp. 158, 164). He also mentioned acute and chronic forms and remittent and intermittent forms.

He indicated that there were three modes of onset, although he added that the first of these was comparatively less frequent. "It may be sudden, as when the immediate consequence of grief, or, gradual and long threatened by premonitory symptoms, and, perhaps the mere exaggeration of the patient's natural character; or, lastly, it may be altogether secondary to other forms of insanity, especially to mania" (pp. 152–153). He noted the following symptoms—disinterest, listless idleness, avoidance of social contacts, sometimes suicidal inclinations, fearfulness, gloominess, groans and sighs, tearfulness, and delusions stemming from the apprehension or from the pessimism (pp. 153–155). He mentioned that the quiet and depressed state, which may be no more than simple depression in many cases, may in some instances be associated with such a "decided inaction of the intellectual faculties" that some authors have termed it *melancholia attonita*.[10] Among a variety of physical symptoms, he mentioned loss of sleep, disturbed dreams, disorders of the digestive system, disordered "uterine functions" in women, and loss of sexual interest in men (pp. 157–158). He cited much to suggest that the prognosis was better for mania than for melancholia, and better for simple melancholia than for melancholia with delusions; but he indicated that the experience at the York Retreat raised questions about these opinions (pp. 156–157).

In the Bucknill and Tuke chapter on "Diagnosis of Insanity," John Charles Bucknill (1817–1897) made the important comment that the symptoms of "uncomplicated melancholia . . . vary in degree, but not in kind, from that normal and healthy grief and sorrow, of which all men have their share in this chequered existence." Further, "some writers on insanity assert that melancholia is frequently a mere growth from a state of normal grief and low spirits," but Bucknill disagreed; he distinguished the predisposed person from the person not predisposed, and indicated that there were occurrences with no effect on "normal emotions" that would cause melancholia in the predisposed person and other occurrences that "would produce normal grief in a person not predisposed" and "melancholia in a person who is so predisposed" (pp. 309–310). He considered the essential predisposition to be a hereditary one. As to precipitating causes, he stated, "it is occasioned by all the moral causes of mental disease; especially by griefs, disappointments, reverses, and anxieties of every kind. It is also caused by long-continued ill-health, occasioned by the infraction of the laws of hygiene; and it is the most frequent form of mental disorder which accompanies the grand climacteric of women" (p. 309). He emphasized that "the symptoms of melancholia are sorrow, despondency, fear, and despair, existing in a degree far beyond the intensity in which these emotions usually affect the sane mind, even under circumstances most capable of producing them; and in numerous instances existing without any commensurate moral cause, and often without any moral cause whatever" (p. 310).

Tuke gave careful attention to hypochondriacal tendencies, acknowledging the "loose, popular" use of the term *hypochondriasis* and then discussing hypochondriacal syndromes both without and with delusions. He indicated that it was often difficult to differentiate these latter two from one another, and he referred to them as *simple hypochondriasis* and *hypochondriacal melancholy*, respectively. He thought of hypochondriacal melancholy as essentially a form of complicated melancholia, with the prominent symptoms, including delusions, being of a hypochondriacal nature (pp. 164–168).

He suggested "hereditary predisposition" as the most important predisposing factor, along with others such as "critical period of life" and parturition. Turning to precipitating factors, he mentioned various "direct moral causes" such as "domestic troubles . . . reverses of fortune and consequent misery . . . disappointed affection" and various acute physical causes (pp. 175–176).

Bucknill dealt with pathogenesis in the chapter "Pathology of Insanity," which focused not on melancholia in particular but rather on insanity in general. Throughout he recognized a dichotomy of disorders with both structural pathology and functional disturbance, and disorders limited to functional disturbance; but he made it clear that he thought that the latter were disorders in which there was subtle, undetected structural harm. After indicating the central role of the brain and the nerves, he bemoaned the limited knowledge of the functions of "the nerve apparatus" and "the laws of nerve-force." He then concluded:

> In default, therefore, of real knowledge respecting the conditions of nerve-function, we must be satisfied with the recognition of the fact, that the great organ of this function is subjected to the general laws of decay and reparation of animal tissues, and to some other laws having special reference to its own degeneration and repair. It is upon this physiological basis only that, in default of more precise and extensive knowledge of the changes in the nerve-cell and the generation of nerve-force, cerebral pathology can be established. *The physiological principle upon which we have to build a system of cerebral pathology is, that mental health is dependent upon the due nutrition, stimulation, and repose of the brain; that is, upon the conditions of the exhaustion and reparation of its nerve-substance being maintained in a healthy and regular state; and that mental disease results from the interruption or disturbance of these conditions.* (p. 342)

Acknowledging the vagueness of his "verbal formulas," Bucknill postulated that various types of "inflammatory action" in the brain might ultimately lead to "irregular excitement of the cerebral functions" and so to insanity (pp. 353–354), an idea reminiscent of Cullen's "irregularity of excitement." He thought that the final "cause and condition of insanity" in this pathogenetic process was a state of "cerebral congestion" or cerebral hyperemia (p. 355). In such "abnormal states of the circulation," the normal "proportioned excitement of function disappears, and is replaced by irregular excitement. Some functions become torpid and oppressed, while others are excited into preternatural activity; and this state affords the basis of insanity" (p. 360). After further consideration of the evidence for "the congestion theory of the pathology of insanity," he concluded that

> insanity is frequently conditioned by a preternatural fulness of the cerebral vessels, which interferes with the uniform and healthy interchange of nutritive plasma, passing from the vessels to the cells, and of the fluid cell-contents in a state of involution or degenerative metamorphosis, passing from the cells to the vessels,—a fulness unaccompanied by exudation tending to become organized, that is, by congestion and not by inflammation. (pp. 360–367 [366])

Bucknill then turned to the more or less opposite condition of cerebral anemia as the other basic "cause and condition" of insanity. Either an insufficient quantity of blood in the cerebrum or a deficiency in the nutritive powers of the cerebral blood supply was involved in this second pathogenetic scheme. In either case, the nutritive defect led to cerebral atrophy and decay, and then to insanity (pp. 368–370). In summing up these two contrasting explanations, he stated:

> In most instances of insanity arising from physical causes, it is probable that the pathological condition of the cerebral cells is subsequent to, if not dependent upon, the pathological condition of the cerebral capillaries. It is unnecessary to go through the roll-call of the physical causes of mental disease; suffice it to say, that, injuries to the head, fever, suppressed discharges, alcohol, and other noxious ingesta, can only influence the cerebral cells through the medium of the capillaries. (p. 373)

He also reasoned that some instances of insanity came about as a result of a sympathetic response to disease in other parts of the body. Although the process was not at all clear, he thought of it as another instance of a functional disturbance, with the implication that there was an undetected pathophysiology at work; and he thought that the nervous system was probably the basis for the communication of such sympathetic responses (pp. 382–383). Recurrently, Bucknill seems to have been implying that any pathogenetic formulations that did not follow his convictions, such as psychological explanations, would be little more than the speculations of metaphysicians.

When it came to applying these formulations, he did not clearly address melancholia in particular, but he seemed to indicate that trends in the direction of cerebral hyperemia and congestion led to excited forms of insanity, and that trends in the direction of cerebral anemia and decay led to depressed or melancholic forms of insanity (p. 370). He thought that the monomanias or partial insanities were functional disorders and thus that the structural damage was so subtle as to be undetected (p. 386).

Bucknill also wrote the Bucknill and Tuke chapter on treatment. He indicated the importance of moral treatment but emphasized that opiate therapy might be crucial in acute melancholia, where it would be difficult to employ moral treatment. Beyond such acute conditions, he recommended tonic and restorative regimens, including tonics, exercise and fresh air, moral treatment, cold sponging or bathing, nutritious food, "and those general appliances of a well-regulated asylum which promote physical health and mental cheerfulness" (pp. 470–471, 484–485).

HENRY MAUDSLEY

Although respectful of and influenced by such authorities as Esquirol, Griesinger, and Morel, Henry Maudsley (1835–1918) gradually broke away from nineteenth-century trends in classification and settled on a relatively simple symptomatological scheme. Among his several "varieties of insanity," he observed that there were "two great divisions—*Affective* and *Ideational*"; and he proceeded to advocate the absence or presence of delusions as his fundamental principle of categorization.[11] The former of these "two well-marked groups" embraced "all those cases in which the mode of *feeling* or the *affective* life is chiefly or solely perverted—in which the whole habit or manner of feeling, the mode of affection of the individual by events, is entirely changed"; and the latter was composed of "those cases in which *ideational* or *intellectual* derangement predominates." In spite of this mode of classification, he thought that "the affective disorder is the fundamental fact; that in the great majority of cases it precedes intellectual disorder; that it co-exists with the latter during its course; and that it frequently persists for a time after this has disappeared." He then emphasized that delusions were not always present in insanity, pointing out that "all writers on insanity, whatever their theories of mental action, are driven by observation of cases" to recognize two important types of insanity in which delusions were absent—"*melancholia simplex,* or melancholia without delusion," and "*mania sine delirio*" (*Physiology and Pathology*, p. 344). These two nondelusional insanities were included among those in the category of "affective or pathetic insanity." His second main category, "ideational insanity," included "those different varieties of insanity usually described as *Mania* or *Melancholia:* the unsoundness affects *ideation,* and is exhibited in delusions and intellectual alienation." Under *melancholia* were those cases in which there was "great oppression of the self-feeling with corresponding gloomy morbid idea," and under *mania* those cases in which there was "excitement or exaltation of the self-feeling, with corresponding lively expression of it in the character of the thoughts or in the conduct of the patient"; and in each group, a case might be *acute* or *chronic*. But his basic subcategories within ideational insanity were not established along these familiar descriptive lines but rather along the conceptual-descriptive lines of *general insanity* where there was "general intellectual derangement" and *partial insanity* where "the alienation seems to be confined to a small number of fixed ideas." Then, under general insanity he placed mania and melancholia, each potentially acute or chronic; and under partial insanity he placed *monomania*, the excited, limited derangements, and *melancholia*, the limited derangements with "a sad and oppressive passion" that Esquirol had termed *lypemania* (p. 365). In spite of all this, he emphasized the provisional nature of his classification, the opinion that "the different forms of insanity are not actual pathological entities," and the tendencies of the various forms of insanity to shift from one into another and to be found intermixed. (pp. 368–369).

Regarding *partial ideational insanity*, Maudsley stated, "Pathologically, there is a systematization of the morbid action in the supreme cerebral centres—the establishment of a definite type of morbid nutrition in them" (p. 370). He thoroughly disagreed with the familiar idea that such a person reasoned satisfactorily or was intellectually sound outside the sphere of his delusion (pp. 370–374). He was of the opinion that the delusion was not the cause of the emotional state, but the other way around. He pointed out that in *simple melancholia* there was no delusion. He outlined the clinical picture in such a condition—the patient felt "strangely and unnaturally changed; impressions which should be agreeable or indifferent are painful; he feels himself strangely isolated, and cannot take any interest in his affairs; he is profoundly miserable and shuns society, perhaps lying in bed all day." The emergence of an idea around which this "vast and formless feeling of profound misery" could become organized might lead to a delusion, and thus an instance of *simple melancholia* would be transformed into an instance of *partial ideational insanity* of the type termed *melancholia* (p. 374). Thus, he conceived of "the affective disorder" as "the fundamental fact," not the delusion (p. 375). Maudsley then cited a number of physical symptoms that often accompanied such cases of melancholia—failed digestion, loss of appetite, constipation, enfeebled circulation, irregular or suppressed menstruation, sleeplessness or disturbed sleep, and sluggish bodily movements (pp. 383–385). Remissions were common; complete intermissions were rare; and the prognosis was better than in excited partial ideational insanity (pp. 385–387). As has been indicated, general ideational insanity reflected a more generalized derangement rather than being restricted to one or a few delusions, and one of its types was melancholic in nature.*

Further as to etiology, Maudsley's basic assumptions stemmed from the Griesinger tradition that mental diseases reflected underlying cerebral diseases, though he was more vehemently committed to this view than Griesinger. Although he was tentative about much in the realms of pathology and pathogenesis in mental disorders, he fairly consistently adhered to a physiological psychology. His inclination toward the Guislain–Griesinger hypothesis of a unitary psychosis meant that he gave little attention to separate causes for melancholia. In approaching the explanation of mental disorders, he advocated a careful case history, and he thought that the causes were multiple. He considered hereditary predisposition to be the most significant predisposing factor; and he emphasized the role of the patient's upbringing and life experiences. At times he leaned toward Morel's theory of degeneration. Among precipitating causes, he mentioned the quality and quantity of cerebral blood flow, which included the familiar anemia and hyperemia or congestion, alcohol, opium, and other poisons; reflex or symptomatic response to irritation in another part of the body; excessive functional activity, such as overwork, depressing passions, and other forms of disturbing emotions; and physical injury to or disease of the brain (pp. 225–291).

Maudsley advocated beginning treatment as early in the illness as possible, removing the patient from the familiar surroundings in which the illness began, and undertaking a sound program of moral treatment. As to "medical treatment," he mentioned the judicious use of baths, the correction of "errors of digestion and secretion," a good diet, and particularly the use of opium (pp. 508–513).

RICHARD VON KRAFFT-EBING

"There is perhaps no other work on psychiatry in any language which has had the vogue, the wide distribution, and the popularity of this of Krafft-Ebing. It has been pre-eminently the clinical text-book of insanity for many years among most of the Continental universities. . . . There is no better practical clinical exposition of the facts of morbid psychology."[12] So wrote Frederick Peterson in 1904 in his introduction to the English translation of Richard von

---

*Although in the third edition of *The Pathology of Mind* (1879) and the fourth edition (1895) Maudsley significantly reorganized his presentation of melancholia, the essentials of his views on the subject remained unchanged—*simple melancholia* and *melancholia with delusion* related to one another, and to other forms of insanity, on a continuum of increasing severity, with the idea that any one form might worsen and be transformed into a severer form.

Krafft-Ebing's (1840–1902) *Text-Book of Insanity*, and there is much to confirm that this work had that degree of influence during the last two decades of the nineteenth century. Krafft-Ebing organized the various psychiatric disorders into two categories: (1) "Mental Diseases of the Adult Brain," and (2) "Arrest of Psychic Development." The second of these dealt with idiocy and with moral insanity as "moral idiocy" and received relatively limited attention. The other category was subdivided into (i) "Diseases without anatomico-pathological lesions: functional psychoses," and (ii) "Diseases which present constant ana-tomico-pathological lesions: brain diseases with predominating mental symptoms; organic psychoses." He then further subdivided these "functional psychoses" into two groups: "(A) *Psychoneuroses:* i.e., *disease-states of the normal and robust brain,*" and "(B) *Psychic degeneration:* i.e., *disease-states affecting the abnormal, predisposed, or weakened brain.*" And among the four "forms of insanity" termed "psychoneuroses" were *melancholia* and *mania.**

After noting the difficulties in establishing "an etiologic classification" for disease-states of the brain, Krafft-Ebing stated: "With few exceptions, insanity is the effect of the combined influence of various causes the individual valuation of which is difficult; the manner of producing the effect is often obscure; the clinical expression is equivocal and, owing to interaction, devoid of clearness" (*Text-Book of Insanity*, p. 278). Nevertheless, he thought that the two categories of "functional psychoses" could be separated from one another, with the "degenerate insanities" differentiated from the "psychoneuroses" on the basis of the prominent role of hereditary predisposition in the "degenerate insanities" and the applicability of Morel's theory of degeneration in explaining their development (p. 279). Further, though, he contrasted the "psychoneuroses" to the "psychic degenerations" on the bases of the former being "acquired diseases in individuals whose cerebral functions were previously normal," being "based upon temporary disposition," tending to be curable and to have infrequent relapses, not having a tendency to periodicity, and manifesting sharp differences between being sane and insane (pp. 280–281). When it came to differentiating the "psychoneuroses" from one another, he indicated that the difficulty in specifying exact causes left one with only "a clinico-functional principle" as a guide. That is, classification had to be based on "the manner of grouping of symptoms and the course"—a clear statement of a principle that guided Kraepelin (p. 281). As he had said in his introduction, "Unfortunately, the uncertain results of pathologico-anatomic inquiry do not enable us to bring the disease-pictures into relation with pathologic and

---

*Text-Book of Insanity, pp. 284–285. The term *psychoneuroses* was *not* used here in the modern sense of nonpsychotic disorders but to refer to the members of that group of "functional psychoses" that occurred in a normal brain. The term *psychoses* implied disordered psychological functions and was synonymous with "forms of insanity."

anatomic findings, and thus do not allow us to replace symptomatic by pathologic and anatomic terms" (p. 46). He acknowledged the possibility that the "psychoneuroses" might worsen and develop into rather deteriorated "secondary states"; but his essential view of them was that they, including melancholia and mania, were "primary disturbances" in which cure was eminently possible (pp. 282–283).

Considering *melancholia* in particular, he stated: "The fundamental phenomenon in melancholia consists of the painful emotional depression, which has no external, or an insufficient external, cause, and general inhibition of the mental activities, which may be entirely arrested" (p. 286). Although he briefly reviewed the current theories of pathogenesis and then elaborated somewhat on his definition, his chapter on melancholia consisted mainly of detailed clinical comments accompanied by case materials, and a short section on treatment. On the other hand, earlier in his textbook he had outlined the nature of the depressed state in melancholia in a way that interwove theoretical assumptions with clinical observations and his particular analogies and metaphors. His comments on the explanatory schemes of the day and his rephrasing of his definition went as follows:

> Concerning the inner basis and relation of these two fundamental anomalies [that is, painful depression and inhibition] of the psychic mechanism in melancholics we have only hypotheses.
>
> While some regard the painful depression as the expression of a disturbance of nutrition in the psychic organ (psychic neuralgia) from which, as a result, arises the inhibition of the mental activities, a more recent theory regards the inhibition as primary, and the psychic pain as a secondary manifestation due to consciousness of the mental inhibition. Both these theories are at best one-sided. The hypothesis that makes psychic pain secondary does not accord with experience. . . . The first manifestation is psychic pain; then inhibition follows, which, of course, becomes a new source of psychic pain. The facts force us to conclude that psychic pain and inhibition are co-ordinated phenomena, between which, of course, a mutual reaction is not excluded. At the same time a common fundamental cause may be thought of: a disturbance of cerebral nutrition (anemia?), which leads to lessened production of vital force.
>
> Melancholia, from a comprehensive, unprejudiced point of view, may be defined as an abnormal condition of the psychic organ dependent upon a disturbance of nutrition, characterized, on the one hand, by a psychic painful emotional state and manner of reaction of the whole consciousness (psychic neuralgia), and, on the other hand, by inhibition of the psychic activities, feelings, intellect, and will, which may go to the extent of arrest. (ibid.)

In the above-mentioned discussion of "the depressed state," he had described matters as follows:

> A painful, depressed state of feeling (psychalgia, phrenalgia), that has arisen spontaneously and exists independently, is the fundamental phenomenon

in the melancholic states of insanity. Here we have a phenomenon analogous to that which occurs in a sensory nerve as a result of disturbance of nutrition, in the form of neuralgia. Disturbance of nutrition in the cerebral cortex leads to mental pain (psychic neuralgia).

While, to the nerve affected with neuralgia, consciousness reacts simply in the form of a general feeling (pain), the result is more complicated when the organ of consciousness itself is diseased. Owing to the solidarity of psychic phenomena, other anomalies necessarily follow from the primary elementary disturbance.

Thus to the organic psychic pain [that is, painful, depressed state] are added other psychologic phenomena. . . .

To the melancholic the external world seems somber and changed—in other colors; even objects which under other conditions would give rise to pleasant impressions seem now, in the mirror of his abnormally changed sense of self, to be worthy of aversion (psychic dysesthesia).

A further source of psychic pain lies in the fact that the intellect is under the impelling influence of feelings, and only such ideas as are in harmony with the state of the emotions can be entertained in consciousness.

Owing to this law, the melancholic is unable to retain in consciousness any other than painful and depressed images and ideas. The immediate result of this is monotony of thought and consequent weariness.

Along with the melancholic depression, the formal activity of the process of thought is also hindered, and there is therefore a notable inhibition of the psychomotor aspect of the mind.

This inhibition of the will, this opposition to the expenditure of psychic force, brings about a great increase in the feeling of depression, which is further augmented by the fact that the patient feels himself overpowered by the disturbance of his psychic mechanism, and powerless to resist it. . . .

Since the disturbance of nutrition is general, along with the psychic neurosis, there are various sensory disturbances (neuralgias, paralgias, paresthesias, anesthesias, and a changed state of general feeling); the vegetative functions and muscular tone suffer as well. These multifarious disturbances of the general state of feeling form another and fruitful source of psychic pain in the depressed consciousness. If the latter elements of painful feeling predominate, the depression takes on hypochondriac features. The abnormal painful depression is in itself objectless. In the milder and more transitory cases of this kind it remains so, and, as a rule, is recognized by the individual as abnormal. As the disease progresses and the disturbance of consciousness increases the patient seeks to explain his depression; and, since it is most natural for him to find the cause of it in anything (external world, earlier experiences, etc.) rather than in an affection of his central nervous system, he at last finds false motives for it (*vide* "Delusions"). In case of hypochondriac depression dependent upon the disturbance of general bodily feeling, resulting from organic anomalies, the effort to find an objective cause is made very early, for in such cases the comprehension of relations to the external world is unclouded, and then the patient develops false ideas concerning his bodily condition, and is apt to imagine that he is afflicted with organic and incurable diseases, when he is subject only to functional disturbances. (pp. 49–51)

Then, in his chapter on melancholia, he elaborated on "psychic symptoms":

> The content of the melancholic consciousness is psychic pain, distress, and depression, as the expression of a nutritive disturbance of the psychic organ. This painful depression in its content does not differ from the painful depression due to efficient causes. . . .
>
> The general result of these painful psychic processes expresses itself clinically in depression and sadness. Psychic dysesthesia causes the patient to be retiring, with desire to avoid people or to assume a hostile attitude toward the external world; psychic anesthesia causes indifference, even to the most important things of life. . . .
>
> The mental need of quiet in the patient is expressed in retiring from society and seeking isolation; the avoidance of sense-impressions and emotional activities.
>
> Disturbances in the intellectual domain are partly those of form and partly those of content. The former consist of retardation of thought and slowness of the association of ideas.
>
> This retardation is part of the general slowing of psychic activities; in part, too, dependent upon the painful feelings with which every psychic act is colored.
>
> The inhibition of the free course of ideas is an important accessory source of psychic pain. This expresses itself clinically in a feeling of fatigue, of mental vacuity, and of lessened mental energy (stupidity, lack of memory of which so many patients complain). Temporary complete stoppage of thought induces despair. The disturbance in the association of ideas is essentially due to the fact that only such ideas are possible as are in accord with the painful feeling, and thus the sum of the ideas that can possibly be reproduced is limited to those of painful content. Inhibition and disturbed association favor the occurrence of imperative ideas.
>
> Formal disturbances of ideas occur in all melancholics. They may be the only anomalies (melancholia without delusions); frequently, however, there is disturbance in the content of ideas: delusions.
>
> In the great majority of cases these arise psychologically and are an attempt to explain the abnormal state of consciousness; but the delusion is not necessarily the product of a logical conscious operation of thought; it may also be merely the conscious result of an unconscious product of association. Delusions arising out of errors of the senses are infrequent in melancholia, and pure primordial delusions are still more infrequent.
>
> The content of melancholic delusions is extremely varied, for they include all varieties of human trouble, care, and fear. Since they are always created out of the ideas peculiar to the individual, it is natural that they should vary infinitely according to individual endowment, sex, position, education, and age, even though certain constant cares and fears of the human race lend to the delusions of innumerable melancholics of all races and all times certain features and characteristics of content which are alike (Griesinger).
>
> The common character of all melancholic delusions is that of suffering, and, in contrast with the similar delusions of paranoia with delusions of persecution, they are referred to personal guilt. . . .

The intensification of mental pain by every kind of mental activity causes laziness, avoidance of work, neglect of occupation, and inclination to retire and take to bed. The want of self-confidence makes the attainment of ambition seem impossible and destroys all effort. The inhibited psychic activity in itself, the difficulty of change of ideas and their coloring by unpleasant feelings, the loss of mental interests which incite to act, find their expression in the complaints of the patient that he would like to act, but that he cannot will himself to act.

The fundamental character of melancholia is that of absence of energy: passiveness. However, in such cases, at least episodically, a very stormy, violent activity, going even to the extent of *furor*, is possible. This is explained by the fact that temporarily the inhibition is overcome by intense emotion. (pp. 286–289)

Under the heading "Other Nervous Symptoms" he completed his section on symptomatology by mentioning insomnia, disturbed sleep, headache, various physical manifestations of a lack of energy, various sensory disturbances, diminished secretions, diminished instinctual impulses, loss of appetite, loss of weight, and anemia (pp. 289–290).

Krafft-Ebing then observed that "melancholic insanity manifests itself clinically in two definite forms, which may be called *simple melancholia* and *melancholia with stupor.*" He commented that "the milder cases of melancholia are those in which the symptoms of mental inhibition are essentially psychic, due to a conscious painful mental process, and not organically induced by arrested activity in the psychomotor nervous paths, shown in its extreme degree by disturbance of muscular innervation (tetany, catalepsy)" (p. 290). He added that those "cases, in which evidently the psychic inhibition is increased and complicated by augmented organic (molecular) resistance in the voluntary paths, constitute transitional forms to the severer forms of melancholia with stupor, in which consciousness is also troubled and the patient sinks into a cloudy mental state" (p. 291). He used *melancholia attonita* and *melancholia stupida* as synonyms for melancholia with stupor, which was akin to the condition that Kahlbaum came to term *catatonia*, although Krafft-Ebing mentioned the "waxy flexibility" (flexibilitas cerea) later associated with catatonia and noted that it was rare (p. 306).

Short of these transitions into melancholia with stupor were the characteristic cases of *simple melancholia*, in which "there is not deep disturbance of consciousness. The inhibition in the emotional life shows itself in anesthesia with despair; in the intellectual life, as painful obstruction to the processes of thought in all directions; in the will, as distressing incapacity to decide upon an action, reaching even to the extent of complete arrest of voluntary acts. The necessary result is a profound diminution of confidence in self" (pp. 290–291). He emphasized that "the fundamental manifestation of the disease-picture is passivity: a distressing arrest of psychic functions," but he added that occasional cases eventuated in a severe degree of distressed restlessness (*melancholia errabunda*) and even in destructive acts (*agitated or active melancholia*) (p. 291). He commented that "simple melancholia is decidedly the most frequent form of mental disease. It presents clinically great variety in the grouping of symptoms and the intensity of the disease" (p. 292). He termed the mildest form *melancholia without delusion* and said that it was "only exceptionally observed in institutions for the insane, but it is extremely frequent in private practice. Often it long escapes the observation of the laity, as well as of physicians, for the patient is able to preserve an appearance of calm and reason." He also observed that "the ordinary medical diagnosis, overlooking the psychic anomaly, is frequently limited to anemia, chlorosis, hysteria, neurasthenia, etc." (p. 293). The next form of simple melancholia along his continuum of severity was *melancholia with precordial distress*, in which delusions were still absent and tension and anxiety might be extreme (pp. 295–298). Then further severity brought on *melancholia with delusions and errors of the senses*, the third stage in his forms of simple melancholia. He thought that "the false ideas" were "almost always the product of efforts to explain the abnormal state of consciousness"; and "the precordial distress and anxious emotional states of expectation" observed in the second form were "very important sources of delusions" (pp. 298–299). He took special note of two "forms of delusions that are especially striking and frequently observed"—*religious melancholia* and *hypochondriac melancholia* (pp. 301–305). In this sequence of stages or forms of simple melancholia and in the relationship of simple melancholia to melancholia with stupor, there was much that was reminiscent of the stages of increasing severity postulated by Griesinger under the influence of Guislain's and Zeller's notion of a unitary psychosis.

In approaching the topics of "course and terminations of melancholia," Krafft-Ebing made some introductory comments that reflected common views in the latter half of the nineteenth century but that were rarely so clearly and succinctly stated.

> The melancholic state occurring at the beginning of the various neuroses and psychoses as an intercurrent disturbance in the initial stages of a disease must be carefully differentiated from melancholia as a form of disease.
> There is very frequently a melancholic symptom-complex as a prodromal manifestation in mania and as an intercurrent phenomenon in senile dementia and dementia paralytica; also in epileptics, hysterics, hypochondriacs, neurasthenics, and sometimes in paranoiacs. It is only melancholia as a form of disease that can be the object of special clinical discussion. (p. 308)

He then discussed the above-mentioned forms as stages in a single disease-process. In each stage, arrest might occur, recovery was a distinct possibility, and worsening into a more serious stage was a danger. He observed that "melancholic insanity in all its stages shows remissions and exacerbations" within the course of a day, remissions in the afternoon and evening, and exacerbations in the earlier hours of the morning (pp. 308–309).

> The disappearance of the disease is gradual, not sudden—at least in chronic and essentially melancholic insanity. Remissions become more pronounced and enduring; sleep and nutrition improve. The patient begins to doubt the reality of his delusions and hallucinations, and the latter gradually disappear. . . .
>
> When the innumerable slight cases that do not reach the hospital for the insane are taken into consideration, the prognosis of melancholia is favorable. Numerous cases of this kind remain at the degree of melancholia without delusion, or have in addition only precordial distress, and pass on to recovery without the occurrence of delusions or errors of the senses.

"Aside from termination in recovery, which takes place in about 60 per cent. of cases treated in insane hospitals, and aside from a fatal result, sometimes due to exhaustion" and sometimes to various intercurrent physical illnesses, "termination in a state of mental weakness" was not uncommon, and "secondary delusional insanity or dementia" might occur (p. 309).

Finally, he laid down "the following general principles for the treatment" of melancholia: (1) "Give the patient complete physical and mental rest." (2) "Surveillance of the patient to protect him from himself and others from him." (3) "Care of the general condition and of the amount of food taken." (4) "Treatment, by proper means, of sleeplessness, which is very exhausting and favors the development of delusions and hallucinations": opium was specially mentioned, and lukewarm baths, mustard-baths, and Preissnitz packs. (5) "Use of symptomatic remedies approved by experience": lukewarm baths and opium were again mentioned (pp. 310–312).

GEORGE H. SAVAGE

Although George H. Savage (1842–1921) was not as influential as most of the other authors cited in this chapter, it is worth taking note of a few passages from his *Insanity and Allied Neuroses* of 1884. In brief form, they provide a representative selection of the types of melancholia, and perspectives on melancholia, that were extant toward the end of the century. He first defined melancholia as "a state of mental depression, in which the misery is unreasonable either in relation to its apparent cause, or in the peculiar form it assumes, the mental pain depending on physical and bodily changes, and not directly on the *environment*." He then stated:

1. Melancholia may be one stage in the mental disorder; thus, it may usher in mania or general paralysis of the insane, it may be present after an attack of mania, as a phase of reaction, or it may be one of the stages in *folie circulaire*.

2. Melancholia may be a complete process in itself.

Melancholia varies greatly in its aspects, just as grief causes an emotional storm in one person while it stuns and stupefies another; so the exaggerated melancholy may be of an emotional or of a dull type.

I shall divide the class of cases which come under the head melancholia as naturally as I can: 1. Into those with *simple* melancholy, *i.e.* those in whom the misery and its expression are simply slight exaggerations of natural states, those cases in whom there is no real delusion, no fiction such as that they are ruined or damned. 2. In contrast to these are those suffering from *active* insanity, those who, instead of suffering in silence, are constantly bemoaning their lot, and, with hand-wringing and hair-tearing, are heaping curses upon themselves. Such cases often resemble patients suffering from mania in aspect.

The cases of most profound misery are classed as suffering from *melancholia attonita*, or *passive melancholy*. . . .

Melancholia may depend for its existence on some delusion, but much more frequently the misery gives rise to the delusion. A saturated solution of grief causes, as it were, a delusion to crystallise and take a definite form.

Melancholia has a *bodily* and a *mental* aspect.[13]

CHARLES MERCIER

A valuable survey of the medical views on melancholia as the nineteenth century was coming to a close—that is, just before Kraepelin's views emerged as the most influential on this subject—was provided by Charles Mercier (1852–1918) in Tuke's *A Dictionary of Psychological Medicine* in 1892. He defined it as "a disorder characterized by a feeling of misery which is in excess of what is justified by the circumstances in which the individual is placed."[14] He also identified this unjustified feeling of misery as one of the cardinal symptoms along with "defects of nutrition and of other bodily processes" and "defect of conduct"; and he added that "commonly there is present, the expression of a delusion." He elaborated at length on the associated behavioral details. He observed that, "in true melancholia—that is to say, in cases in which there is not merely an expression, but an actual experience of misery"—the defect of nutrition is always present "throughout the whole body" and "is always of the nature of a slackening, weakening, diminution of activity in the process of nutrition" (*Dictionary*, 2:788). Mercier's elaborations at this point included the traditional symptoms of constipation and "slowed down" behavior. Then he stated that "delusion is very frequent, though not an invariable accompaniment of melancholia. Many cases begin with a simple feeling of misery without delusion, and, in trifling and mild cases, delusion may not occur, or may not become conspicuous in the whole course of the malady" (pp. 788–789).

Mercier differentiated melancholia "from other varieties of insanity in that it commonly arises *de novo* in a healthy person"; indicated that the prognosis was usually good, much better than it was for most other mental disorders; noted that there was a disposition to relapse; and said:

> Usually the onset of melancholia is gradual. A patient does not suddenly sink into deep melancholia, as he suddenly becomes maniacal or epileptic. He is noticed to be somewhat dull, somewhat lethargic, somewhat uneasy, and in less than his usual spirits, but usually these slight beginnings of the malady attract no notice, and it is not until the disorder has become fully established that it is remembered for how long the symptoms have been gradually increasing. At length the degree of misery and the other symptoms reach a grade at which the limits of the normal are unmistakably exceeded, and it becomes manifest that the patient is suffering from a morbid depression.

In addition to ending frequently in recovery and sometimes in death, "melancholia may merge into mania of more or less acuteness, of which it then appears to have been the initial stage"; and this had occurred frequently enough that some authorities concluded "that all cases of insanity, save of course general paralysis, begin in melancholia" (p. 789).

He then went on to note that "the industry of clinical alienists has rendered perhaps unnecessarily numerous" the varieties of melancholia, "no fewer than thirty varieties having been described by various authors" (ibid.). Parenthetically, the next entry in Tuke's *Dictionary* managed to take note of fifty-four varieties. But Mercier went on in more discriminating fashion to take note of *simple melancholia*, "in which the depression of feeling is unattended by delusion," a phase exhibited by most cases "at the outset, when the depression is not severe" and as severe as the condition became in some cases; of *melancholia with delusion*, "the complement of simple melancholia, and includes all cases which are not included in the previous class"; of *acute melancholia* and *chronic melancholia*, depending on whether the duration was less or more than a few weeks; of *active melancholia*, where "exaggerated gestures, loud cryings and moanings, etc." were involved, and *passive melancholia*, where the patients were "listless, lethargic and languid"; of *suicidal melancholia;* and of "intervals of melancholy," which might "occur in the course of other forms of insanity" and for which he did not think there was any need for separate categories (pp. 789–790).

In approaching the pathogenesis of melancholia, Mercier grounded his considerations in a version of the era's theories of nerve energy and nerve activity (pp. 790–791). Commenting that "we now know enough of the nervous accompaniment of consciousness to know that the feeling of well-being is dependent for its existence on a high state of activity of the nerve-tissue, on a high degree of tension of the nerve energy existing therein."

Through the motor nervous system and "outgoing currents from the central nerve regions," this healthy level of nerve energy and nerve-tissue activity was reflected in the "activity of conduct" and the "activity of all the nutritive processes." Thus, "when feeling is depressed, conduct diminished, and nu- trive processes inactive, we must infer that the opposite condition exists—that the nervous elements are unduly inactive, and the tension of the nervous energy is reduced below the normal"; and "the defect of conduct, the passivity, the indolence, the lethargy of melancholia are dependent upon precisely the same alteration of nerve action as the constipation, the loaded urine, the foul tongue and the other physical symptoms." As to etiology, it then followed that "whatever will produce a lowering in the tension of the nerve energy, and an inefficiency or slackening in the mode of working of the nerve-elements, may produce melancholia" (p. 791). An "hereditary disposition" was first and foremost, with the resultant "undue feebleness of nerve action" predisposing the person to the effects of possible precipitating factors (pp. 791–792). Among these latter, which would make demands beyond the capacity of the hereditarily predisposed system, Mercier mentioned

> puberty, . . . pregnancy, childbirth, suckling, and the climacteric, . . . ex-
> hausting attacks of bodily disease, . . . exhausting exertion, either physical or
> mental, . . . untoward circumstances, the loss of friends, or of fortune, or of
> character; any circumstance which is calculated to produce sorrow, grief, un-
> easiness, anxiety, in an ordinarily constituted person, may, if it act upon a
> person of less than ordinary stamina, produce melancholia. . . . The more
> severe the stress, the greater, naturally, is the chance of melancholia occurring.
> (p. 792)

Mercier's basic theory determined that treatment should be directed to increasing the level of nerve activity and restoring the nerve tension to its normal level. Emphasizing the need to stimulate and increase "the activity of the processes of nutrition," he discussed diet at length, in the face of the loss of appetite and insufficient food intake (p. 793). He considered exercise crucial "in order that the food thus given may be digested and assimilated" (pp. 793– 794). He thought that removal from the home environment could be instru- mental in successful treatment. He indicated that the once-routine use of opium had been largely abandoned, and that the favored drugs were "such as iron, quinine, arsenic, and strychnine" for their tonic effects on "the processes of digestion and of nutrition generally." The improved nutrition would usu- ally bring an end to the constipation, but, if not, he recommended "mineral waters given fasting in the morning" (p. 794). He expected the insomnia to end with improved diet and exercise, but, if not, he mentioned alcoholic beverages with supper and, if all else failed, morphia or chloral. He took note of the possible need of protection against suicidal inclinations (p. 795).

NEURASTHENIA

As we come to the end of considerations of melancholia in the nineteenth century, an addendum on the subject of neurasthenia is in order. Brought to prominence in the last third of the century by George M. Beard (1839–1883), neurasthenia was defined by Beard in 1869 as "exhaustion of the nervous system," or, on analogy with anemia as "want of *blood*," as "want of *nervous force*."[15] In elaborating he stated:

> The diagnosis is obtained partly by the positive symptoms, and partly by exclusion. If a patient complains of general malaise, debility of all the functions, poor appetite, abiding weakness in the back and spine, fugitive neuralgic pains, hysteria, insomnia, hypochondriases, disinclination for consecutive mental labor, severe and weakening attacks of sick headache, and other analogous symptoms, and at the same time gives *no evidence of anaemia or of any organic disease*, we have reason to suspect that the central nervous system is mainly at fault, and that we are dealing with a typical case of neurasthenia.[16]

Reminiscent of the hypochondriacal and nervous disorders of the eighteenth century, neurasthenia also seems to have been a direct descendant of the *asthenic* conditions of John Brown toward the end of that century. Once established, this syndrome had absorbed into it all manner of noninsane nervous and mental disorders that would later come to be termed phobic states, obsessive-compulsive neuroses, and anxiety states—essentially, the twentieth century's *psychoneuroses*. In his study of neurasthenia Bunker effectively summed up much about this disorder in the following:

> For Beard, neurasthenia was a "many-sided and fluctuating" syndrome featured by a multiplicity of subjective symptoms, discoverable in large part only through a painstaking anamnesis, among which fatigue, exhaustion, "lack of nerve force," "nervous bankruptcy," held a cardinal place; attendant manifestations included an array of subjective complaints ranging from various ill-defined aches and pains to phobias and obsessions. In brief, not only was neurasthenia, in Beard's conception, "the centre and type of the family of functional nervous diseases;" it *was* functional nervous disease, was virtually synonymous with it, since scarcely any other sort of so-called functional nervous disorder, hardly even hysteria, was distinguished from it in Beard's formulation—nor, it might be added, in the minds of many later writers.[17]

Although the rise and fall of the syndrome is a complex and lengthy story in its own right and cannot be dealt with here,[18] it is important to note that it frequently served as a nosological home for a variety of nonpsychotic depressive states that earlier would have been diagnosed as hypochondriasis or nervousness, which some authorities even in neurasthenia's heyday would classify as simple melancholia and which would later be thought of as depressive neuroses. Often, too, neurasthenia was thought of as an earlier stage of severer disorders, not unlike the prodromal depressive stage that Griesinger viewed as the beginning of most cases of insanity.

An instructive example of how intermingled ideas on melancholia, depression, and neurasthenia sometimes were in the late nineteenth century was provided by Maurice de Fleury (1860–1931) in a chapter entitled "Melancholy and Its Treatment" in his *Medicine and the Mind*. Drawing on "sound medical observations taken from hypochondriacal or lipaemaniac patients," he reported that "the state of dejection comes from a state of fatigue or exhaustion of the nervous system, of which it is the mental reflex." This affective state was

> nothing else than the vague consciousness of weakness, of powerlessness in our organism, of a diminution, permanent or passing, of the activity of our circulation, and consequently of our vital activity. If we lose some one whom we love, the profound dejection into which we are plunged is not the consequence of our grief, but its cause.
>
> . . . The dread spectacle of death, or the telling of the fatal news, by our eyes or ears, by the optic or the auditory nerve, project strong vibrations to our nerve centres; and these vibrations themselves awaken and rudely destroy notions so firmly fixed, associations of ideas so inveterate, habits of mind so rooted—that the brain is overwhelmed by them and over-wrought. Its vitality becomes exhausted and its tonicity is lessened. Thenceforward the circulation grows languid, respiration becomes weak, the muscles are relaxed and work feebly, and the nerves of sensibility carry to the brain from the whole body the continuous idea of weakness, failure, powerlessness; the mind becomes conscious of this, with a vague and confused consciousness, and that is called grief.
>
> Grief is a special, a lower pitch of brain activity. The mind, if it stays there for a certain time, will form the habit, and henceforward everything will appear to it in a painful, melancholy, pessimistic light.
>
> Melancholy is only a symptom of a disease of the vitality, an impoverishing of the circulation and a slackening of nutrition.[19]

De Fleury then proceeded to equate such conditions with neurasthenia (*Medicine and the Mind*, pp. 265–266). He also referred in a variety of ways to an emotional dichotomy of sadness/melancholy versus joy/gladness and related these to postulated basic physiological states of exhaustion versus excitement—shades of William Cullen and John Brown! He was distinctly optimistic about the treatment prospects for these melancholic-neurasthenic illnesses; he asserted "from having seen it a hundred times, that dull *ennui*, chronic dejection, causeless melancholy, the pessimistic temperament, that tendency to see all things at their worst, to worry one's self perpetually, and to make one's surroundings wretched which is one of the most frequent mind maladies of the present day, may be cured by medicine" (p. 280). His therapeutic program was based on well-chosen tonics and stimulants. Then, when there is a sufficient return of energy, "try to turn aside his fixed ideas by inspiring him with some ambition in proportion to his capacity, and by accustoming him to useful and regular work" (p. 281). He concluded with the comment that "the treatment of melancholy depression exists; as a fact it is efficacious; and that it is so we may well rejoice" (p. 282).

SOME THEMES AND VARIATIONS

Early in this century, the syndrome of melancholia underwent a significant reduction in its content and a sharpening of its outlines as Esquirol separated out a minority group of monodelusional states with exalted mood, and thereafter its descriptive outline was usually restricted to severe depressive disturbances. Melancholia continued to be commonly associated with delusions, but they gradually became less necessary to the accepted clinical description. *Simple melancholia*, or *melancholia without delusion*, emerged as a recognized subtype that might or might not worsen into *melancholia with delusion*. The dejected state with its distressed preoccupation and its concomitant "slowing" of mental and physical functions was increasingly viewed as the descriptive core. As both simple melancholia and the delusional forms were considered to be types of madness or insanity, the presence of a delusion was no longer necessary for a disorder to be an instance of insanity. Although, often enough, the delusional type was described as monodelusional, increasingly the person was described as delusional beyond such limits. Moreover, after Esquirol, melancholia was no longer synonymous with partial insanity; and, with the validity of the notion of partial insanity being increasingly questioned, melancholia gradually lost its status as even one form of partial insanity.

Despite the frequently elaborated theoretical views that were often part of the nineteenth-century presentations on melancholia, the most striking feature of these accounts was the emergence of a strong descriptive tradition, particularly as developed by Esquirol and as carried forward by Griesinger and Krafft-Ebing. Toward the end of the century this tradition was taken up and carried well into the twentieth century by Kraepelin. During the nineteenth century these descriptive contributions increasingly entailed careful attention to the *course* of a disorder, perhaps reflecting the growing populations in psychiatric institutions and the concomitant increase in opportunities to follow the course of these illnesses over longer periods. By the end of the century Kraepelin was bringing the course of an illness into focus as a crucial source of perspective on and understanding of psychiatric conditions.

That a less severe form of melancholia (simple melancholia) might worsen into a severer form (melancholia with delusion) became a common view. The centuries-old observation that melancholia might worsen and become mania continued to be frequently mentioned, and this gradually led to the *melancholia-mania connections* formulated by Baillarger and Falret in the

1850s (see chap. 10). These ideas eventually led to the turn-of-the-century variations on this theme introduced by Kraepelin in the form of the *manic-depressive disease*. A sense of course, of longitudinal development, was crucial to these trends.

A particular longitudinal viewpoint, reflecting the Boerhaavian continuum of severity and originally formulated by Guislain and Zeller, was promulgated by Griesinger in the form of a *unitary psychosis* (*Einheitspsychose*). The influence of this concept continued through the latter half of the century until efforts such as those of Kraepelin toward discrete *disease-entities* considerably reduced its influence. Viewed in another light, the tendency to a "unitarian" view was a version of the efforts toward a simplified nosology (a few diagnostic categories, or perhaps only one), in contrast to the complex nosologies of many mental diseases. In a manner of speaking, there was an ongoing tension or struggle between these two trends throughout the century. As early as the beginning of the century, Thomas Beddoes (1760–1808) alluded to the issue when he wondered *"whether it be not necessary either to confine insanity to one species, or to divide it into almost as many as there are cases."*[20] And Pinel illustrated the issue in his own move from his grand nosological system in which there were many mental diseases to his simplified scheme of only four such disorders.

Still another variant of syndromes being related to one another on a continuum of severity was a system in which there were primary disorders, such as melancholia and mania, that were thought to be curable, and secondary disorders that were thought to have a much worse prognosis, that were often conceived of as a more deteriorated stage of anxiety, and that were often termed dementia. An example of this type of scheme was Krafft-Ebing's *psychoneuroses* and his *psychic degenerations*. In another version of this sort of scheme the former group was composed of disorders of the emotions, or insanities involving the emotions (our affective disorders?), and the latter group of disorders of the intellect, or insanities involving the intellect (our thought disorders?). At times it was likely that the degeneration hypothesis was a basic assumption in such schemes. Further, although Kraepelin conceived of his two categories as discrete diseases without any degenerative drift from one to the other, there is a certain parallel between the former group and his *manic-depressive disease* and between the latter group and his *dementia praecox*.

It has become a commonplace to look back on the nineteenth century and highlight Griesinger's credo, "Mental diseases are brain diseases"; and such an orientation was indeed the prevailing one during the rest of the century. What is often lost sight of, however, is that somatic explanatory schemes of one sort or another had long been prominent and still were in the early nineteenth century. Certainly Heinroth and the other *Psychiker* were inclined toward psychological categories and explanations; and Griesinger may well have been contending with such views in asserting his credo. Also, there was not much firm evidence in favor of somatic explanations of mental diseases. Nevertheless, the traditional assumption of some form of physiological psychology had continued to be prominent, and this had already been joined by convictions about the likelihood of underlying brain pathology on the basis of the growing interest in autopsies of the brain.

These convictions about a basic brain disease were manifested in another interesting way. It became common in the latter half of the century to think in terms of functional nervous and mental diseases versus organic nervous and mental diseases. In contrast to the sometimes loose twentieth-century use of *functional* to mean "non-organic" and "psychological," the nineteenth-century implication was that no organic pathology had been established but that there was surely a physiological dysfunction and, further, that a subtle, undetected structural damage might well be present or might eventually develop.

CHAPTER NINE

Melancholia and Depression in the Twentieth Century

EMIL KRAEPELIN

Although Emil Kraepelin (1856–1926) lived the majority of his years in the nineteenth century and did a significant portion of his work in that century, his influence on matters to do with melancholia and depression is more a twentieth-century story. His impact on the status of such disorders began to be apparent in the 1890s, but he became a central figure on these matters during the early decades of the twentieth century, even up to the middle of the century, and his influence is still with us in important ways. Appearing originally as a *Compendium* in 1883, his famous *Lehrbuch* grew and changed through the second, third, and fourth editions in 1887, 1889, and 1893, but it was only with the fifth and sixth editions in 1896 and 1899 that his far-reaching changes in how to conceive of melancholia and depression really emerged. Turning from neuroanatomical work with Flechsig and experimental psychology with Wundt, Kraepelin developed his own program of clinical investigation with intensive long-range studies of psychiatric disease and worked toward establishing discrete diseases and a new nosological system. Although his views ran counter to Karl Ludwig Kahlbaum's (1828–1899) inclination toward the idea of a unitary psychosis, he was significantly influenced by Kahlbaum's convictions about the importance of detailed clinical-descriptive studies that would justify the establishment of symptom-complexes. Kahlbaum's emphasis on the value of longitudinal study of clinical courses, and the success of others with such an approach in coming to understand general paralysis of the insane, served to shape Kraepelin's work. Kraepelin argued against the limitations of classifying patients on the basis of mental symptoms and in favor of being guided by the longer range course and outcome of both physical and mental symptoms.[1]

In the earlier editions of his *Psychiatrie*—a *Compendium* in 1883, a *Short Textbook* in 1887, 1889, and 1893—Kraepelin categorized melancholic conditions much as most of his contemporaries did. At first, his main category of depressive states included the familiar *simple melancholia* and *melancholia with delusions; melancholia activa*, or *melancholia agitata*, was grouped with the forms of mania; and his periodic psychoses included *periodic melancholia* and *circular insanity* with its depressive phase.[2] In the second, third, and fourth editions, instances of delusional melancholia were reclassified as forms of either the curable *Wahnsinn* (delusional insanities) or the incurable *Verrücktheit* (paranoias). *Agitated melancholia (Angstmelancholie, melancholia activa, melancholia agitata)* became a type within the main category of melancholia, along with *melancholia simplex* and *melancholia attonita*. And he continued to use a category of periodic insanities that included periodic melancholia and a depressive phase in circular insanity.[3]

Then, in the fifth edition of his *Psychiatrie* in 1896, now a *Textbook* rather than a *Short Textbook*, Kraepelin revised his work substantially and introduced a completely new nosological scheme. He began the process of organizing his two, soon to be famous, nosological groups by bringing together in one category psychoses that he considered to be deteriorating in nature and in another category psychoses that he considered to be nondeteriorating. In the first group *(die Verblödungsprocesse)*[4] were those conditions that were to constitute his notion of dementia praecox in his sixth edition in 1899. In the second group *(das periodische Irresein)* he brought together mania, melancholia, and circular insanity, thus discontinuing the presentation of mania and melancholia as separate disorders.[5] Then in the sixth edition he replaced the term *periodic psychosis* with *manic-depressive psychosis (das manisch-depressive Irresein)* to refer to a group that included manic states, depressed states, and mixed states.[6] In these fifth and sixth editions, only *melancholia*, as one of the diseases of the involutional period, remained as a separate melancholic or depressive condition. Kraepelin had here created a category of involutional psychoses that included presenile delusional insanity and senile dementia, along with this melancholia that was to become known as *involutional melancholia* (see pp. 207–211 below). Explicitly borrowing Möbius' dichotomy of exogenous and endogenous etiologies (see pp. 211–212 below), in his fifth edition Kraepelin introduced a category of *acquired* mental diseases that included the *Verblödungsprocesse*, and a category of mental diseases stemming from a morbid *hereditary* or *constitutional predisposition* that included the *periodic psychoses*. But, in his sixth edition, he came to view *both* these sets of diseases—the *Ver-*

blödungsprocesse, now *dementia praecox*, and the periodic psychoses, now *manic-depressive insanity*—as endogenous, while maintaining the contrast of deteriorating and nondeteriorating, respectively.

In his sixth edition Kraepelin introduced manic-depressive disease as follows:

> Manic-depressive insanity comprehends, on one hand, the entire domain of so-called periodic and circular insanity, and, on the other, simple mania usually distinguished from the above. In the course of years I have become more and more convinced that all the pictures mentioned are merely forms of one single disease process. . . . Certain fundamental traits recur in the same shape, notwithstanding manifold superficial differences. Whoever knows the fundamental traits will, with due consideration to certain practical difficulties, always be able to conclude from a single phase that it belongs to the large circle of forms included under manic-depressive insanity. . . . On the other hand, it is, as far as I can see, quite impossible to find any definitive boundaries between the single disease pictures which have been kept apart so far. . . .
>
> *Manic-depressive insanity*, as its name indicates, takes its course in single attacks, which either present the signs of so-called manic excitement (flight of ideas, exaltation, and overactivity), or those of a peculiar psychic depression with psychomotor inhibition, or a mixture of the two states.[7]

The idea of a distinct disease involving both manic and melancholic states was not original with Kraepelin. He had clearly been influenced by the well-established views of this nature that were already part of the psychiatric world of his time. What was really different was the bringing together within the concept of a single, discrete disease almost all the various manic and melancholic disorders. Although various connections had been postulated over the centuries, for Kraepelin his longitudinal studies of the course of many individual disorders suggested affinities that dissolved the distinct disease status of the traditional symptom groups of mania and melancholia. From these studies he concluded that evolution and outcome transcended such symptom groups as a basis for classification; and then, in turn, he offered his new categories as grounds for prognosis.

In surveying the clinical pictures as put forward by Kraepelin, one finds, as Meyer so nicely outlined it, that the diagnosis of manic-depressive insanity was based "on a triad of symptom pairs—exaltation and depression of feelings . . . , flight of ideas or inhibition of thought, and irresistible psychomotor unrest or inhibition."[8] This diagnostic term

> is applied to that mental disorder which recurs in definite forms at intervals throughout the life of the individual and in which a defective hereditary endowment seems to be the most prominent etiological factor.
>
> The greater number of cases usually called recoverable mania, simple mania, simple melancholia, periodical mania, periodical melancholia, and circu-

lar insanity belong to this group. . . . The constant recurrence of certain fundamental symptoms in all the attacks, the uniformity of their course and outcome, and the occasional intimate relation of different forms of the disease, where one form passes over either gradually or rapidly into another, has led to the conclusion that the individual attacks appear in one of three forms, the maniacal, the depressive, or the mixed.

The *maniacal forms* are characterized by psychomotor excitement, flight of ideas with sound associations, great distractibility, pressure of activity, happy though unstable emotional attitude, unstable delusions, some hallucinations, and comparatively little clouding of consciousness.

The *depressive forms* are characterized by psychomotor retardation, absence of spontaneous activity, dearth of ideas, dejected emotional attitude, prominent delusions and hallucinations, and usually clouding of consciousness.

The *mixed forms* present a combination of the symptoms characteristic of each of these conditions.[9]

In considering further Kraepelin's clinical outlines of the depressive forms, one sees what had become of most of the nineteenth-century forms of melancholia and depression, and one is given a view of such disorders that was singularly influential, albeit with occasional modifications, during the first half of the twentieth century.

After presenting the various clinical features of the depressive forms in paired contrast with their opposite number in the manic forms, Kraepelin wrote about "manic states" in a sequence of increasing severity: *hypomania*, *mania*, and *delirious mania*. Then he did the same for "depressive states" in a similar three-part manner: *simple retardation, retardation with delusions and hallucinations*, and *stuporous conditions*. And lastly he dealt with "mixed states." This organizational scheme is a close kin to that which was in common use half a century later.

The first group in the *depressive states* was designated *simple retardation* and was

the mildest form of depression . . . without either hallucinations or prominent delusions. The onset is generally gradual. . . . There appears gradually a sort of mental sluggishness; thought becomes difficult; the patients find difficulty in coming to a decision and in expressing themselves. It is hard for them to follow the thought in reading or ordinary conversation. They fail to find the usual interest in their surroundings.

The process of association of ideas is remarkably retarded; . . . they have nothing to say; there is a dearth of ideas and a poverty of thought. . . . It is hard to remember the most commonplace things. They appear dull and sluggish, and explain that they really feel tired and exhausted. . . . Although mentally retarded, consciousness is unclouded and the environment is correctly apprehended.

In the *emotional attitude* there is a uniform depression. The patient sees only the dark side of life. The past and the future are alike full of unhappiness and misfortune. . . . They are unsuited to their environment; are a failure in their profession; have lost religious faith, . . . frequently express a desire to end their existence, but they seldom make a serious attempt at suicide. Insight is frequently present, the patients appreciating keenly that they are mentally ill. . . .

This form of depression runs a rather uniform *course* with few variations. The improvement is gradual. The duration varies from a few months to over a year. (*Clinical Psychiatry*, pp. 299–300)

The second group in the depressive states was "characterized by hallucinations and varied delusions of persecution and self-accusation," in addition to the psychomotor retardation, difficulty of thought, and dismal emotional state already outlined. "The *onset* of this form is usually subacute or acute, following a period of indisposition, and occasionally even a short period of exhiliration and buoyancy of spirits; a few cases appear after an acute illness or mental shock" (p. 301). Hypochondriacal delusions were also common. "*Hallucinations* . . . groans and moans are heard, disagreeable odors permeate the room, terrible apparitions appear at night, and fearful scenes are depicted." Usually consciousness was unclouded; the patient was correctly oriented and coherent; "but the content of thought and speech shows a constant tendency to revert to their depressive delusions" (p. 302). Possible physical symptoms included

numbness in the head . . . a feeling as if there were weights upon the chest . . . palpitation of the heart. The appetite is poor, the tongue coated, and the bowels constipated . . . usually a strong aversion to food. The sleep is broken and disturbed by anxious dreams. The eyes are lustreless, the skin is sallow and without its accustomed firmness.

The *course* of this form shows variations with partial remissions and very gradual improvement. The duration extends from six to eighteen months.

Termed *stuporous conditions*, "the third group of depressive cases is character-ized by numerous incoherent and dreamlike delusions and hallucinations, with a pronounced clouding of consciousness. This form rarely appears alone, but usually forms an episode in the course of the other forms" (p. 303).

Kraepelin noted that "manic-depressive insanity comprises from ten to fifteen per cent. of admissions to insane hospitals. The disease is more common in women than in men. Of the etiological factors, defective heredity is the most prominent, occurring in from seventy to eighty percent. of cases" (p. 283). He added, "Thus far observation has failed to reveal any characteristic anatomical pathological changes. This fact, together with the recurrence of individual attacks, mostly independent of external causes, has led to the conclusion that the disease depends upon a neuropathic basis, which in the vast majority of cases is hereditary" (p. 284). He observed that the prognosis was "unfavorable in view of the certainty of the recurrence of attacks throughout the life of the individual" but that it was "favorable for recovery from the individual attacks" (p. 309).

Concerned as he primarily was with detailed considerations of course and outcome and essentially convinced of the inevitability of the disease's course, Kraepelin approached treatment mainly in terms of management and symptomatic measures. Except for the milder attacks, treatment was best carried out in an asylum where special precautions could be taken against the danger of suicide. He recommended bed rest, a nutritious diet, outdoor exercise, evening baths, and massage. He mentioned bromides, opium, and morphine. He noted that hypnotic suggestion had brought relief in milder cases. And he cautioned against visits from relatives, long conversations, and letters as possible causes of further emotional disturbance (pp. 314–315).

Although the fifth and sixth editions of his textbook had involved bringing most melancholic disorders together, eventually to be named manic-depressive insanity, in these two editions Kraepelin kept one subgroup of them aside and continued to denominate them *melancholia*. Under the heading of *involutional psychoses* he placed "three forms of mental disease, melancholia, presenile delusional insanity, and senile dementia," and commented that they "seem to stand in a causal relationship to the general physical changes accompanying involution" (p. 254). The first of these three forms was soon to be referred to as *involutional melancholia*. This diagnosis

> is restricted to certain conditions of mental depression occurring during the period of involution. It is to be distinguished from the melancholia of some other writers, who apply the term to any condition of depression, whether it enters into the picture of dementia paralytica, or is a premonitory symptom of acute delirium, or accompanies hysterical insanity, etc. In this broad sense it simply expresses an emotional state. Melancholia, as applied here, represents two groups of cases, which are characterized by *uniform depression with fear, various delusions of self-accusation, of persecution, and of a hypochondriacal nature, with moderate clouding of consciousness and disturbance of the train of thought, leading in the greater number of cases after a prolonged course to moderate mental deterioration.* (pp. 254–255)

He also commented that "a *religious strain* is very prominent in many" and that "other delusions of fear are those of punishment for past misdeeds" (p. 256). He referred to a second, severer group of cases within this diagnostic category that was "characterized by a greater predominance of delusions of fear, which are apt to be extremely silly, and sometimes even nihilistic, many hallucinations, great clouding of consciousness, and some motor unrest" (p. 258). Kraepelin described the course of involutional melancholia as follows:

> a gradual development, a prolonged duration, and a still more gradual convalescence. In cases of recovery the whole course lasts at least twelve months to two years. Short remissions, during which there is only a partial disappearance of the symptoms, occur throughout the whole course. Exacerbations often arise as the result of annoyance, fatigue, and excitation, such as that induced by visits. A gradual improvement of the physical symptoms, especially an increase in weight, may be regarded as a favorable sign. The remissions become longer and

more marked; and the apprehension gives way to irritability and fretfulness; the patients then begin to display interest in work and reading. Even when convalescence is well established, it is not unusual for them to have "bad days," during which they are troubled and apprehensive. (p. 262)

Although one-half improve enough to return home and live comfortably, "the prognosis is not favorable, considering that only one-third of the cases recover, the remaining two-thirds undergoing mental deterioration" (p. 263). He commented that "the anatomical changes which have thus far been noted are only those of arteriosclerosis" (p. 255). As to treatment,

> the first essential is the establishment of a "rest cure," which should include the removal of the patient from irritating persons as well as objects. It is necessary in most cases that the patients be confined in bed with short intermissions, with sufficient and constant attendance. In very light cases a suitable change may be found in removal to a different boarding-place or into the associations of a happy family. It is decidedly not advisable to attempt distractions, such as might be afforded by long journeys, sight-seeing, and constant company.

Careful attention was to be given to diet. It should be "nutritious, given in small quantities and at frequent intervals" (p. 264). For insomnia, he recommended warm baths, avoiding hypnotics if at all possible. If hypnotics were used, he considered alcohol the most valuable, then sulfonal and trional, bromides, or paraldehyde. "The distressing condition of anxious restlessness may be combated with opium or morphin in increasing doses" (p. 265). Careful precautions were to be taken against suicidal tendencies. Finally,

> the psychical influence which may be constantly exerted over the patients by those in attendance is of the greatest value in alleviating distress, modifying the delusions, and relieving the anxiety. For this reason the manner should be gentle, friendly, and assuring, and attempts should always be made to lead the thoughts of the patient away from their depressive ideas. Visits from relatives are deleterious in the height of the disease. Finally, it is of utmost importance that the patients be kept under observation and treatment until thoroughly recovered. A safe index of this may be found in the insight into the disease and the return of sleep and nutrition to their normal state. (pp. 265–266)

The seventh edition of *Psychiatrie* in 1904 did not bring any significant further changes in how Kraepelin dealt with melancholic and depressive disorders. But, in the eighth edition, which appeared in four volumes from 1909 to 1915, the separate category of involutional melancholia disappeared as he accepted Dreyfus' view that the prognosis of such disorders was better than had been alleged and that they should be included in the manic-depressive group.[10] Kraepelin brought them into the sphere of manic-depressive insanity as mixed states.[11] It is from the eighth edition that the following commonly quoted, omnibus definition is drawn:

Manic-depressive insanity, as it is to be described in this section, includes on the one hand the whole domain of so-called *periodic and circular* insanity, on the other hand *simple mania*, the greater part of the morbid states termed *melancholia* and also a not inconsiderable number of cases of *amentia*. Lastly, we include here certain slight and slightest colourings of *mood*, some of them periodic, some of them continuously morbid, which on the one hand are to be regarded as the rudiment of more severe disorders, on the other hand pass over without sharp boundary into the domain of *personal predisposition*. In the course of the years I have become more and more convinced that all the above-mentioned states only represent manifestations of a *single morbid process*. (*Manic-Depressive Insanity*, p. 1)

To this he added that "all the morbid forms brought together here as a clinical entity, *not only pass over the one into the other without recognisable boundaries, but . . . they may even replace each other in one and the same case*" (p. 2). He emphasized that such cases, even if chronic, "never lead to profound dementia"; and he maintained that "the various forms . . . may also apparently mutually replace one another in *heredity*" (p. 3). Other than bringing involutional melancholia into the "family" of manic-depressive insanity, in this eighth edition Kraepelin did little to change the status of the various melancholic and depressive states. His extensive clinical outlines remained much the same. Hereditary predisposition remained at the heart of his comments on etiology. His discussion of treatment was essentially unchanged.

ADOLF MEYER

"The dominant figure in American psychiatry between 1895 and 1940" and influential abroad, Adolf Meyer (1866–1950) was a contemporary of Kraepelin who both valued highly the latter's contributions and came to be critical of them; the views of these two leading figures sometimes seemed to be in competition with each other and sometimes became blended together.[12] Without losing sight of the value of Kraepelin's emphasis on the long-range course of a disease, Meyer emphasized rather the importance of the lifelong history of the person in understanding his unique experience of a disease. Out of this orientation he came to challenge Kraepelin's discrete disease entities and to conceive of psychiatric disorders as maladaptive reaction patterns that depended on constitution and life experiences. Also he introduced a genetic-dynamic approach that, at least in the English-speaking world, came to be interwoven with the emerging contributions of psychoanalysis.

At first favorably disposed toward Kraepelin's nosological innovations as they appeared in the fifth edition of *Psychiatrie*, Meyer gradually developed grave reservations about Kraepelin's discrete disease-entities, although he still thought that manic-depressive insanity and dementia praecox constituted useful paradigms. And he became concerned with the too-inclusive nature of the manic-depressive synthesis. In an annual report for 1904–1905, writing with the manic-depressive insanity and involutional melancholia of Kraepelin's sixth edition in mind, he pointed out that there were

> many *depressions* which command our attention as alienists, without their belonging to the above groups, through the mere fact that depression, of whatever origin, is apt to be dangerous as a foundation for suicide, and tends to shut *in* the patient in self-absorption, so as to exclude the corrective influences of the environment, and so as to allow a cropping out of uncorrected ideas and developments which may take a progressive character, of the nature of a vicious circle, especially where, for some reason, constitutional safeguards are lacking. This seems to be a necessary conclusion from the fact that so many depressions have neither the characteristics of the manic-depressive depression nor those of a definite type of agitated anxiety psychosis belonging more especially to the period of involution.[13]

From there he argued for including in the manic-depressive group only those depressive forms that showed the "classical symptoms" of "subjective feeling of difficulty of thinking and acting, with or without obvious retardation, and with sadness or downheartedness"; and he favored restricting this group to "the cases with recurrence in the same form or with alteration of equivalents" (Winters, *Collected Papers*, 2:143). He was prepared to recognize a category of "conditions akin to the manic-depressive psychoses," but he also proposed a whole category of "depressions" unrelated to that group—"essential depressions not sufficiently differentiated, symptomatic depressions, depressive hallucinosis, agitated depression or anxiety psychosis, depressions with additional symptoms (paranoic traits or other complications)" (pp. 143–144).

In other contexts of approximately the same era, Meyer said more about his own way of conceiving of the melancholias and depressions. In 1902 he had noted that "in its current use melancholia applies to all abnormal conditions dominated by depression" and then added:

> The varieties commonly classified are simple melancholia, stuporous, delusional, homicidal, suicidal, puerperal, acute, chronic melancholia attonita, etc. It is obvious that many dissimilar conditions are thus brought under one heading, simply because they are dominated by depression. A careful analysis leads to the recognition of more essential characteristics; but the nosological interpretation of the various types is still a topic of some controversy. (p. 566)

He outlined in the following manner "the most common symptom-complexes":

> (1) Constitutional depression: a pessimistic temperament that is inclined to see the dark side of everything and is led to gloominess and despondency upon slight provocation. Such moods or periods often present a temporary character in the form of more or less periodic exacerbations, which, however, in distinction from the next group, rather readily pass off with an improvement in the

circumstances of the patient. Such attacks are occasionally accompanied by marked feelings of anxiety.

(2) Simple melancholia proper: an excessive or altogether unjustified depression, often accompanied by defective sleep, precordial pain or uneasiness; a susceptibility for the unpleasant and wearing aspect of things only, and a feeling of self-depreciation, of sinfulness, without insight into the unwarranted morbid nature of the condition. The patient feels himself too bad to live or to be treated kindly. There is usually a feeling of inability and indecision, and especially in the form which is merely a phase of manic-depressive insanity, a difficulty in thinking clearly, and a retardation or inhibition of spontaneous activity.

This may be followed by delusional elaboration; the patient comes to believe that everything, the whole world, will come to a bad end, that it is all the patient's fault; and an occasional hallucination may appear to corroborate and elaborate such feelings and thoughts. This condition is frequently accompanied by a strong affect of fear and anxiety for self and family, or suicidal impulses, or great restlessness, or again self-absorption, or retardation of all activity, leading to a form of stupor.

(3) Other forms are characterized by prolonged "neurasthenic" malaise and a feeling of depression (frequently over moral matters) and by a great tendency to refer the feelings to influence of others, to poison, to hypnotism, to electricity, to nocturnal rape; or there are hypochondriacal complaints, frequently of an absurd character. Hallucinations are common. The whole picture is apt to have a certain resemblance to the paranoic types in later periods of life (after 35), while in earlier periods it undoubtedly belongs usually to the processes of deterioration (dementia praecox), and often presents distinct features of catatonia. (pp. 566–567)

He also took note of "depressive delirium" that might occur "after acute diseases, in pregnancy, etc." and "catatonic melancholia." He went on to state:

The forms (1) and (2) are usually recoverable conditions of greatly varying duration, frequently belonging to the constitutional, recurring, and circular psychoses, the simple depressions being especially prone to occur in several successive generations of a family. In the circular cases, the predominance of an inhibition or retardation of movements and of thought is very striking, while the anxious and agitated forms of (2) are especially characteristic for the climacteric period, and pass without a distinct line into the types of presenile depression with absurd hypochondriacal delusions, shallow affects, and usually poor prognosis. . . .

The individual differences in a large series of cases of melancholia are so great that it would be a grave injustice to the facts to try to describe them as one condition in one connected composite picture.

Clinical experience and experimental psychology show that there are undoubtedly several distinct disease processes which account for the differences of the above types. But definite statements as to their nature and concerning the pathological anatomy seem as yet premature. (pp. 567–568)

In a discussion in 1905 "on the classification of the melancholias" Meyer indicated that he was desirous of eliminating the term melancholia, which implied a knowledge of something that we did not possess, and which had been employed in different specific ways by different writers. If, instead of melancholia, we applied the term depression to the whole class, it would designate in an unassuming way exactly what was meant by the common use of the term melancholia; and nobody would doubt that for medical purposes the term would have to be amplified so as to denote the kind of depression. . . . We might distinguish the pronounced types from the simple insufficiently differentiated depressions. Besides the manic-depressive depressions, the anxiety psychoses, the depressive deliria and depressive hallucinations, the depressive episodes of dementia prae-cox, the symptomatic depressions, non-differentiated depressions will occur. (p. 568)

Eventually Meyer's objections to Kraepelin's disease-entities led him in 1908 to propose the more modest idea of reaction types. Increasingly concerned about the hypothetical anemias, hereditary predispositions, degeneracies, cerebral irritations, depleted nerve energies, defective nerve functions, and nerve cell schemes as the alleged bases for distinct diseases, Meyer argued for the simpler notions of "situation, reaction, and final adjustment," a scheme of "reactions as part of *an adjustment, a response to a demand*" (p. 598). In suggesting his concept of "substitutive reactions," he summed up as follows:

To try and explain a hysterical fit or a delusion system out of hypothetical cell alterations which we cannot reach or prove is at the present stage of histophysiology a gratuitous performance. To realize that such a reaction is a *faulty response* or *substitution of an insufficient or protective or evasive or mutilated attempt at adjustment* opens ways of inquiry in the direction of modifiable determining factors and all of a sudden we find ourselves in a live field, in harmony with our instincts of action, of prevention, of modification, and of an understanding doing justice to a desire for directness instead of neurologizing tautology.

The conditions which we meet in psychopathology are more or less abnormal reaction types, which we want to learn to distinguish from one another, trace to the situation or conditions under which they arise, and study for their modifiability. (p. 599)

Out of this approach he developed six "types of disorders or reaction types": "reactions of organic disorders," "delirious states," "essentially affective reactions," "paranoic developments," "substitutive disorders of the type of hysteria . . . and psychasthenia," and types of defect and deterioration" (pp. 599–600). And, within the *affective reaction types,* he included "the manic-depressive reaction types," the anxiety type," which followed "the series nervousness—uneasiness—anxiety," and "the simple depressions," which were "more or less, excesses of normal depression" (p. 600). As he was to reaffirm periodically over the years, he proposed that "we abandon the prognostic factor as a nosological criterion, replace the term *'manic-depressive'* psychosis by *affective reaction group*, giving in each case the type and the number of the attacks and, wherever present, the admixtures" (p. 476).

Although in 1904 he had commented that "any attempt at inventing too many new names meets a prompt revenge, as the fate of the books of Kahlbaum and Arndt have shown" (p. 333), Meyer did not rest with the simple language of the reaction types. He later introduced the terms *ergasiatry* for psychiatry and *ergasiology* for psychobiology, each derived from his basic concept named "*ergasia* (or psychobiologically integrated 'working')" and covering "both overt and implicit behavior, the functioning of the individual or person" (3:285). In this new scheme, he used the term *pathergasias* to refer to clinical disorders, "malfunctions which are apt to imply functional and even structural damage . . . disturbances of the capacity for self-readjustment" (ibid., p. 287). In the subcategory of "merergasias or kakergasias proper" he included general nervousness, neurasthenia, hypochondriasis, anxiety disorders, and obsessive-ruminative states, which were to become better known as the psychoneuroses (pp. 296–298). And in the subcategory of "holergasic disorders" he grouped most of the conditions that were to become known as the psychoses (pp. 297–308). Included in this latter group were the affective reaction types, now termed the *thymergasias* or *thymergasic reactions*—"in the main equivalent to 'manic-depressive psychosis,'" along with the agitated depressions of the involutional period and various mixed depressive states (pp. 300–302).

Dubious as he was about the contemporary penchant for far-reaching etiological and pathogenetic speculations, Meyer restricted himself to cautious acknowledgments of what might be. He did not develop a systematic theoretical scheme to explain a disease. Instead, he argued for a careful assessment of the patient's situation and pathological reaction, that is, the more or less individual "reaction-set," with an eye to determining how the particular person's disturbed condition might have developed and what might be modified or treated. Endeavoring to avoid deductions from any form of basic theory, he took a distinctly pragmatic approach to understanding and dealing with pathological states.

Regarding treatment, Meyer had reacted against the well-established status of "hereditary predispositions" and the therapeutic pessimism often engendered by an emphasis on constitutional factors. Instead, he emphasized a search of the reactive picture for points of modifiability, for foci for intervention and change. Where in the "experiment of nature," as he conceived of the patient's illness, might one usefully intervene? He did not leave much in the way of writings on treatment, nor did he take special note of the treatment of depression; but in his Salmon Lectures of 1932 he provided an outline of his views on therapy.[14] He conceived of "a psychobiological therapy" as being based on "a study and use of the assets" of the patient. He conceived of therapy as "service in behalf of the patient" but emphasized the importance of the patient as a collaborator in the treatment endeavor. "The psychiatrist—the user of biography—must help the *person himself* transform the faulty and blundering attempt of nature to restore the balance, an attempt which has resulted merely in undermining the capacity for self-regulation" (*Psychobiology*, p. 158). From this general orientation, he outlined his own "common sense" version of psychotherapy, with kindly, humane overtones and involving a searching, practical use of the patient's life history and current situation. He gave careful attention to the hospital milieu and to how the patient might fit into the hospital regime and best be served by it. In the process, he cited such issues as attention to sleep and nutrition, occupational therapy, hydrotherapy, and recreational activities. He followed "a regime of work, rest, and play, socialization and discussion with physicians" (p. 170). On depressive disorders, he commented:

> The physician can offer a patient with a depression a sense of security by communicating an understanding based on his personal knowledge of him and of the situation. He must be able to maintain the patient's contact with a well measured regime, without causing exasperation by futile cheering and urging and without arousing a sense of being misunderstood. He wants to avoid inducing any antagonistic attitude which would interfere with further unburdening and with the rapport that may keep him reasonably in touch with the condition of the patient, alert to the occurrence of suicidal desires and also to those lines of sensitiveness which he hopes to be able to relieve and correct in the prevention of any renewed attack. In the meantime the nutrition and sleep and metabolism and aggravation from somatic and visceral hazards require a special study for correlation of the fluctuations, with attention to the leading or merely incidental role of the changes. (pp. 174–175)

In important yet subtle ways, Meyer continued to influence psychiatry, particularly American psychiatry, after his time, but his language of ergasiology, ergasias, and thymergasic reactions was soon abandoned. After the rare instance of its systematic presentation in Wendell Muncie's (1897–) textbook, *Psychobiology and Psychiatry*, this terminology faded from the scene. Even there, an extensive chapter was devoted to depressions in which the descriptions and discussions could readily be studied without too much interference from the strange, never-quite-accepted, Meyerian terms.[15] Muncie considered simple depressions, anxious depressions, topical depressions, agitated depressions, and involutional melancholias—familiar subtypes that were not much different from many other writings on depression in the same era. And his introductory comments to the chapter on depression touched on many of the dilemmas in considering depressions and expressed views that were shared by many.

Depression is a sweeping reaction in which a dominant and fixed mood of sadness or its equivalent appears as the central issue determining a syndrome whose individual items are best appraised in the light of the mood. The mood may be rather diffuse as sadness, blueness, melancholy, or more topically pointed as worry, or fearful or anxious depression.

The reaction presents general slowing and reduction of useful activity, loss of initiative through a general feeling of inhibition, slowness in thinking, appropriate predominantly autopsychic content as ideas of unworthiness, and self-depreciation, etc., and important physiological concomitants in the direction of a general reduction in the pulse, blood pressure, appetite, weight, bowel action, sleep, and sex functions. The reaction is of great personal and social importance because of the danger of suicide and because of the actual reduction in general efficiency which it entails.

Pathological depression is to be differentiated from normal depression by its greater fixity, depth, and by the disproportion to the causative factors. Depression is the major reaction most easily appreciated since depression of normal proportions is a universal experience.

He stated that depression might occur "in rather pure form (as thymergasic depression)" or "as an accompanying reaction" to a variety of other psychiatric disorders, and that these depressions were clearly more than "the static constitutional depressive type" or than "simple substitutive complaining." They were "major psychoses, historically separable from the minor psychoses by their committability. Hard and fast demarcations of the major from the minor reactions are not possible either on qualitative or quantitative grounds. Neither are they mutually exclusive" (*Psychobiology*, p. 242). Significantly, in a logical extension of Meyer's criticism of Kraepelin's synthesis, Muncie did *not* recognize manic-depressive disease in his nosological scheme but merely made a brief allusion to this Kraepelinian grouping (p. 320).

In another textbook by a less literal Meyerian disciple, Oskar Diethelm (1897–) directly disagreed with the Kraepelinian synthesis, devoted separate chapters to "excitements" and "depressions," and did not address manic-depressive disease as a distinct disorder.

In depressions of any type the mood disturbance is generally accepted as the common feature. Kraepelin grouped them under the term, "manic-depressive psychosis," believing that both elation and depression are part of the same disease entity. This concept was founded on the observation that well-circumscribed depressions and elations (manic and hypomanic psychoses) seem to follow each other directly or with more or less normal intervals between. It is most doubtful that all depressions and elations show this cyclic character. The defenders of the manic-depressive disease entity have to bend clinical observations to force them into this clear-cut group. Many patients have recurrent depressions without elated phases. Other patients have only one depression which, for example, occurs at the time of the menopause or may be frankly situationally determined. The manic-depressive psychoses apparently form a large and well-defined group among the larger group of affective psychoses, but do not embrace all affective reactions. . . .

Many authors stress the influence of heredity and therefore urge strongly against marriage and childbirth, or even demand sterilization. Although in many cases dominant heredity factors play an important role, one should not overlook the fact that dynamic factors enter and that their adjustment may prevent further illnesses. One should never assume a fatalistic attitude because of hereditary tendencies but try to determine what personality features can be utilized to counteract and overcome the hereditary danger. There are certainly few affective illnesses which occur automatically and without being considerably influenced by various dynamic factors. I have never seen one. Dynamic psychiatry has shown that there are always more or less strong dynamic factors.

Depressions are characterized by the depressed mood which is expressed by various individuals, with definite diurnal variations (usually more depressed in the morning), by the attack form of the illness, and by accompanying physical symptoms (loss of appetite and weight, constipation, sleep disturbances, decline of potency and libido, and menstrual disorders). These latter symptoms have led some authors to believe that we deal fundamentally with a metabolic disorder. Others point to specific endocrine factors. This claim is also supported by the frequent disturbance of mood in connection with menstruation, puberty, and menopause. Somatic investigations have not offered much, however, mostly because it is unclear how much is due to various secondary emotional reactions and what is really fundamental.[16]

EUGEN BLEULER

Another important contributor to psychiatry in the first half of the twentieth century was Eugen Bleuler (1857–1939). Although he is better known for his writings on schizophrenia, he also contributed an influential *Textbook of Psychiatry*, which included a lengthy, fairly standard section on "manic-depressive insanity" and a brief section on "reactive depressions." In some disagreement with Kraepelin, Bleuler advocated a more rigorous delineation of the manic-depressive syndrome; he excluded any disorder that entailed symptoms akin to dementia praecox. He outlined "the basic symptoms" of "manic-depressive insanity" or the "group of affective psychoses" as follows:

1. *Exalted or depressive moods.*
2. *Flight of ideas or retardation of the mental stream.*
3. *Abnormal facilitation or retardation of the centrifugal functions of resolution, of acting, inclusive of the psychic elements of motility.* Euphoria, flight of ideas, and pressure activity on the one hand (mania); depression, associative and centrifugal retardation on the other hand (melancholia), are the most frequent combinations. In the cases that reach the psychiatrist these syndromes nearly always occur in the forms of attacks and the intervals seem to be about normal; but it may also be a case of a persistent peculiarity which is then invariably of a lesser degree. *As accessory symptoms there occur also delusions and hallucinations (almost only of hearing and sight), and "nervous" manifestations.*[17]

He went on to say that *"melancholia"* or *"the depressive phase* colors all experiences painfully; often anxiety is added (sometimes in the form of *praecordial anxiety)"* (*Textbook*, p. 472). He briefly mentioned the depressions of the involutional period, disagreeing with Kraepelin's decision to "class them with manic-depressive insanity" (p. 488). Bleuler's views on treatment were essentially similar to those of Kraepelin in that they emphasized a closed asylum, bed rest, and considerable attention to the danger of suicide (pp. 491–493).

In a lengthy chapter devoted to "Psychopathic Forms of Reaction" or "Situation Psychoses," Bleuler included a few lines on *reactive depressions*. The implication of *reactive* was that there was a morbid reaction to an affective experience, in contrast to those psychoses in which there was a morbid process in the brain. "Reactive *depressions*, which become aggravated to a mental disease, are quite rare. . . . In so far as they come to the psychiatrist, they are mostly partial manifestations of other diseases, especially of manic depressive insanity, and naturally of psychopathies and neuroses. Also seniles who are incapable of helping themselves can react with melancholic states of short duration" (p. 537).

HENDERSON AND GILLESPIE

Significantly influenced by Meyer and sharing his objections to Kraepelin's views, David K. Henderson (1884–1965) and Robert D. Gillespie (1897–1945) launched an influential British textbook tradition in 1927 that has continued over several decades and through numerous editions. As Meyer had done, they employed the concept of *reaction-types*, and the various depressive disorders were classified as *affective reaction-types*, with the two main subcategories of *manic-depressive psychosis* and *involutional melancholia*. In considering manic-depressive psychosis, they first described *manic states*, outlining the Kraepelinian triad of basic symptoms (elated mood, flight of ideas, and psychomotor activity) and giving detailed attention to three varieties or stages along a continuum of severity (hypomania, acute mania, and delirious mania). They emphasized that, although readily recognized, these three stages might merge into one another in the actual experience of a particular patient; and they wrote of cases of chronic mania. Then they dealt with *depressive states* in similar fashion as *simple retardation, acute depression*, and *depressive stupor*, again emphasizing Kraepelin's three basic symptoms (depression, difficulty in thinking, and psychomotor retardation) and describing the three varieties as grades of severity with or without distinct boundaries between them. They also wrote about *alternating states* within the manic-depressive category, alternating between depression and elation with little or no interval of remission, and *mixed states*, with mixtures of manic and depressive symptoms.

In their three stages of depression and in the three cardinal symptoms, Henderson and Gillespie were following a tradition that had developed out of Kraepelin's work, that Meyer found meaningful, and that, in spite of objections and variations, continued to be significant during the first half of the twentieth century. They noted that "many other symptoms may be superadded—delusions, hallucinations, irritability, etc." and that suicide was a serious danger. *Simple retardation* "is characterized by depression and by a general slowing, both mental and physical"; and the patient tended to benefit from treatment in a mental hospital, often seeking such care himself.[18] They also mentioned

> *milder forms of depression* . . . which often masquerade under some other guise. Patients will consult the doctor in general practice, or come as out-patients, complaining sometimes of mild depression, but more often of anything but depression. They have vague or emphatic complaints of headache, often of an ill-defined and ill-localised type, and very persistent, of dyspepsia of various kinds, including lack of appetite, feelings of weight in the abdomen, a bad taste in the mouth, constipation, blurring of vision, irritability, especially to noises, lassitude, general weakness and (what is very common) fatigue or actual exhaustion. When thoroughly examined, they present nothing that will satisfactorily account for their symptoms. They are probably continuing at their work, but finding it very difficult, and on closer inquiry it will be found that although their difficulty is at first attributed to the complaints just enumerated or to the exacting nature of their work, as a matter of fact they cannot concentrate, and it is an effort for them to keep to the task at hand. (*Text-Book of Psychiatry*, pp. 133–134)

These patients were commonly treated satisfactorily as out-patients. The authors stated that such cases were frequently "psychogenic" and that often a spontaneous remission occurred (p. 134). In *acute depression* "the retardation is more marked," and hypochondriacal ideas were common (p. 139). And, in *depressive stupor*, the patient had "to be confined to bed," was severely retarded, was "preoccupied with depressive [delusional] ideas of the most devastating kind," and required extensive care for even the most basic needs (p. 140).

Considering the whole range of forms of manic-depressive psychosis, Henderson and Gillespie indicated that there were "no outstanding physical symptoms" that were characteristic, that "the chief physical changes" were "disorder of sleep and emaciation," and that, "particularly in depressed patients," there was "a sluggishness of the whole gastro-intestinal tract" (p. 150–151). None of these symptoms was in any way pathognomonic. These authors followed Kraepelin closely in stating that there was "no doubt that hereditary predisposition is the most important predisposing aetiological factor" (p. 117). And they concluded their section on etiology as follows:

When manic-depressive disorders arise from a clear sky, without any definite precipitating factor, they are termed constitutional or endogenous. In other cases, however, where there seems to have been some fairly adequate precipitating factor, either physical or psychic, we speak of "reactive" excitements or depressions as the case may be. This differentiation is of importance prognostically, "reactive" conditions being on the whole more favourable. The precipitating factor in such cases is usually some present worry or difficulty, and is not necessarily determined by some subconscious complex as are many other types of mental disturbance. (p. 119)

On the whole the prognosis was favorable, better in earlier attacks than in later recurrences, better in younger patients than in those past forty years, and better in cases "determined largely by exogenous factors" than in those "which seem to depend on purely hereditary or constitutional conditions" (pp. 152–153).

They recommended care in a mental hospital, with "a light, nutritious diet," tube feeding if necessary, general measures to promote sleep, hypnotics if such measures were insufficient, precautions against the danger of suicide, careful regulation of bowels and bladder, relaxing baths, occupational therapy, tonics in the convalescent stage, and instructive measures to promote a "better understanding of the factors which have been responsible for the illness, so as to prevent a possibility of recurrence" (pp. 154–157).

As their second category of affective reaction-types, Henderson and Gillespie used the familiar, but sometimes controversial, *involutional melancholia*. Originally established by Kraepelin, but later abandoned by him as a separate disease in favor of Dreyfus's argument that such disorders belonged within the manic-depressive group, involutional melancholia had been reaffirmed as a discrete category of depressive disorders by Kirby, Hoch, MacCurdy, and others. Henderson and Gillespie thought that they had "sufficient evidence that involutional melancholia is a relatively common type of mental disorder, and has certain features of its own. These features are *depression without retardation, anxiety, a feeling of unreality and hypochondriacal or nihilistic delusions*, the last being in the allo-, somato- and auto-psychic fields" (p. 159). Although these authors were somewhat tentative in their arguments for a discrete disorder and although they acknowledged that none of these symptoms was "peculiar to the involutional period," the tendency of these symptoms to occur together, particularly at that time of life, influenced them to give involutional melancholia a separate status (pp. 159–160). In some cases they thought that the involutional period itself was the most important factor, particularly in women; but they suggested that the majority of cases "broke down as the result of psychic factors," the most common of which were "the death of near relatives, financial and business worries, unfortunate home conditions, and the breaking-up of the home" (p. 160). A course of at least six to nine months was common; and the prognosis was better where there was more emotional reaction, particular anxiety, and restlessness, with delusions of death and poverty, but it was poorer where there was peevishness, hypochondriasis, and restriction of affect (p. 178). As to further clinical description, they cited little or no "involvement of the intellectual faculties," the danger of suicide, terrifying hallucinations in the most acute types, a considerable resistance to care and treatment, and physical symptoms such as gastrointestinal distress, loss of appetite and weight, and constipation (pp. 161–163). Regarding treatment, "the average involutional melancholic is best treated in a mental hospital" (p. 180). They emphasized bed rest, a nourishing diet, tube feeding if necessary, fresh air, the promotion of sleep, sometimes a carefully individualized use of hypnotics, occupational therapy, tonics, and precautions against suicide (pp. 180–181). They addressed psychological treatment measures as follows:

> From the psychological point of view, many patients get comfort out of talking over their troubles, but in the acute stages it seems to us that anything in the way of analytic treatment should be avoided, and suggestions and explanations of a psychoanalytic nature should be withheld. Some patients will benefit from talking over their troubles, but others seem to be made worse. The way must be found very gingerly, or a serious catastrophe may be precipitated. Once the patient's condition has sufficiently quieted down to permit a review of the whole illness, and of the causes which have precipitated it, there is not the same danger, and we believe that it is wise to attempt to give the patient a better understanding of how the illness has developed along commonsense non-psychoanalytic lines. By doing so, a recurrence may be prevented. (p. 181)

By 1944, Henderson and Gillespie had changed very little in how they described and dealt with depressive disorders. In the fourth edition in 1936, they added a paragraph on prolonged sleep treatment to their chapter on manic-depressive psychosis, a therapeutic approach about which they had significant reservations.[19] In the sixth edition in 1944, they changed the name of the first of their varieties or stages of depressive states (within the manic-depressive forms) from simple retardation to *simple depression*.[20] In that edition they added the following significant comments to their section on treatment: "The immediate therapeutic outlook in depressions, whether manic-depressive or involutional, has been transformed by the introduction of 'shock' treatment, first by the cardiazol method and now by electricity. These, and leucotomy which is applicable in very chronic cases where the former has failed, are described in the chapter on special methods of physical treatment" (6th ed., p. 261). And they ended that section by stating:

Perhaps the most important thing of all in the way of treatment is to give the patient some better understanding of the factors which have been responsible for the illness, so as to prevent a possibility of recurrence. There are many people who have a cyclothymic temperament, and who, irrespective of treatment and of analysis, will continue to have periodic attacks. But there are many others where the attacks are precipitated by definite exogenous factors, which often can be avoided or corrected. It is important to point this out, not only to the patient, but also to the relatives, for only too often it is injudicious handling and training which are responsible. Social factors must be taken as seriously into account as the more purely medical ones. (ibid., p. 264)

By the ninth edition in 1962, this textbook had been fairly representative for thirty-five years. The presentation of depressive disorders had been somewhat recast, but there had been very little substantive change. Nevertheless, it is of particular interest to note some comments in that edition's chapter "Neurotic Reaction-Types."

There is also a considerable number of cases which may be difficult to classify definitively either as neuroses or affective psychoses: these are the so-called "neurotic depressions," in which reactive emotional features are prominent and the symptoms are often clearly the response of an unstable personality to a situational problem. Some of these reactions are hysterical . . . others, the majority we believe, are to be considered as belonging to the manic-depressive psychoses, the distinction between reactive and endogenous depressions being an arbitrary one.[21]

INVOLUTIONAL MELANCHOLIA

What was later to be known as *involutional melancholia* emerged as an aspect of the nosological reformulations introduced by Emil Kraepelin (1856–1926) in the fifth edition of his famous *Lehrbuch* in 1896.* He had previously taken note of *agitated melancholia (Angstmelancholie, melancholia activa, melancholia agitata)* as a type within the main category of melancholia, along with *melancholia simplex* and *melancholia attonita*, but his fifth edition broke sharply with any such reflections of traditional classifications of melancholic and depressive conditions. While bringing a wide variety of affective disorders together, as periodic psychosis in the fifth edition and as manic-depressive psychosis in the sixth edition in 1899, Kraepelin kept separate as a distinct disorder *melancholia*, one of the diseases of the involutional period. He created a category of involutional

---

*It should be noted, however, that G. Fielding (Blandford (1829–1911) had used the term *climacteric melancholia* in 1871: *Insanity and Its Treatment* . . . (Philadelphia: Henry C. Lea, 1871), pp. 201–202. And melancholia was being referred to as "the most common form of climacteric insanity" before Kraepelin established his involutional psychoses: D. Hack Tuke (ed.), *A Dictionary of Psychological Medicine* . . . , 2 vols. (Philadelphia: P. Blakiston, Son, 1892), 1:235.

psychoses that included presenile delusional insanity and senile dementia, along with this melancholia, which was to become known as *involutional melancholia*. This melancholia "represents two groups of cases, which are characterized by *uniform depression with fear, various delusions of self-accusation, of persecution, and of a hypochondriacal nature, with moderate clouding of consciousness and disturbance of the train of thought, leading in the greater number of cases after a prolonged course to moderate mental deterioration.*"[22] He also referred to a second group within this diagnostic category that was "characterized by a greater predominance of delusions of fear, which are apt to be extremely silly, and sometimes even nihilistic, many hallucinations, great clouding of consciousness, and some motor unrest."[23] Essentially this new category included all anxious depressive insanities of later years that came on then for the first time, that did not have a history of manic-depressive disorder, and that were not merely aspects of some other disorder.

However, by the time of his eighth edition (1909–1915), Kraepelin had accepted Dreyfus's arguments and had brought such disorders into the manic-depressive group as mixed states.[24] Dreyfus had reexamined a significant portion of the cases that Kraepelin had originally studied in setting up this involutional syndrome and concluded that many had a history of previous attacks, that the prognosis was better than had been alleged, and that even those that were truly first attacks should have been diagnosed as manic-depressive disease first occurring in later life.

But the controversy over the status of such disorders was far from ended. In 1909 George H. Kirby (1875–1935) had reviewed Dreyfus's reconsideration of Kraepelin's involutional melancholias and had disagreed with the idea that they all belonged with the manic-depressive group.[25] While he decided that some of those cases were manic-depressive conditions and should never have been given a separate status as melancholias, he concluded that, for a significant number, there was not enough evidence to warrant the diagnosis of manic-depressive psychosis. Thus, even as Kraepelin was abandoning the diagnostic category of involutional melancholia, others were reasserting its validity as a separate disorder. Although Dreyfus's views, and Kraepelin's acceptance of them, were influential for many psychiatrists, especially in Germany, the 1920s saw many reaffirming involutional melancholia as a discrete condition. Even in the German-language literature, the Swiss Eugen Bleuler (1857–1939) in his influential textbook disagreed with Kraepelin's decision to class the depressions of the involutional period with manic-depressive insanity.[26]

In 1922 August Hoch (1868–1919) and John T. MacCurdy (1886–1947) published an influential study in which they noted that Dreyfus, in his attempt to establish a history of earlier attacks in Kraepelin's original cases, had "ferreted out a history of depressions so mild as to seem to be neuroses or merely more or less normal mood swings. Variations of the emotional status are of great theoretic, psychologic importance, but they should not be called 'psychoses' as long as their manifestations remain within certain limits. Otherwise nearly the whole world is, or has been, insane."[27] Among the further points that they emphasized were the more prominent place of anxiety and irritability in cases of involutional melancholia, a stronger inclination to hypochondriasis, and a less sanguine prognosis than Dreyfus, and then Kraepelin, had suggested. Although they were inclined to reaffirm the case for a distinct syndrome of involutional melancholia, they observed that their studies on prognosis seemed to reveal two subgroups, one with a good prognosis and one with a poor prognosis. From this they pointed out that either involutional melancholia might be maintained as a nosological category with both benign and deteriorating variants, or the former group might be included with manic-depressive psychoses and the latter group with dementia praecox.[28] Then, several years later, in his *The Psychology of Emotion*, MacCurdy discussed the same Hoch and MacCurdy data at much greater length in three chapters on "the involutional melancholias." In considering further their original series of cases, he "eliminated the chronic cases and their peculiar symptoms from the general mass of psychotic phenomena lumped together as "involution melancholia," associating the majority of these with dementia praecox and denominating the remainder "organic insufficiency."[29] As to the other group of original cases, the "recoverable cases," he winnowed out some as typical of the depressions of the manic-depressive type and some others as "reactive depressions"; but he concluded that there was a significant residual group that he termed "true involution melancholia." Then he asserted that this latter group represented "a definite manic-depressive reaction type," along with mania and "ordinary depression" (*Psychology*, p. 141). In endeavoring to explain involutional melancholia, he emphasized the lessened adaptive capacities and other predisposing trends set up by the changes of aging, difficult life situations as precipitating factors, and psychological regression in response to these factors (pp. 168–181).

But, in their textbook in 1927, Henderson and Gillespie clearly supported a status for involutional melancholia distinctly separate from manic-depressive insanity, identifying it as one of the two main subcategories among the *affective reaction-types*. Although influenced by MacCurdy, they still thought that they had "sufficient evidence that involutional melancholia is a relatively common type of mental disorder and has certain features of its own. These features are *depression without retardation, anxiety, a feeling of unreality and hypochondriacal or nihilistic delusions*, the last being in the allo-, somato- and auto-psychic fields" (p. 159). Although these authors were in some ways tentative in their arguments for a discrete disorder and although they acknowledged that none of these symptoms was "peculiar to the involutional period," the tendency of these symptoms to occur together, particularly at that time of life, influenced them to give involutional melancholia a separate status (pp. 159–160). They thought that "the most characteristic involutional qualities lie in the content of the psychosis, especially in the apprehension, hypochondriasis and nihilism, and these qualities are the result of the psychological changes associated with advancing years" (p. 160). And Gillespie, in 1929 in an important study entitled "The Clinical Differentiation of Types of Depression," distinguished two main groups of depressions, *reactive* and *autonomous* (endogenous). Within the latter he concluded that there was a distinct subdivision that he termed *involutional depressions*, which involved hypochondriasis, a relatively shallow affect, and a poor prognosis.[30]

Since the 1920s the debate has continued as to whether involutional melancholia was a discrete disorder. To the older arguments based on a distinct clinical picture, there were added those based on a characteristic premorbid personality that was said to distinguish such patients from those with depressions of the manic-depressive type—"narrow range of interests, difficulty in adjusting to change, limited capacity for sociability and friendship, rigid adherence to a high ethical code, marked proclivity for saving, reserve that becomes positive reticence so far as intimate matters are concerned, an ever present anxious tone, profound stubbornness, overwhelming conscientiousness and strained meticulosity as to person and vocation."[31] Parenthetically, this was much like the "anal-erotic character" that had emerged in the psychoanalytic literature.[32] Then some argued that the endocrinological changes of the menopause were responsible for involutional melancholia; some emphasized the psychological changes associated with the climacterium; and these various factors were used in efforts to support the idea of distinctive depressions in the involutional period.[33]

Edition after edition of Henderson and Gillespie's textbook continued to support a separate disease status for involutional melancholia, as did a good many other textbooks. On the other hand, Jelliffe and White in their textbook acknowledged the term *involutional melancholia* but indicated that such cases had "now been pretty generally conceded to belong to the manic-depressive group";[34] and yet they still devoted a section to this condition as one of the presenile psychoses in much the same manner as Kraepelin had earlier when he still conceived of it as distinct from manic-depressive insanity.[35] And others merely abandoned any recognition of such a distinct disorder in their textbooks. For some, particularly in the British literature, the status of involutional melancholia was gradually caught up in the ongoing arguments as to whether there were several discrete depressive disorders, or whether the various depressive conditions were not that distinct from one another and were better thought of as closely related on continua of severity and chronicity.[36]

Recurrently, clinical studies have been put forward to suggest that a discrete involutional melancholia was a valid idea, and, just as often, other studies have argued against this idea. Also, it has been suggested that, whether or not it was ever reasonable to think that they constituted a discrete disease, the cluster of symptoms that was often called involutional melancholia has become less and less common. Gradually, attention to the issues here has diminished as other investigative concerns regarding depressions have become prominent. Two thoughtful and balanced reviews in more recent times have tended toward the conclusion that there is no distinct disease of involutional melancholia, but they each pointed out that it has lingered on in textbooks and classificatory systems.[37] Rosenthal made the following summary statement:

> Involutional melancholia is thus a symptom pattern with an associated premorbid personality and psychodynamic theory, and a corresponding heredity, onset, course, prognosis, and response to therapy which has been described with fair consistency (and some important dissent) as a significant psychiatric illness. It has won itself a place in the textbooks and in the classification systems, but we are still faced with the question of whether it really exists as a clinical entity.
>
> The old debate as to whether involutional melancholia is a subtype of manic-depressive disease has less relevance to us today than it had in the days when all affective disorders were considered variants of manic-depressive illness. The question remaining, however, is whether involutional depression is a distinct syndrome with its own etiology, natural history, and clinical picture, or whether it shades off continuously with milder menopausal neuroses on a vertical severity axis, and with other psychotic depressions on a horizontal descriptive axis.[38]

Kendell was more definitive in his concluding comments:

> Thus the bulk of the evidence, both clinical and genetic, suggests strongly that the depressions of the involutional period differ in no fundamental respect from those of earlier or later periods of life. None the less, involutional melancholia still appears as an independent entity in the majority of current textbooks, European and American, and in the *International Classification of Diseases*.[39]

THE DEPRESSIVE DICHOTOMIES AND VARIOUS CLASSIFICATORY ENDEAVORS

During the same period in which the controversies about involutional melancholia were being played out, there were other arguments revolving around a series of dichotomies in the classifying of melancholic and depressive disorders. In 1893 Paul J. Möbius (1853–1907) had introduced the dichotomy of *endogenous* etiology versus *exogenous* etiology as the basis for classifying psychiatric disorders.[40] The idea of endogenous diseases was derived from the nineteenth-century tradition of hereditary predisposition, a tradition in which Morel's theory of degeneration was prominent as a way of employing the notions of heredity and constitution. The idea of exogenous diseases drew on the whole tradition of traumata, toxins, and other specific etiological agents that, it was hoped, could be correlated with identifiable changes at postmortem.

Taken up by Kraepelin in his fifth edition in 1896, this dichotomous concept soon found its way into common use in German psychiatry. Confusions and disagreements about the meaning of *external* and *exogenous* eventually led to interpreting them as "external to the brain," and gradually *exogenous* came to imply identifiable, and often measurable, causes. Losing sight of the fact that the endogenous and exogenous etiologies had originally been two categories resting on the basic assumption of a biological etiology for all disorders, some included psychogenic causes within the exogenous category, and some made organic etiology equivalent to exogenous causation. At the same time, *endogenous* came to imply "hypothetical, intangible, elusive predispositions, constitutional or hereditary forces which could be conjectured but not demonstrated," and it became "accepted by most authorities that the endogenous concept, though logically requisite, was really a cover for a purely negative approach representing as internal causes what was left when all external causes had been eliminated."[41]

These terms entered the English-language literature only in the late 1920s. Gillespie discussed them, taking note of the problems with Kraepelin's "psychogenic depressions," which were differentiated from his classical (endogenous) depressions of the manic-depressive type, and which implied precipitating causes and fluctuations in the course in response to the physician's visits and other intercurrent stimuli. And Gillespie mentioned two other variants suggested by Kraepelin's student and colleague, J. Lange: "psychically produced melancholias" and "reactive melancholias."[42] Then, on the basis of his own research, Gillespie distinguished two main groups of depressions, *autonomous* and *reactive*. The idea of "reactivity" served him as a central principle: that is, a significant role for precipitating circumstances and a significant variability of the affective state in reaction to intercurrent stimuli. His "autonomous" group showed little or none of this reactivity and was much like Kraepelin's "endogenous" group; and his "reactive" group was crucially characterized by this reactivity, was named with a term borrowed from Lange, and was much like Kraepelin's "psychogenic" group. Out of all this, the dichotomy of "endogenous-reactive" became the more prominent one, assuming many of the attributes of the older endogenous-exogenous dichotomy, including causation being either innate or environmental. Then, from this, some shifted to other dichotomous pairings, such as "endogenous-neurotic," "psychotic-exogenous," and "psychotic-neurotic." A wide variety of arguments arose as to which should be the dichotomy of choice. As Lewis summarized:

> The controversy, so far as British psychiatrists moulded and maintained it, was in part a semantic dispute about the meaning of "endogenous" (equivalent to "cryptogenic" or "hereditary"?); "exogenous" (equivalent to "psychogenic" or to "organic"?), and "psychotic" (fundamentally distinct from "neurotic" and "reactive" or an imprecise term for a phase in a continuum?). "Functional," "biogenic," "autonomous," "idiopathic," and "reactive" contributed also to the semantic uncertainty. But at bottom the dispute (which could as readily have been about "anxiety" as about "depression") turned on discrepant notions regarding the principles and method of psychiatric classification, as well as on assumptions about a necessary association between causes, clinical picture, pathology, course ("natural history"), and response to treatment. . . .
>
> While British and American psychiatrists were disputing about the divisibility of depression into an endogenous and a neurotic form, German psychiatrists were taking for granted an endogenous cyclothymic variety, and a reactive or psychogenic variety, and a somatosis in which the depression was the visible accompaniment or product of (hypothetical) bodily changes.[43]

Meanwhile, in contrast to the various dichotomists, there were a few confirmed unitarians. Expressing relief that psychiatry was "at last losing its passion for multiplying descriptive categories" and believing that "the task of psychopathology" was "to isolate a few fundamental types of anomalous reaction for which a physical basis can be sought," Edward Mapother (1881–1940) at the Maudsley Hospital in London advocated the idea that the various types of depression were related to one another on a continuum rather than being discrete disorders. He favored "the view that neurosis and the depressive psychosis are continuous"; and he argued that "both are associated with lasting bodily anomalies," that "traces of unpleasant experiences are one of the principal causes of both," and that "other mental experiences may be curative" for both.[44] Also at the Maudsley Hospital, in several important studies on depressive disorders, Aubrey Lewis (1900–1975) followed in his senior colleague's footsteps, repeatedly implying that the various ways of differentiating depressions were basically unsound and that a unitarian perspective was preferable.[45]

In a more recent assessment of the "endogenous-reactive" concept, Mendels and Cochrane carefully reviewed a host of previous studies and then concluded that "the so-called endogenous factor might represent the core of depressive symptomatology, whereas the clinical features of the reactive factor may represent phenomenological manifestations of psychiatric disorders other than depression which 'contaminate' the depression syndrome. When depression is present in association with these other features, it might be regarded as just one of several symptoms."[46] Although apparently not prepared to throw out the endogenous-reactive concept, these authors seem to find true syndromic strength in only one of this dichotomous pair, and their conclusions could become the basis for a unitarian viewpoint.[47]

But old dichotomies die hard. In fact, it seems rather that they gradually fade away, only to be replaced by new dichotomies. Acknowledging the attachment of many psychiatrists to the idea of endogenous depression but concerned to find "a terminology without a built-in organic or psychogenic bias," Heron concluded his study of the endogenous-exogenous concept with the suggestion that "the word 'primary' replace 'endogenous,' and that the cluster of affective disorders labelled 'endogenous depressions' be renamed primary depressions."[48] Although himself troubled by what the various dichotomists had wrought, Heron seems here to have sowed the seed for a new dichotomy. Soon afterward the concept of primary depression and secondary depression emerged. Primary depression was defined as "a depressive episode occurring in a patient whose previous history may be described in one of two ways: (a) he has been psychiatrically well, or (b) he has had a previous episode of mania or depression and no other psychiatric illness"; and secondary depression was defined as "a depressive episode occurring in a patient who has had a preexisting, diagnosable psychiatric illness, other than a primary affective disorder."

> A depressive episode is explicitly but minimally (there may be and usually are additional symptoms) defined as a mood change indicative of depressed feelings and expressed by a complaint of depression, sadness, feeling blue, feeling low, feeling gloomy, etc., *plus* at least six of the following 10 symptoms: complaint of thinking slowly, anorexia, insomnia, constipation, feeling tired, decreased ability to concentrate, suicidal ideas, weight loss, decreased sexual interest or activity, and wringing hands or pacing.

Robins and Guze emphasized that "the key to the distinction between a primary and secondary affective disorder is *chronology*,"[49] but it is important to note that it was also a question of a "pure" form of clinical state versus an "impure" form, with the associated advantages for research endeavors. In proposing these categories, Woodruff, Murphy, and Herjanic had added the following clarifying comments:

> Assignment of a patient to either the primary or secondary group does not involve any assumption as to the cause of the depression, or an assessment of the apparent severity of the depression. So-called "endogenous depressions," and "psychotic depressions" would generally be included in our primary group, but the terms are not necessarily synonymous. Many depressions commonly regarded as "reactive" would also be considered primary by the criteria of this study. It is important to note that the term "neurotic depression" is not syn-

onymous with secondary depression. Neurotic depression does not have a generally agreed-upon meaning. It has been used, among other things, to mean a mild depression, a reactive (i.e. psychogenic) depression, a depression with emotional lability, a depression without psychotic features, or a depression occurring in an individual with a neurosis. Depression occurring in the course of a diagnosable neurosis would be a secondary depression in the present scheme.[50]

And still other dichotomous pairs have been proposed in recent times: for example, (a) Pollitt's S (somatic) type versus J (justified) type; (b) Van Praag's vital depression versus personal depression; (c) Leonhard's bipolar depression versus monopolar depression, developed a few years later by Perris and others as bipolar and unipolar depression. Pollitt used the term *depressive functional shift* to refer to a particular cluster of symptoms: "early morning awakening; symptoms worse in the early morning; loss of appetite and loss of weight; loss of sexual desire; constipation; limited emotional facial expression; inability to cry; dry mouth; coldness of the extremities; dryness of the skin."[51] The S type was a "physiological depression" in which symptoms of the depressive functional shift were present. The J type was a "psychological depression" in which such symptoms were absent and was "essentially a 'psychological stress, and understandable in terms of the patient's predicament.'" Van Praag characterized "vital depression" as follows: "It occurs without apparent reason, is motiveless, incomprehensible, and apparently senseless." As to its symptoms, he reported: "In addition to the emotional feelings of depression, symptoms of retardation with a generalized slowing down in intellectual and physical capacity; difficulties in thinking; feelings of indifference; decreased emotional receptivity; and typically loss of appetite, difficulty with sleep, and an overwhelming sense of fatigue." He contrasted this with "personal depression" which was "congruous with the environmental situation" and in which the primary symptoms were "in the emotional sphere." Both Pollitt's "S type" and Van Praag's "vital depression" were close to the traditional descriptions of endogenous depressions. So-called vital depression had been considered by Schneider to be the "cardinal symptom of all endogenous depressions," but Van Praag denied any etiological implications for his use of it, intending it strictly as a descriptive term.[52] Perris proposed that depressive episodes with a history of manic episodes be termed *bipolar depressive illness*, and that major depressions without such a history be termed *unipolar depressive illness*.[53]

On looking back at these various dichotomies, one sees that the Kraepelinian endogenous-exogenous pairing was based on the locus of alleged etiological factors, and that it reflected the familiar nature versus nurture mode of thought. To a considerable extent, its endogenous-reactive offspring had similar implications. In contrast, Gillespie's autonomous-reactive notion was based on the absence or presence of a descriptive-phenomenological factor. The psychotic-neurotic dichotomy, although often loosely used as an equivalent to the endogenous-reactive dichotomy, was given by many a stricter interpretation in which its essential criteria were descriptive-phenomenological: certain symptoms were present or absent. Yet some, perhaps influenced by the nosological unitarianism associated with Mapother and Lewis, used psychotic-neurotic to denote no more than greater or lesser severity. With the emergence of electroconvulsive therapy, many thought that the endogenous-reactive dichotomy had acquired increased validity when it was found that endogenous depressions tended to be ECT-responsive and reactive depressions ECT-unresponsive. For some, this led to an association of endogeneity with somatotherapy and somatic etiology, and of reactivity with psychotherapy and psychogenic etiology, and so a classification originally based on etiological notions became interwoven with issues of therapeutic outcome and found itself correlated with a somatic-psychological dichotomy. A few thought that they had found a similar support for the endogenous-reactive dichotomy in imipramine-responsiveness versus imipramine-unresponsiveness. On the other hand, a variety of more recent clinical research endeavors have challenged the validity of this dichotomy, and yet still others have found support for it in genetic studies. The primary-secondary dichotomy harked back to a Kraepelinian emphasis on a longitudinal perspective but eschewed any etiological implications. It avoided any concern with degree of severity or with therapeutic correlations. It emphasized the symptom picture but focused on syndromic purity or lack of purity, reflecting the interests of the researcher rather than the traditional nosologist or the clinician. With the bipolar-unipolar dichotomy, the emphasis tended to be recurrent illnesses; the longitudinal perspective was important, and the symptom picture along with it; severity characterized both groups; and some therapeutic correlations were suggested. But there were no etiological implications. Throughout the history of these various dichotomies, one finds recurrent evidence of the grand dualisms of nature-nurture and body-mind as underlying assumptions. In turn, there have been efforts to classify and reason about depressions in ways that avoided these assumptions.

More recently, Winokur took up his Washington University colleagues' primary and secondary depression and integrated into that scheme the bipolar-unipolar dichotomy. The result was that *affective disorders* were subdivided into *primary affective disorders* and *secondary depressions; primary affective disorders* were subdivided into *bipolar illness* and *unipolar depressions;* and *unipolar depressions* were subdivided into *familial pure depressive disease, sporadic depressive disease,* and *depression spectrum disease.*[54]

Then Spitzer et al. developed the classification of depressions to be found in the third edition of the *Diagnostic and Statistical Manual of Mental Disorders* (DSM-III) in 1980. Their scheme, within *affective disorders*, included *major affective disorders*, subdivided into *bipolar disorders* (mixed, manic, or depressed) and *major depressions* (single episode or recurrent); *other specific affective disorders*, subdivided into *cyclothymic disorders* and *dysthymic disorders* (depressive neurosis); and *atypical affective disorders*, subdivided into *atypical bipolar disorders* and *atypical depressions*.[55] In an earlier discussion of the process of developing this system, Spitzer et al. had provided the following useful summary of the American experience in classifying depressive disorders and had alluded to past pitfalls and how they were attempting to avoid them.

In 1917 the first official classification system in this country was formulated by the American Medico-Psychological Association (later to become the American Psychiatric Association). It was largely Kraepelinian and was primarily designed for hospital use. Only two mood disorders were listed: manic-depressive psychosis and involutional melancholia. The category of "reactive depression," which reflected Meyerian influence, was added in the 1935 classification and was clearly separated from the psychotic mood disorders by its placement under the category of psychoneurosis. The term affective disorders was first used in 1951 in the Standard Veteran's Administration classification and included manic depressive reaction, psychotic depressive reaction and involutional melancholia. In addition, cyclothymic personality appeared for the first time under a section titled character and behavior disorders. The DSM-I classification of 1952 was essentially the same as the Veteran's Administration classification with only slight modifications. Affective disorders now became affective reactions, and involutional melancholia was reclassified in the general group of disorders of metabolism, growth, and nutrition or endocrine function. DSM-II, published in 1968, was greatly influenced by the eighth edition of the International Classification of Diseases. The DSM-I affective reactions became major affective disorders (corresponding to the ICD-8 term Affective Psychoses), which now included involutional melancholia as well as manic-depressive illness, but excluded psychotic depressive reaction which now was listed separately. This corresponded to the European emphasis on the endogenous-reactive distinction. The depressive reaction of DSM-I became depressive neurosis in DSM-II. Cyclothymic personality remained, even though the ICD-8 corresponding category of thymic personality was a broader concept which included individuals who were characterologically depressed without periods of hypomania.

In developing DSM-III, our first problem was to decide whether to continue the tradition of listing the mood disorders in several areas of the nomenclature. As the historical review indicates, the implication of the assignment of one milder form of the episodic disorder to the category of neurosis was that it was best understood as either reactive or as a defense against anxiety in contrast to the severe forms which were generally conceptualized as endogenous. Also, the implication of categorizing some mild mood swings as personality disorders assumed discontinuity with the severe forms (manic depressive illness) even though most observers have always believed that mild forms are probably related to severe forms in some way.

The general approach towards classification to be taken in DSM-III is to use etiology as a classification axis only if there is convincing evidence to support it. In the absence of such evidence, categories are grouped together if they share important clinical-descriptive features. This approach has the advantage that it groups disorders which share essential and common features without making assumptions as to their etiology. For this reason, we have decided to group together nearly all of the disorders which are characterized by a disturbance of mood. This includes all of the depressions and manias regardless of severity, chronicity, course, or apparent associations with precipitating stress.[56]

Whereas endogenous-reactive has been the most persistent of the many dichotomies, recurrently returning to favor even after apparently effective dismissals, endogenous depression in particular has survived as well as any suggested category of depression in recent times. Gillespie's evidence for his autonomous category was thought to support it. The S (somatic) type of depression, vital depression, and primary depression each seemed similar to it, was suggested to be synonymous with it, and was thought to strengthen the status of endogenous depression; but each type had some who made common use of it maintain that it was not synonymous with endogenous depression. Various statistical techniques have been employed, with results that have been thought to support the idea of endogenous depression as a distinct entity. It has been argued that its symptom pattern is the core of depressive disorders and even that it is the true essence of depression. In one of the many attempts to recognize the central significance of the so-called endogenous symptoms cluster, while avoiding the etiological implications of its name, *endogenomorphic* was introduced as another name for it.[57] And, phoenix-like, *melancholia* has recently arisen as a new synonym for it. As the architects of DSM-III put it: "A term from the past, in this manual used to indicate a typically severe form of depression that is particularly responsive to somatic therapy. The clinical features that characterize this syndrome [that is, melancholia] have been referred to as 'endogenous.'" Since the term "endogenous implies, to many, the absence of precipitating stress, a characteristic not always associated with this syndrome, the term 'endogenous' is not used in DSM-III" (Spitzer et al., *DSM-III*, p. 205). Although the authors of DSM-III put forward a good number of depressive categories, within their *major affective disorders* there are but two basic categories of depression, *bipolar disorder, depressed* and *major depression*. Within major depression, "psychotic features" may or may not be present, *and* "melancholia" may or may not be present (ibid., pp. 205–224). As aptly expressed in a recent study, "the *DSM-III* criteria for melancholia are intended to define an endogenomorphic subcategory of major depressive episode for which somatic treatment is usually required."[58]

After many twentieth-century decades of considering and arguing about depressive disorders, of organizing the data on them, and of proposing classifications, matters are far from settled. There are a number of judicious and useful surveys of the issues and arguments, each of which I am indebted to in endeavoring to trace the more recent history of depressive conditions;[59] and each of these has been provided by an author (or authors) experienced and wise in the study of depression. It is impressive to see how careful these authors have been in weighing and assessing this area of study, and it is sobering to realize how well warranted this carefulness has been. Although many an investigator of depression has followed the time-honored practice of attacking and attempting to tear down the work of his predecessors, few have been able effectively to sustain any sort of rigid position or continue for very long with any sort of dogmatic assertion.

SIGMUND FREUD AND OTHER PSYCHOANALYSTS

Another author of considerable significance regarding melancholia and depression in the twentieth century was Sigmund Freud (1856–1939), the originator of psychoanalysis. Of particular influence was his paper "Mourning and Melancholia," discussed by him as early as 1914, written and revised into its final form in 1915, and finally published in 1917.[60] In this study's immediate background were Freud's earlier views on melancholia and depression and some important observations by his colleague Karl Abraham (1877–1925).

In his earlier writings Freud sometimes used the term *melancholia* to refer to the range of clinical conditions that the modern psychiatrist would refer to as *depression*, and at other times he was referring only to what today might be termed *psychotic depression*. And he used the term *depression* sometimes as a synonym for melancholia in either of these two meanings just cited, but more often as a descriptive term for that particular affective aspect of a person's state of mind, whether pathological or not, that might also be called dejection. This latter trend was manifested in a work written in 1892–1893 in which he stated, "Where a neurosis is present—and I am explicitly referring not to hysteria alone but to the *status nervosus* in general—we have to assume the *primary presence* of a tendency to depression and to a lowering of self-confidence, such as we find very highly developed and in isolation in melancholia" (*Standard Edition*, 1:121). Further instances of *depression* used as a descriptive term, rather than as a diagnostic term, were scattered through the case histories that were brought together in 1895 as *Studies on Hysteria;* and, at one point in the case history of Frau Emmy von N., Freud mentioned "neurotics, in whose self-feeling we seldom fail to find a strain of depression or anxious expectation" (2:92).

In the various "Drafts" of his developing views in the 1890s that culminated in his *Project for a Scientific Psychology* and that were brought together as *The Fliess Papers*, to use the names bestowed by editors in more recent times, Freud made a number of references to depression and melancholia in contexts dealing with his idea of *actual neuroses*. In contrast to *psychoneuroses* (hysteria, obsessional neurosis), in which the symptoms were thought to stem from unconscious conflicts derived from traumatic experiences that had disrupted early sexual development, *actual neuroses* (neurasthenia, anxiety neurosis) had their origins in faulty sexual practices in current life—such as excessive abstinence, excessive masturbation, unduly prolonged intercourse, and coitus interruptus—that might lead to a depleted state of somatic sexual excitation and associated weakness, or to an excessive accumulation of somatic sexual excitation and associated transformation of the dammed-up excitation into anxiety. The psychoneuroses involved psychical mechanisms, whereas the actual neuroses were organically conditioned. Freud referred to *periodic depression* as "a form of anxiety neurosis" (later termed an *actual neurosis*), with *phobias and anxiety attacks* as two other forms of anxiety neurosis (1:178). He mentioned "depressive affects" as *one* of the precipitating factors that, in necessary conjunction with the predisposing factor of "sexual exhaustion," could lead to neurasthenia (later termed an *actual neurosis*) (p. 180). And then, more in analogy to rather than as an instance of an actual neurosis, he commented that melancholics, although often without any need for coitus and sexually "anaesthetic," "have a great longing for love in its psychical form—one might say, psychical erotic tension. Where this accumulates and remains unsatisfied, melancholia develops. Here, then, we should have the counterpart to anxiety neurosis. Where physical sexual tension accumulates—anxiety neurosis. Where psychical sexual tension accumulates—melancholia" (p. 192). Finally, in a "Draft" devoted to melancholia in particular, he elaborated on these various themes. He stated:

> The facts before us seem to be as follows:
> (A) There are striking connections between melancholia and [sexual] anaesthesia. This is borne out (1) by the finding that with many melancholics there has been a long previous history of anaesthesia, (2) by the discovery that everything that provokes anaesthesia encourages the generation of melancholia, (3) by the existence of a type of women, very demanding psychically, in whom longing easily changes over into melancholia and who are anaesthetic.
> (B) Melancholia is generated as an intensification of neurasthenia through masturbation.
> (C) Melancholia appears in typical combination with severe anxiety.
> (D) The type and extreme form of melancholia seems to be the periodic or cyclical hereditary form.

Noting that "the affect corresponding to melancholia is that of mourning—
that is, longing for something lost," he reasoned that "in melancholia it must be
a question of loss—a loss in *instinctual* life"; and, from "careful observation" he
suggested that "the famous *anorexia nervosa* of young girls" was "a melancholia
where sexuality is undeveloped" (p. 200). From there he put forward the
hypothesis that *"melancholia consists in mourning over loss of libido"* (p. 201; see also
p. 255). In a physicalistic scheme, with a complex neurophysiological diagram
and reasoning in terms of amount and distribution of somatic sexual excitation,
Freud went on to discuss "the three forms of melancholia, which must in fact
be distinguished": (1) the production of somatic sexual excitation decreased or
ceased, and this "is probably what is characteristic of *common severe* melancholia proper, which recurs periodically, or of cyclical melancholia, in which
periods of increase and cessation of production alternate"; (2) "neurasthenic
melancholia" was the result of "excessive masturbation" bringing about "a
lasting reduction" in somatic sexual excitation; (3) "anxious melancholia, a
mixed form combining anxiety neurosis and melancholia," was the outcome of
"sexual tension" being diverted from the ideas with which it had been connected, without any diminution in the production of somatic sexual excitation,
and this excitation or tension was transformed into the "psychical" experience
of anxiety (pp. 201–203). There then followed several pages of reasoning in
terms of his neurophysiological theory in which he endeavored to account for
melancholia being "but a sign of a disposition to" sexual anaesthesia in some
cases, for melancholia being caused by the anaesthesia in other cases, for
women being more prone to sexual anaesthesia and thus to melancholia, and
for "the effects of melancholia" being best described as *"psychical inhibition with
instinctual impoverishment and pain concerning it"* (pp. 203–206). Continuing with
the reasoning that had conceived of the three forms of melancholia as actual
neuroses, he noted that "whereas potent individuals easily acquire anxiety
neuroses, impotent ones incline to melancholia" (p. 204).

Another theme in Freud's writings in the 1890s suggested that there was
often considerable common ground between neurasthenia and melancholia, a
view not uncommon in those years. He commented that "a number of neuroses which are today described as neurasthenia—in particular, neuroses of an
intermittent or periodical nature—ought rather to be included under melancholia" (3:90). And he observed that the symptoms of neurasthenia were often
"accompanied by severe depression" (3:275). In 1905 he took particular note of
the extent to which "depressive affects" might lead to various physical symptoms, cause distinct physical diseases, increase susceptibility to physical illness, or worsen already existing physical diseases (7:287–288).

In 1911 Karl Abraham (1877–1925) addressed the subject of severe
depressive illnesses in more detail, providing the first extensive clinical-psy-
choanalytic data on such disorders. He first commented that "the affect of

depression is as widely spread among all forms of neuroses and psychoses as is that of anxiety. The two affects are often present together or successively in one individual; so that a patient suffering from an anxiety-neurosis will be subject to states of mental depression, and a melancholic will complain of having anxiety." Just as "neurotic anxiety" was differentiated from "ordinary fear," "neurotic depression" was to be distinguished from "the affect of sadness or grief." Whereas fear and grief were normal affects with their causes quite apparent, anxiety and depression were "unconsciously motivated and a consequence of repression."[61]

> We fear a coming evil; we grieve over one that has occurred. A neurotic will be attacked with anxiety when his instinct strives for a gratification which repression prevents him from attaining; depression sets in when he has to give up his sexual aim without having obtained gratification. He feels himself unloved and incapable of loving, and therefore he despairs of his life and his future. This affect lasts until the cause of it ceases to operate, either through an actual change in his situation or through a psychological modification of the displeasurable ideas with which he is faced. Every neurotic state of depression, just like every anxiety-state, to which it is closely related, contains a tendency to deny life. ("Notes," pp. 137–138)

From his clinical work with a series of depressive disorders which belonged to that era's Kraepelinian category of manic-depressive insanity,* he noted that these patients shared some important features with obsessional neurotics: "an attitude of hate . . . was paralyzing the patient's capacity to love"; ambivalence, uncertainty, and doubt plagued them with the result that "in every situation" they suffered "from feelings of inadequacy" and stood "helpless before the problems of life" (pp. 139, 143). Beyond this, he formulated the depressive patient's dilemma differently. From "an attitude of the libido in which hatred predominates," his conflict could be expressed "in the following formula: 'I cannot love people; I have to hate them' " (pp. 144–145). Beginning with the person's nearest relatives, this attitude gradually became generalized. "The pronounced feelings of inadequacy from which such patients suffer arise from this discomforting internal perception." With "the content of this perception . . . repressed and projected externally" and "brought into association with other—psychical and physical—deficiencies," the patient came to the view: "People do not love me, they hate me . . . because of my inborn defects. Therefore I am unhappy and depressed." This repressed hostility tended to

---

*"Notes," pp. 138–139. Abraham indicated that, while he would group all the cases under this heading, one of them would be diagnosed by Kraepelinian standards as involutional melancholia. These comments were appropriate for the seventh edition of Kraepelin's textbook, but Kraepelin's eighth edition, in process as Abraham wrote, was to bring the involutional melancholias into the manic-depressive category.

reveal itself in dreams, symptomatic acts, an inclination to annoy other people, and violent desires for revenge (p. 145). "The more violent were the person's unconscious impulses of revenge the more marked is his tendency to form delusional ideas of guilt" (p. 146). Although the depression, anxiety, and self-reproach led to considerable suffering, the patient often obtained "pleasure from his suffering and from continually thinking about himself" (p. 147). After thus discussing the depressive phase of the manic-depressive disease in terms of the patient being weighed down by his complexes, being unable to love, and being melancholic in the face of inadequate libido, not having libido available, or suffering a loss of libido as Freud had briefly suggested, Abraham gave some attention to the manic phase in terms of the patient becoming overwhelmed by the surge of the no longer repressed instincts (pp. 149–151).

As already noted, Freud had made brief allusions to connections between mourning and melancholia in his "Drafts" in the 1890s (*Standard Edition*, 1:201, 255). And, in a discussion on suicide in 1910, he suggested that it might be valuable to undertake "a comparison between it [that is, melancholia] and the affect of mourning" (11:232). Abraham's views, following the spirit of these earlier hints, gave Freud both clinical data and considered interpretation for his developing ideas. Then, in "Mourning and Melancholia," he undertook "to throw some light on the nature of melancholia by comparing it with the normal affect of mourning." Observing that its definition fluctuated "even in descriptive psychiatry," he stated that melancholia "takes on various clinical forms the grouping together of which into a single unity does not seem to be established with certainty; and some of these forms suggest somatic rather than psychogenic affections." Here Freud was likely alluding to the controversial inclusion by Kraepelin of all manner of depressive conditions, from the mildest to the severest, within the single category of manic-depressive disease. Kraepelin's final step in this direction—bringing involutional melancholia into the fold in his eighth edition (1908–1913)—had sparked considerable controversy, and gradually led to separating out various depressive disorders and leaving the narrower definition of manic-depressive psychosis as we have come to know it in more recent times. Also Freud carefully "warned against any over-estimation of the value of our conclusions" and indicated that "our material, apart from such impressions as are open to every observer, is limited to a small number of cases whose psychogenic nature was indisputable" (14:243).

> The correlation of melancholia and mourning seems justified by the general picture of the two conditions. Moreover, the exciting causes due to environmental influences are, so far as we can discern them at all, the same for both conditions. Mourning is regularly the reaction to the loss of a loved person, or to the loss of some abstraction which has taken the place of one, such as one's

country, liberty, an ideal, and so on. In some people the same influences produce melancholia instead of mourning and we consequently suspect them of a pathological disposition. It is also well worth notice that, although mourning involves grave departures from the normal attitude to life, it never occurs to us to regard it as a pathological condition and to refer it to medical treatment. We rely on its being overcome after a certain lapse of time, and we look upon any interference with it as useless or even harmful.

The distinguishing mental features of melancholia are a profoundly painful dejection, cessation of interest in the outside world, loss of the capacity to love, inhibition of all activity, and a lowering of the self-regarding feelings to a degree that finds utterance in self-reproaches and self-revilings, and culminates in a delusional expectation of punishment. This picture becomes a little more intelligible when we consider that, with one exception, the same traits are met with in mourning. The disturbance of self-regard is absent in mourning; but otherwise the features are the same. Profound mourning, the reaction to the loss of someone who is loved, contains the same painful frame of mind, the same loss of interest in the outside world—in so far as it does not recall him—the same loss of capacity to adopt any new object of love (which would mean replacing him) and the same turning away from any activity that is not connected with thoughts of him. It is easy to see that this inhibition and circumscription of the ego is the expression of an exclusive devotion to mourning which leaves nothing over for other purposes or other interests. It is really only because we know so well how to explain it that this attitude does not seem to us pathological. (14:243–244)

Here were clear indications of the centuries-old theme that in melancholia the sadness or dejection was "without cause" or "without apparent cause," whereas in grief the cause was quite apparent. Freud observed that in grief and mourning "it is the world which has become poor and empty" due to the quite apparent loss, whereas "in melancholia it is the ego itself" (p. 246). In mourning the sufferer slowly withdrew the emotional attachment from the now-lost object and gradually freed himself from this painful state. In melancholia, however, matters were much subtler, the nature of the loss much less clear or very unclear.

This would suggest that melancholia is in some way related to an object-loss which is withdrawn from consciousness. . . . In melancholia, the unknown loss will result in similar internal work [to that of mourning] and will therefore be responsible for the melancholic inhibition. The difference is that the inhibition of the melancholic seems puzzling to us because we cannot see what it is that is absorbing him so entirely. The melancholic displays something else besides which is lacking in mourning—an extraordinary diminution in his self-regard, an impoverishment of his ego on a grand scale. . . . The patient represents his ego to us as worthless, incapable of any achievement and morally despicable; he reproaches himself, vilifies himself and expects to be cast out and punished. . . . He is not of the opinion that a change has taken place in him, but extends his self-criticism back over the past; he declares that he was never any better. This picture of a delusion of (mainly moral) inferiority is completed by sleeplessness and refusal to take nourishment, and—what is psychologically very remarkable—by an overcoming of the instinct which compels every living thing to cling to life. (pp. 245–246)

Whereas the grief-stricken person complained of the loss of a loved one, the melancholic bemoaned his own limitations and inadequacies. But Freud reasoned that there might well be some truth to the melancholic's self-criticism, that "he must surely be right in some way," that at least "he is giving a correct description of his psychological situation" (pp. 246–247). He then went on to say,

> If one listens patiently to a melancholic's many and various self-accusations, one cannot in the end avoid the impression that often the most violent of them are hardly at all applicable to the patient himself, but that with insignificant modifications they do fit someone else, someone whom the patient loves or has loved or should love. . . . So we find the key to the clinical picture: we perceive that the self-reproaches are reproaches against a loved object which have been shifted away from it on to the patient's own ego. (p. 248)

This lost "loved object," or aspects of that person, had been "taken into" the melancholic by a process of introjection, and an identification with that person had occurred, that is, aspects of the lost object had become internalized aspects of the person who has now become the melancholic sufferer. "The shadow of the object" had fallen "upon the ego," and a critical inner agency judged the ego as though it were "an object, the forsaken object" (p. 249). Thus the self-reproaches of the melancholic amounted to both overt attacks on himself and unconscious attacks on the lost "loved object" (pp. 248–249). Freud characterized the relationship of such a person to the "loved object" as a narcissistic object-choice, and indicated that melancholia borrowed "some of its features from mourning, and the others from the process of regression from narcissistic object-choice to narcissism" (p. 250). Such relationships also involved a significant ambivalence, and this ambivalence tended to manifest itself in the form of hatred and sadism toward the ego (and the introjected object) in the melancholic state (pp. 250–252). In concluding, Freud stated that "the three preconditions of melancholia" were "loss of the object, ambivalence, and regression of libido into the ego" (p. 258). All three factors were deemed necessary, but only the regression of emotional investment was considered specific to melancholia.

Toward the end of "Mourning and Melancholia" Freud briefly attended to the subject of mania; he suggested that "in mania, the ego must have got over the loss of the object (or its mourning over the loss, or perhaps the object itself)" and that there was thus a substantial release of energy that led to the unfettered behavior of the manic person (p. 255). He noted that some cases of melancholia manifested this shift into mania by displaying "the regular alternation of melancholic and manic phases which has led to the hypothesis of a circular insanity"; in other cases the signs of mania were only very slight; and there were still other melancholics in which this did not occur at all (p. 253). Threaded through these considerations that there were different types of melancholia were recurrent indications of Freud's uncertainty as to the role of somatic or constitutional factors in the melancholias. For example, as noted above, he questioned whether all the various melancholias should really be grouped together (as Kraepelin had done); Freud commented that "some of these forms suggest somatic rather than psychogenic affections" (p. 243). At another juncture, he stated that it was "probably a somatic factor, and one which cannot be explained psychogenically," that led to "the regular amelioration in the condition that takes place towards evening," and he wondered whether "toxins may not be able to produce certain forms of the disease." He thought that the cyclical nature of some cases suggested a "non-psychogenic" nature, and yet he found his psychogenic notions applicable in some such cases (p. 253). In 1921 he returned to these themes toward the end of *Group Psychology and the Analysis of the Ego*, where he indicated that, in typical cases of "cyclical depression" (that is, manic-depressive disorders), "external precipitating causes do not seem to play any decisive part" and thus that it was customary "to consider these cases as not being psychogenic." He added, though, that "a change into mania is not an indispensable feature of the symptomatology of melancholic depression. There are simple melancholias, some in single and some in recurrent attacks, which never show this development" (18:132). Then, in contrast to his just-mentioned conclusion regarding somatogenesis, he stated:

> There are melancholias in which the precipitating cause clearly plays an aetiological part. They are those which occur after the loss of a loved object, whether by death or as the result of circumstances which have necessitated the withdrawal of the libido from the object. A psychogenic melancholia of this sort can end in mania, and this cycle can be repeated several times, just as easily as in a case which appears to be spontaneous. Thus the state of things is somewhat obscure, especially as only a few forms and cases of melancholia have been submitted to psycho-analytic investigation. So far we only understand those cases in which the object is given up because it has shown itself unworthy of love. It is then set up again inside the ego, by means of identification, and severely condemned by the ego ideal. The reproaches and attacks directed towards the object come to light in the shape of melancholic self-reproaches. (18:133)

Originally, in "Mourning and Melancholia," Freud had referred to "the disturbance of self-regard" and inordinate "self-criticism" in melancholia, and postulated an inner "critical agency," acknowledging its kinship with the traditional notion of conscience (14:244, 246, 247). In the passage above, his evolving concept of the *ego ideal* had come to include these self-critical activities and thus to be responsible for the melancholic's self-reproaches. Then, as the *ego ideal* became the *super-ego* in Freud's system, the superego replaced the ego ideal as this self-critical agency (19:28); the tension between the ego ideal and the ego that manifested itself as the inner sense of guilt came to be between the superego and the ego; and the superego became responsible for the "cruel suppression of the ego" in melancholia (21:165). Gradually the emphasis had come to be less on the disappointing introject and more on the harsh superego. Freud summed up his final form of these views in 1933 in his *New Introductory Lectures on Psycho-Analysis* as follows:

> The most striking feature of this illness [melancholia] . . . is the way in which the super-ego—"conscience," you may call it, quietly—treats the ego. While a melancholic can, like other people, show a greater or less degree of severity to himself in his healthy periods, during a melancholic attack his super-ego becomes over-severe, abuses the poor ego, humiliates it and ill-treats it, threatens it with the direst punishments, reproaches it for actions in the remotest past which had been taken lightly at the time—as though it had spent the whole interval in collecting accusations and had only been waiting for its present access of strength in order to bring them up and make a condemnatory judgment on their basis. The super-ego applies the strictest moral standard to the helpless ego which is at its mercy; in general it represents the claims of morality, and we realize all at once that our moral sense of guilt is the expression of the tension between the ego and the super-ego. It is a most remarkable experience to see morality, which is supposed to have been given us by God and thus deeply implanted in us, functioning [in these patients] as a periodic phenomenon. For after a certain number of months the whole moral fuss is over, the criticism of the super-ego is silent, the ego is rehabilitated and again enjoys all the rights of man till the next attack. In some forms of the disease, indeed, something of a contrary sort occurs in the intervals; the ego finds itself in a blissful state of intoxication, it celebrates a triumph, as though the super-ego had lost all its strength or had melted into the ego; and this liberated, manic ego permits itself a truly uninhibited satisfaction of all its appetites. (22:60–61)

In 1924, on the basis of additional clinical studies, Abraham contributed further to the subject of melancholia. In his review of his experience with "melancholic depression," he concluded that several factors were crucial to the emergence of such an illness. Although he did not find any indication of "direct inheritance" in manic-depressive states, he regularly found "a constitutional factor" in the sense that "neuroses of other kinds abounded" in the family history.[62] Second, there was a fixation of emotional development at the oral stage that derived from a withdrawal of love during infancy and that led to a strong inclination toward direct oral gratification and an excessively dependent relationship with key persons in later life.[63] Finally, a "repetition of the primary disappointment in later life" became "the exciting cause of the onset of a melancholic depression."[64]

Prominent among the later psychoanalysts who contributed to the subject of melancholia and depression was Sandor Rado (1890–1972). In two early articles in 1927 Rado accepted Freud's idea of an inordinately self-critical superego but added another important theme, namely, that "this disease" of melancholia could be described "only as a great despairing cry for love."[65] In "The Problem of Melancholia" he declared that "the most striking feature" among "the symptoms of depressive conditions" was "the fall in self-esteem and self-satisfaction." He differentiated *depressive neurosis* from *melancholia*, noting that in the former there was an attempt to conceal this "fall in self-esteem," whereas "in melancholia it finds the clamorous expression in the patients' delusional self-accusations and self-aspersions, which we call 'the delusion of moral inferiority'" (*Psychoanalysis of Behavior*, 1:48). The depressive person, like a small child, was unusually dependent on the approval and affection of others for maintaining his self-esteem. Whereas the healthier person would have achieved a degree of independence in which his self-esteem had "its foundation in the subject's own achievements and critical judgment," the depressive had retained a more primitive or narcissistic dependence on others for the assurance of his own worth (pp. 48–49). Rado observed that "we find in them, above all, an intensely strong craving for narcissistic gratification and a very considerable narcissistic intolerance. We observe that even to trivial offences and disappointments they immediately react with a fall in their self-esteem" (p. 48). Further, "such persons are never weary of courting the favour of the objects of their libido and seeking for evidence of love from them; they sometimes expend an astonishing skill and subtlety in this pursuit." However, once they were sure of the affection and regard of the other person, they were inclined to take the person for granted and to "become more and more domineering and autocratic, displaying an increasingly unbridled egoism, until their attitude becomes one of full-blown tyranny." Unaware as they were of this needy and demanding attitude, they reacted with bitter anger if the other person reacted aggressively or withdrew his love (p. 49). It was against this background, and in the wake of this earlier stage of bitter resentment, that the depressive turned to "contrition," to "remorseful self-punishment and expiation," and to a full-blown depressive state as "a great despairing cry for love." "The ego does penance, begs for forgiveness and endeavours in this way to win back the lost object" (p. 50). Rado conceived of this interpersonal drama as having become internalized and played out within the person, as an intra-psychic drama between the ego and the superego. And from there he empha-sized a sequence of *"guilt, atonement* and *forgiveness"* as crucial in the emergence and resolution of states of depression. He went on to say,

> I think that if we trace the chain of ideas, *guilt-atonement-forgiveness*, back to the sequence of experiences of early infancy: *rage, hunger, drinking at the mother's breast*, we have the explanation of the problem why the hope of absolution and

love is perhaps the most powerful conception which we meet with in the higher
strata of the mental life of mankind.

According to this argument, the deepest fixation-point in the melancholic
(depressive) disposition is to be found in the "situation of threatened loss of love"
[Freud], more precisely, in the hunger-situation of the infant. (p. 53)

Rado summed up "the process of melancholia" as representing "an attempt at
reparation (cure). . . . It is designed to revive the ego's self-regard, which has
been annihilated by the loss of love, to restore the interrupted love-relation, to
be as it were a prophylactic measure against the ego's ever suffering such severe
injury again" (p. 60). At the end of this study Rado returned to the differences
between "*neurotic* depression" and "true melancholia." In the former, the ego
was more or less intact, and the relations to the object and to reality were
preserved. The neurotic depression was "a kind of partial melancholia of the
(neurotic) ego; the further the depressive process extends within the ego at the
cost of its relations to the object and to reality, the more does the condition"
approach true melancholia, that is, become a psychotic depression (p. 62).

Some years later, in 1950, having revised his thinking to produce his
"adaptational psychodynamics," Rado modified his ideas on depression. He
continued to hold the following views: (1) "the depressive spell is a desperate
cry for love, precipitated by an actual or imagined loss which the patient feels
endangers his emotional (and material) security"; (2) "the emotional overreac-
tion to this emergency unfolds, unbeknown to the patient himself, as an
expiatory process of self-punishment"; and (3) the patient's efforts are in the
direction of restoring to himself his sources of emotional sustenance, love, and
security (p. 236). Among Rado's newer views was that of the patient's dilemma
between being guided by his coercive rage at the beloved person or by his
guilty fear in the face of his own feelings and inclinations. Was the lost love
object to be regained by the power of the coercive rage or by virtue of the self-
punishment and atonement? From this he concluded:

The extreme painfulness of depression may in part be explained by the fact
that in his dependent craving the patient is torn between coercive rage and
submissive fear, and thus strives to achieve his imaginary purpose, that of
regaining the mother's love, by employing two conflicting methods at the same
time.

The struggle between fear and rage underlies the clinical distinction
between retarded depression and agitated depression. If rage is sufficiently
retroflexed by the prevailing guilty fear, the patient is retarded; if the prevailing
guilty fear is shot through with straight environment-directed rage, he is agitated. (pp. 237–238)

He now thought that "the entire depressive process must be evaluated from the
adaptational point of view, and interpreted as a process of miscarried repair"

(p. 238). Finally, he observed that "the incidence of depressive spells is not limited to the class of moodcyclic phenotypes. Such spells also occur in almost every other pathogenic type." He questioned "whether or not significant psychodynamic differences exist between depressive spells that occur in different pathogenic contexts" (p. 241).

The various themes developed by Abraham, Freud, and Rado were reviewed in some detail in 1945 by Otto Fenichel (1898–1946) in his encyclopedic survey of psychoanalytic thought up to that time.[66] He introduced the subject of depression by commenting that, "to a slight degree, depression occurs in nearly every neurosis (at least in the form of neurotic inferiority feelings); of high degree it is the most terrible symptom in the tormenting psychotic state of melancholia" (*Psychoanalytic Theory*, p. 387). Although he accepted the main elements in the views of these three predecessors, and he integrated them effectively, he particularly emphasized the dependent, narcissistic orientation that made some persons vulnerable to depressive disorders, and he placed the loss of self-esteem at the heart of the pathogenic process. He commented: "A severe depression represents the state into which the orally dependent individual gets when the vital supplies are lacking; a slight depression is an anticipation of this state for warning purposes" (p. 388). And he "stressed that the borderline between neurotic depressions, with ambivalent struggles about narcissistic supplies between the patient and his objects, and psychotic depressions, where the conflict has become internalized, is not a sharp one" (p. 392).

Less extensively influential, yet interesting and valuable or at least provocative to many, were the views of Melanie Klein (1882–1960) on depression. She conceived of a series of basic "positions" as phases in normal development, with the child passing through a depressive phase, the *depressive position*, in the latter half of the first year: "The baby experiences depressive feelings which reach a climax just before, during and after weaning. This is the state of mind in the baby which I termed the 'depressive position,' and I suggested that it is a melancholia in *statu nascendi*."[67] This phase was associated with anger, anxiety, guilt, and sadness, which reflected the infant's frustration and rage in the face of his less than total control of the resources represented by the mother/love-object, his concern for the safety and intactness of the love-object, his guilt and remorse about his own dangerous demandingness and growing ambivalence toward it, and his "sadness relating to expectations of the impending loss of it" (*Contributions*, p. 290). Depending on the vicissitudes of this normal depressive phase, it could become the basis for some persons to regress to it as a fixation point and to experience a clinical depression in later life. She stated that "wherever a state of depression exists, be it in the normal, the neurotic, in manic-depressives or in mixed cases, there is always in it this specific grouping of anxieties, distressed feelings and different varieties of these defences, which I have here described and called the depressive position" (p. 296). And she reasoned that it was intimately associated with mourning, contending that "the child goes through states of mind comparable to the mourning of the adult, or rather, that this early mourning is revived whenever grief is experienced in later life" (p. 311). With normal development, the infant learned that the mother he hated (the mother who frustrated, the "bad object") and the mother he loved (the mother who gratified, the "good object") were one person (the actual mother, the "whole object"), and the depressive phase was lived through, and its issues were reasonably well resolved. If the anger and hate were disproportionately stronger than the love toward the love-object, the child might fail to integrate these two "part-objects" and thus fail to establish a "good internal object." The stage would then be set for the occurrence of depressions in adult life. In other words, the early mother-child relationship needed to be such that the child came to feel that he was loved and was worthwhile. Without this, he would fail to resolve the normal ambivalence toward the mother; he would be at risk to fail in overcoming the anxiety and depression of the depressive position; he would not achieve a satisfactory level of self-esteem; and he would be predisposed to depressions in adult life. As Klein put it in concluding a study on mourning,

> The fundamental difference between normal mourning on the one hand, and abnormal mourning and manic-depressive states on the other, is this: the manic-depressive and the person who fails in the work of mourning, though their defences may differ widely from each other, have this in common, that they have been unable in early childhood to establish their internal "good" objects and to feel secure in their inner world. They have never really overcome the infantile depressive position. (pp. 337–338)

In the early 1950s Edward Bibring (1895–1959) added a particularly thoughtful contribution to the psychoanalytic literature on depression. He harked back to Freud's emphasis on "an extraordinary fall of self-esteem" in melancholic depressions, in contrast to grief in which there was no such fall in self-esteem.[68] Then he referred to Fenichel's view that a decrease in self-esteem was common to both grief and melancholia: "The simple as well as the melancholic forms of depression have in common a decrease in self-esteem. The clinical differences are viewed as stages in the course of the struggle to regain the lost self-esteem by various recovery mechanisms ("Mechanism of Depression," p. 17). Bibring went on to subscribe to the idea that "a loss of self-esteem is common to all types of depression" and to conceive of depression as "an ego-psychological phenomenon, a 'state of the ego,' an affective state." He noted that this latter referred to "all 'normal' and 'neurotic' depressions, and probably also to what is called 'psychotic' depression" (p. 21). He conceived of depression as "the emotional expression (indication) of a state of helplessness and powerlessness of the ego, irrespective of what may have caused the breakdown of the mechanisms which established his self-esteem" (p. 24). But, in addition to the feelings of helplessness,

> one invariably finds the condition that certain narcissistically significant, i.e. for the self-esteem pertinent, goals and objects are strongly maintained. Irrespective of their unconscious implications, one may roughly distinguish between three groups of such persisting aspirations of the person: (1) the wish to be worthy, to be loved, to be appreciated, not to be inferior or unworthy; (2) the wish to be strong, superior, great, secure, not to be weak and insecure; and (3) the wish to be good, to be loving, not to be aggressive, hateful and destructive. It is exactly from the tension between these highly charged narcissistic aspirations on the one hand, and the ego's acute awareness of its (real and imaginary) helplessness and incapacity to live up to them on the other hand, that depression results. . . . These three sets of conditions are, of course, not exclusive of each other but may, under certain circumstances, coexist in varying combinations in the same individual and at the same time. Though the persisting aspirations are of a threefold nature, the basic mechanism of the resulting depression appears to be essentially the same. . . . Depression can be defined as the emotional correlate of a partial or complete collapse of the self-esteem of the ego, since it feels unable to live up to its aspirations (ego ideal, superego) while they are strongly maintained. (pp. 24–26)

To the decreased self-esteem, the state of helplessness, and the emotional correlate he added "a more or less intensive and extensive inhibition of functions" (p. 27). Rather than emphasizing "the oral frustration and subsequent oral fixation" cited by his psychoanalytic predecessors, Bibring thought that the "early self-experience of the infantile ego's helplessness, of its lack of power to provide the vital supplies, is probably the most frequent factor predisposing to depression" (p. 37). Depression in adult life thus occurred when "the painful discovery of not being loved" or not having the needed "supplies" regressively reactivated this early awareness of helplessness (pp. 37, 39). Finally, Bibring assumed that "all other factors which determine the different clinical pictures of depression represent accelerating conditions or 'complications' superimposed on the basic mechanism." In addition to the basic mechanism and predisposing conditions, he identified "the attempt at restitution associated with depression," "conditions which complicate the basic type of depression such as aggression and orality," and "the secondary use which may be made—consciously or unconsciously—of an established depression (e.g., to get attention and affection or other narcissistic gratification)" (p. 40).

Another significant contributor to the psychoanalytic literature on depression has been Edith Jacobson (1897–), whose sustained attention to such disorders over some forty years has led to a series of valuable studies.[69] In contrast to Fenichel and Bibring, she was not so ready to group the various types of depression together, and she differentiated neurotic depressions from psychotic depressions differently and more sharply than Rado had done. Jacobson emphasized that the depressions of the manic-depressive group were psychotic in nature and quite distinct from neurotic depressions; and, within this group, she followed a practice of many predecessors in differentiating "simple depressions" from "acute psychotic types of depression." In contrast to the "acute psychotic depressions," the "simple depressions" did "not manifest psychotic symptoms in the sense of delusional ideas or hallucinations." In them she noted "anxieties, feelings of blankness and detachment, of inner weariness and apathy, a mental and physical inability to enjoy life and love, sexual impotence (or frigidity), and feelings of deep inferiority, inadequacy, and general worthlessness"; she variously referred to these feelings as corresponding to "the impoverishment of their egos, their inability to relate to people, and their general loss of interest" and as reflective of the basic "ego disturbance expressive of the psychotic process." Such symptoms indicated "an endogenous process," were "expressive of the psychotic-depressive process proper," and were thought to be associated with "underlying constitutional, hereditary, somatic" factors, although "psychological causal factors" might additionally be present and play a quite different role in different individuals. She then mentioned "symptoms ensuing from a psychotic guilt conflict, such as ideas of sinfulness, (delusional) self-accusations, suicidal impulses and actions" as additional symptoms that would be present in the "acute psychotic depression" and as indicative of "secondary attempts at defence and restitution." Finally, Jacobson observed that "in blatant delusional cases we usually do not question the psychotic nature of the illness but that the "simple depression" might be mistakenly "regarded as neurotic or may even be equated with grief," particularly in those cases that developed in reaction to "experiences of loss or disappointment" (*Depression*, pp. 171–175). She emphasized, however, that the term *reactive* was not to be equated with *neurotic*, as some authors loosely did. Rather, it referred to "the kind of psychotic depression that, in contrast to 'endogenous' depression, clearly develops in 'reaction' to a precipitating event." Thus it was essentially a descriptive term indicating the presence of such "a precipitating event" (p. 168). Regarding *neurotic depressives*, "in contrast to psychotic depressives," they "do not tend to regress to such an early developmental level" (p. 177). And she held the view that the nature of psychotic depressions was crucially determined by "underlying neurophysiological pathology," by "constitutional neurophysiological processes" (pp. 183–184).

As to how a clinical depression came about, Jacobson thought that a diminished self-esteem was the essential feature. "A lack of understanding and acceptance by the mother . . . reduces the child's self-esteem." The resultant ambivalence and the interaction with the parents led to "a turning of aggression against the self" and "a feeling of helplessness, which . . . creates the basic depressive affect" (p. 180). She wrote of an "underlying" condition:

> This basic conflict seems to be of the same order in all depressed states: frustration arouses rage and leads to hostile attempts to gain the desirable gratification. When the ego is unable (for external or internal reasons) to achieve this goal, aggression is turned to the self image. The ensuing loss of self-esteem is expressive of the narcissistic conflict, i.e., a conflict between the wishful self image and the image of the deflated, failing self. The nature of the mood condition that then develops depends on the intensity of the hostility and the severity and duration of frustration and disappointment. (p. 183)

The various themes set in motion by Freud in "Mourning and Melancholia" have continued to reverberate in many subsequent considerations of melancholia and depression, often beyond the limits of the psychotic depressions that Freud had under consideration. The majority of his successors have joined him in the careful differentiation of melancholia and depression from mourning and grief, although it should be noted that here he was treading in the footsteps of many predecessors over the centuries. But his emphasis on the "lowering of the self-regarding feelings" as a differentiating factor was an original contribution. This led to Rado's "fall in self-esteem," Fenichel's central emphasis on the loss of self-esteem, Klein's developmental failure to achieve a satisfactory level of self-esteem, both Bibring's and Jacobson's recurrent emphasis on diminished self-esteem, and the frequent attention of later authors, whether or not they were psychoanalysts, to issues of self-esteem in depressed patients. Freud's emphasis on self-criticism, an inner "critical agency," and the melancholic's self-reproaches led some to follow in his footsteps and focus on early love-objects who had been less than satisfactory, who had been internalized and thus "carried" with the person into adult life, and who, as the true targets of the melancholic's criticism, thus accounted for its self-directed nature. But others thought of the self-criticism more as an unhappy correlate of the low self-esteem, although they still associated the low self-esteem with unfortunate early experiences. Freud's view that the hostility of the self-reproaches reflected palpable, although often unrealized, complaints toward the earlier, disappointing love-objects influenced many to the conclusion that a central issue was an inner-directed anger that needed to be redirected outward, an interpretation that made sense for some depressives and yet proved quite misleading for others. The theme of loss so central to grief and mourning had, over the centuries, been intermittently cited as a precipitant in some cases of melancholia. But Freud and Abraham argued for a subtler type of loss in the child's early development that then predisposed the person to later melancholic episodes in reaction to disappointments or losses, however mild these might seem, and this view has been subsequently subscribed to by many. Gradually, however, there was a shift away from emphasis on the lost love-object toward the idea of diminished self-esteem. Freud was not introducing anything new in discussing melancholia and depression as reactions to life events, as perhaps psychologically or socially determined, at least in part, rather than essentially the outcome of underlying somatogenic processes. But his concept of a complex developmental process, with sociopsychological events that became potential precipitants of later depression, was very different. And, against this backdrop, his detailed attention to possible intrapsychic reactions set in motion by later life events was again very different. From Freud and Abraham came notions such as narcissistic needs, oral erotism, orality, oral dependency, neediness, and demandingness, among others, which were thought of as reflections of the predisposing events of infancy and which were often a part of subsequent psychoanalytically influenced considerations of melancholia and depression. From Abraham came the idea of an early developmental stage when the child was specially vulnerable to problematic experiences with primary "caregivers," and thus when a fixation point might be established to which the person might regress in the face of later disappointments and frustrations, or a predisposition might be established that would leave the person prone to clinical depression in later life. This was discussed by various authors in varying ways, such as the oral phase of development not being properly transcended due to difficulties in the mother-child relationship or the nursing situation, or the issues of the depressive position not being adequately resolved, or the separation-individuation stage not being satisfactorily negotiated, or the infant's experience of natural helplessness and neediness being associated with less than satisfactory response from the key "caregiver." Some emphasized that the person was left with a disposition to low self-esteem, and thereafter his regulation of self-esteem was precarious. Others emphasized rage and hostility toward the "caregiver," and associated guilt, which became an internalized drama that could all too easily be set in motion, with intense self-criticism, or a palpable but unacknowledged hostility toward others, or a litany of complaints. Having much earlier shifted away from his neurophysiological explanations of depression, in "Mourning and Melancholia" Freud discussed the cases on which it was founded in terms of their psychogenesis, but he several times alluded to the likelihood of a somatogenetic basis for many melancholias. Later psychoanalysts have varied a great deal in where they stood on such questions. It has been common enough for them to take into account constitutional or hereditary factors and somatic factors in etiology, but many have been inclined toward a primarily psychogenic orientation. Jacobson, in particular, placed considerable emphasis on the role of constitutional factors and somatic etiology in psychotic depression, and she has influenced many psychoanalytic thinkers. In the process, she opened up the question as to whether the low self-esteem was determined by the inadequate nurturance of unfortunate early experiences, or whether the early nurturant experiences merely fell short of the constitutionally determined, inordinate early demands of the infant. Furthermore, whether the emphasis was basically on nurture or nature, whether the predisposition was psychologically or somatically determined, the precipitants of a later clinical depression might be psychological or somatic.

RECENT BIOLOGICAL THEMES

From the long reign of the humoral theory and its black bile to modern biochemical concepts, biological themes have always been prominent among the attempts to explain melancholia and depression.[70] Whether iatrochemical explanations or mechanical explanations, whether constitutional factors or hereditary factors, whether disordered nerves or an irritated cerebrum, whether cerebral congestion or a nutritional disorder of the brain, the recent centuries' successors to the humoral theory have continued to be central among theories of the etiology and pathogenesis of such disorders. During the twentieth century, for many observers familial incidence continued to suggest that a hereditary factor was crucial, especially where manic-depressive conditions were concerned. Premenstrual depression, postpartum depression, and depression associated with the menopause or the climacterium have led to hormonal theories. The frequent association of depression with a physical illness has been a cause for wondering about a biological explanation. And the precipitation of a depressive episode by various pharmaceutical agents, for example, reserpine, has been another source of suggestive evidence.

The sharpening of method in genetic investigation, via twin studies and more sophisticated family studies, has strengthened the conviction that there is a genetic factor in manic-depressive disorders. Recent decades have seen numerous studies suggesting the association of various endocrine changes with depressive disorders, particularly changes involving the hypothalamic-pituitary-adrenal, the hypothalamic-pituitary-thyroid, and the hypothalamic-pituitary-growth hormone axes. Most commonly cited are the studies of the first of these, which stem from the observation that the hypersecretion of cortisol by the adrenal cortex occurs in many psychotic depressions and subsides with improvement. The realm of electrolyte metabolism is another area of recent focus in the study of depressions, with attention to the metabolism of sodium, potassium, and calcium. Most extensively studied and most suggestive has been sodium metabolism; it has been observed that sodium retention is greater during depressions than after recovery. And these few observations barely hint at the vast accumulation of empirical biological data that has emerged in recent research on affective disorders. As one authority has stated it, these various "new data . . . make for a confusing and certainly incomplete picture" and "cannot be encompassed within any one theoretical framework."[71]

Particularly prominent in this extensive and complex mass of recent data have been the themes and variations associated with the biogenic amine hypotheses. The catecholamines (epinephrine, norepinephrine, and dopamine) and the indole amines (serotonin and histamine) have been extensively studied, and there is much to suggest that they are seriously implicated in the pathophysiology of depression. Out of the clinical and laboratory pharmacology associated with these neurotransmitters and depression have come the following conclusions: "(1) Drugs used in the treatment of depression increase the level of available amines in the brain; (2) drugs known to increase the level of brain amines produce overactivity and alertness in experimental animals; (3) drugs (such as reserpine) known to deplete brain amines produce sedation and inactivity in experimental animals; (4) drugs that deplete brain amines cause depression in man."[72] Zis and Goodwin have outlined matters as follows:

> Historically the biogenic amine hypothesis of affective disorders grew out of associations betwen serendipitous observations of the clinical effects of certain drugs and the neurochemical effects of these drugs in animal brain. The "classical" biogenic amine hypothesis of affective disorders states that depression is associated with a functional deficit of one or more neurotransmitter amines at critical synapses in the central nervous system and conversely mania is associated with a functional excess of these amines. . . . Attempts to evaluate this hypothesis have involved the study of the levels of biogenic amines and their metabolites in various tissues and fluids obtained from depressed and manic subjects, the study of the activity of various amine synthesising and degrading enzymes, the study of the relationship between the neuropharmacological effects of various drugs in animals and their respective behavioral effects in man and the results of various neuroendocrine and pharmacological challenge tests. ("Amine Hypothesis," p. 175)

But more recent investigations have indicated that "the initial formulations involving too little or too much neurotransmitter have not been very well substantiated" (ibid., p. 186). Rather, "it has become evident that complex interactions exist between the monoaminergic systems and other neurotransmitter or neuromodulator systems such as the cholinergic and the endorphin systems" (p. 175). Further, "phase of illness, phase of homeostatic balance and phase of circadian periodicity . . . represent additional sources of variation that only lately have been coming into focus" (p. 186). In short, the earlier formulations of the biogenic amine hypothesis appear to have been too simplistic, but, in one more sophisticated form or another, such a hypothesis seems likely to remain significant for the understanding of affective disorders. Schildkraut et al. too made it clear that the accumulating data on the biochemistry of depressive disorders had become so complex as to burst the bounds of any reasonably simple hypothesis; but they concluded that "two facts seem clear: The depressive disorders seem to be a group of interrelated neuroendocrinometabolic disorders, and biochemical procedures will be required to subdivide and classify these disorders" ("Affective Disorders," p. 777).

RECENT PSYCHOLOGICAL THEMES

Whether adding to it, confirming it, or actively disputing it, more recent psychological considerations of depressive disorders have frequently reflected the heritage left by Freud and other psychoanalysts taken note of above: themes such as disappointment and loss, diminished self-esteem, oral dependency, needy demandingness, anger toward self and/or others, guilt and punishment. Among the additional contributions of significance have been those coming from intensive studies of deprived infants and young children, animal studies of the effects of separation in the very young, extensive studies of the cognitive correlates of depression, further psychoanalytic contributions, and experimental investigations of "learned helplessness."

Unfortunate natural experiments affecting the very young allowed some investigators access to valuable data on depressive-type syndromes. In the course of a long-term study of infant behavior in a nursery, René A. Spitz (1887–1974) noted a syndrome of severe distress that he named *anaclitic depression*.[73] Emerging in the second half of the first year and stemming from an abrupt separation of the infants from their mothers, who had been actively involved in their care, and their replacement by unfamiliar caretakers, this syndrome entailed (1) apprehension, sadness, weepiness; (2) lack of contact, rejection of environment, withdrawal; (3) retardation of development, retardation of reaction to stimuli, slowness of movement, dejection, stupor; (4) loss of appetite, refusal to eat, loss of weight; (5) insomnia; and (6) facial expressions similar to those in depressed adults ("Anaclitic Depression," p. 316). The return of the mother within three months led to a marked improvement, although occasionally with an initial period of unresponsiveness; otherwise the syndrome worsened and threatened to become irreversible. With the return of the mother, there was also a significant period of excessive dependency on her, severe distress with any separation, and marked fear of strangers and unfamiliar environments. When the return of the mother was impossible, the timely introduction of a satisfactory surrogate mother was a crucial antidote against severer problems. Spitz argued against any association of this syndrome with Klein's depressive position; he disagreed that there was such a developmental stage and maintained that this syndrome reflected unfortunate experiences that established a fixation point that might lead to later regression and adult melancholia (pp. 322–324).

Engel and Reichsman studied extensively and intensively the single case of a similarly troubled child.[74] Studied from infancy, this child had a congenital atresia of the esophagus and surgically produced gastric and esophageal fistulas; her mother responded to the resultant difficulties by being unable to care for her with ordinary warmth; and the infant failed to flourish, lost weight in spite of adequate food intake, and became marasmic and apparently depressed. The investigators concluded that her inadequate relationship with her mother accounted for her retarded development, her marasmus, and her depression. She was studied at length in a context of intensive, loving care from the hospital staff; she recovered from her marasmic state and depression; and she made up her developmental deficits. There then occurred "a striking behavioral pattern" that they termed *"the depression-withdrawal reaction."* "This reaction typically occurred when the infant was confronted alone by a stranger and was characterized by muscular inactivity, hypotonia, and sad facial expression, decreased gastric secretion, and eventually a sleep state. It vanished as soon as the baby was reunited with a familiar person" ("Induced Depressions," pp. 428–429). As Engel and Reichsman noted, there were many similarities between their *depressive-withdrawal reaction* and Spitz's *anaclitic depression*, and they conceived of it as a *"depression of infancy"* (pp. 440–441). They associated their findings with Freud's and Abraham's views of "the importance of object loss and of the oral receptive phase in the genesis of depression," and they recognized affinities with the views of Rado, Jacobson, and Bibring (pp. 441–443). After asking why muscular hypotonia and inactivity occurred, why oral activity and gastric secretion decreased or ceased, and why sleep was the eventual outcome, these investigators concluded that these were basic biological aspects of the depressive pattern that reflected "reduced activity and reduced interaction with the environment," or a "pattern of biologic withdrawal, essentially the organism's recognition of the need for reduced activity and metabolism in the face of actual or threatened exhaustion or unavailability of external supplies" (pp. 445–449). When an earlier response of distress and crying failed to bring the departed mother and led to severe anxiety and eventual exhaustion, the infant gradually learned that "the depression-withdrawal reaction was the more economic, energy-conserving process" (p. 449).

Similar trends have been reported in animal studies where the infant and the mother have been separated. An illuminating example is the work of Kaufman and Rosenblum, who studied infant monkeys and their mothers.[75] They observed that the infants initially responded to separation with "agitated searching and calling and a fall in peer-directed behaviors" and then "a deep depression similar to the anaclitic depression of human infants described by Spitz"; that interest and activity gradually returned, first involving the inanimate environment and then the social environment; and that the return of the mother brought on clinging, overdependent behavior with complementary responses from the mother ("Reaction to Separation," pp. 671–672). The various reactions in this pattern were noted to have "apparent survival value, in part through their communicative significance" (p. 648). These investigators found much in their work to support Engel's views, and borrowed from both Spitz and Engel to refer to the infants' reactions as "anaclitic depression and conservation-withdrawal."

In contrast to these various studies of the very young, Beck started from studies of depressed patients in psychological treatment and eventually came to some very different conclusions about clinical depressions.[76] Instead of the standard twentieth-century view that depressive states were essentially affective disorders, he concluded that significant cognitive distortions were at the heart of the matter. Rather than the more usual view that any deviations in thought stemmed from the disordered affect, he conceived of the cognitive distortions as primary in depressions and the disordered mood and behavior as secondary. He concluded that an individual structured his experience in a characteristic way, and this characteristic way, his particular schema, determined his affective response to any particular experience (*Depression*, pp. 228–240). "If the patient incorrectly perceives himself as inadequate, deserted, or sinful, he will experience corresponding affects such as sadness, loneliness, or guilt" (p. 239). Characteristic of depressed patients, and not of nondepressed patients, was the prominence of certain ideational themes: low self-evaluation, ideas of deprivation, exaggeration of problems and difficulties, self-criticism and self-commands, and wishes to escape or die (pp. 230–233). Beck conceived of these themes as "derivatives of certain basic cognitive patterns which are activated in depression." He identified "a set of three major cognitive patterns," his "primary triad in depression": (1) "construing experiences in a negative way"; (2) "viewing himself in a negative way"; and (3) "viewing the future in a negative way." He saw these three patterns—negative view of world, of self, and of future—as leading to depressed mood, paralysis of will, avoidance wishes, suicidal wishes, and increased dependency. And he considered these formulations to be "applicable to the various types of depression, including those that might be classified as neurotic or psychotic, endogenous or reactive, involutional or manic depressive" (pp. 255–256). As to how all this came to be, Beck stated: "During the developmental period the depression-prone individual acquires certain negative attitudes regarding himself, the outside world, and his future." Thus, carrying with him the latent disposition embodied in "the primary triad," the person is "especially sensitive to certain specific stresses such as being deprived, thwarted, or rejected." To such stresses he would then respond "disproportionately with ideas of personal deficiency, with self-blame, and with pessimism," and this would lead to "the typical depressive feelings of sadness, guilt, loneliness, and pessimism" and even to some of the physical symptoms, such as retardation. He also thought that these schemas were "largely inactive during the asymptomatic periods"; and he reasoned that, once these schemas were activated, "the affective reactions may facilitate the activity of these idiosyncratic schemas and, consequently, enhance the downward spiral in depression" (p. 290).

In addition, Beck developed a treatment approach based on these findings, which he named "cognitive psychotherapy" and "cognitive therapy of depression" (pp. 318–330). It is of particular interest to add a note on the variations in the role of loss in Beck's formulations. So prominent in many psychological views on depression, this theme was hardly taken into account in Beck's first extended presentation of his ideas, either in considering the predisposition to or the precipitation of depression (pp. 275–281). Yet, in a book-length presentation of his cognitive therapy less than a decade later, the theme of loss had acquired a considerable prominence in his thought on both predisposing and precipitating factors.[77]

On the basis of animal studies Seligman developed the concept of *learned helplessness*, which was then applied to depressive disorders in humans.[78] After beginning with inescapable electric shocks to dogs, extending the findings to several other species, establishing that the findings were valid for other traumatic experiences, and determining that the helplessness acquired in traumatic circumstances had effects on the nontraumatic aspects of life (*Helplessness*, pp. 21–44), Seligman and various colleagues concluded that helplessness was "a disaster for organisms capable of learning that they are helpless," that "the motivation to respond is sapped, the ability to perceive success is undermined, and emotionality is heightened," and that "these effects hold across a wide variety of circumstances and species, and are prominent in *Homo sapiens*" (p. 44). From this Seligman developed his

> theory of helplessness which claims that organisms, when exposed to uncontrollable events, learn that responding is futile. Such learning undermines the incentive to respond, and so it produces profound interference with the motivation of instrumental behavior. It also proactively interferes with learning that responding works when events become controllable, and so produces cognitive distortions. The fear of an organism faced with trauma is reduced if it learns that responding controls trauma; fear persists if the organism remains uncertain about whether the trauma is uncontrollable; if the organism learns that trauma is uncontrollable, fear gives way to depression. (p. 74)

Having accounted for the disturbances in motivation, cognition, and emotion with his theory of helplessness, Seligman proceeded to apply it to the understanding of depressive disorders in humans. He reasoned that

> what produces self-esteem and a sense of competence, and protects against depression, is not only the absolute quality of experience, but the perception that one's own actions controlled the experience. To the degree that uncontrollable events occur, either traumatic or positive, depression will be predisposed and ego strength undermined. To the degree that controllable events occur, a sense of mastery and resistance to depression will result. (p. 99)

Depression was essentially "learned helplessness," and the cure of depression was rooted in new learning for the patient, in his "regaining his belief that he can control events important to him" (p. 105). Seligman suggested that "early experience with uncontrollable events may predispose a person to depression, while early experience with mastery may immunize him" (pp. 105–106). While he was more sure of the application of his "learned helplessness model" to reactive depressions, he thought that "endogenous depressions have much in common psychologically with reactive depressions" (p. 79).

As we come to a close in considering the seemingly endless variety of psychological explanations of depression, Bemporad's "critical review" serves well in briefly identifying a few other themes. On the subject of melancholic patients, he drew the following quotations from the work of Alfred Adler: "Such individuals will always try to lean on others and will not scorn the use of exaggerated hints at their own inadequacy to force the support, adjustment, and submissiveness of others. . . . Actually there is no psychological disease from which the environment suffers more and is more reminded of its unworthiness than melancholia."[79] From the perspective of Adler's individual psychology, Kurt Adler summed up his views on depressive patients as follows: "This then is the relentless effort of the depressed: To prevail with his will over others, to extort from them sacrifices, to frustrate all of their efforts to help him, to blame them—overtly or secretly—for his plight, and to be free of all social obligation and cooperations, by certifying to his sickness" ("Critical Review," p. 41). Bemporad cites Bonime at length as "the most persuasive exponent of the culturalist [psychoanalytic] position on depression." His contention is that

> depression is not simply a group of symptoms that make up a periodic illness, but that it is a *practice*, an everyday mode of interacting. Any interference with this type of functioning leads to an outward appearance of clinical depression in order to coerce the environment into letting the individual reinstate his usual interpersonal behaviors. The major pathological elements in this specific way of life are manipulativeness, aversion to influence by others, an unwillingness to give gratification, a basic sense of hostility, and the experience of anxiety. (ibid.)

Bonime holds that "the etiology of adult depression can be found in a child-hood that lacked the needed nurturance and respect from parents," and that "a constant underlying dynamic factor" for such patients is "the grim pursuit of the unrealized (or incompletely realized) childhood." In reviewing the thought of these and other authors whom he associates with "culturalist" perspectives on depression, Bemporad noted that their emphasis has been "on the interpersonal aspects of the disorder as well as on the depressive's unrealistic yet desperately needed personal goals (and the appearance of clinical depression either when interpersonal responsiveness is not elicited or when there is a failure to achieve the grandiose goals)" (p. 42). He went on to say that "the culturalist sees depression as part of the fabric of sociocultural intercourse, and not as an isolated phenomenon" (p. 43). But, perhaps in some recognition of the less than benevolent aspect of these culturalist views, he added,

> At the same time there is a relative lack of appreciation for depression as a personal experience, or of how the patient actually suffers in his melancholic sorrow. So much attention is given to what the depressive wishes to achieve, evade, or manipulate that one senses that the actual individual and his inner life have been overlooked. The interpersonal and culturalist orientations have served as significant correctives to the excessive concern for the internal dynamics that the early psychoanalytic writers had with depression. However, they often appear equally limited in their zeal to point out the external aspects of depression as the very "internally oriented" theorists that they criticize. (ibid.)

RECENT SOCIOCULTURAL THEMES

In his valuable survey volume on depression Mendels summed up his review of "Social and Cultural Studies" on depression as follows:

> A variety of social, cultural, religious, and educational factors may exert some influence on the incidence and form of the affective disorders. It is apparent that child-rearing practices, religious training, cultural patterns of mourning, the presence of socially acceptable outlets for aggression and other drives, the extent to which a culture inculcates guilt or diffuses personal responsibility, and specific genetic traits in any group of people will influence the development and form of psychopathology.[80]

He remarked on the differential incidence and the differential manifestations of depression across cultures; he described Eaton and Weil's studies of the Hutterites, which showed a markedly higher incidence of depression in a subculture within the larger cultures of the United States and Canada; and he mentioned various other studies of differential incidence across ethnic subgroups and socioeconomic subgroups in the United States.[81]

But there is a significant scholarly world of cross-cultural studies on depression that extends well beyond such limits. This world has been effectively surveyed by Marsella, who brought out clearly how much depressive experience and disorder vary as a function of sociocultural factors.[82] While cross-cultural studies have indicated that the frequency of depression is higher in Western societies, and "many non-Western cultures do not even have a concept of depression that is conceptually equivalent to that held by Western mental health professionals" ("Depressive Experience," p. 274), there is also considerable evidence to suggest that the experience and manifestation of depression vary according to how much a culture is Western (objective epistemic orientation, internal locus of control) or non-Western (subjective epistemic orientation, external locus of control). Rather than depression assuming a universal form,

> the psychological representation of depression occurring in the Western world is often absent in non-Western societies. However, somatic aspects do appear quite frequently regardless of culture. Oftentimes, it is only when individuals in non-Western societies become more Westernized that we find similarities to the patterns of depression found in the Western world. This psychological representation involves reports of depressed mood, guilt, and feelings of self-depreciation. The fact that this is absent in many cultures suggests that the epistemic framework of a culture must be considered in evaluating psychiatric disorders. "Depression" apparently assumes completely different meanings and consequences as a function of the culture in which it occurs.
>
> . . . Depressed somatic functioning does not have to have psychological implications! If a culture tends to label experience in psychological terms, then the picture of depression known in the West may emerge. Once this occurs (i.e., feelings of despair, guilt, unworthiness, lack of purpose), suicide may be an inevitable consequence because the perception of the world becomes dramatically altered. In many non-Western cultures this does not occur and suicide is rare. (p. 261)

In commenting on the various cultural theories of depression, Marsella stated that

> depression appears to be related to both the quantity and quality of stresses present in a culture, especially during critical periods of childhood when object attachments are being formed. Certain types of family structures seem to foster child-rearing patterns that can innoculate individuals against the risk of depression. Further, certain patterns of mourning rituals and aggression outlets seem to be able to reduce the threat of depression that might be precipitated by deaths and other losses. (p. 274)

However, he pointed out that these conclusions were based largely on anecdotal material.

Also prominent in the more recent literature on sociocultural variables have been studies suggesting that the greater incidence of depression in women over men was derived from such factors. Judging women to be socially

disadvantaged and so more prone to depression, some have argued that preju-
dicial social factors constituted the essential cause, and others have thought
that the socialization of young girls brought about a form of learned helplessness that predisposed them to depression later.[83]

RECENT TREATMENT TRENDS

Psychological treatment of one form or another has long had its place in the
treatment of depressive disorders, and that continues to be the case. Psychological measures had long been considered adjuvant to physical therapies for
melancholia and depression, and, in more recent times, there has hardly been a
psychological theory of depression that has not given rise to a related variant in
the psychological treatment of such disorders. Behavioral therapists approach
the treatment of depression in their way, and psychoanalysts do so in their
way. And numerous other psychotherapeutic approaches, many of which
have evolved from psychoanalysis, frequently have their own variations.
Among the many themes that might be operative are reassurance and other
supportive measures; avoiding the depressed patient's expectation of rejection,
and not playing into his self-criticism; dealing carefully with the undercur-
rents of anger; easing a sense of despairing loneliness; modifying the disposition to feel helpless; bringing hope where the trend is toward hopelessness;
easing the sense of guilt; resolving the various underlying conflicts; correcting
the cognitive distortions; coping with the helplessness or frustration that the
patient might induce in the psychotherapist; being undespairing in the face of
the patient's despair and hopelessness and helping to protect him from suicidal
inclinations.

There have always been medications for depressed patients prescribed
to stimulate, to lift the mood, or otherwise to right the imbalance in which the
patient finds himself. The antidepressants of our day seem to be particularly
effective, although not necessarily in every case. The two main groups are the
monoamine oxidase inhibitors and the tricyclics, and each of these groups has
come to be significantly connected to the biogenic amine theory of etiology.
When the depression is an aspect of a bipolar disorder, lithium carbonate is
often used. Also, it has become quite common to combine the use of an
antidepressant medication with one or another of the psychotherapeutic approaches.

Since the 1930s electroshock or electroconvulsive therapy has had an
important place in the array of approaches to the treatment of depression.
Over the years its technology has been refined, and various adjuvant medications have been introduced to ease risk, side effects, and discomfort. It is less

frequently used than it once was, but it is still thought to have its place for some severe depressions or in depressions refractory to other treatments.

The evaluation of a depressed patient regularly involves the assessment of the place of suicidal thoughts, suicidal inclinations, and suicidal risk. The severity of such inclinations, or an actual suicidal attempt, is often the basis for arranging that the patient's treatment take place in a hospital setting. At times, pathological interactions with family members might be the basis for hospitalization. And a hospital is commonly the preferred site for electroconvulsive therapy.

III

Some Special Connections

CHAPTER TEN

The Various Relationships of Mania and Melancholia

That mania and melancholia might be connected, even intimately connected, is a notion that goes back many centuries indeed. That they might at times constitute some sort of cyclical disorder is a much newer idea, and yet one that is well over a hundred years old. Whether it is *la folie à double forme* of Baillarger, *la folie circulaire* of Falret père, or *the circular insanity* as these conditions came to be termed in English—whether it is *das manisch-depressive Irresein* of Kraepelin, or the *manic-depressive psychosis* as this came to be translated—or whether it is *the bipolar disease* of more modern psychiatrists, this newer idea has been suggested as a possibility by some and asserted as a fact by others for a long time now. The earlier history of associating melancholic conditions with manic conditions has surely played a part in these later suggestions and assertions that they were essentially phases in a single disorder. And both the earlier and later history probably reflect observations of the transition in the same person from melancholic state to manic state, or vice versa.

Although the mania and the melancholia of ancient medicine were not the same as the conditions denoted by those terms today, disorders similar to our mania and our melancholia constituted significant portions of the larger groupings of mental disorders that were subsumed under those rubrics in ancient times. In classical Greece mania often seems to have meant madness in a relatively loose and general sense, but at times it had the more specific meaning of raving madness; and melancholia and its cognates were often used to mean crazy or nervous but also had the more clearly defined meaning of a disorder involving "fear and sadness" that had lasted a long time.[1] Gradually mania and melancholia, joined by phrenitis, became the three traditional forms of madness in ancient medicine. They came to be categorized under diseases of the head, with the former two being characterized as chronic diseases without fever and contrasted with phrenitis as an acute disease with fever. Mania came to be thought of as a state of mental derangement associated with severe excitement and often wild behavior. Melancholia came to mean fear and despondency, usually associated with aversion to food, sleeplessness, irritability, and restlessness; often associated with one or another particular delusion, with being misanthropic and tired of life, and with costiveness; and, in a particular subtype, with flatulence and digestive disturbances as well.

Suggestions that these two disorders were intimately connected date back to at least the first century B.C. Soranus (early second century) tells us that "the followers of Themison, as well as many others, consider melancholy a form of the disease of mania."[2] Themison was the father of the Methodist School of medical thought that emerged in the first century B.C., but Soranus, himself of a Methodist orientation, promptly added that he considered these two conditions to be two distinct diseases. He also noted that Apollonius Mys (first century, B.C.), a follower of Herophilus, had said that "melancholy should be considered a form of mania,"[3] but he again expressed the opinion that they were two separate diseases. Parenthetically, it is of some significance that he saw these two conditions as having much the same prodromal symptoms and that he recommended much the same treatment, and yet he clearly differentiated them from each other. For Soranus, mania involved an impairment of reason with delusions; fluctuating states of anger and merriment, although sometimes of sadness and futility and sometimes "an overpowering fear of things which are quite harmless"; "continual wakefulness, the veins are distended, cheeks flushed, and body hard and abnormally strong"; and a tendency for there to be "attacks alternating with periods of remission."[4] Melancholia involved being "downcast and prone to anger and . . . practically never cheerful and relaxed"; "signs . . . as follows: mental anguish and distress, dejection, silence, animosity toward members of the household, sometimes a desire to live and at other times a longing for death, suspicion . . . that a plot is being hatched against him, weeping without reason, meaningless muttering, and, again, occasional joviality"; and various somatic symptoms, many of them gastrointestinal.[5]

Aretaeus of Cappadocia (ca. 150) has left us a comment that seems to belong to the very tradition alluded to by Soranus, a comment that has been quoted by many and mistakenly said by some to be the first suggestion that there might be a close association between mania and melancholia. He stated, "It appears to me that melancholy is the commencement and a part of mania."[6] The context for this was his chapter on melancholia, which is found immediately ahead of his chapter on mania in his book on chronic diseases. This arrangement as adjacent chapters, either in works on chronic diseases or in sections on diseases of the head, was to become a long-standing tradition; and the commonest exception was when they were treated in a single chapter, with the two accounts interwoven to varying extents and the title sometimes mania, sometimes melancholia, and sometimes a combination.

In this account of melancholia Aretaeus described it as

> a lowness of spirits from a single phantasy, without fever; . . . the understanding is turned . . . in the melancholics to sorrow and despondency only. . . . Those affected with melancholy are not every one of them affected according to one particular form; but they are either suspicious of poisoning, or flee to the desert from misanthropy, or turn superstitious, or contract a hatred of life.
>
> . . . The patients are dull or stern, dejected or unreasonably torpid, without any manifest cause: such is the commencement of melancholy. And they also become peevish, dispirited, sleepless, and start up from a disturbed sleep.
>
> Unreasonable fear also seizes them, if the disease tend to increase, when their dreams are true, terrifying, and clear: for whatever, when awake, they have an aversion to, as being an evil, rushes upon their visions in sleep. They are prone to change their mind readily; to become base, mean-spirited, illiberal, and in a little time, perhaps, simple, extravagant, munificent, not from any virtue of the soul, but from the changeableness of the disease. But if the illness become more urgent, hatred, avoidance of the haunts of men, vain lamentations; they complain of life, and desire to die. In many, the understanding so leads to insensibility and fatuousness, that they become ignorant of all things, or forgetful of themselves, and live the life of the inferior animals. . . . They are voracious, indeed, yet emaciated; for in them sleep does not brace their limbs either by what they have eaten or drunk, but watchfulness diffuses and determines them outwardly. (*Extant Works*, pp. 299–300)

In his next chapter Aretaeus gave us what is, next to that of Soranus, probably the earliest extant account of mania that provides any significant detail. He noted that "it is altogether a chronic derangement of mind, without fever" (p. 301), having previously indicated much the same for melancholia (pp. 298–299). He differentiated it from "delirium in drunkenness," madness induced by "edibles, such as mandragora and hyoscyamus," and "the dotage which is the calamity of old age" (p. 301).

> But mania is something hot and dry in cause, and tumultuous in its acts. . . . Mania intermits, and with care ceases altogether. And there may be an imperfect intermission, if it takes place in mania when the evil is not thoroughly cured by medicine, or is connected with the temperature of the season. For in certain persons who seemed to be freed from the complaint, either the season of spring, or some error in diet, or some incidental heat of passion, has brought on a relapse.
>
> Those prone to the disease, are such as are naturally passionate, irritable, of active habits, of an easy disposition, joyous, puerile. . . . In those periods of life with which much heat and blood are associated, persons are most given to

mania, namely, those about puberty, young men, and such as possess general vigour. . . . The diet which disposes to it is associated with voracity, immoderate repletion, drunkenness, lechery, venereal desires. Women also sometimes become affected with mania from want of purgation of the system, when the uterus has attained the development of manhood. . . . they stir up the disease also, if from any cause an accustomed evacuation of blood, or of bile, or of sweating be stopped. (pp. 301–302)

He then proceeded to lively descriptions of excited clinical states, some of them joyous and grandiose, and some of them angry and dangerous; noted that delusions were common; and mentioned insomnia (pp. 302–303).

At the height of the disease they have impure dreams, and irresistible desire of venery, without any shame and restraint as to sexual intercourse; and if roused to anger by admonition or restraint, they become wholly mad. Wherefore they are affected with madness in various shapes; some run along unrestrainedly, and, not knowing how, return again to the same spot; some, after a long time, come back to their relatives; others roar aloud, bewailing themselves as if they had experienced robbery or violence. Some flee the haunts of men, and going to the wilderness, live by themselves. (p. 304)

For both Soranus and Aretaeus, it is clear that mania and melancholia each included a wider range of conditions than the twentieth century would group under those terms, and yet they clearly included syndromes akin to our mania and melancholia. Mania was predominantly a matter of excited states, delusions, wild behavior, grandiosity, and related affects; and melancholia was primarily dejected states, delusions, subdued behavior, insomnia, discouragement, and fear. Yet, as we are studying the relationship of mania and melancholia to one another, it is important to note that minor themes were sounded: dejection sometimes occurred in mania, grandiosity and related affects were sometimes preeminent in melancholia. Finally, in considering Aretaeus's view that melancholia was an early stage of mania, we must keep in mind just how different a notion this is from the suggestion that the two conditions are parts of a single disease with a cyclical character.

In the writings of Galen of Pergamon (131–201) melancholia was clearly established as a chronic disease without fever. Following Hippocrates, he considered fear and sadness the basic symptoms; a particular, fixed delusion was common, though varying in content from person to person; some melancholiacs were misanthropic and tired of life, although not all wished to die and some even feared death; and some suffered from a specific type, melancholia hypochondriaca, which included a variety of gastrointestinal symptoms.[7] Galen's writings contain only fragmentary passing comments regarding mania. As with melancholia, it was a chronic disease without fever, and the psychic functions were damaged; the condition might be a primary disease of the brain or one in which the brain was affected secondary to disease else-where.[8] Mania was a pathological excitement caused by a biting and hot humor, the yellow bile, in contrast to melancholia as a pathological dejection caused by a cold and dry humor, the black bile.[9]

In examining the relationship between pathological excitements and pathological dejections, we should remember that Galen held that there were two types of black bile. Earlier Rufus of Ephesus (fl. 98–117) had said that black bile could be formed by the chilling of blood or by the overheating of other bodily humors.[10] Influenced by Rufus, Galen mentioned "the other atrabilious humor which is [generated] by combustion of yellow bile and provokes violent delirium . . . because it occupies the substance of the brain itself."[11] From this he developed a scheme in which ordinary black bile was thought to cause the melancholic states associated with fear and sadness, and this second type of black bile was thought to cause a different type of melan-cholia, a violent form of madness; eventually this second black bile came to be referred to as unnatural, adust, or burnt. These lines of thought led to a tradition of dejected states due to natural black bile and excited states due to unnatural black bile, sometimes considered to be two separate diseases and sometimes two variants within melancholia.

In his section on melancholia, Alexander of Tralles (525–605) included a broader range of deranged states than was usual, among them the familiar dejected states.[12] When he attributed the condition to an excess of black bile, his description was much like Galen's, with the addition of certain delusions that, like some mentioned by Galen, were cited by many later writers on melancholia. He did not leave a separate discussion of mania, but interwove with his discussion of the dejected forms of madness considerations of cheerful forms attributed to a plethora of blood and of rageful forms attributed to blood transformed into black bile. While this is in keeping with the often broader use of the term *melancholia* in ancient times, it also seems to imply that pathological excitements and pathological dejections were closely connected for Alexander, as they were for some other ancient authorities. After indicating that unremit-ting cases of melancholia of some duration may worsen to the point of raving madness, he stated that mania was nothing but an exaggeration of the melan-cholic state to the point of extreme wildness,[13] a view akin to that of Aretaeus.

Paul of Aegina (625–690) continued the emerging tradition of describing melancholia much as Galen had, with an admixture that may well have been drawn from Alexander of Tralles.[14] For Paul mania was a separate disease, but he discussed it only briefly in conjunction with melancholia. It "occasions ungovernable madness, so that those affected with it will destroy persons who come near them unguardedly." Of particular interest was his etiological scheme, in which melancholia was caused by ordinary black bile and mania "by yellow bile, which, by too much heat, has been turned into black" bile.[15]

For the rest of the medieval era the relationship of mania and melancholia remained much the same. They continued usually to appear together among the diseases of the head, to be grouped together as the two chronic forms of madness, to be described as being without fever, and to be presented in adjacent chapters or sections, if not in the same chapter. Mania continued to imply primarily excited psychotic states, and melancholia dejected psychotic states. And the basic clinical descriptions changed very little.

Although most authorities continued to conceive of them as two separate diseases, the occasional author cited Aretaeus or Alexander of Tralles as a basis for asserting a more intimate connection between them; but the connection suggested was usually that of melancholia as the earlier stage and milder form of madness, and mania as the later stage and more serious or advanced form. Yet even those who presented them as quite distinct diseases often employed humoral explanations that seemed to hint at unstated connections. Some maintained that adust, or burnt, black bile (with its associated hotness) was the cause of mania, in contrast to natural black bile (with its coldness and dryness) being the cause of melancholia. And others conceived of a raving or furious form of melancholia attributed to this adust black bile, and contrasted this with the commoner form of melancholia caused by the natural black bile. That is, excited and dejected psychotic states were clearly differentiated from each other clinically and yet were given interestingly connected explanations in terms of the humoral theory.

Although matters continued much as just described during the sixteenth and seventeenth centuries, the occasional author would, as Burton put it, "make *madness* and *melancholy* but one disease, which Jason Pratensis [1486–1559] especially labours, and that they differ only in the more or less, in quantity alone, the one being a degree to the other, and both proceeding from one cause." Burton went on to say, "But most of our neotericks do handle them apart, whom I will follow in this treatise."[16]

Then, in the latter half of the seventeenth century, Thomas Willis (1621–1675) dealt with the notion of a close connection between melancholia and mania in eloquent fashion, and it became increasingly common to assert just the sort of relations between these disorders that he suggested. Although Willis followed the common practice of presenting them as two distinct diseases, he employed a metaphor that could be taken to imply two aspects of a single process. In his *De anima brutorum* (1672) he discussed these two conditions in adjacent chapters and used the traditional names for them while his translator termed them *melancholy* and *madness* in English. He grouped together *melancholy*, *madness*, *phrensie*, and *foolishness* or *stupidity* as "Distempers of raving," using raving as the generic term much as many predecessors had used madness. Willis defined melancholy (melancholia) as "a raving without a Feavour or fury, joined with fear and sadness."[17] Like melancholy, madness (mania) was "without a Feavour," and it was categorized as a raving or a delirium; but, in contrast to melancholy, madness entailed "a Fury . . . add Boldness, Strength, and that they are still unwearied with any labours, and suffer pains unhurt. . . . *Madmen* are not as *Melancholicks*, sad and fearful, but audacious and very confident, so that they shun almost no dangers, and attempt all the most difficult things that are" (pp. 188, 201, 205). Thus distinguishing these conditions as separate diseases, he indicated in his chapter on melancholy that "*Melancholy* being a long time protracted" may "pass into" various other diseases, including "sometimes also into Madness" (p. 193). Then, at the beginning of his chapter on madness, he went much further:

> . . . Both which are so much akin, that these Distempers often change, and pass from one into the other; for the *Melancholick* disposition growing worse, brings on *Fury;* and *Fury* or *Madness* growing less hot, oftentimes ends in a *Melancholick* disposition. These two, like smoke and flame, mutually receive and give place one to another. And indeed, if in *Melancholy* the Brain and Animal Spirits are said to be darkened with fume, and a thick obscurity; In *Madness*, they seem to be all as it were of an open burning or flame.*

Nearly ten years earlier (1663 or 1664), in lectures that were later to be developed into *De anima brutorum*, Willis had briefly alluded to such connections between melancholia and mania when he stated that "chronic melancholy not infrequently degenerates into mania."[18] Still earlier (1650), in his case records he cited the case of "a countrywoman, aged about 45, for long melancholic" who "was seized by mania" to the extent that "it was necessary to bind her with chains and ropes to keep her in bed" and the next day "was now shouting wildly, now singing, now weeping."[19] Dewhurst suggests that this was an instance of what today would be called manic-depressive psychosis.[20] Also of particular interest is a collection of medical reports from the 1670s found among the papers of Willis's student John Locke in the Bodleian Library at Oxford. In these reports one learns of a serious disorder suffered by Anne Grenville that entailed recurrent episodes of both a manic and a melancholic nature. In an interesting study of these materials Dewhurst has reasonably suggested that this illness would today have been diagnosed as manic-depressive psychosis. In 1679 one of the consultants on this case, Dr. Brouchier of Aix in France, in a mode closely akin to that of Willis, stated that Mrs.

---

*Willis, *Soul of Brutes*, p. 201. This passage found its way into the compilations of Théophile Bonet (1620–1689) under his heading of mania: Theophili Boneti, *Sepulchretum* . . . (Geneva: Leonardi Chouët, 1679), p. 176, and Théophile Bonet, *Polyalthes* . . . , 3 vols. (Geneva: L. Chouët & Socii, 1691–1693), 1:701. Misreadings of Bonet's Latin have allowed the occasional author to find a terminological anticipation of "manic-depressive" in these works, although they contain only a conceptual anticipation of circular insanity, and that borrowed from Willis.

Grenville experienced "twin symptoms, which are her constant companions, Mania and Melancholy, and they succeed each other in a double and alternate act; or take each other's place like the smoke and flame of a fire."[21]

By the early 1700s the iatrochemical perspectives of Willis had given way to the mechanical perspectives of Hoffmann and Boerhaave for explaining disease, but opinions on the relationships between melancholia and mania continued in Willis's mode, and often enough they directly reflected his views. Using *delirium* to mean disordered thought or derangement and as his generic term equivalent to many predecessors' use of *madness*, Friedrich Hoffmann (1660–1742) stated that "delirium is either melancholic or maniacal, both without fever; the former is associated with sadness and fear not having any manifest cause, the latter with fury and violence."[22] He went on to say that "mania can easily pass over into melancholy, and conversely, melancholy into mania."[23]

Herman Boerhaave (1668–1738) used the traditional terms of melancholia and mania, and once again a translator used melancholy and madness, respectively; and he followed the established custom of presenting these two conditions as separate diseases but adjacent to each other in his text. He stated that "physicians call that Disease a Melancholy, in which the Patient is long and obstinately delirious without a Fever, and always intent upon one and the same thought";[24] and, in his various elaborations, he mentioned most of the other familiar symptoms. Then he began his section on madness by saying that "if Melancholy increases so far, that from the great Motion of the Liquid of the Brain, the Patient be thrown into a wild Fury, it is call'd *Madness*. Which differs only in Degree from the sorrowful kind of Melancholy, is its Offspring, produced from the same Causes, and cured almost by the same Remedies." To these comments he added a, by then, familiar list of symptoms: "The Patient generally shews a great Strength of the Muscles, an incredible Wakefulness, a bearing to a wonder of Cold and Hunger, frightful Fancies, Endeavors to bite Men like Wolves, or Dogs, etc." (*Aphorisms*, pp. 323–324). Boerhaave discussed the three traditional types of melancholia, but as though they were three degrees of severity within a single illness rather than three types affecting three different sites. The first degree involved the general mass of the blood and entailed the familiar physical symptoms and affective changes; the second degree meant the various gastrointestinal symptoms long associated with his predecessors' hypochondriacal melancholia; and only with the third form or stage did he add the disturbances in mental functioning or deranged thought (pp. 313–317). Although he presented mania or madness as a separate disease, he clearly suggested that it was essentially the outcome of still another stage of worsening.

Versions of these ideas appeared in the writings of many eighteenth-century medical authorities, sometimes reflecting the influence of Willis, sometimes that of Hoffmann, and often that of Boerhaave, "the teacher of all Europe."[25] In his commentary on Boerhaave's aphorisms on melancholia Gerard Van Swieten (1700–1772) said that this disease was "distinguished from the mania, or raving madness, in as much as it is not attended by those furious outrages which are observed in maniacal persons: and yet an increasing melancholy may degenerate into a mania."[26] To Boerhaave's sections on mania he added similar comments, this time elaborating on views expressed directly by Boerhaave. "*Mania* . . . usually follows after a long continued melancholy has preceded" (*Commentaries*, 11:132). After carefully distinguishing the "maniacal or raving-madness" from the "melancholy-madness," Van Swieten stated that "the mania springs from the melancholy which went before it, and is, both as to its matter and causes the very same distemper; and differs from that only by the violent ravings." And he believed that there was support for his views in those of Alexander of Tralles (pp. 134–135).

Particularly influenced by Boerhaave, and also drawing extensively on Hoffmann and other authorities of the time, Robert James (1705–1776) assembled an influential medical encyclopedia in which mania or madness was dealt with at length in an entry that also contained the primary account of melancholia. He quoted Boerhaave's statements about the close connection between melancholia and mania, cited Galen as his authority for the observation that "violent Anger" was the likeliest among the causes that might convert "Melancholy into Madness," and introduced the entry with a vigorous assertion that these two disorders were really one.

> There is an absolute Necessity for reducing Melancholy and Madness to one Species of Disorder, and consequently of considering them in one joint View, since, from daily Observation and Experience, we find, that they both arise from the same common Cause and Origin, that is, an excessive Congestion of the Blood in the Brain, which is a weak and tender Part of the Body; and that they only differ in Degrees, and with respect to the Time of Invasion; so that Melancholy may be justly taken for the primary Disorder, and Madness for an Augmentation, or an accidental Effect of it. This was the Opinion of the ancient Physicians. Thus *Alexander Trallian*, in *Lib. I. Cap. 16.* informs us, that Madness is nothing but Melancholy arrived at a higher Degree, and that the Connection between these two Disorders is so great, that a Transition from the one to the other easily happens. *Aretaeus* also, in *Lib. 3. Cap. 5.* tells us, that Melancholy is the Beginning and Origin of Madness, which is brought on rather by the Increase of Melancholy than by any other Cause. This Doctrine is confirm'd by daily Experience and accurate Observation, since we find that melancholic Patients, especially if their Disorder is inveterate, easily fall into Madness, which, when removed, the Melancholy again discovers itself, though the Madness afterwards returns at certain Periods: Nor are the Measures to be taken for the Cure of these two Disorders greatly different from each other, since the Physician, who knows how to remove or lessen the immediate Cause of Melancholy is by this very Means qualified either for preventing or curing Madness.[27]

But James and Van Swieten were far from the only medical authorities to present such views during the middle decades of the eighteenth century. In fact, opinions of this sort became commonplace. The following are merely telling examples from among the numerous available instances.

Richard Mead (1673–1754), in his *Medical Precepts and Cautions* in 1751, dealt with these two conditions in his chapter "Of Madness." He said:

> But these two disorders sometimes take each other's place, and undergo various degrees of combination. . . . Medical writers distinguish two kinds of Madness, and describe them both as a constant disorder of the mind without any considerable fever; but with this difference, that the one is attended with audaciousness and fury, the other with sadness and fear: and that they call mania, this melancholy. But these generally differ in degree only. For melancholy very frequently changes, sooner or later, into maniacal Madness; and, when the fury is abated, the sadness generally returns heavier than before.[28]

In 1761 in his invaluable contribution to the development of clinical-anatomic correlations, Giovanni Battista Morgagni (1682–1771) presented madness and melancholy together in his eighth letter, a section in his book devoted to diseases of the head. Quoting from Willis, he argued for the close relationship of these two disorders. In support of this, he went on to say:

> And you often see physicians doubting, on the one hand, from taciturnity and fear, and on the other, from loquacity and boldness, every now and then alternately appearing in the same patient, whether they should pronounce him to be afflicted with madness, or with melancholy. And this consideration made me endure, with more patience, the answers which I have frequently receiv'd, when, upon dissecting the head of persons who had been disorder'd in their senses, I have enquir'd with which of the two deliria they had been affected; answers, which were frequently ambiguous, and often repugnant to each other, and yet perhaps true in the long course of the disease.[29]

These views are a fair indication of those generally accepted during the remaining decades of the eighteenth century and into the early decades of the nineteenth century, both within and beyond the boundaries of medicine. For example, in a work by Richard Brookes (fl. 1750) they appeared in the following form: "*Melancholy* and *Madness* may be very properly considered as Diseases nearly allied; for we find that they have both the same Origin; that is, *an excessive Congestion of Blood in the Brain:* They only differ in Degree, and with Regard to the Time of Invasion. *Melancholy* may be looked upon as the *primary Disease*, of which Madness is only the Augmentation."[30] He cited Hoffmann as the authority for this passage and further on used Boerhaave's scheme, in which hypochondriasis, melancholia, and mania were related to one another in terms of stages of severity (*Practice of Physic*, p. 141). Brookes presented these opinions in a text based on "the Writings of the most Celebrated Practical

Physicians, and the Medical Essays, Transactions, Journals, and Literary Correspondence of the Learned Societies in *Europe*" (title page), which appeared in a series of editions, was widely read by medical practitioners and students in the English-speaking world, and became the basis for the entry on "Medicine" in the first edition of the *Encyclopaedia Britannica*, 1768–1771. The section "Of Melancholy and Madness" was taken verbatim from Brookes's work.[31]

By this time it had also become usual to conceive of melancholia as partial insanity, that is, the derangement limited to a single idea or small number of related ideas, and of mania as universal sanity, that is, the derangement extended through much of the person's thinking.[32] Thus a continuum of increasingly disordered intellectual functioning became another representation of the idea of melancholia degenerating into mania or worsening to become mania.

William Cullen (1710–1790), one of the most influential medical men in the latter half of the eighteenth century, took note of these traditional connections between mania and melancholia. In his chapter on mania he mentioned "those causes of mania which arise in consequence of a melancholia which had previously long subsisted."[33] Then, in his chapter on melancholia, he referred to mania as "often no other than a higher degree of melancholia." Having suggested that melancholic tendencies were the result of "a drier and firmer texture in the medullary substance of the brain," he went on to say that "it does not appear to me any wise difficult to suppose, that the same state of the brain may in a moderate degree give melancholia; and in a higher, that mania which melancholia so often passes into."[34]

In a work based on Cullen's nosology and purportedly directed toward students and country clergy, Reverend Joseph Townsend (1739–1816) carefully differentiated melancholia and mania from each other in customary fashion as, respectively, "insanity accompanied by sadness" with fear prevailing and "insanity attended by rage" with anger prevailing.[35] Then, among his "species of mania," he included a form that he termed *mania melancholia* and described it as a mania that was "commonly preceded by and alternates with *melancholia*" (*Guide to Health*, p. 135).

Townsend mentioned Hoffmann and Boerhaave as authorities who conceived of mania as differing only in degree from melancholia, and then promptly disagreed with them and referred to Cullen in support of his own view that they were quite separate diseases (p. 132). Although he found some support for his category of mania melancholia in Hoffmann, Boerhaave, and De Sauvages, he drew primarily on Cullen's chapter on mania in his *First Lines*, where he had identified two types of mania, one occurring in persons with a sanguine temperament and the other in those with a melancholic temperament

(p. 492). Townsend based his assertions on these latter, where the person before and after the attack of mania was of a melancholic temperament (but not suffering from an attack of melancholia). As to the term *mania melancholica*, it had not been used by any of these earlier authors to whom Townsend paid particular attention; but he could have come across an occasional eighteenth-century use of it derived from Bonet.*

In his important *An Inquiry into the Nature and Origin of Mental Derangement* Alexander Crichton (1763–1856) touched briefly on possible connections between melancholia and mania. He stated that, in some cases, "melancholy" was "succeeded by a very mild aberration of reason, in which not only the thoughts, but the actions of the man are inoffensive," while other cases "terminate in, or at least alternate, with a state of furious delirium, having all the true character of mania."[36] Although expressed in terms essentially familiar in their own time, these comments included the unfamiliar suggestion that there might be instances where a melancholic state alternated with a manic state.

John Haslam (1764–1844), who was long connected with Bethlehem Hospital and was respected by Pinel, also made brief references to the possible connections between melancholia and mania. He differentiated these two disorders and noted that they were the two basic forms of madness. But he took pains to emphasize their common ground by stating, "I would strongly oppose their being considered as opposite diseases. In both, the association of ideas is equally incorrect, and they appear to differ only, from the different passions which accompany them. On dissection, the state of the brain does not shew any appearances peculiar to melancholy; nor is the treatment which I have observed most successful, different from that which is employed in Mania."[37] Further, in discussing the alleged tendency for the melancholiac to have his mind "strongly fixed on" or frequently returning to a particular "set of ideas," he commented, "But this definition applies equally to mania, for we every day see the most furious maniacs suddenly sink into a profound melancholy; and the most depressed, and miserable objects, become violent and raving. We have patients in Bethlehem Hospital, whose lives are divided between furious and melancholic paroxisms; and who, under both states, retain the same set of ideas."[38]

Philippe Pinel (1745–1826) made the traditional observation that some

*See n. * on p. 255. In contrast to Townsend's use of the term, Heinroth testified to the occasional eighteenth-century use to mean an angry melancholia of a despairing, suicidal nature: Johann Christian Heinroth, *Textbook of Disturbances of Mental Life: Or Disturbances of the Soul and Their Treatment*, trans. J. Schmorak and intro. George Mora, 2 vols. (Baltimore: Johns Hopkins University Press, 1975), 1:205–206. At the end of the nineteenth century, Tuke indicated that the term was merely a synonym for melancholia: D. Hack Tuke (ed.), *Dictionary of Psychological Medicine*, 2:760.

cases of "melancholia of several years standing" may "degenerate into mania."[39] Also familiar was the statement made by his English translator, D. D. Davis, in his introduction to *A Treatise on Insanity*, that "it was believed by most of the physicians of antiquity, that mania and melancholia are only degrees or varieties of one and the same affection" (p. xxxiv). And, in his own introduction to the original French edition, like a number of eighteenth-century predecessors, Pinel had alluded to a sequence of conditions ranging along a continuum of increasing severity, from a mildly dejected state through melancholia to mania.[40]

In 1818 Johann Christian Heinroth (1773–1843) made some novel comments on the possible connections between melancholia and mania. Within his own complex nosological system he clearly differentiated them as two distinct diseases. Then he briefly referred to Boerhaave as holding, "like so many ancients," the view that mania was "merely a more acute grade of melancholia,"[41] but he himself subscribed neither to this notion nor to the related idea that melancholia might deteriorate into mania. Instead he suggested other forms of occasional connection between these two disorders; in one instance he stated that mania was "apt to give way to melancholia" as a result of remorse for the violence done, and in another instance that one of the outcomes of an attack of mania might be that the patient "sinks into melancholia or general confusion, which is interrupted by attacks of mania."[42]

In 1828 George Man Burrows (1771–1846) indicated that he was familiar with a number of the earlier authorities who had suggested that mania and melancholia were either one disease or closely connected, although he mistakenly included Caelius Aurelianus among them.[43] He also mentioned that "in canine madness there are two species: one, raging, in which all the symptoms denote high excitement; the other, in which the animal is dull; and that these conditions vary, and sometimes interchange." And then he went on to draw a parallel with the two types of human madness, mania and melancholia. On these grounds, he concluded that "mania and melancholia have one common physical origin, and are one and the same disease." Although thus disposed to see them as aspects of one disease, he finally advised that "a distinction between them should be recognized and preserved; not only for convenience, but because the moral, if not the medical, treatment applicable to the one is not always so to the other" (*Commentaries*, p. 252).

Jean-Etienne-Dominique Esquirol (1772–1840), like Cullen and Pinel, did not give systematic attention to the possible connections between melancholia and mania but did make scattered brief comments along the lines of the traditional views about such connections. In his chapter on melancholia, he noted that "Frederic Hoffmann and Boerhaave, regard melancholy as the first degree of mania" and that Fodéré "gives the name of mania to melancholy, when the latter passes into the state of excitement or fury," without indicating whether or not he shared such views.[44] He followed these comments by carefully differentiating melancholia, monomania, and mania from one another as separate diseases, stating that melancholia or lypemania was a partial insanity of a "sad, debilitating or oppressive" nature, that monomania was a partial insanity of an excited and expansive nature, and that mania was a generalized insanity with excitement and exalted affect (*Mental Maladies*, p. 203). In the chapter on monomania, representing his own views this time, he said that monomania was "sometimes preceded by melancholy and lypemania" and that "monomania sometimes passes into mania, and sometimes alternates with lypemania" (p. 333). In his chapter on mania, again reflecting his own views, he elaborated:

> Melancholy and hypochondria have, in all times, been signalized, as predisposing causes of mania. Several distinguished masters, Alexander de Tralles, and Boerhaave himself, were of the opinion, that melancholy (lypemania), was only the first degree of mania. This is in some cases true. There are in fact, some persons who, before becoming maniacs, are sad, morose, uneasy, diffident and suspicious. Some suffer from a partial delirium, attended with excitement. Others, feel that they are sick, suffer from cephalalgia and soreness of the limbs, and have a presentiment, that they are threatened with a grave malady, and even entertain a fear of becoming insane. They are restless, and disturbed in mind; demand remedies, and take many of them. In these cases, melancholic and hypochondriacal symptoms are the precursors of mania. (pp. 381–382)

Thus the essence of Esquirol's views was that, in some instances, melancholia was a milder form of derangement on a continuum of severity and might worsen to become monomania or, further, to become mania.

Around mid-century two leading French alienists, each a student of Esquirol, played key roles in influencing nineteenth-century views on how melancholia and mania might be related to each other. Jules Baillarger (1809–1890) in 1854 asserted the existence of a distinct and separate disease with both melancholic and manic phases and characterized by regular periods of each.[45] He termed this disorder *la folie à double forme* and distinguished it from melancholia and mania. In response to his presentation, two weeks later Jean-Pierre Falret (1794–1870) described a similar condition that he termed *la folie circulaire;* he stated that he had been discussing such a condition with his students at the Salpêtrière for the past ten years and cited his own published description of this disorder in 1851.[46]

Although there was controversy then and there have been arguments since as to who should be credited with the priority for this formulation, nineteenth-century authorities tended to grant this status to Baillarger. On the other hand, a careful examination of the original materials makes it difficult to take sides. In his 1851 publication Falret had made reference to the long established observation that some cases of mania were changed into melancholia, and vice versa, and then went on to make brief mention of a discrete type of limited alienation in which excited states and depressed states alternated with each other, the depressed state usually being somewhat longer. While connecting the two states as "a special form [of mental illness] which we call circular," he emphasized that neither the excited state nor the depressed state was a fully developed state of derangement of the sort ordinarily associated with mania and melancholia.[47] The term *la folie circulaire* was not used in this earlier publication.

In his presentation Baillarger went further than Falret in describing the two stages as periods of fully developed madness within a single disease, and then he summarized his views in the form of the following conclusions.

(1) In addition to monomania, melancholia and mania, there exists a special type of insanity characterized by two regular periods, the one of depression and the other of excitement.

(2) This type of insanity presents itself in the form of isolated attacks; or, it recurs in an intermittent manner; or, the attacks might follow one another without interruption.

(3) The duration of the attacks varies from two days to one year.

(4) When the attacks are short, the transition from the first to the second period occurs suddenly and usually during sleep. On the contrary, it occurs very slowly and gradually when the attacks are prolonged.

(5) In the latter case the patients seem to enter into a convalescent state at the end of the first period; but if the return to health is not complete after fifteen days, a month, six weeks at most, the second period breaks out.[48]

In his paper that replied to Baillarger's presentation, Falret extended his definitional comments to include a nearly lifetime history and the alternation of excitement and depression in an almost regular manner, and he introduced an emphasis on the role of heredity and the more frequent incidence in women.[49] And he vigorously argued his claim to priority. Then, in responding to this claim, Baillarger in turn argued for his own originality and for the differences in their views, and he repeatedly pointed out that Falret's "Mémoire" had been presented only after the latter had the benefit of Baillarger's "Note."[50]

However one might judge the respective claims to priority, these two clinical descriptions were remarkably similar, and they seemed to stem from the same basic type of clinical data. Each author insisted on a single manic-melancholic circular disease distinct from both mania and melancholia. Together they exerted a very strong influence for the remainder of the nineteenth century, and their basic notion has persisted, however modified.

Again around the middle of the nineteenth century, an important work by Wilhelm Griesinger (1817–1868) included an exhaustive and significant presentation of ideas on melancholia and mania accompanied by extensive clinical accounts. A leader in German psychiatry and general medicine, internationally respected, controversial at home, and a formative influence on the emerging university psychiatry, Griesinger in his *Mental Pathology and Therapeutics* both gave significant attention to psychological factors and was a crucial influence on the biological psychiatry of the latter half of the century.[51] In his section "Forms of Mental Disease" he followed the long-standing practice of presenting melancholia and mania in adjacent chapters, respectively titled "States of Mental Depression" and "States of Mental Exaltation." And he was crucially influenced by the emerging nineteenth-century notion of a unitary psychosis (*Einheitspsychose*), for which he cited his teacher, Ernst A. Zeller (1804–1877), who in turn had taken up the idea from Joseph Guislain (1797–1860), the famous Belgian alienist. From this he derived his basic thesis that the various forms of mental illness were essentially stages in a single disease process: "a certain definite *succession* of the various forms of emotional states, whence there results a method of viewing insanity which recognizes in the different *forms*, different *stages* of one morbid process."[52]

Under "States of Mental Depression" he identified "a state of profound emotional perversion, of a depressing and sorrowful character" that he termed the "*stadium melancholicum*," or initial melancholic stage, which he considered "the initiatory period" in "the immense majority of mental diseases." This "melancholia which precedes insanity" was commonly "the direct continuation of some painful emotion dependent upon some objective cause (moral causes of insanity), *e.g.*, grief, jealousy; and it is distinguished from the mental pain experienced by healthy persons by its excessive degree, by its more than ordinary protraction, by its becoming more and more independent of external influences" (*Mental Pathology*, p. 210).

He then went on to discuss hypochondriasis as the next stage in his sequence of "States of Mental Depression" ranged along a continuum of gradually increasing severity. He said:

> The hypochondriacal states represent the mildest, most moderate form of insanity, and have many peculiarities which essentially distinguish them from the other forms of melancholia. While they, of course, share with the others the generic character of dejection, sadness, depression of mind, diminution of the activity of the will, and of a delirium which corresponds to this mental disposition, they yet differ from them in this characteristic manner—that in these states the emotional depression proceeds from a strong *feeling* of BODILY *illness* which constantly keeps the attention of the patient concentrated upon itself; that, consequently, the false opinions relate almost exclusively to the *state* of *health* of the subject, and the delirium turns constantly upon apprehensions of some grave malady—upon unfounded and curious ideas regarding the nature, the form, and

the danger of this his disease. This feeling of bodily illness is sometimes general and vague, sometimes it resolves itself into particular anomalous and disconnected sensations. (p. 211)

He noted that such conditions were essentially emotional disorders with the intellect unaffected:

> In spite of this emotional disorder and of the false conceptions, the association of ideas is usually unimpaired; the abnormal sensations and ideas are logically connected throughout, and justified by reasons which are still within the bounds of possibility. And just because of this absence of actual derangement of the understanding, hypochondria appears to be essentially a *folie raisonnante mélancholique*. (ibid.)

He added that hypochondriasis had "exactly the same origin—the same objective groundlessness and subjective foundation of the delirious conceptions as in the other forms of melancholia and more advanced insanity" (p. 213). The bodily sensations were real but somatically unfounded; the intellect functioned soundly but started from false premises; and the derangement was limited to the sphere of the false premises. Although the condition might well remain circumscribed or be reversed, it was not uncommon for it gradually to worsen. In such instances the patient frequently became more dejected, more preoccupied with his various bodily sensations, and more indecisive, and so eventually a disorder of the will compounded the basic emotional disorder. Then "the higher degrees of hypochondria" might "gradually pass, partly through increase of the feeling of anxiety, partly through the fixing of certain attempts at explanation, not only into true melancholia, but even complicated with delusions" (p. 215).

From there Griesinger proceeded to introduce melancholia proper as follows:

> In many cases, after a period of longer or shorter duration, a state of vague mental and bodily discomfort, often with hypochondriacal perversion, depression and restlessness, sometimes with the dread of becoming insane, passes off, a state of mental pain becomes always more dominant and persistent, but is increased by every external mental impression. This is the essential mental disorder in melancholia, and, so far as the patient himself is concerned, the mental pain consists in a profound feeling of *ill-being*, of inability to do anything, of suppression of the physical powers, of depression and sadness, and of total abasement of self-consciousness. (p. 223)

He went on to describe a tendency toward increased unhappiness and dejection, irritability, either discontent or withdrawal from others, preoccupation with self, sometimes hatred of others, sometimes contrariness. And a tendency toward indecisiveness and inactivity was thought to reflect a worsening of the disorder of the will (pp. 223–226). Eventually a variety of "melancholic insane ideas" would appear, false ideas and judgments "corresponding to the actual disposition of the patient" (p. 227). Physical activity lessened and slowed (p. 230). "Usually . . . the course of melancholia is chronic, with remissions; more rarely with complete intermissions, of variable duration." In some cases the melancholia was acute, and "a very short period of painful perversion of the feelings, accompanied with profound anxiety, precedes the development of mania, particularly of intermittent mania" (p. 234). It was in this section on melancholia that, in his revised edition of 1861, Griesinger added a brief consideration of the contributions of Baillarger and Falret from the 1850s. His chapters on melancholia and mania were otherwise essentially unchanged from the original edition of 1845, including the very context in which he acknowledged their work. He merely added his comments on them to a preexisting paragraph on the transformations of melancholia into mania, and vice versa.

> Transformations into mania, and the passage from this again into melancholia, are phenomena by no means rare. Sometimes the disease represents a cycle of these two forms, which often regularly alternate with each other—"la folie circulaire," which the French alienists have recently been discussing. Other observers, including myself, have seen cases where regularly at one particular season—for example, in winter—a profound melancholia has supervened, which in spring passes into mania, which again in autumn gradually gives way to melancholia.[53]

In acknowledging these French authors, he recognized their insistence that such combinations constituted a separate disease distinct from both melancholia and mania; but this was quite a different notion from Griesinger's own view that the various forms of insanity were phases in a single disease process. His alternating states of melancholia and mania reflected the idea of shifts back and forth between stages on a continuum, and his conception of them as aspects of one disease was only a part of his larger notion of a unitary psychosis. In contrast, Baillarger and Falret brought *some* states of melancholia and mania together in the idea of a circular insanity as part of the larger French trends that were working to crystallize out separate disease-entities, as had been done with general paralysis. Griesinger then continued on to comment on a variety of "sub-forms" of melancholia that might occur; and, as he described types that involved violence and "excitement of the will," he stated that "the more vague and permanent the excitement, the less are we inclined to regard this condition as one of melancholia, and the nearer does it approach to the form of mania," and then added that there were a variety of "intermediate forms through which this transition from melancholia passes into maniacal excitement" (p. 271).

He dealt with mania at length in the next chapter. He referred back to the depressed activity and incapacity for exertion characteristic of so many melancholics, alluded to the increasing inclinations to activity in the form that began to approximate mania, and then said,

> The possibility of exhibiting the emotion by actions, and of thereby obtaining relief, shows that the affective sphere of the mind and the will have become more free; indeed, the stronger and more persistent these impulses are, and the more extended and independent this aspiration to freedom becomes, the more there result states of *persistent excitement and exaltation of will*, with which also there is easily united *an increase of the self-sensation and of self-confidence*. Such conditions, which have been appropriately designated, in opposition to melancholia, morbid states in which the patients are *out of themselves*, are comprised under the name of mania. (p. 273)

To this he added that "there ensues a state of great physical restlessness, the patient keeping his muscles in constant play (speech, gestures, movements of the body generally), and perpetually speaking, shouting, weeping, dancing, leaping, storming, etc.; and thus is constituted the form generally called mania (p. 274). And these inclinations may also lead to inordinate vanity and grandiose delusions. Emphasizing once again the connection between melancholia and mania, he commented that "we have more than once had occasion to remark that, in the majority of cases, melancholic states precede the maniacal, and that the latter is engendered by the former" (p. 276). Although the concept of a unitary psychosis had provided a very different context for Griesinger's discussions of melancholia and mania, his continuum of severity was reminiscent of Boerhaave's continuum of hypochondriasis-melancholia-mania; and, if for each author one considers the relationship of melancholia and mania apart from his larger scheme, there was very little difference.

In the latter half of the nineteenth century there were some who continued in the older tradition of commenting on how *some* cases of melancholia might change into mania and vice versa, some who used the well-established idea of *some* cases of melancholia deteriorating into mania, some who merely asserted that melancholia and mania were one disease, some who followed the Boerhaavian tradition of conceiving of them on a continuum of increasing severity, more who took up the Guislain–Zeller–Griesinger version of a continuum of severity and espoused the idea of their being stages in a unitary psychosis, and probably the largest number who followed the Baillarger–Falret tradition of circular insanity, melancholia, and mania as discrete diseases as they pursued the goal of establishing an array of separate disease-entities. *Circular insanity* became the common English term in this latter frame of reference, which had become the prevailing one by the 1890s.* In 1892 Antoine Ritti (1844–1920) provided an excellent review of contemporary thought on this disorder in Tuke's *A Dictionary of Psychological Medicine*. In noting the various synonyms for circular insanity, Ritti mentioned both Baillarger's and Falret's terms, and "Folie à double phase (Billod); Folie à formes alternes (Delaye); Délire à formes alternes (Legrand du Saulle); Die cyclische Psychose (Ludwig Kirn); Das circulaere Irresein (von Krafft-Ebing), etc."[54] As a definition, Ritti offered:

> By circular insanity, or *folie à double forme*, we understand a special form of mental derangement, the attacks of which are characterised by a regular sequence of two periods—one of depression, and another of excitement, or inversely. With regard to its course, this disorder may present itself under two distinct forms: (1) When the attacks are isolated or repeat themselves after more or less long intervals only, we have insanity of double form, properly speaking, or the periodical type; (2) if the attacks follow each other without having a lucid interval between them, we have continuous insanity of double form or of the circular type.
>
> Circular insanity presents the general characters of intermittent mental disorders; all the attacks resemble each other, so that if we have observed one of them carefully, we find again in all the following ones the same symptoms, the same delirious conceptions, the same actions, the same course, etc.; moreover, the duration of such attacks shows but little variation. ("Circular Insanity," pp. 214–215)

Ritti went on to provide detailed clinical pictures of the two phases of this disease. For the "period of depression" he described three types, "(1) mental depression, (2) melancholia, (3) melancholia *cum stupore*," so ranked on a continuum of severity. By *mental depression* he meant that the patient showed "symptoms of depression of all physical and intellectual powers only," looking "sad without having melancholy delusions." In that era this constituted the syndrome termed "simple melancholia" in persons who did not show a cyclical disposition. They were easily fatigued, showed a marked reduction in physical activity, were anergic, felt depressed and miserable, seemed largely indifferent to those around them, and had "the look of sadness and weariness" (p. 216). Although the majority of "patients labouring under the insanity of double form remains within the limits of this physical and moral depression," some went on to develop "delusions of a melancholy nature" in addition (p.

---

*Although the distinction was not always well maintained, *circular insanity* meant disorders in which the emotional state shifted back and forth between mania and melancholia, with or without normal intervals; whereas *periodic insanity* merely meant the alternation of morbid and normal states, sometimes at more or less regular intervals and sometimes not. Periodicity was thus characteristic of many affective disorders but not restricted to them. For some interesting observations on these themes, see Aubrey Lewis, "Periodicity," in [Aubrey Lewis], *The Later Papers of Sir Aubrey Lewis* (Oxford: Oxford University Press, 1979), pp. 113–120.

217). These came under the second heading of *melancholia*, which he also referred to as "actual melancholia" and "true melancholia" (pp. 216–217). These delusions were classified into four groups: disgust with life, often to the point of suicidal thoughts and attempts; delusions of "ruin, incapacity, culpability, and condemnation"; delusions of persecution, often with auditory hallucinations; and various hypochondriacal delusions. The third or "highest stage" of the melancholic period was *melancholia cum stupore*, essentially what would be called a catatonic state today (p. 217). For the other phase of this disease, the "period of excitement," Ritti again described three types: "(1) mental agitation, (2) maniacal excitement, (3) mania with ideas of exaltation." By *mental agitation* he meant "the general over-excitation of all the faculties, the exaggerated and abnormal activity of sensibility, intellect and will, and also the disorder of conduct without decided derangement of intellect and without incoherency of speech" (p. 218). He went on to describe a marked increase in physical activity, a pressure of ideas and memories, a pressure of speech, a state of exaltation, being "rash and enterprising," being easily irritated if crossed, and sexual excesses (pp. 218–220). The second type, *maniacal excitement with incoherence*, referred to either paroxysmal attacks of violence in the course of the milder excited state or "a genuine attack of acute mania." And the third type, *mania with ideas of exaltation*, referred to maniacal excitement accompanied by a pervasive grandiosity and delusions of an exalted nature (p. 220).

In addition to presenting these clinical outlines, Ritti stated that the disease might begin with either a depressive phase or a maniacal phase, but the commonest pattern was for it to begin with "a more or less prolonged initial stage of melancholia" (p. 221). He went into extensive detail as to the various modes of transition from one phase to another, the various degrees of severity, and the various possible durations (pp. 221–222). He termed it "an essentially chronic disease" in the sense that there was a pattern of remissions and recurrences, and then emphasized that this disorder did not tend to deteriorate into a frank dementia (pp. 223–224).

The late nineteenth century also saw some interesting considerations of milder forms of circular mental disturbance, disturbances that the trained observer might conceive of as being on a continuum with the more commonly recognized circular clinical disorders and yet that many did not think of as psychiatric illnesses at all.[55] Jules Falret (1824–1902) wrote about such cases as attenuated forms of his father's *folie circulaire*. Karl Ludwig Kahlbaum (1828–1899) wrote about them as *cyclothymia* and contrasted them to the severer disturbances of *typical circular insanity*. Parenthetically, Kahlbaum also mentioned depressions that were not merely the depressed phase of a circular insanity and termed them *dysthymia*. Then Ewald Hecker (1843–1909), Kahlbaum's student, gave more extended attention to these milder forms under the rubric *cyclothymia* and indicated that many of his contemporaries were attending to them as cases of *neurasthenia*.

In a psychiatric world influenced by the views of Baillarger and Falret on the subject of circular insanity and in which a sustained effort to describe and delimit distinct and separate mental diseases had been under way for some time, Emil Kraepelin (1856–1926) began his studies on the course of psychiatric disease and his work toward establishing discrete diseases and a new nosological system. But it was only in the later editions of his influential textbook, *Psychiatrie*, that his notion of *manic-depressive psychosis* was to emerge. By the third edition of 1889 there was no special indication of his eventual views. In fact, he presented mania, melancholia, and the periodic psychoses (circular insanity and the periodic manias and melancholias) in much the same way as most of his contemporaries. In spite of certain modifications in his nosological scheme in the fourth edition in 1893, his view of these particular conditions was not significantly different. By the time of his fifth edition in 1896 with its important changes and his sixth edition of 1899 with the category of manic-depressive psychosis, the idea of circular insanity had long been established, and Ritti's account of it in 1892 was a representative one for the times ("Circular Insanity," pp. 214–229). In the fifth edition Kraepelin began the process of organizing his two, soon to be famous, nosological groups, bringing together in one category psychoses that he considered to be deteriorating in nature and in another category psychoses that he considered to be nondeteriorating. In the first group (*die Verblödungsprocesse*)[56] were those conditions that were to constitute his notion of dementia praecox in his sixth edition. In the second group (*das periodische Irresein*) (pp. 595–653) he brought together mania, melancholia, and circular insanity, and he discontinued the presentation of mania and melancholia as separate, nonperiodic disorders. Then in the sixth edition he replaced the term *periodic psychosis* with *manic-depressive psychosis* (*das manisch-depressive Irresein*) to refer to a group that included manic states, depressed states, and mixed states,[57] with no separate status for mania and only involutional melancholia as a separate category of melancholia.

In this sixth edition he described manic-depressive illness as follows:

> Manic-depressive insanity comprehends, on one hand, the entire domain of so-called periodic and circular insanity, and, on the other, simple mania usually distinguished from the above. In the course of years I have become more and more convinced that all the pictures mentioned are merely forms of one single disease process. . . . The reason for my taking this position is the experience that in all the disease types mentioned certain fundamental traits recur in the same shape, notwithstanding manifold superficial differences. Whoever knows the fundamental traits will, with due consideration to certain practical difficulties, always be able to conclude from a single phase that it belongs to the

large circle of forms included under manic-depressive insanity. . . . On the other hand, it is, as far as I can see, quite impossible to find any definitive boundaries between the single disease pictures which have been kept apart so far. From "simple" mania, the numerous cases with two, three, four attacks in a lifetime lead over quite gradually to periodic forms, and from these we reach circular insanity, through those cases in which a more and more marked initial or terminal stage of depression gradually complicates the pure picture of mania, or in which the long series of maniacal attacks is unexpectedly interrupted by a state of depression. . . . *Manic-depressive insanity*, as its name indicates, takes its course in single attacks, which either present the signs of so-called manic excitement (flight of ideas, exaltation, and overactivity), or those of a peculiar psychic depression with psychomotor inhibition, or a mixture of the two states.[58]

The development and clear use of the idea of a distinct disease involving both manic and melancholic states was not original with Kraepelin. He was obviously influenced by the well-established views of this nature that were already part of the psychiatric world of his time. What was really different was the bringing together of a variety of manic and melancholic disorders under one conceptual roof, with the accompanying abandonment of a separate status for mania and for melancholia, and with involutional melancholia being the only separate condition remaining. A further change was the definitive breaking away from any sense that a tidy alternation between manic and melancholic phases was the rule for this periodic psychosis.

The seventh edition of his textbook in 1904 did not bring any significant further changes in Kraepelin's presentation of manic-depressive insanity. Then, in the eighth edition, which appeared in four volumes from 1909 to 1915, the separate category of involutional melancholia disappeared as he accepted the view of Georges Louis Dreyfus (1879–?) that the prognosis of such disorders was better than had been alleged and that they should be included in the manic-depressive group;[59] and Kraepelin included them as mixed states. It is from this edition that the following commonly quoted definition is drawn.

> Manic-depressive insanity, as it is to be described in this section, includes on the one hand the whole domain of so-called *periodic and circular* insanity, on the other hand *simple mania*, the greater part of the morbid states termed *melancholia* and also a not inconsiderable number of cases of *amentia*. Lastly, we include here certain slight and slightest colourings of *mood*, some of them periodic, some of them continuously morbid, which on the one hand are to be regarded as the rudiment of more severe disorders, on the other hand pass over without sharp boundary into the domain of *personal predisposition*. In the course of the years I have become more and more convinced that all the above-mentioned states only represent manifestations of a *single morbid process*.[60]

To this he added that "all the morbid forms brought together here as a clinical entity, *not only pass over the one into the other without recognisable boundaries, but . . . they may even replace each other in one and the same case*" (*Manic-Depressive Insanity*, p. 2). He emphasized that such cases, even if chronic, "never lead to profound dementia"; and he maintained that "the various forms . . . may also apparently mutually replace one another in *heredity*" (p. 3).

Although the manic-depressive synthesis and the idea of a manic-depressive disease are still with us, it is not for any lack of challenge to their status. No sooner had Kraepelin bowed to critics such as Dreyfus, and brought involutional melancholia into the family of manic-depressive disorders, than others challenged this move. During the second decade of this century, these criticisms grew, and eventually August Hoch (1868–1919), along with John T. MacCurdy (1886–1947), made crucial contributions to the return of involutional melancholia to its earlier position as a psychotic disorder separate from manic-depressive psychosis. Among the points that they emphasized were the more prominent place of anxiety and irritability in cases of involutional melancholia, a stronger inclination to hypochondriasis, and a less sanguine prognosis than Dreyfus, and then Kraepelin, had suggested. In fact, Hoch's studies on prognosis revealed two subgroups, one with a good prognosis and one with a poor prognosis, and thus served to challenge the unity of the very syndrome whose separate status was being reasserted. From this they pointed out that either involutional melancholia might be reestablished as a nosological category with both benign and deteriorating variants, or the former group might be included with manic-depressive psychoses and the latter group with dementia praecox.[61]

But there were other critics of Kraepelin's views who were concerned more with his systematic efforts to establish distinct disease-entities. Adolf Meyer (1866–1950) was an early critic of this sort, and during the first decade of the century he urged the use of the more modest idea of reaction types rather than that of disease-entities.[62] Regarding manic-depressive insanity in particular, although he thought of the status given it by Kraepelin as a significant contribution, he stated: "I should like to propose that we abandon the prognostic factor as a nosological criterion, replace the term '*manic-depressive*' psychosis by *affective reaction group*, giving in each case the type and the number of the attacks and, wherever present, the admixtures."[63] Others in this group of critics saw Kraepelin's taking away a separate disease status from involutional melancholia as one more step in creating such an unwieldy group under the rubric of manic-depressive insanity that it merely affirmed their conviction that the idea of distinct diseases was not supportable. Along this line, Alfred E. Hoche (1865–1943) maintained that, in the manic-depressive insanity of Kraepelin's eighth edition, "it no longer mattered whether there was mania or melancholia, occurrence once in life, or many times, at irregular or at regular intervals, whether late or early, with predominance of these symptoms or those."[64] Arguing instead for a recognition of "certain regular recurring symptom-complexes," Hoche stated, "If the term 'manic-depressive' is meant as a theoretical expression of the close internal relationship of the two opposite poles of affectivity, then there are no objections to raise against it. But the name is to be rejected as a disease-entity and consequently as a designation of diagnostic and prognostic value."[65]

In the wake of the reestablishment of involutional melancholia as a discrete disorder, the distinction emerged between still other psychotic depressions and manic-depressive psychoses, although a separate manic psychosis was *not* an outcome of this process. And, after Kraepelin's time, his omnibus category of manic-depressive disease was gradually pared down further. Nonpsychotic depressive disorders were separated out, and, later, schizo-affective psychoses. More recently, the traditional, "circular" manic-depressive disorder has come to be termed *bipolar affective disorder*, and those with recurrent disturbances, but of a depressive nature only, have been said to suffer from *unipolar affective disorder* (originally, monopolar). During the many arguments and debates associated with these various changes of the last sixty years, the narrower notion of a discrete manic-depressive disease has frequently been questioned, and yet the manic-depressive synthesis, at least in the form of a symptom-complex, has somehow survived.

CHAPTER ELEVEN

Hypochondriasis and Melancholia

As with so many of our modern labels for a disease or a syndrome, hypochondriasis has come to mean something quite different from what it once did. Today it denotes "the subjective preoccupation with suffering a serious physical illness which cannot be verified objectively on a physiological or organic basis," or it refers to "a chronic tendency of being morbidly concerned about one's health and of dramatically exaggerating trifling symptoms, as if they were a dreaded disease."[1] It may occur as an aspect of various forms of psychiatric illness; it may be viewed as a disorder in its own right; it may appear in severer instances in the form of somatic delusions; and it may be, in some instances, little more than a label given to a chronic complainer. But its roots are to be found in the history of melancholia. Derived from the Greek word referring to the area immediately below the lower ribs, *hypochondrium* became the term for the anatomical region, and *hypochondria* the term for the viscera located there. It was probably first adapted to the name of a disease by Galen when he referred to one of the three types of melancholia as the *hypochondriacal affection*, the type in which the primary site of the disease was thought to be in the hypochondria. These three forms of melancholia, including this one that came to be known as melancholia hypochondriaca or hypochondriacal melancholia, continued to be part of medical thought until well into the seventeenth century. Then, in the latter part of that century, the terms *hypochondriasis* and *hypochondria* emerged as synonyms for hypochondriacal melancholia, and gradually this disorder was differentiated from melancholia as a separate, though related, disease.

Prior to Galen, Rufus of Ephesus had mentioned gastrointestinal symptoms in his discussion of melancholia and had originated the triadic classification of melancholias that included the form in which "the hypochondria" were "primarily affected" (see chap. 2). Soranus of Ephesus too referred to gastrointestinal symptoms, as did Aretaeus of Cappadocia, who also referred to the cause of melancholia as at times being "in the hypochondriac regions" (see chap. 2). Galen discussed this type of melancholia at greater length and referred to it as "a hypochondriac or gassy disease" and "the flatulent and hypochondriac affection."[2] This was one of the two secondary forms of melancholia; in this case the primary disease was in the upper abdominal area with resultant flatulence and digestive disturbances, and the brain was affected secondarily with a dejected state as a result. He stated: "It seems that there is an inflammation in the stomach and that the blood contained in the inflamed part is thicker and more atrabilious," with the result that "an atrabilious evaporation produces melancholic symptoms of the mind by ascending to the brain like a sooty substance or a smoky vapor" (*Affected Parts*, pp. 92–93). He also explained it in terms of the patient's suffering from an affection of the spleen that led to a "noxious serum" flowing "from this organ into the stomach" and resulted in this "gassy or hypochondriac disease" that rendered "people despondent, hopeless and sad" due to the "evaporation of toxic humors" that ascended to the brain (p. 153).

Perhaps the earliest extant description of this disorder is that of Diocles (ca. 350 B.C.), but it is known to us only through Galen's quotations from it and discussions of it, and Diocles apparently did not use any of the "hypochondriacal" names for it that were to become so familiar after Galen. Diocles stated:

> Another disease arises in the cavity of the stomach, unlike those previously mentioned; some [physicians] call it melancholic (*atra-bilious*), other [*sic*] gassy. After meals, and especially after food which is difficult to digest and feels hot, this condition is accompanied by much watery spitting, sour eructations, gas and heartburn [literally: burning in the hypochondria], also by splashing noises [in the abdomen] which do not occur instantly but after some delay. Sometimes there are severe pains of the [gastric] cavity which in a few persons extend toward the broad of the back. These pains abate by [the use of] well-cooked food but return when the same [heavy] food is eaten again. The pain often becomes annoying during fasting and after the principal meal. Those who suffer from vomiting bring up undigested food and mucus which is not very bitter but hot and so acid that even the teeth become bloody. This befalls mostly young people and quite suddenly. But in whatever form it may start, it can persist in all cases. (p. 91)

In the references made to his etiological notions it is clear that he thought that undue heat was involved, in contrast to the later tradition, which held that melancholic disorders were usually cold and dry. Galen made special mention of the fact that Diocles had omitted from his clinical description the fear and dejection that he [Galen] considered essential symptoms of melancholic conditions, including "the flatulent and hypochondriac affection" (p. 92).

The group of three types of melancholia put forward by Rufus and developed further by Galen was to become the standard way of presenting this disease in medical thought. Schematized somewhat, the Galenic picture was transmitted by the Byzantine medical compilers—Oribasius of Pergamon, Alexander of Tralles, and Paul of Aegina; it was this schematized Galenism that then served the Arabic medical world in its considerations of melancholia, including the hypochondriacal type. There was the primary type in which only the brain was affected; and there were two types in which the brain became affected secondarily, one stemming from a primary condition affecting the entire mass of the blood, and the other, the hypochondriacal melancholia outlined above, with the primary condition in the hypochondriacal region. Melancholic patients were fearful, sad, misanthropic, and often tired of life; an aversion to food, sleeplessness, irritability, and restlessness were common symptoms; and often, but not necessarily, the person was troubled by a circumscribed delusion. In the case of melancholia hypochondriaca the depressive symptoms were also accompanied by flatulence and digestive disturbances. With the humoral theory as the main explanatory system, melancholia was thought to be a disease of the substance of the brain due to an excess of black bile. As the black bile was associated with the qualities of coldness and dryness, melancholia was also known as a cold and dry disease. In hypochondriacal melancholia additional explanation was usually offered to the effect that subtle emanations from the black bile made their way from the hypochondriac region to the brain in the form of toxic vapors.

It was essentially this same picture that appeared in the Latin medical writings of the late medieval era and the Renaissance and is to be found in representative medical works through the sixteenth century and into the seventeenth century. Taking due note of "the Greek, Arabian, and Latine" authorities, André Du Laurens (1560?–1609) provided an important review of medical thought on melancholia from Galen to the late sixteenth century. He thought in terms of the three traditional types of melancholia, and he stated that "the third kinde" was "commonly called *Hypochondriake* or flatuouse, because it hath his seate universally in the region of the bodie, called *Hypochondria*: it is called the windie or flatuouse melancholie, because it is alwaies accompanied with windines."[3] Contrasting this condition to the primary melancholia of the brain, he said that it "doth handle the grieved nothing so roughlie, it hath his periods, oftentimes making truce with the diseased" (*Discourse*, p. 89); and he also declared that it was "the sleightest and least dangerous of all the rest [of the melancholias], but the most difficult and hard to be thoroughly knowne" (p. 125). He went on to say that "the most learned Phisitions of our time, have defined the *Hypochondriake* melancholie, to be a drie and hote distemperature of *Mesenterium,* the liver and spleene, caused by an obstruction, comming of grosse humours, which being heated, doe breath abroad many vapours" (pp. 125–126). He outlined the way in which "the *Hypochondriake* disease" would develop in each of these three sites, naming them the "three kindes . . . *Hepatike, Splenetike,* and *Meseraicke";* and he indicated that, in each kind, an obstruction developed and "the veines of these parts" became "stuffed and filled of some kinde of humour" that "doth there take an unnaturall heate, and maketh a marveilous hurlie-burlie in the whole order of nature" (pp. 126–128). Then, addressing the role of the humors in his pathogenetic scheme, Du Laurens spoke of another way in which there might be said to be three kinds of hypochondriacal melancholia: "There is one kinde which is made of that melancholie, which is cold and naturall, which keeping it selfe within the veines, and being there pinched for lacke of roome, groweth hote: another is caused of an adust and burnt humour; and the third of fleagme, and other raw crudities mixed with some quantitie of choler" (p. 128). Whether due to natural black bile, adust or unnatural black bile, or the mixture of phlegm and yellow bile, he conceived of the obstruction as leading to the humor becoming heated and giving off the vapors that caused the various symptoms. It was a dry condition, with the heat developing rapidly where hot adust black bile was involved and slowly where cold natural black bile or cold phlegm was involved (p. 127).

Regarding the clinical picture, he noted:

> Besides the feare and sadness they suffer, as common accidents to all manner of melancholie, they feele a burning in the places called *Hypochondria,* they heare continually a noyse and rumbling found throughout all their bellie, they are beaten with winde on both sides, they feele a heaviness in their breast, which causeth them to fetch their breath double, and with a feeling of paine; oftentimes they spit a cleere and thinne water; they have a swilling in their stomacke, as though it did swimme all in water; they feel an extraordinarie and violent kind of moving of the heart, called the beating of the heart, and on the side of the spleene, there is something which biteth and beateth continually; they have some little cold sweats, accompanied sometimes with a little sowning; their face is oftentimes very red, and there appeareth to them in maner of a flying fire or flame which passeth away; their pulses doe change and become little and beating thicke; they feel a wearisomnes and feeblenes all over their bodie, and yet more specially in their legs; the bellie is never loose; in the end they grow leaner and leaner by little and little. (p. 129)

Then he proceeded to explain these various symptoms in terms of the wind and the vapors from the obstructed sites "running to and fro" in the various affected parts of the body (pp. 129–131). Although it was not typical to include quite this much clinical or theoretical detail in a presentation of hypochondri-acal melancholia, in so doing Du Laurens seems to have been bringing together all the different clinical possibilities that had been recorded by his many predecessors, all the various ways of categorizing cases, and all the variants of explanation as to their pathogenesis.

Another prominent sixteenth-century medical authority, Felix Platter (1536–1614), addressed the subject of melancholia at some length and with useful clinical detail in a textbook, *Praxeos Medicae Tomi Tres,* which was first published in 1602 and which remained a valued work during the seventeenth century. He included a brief section on *"Melancholy Hypochondriacal"*:

> There is also another species of it which they denominate from the place affected *Hypochondriacal Melancholy,* in which the forementioned accidents [that is, the general clinical picture of melancholia] do often intermit and again return upon the same day, and those who are sick of it, as oft as they come to themselves, otherwise then the rest (who unless some other things be joyned, do only complain of *a pain of the Head,* or sometimes of *a Heaviness*) do acknowledg that they are truly sick, and though they scarce or seldome lie by it, and notwithstanding are able to undergo other duties, yet they complain perpetually *of a pain of the Hypochondries* especially in the left side (which they call *a pain at the Heart*) a Heat, Pulse, *Murmur, Belchings, Vomiting, Spitting, pain of the Head, Vertigo, a ringing in the Ears, beating of the Arteries,* and innumerable other affects which they feel, and sometimes Phansie to themselves; and they trie Physitians, desire Cure, and trie divers Remedies, and unless they be eased presently, they change Physitians and Medicines.[4]

As with Du Laurens, one sees here hints that this disorder tended to be intermittent and less severe than other forms of melancholia. There also seems to be some indication that the wide variety of complaints were coming to be viewed in a manner akin to the modern view of the hypochondriacal patient. Diethelm brings out this point well with a quotation from another of Platter's works.

> These patients are convinced that they have various diseases, and some are true, others imaginary. This is especially true of men who are intelligent and delve into matters deeply, especially physicians that study the causes of diseases. They suppose they have these diseases, and tire out the physicians by telling about them, some write and talk that every part of their body, internally and externally, was diseased when, however, they can eat, sleep and drink well. They also may persuade themselves that they have lost all their natural heat and have many imaginary diseases in their brain, stomach, lungs, liver, kidneys. Some patients have complained that they cannot sneeze, perspire or dream. Others complain of some true diseases but in addition they imagine many others. This is what I saw happen to a certain nobleman who for forty years tortured himself almost continuously with this kind of thoughts and used many remedies and who, nonetheless, lived to an advanced age.[5]

In discussing this illness further in his textbook, Platter outlined his views on its pathogenesis as follows:

A Melancholick filthy Vapor troubling the Spirits and affecting the Head breeds that Species of *Melancholy* which they call *Hypochondriacal*, because they chiefly complain of that place affected; for the cause of this evil lurkes in the parts of the Belly under the Ribes or Hypochondries, which the *Arabians* call *Mirach* and from thence denominate this Species *mirachal melancholly*, and from that part a vapor raised upwards to the Head at a certain time, then when it assails it, it makes this melancholly exert itself. Most men write that the sewel of this is the *Spleen* because it is the natural seat of *melancholly* and because they are most troubled in the left side, but others affirm that this matter is contained in the *stomach* also which doth most possess the left hypochondria, and in its neighboring part: others also place in *the Liver* and *Mesentary* and the *Veins* of that called *mesaraicks:* which we also affirm is heaped and lies hid in the *mesarick Veins* not only those that through the mesentery and call, but also the other natural bowels, especially in those places where these branches of the *Vena porta* being more and greater do tend towards the Spleen and Stomach in the left side, although this matter may be heaped up also in other places, upon which account they feel their pain most commonly in the left side, yet sometimes in the right part of the hypochondries and back, where the Spleen and chief bowels lie hid.

But most do give out that the *matter* lying there, from which this evaporation rising doth affect the mind, to be *melancholly blood*, which we also can no waies deny, but we deny it to be cold, seeing that burning which the Patient feels in that place where the humor lurks doth sufficiently declare the acrimony and heat of the humor: for as it was said in *Feavers* that the blood in the *Vena cava* did cause *continual Feavers*, but that in the branches of the *Vena porta*, being more cholerick and excrementitious which is continually heaped up from the meat and drink lately changed into chyle, when it putrefies it doth by its evaporation cause *intermitting Feavers;* so also it happens in this case, as we shall by and by shew, that as from *melancholly blood* contained in the branches of the *Vena cava* the *true melancholly* is caused, so from that which is accumulated in the branches of the *Vena porta* and there fils up the Veins in certain places, yet doth not putrefie, but is adust, faeculent, and hath also some malignity; if the vapors of that raised up, keeping the condition of the humor from whence they proceed, do assail the brain they wil cause *a melancholly returning by course* which lasts so long, til they being discust again do grant some ease to the Patient, so long til new vapors arise, which for the most part is every day.

And hence it comes to pass that this *melancholly* otherwise than the true, hath its *intermissions*, then especially when some *excretion* of *wind* chiefly, with which this evaporation doth fil the Stomach and Guts, is made by *belching;* which carries with it a heat by reason of the humor from whence it proceeds, and an acidity by reason of the Stomach, in which that a certain acidity is alwaies contained we shall declare in its proper place, or when these vapors which tend upwards are partly emptied by *vomiting* or partly reveld by *Farts* and *Stools*, or when by *cold meat* yet moderately taken, those heats being mitigated and vapors represt they do a little ease the evil, as by taking that which is hot and plentiful, that affect by reason of the boyling of those parts and plenty of wind, is exasperated: because the stomach is comprest with these and pained puft up, and together with the Guts makes a murmuring, rumbling and waving the aforesaid *Windes* are so frequent in this affect, that it is called also *the windy melancholly* and divers Excrements thrust thither from *the mesaraick Veins* are the Causes, by reason of which also they then feel heats in those places where this matter principally lurks, as hath been said: but also these *filthy vapors ascending* upwards, because the heart also by the way is oftentimes grievously affected they complain of *a palpitation of the heart, and beating of the Arteries* and the *Midriff* being somewhat *hindred* of some *suffocation:* so that scarce any other evil doth so long torment a man as this affect doth, if he lie not down by the Disease, with so many *accidents* in *the hurts of the natural, vital, animal parts* infinite of which they continually complain.[6]

Again, Platter's views were similar to those of Du Laurens in many ways, including his assertion that it was a hot condition.

With Du Laurens and Platter particularly prominent among the Renaissance authorities from whom he drew, Robert Burton (1577–1640) surveyed the medical literature on melancholia in considerable detail in *The Anatomy of Melancholy* in 1621. On "Windy Hypochondriacal Melancholy" he indicated that the symptoms were "so ambiguous" that it was extremely difficult to determine "the part affected."[7] He sided with the small minority of predecessors who thought that, although fear and sorrow were common symptoms in this type of melancholia, they were not always present. Among numerous other symptoms, he noted:

> *sharp belchings, fulsome crudities, heat in the bowels, wind and rumbling in the guts, vehement gripings, pain in the belly and stomack sometimes, after meat that is hard of concoction, much watering of the stomach, and moist spittle, cold sweat, unseasonable sweat all over the body.* . . . Their ears sing now & then, *vertigo* & giddiness come by fits, turbulent dreams, dryness, leanness; apt they are to sweat upon all occasions, of all colours and complexions. . . . sometimes their shoulders and shoulder-blades ache, there is a leaping all over their bodies, sudden trembling, a palpitation of the heart, and that grief in the mouth of the stomack, which maketh the patient think his heart itself acheth, and sometimes suffocation, short breath, hard wind, strong pulse, swooning. (*Anatomy,* pp. 350–351)

After enumerating the various abdominal sites where this condition might have its beginnings, he stated:

> And from these crudities windy vapours ascend up to the brain, which trouble the imagination, and cause fear, sorrow, dullness, heaviness, many terrible conceits and chimeras, as Lemnius well observes; *as a black and thick Cloud covers the Sun, and intercepts his beams and light, so doth this melancholy vapour obnubilate the mind, enforce it to many absurd thoughts and imaginations,* and compel good, wise, honest, discreet men (arising to the brain from the lower parts, *as smoke out of a chimney*) to dote, speak and do that which becomes not them, their persons, callings, wisdoms. (p. 351)

He noted a tendency to intermissions or lucid intervals. And he observed that they were "prone to Venery, by reason of wind," that they fell in love easily, and that coitus often benefited them (p. 352).

Although agreeing with Du Laurens on many other matters to do with hypochondriacal melancholia, Burton thought that he was wrong in viewing it as the "least dangerous, and not so hard to be known or cured," and maintained that it was "the most grievous and frequent" type. He wrote of the "inward" causes, mentioning the various hypochondriacal organs as sources of the disorder and favoring the idea of local obstruction leading to a hot condition and "gross vapours sent to the heart and brain" (p. 323). Then he declared that "outward causes are bad diet, care, griefs, discontents, and, in a word, all those six non-natural things," and added that "most commonly fear, grief, and some sudden commotion or perturbation of the mind, begin it, in such bodies especially as are ill-disposed." He also mentioned that "Melancthon will have it as common to men, as the mother to women, upon some grievous trouble, dislike, passion or discontent" (p. 324). In drawing this parallel between hypochondriacal melancholia in men and hysteria in women, Burton may have been taking a step down the path that was to lead to these disorders being viewed as equivalents later in the same century.

In the latter half of the seventeenth century the idea of some sort of parallel between hypochondriacal melancholia and hysteria was developed considerably further in the writings of Thomas Willis (1621–1675). Although he made brief mention of hypochondriacal melancholia as one of the three traditional types in his chapter on melancholia in *Two Discourses Concerning the Soul of Brutes* . . . in 1672, Willis referred the reader to his earlier "Tract of Convulsive Diseases" for a detailed consideration of this disorder. In this brief mention he noted that "sometimes *Melancholy* is either primarily excited, or very much cherished from the Spleen, being evilly affected," but he favored the view that it originated in the blood, which deposited "*Melancholick* foulnesses" in the spleen, which in turn "exalted" these materials "into the nature of an evil Ferment" and returned this result to the blood, whose condition was then such that it tended to cause this form of melancholia.[8] In *Pathologiae Cerebri et Nervosi Generis Specimen* in 1667 he had included the "Hypochondriack Distempers," along with hysterical disorders, among the convulsive diseases. His description of these "Distempers," interwoven with elements of his pathogenetic theory, was as follows:

> The symptoms which are imputed to this Disease, are commonly very manifold, and are of a divers nature; neither do they observe in all the like beginning, or the same mutual dependency among themselves: for they seem in these most to affect the Inwards of the lower belly, in those the *Praecordia*, in others the confines of the brain: and in most, though not in all, the ventricle [that is, the stomach] labours much; concerning the appetite it is often too much, but presently burthened with what it hath taken in; and when the food, staying longer in it, by reason of slowness of concoction, their Saline particles being carried forth into a flux, pervert the whole mass of the Chyle into a pulse or

pottage, now sour or austere, now salt or sharp: from hence pains in the heart, great breakings forth of blasts, rumbling of wind, and often vomiting succeed; and because of a pneumatick defect, or of spirits, the chyme or juice is not wholly made volatile, and carried forth of doors, but that the ballast of the viscous or slimy matter, sticking to the coats of the ventricle, is left behind; an almost continual spitting infests them; a distention in the *Hypochondrium*, and often there, and under the ventricle, a cruel pulsation is felt: also there pains ordinarily arise, which run about here and there, and for many hours miserably torment with a certain lancing: in the mean time, from the contractures of the Membranes, and from the fluctuation of winds, stirred up by that means, rumblings and murmurs are produced: Also in the *Thorax*, oftentimes there is a great constriction and straitness, that the respiration becomes difficult and troublesome upon any motion: also, most grievous asthmatical fits fall upon some: moreover, the sick are wont to complain of a trembling and palpitation of the heart, with a noted oppression of the same: also a sinking down or melting away of the spirits, and frequent fear of a trance comes upon them, that the sick think Death is always seising them: In this Region, about the membranes, and chiefly the *mediastinum*, or that divides the middle of the belly, an acute pain, which is now circumscrib'd to one part, now extended to the shoulders, is a familiar symptom of this Disease. But indeed in the head an iliad of evils doth for the most part disturb Hypochondriacal people, to wit, most cruel pains returning at set times do arise; also the swimming of the head, and frequent *Vertigoes*, long watchings, a Sea, and most troublesome fluctuation of thoughts, an uncertainty of mind, a disturbed fancy, a fear and suspition of every thing, an imaginary possession of Diseases, from which they are free; also very many other distractions of spirits, yea, sometimes melancholly and madness accompany this sickness: besides these interior Regions of the Body beseiged by this Disease, wandring pains, also Convulsions, and numbness, with a sense of pricking, invade almost all the outward parts; nightly sweats, flushings of the blood in the face, and the palms of the hands, eratick Fevers, and many other symptoms of an uncertain original, do every where arise.[9]

In approaching his views on the pathogenesis of these conditions, Willis made it clear that he disagreed with Highmore's idea that they were caused by a weakness of the stomach (*Practice of Physick*, pp. 82–83), and he acknowledged the common view that they stemmed from the spleen, from which "vapours" were thought to arise and cause the symptoms by "variously running up and down here and there." Although he thought that the spleen had a significant role, he conceived of that role as a more indirect one, and he emphasized that the essential elements of such diseases were "convulsions and contractions of the nervous parts" (p. 81), that the main symptoms "depend immediately upon the irregularities of the animal spirits, and the nervous juice, rather than on the evil disposition of the *Viscera*" (p. 82). Preparatory to outlining the spleen's role in hypochondriacal conditions, he then described aspects of its normal physiology. He referred to the blood as depositing certain "dregs" in the spleen that were "composed of a fixed Salt, and an earthly matter"; these materials were then transformed into "a juice very fermentive" in the spleen; and this was returned to the blood to give it "a certain austerity and sharpness, with vigour of motion." Then, in addition to thus influencing "the Brain and nervous stock" indirectly via the blood, the spleen more directly had an invigorating effect on the brain, the nerves, and the animal spirits via its intimate nervous connections. In summary, the spleen exercised a "fermenting virtue," which, when things went normally, had an enlivening effect on "the Blood and nervous Liquor" and the animal spirits for which the latter was the vehicle (p. 84). Against this background Willis went on to indicate that, if the spleen was not functioning normally, both the blood and the nervous juice may be either sharper or duller than usual, with resultant disorders. This may occur either when the spleen "doth not strain forth the melancholy Recrements of the Blood" or when it failed to "Cook them into a fermentative matter" once they were in the spleen (p. 85). Then, elaborating on these basic notions, he outlined how the various mental and physical symptoms might come about in the hypochondriacal disorders (pp. 85–86). In view of the blood's direct effect on the brain, he thought that such disorders may have been "chiefly derived from the Head" in many instances, and yet a basic fault in those cases would still lie with the spleen for its failure to "strain forth the atrabilarie dregs from the blood." Whether the disorder began in the head or in the spleen, Willis thought that the nervous connections between the two provided the means whereby the animal spirits could readily pass from the afflicted primary site to stir up symptoms in the other site; and he conceived of the disturbed animal spirits moving about in the hollow nerves having the convulsive effects that he thought were the cause of many of the hypochondriacal symptoms (pp. 86–87).

At the same time as he disputed the traditional role for the spleen in hypochondriacal disorders, Willis challenged the traditional role for the womb in explaining hysterical disorders. As he had concluded with the former group, so he concluded that hysterical conditions were "primarily Convulsive" (that is, light spasms and milder convulsive movements, as well as classical convulsions) in nature and that they mainly stemmed from "the brain and nervous stock being affected" (p. 71). He saw the two types of illness as similar in the wide variety of vague symptoms, in the clinical descriptions having many symptoms in common, in the tendency to a fluctuating clinical picture, and in the tendency to imagine various recognized physical disorders (pp. 69–81). While he thought that hysteria was more common in women, he noted that it sometimes afflicted men (pp. 69, 74). He found hypochondriacal conditions to be more common in men, particularly those "of a melancholly temperament . . . about the height or midst of their Age"; but he reported that they also occurred in women, in whom they were "accompanied by a great many more Convulsive Distempers" and in whom it was more difficult to achieve a cure. Further, he thought that frequently in women "the Hysterical" was "joyned with the *Hypochondriacal* Passion" (p. 81).

Probably influenced by Willis's views, Thomas Sydenham (1624–1689) wrote about hypochondriacal disorders in ways reminiscent of Willis and brought these conditions into an even closer connection with hysterical disorders. In his *Epistolary Dissertation to Dr. Cole* (1681/1682) Sydenham devoted the latter part to a thoughtful presentation of "hysteric Diseases," which said a good deal about hypochondriacal conditions, some of it explicit, but much of it conveyed indirectly through his equating hypochondriacal conditions with hysterical conditions. After asserting that "hysteric disorders" made up a significant proportion of chronic illnesses, and noting as Willis had done that such illnesses also occurred in men, he stated that there was a considerable similarity between "hypochondriac complaints" and "those symptoms which seize hysteric women."[10] Then he proceeded with his discussion as though hypochondriacal disorders in men were essentially equivalent to hysterical disorders in women, at times making this underlying assumption explicit (*Works*, pp. 416, 422) and at times citing clinical examples of hypochondriacal conditions to illustrate the whole group (p. 421). In a letter written in 1687 he summed up his views in a sentence: "Your case is only that which in men we call Hypochondriacall, in women Hystericall proceeding from an Ataxy of Shatterednesse of the Animall Spirits";[11] and in *Processus Integri*, a work that appeared posthumously in 1693, he provided prescriptions for "that disorder which is called the hysteric passion in women, and the hypochondriac disease in men" (*Works*, p. 603). Using the same phrasing as Willis had earlier, he attributed both types of disorder to the same pathogenetic factors, namely, "irregular motions of the animal spirits." With these "irregular motions" as "the internal efficient causes," he wrote that "the *procatarctic* or *external cause* thereof are either violent motions of the body, or, more frequently, some great commotion of mind, occasioned by some sudden fit, either of anger, grief, terror, or the like passions" (p. 416).

Regarding the clinical manifestations, Sydenham described a wide variety of aches, pains, symptom complexes resembling other recognized disorders, and labile emotions. He specially emphasized "making great quantities of urine as clear as rock water" (p. 414). And he interwove references to melancholic and despairing tendencies. It is of particular interest that he presented the numerous clinical details and variations in such a way as to suggest that these disorders were not forms of madness, in contrast to the more traditional view of hypochondriacal conditions constituting a form of melancholia and thus of madness.

Friedrich Hoffmann (1660–1742) objected to this growing trend to equate hypochondriacal disorders with hysteria. As John Swan put it in his edition of Sydenham's works, "The *hysteric passion*, says *Hoffman*, is falsely held by several modern writers to be the same with the *hypocondriac disease*, or to differ only with respect to the sex, and not in nature; the latter only seizing men, and the former women"; and Swan himself clearly shared Hoffmann's view (pp. 408–409). Or, as stated in Hoffmann's system of medicine, "the hysterical and hypochondriacal disease have been erroneously confounded: though they have several symptoms in common, there are several also peculair to each."[12] With a terminology somewhat reminiscent of Willis's language of spasms and convulsions for these two disorders, he defined "the hysteric disease" as "a spasmodico-convulsive affection of the nervous system, arising from a disorder of the uterus," and "the hypochondriacal disease" as "a spasmodico-flatulent indisposition of the stomach and intestines, affecting, by consent, the whole nervous system, and disordering all the animal functions" (*System*, pp. 43, 60). Thus he restored the uterus to its traditional place in the pathogenesis of hysteria but did not return the spleen to its traditional role in explaining hypochondriacal disorders, indicating instead that "the true seat of the disease appears to be in the membranous and nervous coats of the alimentary canal" (p. 63). Like Willis and Sydenham, Hoffmann suggested that disordered functioning of the nervous system was a key factor in both types of illness, but he did not follow them in assigning it the primary role. As one might expect with the womb as the organ primarily affected, he portrayed hysteria as though it were limited to women, and yet he indicated that an occasional case occurred in pubertal boys and celibate adult men (pp. 53–54). But he thought that the hypochondriacal disease was "as common to women as to men, though in the former it is confounded very improperly with the hysteric passion" (p. 62).

Regarding the clinical description of the hypochondriacal disease, he reaffirmed the traditional picture of a wide variety of gastrointestinal symptoms and mentioned oppressive symptoms referable to the lungs and the heart, certain visual symptoms, a languid, weak state, and a "propensity to anger, fear, grief, despair; vain imaginations, loss of memory, failure of reason, turbulent sleep" (pp. 60–61). Despite this hint that mental derangement might be a feature of such disorders, the cases he cited were not instances of madness. And he apparently differentiated the hypochondriacal disease as a nonpsychotic condition from melancholia as a form of madness; he suggested that melancholia, and even "maniacal paroxysms," might follow on a hypochondriacal illness, somewhat like the series of disorders on a continuum of severity that Boerhaave outlined (p. 69).

Although significantly influenced by Sydenham in many matters, including the natural history of diseases, Herman Boerhaave (1668–1738) barely mentioned hysteria in his writings,[13] and he discussed hypochondriacal disorders quite separately in his sections on melancholia. This was the traditional place for such a discussion, but he gave these illnesses a different status there than had his predecessors.[14] He portrayed three categories of melancholia much like the three traditional types, but he discussed them more as though they were three degrees of severity within a single illness than as three types of melancholia affecting different sites. After describing the first degree of melancholic illness much like the traditional type that affected the entire mass of blood, he used the terms "an *Hypochondriac Disease*" and "the Spleen" in describing the second degree of this condition. Influenced by mechanical principles and employing the hydrodynamics of circulatory physiology, he saw each degree of these conditions as the result of a further slowing in the movement of the blood. He saw this particular condition as being the result of the pathogenic material growing "thicker, tougher, and [even] less moveable" and so being driven "into the Hypochondriac Vessels; . . . Here it will gradually stop, be accumulated and stagnate" (*Aphorisms*, p. 315). In addition to a worsening of the symptoms associated with the first stage in the sequence of melancholic diseases (p. 314), there was "a sense of a constant Weight, Anguish, Fulness, chiefly after eating and drinking; a difficult Breathing from the Bowels of the Abdomen being burthened," along with other symptoms associated with the hypochondriacal region (pp. 315–316). The third form or stage of melancholia was the outcome of still further worsening, and it was only then that Boerhaave cited disturbances in mental functioning (p. 317).

Like Hoffmann, Boerhaave largely abandoned the humoral theory, favored the newer mechanical explanations, and conceived of the hypochondriacal disease as resulting from a circulatory slowing; but his view that there was a slowing of blood flow and a stagnation in the hypochondriac region was reminiscent of the earlier obstruction-stagnation ideas that had explained hypochondriacal disorders in traditional humoral theory. And his theory was vasocentric in nature, in contrast to the emphasis placed on a dysfunction of the nervous system by Willis, Sydenham, and, to a lesser extent, Hoffmann.

On the basis of his *Aphorisms*, Boerhaave would not seem to have grouped hypochondriacal and hysterical conditions together, either as two types of convulsive diseases as Willis had indicated, or as essentially the same disease as Sydenham had maintained. Yet, on the basis of Gerard Van Swieten's (1700–1772) famous *Commentaries* on the *Aphorisms*, Boerhaave may have been closer to Sydenham's views than it might seem from his writings. In a way that suggests that he was extending the presentation in the *Aphorisms* in the spirit of his master's own views, Van Swieten several times endorsed Sydenham's ideas about hypochondriacal conditions. Citing Sydenham, he referred to "that wonderful and multiform disease, which is by Physicians usually termed an hysterical or hypochondriacal fit," indicated that it occurred in both women and men, described a clinical picture much like Sydenham's, and followed him again in stating that "the nature or essence of this disease consists in the nervous system being too easily moveable, and in spirits being less firm."[15] In his commentary on another of the aphorisms, Van Swieten identified two kinds of "hypochondriacal malady"; he referred to one as "the *hypochondriacal malady without an offending matter*" and indicated that the other was associated with "an offending matter" (*Commentaries,* 9:185–186; see also 11:101). Regarding the first kind, he cited Sydenham once again and clearly identified the condition as the one just mentioned above.

> Their whole nervous system [is] so very moveable or irritable, that even from slight passions of the mind they are troubled with great oppressions, convulsive motions, pains, and the like. . . . Such men have been usually termed hypochondriacal, as the women have been denominated hysterical, from the same malady; which in them has been wrongly ascribed to the womb. . . . This malady arises only from too great a tenderness, or irritability of the nerves, causing inordinate distributions of the spirits. (9:185–186)

And he mentioned Sydenham's allegedly pathognomonic sign of "the very copious flux of most thin and limpid, or watery urine" (p. 186). Then, in his commentary on still another aphorism, Van Swieten stated that "this is in reality the very same affection with the hysteric passion" (11:101). The second kind of "hypochondriacal malady" resulted from the slowing of blood flow and resultant thickening effect that caused a "gross atrabiliary matter" to collect "in the abdominal viscera" (9:185). This was the second degree or type in Boerhaave's sequence of melancholic disorders, "the hypochondriac malady, with matter atrabiliary, or biliary" (11:54).

During the early decades of the eighteenth century, in the same era in which Hoffmann and Boerhaave were each in his own way making use of Sydenham's ideas, and perhaps Willis's, a number of other authors gave special attention to the topic of hypochondriacal disorders. Influences from Willis and Sydenham were usually significant for them, whether they were following their views, disputing them, or merely taking them into account.

In 1711 Bernard de Mandeville (1670?–1733) published *A Treatise of the Hypochondriack and Hysterick Passions, Vulgarly call'd the Hypo in MEN and Vapours in WOMEN . . .* , arranged as an imaginary dialogue between a patient and a physician, and approached more as "Information to Patients" than "to teach other Practitioners."[16] Reflecting a clinical practice in which he had become somewhat of a specialist in these disorders, de Mandeville left us one of the earliest works on what we might term nonpsychotic mental disorders today and what were then receiving increasing attention as "nervous diseases."

From a beginning of "Heart-burning," "flushings in my Face" after meals, "Wind and sowre Belches," and "a clear insipid Water" coming off his stomach in the morning (*Treatise*, p. 7), the hypothetical patient gradually developed the profusion of symptoms that, by then, was considered characteristic of the hypochondriac disease. These included constipation, headaches, vertigo, various gastrointestinal symptoms, and, "when the Disease was got up into my Head," severe sleeplessness and frightening dreams (pp. 21–23). Over the years he became "an *Hypochondriacus Confirmatus*" who made his way from physician to physician. He emphasized that he was sorely troubled "both to Body and Mind," and he summed up his psychological distress by stating that "I am full of Doubts and Fears, I'm grown peevish and fretfull, irresolute, suspicious, every thing offends me, and a trifle puts me in a Passion" (p. 42). Although a reader of this work might wonder in view of some of the suspicions and extreme somatic worries, the patient carefully contrasted himself to those who suffered from melancholia, indicating that his reason was not impaired and thus that he was not mad (pp. 44–45).

In several places de Mandeville made it clear that he thought that "the *Hypochondriack* and *Hysterick* Passions proceed from the same Original" (p. 100). Then, regarding the pathogenesis of "Hypochondriacism" in particular, the theories of the ancients were intermittently ridiculed and eventually set aside, including the humoral theory and the traditional role of the spleen (pp. 78–79). He went on to "absolve" most of the other hypochondriac organs that had been "faulted" in various theories of such disorders, and he concluded that "the cause of Hypochondriack and Hysterick Diseases is in the Stomach" (pp. 81–82). He indicated some sympathy with those who had previously suggested a crucial role for the stomach, such as Diocles, Sylvius de le Boë, and Highmore, but he disagreed with their theories (pp. 79, 82). Then, despite his assertion that he did not make use of any hypotheses (p. 47), de Mandeville extended his view that the stomach was the primary site to include a disordered chylification or digestion as the essential pathogenic factor (p. 121). He criticized at considerable length Willis's views on the role of the spleen in normal functioning as well as in the pathogenesis of hypochondriacal conditions (pp. 82–100). Despite presenting Willis's views as though a dysfunctional spleen was the essential factor, he did seem aware that both Willis and Sydenham thought that irregular motions of the animal spirits were primary, and he registered disagreement with that notion as well (p. 102). Yet he still allowed a significant place for the nervous system in the pathogenesis of these disorders when he asserted that the animal spirits crucially affected "the

Stomachick Ferment" toward either health or hypochondriac disorders; a deficiency of these spirits was basic to both hypochondriacal and hysterical illnesses (pp. 134–136).

In the process of criticizing Willis, de Mandeville satirically questioned the idea that the spleen might serve to sharpen the animal spirits and thus, where it was functioning well, account for superior mental abilities; and he contrasted such a view with the popular use of "the word Spleen in its Figurative Sense . . . to express Passion, Malice, Rancour, and a Perversly Satyrical Temper, rather than Sharpness and Sagacity . . . for being Touchy, Waspish, and Unsociable, always denoting a Vice, and not a Virtue of the Mind" (p. 94). But he then agreed that there was merit in denominating "the Passio Hypochondriaca . . . the Disease of the Learned," although without any place for the spleen in the reasons why (pp. 94–95).

When it came to the "Procatartik" [meaning predisposing, in this instance] causes of the disease, he specially emphasized "immoderate Exercise of the Brain, and Excess of *Venery*" through their tendency to deplete the animal spirits (pp. 142–146). As to the "Concomitant" or accessory causes, he mentioned "Immoderate Grief, Cares, Troubles, and Disappointments," as well as "the leaning the Stomach and *Praecordia* against large Books, Desks, and Tables" that might occur with a scholar (p. 150).

In summing up toward the end of the book, the author mentioned two other features of these disorders that are of interest. First, he emphasized the variability of the clinical picture: "I never saw yet two Hypochondriacal Cases exactly alike" (p. 258). Second, he said that he generally observed that "People troubled with either *Hypo*, or *Vapours*, to a considerable degree, never think others as bad as themselves, and yet are always wonderfully offended, if their own Distemper be any ways slighted" (p. 264).

Richard Blackmore (1653–1729) was another who wrote an important treatise on "the Spleen and Vapours: or, Hypochondriacal and Hysterical Affections" and considered them "one and the same under different Denominations."[17] For him, too, they were essentially "nervous diseases." He prefaced his clinical description of "the Spleen" with the statement that "this *Proteus*, this Posture-Disease, can assume the Shape and Figure, and the Part of many others of different Denominations" (*Treatise*, p. 16). He noted that "this Disease . . . is attended with a long Train of Complaints, and a sad Variety of Sufferings" (pp. 16–17).

> First, a deprav'd Disposition of the Stomach, and an impair'd digestive Faculty, . . . great Oppressions and grievous Pain of the Stomach; which likewise is sometimes so fill'd and distended with Storms of Hypocondriacal Winds, that this Receptacle, and the inferior neighbouring Parts, seem a dark and troubled Region of animal Meteors and Exhalations, where opposite

Steams and rarify'd Juices contending for Dominion, maintain continual War. These Ferments and flatulent Effluvia, while they infest the Cavity of the Stomach and Colon, to the great Disturbance and Suffering of the Patient, strive and struggle for Vent with great Noise, like Vapours and Reeks imprison'd in Caverns under ground: hence proceed those tumultuous Belchings and loud Eructations that accompany this Contention. (p. 17)

He then described numerous "terrible Disorders in the Colon" and added that "sometimes a great Agitation is perceived in the Cavity of the Abdomen, in the Mesentery, and the Neighbouring Parts" (p. 19). He mentioned various symptoms and fears referable to the Heart, including "Palpitation and Trembling, Faintness and Sinking of Spirit" (pp. 20–21). Then there were symptoms in the chest, "cold clammy Sweats in their Legs and Thighs," and various symptoms of muscular distress (pp. 21–23). "But the Symptoms that accompany this Distemper in the Head, are more various and surprising"— including pains, aches, vertigo, dizziness, dullness and melancholy, drowsiness or insomnia, and "sometimes tumultuous, sad and monstrous Dreams" (p. 23). To these he added "many besides that affect the Mind, and disturb the superior commanding powers"—"at times forgetful and unreflecting"; "very various and changeable in their Judgment, and unsteady in their Conceptions of Persons and Things"; "a constant Diffidence and groundless Suspicion of all Men, a captious Inclination to take things amiss"; an "unfortunate Inconstancy and Fluctuation of their Judgment" and resolve; and "no less Diversity and Inconstancy in their Temper and Passions" (pp. 24–27). Blackmore concluded by saying, "not that all these are found in every Individual afflicted with this Evil, or in so high a degree, as what has been described; but they are all found in some measure in one or other Branch of the Species" (p. 27).

Considering who might be particularly prone to these disturbances, he said: "Hypocondriacal Men are, for the most part, meagre, thin, and unmuscular; of a pale, almost livid, and saturnine Complexion, and a dark, suspicious and severe Aspect; nor unlike to this is their Temperament and Disposition, such Persons being very scrupulous, touchy, humoursome, and hard to please: their Pulse is usually weak, and below the Standard of Nature in other Men, and often too swift, like that in a hectick Fever" (p. 15). He also maintained that "the Natives of this Island were specially prone to these disorders" to the extent that he termed it "the *English* Spleen" (pp. iii–vi).

As to how "Hypocondriacal Sufferings" should be explained, Blackmore disagreed with any idea that the spleen had a significant role in their pathogenesis, including even the auxiliary role assigned to it by Willis (pp. 1–2, 13–14). He also disagreed with Highmore's idea that the basic problem was in the stomach (p. 13). Instead he indicated explicitly that he was following Willis and Sydenham in holding the view that such disorders stemmed from "the irregular and disturbed Motions of the Spirits, and the irritable Disposition of the Nerves" (pp. 11–12). Elaborating on this, he stated:

> A tender and delicate Constitution of the Nervous System, and an inordinate Fineness and Activity of their Inmates, the Animal Spirits being first supposed, it may be easily conceived how these volatile Guests may, by various Impressions made upon them, be driven into disorderly Motions and convulsive Spasms and Contractions in any Bowel or Part of the Body: for instance, if they are disturbed or agitated by any noxious Humours lodged in the Brain, or by any sudden and violent Impressions made upon them by outward, surprizing Objects; for it often happens, that by the relation of unwelcome News, sad Accidents, sudden Outcry, or the very opening of a Door, or disagreeable and frightful Ideas presented to the Fancy or Imagination, when the Patient is awake or asleep, the Spirits are stimulated, and impelled into confused Motions, and their Ranks and Connexion being broken or ruffled, they produce the Symptoms before enumerated belonging to the Head; and if their Motion is continued and communicated to the inferior Parts, through which these active Instruments of Sense and Motion are dispersed, it occasions the Complaints and hurtful Sensations that are perceived in those Organs, such as short-breathing in the Chest, Palpitation of the Heart, Trepidation, or Trembling of the Limbs, and a Profusion of pale Water from the Kidneys.
>
> But the Spirits are more frequently vexed and provoked by some noxious and peccant Juices, either austere, sowre, or bilious, in an adust Degree, harbouring in the Bowels, or other Repositories in the Body, which prick the Nerves and provoke the Spirits communicated to those Parts, and so drive them into involuntary convulsive Agitations. (pp. 30–31)

And Blackmore made it clear that he so conceived of the nerves and animal spirits being disordered in "Hypochondriacal, as well as Hysterick Patients" (p. 52).

In comparing the "Hypochondriack Affections" with melancholia, he asserted that they were closely related, and that "indeed the Limits and Partitions that bound and discriminate the highest Hypochondriack and Hysterick Disorders, and Melancholy, Lunacy, and Phrenzy, are so nice, that it is not easy to distinguish them, and set the Boundaries where one ends, and the other begins (pp. 154, 163–164). But he described melancholia as the more serious disorder, as tending more to be a chronic condition, as involving more of a tendency to dwell on the "same Set of Objects," and as more consistently entailing "Sadness, Dejection, and Fear" (pp. 157, 164). Furthermore, it involved more serious dysfunctions of the imagination and the reason, including frank delusions, and it was essentially a form of madness (pp. 161–162, 165–166).

Another significant author on these various "nervous diseases" was Nicholas Robinson (1697–1775), who in 1729 published an influential volume on "the Spleen, Vapours, and Hypochondriack Melancholy." He addressed the close connections thought to exist between these three conditions as follows and briefly outlined the clinical picture at the same time:

> From the best and nicest Observations I have been able to make, I cannot discover any other Difference between the Spleen and Hypochondriack Melancholy, than that the Hip. is the Spleen improv'd on the Constitution, through a longer Continuance of the Disease: The Vapours are so nearly related to the Spleen, that whatever can, with any Propriety, be alleg'd of the one; with a very little Variation, may be inferr'd of the other. Both Men and Women, subject to the foregoing Disorders, are liable to be affected with a Lowness of Spirits; both are subject to generate Wind, to a costive Body; both also are incident to be affected with a sudden Failure of the Senses, a casual Absence of Reason; whereby the regular State of the Animal Œconomy is sometimes greatly interrupted: So that these Disorders receive their different Natures from their affecting different Sexes; for what the Vapours are in Women, that the Spleen is in Men, and if the Vapours are subject to Histerick Fits, the Spleen is sometimes incident to be affected with the Epilepsy, or at least Disorders of the Convulsive kind.[18]

The close kinship of the vapors in women and the spleen in men was much like Sydenham's views, and the parallel between them in terms of fits and convulsions was reminiscent of Willis. Relating the spleen and hypochondriacal melancholia to each other on a continuum of severity reflected an emerging trend influenced by Boerhaave, although he had used "the spleen" and "the hypochondriac disease" as synonyms to refer to hypochondriacal melancholia as a disorder short of the madness associated with melancholia, which was, in turn, the next stage of severity. Robinson then added that, "as the Hypochondriack Melancholy is only the Progress of the Spleen and Vapours, so melancholy Madness is only the Hyp. improv'd upon the Constitution from Length of Time, and a Continuance of the Disease; which is the Reason why . . . I only handle it as the Progress of the Symptoms, when they degenerate into melancholy Madness" (p. 227). Following Boerhaave closely in each regard, he had viewed hypochondriacal melancholia as short of madness; he here indicated that melancholia was a form of madness and the next stage on a continuum of severity; and he later referred to mania as still a further stage of worsening (p. 241).

Robinson described "the Spleen" in men at considerable length, first noting early symptoms such as complaints of declining health, "the Constitution of the Mind . . . dull, heavy, and uneasy," yawning, "the Complexion . . . wan, pale," and loss of appetite (pp. 203–204). "To these Symptoms succeed a Lowness of Spirits, accompany'd with a Faintness and Dizziness of the Head"; indigestion led to "Crudities, that being chang'd into Wind, furnish out the greatest Part of Splenetick Symptoms," which included the passing of such wind up and down the gastrointestinal system; weakness, discomfort in the hypochondriac region, and various signs of local distress elsewhere were mentioned; disturbed sleep might occur, and various "impertinent and groundless Fears, that render Life not only uneasy to themselves, but greatly perplexing to all their Friends about them" (pp. 204–209). "And under lesser Disturbances of the Imagination, they are continually complaining of their unhappy State of Life, oppress'd and overborn with Calamities and Afflictions; no Bodies Pains are equal to their Pains; none knows what they feel and suffer" (pp. 209–210). With some additions, the symptoms were much the same for "the Vapours" in women (pp. 211–225). When it came to "Hypochondriack Melancholy," the various bodily symptoms were worsened, and the psychological symptoms were more extensive as well as severer (pp. 226–233).

Strongly influenced by Newton and the mechanical philosophy, Robinson endeavored to account for normal psychological functions and psychological disorders in mechanical terms as reflections of bodily events; he presented his book as one "Wherein all the Decays of the Nerves, and Lownesses of the Spirits, are mechanically Accounted for" (title page). He wrote of a refined material substance, "a most subtle fine Animal Aether, of different Elasticities, agreeable to the different Springynesses of the nervous Fibres" (p. 79). He conceived of this aether as the "instrument" that the mind employed to excite the passions, and as the "medium" it used to alter the "Vibrations of the Nerves" and influence other bodily activities (pp. 78–79). The "Force or Elasticity in the Animal Aether" served "to support the Faculties, balance the Mind, and keep the Passions steady" (p. 80). He thought of the brain and the nerves as being composed of "*Machinulae* . . . little small corpuscles of Matter"; and he developed a scheme that involved greater and lesser distances between these particles, lesser and greater tensions in the fibres as the respective results, and, again respectively, slower motions with duller functioning and speeded up motions with overstimulated functioning (pp. 18, 102–105). As Willis and Sydenham had written of "irregular motions of the animal spirits," so Robinson then proceeded to use the idea of "irregular Motions of the Nerves" with "Uneasiness and Pain . . . in Proportion to the Tension of the Fibres" (pp. 256–257). He conceived of many of the symptoms of "the Spleen, Vapours, and Hypochondriack Melancholy" as resulting from the "Machinulae" coming to be "at too great a Distance from each other" with a resultant pathological decrease in the natural tension of the nerves and muscles, and thus weariness, weakness, disinclination to activity, and dejection (pp. 258–259). In contrast, "the Fits or Paroxysms" and other symptoms reflecting excessive activity stemmed from the "Machinulae" being too close together and the tensions too great (pp. 259–262). For him, "Every Change of the Mind . . . indicates a Change in the Bodily Organs" (pp. 178–179).

Robinson took some pains to establish the idea that "the Spleen, Vapours, etc. are real Diseases, and no Ways depending on the imaginary Whims of Fancy" (pp. 185–188, 192). At the same time, he acknowledged the question that "if our Perceptions be such certain Indications of the Existence of a real Affection in the Body, how comes the Patient so often mistaken in judging of the Danger attending these Perceptions in this Disease" (pp. 182–183). He then answered this by remarking that "the Perception of Pain or Uneasiness" always reflected an actual bodily disorder, but the patient's judgment might be faulty in assessing the degree of danger (pp. 182–184).

Influenced by his own case as well as the trends of the times, George Cheyne (1671–1743) published *The English Malady* in 1733, a treatise on the "Spleen, Vapours, Lowness of Spirits, Hypochondriacal, and Hysterical Distempers, etc." His title is reminiscent of Blackmore's "the *English* Spleen," and "Nervous Diseases" in his subtitle clearly reflects the developing emphasis on "nervous disorders" that stemmed from the works of Willis and Sydenham.

In outlining the clinical picture, Cheyne took some pains to point out that "the *Spleen* or *Vapours*" were terms often used rather loosely to refer to "*All Lowness of Spirits, Swelling of the Stomach, frequent Eructation, Noise in the Bowels or Ears, frequent Yawning, Inappetency, Restlessness, Inquietude, Fidgeting, Anxiety, Peevishness, Discontent, Melancholy, Grief, Vexation, Ill-Humour, Inconstancy, lethargick* or *watchful Disorders*, in short, every Symptom, not already classed under some particular limited Distemper."[19] He stated that any of these various symptoms might be caused by the "Vapours" and be "*Symptomatick*" of some other, well-established disease; or some cluster of such symptoms might themselves constitute the disease, that is, they might constitute a "genuine, simple, and original" case of the "*Spleen*" or "*Vapours*" (*English Malady*, pp. 194–195). He went on to say:

> To enumerate all the almost infinite Symptoms, Degrees, and Kinds of *Vapours* is impossible, and perhaps very little to the Purpose. In general, when the Symptoms are *many, various*, changeable, shifting from one Place to another, and imitating the *Symptoms* of almost every other Distemper. . . . Then they may be properly called *Vapours;* for Distinction's Sake, I will divide them into three Degrees, though the Reader is neither here to expect Accuracy nor Certainty, that may be depended upon, in such a *Proteus-like* Distemper. (pp. 195–196)

He thought of "the *first Degree*" as encompassing those conditions for which the names "Vapours" and "Spleen" should ordinarily be reserved.

> The Symptoms then, besides Lowness of Spirits, are *Wind, Belching, Yawning, Heart-burning, Croaking of the Bowels, . . .* a *Pain* in the *Pit of the Stomach . . .* and sometimes there is an *Inflation . . .* in the Stomach to be seen, especially in the *Sex;* a *Coldness* or *Chilliness* upon the Extremities and sometimes

Flushing . . . and Burning in the Hands and Feet, *Cold damp Sweats, Faintings*, and Sickness . . . the Stools being sometimes very *costive*, sometimes *loose* and slimy, a *Feeling* like that of *cold Water* poured over several Parts of the Body, *Head-Aches* either behind or over the Eyes, . . . a *Noise* . . . in the Ears; *Yawning*, and *Stretching*, and sometimes a Drowsiness or *Lethargy*, at other times *Watching* and Restlessness. . . . Some have but a few of these *Symptoms*, and some all of them, and a great many more. (pp. 197–198)

And he also included Sydenham's sign, noting that "One of the most *dispiriting* Symptoms of this Distemper, and one of the most certain Signs of it, is a frequent Discharge of thin, limpid, pale Water, by *Urine*" (pp. 210–211). He went on to say that "the *second* Stage of this Distemper" was

attended with all these Symptoms, in a much higher and more eminent Degree, and some new ones . . . such as are instead of Lowness of Spirits: a deep and fixed *Melancholy, wandering* and *delusory Images* on the Brain, and *Instability* and *Unsettledness* in all the intellectual Operations, *Loss of Memory, Despondency, Horror* and *Despair*, a *Vertigo, Giddiness* or *Staggering, Vomitings* of *Yellow, Green,* or *Black Choler:* sometimes unaccountable Fits of *Laughing*, apparent *Joy, Leaping* and *dancing;* at other Times, of *Crying, Grief* and *Anguish;* and these generally terminate in *Hypochondriacal* or *Hysterical Fits* (I mean *Convulsive* ones) and *Faintings*, which leave a Drowsiness, *Lethargy*, and extream Lowness of Spirits for some Time afterwards. (p. 199)

He then mentioned briefly "the *third* State . . . which is generally some *mortal* and incurable Distemper, such as *Dropsy, Black Jaundice, Consumption, Palsy, Epilepsy,* or *Apoplexy*, etc." (p. 200).

Although at times Cheyne seemed to suggest that all three of these degrees of illness came under the rubric *Spleen* or *Vapours*, his use of these terms was primarily for the first stage; and his book was essentially devoted to the disorders of that stage which were by then well established as *the Spleen, the Vapours,* or *hypochondriacal melancholia* and were not usually thought of as instances of madness, in contrast to melancholia proper, which was still a form of madness. Moreover, almost all the cases that he outlined, including his own, were instances of this milder, nonpsychotic form of "nervous disorder," and he explicitly concerned himself with differentiating them from madness (pp. 260–261). Also, Cheyne's "Spleen" or "Vapours" was somewhat reminiscent of Boerhaave's hypochondriacal melancholia in that each involved dejection, anxiety, and a protean complex of physical complaints; none of them was described in a way that suggested a form of madness; and each was conceived of within a sequence of stages as a milder type that might worsen and develop into classical melancholia, a form of madness.

When it came to explaining these various disorders, Cheyne was much influenced by Newton as he strove to account for the normal and the abnormal in mechanical terms. He conceived of the nerves as solid and possessed of an "elastick Force" and as having "innate Mechanick Powers" that allowed them to serve sensation and motion by transmitting vibrations or undulations; and he thought it likely that the Newtonian aether played a crucial role (pp. 4–5, 63–64, 70–72, 75–76, 87–89). It was against this background that he then considered the pathogenesis of these "nervous disorders." Their various symptoms "will naturally and readily be deduced from too thick and glewy or sharp Juices, some great Bowel spoil'd, or strong Obstructions form'd, and the regorging Fluids thereby brought on, struggling and labouring under the *Animal Functions*, in relaxed feeble, and unelastick Solids" (p. 193). Rather than the "free Spirits" or "strong Spirits, and firm fibres" of sound nervous function and good health, these nervous disorders involved "Lowness of Spirits" or being "dispirited by Weakness of Nerves" (pp. 1, 193–195). The nerves in such conditions were weak and too "loose and relaxed," notions akin to the "*Laxum* . . . of the antient *Methodists*" (p. 227).

> When by the mentioned Circumstances, all these [that is, the Animal Functions] become forced, labour'd, and uneasy, the Symptoms we commonly ascribe to the *Spleen*, must necessarily arise: even tho' they be attended with no really form'd Disease, or no noble Organ entirely spoil'd; and the true Reason of the Multiplicity, Variety, and Inconstancy of these Symptoms, is the vast Multitude of the Combinations possible, of these natural Functions, every one of which makes a new *Symptom*, and whose uniform, equable Performance is so necessary to Health. (p. 193)

As these several examples illustrate, with the various writings on "nervous disorders" during the first half of the eighteenth century hypochondriasis continued to entail sadness, dejection, or "lowness of spirits" in most instances, although sometimes this was nearly lost in the plethora of other symptoms included in the descriptive accounts. Usually such disorders were not cases of madness, and thus they were differentiated from melancholia, which also entailed sadness or dejection but was a form of madness. And it had become common to relate hypochondriasis as the milder disorder to melancholia as the severer disorder on a Boerhaavian continuum of increasing severity.

In 1764 Robert Whytt (1714–1766) wrote about those disorders that "have been treated of by authors, under the names of Flatulent, Spasmodic, Hypochondriac, or Hysteric," and that had come to be called "Nervous." In using this latter term he commented, "Which appellation having been commonly given to many symptoms seemingly different, and very obscure in their nature, has often made it to be said, that physicians have bestowed the character of *nervous*, on all those disorders whose nature and causes they were ignorant of"; but, while acknowledging that there were "few disorders which may not, in a large sense, be called *nervous*," he proposed only "to treat of those disorders which in a *peculiar* sense deserve the name of *nervous*, in so far as they are, in a great measure, owing to an uncommon delicacy or unnatural sensibility of the nerves, and are therefore observed chiefly to affect persons of such a constitution."[20] Although Whytt was following a path well trodden by such as De Mandeville, Blackmore, Robinson, and Cheyne, his own presentation probably had a greater impact than any since those of Willis and Sydenham.

Regarding clinical features, he prefaced his observations as follows:

> As the sagacious Sydenham has justly observed, that the shapes of proteus, or the colours of the chamaeleon, are not more numerous and inconstant, than the variations of the hypochondriac and hysteric disease; so those morbid symptoms which have been commonly called *nervous*, are so many, so various, and so irregular, that it would be extremely hard, either rightly to describe, or fully to enumerate them. They imitate the symptoms of almost all other diseases. (*Works*, p. 530)

Then he proceeded to a listing of "the most common and remarkable" of the many symptoms which might occur, including "wind in the stomach and intestines, heart-burning" and numerous other symptoms referable to the stomach and other abdominal organs; "an uneasy, though not painful sensation about the stomach, attended with low spirits, anxiety, and sometimes great timidity"; flushings and chills; shifting muscular pains; "cramps, or convulsive motions of the muscles" or even "a general convulsion"; "long faintings"; "palpitations, or trembling of the heart"; a variable pulse, occasional breathing difficulties, "yawning, the hiccup, frequent sighings, and a sense of suffocation"; "fits of crying, and convulsive laughing"; giddiness, pains in the head, occasional disturbances of sight, sound or smell; "obstinate watchings, attended sometimes with an uneasiness which is not to be described, but which is lessened by getting out of bed; disturbed sleep, frightful dreams, the night-mare; sometimes a drowsiness, and too great inclination to sleep; fear, peevishness, sadness, despair, at other times high spirits; wandering thoughts, impaired memory, ridiculous fancies; strange persuasions of their labouring under diseases of which they are quite free; and imagining their complaints to be as dangerous as they find them troublesome; they are often angry with those who would convince them of their mistake" (pp. 530–532).

After these details, he stated that the patients who were liable to these disorders

> may be distinguished into three classes:
> 1. Such as, though usually in good health, are yet, on account of an uncommon delicacy of their nervous system, apt to be often affected with violent tremors, palpitations, faintings, and convulsive fits, from fear, grief, surprise, or other passions; and from whatever greatly irritates or disagreeably affects any of the more sensible parts of the body.

2. Such as, besides being liable to the above disorders from the same causes, are almost always, more or less, troubled with indigestion, flatulence in the stomach and bowels, a lump in the throat, the *clavus hystericus*, giddiness, flying pains in the head, and a sense of cold in its back part, frequent sighings, palpitations, inquietude, fits of salivation, or pale urine, etc.

3. Such as, from a less delicate feeling or mobility of their nervous system in general, are scarce ever affected with violent palpitations, faintings, or convulsive motions, from fear, grief, surprise, or other passions; but, on account of a disordered state of the nerves of the stomach and bowels, are seldom free from complaints of indigestion, belching, flatulence, want of appetite, or too great craving, costiveness, or looseness, flushings, giddiness, oppression or faintness about the *praecordia*, low spirits, disagreeable thoughts, watching or disturbed sleep, etc.

The complaints of the first of the above classes may be called *simply nervous;* those of the second, in compliance with custom, may be said to be *hysteric,* and those of the third, *hypochondriac.* (pp. 532–533)

As had most recent writers except "the learned Hoffmann," Whytt then indicated that he deemed the hypochondriac and the hysteric disorders, commonly associated with men and women, respectively, to be essentially the same disease (p. 533). He also commented that patients who had "been long afflicted" with such conditions "sometimes fall into melancholy, madness" and other more serious diseases (p. 532). Here, and elsewhere, he made it clear that hypochondriasis was not a form of madness and was to be differentiated from melancholia.

With his important contributions to neurology and neurophysiology as a background, Whytt outlined the coordinating role of the nervous system, including the role of the nerves in conveying sensory messages ("the sensibility of the nerves") and in causing reaction or distress in bodily parts distant from a site of primary activity or pathology ("the sympathy of the nerves") (preface, pp. 489–524). He then conceived of hypochondriac and hysteric disorders as "nervous" in that they "proceed, in a great measure, from a weak or unnatural constitution of the nerves" (pp. 529–530). He elaborated on this by outlining two main categories of "predisposing causes." First, "a too great delicacy and sensibility of the whole nervous system," which "may be either natural, that is, an original defect in the constitution, or produced by such diseases, or irregularity in living, as weaken the whole body, especially the nerves" (p. 537). Second, "there is often an uncommon weakness or delicacy, or an unnatural or depraved feeling in various parts of the body, which exposes certain persons to violent, and sometimes very extraordinary affections, from causes which would scarce produce any disturbance in people of a sound constitution" (p. 543). Turning to precipitating causes, he described three "general occasional Causes": (1) "Some morbid matter bred in the blood"; (2) "The diminution or retention of some accustomed evacuation"; (3) "The want of a sufficient quantity of blood, or of blood of a proper density" (p. 551). And then he listed six "particular occasional Causes": (1) "Wind"; (2) "A tough phlegm"; (3) "Worms" [each of these three, "in the stomach and bowels"]; (4) "Aliments improper in their quantity or quality"; (5) "Scirrhous or other obstructions in the *viscera* of the lower belly"; (6) "Violent affections of the mind" (p. 570).

With William Cullen (1710–1790) the tradition of "nervous disorders" was extended, and the term *neurosis* was introduced as the generic name for such conditions. He developed an extensive nosological system in which he arranged diseases into four *Classes*, one of which was Nervous Disorders or Neuroses. This class was, in turn, divided into four *Orders:* Comata (deprivations of voluntary motion), Adynamiae (deprivations of involuntary motions, whether vital or natural), Spasmodic Affections (irregular motions of the muscles), and Vesaniae (disorders of the intellectual functions). In this scheme he reasserted the older tradition that hypochondriasis and hysteria were quite separate diseases, and this became the common view once again. Each was considered to belong to the large class of diseases that he termed "Neuroses," but hysteria was categorized among the Spasmodic Affections and hypochondriasis among the Adynamiae. Although he acknowledged some similarities, he carefully differentiated these two disorders, commenting that hysteria had been "improperly considered by physicians as the same with some other diseases, and particularly with hypochondriasis."[21] He also noted that there had been an unfortunate tendency to consider almost any "nervous symptoms" as attributable to one or the other of these two conditions (*First Lines*, p. 471).

On the other hand, he stayed with another eighteenth-century opinion when he carefully differentiated hypochondriasis from melancholia. He noted that both diseases tended to occur in persons of a melancholic temperament but that dyspeptic symptoms would usually be present in hypochondriasis and absent in melancholia, and "mistaken judgment" or "false imagination" was restricted to "the state of the person's own health" in hypochondriasis and either not so restricted or "groundless and absurd" in melancholia (pp. 495–496). And he categorized melancholia as a type of madness or insanity, while judging hypochondriasis, for all its troubled state of mind, not to be a form of madness (pp. 385–392, 492–499).

As he proceeded to describe "Hypochondriasis, or the Hypochondriac Affection, Commonly Called Vapors, or Low Spirits," Cullen put it as follows:

> In certain persons there is a state of mind distinguished by a concurrence of the following circumstances: A languor, listlessness, or want of resolution and activity with respect to all undertakings; a disposition to seriousness, sadness and

timidity; as to all future events, an apprehension of the worst or most unhappy state of them; and therefore, often upon slight grounds, an apprehension of great evil. Such persons are particularly attentive to the state of their own health, to even the smallest change of feeling in their bodies; and from any unusual feeling, perhaps of the slightest kind, they apprehend great danger, and even death itself. In respect to all these feelings and apprehensions, there is commonly the most obstinate belief and persuasion. (p. 385)

He took note of the long-standing practice of using *"Low Spirits"* and *"Vapors"* as synonyms for hypochondriasis and, after acknowledging that "the term *Vapors"* was "founded on a false theory," begged leave to employ it nonetheless. Then, using "vapors" and "dyspepsia" as general terms for two groups of symptoms, the former for the dejected, weakened, and worried state just outlined and the latter for a complex of indigestion and various other gastrointestinal symptoms, he proceeded to differentiate *Hypochondriasis* the disease from *Dyspepsia* the disease, the latter having been dealt with at length in the previous chapter as another disorder belonging to the class Adynamiae. The combination of vapors with dyspepsia "in young persons of both sexes, in persons of a sanguine temperament, and of a lax and flaccid habit" was what constituted *Dyspepsia* the disease; and the combination of vapors with dyspepsia "in elderly persons of both sexes, of a melancholic temperament, and of a firm and rigid habit" was what constituted *Hypochondriasis* the disease. Dyspepsia was more a "primary and topical affection of the stomach" with the dejected, weakened, and worried features as sympathetic or secondary symptoms; and hypochondriasis was a pathological "turn of mind peculiar to the [melancholic] temperament" with the symptoms of digestive upset as secondary (p. 386). Further, he noted that "the affection of the mind is commonly different in the two diseases. In dyspepsia, it is often languor and timidity only, easily dispelled; while, in hypochondriasis, it is generally the gloomy and rivetted apprehension of evil" (p. 387).

In the background of Cullen's views on hypochondriasis were his neural explanations involving a system of forces, solid nerves, and a nerve fluid reflecting elements of both Haller's physiology and Newton's speculative mechanics for the nervous system.[22] This fluid was inherent in the nerves and mediated the transmission of oscillatory or vibratory motions; and he conceived of it as one of a group of imperceptible and imponderable fluids that were modifications of Newton's aether.[23] On these foundations he constructed a theory of disease in which the ideas of "excitement" and "collapse" were used in the discussion of both normal and abnormal states. He conceived of excitement and collapse as states of increased and decreased mobility of the nervous power or nervous fluid in the brain whose effects were felt throughout the nervous system.[24] The "collapse" end of the spectrum referred to conditions ranging from the normal state of sleeping to pathological extremes such as syncope and death, and included the various forms of dejected states such as hypochondriasis and melancholia. Regarding hypochondriasis in particular, he stated that "the state of the mind which attends, and especially distinguishes hypochondriasis, is the effect of that same rigidity of the solids, torpor of the nervous power, and peculiar balance between the arterial and venous systems which occur in advanced life, and which at all times take place more or less in melancholic temperaments" (*First Lines*, p. 387).

The reestablishment of the hypochondriac affection and the hysteric affection as separate disorders was hinted at in the nosological contributions of Sauvages and was argued in some detail by Cullen; this then became the accepted view once more and continued as such into the modern era. However, the relationship of hypochondriac disorders to melancholia was more problematic. The trend through the various eighteenth-century writings on "nervous disorders" had been to consider hypochondriac conditions as tending to occur in persons of a melancholic temperament (as was the case with melancholia), as being associated with dejection, worry, and weakness (much like melancholia), and yet as needing to be differentiated from melancholia. Although the occasional medical author thought of hypochondriac disorders as including instances of melancholic madness, most of the time these disorders were differentiated, as not being instances of madness, from melancholia as one of the forms of madness. But this picture was confounded at times by certain colloquial usages. In addition to the tendency to employ the term *melancholy* loosely for any sort of dejected state, sometimes melancholy was used as a synonym for hypochondriasis without implying madness, and at other times hypochondriasis was referred to as madness; but these were contrary to usual medical usage. For the most part such colloquial practices were akin to the modern casualness often evidenced in the use of the terms *depression* and *crazy*.

The problems of conceiving of and categorizing hypochondriacal disorders were approached in still another way by Thomas Arnold (1742–1816), a student of Cullen's, in his *Observations on . . . Insanity* toward the end of the century. Although he thought of such conditions as quite distinct from melancholia, he carefully differentiated an insane form of hypochondriasis from a noninsane form.

In contrast to Cullen and many other eighteenth-century authorities, he presented a section on "hypochondriacal insanity" unchanged from the original edition of 1782–1786 to the second edition of 1806.

> In HYPOCHONDRIACAL INSANITY the patient is for ever in distress about his own state of health, has a variety of disagreeable, and sometimes painful feelings, to which he is ever anxiously attentive, and from which he can rarely divert his

thoughts, either to business, or amusement: and though the causes of these disagreeable, and painful feelings, are usually obstinate, and sometimes incurable, yet his fear, anxiety, and conceits, are such as at best indicate an irrational, and insane imbecility of mind; and often lead him to fancy himself threatened, or wasting, with dreadful diseases, which exist only in his distressed imagination.

Some, when the disease has gained ground, and become much exasperated; when unremitted brooding over their own unhappy state, and miserable apprehensions, has produced an habitual gloom and dejection of mind; are afflicted with a constant impression of melancholy, which neither business nor amusement can obliterate, which no efforts, of themselves, or their friends, can overcome; which yet they can ascribe to no particular cause, and which seems to have no fixed, or determinate object; and, while they scarcely can describe, or even distinguish, what it is that distresses them, experience a perpetual depression of spirits, a *taedium vitae*, which destroys all power of enjoyment, and often, amidst a profusion of every earthly blessing, renders life an insupportable burden, from which death alone affords any prospect of relief.

In proportion as this gloom continues, and increases, life becomes daily more and more intolerable; and they complain of a frequent intrusion of momentary temptations to destroy themselves, and to quit a wretched state of being, in which they not only no longer have the smallest hope of happiness, but experience an hourly increase of the most grievous present misery, and still more grievous future apprehensions.—Such temptations recur with more frequency, and violence, as the disorder acquires strength; and too often end in actual suicide.[25]

To this he added that, commonly but not universally, the condition was "accompanied with flatulency, and such other symptoms of a disordered state of the stomach and bowels, as are commonly esteemed by medical writers, both ancient and modern, to be inseparable companions of what they call *melancholia hypochondriaca*, or *hypochondriac melancholy*" (*Observations*, 1:177). But he thought that Sydenham had been quite mistaken "in confounding it with the hysterical disease, from which it appears to be perfectly distinct" (p. 180).

In dealing with his critics in the preface to his second edition, Arnold provided some useful further thoughts on hypochondriacal conditions. He reaffirmed his view that there was a species of insanity fairly termed "hypochondriacal insanity" and made it clear that this ailment was essentially the same as the form of melancholia referred to as *melancholia hypochondriaca* by so many earlier writers (pp. xxv–xxvi). Then he carefully distinguished another type of hypochondriacal condition that he did not consider to be a form of madness. He called it "simple hypochondriasis, unaccompanied with insanity" (p. xxxiii).

The lower degrees of hypochondriasis, before erroneous notions are become singularly absurd, invariable, and intense, I do not consider as coming under the character, and denomination, of insanity; but merely as being afflictive bodily disorders, which powerfully affect, and are peculiarly apt to discompose, and derange, the mind. To these I leave their ancient, and very general name, of *morbus hypochondriacus*, or *malum hypochondriacum*, or, as it has been termed by modern writers, *hypochondriasis*. (p. xxvi)

Belonging with this milder disorder were such symptoms as "indigestion, wind, pain and noise in the bowels, acid eructation, and a variety of distressful feelings, acute pains, debility, and even low spirits and dejection of mind" (p. xxvii). And the relationship of this condition to hypochondriacal insanity was no more than "that of an attendant symptom, and occasional cause" (pp. xxvii–xxviii). Further, with the support of quotations from Erasmus Darwin, he noted that hypochondriacal insanity was often "*confounded with hypochondriasis*, in popular conversation," and then he again emphasized that the former was a type of insanity and the latter was not (pp. xlviii–xlix). In drawing this distinction and in considering hypochondriasis, hypochondriacal insanity, and worse to be related to one another on a continuum of severity, Arnold saw himself as following in the footsteps of Hoffmann and others.

Although inclined to Hartley's views and his language of motions and vibrations, Arnold did not use any sort of systematic pathophysiological scheme to explain the various forms of insanity. His conceptual efforts were directed more toward the construction of a grand nosological system in the eighteenth-century tradition associated with Sauvages, Cullen, and others and reflected his high regard for Sydenham's ideas on the arrangement of diseases. He developed "A Table of the Species of Insanity," in which there were two main categories, *Ideal Insanity* and *Notional Insanity*, that approximated what we might call hallucinatory insanity and delusional insanity; and the types within these two divisions were based on the outlining of symptom clusters "drawn with some care and exactness immediately from nature" (p. liii). Hypochondriacal insanity was grouped with the "notional" or delusional insanities.

He then organized his explanatory notions into an elaborate system of *remote causes* and *proximate causes*. He divided the remote causes into *bodily causes* and *mental causes*. The bodily causes included (1) "such internal causes as are immediately seated in the brain, its vessels, and membranes," (2) "such external causes as operate mechanically upon that organ," (3) systemic causes that might include the brain directly among the sites affected or might gradually affect it indirectly, and (4) causes that affect other sites primarily and the brain by sympathy (2:5); and the mental causes included (1) inordinately "intense application of mind," (2) "passions of various kinds, when sudden, violent, or habitual," (3) "too great activity of imagination," and (4) "the imbecillity of mind" (2:10–11). As to "the proximate causes of insanity, from whatever remote cause, or causes, it may derive its origin, is, without doubt, seated in the brain" (2:274). They included (1) "the small arteries of the brain may be in too active a state"; (2) "the brain may be compressed by a gradual accumulation in its veins, and sinuses, without any increased activity of the arteries"; (3) "water, or other preternatural substances . . . or parts enlarged by disease" may serve to compress the "medullary substance" of the brain; and (4) "there may be a change in the intimate, and invisible texture, in what HARTLEY calls the infinitesimal particles, of the medullary substance of the brain" (2:279–280). Arnold then addressed the causes of hypochondriacal insanity in particular.

> (a) the alimentary canal, and the whole apparatus of the instruments of chylification, are, sometimes, the parts that first suffer; and the head is only affected in consequence of the disorder of these important organs. . . . (b) Often, however, the head seems to be primarily affected. . . . In these cases, the nervous, and other symptoms, affecting other, and distant, parts of the body, are only the consequences of the disordered state of the brain. (c) In other cases, the head, and the rest of the body, seem to suffer at the same time, and from the same common cause: as when the disorder proceeds from much and fatiguing dissipa-tion, and late hours, from a studious and sedentary life, or from habitual excesses in eating, drinking, or venery. In all cases, however, the nerves suffer much; and uncomfortable, and distressing, feelings, are a predominant symptom. (2:309–310)

Another of Cullen's students, Benjamin Rush (1745–1813), dealt with hypochondriasis in a somewhat unusual fashion. Using the term *partial de-rangement* as a synonym for it, he employed the notion of *partial insanity*, which many had previously mentioned in defining and describing melancholia.[26] After observing that "partial derangement consists in error in opinion and conduct, upon some one subject only, with soundness of mind upon all, or nearly all other subjects," he stated that the nosologists of the day had identified two forms of partial insanity, as follows: "When it relates to the persons, affairs, or conditions of the patient only, and is attended with distress, it has been called hypochondriasis. When it extends to objects exter-nal to the patient, and is attended with pleasure, or the absence of distress, it has been called melancholia. They are different grades only of the same morbid actions in the brain, and they now and then blend their symptoms with each other."[27] Rush was dissatisfied with these names for these two condi-tions, and he coined the terms *tristimania* for the former and *amenomania* for the latter (*Diseases of the Mind*, pp. 73–74). His objections to the term *hypochondriasis* stemmed from its allusion to an area of the body and from the association that had developed between the name and the idea of an imaginary disease. He also noted that "the hypochondriasis, or tristimania, has sometimes been con-founded with hysteria" and then proceeded to differentiate them on a number of counts (pp. 74–76). He emphasized that hypochondriasis was "induced chiefly by mental causes, and particularly by such of them as act upon the understanding, through the medium of the passions and moral faculties," whereas hysteria was "produced chiefly by corporeal causes" (p. 74).

His description of *"hypochondriasis* or *tristimania"* included all the familiar symptoms:

> as they appear in the body . . . dyspepsia; costiveness or diarrhoea . . . flatu-
> lency . . . a tumid abdomen, especially on the right side; deficient or preter-
> natural appetite; strong venereal desires accompanied with nocturnal emissions
> of semen; or an absence of venereal desires, and sometimes impotence; insen-
> sibility to cold; pains in the limbs at times, resembling rheumatism; cough; cold
> feet; palpitation of the heart; head-ach; vertigo; tenitus aurium; . . . a disposition
> to faint; wakefulness, or starting in sleep; indisposition to rise out of bed. . . .
>
> The characteristic symptom of this form of derangement, as it appears in
> the mind, is *distress,* the causes of which are numerous, and of a personal nature.
> (pp. 76–78)

He then detailed examples of these "causes," which turned out to be delusional beliefs about bodily afflictions and various delusions akin to those often cited in earlier accounts of melancholia; and he noted that these various delusional beliefs were consistently degrading to the sufferer (pp. 78–80). He observed that such patients were "peevish and sometimes irascible. . . . They quarrel with their friends and relations. They change their physicians and remedies," and some of them made frequent changes in their place of habitation (pp. 81–82). He concluded his descriptive account by stating that more extreme symptoms might occur, such as despair, the wish to die, and even suicide (pp. 93–95).

Several issues merit special attention here. In seeing hypochondriasis as "the lowest grade of derangement," Rush seems to have been following the eighteenth-century trend that conceived of this condition on a continuum of severity extending to melancholia and then mania (p. 73). But even a cursory examination of his clinical outline makes it clear that he had collapsed the picture of hypochondriasis and the picture of melancholia that were typical for the eighteenth century into one clinical entity that he termed "hypochon-driasis"; and, for Rush, there was no longer a distinct condition by that name which was not a type of insanity. Furthermore, while the clinical contents of his syndrome of hypochondriasis or tristimania included all that had been subsumed under the older term *hypochondriacal melancholia* and that Arnold had termed "hypochondriacal insanity," they also included most of what had long been meant by melancholia as the generic term for one of the main categories of madness. On the other hand, Rush separated out the monodelusional states that were either exalted or merely nondejected in nature from their eighteenth-century context as a minority group among the melancholic madnesses; and he asserted, surprisingly, that they constituted what was usually meant by "melancholia" and that they should be renamed "amenomania." He also commented that such a disorder was "a higher grade of hypochondriasis, and often succeeds it" (p. 133).

In explaining disease in general Rush had developed his own unitary theory of disease, shifting from Cullen's primary emphasis on the nervous system to an emphasis on a "primary disease in the sanguiferous system," mainly the arteries.[28] His theory entailed the reduction to pathological levels of the "motion" and "the excitement of the system," with "irregular" or "convulsive" motions occurring that were also termed "morbid excitement." This activity was "mechanical" in nature and was a result of the "elastic and muscular texture" of the blood vessels. Disorders of the mind constituted one more set of illnesses with basically the same proximate causes and pathogenesis as other illnesses. "The cause of madness is seated primarily in the blood-vessels of the brain, and . . . depends upon the same kind of morbid and irregular actions that constitutes other arterial diseases" (*Diseases of the Mind*, pp. 15–16).

Several recurrent themes were significant as various authorities addressed issues regarding hypochondriasis over the course of the nineteenth century.[29] First, it continued to be common to recognize a distinct condition that was noninsane and entailed the symptoms that had been traditionally associated with hypochondriasis. Most commonly these were dyspepsia and other abdominal complaints, dejection, and a worried and exaggerated preoccupation with almost any bodily sensation or minor ailment; and, less frequently but commonly, palpitations and other complaints related to the circulatory system, a sense of weakness, and inertia. With considerable frequency, it would be emphasized that hypochondriasis was a noninsane disorder, that it was to be differentiated from hypochondriacal insanity or hypochondriacal melancholia, that it was to be differentiated from melancholia, and that it was distinct and separate from hysteria.* Further, it was often grouped with or merged into other noninsane disorders, at times denominated as "nervous disorders" or "mental disturbances," a trend that eventually led to the *neurasthenia* of Beard and the *neuroses* of Freud.[30]

Second, hypochondriacal insanity, or hypochondriacal melancholia, was usually differentiated from hypochondriasis and was viewed as a more serious disorder and a form of insanity; and it was often thought to reflect a worsening of hypochondriasis and to be the next stage on a continuum of

---

*Occasioned by the arguments surrounding the denied plea of insanity in the case of Luigi Buranelli, an interesting and careful differentiation between hypochondriasis and melancholia was made by the editor, John C. Bucknill, in *Asylum J. Ment. Sci.*, 1855, *1*, 213–215. Borrowing from the trial's proceedings the felicitous phrase that the prisoner's "unfounded and absurd ideas" were *illusions the result of hypochondriasis, and not delusions the result of insanity.*" Bucknill followed the lead of Cullen and others in maintaining that *all* hypochondriacal conditions were noninsane disorders and thus to be differentiated from melancholia, a form of insanity.

severity. In addition to the symptom complex associated with hypochondriasis, it usually involved a worsening of the various somatic complaints and
an increase in the worried preoccupation with actual and possible symptoms to
the level of delusional beliefs.

Some authors were less concerned with a careful differentiation of
hypochondriasis and hypochondriacal melancholia from each other as just
outlined. Some lumped them together and did not consider the disease a form
of insanity; they usually played down the unrealistic or delusional trends in the
patient's somatic concerns. Others lumped them together as a form of insanity,
usually making more of the unrealistic nature of the patient's somatic concerns.

Whether carefully differentiated or lumped together, these various hypochondriacal conditions frequently stood next to melancholia on a continuum
of severity, with the latter as a form of insanity and the outcome of a further
degree of worsening. Then there were some authors, such as Griesinger, who
conceived of these disorders on just such a continuum but as stages in a single
disease rather than as distinct diseases.

As to the trends in the explanations of hypochondriacal conditions,
vascular circulation notions such as those of Rush did not find much favor with
succeeding generations. Explanations involving the gastrointestinal system or
various abdominal organs as the primary site were still put forward by some,
but such views were more and more in a minority, even in the earlier part of the
nineteenth century. By that time the predominant view was that the primary
site was in the nervous system. In reviewing these matters, Tuke, although
subscribing to this view as "undoubtedly the more correct one," stated that "at
the same time universally applied, it is too exclusive; for in many instances
disorder of the digestive system is the origin of the mental affection, which
latter is cured by the relief of the former" ("Mental Disorder," p. 231). Of
particular influence in the early part of the century were Etienne-Jean Georget
(1795–1828) and Jean-Pierre Falret (1794–1870). Georget maintained that
hypochondriasis was essentially "an affection of the brain" rather than the
nervous system in general, with other organs affected secondarily (ibid.).
Shortly afterward, with due consideration of Georget's views, Falret argued
even more vigorously that this disease stemmed from a primary disorder in the
brain.[31] With a varying emphasis on the brain itself versus the nervous system
in general, this was the prevailing view over the remainder of the century;
those who still espoused a theory of some other primary site considered the
nervous system to be affected secondarily. Moreover, those who held views
that we would term "psychosomatic" usually thought of intellectual, moral, or
emotional factors as causing a pathological condition in the nervous system.
And then there were notions such as *hypochondria sine materia* as distinct from

hypochondria cum materia, which were nineteenth-century forerunners of modern psychogenic theories.

A brief, yet judicious and representative, overview of hypochondriasis was provided by Joseph Jastrow (1863–1944) at the end of the century. Hypochondria, or hypochondriasis, was discussed as follows:

> A condition of nervous origin characterized by consciousness and morbid anxiety about the physical health and functions.
>
>   . . . As a symptom variable in degree, it is characteristic of certain temperaments and of weakened conditions of the nervous system; but in its extreme development it becomes a symptom of insanity, and frequently constitutes the main factor of diagnosis of the insanity, which is then termed hypochondriacal insanity or hypochondriacal melancholia.
>
> It is closely allied to melancholia, with its depression of spirits and concentration of mind upon self, but it differs from it in that the melancholic is absorbed in his own thoughts, often to indifference regarding his health and food, while the hypochondriac is constantly busy with his bodily sensations. These may be vague and general, or formulated with regard to certain organs. The hypochondriac reads medical literature, consults various physicians, examines his own secretions, fears this or that trouble, analyses and exaggerates every minute symptom, is conscious of his digestion, respiration, or circulation, administers endless remedies, and changes them as rapidly for others. He may entertain definite delusions as to the specific cause of his ill health, but he may be free from delusions and simply absorbed in his bodily feelings and misery.[32]

Thus, at the turn of the twentieth century, the long-standing tendency to consider hypochondriasis as "closely allied" to melancholia, "into which it often develops," was still active; and depressive features were still a significant part of the clinical picture.[33] During this century there has continued to be a basic constellation of symptoms associated with the name *hypochondriasis* or *hypochondria*—an unusual preoccupation with bodily sensations and physical symptoms; worries or beliefs that such manifestations reflect physical diseases for which neither organic nor physiological bases can be found; and an unusual tendency to complain about these symptoms and concerns. Associated depressive features have been common, but gradually less frequent, in the description presented in twentieth-century psychiatric textbooks. Although not a necessary accompaniment, there have been instances enough where the worries and beliefs have developed to the point of being delusional in nature.

With or without these associated depressive features, this symptom complex has often been viewed as a distinct disease of a nonpsychotic nature. In the earlier part of the century such instances were commonly termed "hypochondriasis" or "hypochondria," but eventually the term "hypochondriacal neurosis" became fashionable, probably influenced by Freud in his designation of such a condition as an *actual neurosis.** When neurasthenia was still considered to be a disease, some authors concerned themselves with differentiating this disorder from hypochondriasis, while others suggested that they were related disorders or that both were closely related to depression.[34] And more recently some have suggested that many instances of hypochondriasis without apparent depression were cases of *masked depression.*[35] When the somatic concerns were exaggerated to the point of delusions, in the earlier part of the century some still used the older names of *hypochondriacal insanity* and *hypochondriacal melancholia.* Increasingly, however, hypochondriacal trends, including the somatic delusions, came to be considered aspects of some cases of schizophrenia and of some cases of melancholia in the sense of psychotic depression. Regarding the association with melancholia, hypochondriacal features were viewed as integral to the syndrome of involutional melancholia, a type of psychotic depression that emerged and faded again as a distinct disease during this century. All these various issues were nicely captured in brief compass by David K. Henderson (1884–1965) and Robert D. Gillespie (1897–1945) as follows:

> As a symptom it occurs in many forms of mental illness. It is most common in depressions, especially in the depressions of the involutional period. It also occurs as part of a schizophrenic syndrome, when the hypochondriacal ideas are of the most grotesque kind. Sometimes hypochondria is hysterical in origin, and not infrequently what appears on superficial examination to be hypochondriasis is actually a chronic anxiety state. But a hypochondriacal conviction and preoccupation is sometimes found in which it is impossible to demonstrate that it is part of one of the larger syndromes.[36]

As one might gather from the above, it has been argued back and forth as to "whether hypochondriasis exists as an entity in its own right or whether it is always part of another syndrome," but careful studies of extensive series of cases have recently suggested that "there is no such entity as primary hypochondriasis, it always occurring as part of another syndrome, usually a depressive one."[37] Then, from the vantage point of research on depressive states, Schuyler has drawn on the factor pattern studies of Grinker et al. to outline four types of depression, one of which was the hypochondriacal type.[38] But such a careful student of hypochondriacal syndromes as Ladee would minimize the connections between them and depression.[39]

*[Sigmund Freud], "On Narcissism: An Introduction," in *The Standard Edition of the Complete Psychological Works of Sigmund Freud*, ed. James Strachey et al., 24 vols. (London: Hogarth Press, 1955–1974), 14:83–84. While not being much used as a diagnosis, the notion of hypochondriacal neurosis has persisted in various modern textbooks and has been given a place in *Diagnostic and Statistical Manual of Mental Disorders II* (1968) and *DSM-III* (1980) after having been abandoned in *DSM-I* (1952).

Still another way of considering the relationship of hypochondriasis and depression was very recently reviewed in detail in a valuable study by Katon, Kleinman, and Rosen.[40] They conceive of depression as "the prototype bio-psychosocial illness with characteristic biologic or vegetative symptoms, psychological changes in affect and cognition and often antecedent social stressors as well as consequences for the social support system as a result of the illness."[41] The tendency of any sufferer from such a disorder to focus on the somatic complaint aspect of his condition is an important form of somatization. Terming somatization "a metaphor for personal distress," these authors demonstrate the extent to which turning away from the affective changes and focusing on the somatic and vegetative complaints is the favored mode of expression for many such sufferers in various non-Western cultures and in certain subgroups within Western cultures. And they conceive of a major depressive disorder as a conglomerate of affective trends and somatic features with the potential of being perceived by the sufferer or by others in terms of the affective changes, in terms of the somatic complaints, or in terms of some combination thereof, depending on the determining effects of various individual and sociocultural factors.

CHAPTER TWELVE

Grief, Mourning, and Melancholia

With Old French and Old English roots, *grief* long meant hardships, harms, ailments, mental pain or distress, as well as sorrow or sadness.[1] Also stemming from Old English roots, *sorrow* tended to have a narrower range of meanings than grief but shared the implication of sadness, of mental distress or suffering, particularly that of a dejected state in response to loss. Again with Old English roots, *sadness* had much the same meanings as sorrow. With meanings of sadness, sorrow, grief, mournfulness, or dejection, the Latin *tristitia* was closely akin to these three terms. It carried these meanings in classical, medieval, and renaissance literature, regularly appearing in medical contexts (as a basic symptom in melancholia), in theological contexts (as a cardinal sin), and in writings on the passions (as one of the basic affects). It was the root for the now obsolete *tristesse* in English and for the still used *tristesse* in French.

Although grief, sorrow, and sadness were often used to refer to unhappy affective states in general, they commonly referred to dejected states in particular. And, while grief and sorrow eventually came to denote the emotional states that followed bereavement, they long referred to dejected states associated with melancholia as well as with mourning.

Originally from Old English roots, the verb *to bereave* meant to deprive, rob, or dispossess a person of a possession. After about the middle of the seventeenth century, this mostly referred to immaterial possessions, such as life and hope, except for loss of relatives by death; *bereft* came to be usual for being deprived of the former, and *bereaved* for being deprived by death of loved ones. In the eighteenth century, *bereavement* emerged to mean the fact or state of being bereaved or deprived of anything, but especially of loved ones by death. Still again with Old English roots, *mourning* stems from a verb meaning

311

to feel sorrow, grief, or to sorrow, grieve, lament, particularly for the death of a person. As a noun, it has long meant the feeling or the expression of sorrow or grief for someone's death.

In the modern literature on bereavement, grief, and mourning, *bereavement* has come to be defined usually as the reaction to the loss of a close relationship, particularly by death. *Grief* is also used to refer to this reaction but more commonly to denote the emotional response to the loss. And *mourning* has meant much the same as grief but has more recently come to mean the psychological processes that occur in bereavement, the processes of gradually working toward accepting the loss or giving up the person.[2]

There are some paradoxical themes in the many centuries of relationship between the sadness and grief associated with bereavement and the sadness of melancholia the disease. Among the cardinal symptoms of melancholia were fear and sadness, frequently stated to be *without cause* or *without apparent cause*. And yet, many an author noted that one of the possible precipitating causes of melancholia was the grief and sadness occasioned by the loss of a loved one, clearly a sadness with a cause. On the other hand, such losses and the resultant grief and sadness did not necessarily lead to melancholia. Commonly, the experience of bereavement, followed by sadness and a process of mourning, was lived through without leading to melancholia the disease. Mourning and its affects clearly constituted an unusual mental state, but, however distressing, it was usually not found in the medical lists of diseases. Occasionally it was mentioned that a melancholic disposition or temperament was a key factor in those cases of sadness following bereavement that progressed to melancholia.

GRIEF, MOURNING, AND CONSOLATION

In the literature of classical Greece and Rome are to be found the roots of the *consolatio*. Themes of comfort and consolation were developed into a set repertoire of arguments that would be offered to the troubled in the form of simple letters or philosophical treatises. These *consolationes* were addressed to those distressed as a result of various misfortunes, mainly the loss of loved ones through death.

> Of the stock arguments (*solacia*), one group is applicable to the afflicted person, the other to the cause of the affliction. Among the former the commonest thoughts are: Fortune is all-powerful—one should forsee her strokes (*prae-meditatio);* has a loved one died?—remember that all men are mortal; the essential thing is to have lived not long but virtuously; time heals all ills; yet a wise man would seek healing not from time but from reason, by himself putting an end to his grief; the lost one was only "lent"—be grateful for having possessed him. As to death, the cause of the affliction, it is the end of all ills: the one who is

lamented does not suffer; the gods have sheltered him from the trials of this world. To these *loci communes* consolers sometimes add eulogy of the dead, and almost always examples of men courageous in bearing misfortune.[3]

All this was usually presented in a rather intellectualized manner, with reason considered to be the supreme consoler. However, Seneca viewed "family affections as precious sources of comfort," and the early Christian consolers, "while resorting to pagan arguments, were enabled to renew the genre by the stress laid upon feeling and by the character of their inspiration, which was at once biblical, ethical, and mystic."[4]

In a tradition stemming from the lost *On Grief* by Crantor (ca. 335–ca. 275 B.C.), which he had written for a friend whose children had died, the literature of consolation became an established body of writings and principles to be drawn upon to console the bereaved.[5] Commonly cited in tracing this tradition are the lost *Consolatio* of Cicero (106–43 B.C.), written to console himself for the loss of his daughter Tullia and portions of his *Tusculan Disputations*, in each of which he drew from Crantor's work with appreciation;[6] several of Seneca's (ca. 4 B.C.–65 A.D.) *Epistulae Morales ad Lucilium* and two of his *Consolationes*, those known as *Ad Marciam* and *Ad Polybium*;[7] and, again with an appreciative acknowledgment to Crantor, two of Plutarch's (ca. 46–120 A.D.) essays in his *Moralia*, *Consolatio ad Apollonium* and *Consolatio ad Uxorem*, the latter written to his wife on learning of the death of their two-year-old daughter, Timoxena.[8] In contrast to the Stoics, who held grief and sorrow to be reprehensible affects that should be eliminated, Crantor is reputed to have viewed them as quite natural but needing to be kept in bounds. Although less harsh than was typically Stoic, Cicero followed in the Stoic tradition that conceived of the passions or affects as disorders of the soul and of those persons thus distressed as being distinctly unwise. He subscribed to the view that philosophy was the medicine for souls thus distressed, and that wise men or philosophers should serve as physicians of the soul by employing the wisdom of philosophy to heal such souls. As with other affects, the philosopher was to enlist the bereaved person's reason through consolatory counsel in an effort to do away with, or at least subdue, the grief and sorrow. With a modified Stoic orientation, Seneca urged a modest sorrow, rather than an absence thereof, in one of his *Epistulae* on bereavement and grief; but he turned to vigorous admonitions against grief in another. Although manifesting a kindlier tone than was typically Stoic, Seneca used the standard consolatory rationalizations in his *Consolationes:* "All men must die; there is no need to grieve on our own account or that of the dead; time will ease the sorrow, but let reason do it first" (*Moral Essays*, 2:viii). In his *Consolatio ad Apollonium*, while striving for "the mitigation of grief" and an end to the mourning process, Plutarch appreciated the naturalness of grief in the face of loss. He thought that there was a time for sorrowing and a time to console in an effort to bring the grief to an end; and he allowed that consolation might be offered prematurely. He was opposed to any Stoic extremes, but he took the view that "sensible is he who keeps within appropriate bounds." "Reason therefore requires that men of understanding would be neither indifferent in such calamities nor extravagantly affected" (*Moralia*, 2:113). In this spirit Plutarch then gave attention to the various traditional consolatory themes and provided an extensive anthology of extracts from the literature of consolation. In his *Consolatio ad Uxorem*, the themes were much the same, but the tone and manner were much more personal, reflecting both his relationship to the person being comforted and the fact that he shared in the loss (7:575–605).

Out of this background, albeit often mellowed somewhat, were handed down the standard Stoic themes: death was everyone's ultimate fate, life was a loan from the Deity, immoderate sorrow was not natural and profited neither the mourner nor the dead, and the sorrowing of the bereaved should be checked by reason. Retaining much of both the form and the substance of its classical origins, the Christian *consolatio* developed in the direction of adding religious counsel in the service of comfort, encouragement, and support to see the bereaved person through a difficult time.[9] Comfort was offered in the form of emphasizing the treasured memories of the dead person, assuring the bereaved person that they would be together again in the hereafter, and reawakening the sufferer's awareness of belonging to the hopeful living. That a period of grief was normal, and probably necessary, before consolation was appropriate or potentially helpful, though not a new idea, came increasingly to be an accepted view. In a trend already apparent in the classical consolatory literature, there was a shift away from vigorous admonitions and exhortations to cease sorrowing, and toward comforting appreciations of the person's grief and rationalizations to aid in relieving it. The emphasis changed from admonishing the sufferer to cease being distressed toward providing relief from distress. And consolation became a prominent theme in Christian literature.

Over the many subsequent centuries consolation has continued to be prominent in the Christian tradition, particularly for bringing comfort to the grief-stricken. With variations and adaptations for different eras and for different cultures, the literature of consolation has evolved and yet has retained much from its past in its form and themes. The prominence of such literature has waxed and waned. Influences from the classical world and from Patristic literature continued to be significant. Philosophers and poets have played interesting variations on the familiar themes, with the Renaissance a time of plenty in these regards. There have been innumerable mourner's manuals and guides to consolers in the various religious literatures, and theologians have recurrently argued about what was best for grievers and what variations on consolatory themes should be brought to them. This rich tradition has revolved around those who have suffered the loss of loved ones—the bereaved, the grief-stricken. And usually they have been conceived of as a distinct group suffering from a prime misfortune among the world's array of misfortunes: distressed, saddened, sorrowing, burdened by an unusual mental state; but not abnormal, not suffering from a disease or an illness, except in that minority for whom the distress became inordinately protracted or made them quite mad.

"SADNESS WITHOUT CAUSE"

Sadness without cause, or some similar phrase, emerged as a common element in descriptive outlines of melancholia during the sixteenth century, but the notion was by no means new at that time. It was not to be found in most of the early accounts of melancholia. But, in the famous Aristotelian *Problem XXX*, in his discussion of the melancholic temperament the author commented that, where the temperament was "cold beyond due measure, it produces groundless despondency."[10] Celsus, in his therapeutic advice for melancholia, seems to have implied such a concept when he recommended that the patient's dejected state "be gently reproved as being without cause."[11] Then in the sixth century Alexander of Tralles included "sadness without reason" among the symptoms of melancholia; and, for monitoring the patient's progress in treatment, he specially advised attention to whether or not his "groundless sadnesses" were being eased.[12] It is important to note, however, that these authors conceived of melancholia as being caused by the black bile. Rather than suggesting a total "causelessness," their "without cause" clearly referred to an absence of the sort of events commonly thought to have the potential to precipitate a state of sadness, such as losses, disappointments, failures, and the like.

During the sixteenth century it gradually became conventional to indicate that the sadness of melancholia was without cause. By the end of the century Du Laurens was following the common practice when he said of melancholia, "Wee will define (as other good authors doe) a kinde of dotage without any fever, having for his ordinarie companions, feare and sadnes, without any apparant occasion."[13] Bright, a contemporary of Du Laurens, effectively illustrated the idea of "without cause" for the "fear and sadness" of melancholia.

> We do see by experience certaine persons which enjoy all the comfortes of this life whatsoever wealth can procure, and whatsoever friendship offereth of kindnes, and whatsoever security may assure them: yet to be overwhelmed with heavines, and dismaide with such feare, as they can neither receive consolation,

nor hope of assurance, notwithstanding ther be neither matter of feare, or discontentment, nor yet cause of daunger, but contrarily of great comfort, and gratulation. This passion being not moved by any adversity present or imminent, is attributed to melancholie the grossest part of all the blood.[14]

After indicating how very typical it was, in the early seventeenth century Burton used Du Laurens's definition as his own and provided a series of glosses on its various elements. Regarding the by then traditional phrase *fear and sadness, without any apparent occasion*, Burton stated that "*without a cause* is lastly inserted, to specify it from all other ordinary passions of *Fear* and *Sorrow*."[15] And, in discussing melancholia's "signs in the mind," he made particular mention of "*Sorrow* . . . without any evident cause; grieving still, but why they cannot tell" (*Anatomy*, p. 331).

By the late seventeenth century the practice of citing melancholia's cardinal symptom of sadness as being "without cause" had become much less common, and this change became the common practice in its turn. In the 1690s Hoffmann described melancholia as being "associated with sadness and fear not having any manifest cause";[16] but he was already in the minority, and during the eighteenth century it was infrequent to find any such comment in medical writings on melancholia. In light of the fact that most of the authors who abandoned the idea of "sadness without cause" in this era took up the concept of partial insanity as being characteristic of melancholia,[17] it appears that there was a shift away from the affective disturbance as a central feature toward conceiving of melancholia as an intellectual disorder, with the affective symptoms present but secondary.

In the late nineteenth century, phrases reminiscent of the traditional *without cause* or *without apparent cause* once again appeared in medical texts dealing with melancholia. Reflecting a trend back to conceiving of melancholia as an affective disorder, Krafft-Ebing stated that "the fundamental phenomenon in melancholia consists of the painful emotional depression, which has no external, or an insufficient external, cause."[18] In Tuke's *A Dictionary of Psychological Medicine* in the 1890s Mercier represented the views of many when he said that melancholia was "a disorder characterized by a feeling of misery which is in excess of what is justified by the circumstances in which the individual is placed."[19]

With Kraepelin, and others later, the tendency was to conceive of many cases of melancholia and depression as "mostly independent of external causes."[20] This developed into the concept of *endogenous depression*, which carried on the tradition of "without apparent cause" accompanied by the assumption of underlying organic or biological factors as causal. There have been numerous related phrases, such as "excessive depression," "unjustified depression," and "depression disproportionate to causative factors," to name just a few.

All these various phrases, from *sadness without cause* to the modern variants, assume or imply a category of sadnesses where the cause is apparent and readily agreed upon by most: sadnesses in response to losses, disappointments, failures, and the like. Many times these sadnesses have been categorized as melancholias and depressions, especially when the unhappy state has seemed disproportionate to the cause. The twentieth century's category of *reactive depression* came to be used for many such sadnesses, particularly where the sadness or depression was fairly severe and yet seemed reasonably proportionate to the apparent cause. Nevertheless, there are, and always have been, unhappy states of a distinctly sad nature that have not been conceived of as clinical disorders. Rather, they have been thought of as merely episodes, albeit unusual ones, within the normal range of the human condition. Instances of the sadness, grief, and mourning associated with the loss of loved ones have found their way into each of the clinical categories just noted; but the majority of these sadnesses from bereavement, however unhappy, have usually been thought of as being within the normal range of human experience. And they have constituted a portion of the "sadnesses with cause" assumed by the literature on melancholia.

BEREAVEMENT AS A CAUSE OF MELANCHOLIA

For a long while the etiology of melancholia was discussed primarily in terms of an excess of black bile, with the six non-naturals gradually emerging to account for the factors that could engender such an excess. In Ishaq ibn Imran's work on melancholia, psychological factors were given more attention as possible causes than had previously been the case. He mentioned the loss of loved ones, the loss of treasured possessions, and excessive scholarly activity, each of which was mentioned by Constantinus Africanus in his *De Melancholia* derived from Ishaq's work and each of which became common in later lists of possible causes.[21] As Ishaq's views were essentially drawn from those of Rufus of Ephesus, it may be that these psychological factors were raised as possible causes by Rufus, but the surviving fragments of the latter's writings do not allow us to know one way or the other.

Gradually the mention of losses, disappointments, failures, and excessive mental activity as events that might lead to melancholia the disease became commonplace. At the beginning of the seventeenth century Platter took especially thoughtful note of these factors. He stated that "*Sadness* or *vehement Grief* lasting long" could "beget a *Melancholick Perturbation of the Mind*" that might degenerate into a true melancholia "if it take deeper roote and disturb the Spirits, and change the Temperament of the Body." This "*Sadness of Mind*" that might thus develop into a true melancholia "proceeds from grief or mourning most commonly for some things lost of Money, Honour, or any other thing, as the Death of Children, Parents, Friends."[22] That is to say, such events were associated with grief or mourning; but such a sadness might or might not become protracted and develop into melancholia the disease. Furthermore, however, all this did not preclude Platter from defining melancholia as "a kind of mental alienation in which imagination and judgment are so perverted that without any cause the victims become very sad and fearful. For they cannot adduce any certain cause of grief or fear except a trivial one or a false opinion which they have conceived as a result of disturbed apprehension."[23] Also, in the light of twentieth-century views, it is interesting to note Platter's emphasis on the role of loss.

Napier, the physician and clergyman who left extensive records covering nearly forty years of his medical practice in rural England, has provided us with a particularly valuable perspective on the relationship of grief and mourning to melancholia in the early seventeenth century. Although there is no indication that Napier was influenced by Platter, his materials provided a very similar orientation to that outlined above from Platter's writings. The loss of close family members was prominent among the causes of severe mental distress among Napier's patients. Bereavement was the third most common stress recorded by Napier, and almost one-third of such patients had suffered the loss of their spouse.[24] Sorrow and grief were familiar to most people. "Sorrowful occasions were so common that the causes of such misery and the mood they provoked were both described with a single word, *grief.* The supple phrase *to take a grief* meant more than to have felt some sudden sadness; it also implied that one had been assailed by a sickness or a loss, a *grief.*"[25] But, in addition to the grief and sorrow occasioned by losses and other distressing circumstances, there were instances of "baseless sorrow"—the traditional "sadness without cause"—which meant a diagnosis of melancholia.[26] Besides this unprovoked sorrow, though, not infrequently the death of a loved one provoked a sadness of such intensity and duration that the diagnosis of melancholia was made. In summary, the grief or sorrow provoked by the loss of loved ones characteristically led to a dejected state of some seriousness; but this was not conceived of as abnormal, and, after a period of mourning, it usually passed. On the other hand, a large number of such cases continued at such length or to such a level of intensity that mental derangement ensued, and a diagnosis of melancholia was made. Thus, although melancholia commonly occurred in association with unprovoked sorrow, it could also stem from a disproportionate response to the death of loved ones. Grief and mourning were clearly recognized as distinct from melancholia, and yet there was a possible intimate relationship.

As had others before him, Burton both emphasized "sadness, without any apparent occasion" in his definition of melancholia and took account of the loss of loved ones through death, and the associated grief, sorrow, and bereavement, as one among the many possible causes of melancholia. In fact, he thought that, "in this Labyrinth of accidental causes, . . . loss and death of friends may challenge a first place" (*Anatomy*, p. 305). And he placed this sorrow in close association with the sorrow and distress brought on by more modest, even quite temporary, partings and separations. He went on to say,

> If parting of friends, absence alone, can work such violent effects, what shall death do, when they must eternally be separated, never in this world to meet again? This is so grievous a torment for the time, that it takes away their appetite, desire of life, extinguisheth all delights, it causeth deep sighs and groans, tears, exclamations, . . . howling, roaring, many bitter pangs, and by frequent meditation extends so far sometimes, *they think they see their dead friends continually in their eyes*, ... What the wretched overmuch desire, they easily believe; still, still, still, that good father, that good son, that good wife, that dear friend runs in their minds; a single thought fills all their mind all year long, ... They that are most staid and patient are so furiously carried headlong by the passion of sorrow in this case, that brave discreet men otherwise oftentimes forget themselves, and weep like children many months together. (pp. 305–306)

Burton illustrated such matters further with numerous accounts of persons distressed beyond consolation by their losses, grieving to the point of despair, and sometimes suicidally inclined or even killing themselves (pp. 306–307).

Within his many pages on "The Cure of Melancholy" Burton included a lengthy "Consolatory Digression." After having "made mention of good counsel, comfortable speeches, persuasion, how necessarily they are required to the cure of a discontented or troubled mind, how present a remedy they yield, and many times a sole sufficient cure of themselves," he drew on the consolatory writings of many predecessors as "Remedies" for "all manner of Discontents" that might lead to melancholia, among those "Discontents" being "death of friends" and "orbities" [that is, bereavements] (pp. 491–492). In the particular portion for remedies "Against Sorrow for Death of Friends" he noted that "death and departure of friends are things generally grievous . . . a man dies as often as he loses his friends. . . . But howsoever this passion of sorrow be violent, bitter, and seizeth familiarly on wise, valiant, discreet men, yet it may surely be withstood, it may be diverted" (pp. 532–533). Consolatory counsel was offered to the grief-stricken to the effect that their dead loved one was better off. They were advised that grief, among other passions, should be experienced in moderation. They were reminded that all of us must eventually die; and comfort was offered through the belief in life hereafter. A rationalization was provided for nearly every form of loss of someone close and dear. Diversions in thought and action were suggested to turn the sorrowing person's mind away from preoccupation with his loss (pp. 532–540).

Toward the end of the seventeenth century, Rogers made some interesting comments about the relationship of bereavement to melancholia in the course of writing at length about the trials and tribulations of those afflicted with melancholia. He indicated that many who suffered from this disease had harbored some disposition to such a disorder, but "many that are far from being naturally inclined to Melancholly, have been accidentally overwhelmed with it." Among the causes that might precipitate melancholia in those not naturally inclined to it was "the loss of Children."[27] On the other hand, in his dedication to Lady Mary Lane, he made it clear that such losses of loved ones did not necessarily lead to melancholia; he carefully differentiated from melancholia the disease Lady Mary's grief and sorrow in response to the deaths of her father, her mother, and several children (*Discourse*, pp. A3–A4).

Mention of the loss of loved ones as a possible cause of melancholia became relatively infrequent in eighteenth-century medical writings. But it became somewhat more common again in the nineteenth century, periodically being listed as one of the possible precipitating factors in the etiology of melancholia. The twentieth-century medical literature on melancholia and depression has continued this trend of periodic mention of bereavement as one among a number of possible precipitants. Implicit in most medical literature, and quite explicit in other forms of literature, in the background of these nineteenth- and twentieth-century patterns stood the commonly accepted view that the grief and sorrow of bereavement were quite natural and normal, not to be considered pathological in most cases.

The emergence of the twentieth-century category of reactive depression made a nosological home for a substantial number of depressions that occurred in the wake of bereavements, perhaps a higher percentage being classified as pathological than previously as a result of a too inclusive use of the category. But psychiatric studies of the last thirty years or so have served to reaffirm the common man's view that grief and mourning were certainly unusual, and yet did not necessarily constitute a psychiatric illness. Although modern authorities on bereavement have effectively illustrated how very much at risk the grief-stricken are for the development of a variety of illnesses, they have also shown that only a relatively small percentage go on to develop serious depressive disorders. On the other hand, at least one study has suggested that the experience of bereavement may well increase the probability that an individual will develop a clinical depression.[28]

MOURNING AND MELANCHOLIA

Twentieth-century thought on the relationship of grief and mourning to clinical melancholia or depression tends to be presented as though it dated from Freud's *Mourning and Melancholia* in 1917. And, in a manner of speaking, perhaps it did. Prior to that work, the familiar relationships obtained, as outlined above. Bereavement occurred; people grieved and sorrowed as a result; in most cases their mourning gradually subsided without the development of clinical melancholia or depression; but for a few the loss of a loved one eventually led to a depressed condition of such intensity or duration, sometimes entailing a delusional state, that it was concluded that bereavement had precipitated an instance of melancholia or depression. Thus Freud did not initiate the practice of differentiating mourning from melancholia. Nor did he challenge the well-established view of both the common man and the expert that mourning and melancholia were different. He merely shared the common view but then went on to ask: "With these different conditions being as similar as they are, just what *is* the nature of the difference?"

In *Mourning and Melancholia* Freud undertook "to throw some light on the nature of melancholia by comparing it with the normal affect of mourning."[29] He then outlined the relationship of the two conditions in a way that reflected well the common view.

> The correlation of melancholia and mourning seems justified by the general picture of the two conditions. . . . Mourning is regularly the reaction to the loss of a loved person, or to the loss of some abstraction which has taken the place of one, such as one's country, liberty, an ideal, and so on. In some people the same influences produce melancholia instead of mourning and we consequently suspect them of a pathological disposition. It is also well worth notice that, although mourning involves grave departures from the normal attitude to life, it never occurs to us to regard it as a pathological condition and to refer it to medical treatment. We rely on its being overcome after a certain lapse of time, and we look upon any interference with it as useless or even harmful.
>
> The distinguishing mental features of melancholia are a profoundly painful dejection, cessation of interest in the outside world, loss of the capacity to love, inhibition of all activity, and a lowering of the self-regarding feelings to a degree that finds utterance in self-reproaches and self-revilings, and culminates in a delusional expectation of punishment. . . . With one exception, the same traits are met with in mourning. The disturbance of self-regard is absent in mourning; but otherwise the features are the same. Profound mourning, the reaction to the loss of someone who is loved, contains the same painful frame of mind, the same loss of interest in the outside world—in so far as it does not recall him—the same loss of capacity to adopt any new object of love (which would mean replacing him) and the same turning away from any activity that is not connected with thoughts of him. It is easy to see that this inhibition and circumscription of the ego is the expression of an exclusive devotion to mourning which leaves nothing over for other purposes or other interests. It is really only because we know so well how to explain it that this attitude does not seem to us pathological. (14:243–244)

Freud then outlined what he called "the work of mourning." As reality makes clear to the bereaved person, the loved one is gone, not to return. With objections, with pain, and with stops and starts, the grief-stricken person gradually works over the memories and attachments to the lost loved one, clinging to the person and yet slowly giving him or her up, and eventually accepting the realities of the loss. Remarkably, "this painful unpleasure is taken as a matter of course by us" (pp. 244–245). To varying extents, the person is eventually free to go on with his or her life, to reinvest interest and energy in other activities and other people. This "work of mourning" is an important process of adaptation whereby the bereaved person, to varying degrees, withdraws feelings from the mental image of the loved one who is gone.

Freud noted that in grief and mourning "it is the world which has become poor and empty" due to the quite apparent loss, whereas "in melancholia it is the ego itself" which is experienced as "poor and empty" (p. 246). He then proceeded to account for the key difference—the low self-regard, the diminished self-esteem, in melancholia—as an inner sense of loss derived from crucial losses or disappointments in childhood. An episode of clinical depression in adult life may have a significant actual loss as a precipitant, a trivial actual loss, or no apparent precipitant, depending on the extent of this underlying predisposition; but, whatever the case, the severity or duration of the depressive state is disproportionate to the precipitant.

After having been made so explicit by Freud and having been expressed in such distinctive terms, the differentiation of mourning and grief reactions from melancholia and clinical depressions continued to be viewed in much the same way by many who followed. Yet as Siggins has pointed out, a number of psychoanalytic authors came to favor a lessening of Freud's distinction between the symptoms of mourning and those of melancholia[30] and held that a lowered self-esteem, ambivalence, and identification with the lost love object were present in both conditions.[31] But, however close to his formulation, and whether connecting mourning and melancholia intimately or contrasting them sharply, in the years since Freud's contribution many authors have attended to both types of distress in a single context. It is noteworthy, however, that for the first few decades after *Mourning and Melancholia* the primary attention in such studies was directed toward melancholia and clinical depression, with mourning and grief reactions dealt with secondarily to sharpen the boundaries between what was and what was not a clinical depressive illness, or to contribute in some other way to the understanding of clinical depression. In an interesting exception to this trend, Klein gave more attention to mourning in its own right and brought mourning and melancholia into a more intimate connection than had usually been the case.

Klein conceived of the child as passing through a normal developmental phase, *the depressive position*, which occurred during the latter half of the first year and was associated with weaning;[32] and she thought of this as a state of mourning, for she maintained that "the child goes through states of mind comparable to the mourning of the adult, or rather that this early mourning is revived whenever grief is experienced in later life."[33] From this it followed that a problematic outcome in this early depressive phase predisposed the child to clinical depression in adult life and to pathological versions of mourning in response to the death of a loved one. Normal mourning, pathological grief, and clinical depression were thus related to one another on a continuum, with the differences stemming from the degree of unresolved difficulties carried into adult life from that early depressive phase. As Klein put it in concluding a study on mourning,

> The fundamental difference between normal mourning on the one hand, and abnormal mourning and manic-depressive states on the other, is this: the manic-depressive and the person who fails in the work of mourning, though their defences may differ widely from each other, have this in common, that they have been unable in early childhood to establish their internal "good" objects and to feel secure in their inner world. They have never really overcome the infantile depressive position. ("Mourning," pp. 337–338)

In more recent times, following on the pioneer work on grief reactions by Lindemann and the important contributions of Bowlby on attachment and loss,[34] studies addressing both mourning and clinical depression have much more frequently had a primary emphasis on bereavement, grief, and mourning, with clinical depression being contrasted to grief as one type of pathological outcome that might occur in a minority of bereavements. In fact, with the continuing work of Bowlby and the valuable contributions of Parkes, Raphael, and others,[35] this trend has brought into being a particularly fruitful field of specialized endeavor: the study of grief and mourning as a constellation of phenomena significant in its own right, and the ministering, clinical or otherwise, to the grief-stricken. In the last several decades, as this specialized field of study has been taking shape, the concept of the *grief reaction* has been viewed in ways ranging from, at one extreme, "a pattern of behavior which is not intrinsically a mental illness at all . . . but a recurrent, culturally molded response to drastic change in life circumstances"[36] to, at the other extreme, "a disease state."[37] Although showing a tendency to equivocate somewhat as to just how a grief reaction should be classified, the experts on grief have gradually separated out the grief reaction from the category of reactive depression and have carefully defined it as different from any other clinical depressive category, whether melancholia, neurotic depression, affective disorder, major depressive disorder, or whatever. Variously referring to normal grief, normal grief reaction, or uncomplicated grief reaction, these authorities have differentiated a normal variant from pathological variants. Although the descriptive details of this normal variant have varied somewhat from authority to authority, the following outline is roughly representative: "(1) somatic distress, (2) preoccupation with the image of the deceased, (3) guilt, (4) hostile reactions, and (5) loss of patterns of conduct," and for some (6) "appearance of traits of the deceased in the behavior of the bereaved" (Lindemann, "Acute Grief," p. 142). Then, among the pathological variants are recognized delayed grief reactions, distorted grief reactions, and chronic grief reactions; as other pathological outcomes, various psychosomatic disorders might occur, and various other physical illnesses might be precipitated; and in a minority who are so predisposed a major depressive disorder might occur. But none seems to be in doubt that grief reactions (or mourning) are quite different from clinical depressions (or melancholia), however much they might share symptoms such as sadness and depression.

CHAPTER THIRTEEN

Religion, the Supernatural, and Melancholia

Over the centuries melancholia the disease, and related melancholic matters, have often been conceived of as having a significant relationship to religious themes or to supernatural factors in some form or other. From even the earliest times, and in almost every era, there have been instances of mental disturbances being explained as punishment for sin. Whether the gods, a god, or the God, the supernatural being (or beings) visited the distressing state on the sufferer as punishment for his sin or because of his lack of repentance for his sin. A variation on this theme involved the view that the god had used the infliction of the disease to improve the person by purging him of his sins; and thus the disease might, at the same time, be a sign of sin, a punishment for sin, and a means of expiation. Another variation conceived of the sufferer as, for his sins, having been left unprotected by the supreme being, who thus "allowed" some demon, a devil, or the Devil to afflict him with the disease. Still another variation did not involve punishment for sin, but rather the supreme being visited the disease upon a good person as a test for the righteous and a way to increase their merit, or as a way of tempering the moral steel of the believer in the fires of suffering and temptation. Dejected states, in many instances melancholia, were prominent among the mental disturbances conceived of in these various ways.*

---

*Although such explanations certainly existed, at least for the pre-Crusade medieval era serious question has been raised as to their place in the array of explanations put forward to account for the experience of an actual sufferer. Kroll and Bachrach have argued that there was *not* a "significant reliance upon a belief that sin was the major causative factor of mental illness." They have presented persuasive evidence from pre-Crusade sources that supernatural explanations were used for only a distinct minority of cases. At least when it came to proximate causes, natural explanations were preferred: such as humoral imbalance, intemperate diet or alcohol intake, overwork, and grief: Jerome Kroll and Bernard Bachrach, "Sin and Mental Illness in the Middle Ages," *Psychol. Med.*, 1984, *14*, 507–514.

In medieval Christendom in particular, although God might cause mental disorders directly, He more commonly was thought of as being in the role of ultimate cause, with more mundane factors serving as the immediate causes. With the background of Original Sin as a predisposing factor and God as the ultimate cause of disease, the immediately effective causes were then usually thought of in terms of the humoral theory. The perfect sanguine temperament of man before the Fall was lost, and the unending humoral strife that caused disease and could predispose to sin began. Original Sin had changed every man's constitution, and individual sin then led to further mental and physical disorder.[1] St. Hildegard of Bingen (1098–1179) related the origin of the black bile or "humor melancholicus" to the Fall of Man.[2] Adam's eating of the apple led to the melancholy humor "curdling in his blood . . . as when a lamp is quenched, the smouldering and smoking wick remains reeking behind . . . the sparkle of innocence was dulled in him, and his eyes, which had formerly beheld heaven, were blinded, and his gall was changed to bitterness, and his melancholy to blackness."[3] Hildegard portrayed melancholia as the original disease and the melancholy temperament as particularly unfavorable among the temperaments, with humor, disease, and temperament all stemming from Original Sin. Melancholia was Adam's punishment "and had to be borne by the whole race, and only a physician (and the saint herself spoke in *Causae et curae* no less as a physician than as a theologian) could ease the worst symptoms of this essentially incurable hereditary evil."[4]

Apart from any question of sin and punishment, melancholia and other dejected states have been among the many types of misfortunes and miseries that human beings have explained in terms of the evil, or the vengeful, or the otherwise nefarious doings of demons, devils, the Devil, Satan, witches in association with demons or the Devil, and so forth. As noted above, sometimes these demon-related ideas became interwoven with ideas of sin and punishment. And sometimes misfortunes were explained in demon-related terms or as the outcome of sorcery, with someone else's revenge or envy at the heart of the matter rather than the sufferer having committed any wrong. But in many instances they were thought of as merely unexpected and unjust visitations from supernatural beings who populated the netherworld or the unseen world of a particular culture. Being plagued by devils or being possessed by a demon has been an explanatory scheme with many variations in many different cultures for many different misfortunes, and many melancholic or dejected states have been explained in this way.

These various supernatural explanations for melancholic states have led sufferers, and those concerned on their behalf, to offer prayers and pleadings to various gods, to God, to supernatural intermediaries and other lesser spiritual powers, to saints, and so on in the search for relief and cure. The Christian Church's sacrament of confession for sins and the assignment of penance were often significant approaches to relieving distressing mental states, including sad and dejected states. Exorcism was often undertaken as a way of getting rid of a demon or devil that had possessed a melancholic sufferer. Various other rituals, incantations, rites of purification, and ways of putting right moral and interpersonal imbalances have had their place in seeking to relieve the sufferings of melancholics.

Another connection between supernatural themes and melancholia entailed the issue of prophecy. The data from antiquity indicate that divine possession and demonic possession were competing supernatural explanations in considering alleged prophecies, the choice depending on whether the utterances were viewed as truly prophetic.[5] Then, in the Aristotelian view that the melancholy temperament disposed the person to creativity and superior accomplishments, there had been included the idea that he may have prophetic powers. Perhaps derived from the divine madness of Plato, this explanation of the gift of true dreams and prophecies in terms of the humoral theory and a melancholic disposition may well have been a secularization of the supernatural origins of Plato's inspired madness (see pp. 31–33 above). Thereafter, references to prophecy occurred at times as suggestions that a melancholic temperament had allowed such an accomplishment. Medical authors on melancholia occasionally made such comments, but they also occasionally suggested that prophesying was a reflection of delusional trends in the person afflicted with melancholia. For example, Rufus of Ephesus thought that some melancholics manifested the gift of prophecy rather than conceiving of this as delusional (see p. 36); Alexander of Tralles mentioned that some melancholics believed that they could foretell the future, with the implication that such notions were delusional (see p. 52); and Paul of Aegina referred to some melancholics who considered themselves to be divinely inspired and foretelling the future, apparently implying that such ideas were delusional (see pp. 54, 56). And such brief references to prophecy intermittently appeared in discussions of melancholia in medical works during the Renaissance. For example, Du Laurens mentioned that the melancholic humor sometimes grew hot and caused "a kinde of divine ravishment, commonly called *Enthousiasma*, which stirreth men up to plaie the Philosophers, Poets, and also to prophesie"; and, although it is not fully clear, he seems to have been inclined to accept such a manifestation as true prophecy rather than delusion (see p. 89). Renaissance authors, both medical and nonmedical, came down on both sides of this question, some favoring the idea that some melancholics were gifted with prophetic powers and some certain that such behavior was delusional in origin.[6] The former view reflected the Aristotelian regard for a melancholy temperament, and the latter reflected the more mundane Galenic-medical view.

As we have seen in the chapter dealing with acedia (chap. 4), there was a long history, first among ascetics and monks and later among Christians in general, of some dejected states being conceived of and dealt with as the cardinal sins *acedia* and *tristitia* rather than as melancholia the disease. Such dejected states were sometimes attributed to the work of demons; sometimes they were viewed as the result of the sinfulness or merely the weakness of the sufferers; and sometimes the very existence of the dejected state was conceived of as the sinfulness itself.

As one can see from these various comments, sinful actions, guilty concerns, and dejected states in consequence thereof had long been common, but traditionally guilt had not appeared in the catalogues of symptoms associated with melancholia the disease. But, in the sixteenth century, whether or not guilt was an aspect of melancholia emerged as a matter of some concern. This issue was of such consequence that Bright devoted several chapters of *A Treatise of Melancholie* to differentiating those who suffered from dejection due to a guilty conscience from those who suffered from true melancholia (see pp. 83–86 above). During the seventeenth century, some continued this careful differentiation, and others began to include guilt as one of the possible symptoms in melancholia the disease or to conceive of guilt-ridden dejected states as a type of melancholia. This latter trend was significantly furthered when Burton introduced the term *religious melancholy* for distinct subtypes of melancholia in which religious concerns were prominent and guilt was often present.

Another way in which religious concerns became intertwined with melancholia the disease is seen in the history of *enthusiasm* from the sixteenth to the eighteenth century.[7] The original meaning of this word and its cognates—derived from the Greek ἔνθεος—was "being possessed by a god," or "divine possession," or the person possessed was thought to have taken in or been entered by the spirit, knowledge, or power of a god, hence the term *divine inspiration*. And these meanings were still current in the sixteenth and seventeenth centuries. Enthusiasm, as it concerns our account here, began to take shape in Luther's wake. One effective challenge to the accepted ways seems to have set the stage for the many others that followed. But it became a prominent theme only in the seventeenth century. It entailed a revivalism, a reaffirmation of the purity of religious beliefs and ways that its followers thought ought to obtain, often associated with prophecies and at times with millenarian beliefs, ecstasy, speaking in tongues, or holy trances. They commonly believed themselves to have been "born again," to have been "saved," to have found grace, to have reasserted the purity that the weaker ones, the sinful ones around them had fallen away from. "All these movements were cradled in Reformation

Protestantism" (Knox, *Enthusiasm*, p. 5). Such religionists claimed divine inspiration and were self-appointed to the status of enthusiast, but the seventeenth century gradually came to view enthusiasm as a derogatory label. Originally challenged mainly on theological grounds, challenged by some as being afflicted with demonic or diabolical possession, occasionally alleged to be hysterics, enthusiasts eventually came to be "diagnosed" with some frequency as suffering from melancholia, with their beliefs and enthusiastic behaviors as symptoms of that disorder. From medical writings and their scattered references to prophecy and divination as reflections of the delusions of melancholics, those contending with the deviant beliefs of enthusiasts and sectarians brought such views into the realm of religious controversy, aiming to explain away such beliefs as symptoms of melancholic illness. Burton was central in this transition, including enthusiasm as he did among the forms of *religious melancholy in excess* in *The Anatomy of Melancholy*. He brought together references and trends from Renaissance literature, both medical and nonmedical, to construct this category of melancholia, which in turn had a strong influence on many who came after him.

The diagnosis of melancholia was introduced in this same era with regard to another issue with supernatural associations. The witchcraft craze of the sixteenth and seventeenth centuries subjected many unfortunates in Western Europe to accusations of malevolent activities as witches and to persecution, torture, and often death. In their defense, some suggested a medical explanation for the behavior of alleged witches in arguing that they suffered from melancholia and so experienced delusions and hallucinations and were prone to be influenced to give false confessions. Two of the more famous names in the late sixteenth-century witchcraft debates, Johann Weyer (1515–1588)[8] and Reginald Scot (1538–1599),[9] made such suggestions. Anglo has discussed several such instances from earlier in the century and then has given careful attention to these two authors in particular.[10] He pointed out that Weyer made his case rather badly, doing a poor job of fitting his clinical observations concerning melancholia to his efforts to refute the witch persecution. Clearly, Weyer did not suggest that there were no such things as witches or that witches were really only melancholics. Instead, he argued that witches were usually female and thus unusually prone to melancholic vapors, suffered from melancholia, and passively experienced being actively used by the Devil, who led them into their delusions. Scot accepted the idea that an alleged witch might well have been suffering from melancholia, but, rather than fitting this idea to a supernatural explanation, he saw it as the basis for a natural explanation. That is, rather than viewing such a mental disorder as rendering the sufferer an easy prey for the Devil, he argued that the person merely suffered from delusions as an aspect of a melancholic illness.[11]

ROBERT BURTON AND RELIGIOUS MELANCHOLY

As just outlined, during the sixteenth century there was a gradually increasing tendency to associate unusual religious preoccupations with mental derangement of one sort or another, and with melancholia in particular. Extreme guilty concerns with fears of being beyond salvation, of being in serious danger of damnation, of having been abandoned by God, and so forth seem to have become increasingly common, led to varying degrees of despair, and were often associated with melancholia by both medical and nonmedical observers. At the same time, various forms of extreme religious beliefs, religious fanaticism, and enthusiastic religious outpourings, sometimes considered schismatic or heretical and sometimes not, began to be thought of as indications of melancholia. These latter trends sometimes took the form of a dismissive view of someone who disagreed with more standard religious views, and sometimes amounted to a charitable approach to someone who might otherwise be condemned for his deviant religious views.

It is against this background, and out of its many and varied associations of melancholia with atypical religious concerns, that Robert Burton (1577–1640) developed his lengthy presentation of *religious melancholy*. In introducing this subtype of melancholy, Burton noted that, in contrast to much that he had written on melancholy, here he had "no pattern to follow . . . no man to imitate. No Physician hath as yet distinctly written of it . . . all acknowledge it a most notable symptom, some a cause, but few a species or kind" (*Anatomy*, pp. 866–867). Citing a series of medical authorities who had briefly alluded to unusual religious preoccupations as symptoms, he indicated that a variety of religious delusions, aberrant religious convictions, and excessive religious concerns might reasonably be grouped together and conceived of as instances or aspects of religious melancholy. And he gathered in under this rubric just about any case of melancholy that involved symptoms associated with religion or had alleged causes of a religious nature. Noting that the occasional predecessor had divided "Love-Melancholy" into two species—"that whose object is women" and that "whose object is God"—he introduced "Religious Melancholy" as the name for the latter (p. 867). He devoted the third and last "Partition" of *The Anatomy of Melancholy* to "Love-Melancholy," with three species within this genus, love-melancholy proper, jealousy, and religious melancholy.

After an extended paean to God and "True Religion" (pp. 868–875), Burton wrote of the many aberrant religious views and misguided religious preoccupations as instances of "Superstition," which had become the common term for deviant religious notions. He stated that "the part affected of superstition, is the brain, heart, will, understanding, soul itself, and all the faculties of it, all is mad, and dotes" (p. 875). In the diatribe against superstition that followed, he seemed to imply that most men were guilty of superstition, except for a small portion of the purer Christians (pp. 875–878). As to the causes of superstition and so of religious melancholy, "the first mover . . . is the Devil" (p. 879). Further, he indicated those functionaries and leaders who induce superstition in others, gull them, and use their credulousness, among whom he included politicians and various types of priests and religious leaders of persuasions different from his own (pp. 881–888). He was sternly critical of false prophets and of such ubiquitous problems as "Atheism, Superstition, Idolatry, Schism, Heresy, Impiety" (p. 888). He attributed the troubled mental states of solitaries, anchorites, monks, and contemplatives to solitariness, fasting, and religious melancholy (pp. 893–894). After considering a host of religious delusions, religious sects and their beliefs, and unusual religious behaviors, he maintained that such men, however reasonable and sound in other matters, were, in these restricted spheres of their beliefs, showing that they suffered from "a diseased imagination." In fact, "they are certainly far gone with melancholy, if not quite mad, and have more need of physick than many a man that keeps his bed, more need of Hellebore than those who are in Bedlam" (p. 919).

Indicating by implication that fears for one's soul, excessive concerns about damnation, and so on were reflections of *religious melancholy in excess*, Burton then emphasized that there was also *"religious melancholy in defect."* This was "that other extreme, or defect of this love of God," a "monstrous Melancholy; or poisoned Melancholy"; he would so diagnose "all manner of Atheists, Epicures, Infidels, that . . . fear not God at all." Also included here, however, were those who were "too distrustful and timorous, as desperate persons be" (p. 925). By this Burton meant those who, as a result of the weakness or defective nature of their belief in God, were given to various kinds of despair or desperation. He defined desperation as "a sickness of the soul without any hope or expectation of amendment: which commonly succeeds fear; for whilst evil is expected, we fear; but when it is certain, we despair." Because such persons "cannot obtain what they would, they become desperate, and many times either yield to the passion by death itself, or else attempt impossibilities, not to be performed by men" (p. 936). He further characterized the condition as "opposite to hope," as "a most pernicious sin," and as often inclining the sufferer toward suicide (p. 937). "The heart is grieved, the conscience wounded, and the mind eclipsed with black fumes arising from those perpetual terrors." Turning to the causes of despair, Burton stated that "the principal agent and procurer of this mischief is the Devil; those whom God forsakes, the Devil, by his permission, lays hold on" (p. 938). The Devil "produceth this effect" by means of the melancholy humour itself, which is the Devil's bath; . . . those evil spirits get in, as it were, and take possession of us. Black choler is a shoeing-horn, a bait to allure them insomuch that many writers make melancholy an ordinary cause, and a symptom of despair, for that such men are most apt by reason of their ill-disposed temper, to distrust, fear, grieve, mistake, and amplify whatsoever they preposterously conceive, or falsely apprehend. . . . The body works upon the mind, by obfuscating the spirits and corrupted instruments. (pp. 938–939)

Burton then addressed himself to a comparison of melancholy and despair. Though he found them to be similar in many ways and often difficult to differentiate, he emphasized that they were basically different. Melancholy usually entailed "fears without a cause," was associated with fear and grief, and was often "without affliction of conscience." Despair, in contrast, was associated with extremes of "bitterness." Yet "melancholy alone" was at times "a sufficient cause of this terror of conscience" (p. 939). And melancholy and despair were much the same in many instances. Melancholic persons, out of "fear of God's judgment and hell fire," may be driven to despair; and

> fear and sorrow, if they be immoderate, end often with it. Intolerable pain and anguish, long sickness, captivity, misery, loss of goods, loss of friends, and those lesser griefs, do sometime effect it. . . . When the humour is stirred up, every small object aggravates and incenseth it. . . . Solitariness, much fasting, divine meditations, and contemplations of God's judgments, most part accompany this melancholy, and are main causes . . . ; to converse with such kind of persons so troubled, is sufficient occasion of trouble to some men. (ibid.)

After taking note of troubling religious writings and "hell fire and damnation" preachers as influences that might induce this type of religious melancholy, Burton declared that "the last and greatest cause of this malady, is our own conscience, sense of our sins, and God's anger justly deserved, a guilty conscience for some foul offence formerly committed" (p. 942). Although he cited Bright when he first mentioned the importance of differentiating melancholy and a guilty conscience, remarking that "much melancholy is without affliction of conscience," Burton did not consistently separate the two as Bright had done (p. 939).[12] At times he blurred the distinction, and, even when he was more careful, the guilty conscience remained one of the origins of one of the types of religious melancholy, namely, the type associated with a *deficit* of belief and tending to lead to despair.

Discussing the symptoms of despair further, Burton let loose a flow of discouraging, worrisome observations such that a sinful reader might well have sought confession, forgiveness, and penance forthwith.

> Of those melancholy Symptoms, these of Despair are most violent, tragical and grievous; far beyond the rest, not to be expressed, but negatively, as it is privation of all happiness, not to be endured; *for a wounded spirit who can*

bear? . . . Imagine what thou canst, fear, sorrow, furies, grief, pain, terror, anger, dismal, ghastly, tedious, irksome, etc., it is not sufficient, it comes far short, no tongue can tell, no heart conceive it. 'Tis an Epitome of hell, an extract, a quintessence, a compound, a mixture of all feral maladies, tyrannical tortures, plagues and perplexities. There is no sickness, almost, but Physick provideth a remedy for it; to every sore Chirurgery will provide a salve: a friendship helps poverty; hope of liberty easeth imprisonment; suit and favour revoke banishment; authority and time wear away reproach: but what Physick, what Chirurgery, what wealth, favour, authority can relieve, bear out, assuage, or expel a troubled conscience? . . . All that is single in other melancholy, horrible, dire, pestilent, cruel, relentless, concur in this, it is more than melancholy in the highest degree. (p. 946)

He went on to mention that these sufferers were "in great pain and horror of mind, distraction of soul, restless, full of continual fears, cares, torments, anxieties"; "they can neither eat, drink, nor sleep . . ."; they were "subject to fearful dreams and terrors"; "they are generally weary of their lives"; and "most part, these kind of persons make away themselves, some are mad, blaspheme, curse, deny God, but most offer violence to their own persons, and sometimes to others" (pp. 946–947, 949).

As to treatment, in his section on *religious melancholy in excess* Burton first chronicled numerous extremely harsh approaches to "Hereticks," but he seemed to favor gentler efforts to persuade and admonish, with excommunication if those measures failed (pp. 922–924). For "Prophets, dreamers, and such rude silly fellows, that through fasting, too much meditation, preciseness, or by Melancholy are distempered: the best means to reduce them to a sound mind is to alter their course of life, and with conference, threats, promises, persuasions, to intermix Physick" (p. 924). He briefly alluded to some "Prophets and dreamers" who were persecuted "with fire and fagot," adding that he thought "the most compendious cure for some of them at least, had been in Bedlam" (pp. 924–925). When he later considered the treatment of *despair* separately, he emphasized that it was inadequate to treat the person with "Physick" alone or with "good advice" alone, that "they must go hand in hand to this disease." But it should be noted that "Physick" was not synonymous with medications, but, instead, it meant a range of things that physicians do; and "good advice" meant entering the realm of what the religious functionary might do. Burton then summarized as follows:

> For Physick, the like course is to be taken with this, as in other Melancholy: diet, air, exercise, all those passions and perturbations of the mind, etc., are to be rectified by the same means. They must not be left solitary, or to themselves, never idle, never out of company. Counsel, good comfort is to be applied, as they shall see the parties inclined, or to the causes, whether it be loss, fear, grief, discontent, or some such feral accident, a guilty conscience, or otherwise by frequent meditation, too grievous an apprehension, and consider-

ation of his former life; by hearing, reading of Scriptures, good Divines, good advice and conference, applying God's Word to their distressed souls, it must be corrected and counterpoised. (p. 950)

Then, in briefly citing the approaches suggested by various authorities, Burton made much reference to sin, guilty conscience, and dealing with the sufferer's distress in that framework, with brief references to "Physick"; and he emphasized at length that God's goodness, mercy, and forgiveness were more than equal to the sufferer's sins (pp. 950–956). "Faith, hope, repentance, are the sovereign cures and remedies, the sole comforts in this case; confess, humble thyself, repent, it is sufficient" (p. 966). Interwoven in the lengthy discussions of such spiritually troubled persons were recurrent uses of a medical metaphor: the religious melancholic was "spiritually sick." Burton advocated various "Excellent Exhortations" by other authors for the despairing melancholic, and he provided a lengthy consolatory discourse of his own. Closing with more general advice and urging such a sufferer to "submit himself to the advice of good Physicians, and Divines," he advised for religious melancholy, and for all other types of melancholy, "give not way to solitariness and idleness. Be not solitary, be not idle" (p. 970).

RELIGIOUS MELANCHOLY AFTER BURTON

In the latter half of the seventeenth century and into the eighteenth century, the diagnosis of religious melancholy as an explanation for enthusiasm and other aberrant religious preoccupations continued to be an active theme. Increasingly there was a rejection of magical beliefs and practices, a growing skepticism toward witchcraft, and a decline in the belief in Hell and in the power of Satan, at least in the case of the educated classes; this was associated with a gradual turning away from supernatural explanation and toward natural explanation. There was a steady rise in objection to enthusiasm, prophesying, divinations, and other superstitions. But there was less and less tendency to explain such phenomena in terms of demonic or diabolical activity, and a continuing tendency to reject the divine explanations for them suggested by their proponents. Instead, and increasingly, natural explanations in terms of the psychological notions and medical theories of the day were put forward in their place, often with melancholia as the suggested diagnosis.[13] The trend that had been crystallized by Burton in his introduction of *religious melancholy* continued to serve the concerns about and attacks on those given to enthusiasm and related atypical experiences. Whether clergyman, physician, or layman, those who reacted against religious enthusiasm and other challenges to the established religious order explained many of these phenomena as aspects of mental disorders, particularly of melancholia.[14] During the eighteenth century, though, there was a shift toward more allegations that the diagnosis should be mania, madness (= mania), or lunacy, and fewer that it should be melancholia.

This use of an allegedly medical diagnosis of melancholia to deal with deviant religious views and practices was more commonly a practice of medically informed nonmedical persons rather than a common practice among physicians. And, where indulged in by a physician, it does not seem to have been done in the service of a patient. Nevertheless, although the category of religious melancholy never acquired a prominent place in the medical classifications or in the formally medical writings of these times, it did occasionally find a modest place in such contexts. An interesting instance is found in Thomas Willis's (1621–1675) chapter on melancholy in his *Two Discourses Concerning the Soul of Brutes*. Although he did not use the term *religious melancholy*, among his several types of *special melancholy* or *particular melancholy* he listed those to do with "*furious Love, Jealousie, Superstition, despair of Eternal Salvation.*"[15] Each of these appears to have been drawn directly from the three species—melancholy, jealousy, and religious melancholy—which Burton had grouped together under love-melancholy as a generic term. *Superstition* and *despair of Eternal Salvation* were clearly the *religious melancholy in excess* and *religious melancholy in defect* of Burton. In keeping with his dismissal of the black bile as the essential cause of melancholy, Willis did not use the humoral theory but instead discussed these conditions in terms of the vicissitudes of the animal spirits (*Soul of Brutes*, p. 200). And there was no hint here of the religious polemics in which religious melancholy had found such lively use.

In his section on melancholy Richard Blackmore (1653–1729) took note of "religious Melancholy" but in a different fashion from what had become customary. He was *not* discussing a diagnosis that might explain away a person's enthusiasm or other atypical religious behavior, *nor* was he attending to either superstitious or despairing melancholy in the spirit of Burton. The melancholic sufferers whom he had in mind were preoccupied with religious concerns, but Blackmore conceived of this as merely another variant of the tendency of the melancholic to be preoccupied with some particular subject that was of special significance to him. He emphasized that "the Thoughts of melancholy Persons . . . generally pore and muse upon such as have been the ordinary Entertainment of their Minds before they fell into this distempered State"; and so "when the Imaginations of religious Persons receive a melancholy Turn, they are always taken up about the important Affairs that concern the Performance of their Duty here, and their Happiness hereafter." He strongly objected to such disorders being termed "superstitious Madness" and to the idea that "Religion" might be "the Cause of this Effect."[16] He further objected that such reasoning tended to lead to viewing "all pious and devout

Men" as "only Hypochondriacal Enthusiasts, or whimsical Visionaries" (*Treatise*, pp. 158–159). He then pointed out that there were equally pious persons who neither suffered from melancholy nor were of a melancholy disposition, and that many sufferers from melancholy were not preoccupied with religious concerns (p. 159). Rather than religion being a cause of such disorders, "religious Melancholy" was "as much a bodily Disease, as any other Class and a different Nature"; and thus such cases "must more depend upon the Art of the Physician, and the Force of Medicine, than the Skill and Reasonings of the Casuist, for their Recovery" (pp. 159–160).

Later in the eighteenth century, as the great systems of disease classification were developed, religious melancholia assumed a relatively consistent place as one of the subtypes of melancholia. François Boissier de Sauvages (1706–1767), citing Willis's *melancolia superstitiosa* as one of his precedents, wrote briefly of *religious melancholy*, or *melancolia religiosa*. This melancholia consisted of severe sorrow in which one experienced fear of God's judgments and, owing to a defect of conscience, had need of his forgiveness. This disease ordinarily attacked those whose spirits were low due to some misfortune or due to weariness from bodily pleasures. In contrast to truly pious men, the melancholics did not know the true religion and were uncertain, superstitious, constantly fearful, and reduced to despair. Here De Sauvages was clearly following the tradition of Burton's *religious melancholy in defect* and Willis's *despairing* type of melancholy. But he also mentioned the early desert ascetics and their melancholic religiosity in a way that suggested Burton's *religious melancholy in excess* and Willis's *superstitious* type.[17] Then, in a separate section as another subtype of melancholia, he took note of *enthusiastic melancholy*, or *enthusiasm*, which he also referred to as the *melancolia enthusiastica* of Paul of Aegina. Such persons were melancholics who thought that they were stirred by divine inspiration and could predict the future. The implication was obvious that De Sauvages viewed them as deluded (*Nosologie*, 2:738–739).

In his nosological system William Cullen (1710–1790) stated that melancholia "varies according to the vanity of things, about which the man is insane." One type entailed "a superstitious fear of future circumstances," and there he cited De Sauvages's *religious melancholia*. He also mentioned another type associated with "a false conception about the agreeable state of his affairs," citing several of De Sauvages's types of melancholia, including *enthusiastic melancholia*.[18] But he did not take up these subtypes in his *First Lines of the Practice of Physic*, where he discussed melancholia at some length.

An interestingly different perspective is found in William Buchan's (1729–1805) *Domestic Medicine*, a household medical handbook by an author who was Cullen's contemporary and an Edinburgh physician himself. In his section on *melancholy*, within a chapter on "nervous diseases," he did not mention religious melancholy as a type of melancholy, but he included "gloomy and mistaken notions of religion" among the possible causes of this disease.[19] Buchan devoted the first part of his book to "the general Causes of Diseases." One category among those "general Causes" was "the Passions, which he observed to "have great influence both in the cause and cure of diseases" (*Domestic Medicine*, p. 101). Under the rubric of "the Passions," he discussed anger, fear, grief, love, and *religious melancholy*, the last of which he treated as follows:

> Many persons of a religious turn of mind behave as if they thought it a crime to be cheerful. They imagine the whole of religion consists in certain mortifications, or denying themselves the smallest indulgence, even of the most innocent amusements. A perpetual gloom hangs over their countenances, while the deepest melancholy preys upon their minds. At length the fairest prospects vanish, every thing puts on a dismal appearance, and those very objects which ought to give delight, afford nothing but disgust.—Life itself becomes a burthen, and the unhappy wretch, persuaded that no evil can equal what he feels, often puts an end to his miserable existence.
>
> It is great pity that ever religion should be so far perverted, as to become the cause of those very evils which it was designed to cure. Nothing can be better calculated than *True Religion*, to raise and support the mind of its votaries under every affliction that can befal them. It teaches men that even the sufferings of this life are preparatory to the happiness of the next; and that all who persist in a course of virtue shall at length arrive at complete felicity.
>
> Persons whose business it is to recommend religion to others, should beware of dwelling too much on gloomy subjects. That peace and tranquility of mind, which true religion is calculated to inspire, is a more powerful argument in its favor than all the terrors that can be uttered. Terror may indeed deter men from outward acts of wickedness, but can never inspire them with that love of God, and real goodness of heart, in which alone true religion consists. (p. 106)[20]

The Burtonian categories of *religious melancholy* handed down by Willis, De Sauvages, and others have been abandoned here. From Burton's, and others', use of the diagnosis of melancholy to explain away deviant religious views and practices, *religious melancholy* had gradually become a standard subtype of melancholy in medical nosologies and now was undergoing a further change to where it reflected the alleged role of religion in causing a mental disorder, despite the strong protest of Blackmore and others against such a trend. With Buchan at least, it was not a criticism of religion. He was quite clear that religion might well be a comfort and a support. Instead, he thought that it reflected a perversion of *true religion*, a serious degree of imbalance or intemperance in the religious orientation of some persons. Buchan's perspective also represented a shift from the humoral theory of Burton's time in explaining a type of melancholy, and from the later physicalistic explanations of such as Blackmore, to a psychological explanation apparently derived from the tradition of the six non-naturals, according to which the passions constituted one category of factors that might become unbalanced and so lead to disease.

Later still in the eighteenth century, Thomas Arnold (1742–1816) gave renewed life to the Burtonian tradition in the consideration of melancholic conditions and religious concerns. In contrast to De Sauvages and other medical authors who had made modest use of Burton's categories, he gave extended, even intemperate, attention to types of mental disorder that were clearly "descendants" of Burton's religious melancholy, but without using that term. Also, his vigorous criticism of religious views not his own was more in the Burtonian tradition than the more restrained use of Burton's categories which had characterized the eighteenth-century medical writings that used them. In Arnold's nosological scheme his two main categories were *Ideal Insanity* and *Notional Insanity*, which approximated what we might call hallucinatory insanity and delusional insanity. Among the types in this second category was *pathetic insanity*, which included the various forms of insanity in which a particular passion strongly predominated, affective disorders as we might say. Among the sixteen varieties of pathetic insanity were most of the types that predecessors had included under melancholia. Of special interest are three of these types: *superstitious*, *enthusiastic*, and *desponding*. In approaching these three types he provided a joint preface that was essentially a lengthy criticism of the Roman Catholic Church. He concluded this preface with the following:

> From the abuse, diminution, and rejection, of reason, in various degrees and combinations, have proceeded three kinds of deviation from the spirit, and wisdom, of true religion; superstition, enthusiasm, and despondency.
>
> Superstition considers the Deity as an unreasonable, fantastical, and capricious being, whose favour is to be obtained, or anger averted, by idle ceremonies, ridiculous observances, or partial mortifications.
>
> Enthusiasm views GOD as the friend, and his spirit as the guide, of the happy individual, who experiences his favour, and is sensible of his influence; and acting by the impulse of internal feeling, conviction, and illumination, and of an ardent zeal for the cause, and honour, of GOD, and the advancement of his kingdom, is prepared to believe every suggestion of a wild imagination to be the suggestion of the Holy Spirit, and every impulse of a foolish, or frantic zeal, to be an intimation of the will of Heaven, which ought to be attended to, and obeyed.
>
> Despondency represents the Deity in the same ignoble light in which he is exhibited by superstition; and is as little governed by reason, and as much by feeling, as enthusiasm; but paints him at the same time, not only as capricious, but inexorable; not merely as void of friendship, but as an enemy, and a tyrant.[21]

After indicating that it was only the more extreme forms of these tendencies that should be considered to have proceeded "from a disordered brain" and thus to be instances of insanity (*Observations*, p. 219), he then devoted separate sections to *superstitious insanity*, *fanatical* or *enthusiastic insanity*, and *desponding insanity* (pp. 219–241). Arnold said that both the superstitious and the enthusiastic types of insanity were prone to worsen and become maniacal insanity, and that the desponding type was strongly inclined to suicide.

Early in the nineteenth century Johann Christian Heinroth (1773–1843) included *religious melancholia* among the "subspecies, variations, and modifications of melancholia." He noted that, in contrast to pure melancholia, "this form is . . . determined by its object, and does not differ from pure melancholia in any other respect, unless accompanied by a tendency to suicide or murder, in which case it properly belongs" with the mixed disorders.[22] Then, in considering its treatment, he elaborated significantly on his sense of this disorder.

> Nothing helps in such cases: reasonable persuasion, consolation, hope, or any other balm or spiritual life. The faith has gone; what can be put in its place? The most important thing is for the physician to have a thorough knowledge of human nature. True religious feeling never results in religious melancholia; on the contrary, it offers a protection from it and from all other morbid conditions of the psyche. However, if this feeling is not there, it cannot help. It is therefore quite useless, not to say foolish, to attempt to cure a so-called religious melancholic by way of a divine speech on religion. The patient is deaf to it, and it is indeed his very lack of religion that has made him sick in the first place. It may sound paradoxical, nevertheless, the way to the recognition and cure of this evil lies in a different way of healing. Worldly life, worldly errors, sinking in its quagmire, and the finally awakened voice of conscience, which arouses terror in the degenerate spirit and disposition, are the moments of religious melancholia. A life consisting of excesses, vital forces which have become exhausted, devotion to passions of all kinds, a crime or a number of serious offenses, this is the swampy pond, the sediment of which is now sent to the surface by the storm, these are the terrors of the deep which are now exposed to daylight. Religious melancholia is caused by a disturbed soul dwelling in a disturbed body; this is why it is so difficult to cure and why it often cannot be cured at all. Nobody should be deceived by its appearances; the air of religious sensations is spurious. They are in fact not religious sensations at all but are upheavals of the tortured imagination of an impure heart sunk into worldly life and into self-life. Who can look into the human heart? The apparently innocent life is often but a sin retained in the innermost soul and cloaked by a veil of exterior shame so that it might pose as innocence. There are such things as "whitewashed sepulchres." Why are we saying all this? In order to reject any attempt at a moralizing or religious treatment. The *immediate* business of the physician is *deflection by counterstimulation* and *relief of oppressive feeling* by a *counterpressure;* while his *next* task is to *strengthen* the fallen, *excite* and *revive* the petrified, dead spiritual and somatic life. (*Disturbances*, 2:362–363)

As to the treatment itself, Heinroth stated:

> All appropriate medicaments of the deflecting genus must be employed: douching the shorn scalp, the nausea cure, rubbing tartar emetic ointment into the head, moxa, the swing machine. The exterior pain calms the inner pain; fear

and anxiety directed at the outside make the patient forget his inner fears. Since the suffering of the disposition is broken in this manner again and again, day after day, there eventually appear prolonged intervals in the internal pain of the soul, that is, moments arise which can be utilized to bring the patient back to his senses. (p. 363)

He then advised suitable diet, with emphasis on "nourishing broths" and light, soft foods; "above all genuine wine if the patient can stand this"; various medicaments that were thought to reinforce the nervous energy; the occasional use of narcotics; and "exercise in the open air, warm baths, frictions, the charm of music"; with the goal in these measures of improving the patient sufficiently "that moral treatment proper can be considered" (pp. 363–364).

For a perspective on trends in the relationships between melancholia and religion later in the nineteenth century, D. Hack Tuke (1827–1895) is a useful guide. In Bucknill and Tuke's textbook in the 1850s, in his section on melancholia he briefly discussed "the connection between religion in its various forms, regarded as a *cause*, and the production of religious melancholy."[23] To illustrate his views on the subject, Tuke quoted a passage from Andrew Combe (1797–1847) that followed familiar lines: true religion was a comfort and a support; "the true dictates of religion" were in harmony with "the practical duties of life" and did not lead to mental disorders; and it was only religious excesses and the abuse of religious feelings that led to disease, despair, and insanity. He also added that "the exciting cause of religious melancholia is sometimes to be traced to the fiery denunciations of a well-meaning but injudicious preacher" (*Manual*, p. 173). Although arguing, via the quotation from Combe, that "true religion" was not a cause of insanity, Tuke also pointed out that Pinel, "at an early period of his observation—before the spread of infidel principles in France," had "calculated that about one-fourth of the cases of insanity with the causes of which he was acquainted, were due to excessive religious enthusiasm"; but, a generation later, Esquirol "found that, in upwards of 600 lunatics in the Salpêtrière, this was the cause in only eight cases, and, in 337 admitted into his private asylum, this was supposed to be the cause in only one instance. In the place of religion, political excitement was a fruitful cause of insanity" (pp. 172–173).

In the 1890s, though, in his *Dictionary of Psychological Medicine*, Tuke merely offered a brief definition of *melancholia religiosa*: "the form of melancholia in which the patient has great despondency as to his future salvation, or in which a morbid religious emotionalism tinges the mental aberration."[24] But he also provided a long entry by one of this contributors on "the relations of religion to insanity" in which the author judiciously dealt with these relations under the following three headings: "Religion may, on the one hand, produce unsoundness of mind, or, on the contrary, hinder its development; secondly, it may cause certain symptoms of insanity, or modify them; finally, it may be employed as a means of moral prevention and treatment" (*Dictionary*, 2:1088–1091). This entry contained only the briefest allusions to melancholiacs with religious delusions. Then, in an entry of his own on "religious insanity," Tuke dealt with religious delusions at some length, those associated with melancholia being but one type (pp. 1091–1092).

Dealing briefly with religious melancholia still occurred periodically in medical writings during the last half of the nineteenth century, but it was less and less the case, and those who did so were increasingly circumspect and limited in what they had to say. Wilhelm Griesinger (1817–1868), with obvious reluctance, indicated that he ought to acknowledge a few of the traditional subtypes of melancholia, although he thought that such variations reflected only differences in "the *form* and *subject* of the *delirium*" rather than any basic difference in the disease. One such subtype was *melancholia religiosa*, "that form of melancholia in which the delirium centres chiefly upon religious ideas, the patient's principal delusions being that he has committed fearful sins, the terror of being punished by hell, and that he is a castaway, etc." He thought that the "religious delusions of the melancholic are to be regarded as symptoms merely of an already existing disease, and not as the causes of the affection."[25] Richard von Krafft-Ebing (1840–1902) took note of *religious melancholia* as merely one example of the fact that "certain forms of delusions" in melancholia were "especially striking and frequently observed."[26] He outlined a prototypical history as follows:

> A patient naturally religious that has fallen a victim of melancholia takes refuge from his depression and fear in prayer. The failure to obtain the uplifting and comforting feeling that prayer formerly gave makes prayer seem ineffectual. The patient realizes this with horror, and falls into despair. He sees that he is abandoned by God, and has lost eternal happiness. He deserves this fate because he is a sinner, has prayed too little, and not honored God enough. (*Text-Book of Insanity*, pp. 301–302)

By the turn of the century, religious melancholia as a distinct disease, or even as a subtype of melancholia, had essentially disappeared. It was still occasionally acknowledged as a theme from the past. But all that was really left from this "disease" of earlier times was the recognition that some clinically depressed persons suffered from religious delusions.

IV

Some Melancholic Variants

CHAPTER FOURTEEN

Lycanthropy

Although the term *lycanthropy* was originally derived from the notion of a man taking the form of a wolf, lycanthropy, lycanthropia, or wolf-madness became the name for a form of madness in which the afflicted person suffered from the delusion that he had been turned into a wolf and tended to behave accordingly. Further, this name came to be the generic term for any delusional belief of having been turned into an animal, with cynanthropy (dog-madness) relatively common among the various other possibilities. This use of the term must be differentiated from lycanthropy in the extensive folklore concerning were-wolves and the like, where it referred to the assumption by a human of the form and traits of a wolf as a result of witchcraft, magic, or other supernatural influence.

Oribasius of Pergamon (325–403) recognized a syndrome that he termed "lycanthropy" and described as follows. Such persons went out at night, imitating wolves in every way and staying around tombs until daytime. The signs were paleness, languid expression, eyes dry and without tears; the eyes were hollow, the tongue was extremely dry, and no saliva escaped the mouth; the sufferers were dry and had incurable ulcers on their legs from frequently running into things.[1] He commented that this condition was a type of melancholia, but he gave no indication as to how he might relate it to etiological views about melancholia.

Much the same account became appended to Galen's writings as part of the treatise *De Melancholia*, which is now termed "pseudo-Galenic" and probably was written by Aetius of Amida (sixth century).[2] This discussion also commented that lycanthropy tended to have its onset in the month of February; it made references to cynanthropy in such a way as to suggest that these two disorders were versions of a single disease; and it indicated that this disease was a form of melancholia. Both Oribasius and Aetius are said to have drawn their accounts from the writings of Marcellus of Side (second century). Then Paul of Aegina (625–690) in a section on lycanthropy among the diseases of the head described it in practically identical terms and referred to it as "a species of melancholy."[3]

Drawing directly on Oribasius, Aetius, and Paul, various Arabic medical authors (for example, Rhazes, Haly Abbas, and Avicenna) gave lycanthropy the status of a distinct disease, described it in almost identical terms to those of these Byzantine compilers, and thought of it as a special form of melancholia. In referring to these matters, Ullmann notes that even their term for it, "al-quṭrub, is only a clumsy reproduction of the Greek word *lykanthropia*."[4]

During the later Middle Ages and the Renaissance, there was both a flowering of the folklore on werewolves and a frequent, brief mention of lycanthropy the disease in medical works.* The latter commonly referred to this condition as a type of melancholia, but gradually some came to view it as a form of mania. As the witchcraft craze took shape during the Renaissance, the concern of theological and legal authorities with witchcraft and sorcery came to include an increased conviction of the reality of werewolves, and many alleged werewolves were put to death. Some medical authors protested that anyone who thought that he was a wolf (or other animal) was a melancholic rather than a candidate for theological or legal judgment. Others wrote of such delusions as being symptoms of demonomania, thus wedding the idea of this disorder as a form of madness with etiological notions related to the devil or demons.

Toward the end of the sixteenth century the Italian monk Tommaso Garzoni (1549?–1589) provided the following description, which fairly reflects the views to be found in many Renaissance medical writings. Among the types of melancholia,

> the Phisitions place a kinde of madness by the Greeks called *Lycanthropia*, termed by the Latines *Insania Lupina;* or wolves furie: which bringeth a man to this point . . . that in Februarie he will goe out of the house in the night like a wolfe, hunting about the graves of the dead with great howling, and plucke the dead mens bones out of the sepulchers, carrying them about the streetes, to the great

---

*Although one might suggest that those who suffered from the delusion of being a wolf contributed to the developing lore about werewolves, it is at least as likely that the lore about werewolves provided the delusional content for some who were inclined to be delusional, much as the delusions of many psychotic persons have been noted to have a correlation with current topics in more recent times. For an overview of the folklore and other developments in this era, see J. A. MacCulloch, "Lycanthropy," in *Encyclopaedia of Religion and Ethics,* ed. James Hastings, 13 vols. (Edinburgh: T. & T. Clark, 1908–1927), 8:206–220.

feare and astonishment of all them that meete him. . . . Melancholike persons of this kinde, have pale faces, soaked and hollow eies, with a weake sight, never shedding one teare to the view of the worlde, a drie toong, extreme thirst, and they want spittle and moisture exceedingly . . . suffering this madnes in his imagination and cogitative parts (for all men agree not touching the memorie).[5]

Several decades later Robert Burton (1577–1640) provided a version of the familiar description, citing a long list of Renaissance medical authors who had written about this disease.

> *Lycanthropia*, which Avicenna calls *Cucubuth*, others Wolf-madness, when men run howling about graves and fields in the night, and will not be persuaded but that they are wolves, or some such beasts. Aetius and Paulus call it a kind of *Melancholy;* but I should rather refer it to *Madness*, as most do. Some make a doubt of it whether there be any such disease. Donatus Altomarus saith, that he saw two of them in his time: Wierus tells a story of such a one at Padua, 1541, that would not believe to the contrary, but that he was a wolf. He hath another instance of a Spaniard, who thought himself a bear: Forestus confirms as much by many examples; one amongst the rest of which he was an eyewitness, at Alkmaar in Holland, a poor husbandman that still hunted about graves, & kept in churchyards, of a pale, black, ugly, & fearful look. Such belike, or little better, were King Praetus' daughters, that thought themselves kine. And Nebuchadnezzar in Daniel, as some interpreters hold, was only troubled with this kind of madness. . . . This malady, saith Avicenna, troubleth men most in February, and is now-a-days frequent in Bohemia and Hungary, according to Heurnius. Schernitzius will have it common in Livonia. They lie hid most part all day, and go abroad in the night, barking, howling, at graves and deserts; *they have usually hollow eyes, scabbed legs and thighs, very dry and pale*, saith Altomarus.[6]

Burton exaggerated the trend toward considering lycanthropy a form of mania. Actually the majority of Renaissance authorities still considered it a form of melancholia, but, by Burton's time, some had come to think otherwise. It is also of note that the sixteenth century had brought an increasing trend toward citing actual cases rather than merely quoting the standard description and sometimes making a retrospective diagnosis on some figure from classical lore.

During the later seventeenth century and the eighteenth century, lycanthropy was more consistently viewed as a form of melancholia, but it gradually became less prominent in medical writings. From the brief, almost stereotyped, account that was so often found in Renaissance medical works, its place changed to one of being mentioned even more briefly in a section on melancholia, or else it was not mentioned at all. In his lectures at Oxford in the early 1660s Thomas Willis (1621–1675) included the topic "Occasional Melancholy," within which he referred to "lycanthropy and those melancholic conditions associated with the imagination of a metamorphosis, examples of which occasionally occur"; and he then briefly remarked that "these conditions do not seem to consist so much in the contraction or dilation of the *anima sensitiva* as in the changing and deterioration of its shape."[7] This latter comment reflected Willis's view that man had a *rational soul* that was immaterial, immortal, and peculiar to him and a *corporeal soul* that was material, mortal, bipartite, and similar to that of other animals. The two aspects of the latter were (1) the *vital soul*, which inhabited the blood and "inkindled" it, being flame-like in nature, and (2) the *sensitive soul*, whose extremely subtle, yet material, substance was "an heap of Animal Spirits every where diffused thorow the Brain and Nervous Stock" and which was coextensive with the body and its parts.[8] This sensitive soul "sometimes expands beyond our body," as in joy and related emotions, and sometimes "contracts so as not to be coextensive with our body," as in sorrow and melancholia; and it "occasionally changes its shape, undergoing metamorphoses, as it were, and taking on various forms," and so lycanthropy or other delusions of metamorphosis might occur.[9] Then, in 1672 in his *Two Discourses Concerning the Soul of Brutes*, Willis stated that

> some *Melancholick* persons undergo imaginary *Metamorphoses*, as to their fortunes, or as to their bodies, *viz.* whilst one imagines himself, and plays the part of a Prince, and another a Beggar; another believes that he has a Body of Glass, and another that he is a Dog, or a Wolf, or some other Monster; for after the Corporeal Soul's being distemper'd with a long *Melancholy* and the mind blinded, it wholly departs both from it self, and also from the Body, and affects, and as much as in it lyes, truly assumes a new image or condition. (pp. 200–201)

Thus the various delusions of bodily change were now grouped with other delusions about the self drawn from the traditional list of delusions associated with melancholia.[10] Delusions of bodily metamorphosis were clearly retained within the boundaries of melancholia, but now as symptoms that might afflict some melancholiacs rather than as indications of a distinct subtype of melancholia. Furthermore, although Willis had used the term *lycanthropy* in his lectures a decade earlier, he abandoned it in this context. Interestingly, some later authors referred back to Willis as having employed the nosological category of *melancholia metamorphosis* rather than lycanthropy.

Shortly after Willis's time, Stephen Blankaart (1650–1702) developed a medical dictionary in which he defined *lycanthropia* as "a Madness proceeding from a mad Wolf, wherein Men imitate the howling of Wolves."[11] He also indicated that another name for this condition was "*rabies Hydrophobica.*" The occasional author had similarly associated lycanthropy with rabies even while describing it in its traditional terms, but this was not usual.

Lycanthropy was again taken note of in a medical dictionary in the encyclopedic work of Robert James (1705–1776) in the 1740s. He merely cited the usual earlier authors, referred to it as a type of melancholia, and provided the traditional description but added nothing from any eighteenth-century sources.[12]

Herman Boerhaave (1668–1738) was probably alluding to this disorder when he mentioned the "frightful Fancies, Endeavours to bite Men like Wolves, or Dogs, etc.,"[13] but he made this mention in one of his aphorisms on mania, rather than melancholia, and made no use of the traditional names. In his famous *Commentaries* on Boerhaave's *Aphorisms*, Gerard Van Swieten (1700–1772) took this allusion to mean the historical "*lycanthropia* and *cyanthropia*, when the raving persons imitate wolves or dogs, and sometimes believe themselves transformed into those animals."[14] Beyond such very brief comments, the century's medical texts had little to say about this condition.

Important eighteenth-century nosologists like Boissier de Sauvages and Cullen mentioned it very briefly, each finding a place for it in his exhaustive system of diseases toward the end of a long list of types of melancholia and each abandoning its traditional name. François Boissier de Sauvages (1706–1767) termed this disorder *melancolia zoantropia*, thus developing a generic term for instances of madness with the delusion of being transformed into an animal rather than continuing with the name associated with the wolf in particular.[15] He made it clear that he was dealing with the disorder traditionally called lycanthropy, although he emphasized sixteenth- and seventeenth-century authorities instead of the ancients in his citations. Like Willis, however, he also included brief references to some of the delusions from the traditional list so often associated with accounts of melancholia. And he acknowledged those authors who had cited instances of people believing that they were wolves or dogs after being bitten by a rabid wolf or dog, but he stated that this was only rarely a symptom of rabies.

William Cullen (1710–1790) recognized this condition in his *Nosology*, where he identified it as a type of melancholia and defined it as "with false conception about the nature of his species."[16] Rather than citing any other authorities or making any reference to the term *lycanthropy*, Cullen merely drew from Boissier de Sauvages. Indicating that they were both from Sauvages, he included within this category "zoantropic melancholia" and "hippantropic melancholia," the latter having been a separate type for Sauvages and meaning a person with the delusion of being a horse. Interestingly, he also included a third of Sauvages's types of melancholia in this category, "Scythian melancholia," in which a man had the delusion of having been transformed into a woman.

By the nineteenth century, references to lycanthropy were even less common in medical writings. In those on mental disorders in particular, the disorder was rarely given a separate status, the delusions were occasionally taken note of under some other heading, and the name tended to be mentioned only as a matter of historical interest. Thomas Arnold (1742–1816) grouped together under the term "*sensitive insanity*" those conditions "in which the disorder shows itself chiefly, or remarkably, in the erroneous images which are excited in the mind, relative to the person's own form, substance, or other sensible qualities, or contents; and which are not only contrary to truth, but often inconsistent with the nature of things, and almost always contradictory to the testimony of the senses of those about them. . . . Such erroneous images are presented to the mind, for the most part, if not altogether, in consequence of erroneous sensation."[17] Among the "persons afflicted with this species of insanity," Arnold found a place for those who "thought themselves transformed into wolves, dogs," and other animals (*Observations*, 1:122).

Johann Christian Heinroth (1773–1843) included *melancholia metamorphosis* among his types of melancholia, with subgroups according to the animal in the delusion.[18] He commented that "these forms are very seldom heard of nowadays, but were frequent in antiquity" (*Disturbances*, 2:372). Jean-Etienne-Dominique Esquirol (1772–1840) briefly referred to "zoanthropy" as a form of lypemania or melancholia and described it as "a deplorable aberration of the mind, which perverts the instinct even, and persuades the lypemaniac that he is changed into a brute."[19] Wilhelm Griesinger (1817–1868) alluded to such delusions as being among "the elementary disorders of sensation."[20] These delusions, along with numerous others, were listed by John Charles Bucknill (1817–1897) and Daniel Hack Tuke (1827–1895) under the heading "delusional insanity" (*Manual*, p. 136).

As these brief references suggest, lycanthropy had essentially disappeared as a syndrome, and there was no tendency for it to return in the nosologies of the late nineteenth and twentieth centuries. By the early nineteenth century the delusion of being a wolf, or other animal, was still accounted for by some authors either as an uncommon subtype of melancholia or as an uncommon delusion among the many different delusions that might be associated with a particular case of melancholia. But, during the early nineteenth century, the clinical content of melancholia was reduced somewhat and sharpened in its outlines. While melancholia continued to be associated with depressive features, apprehensive tendencies, and delusions, the inclusion within its boundaries of a minority group of delusional states with exalted mood gradually came to an end. Moreover, instances of the wild behavior traditionally associated with the raving madness or mania had less and less chance of occasionally being categorized with the melancholias, and the same was true for the, by then, rare instances of zoanthropic delusions and their associated wild behavior.

In the past hundred years terms such as *insania zoanthropica* and *zoanthropy*, as well as *lycanthropy* or *cynanthropy*, have continued to turn up occasionally in psychiatric writings, but their contexts have been either a brief reference to a syndrome rarely seen any more or a historical touch added to the report of a rare case in which a psychotic person suffered the delusion of being a wolf or other animal. Such case reports have also tended to excite the author's interest in the lively folklore concerning the werewolf and related matters. Delusions of this sort have become merely rare instances among the wide range of delusions from which a particular person might suffer, and the differential diagnosis has become a consideration among the categories of insanity or psychotic disorder to be found in more recent nosologies.[21] Further, twentieth-century encyclopedias often have an entry for lycanthropy, with their accounts primarily dealing with the folklore but with some brief comments about the historical mental disorder.

CHAPTER FIFTEEN

Love-Melancholy

The relationships of disturbed mental states to love have been conceived of in many different ways and have been given many different names. *Love-melancholy* came into prominence with Robert Burton's (1577–1640) use of the term in his lengthy section on such matters. But over the centuries there have been terms such as *love-sickness, love-madness, amor hereos, amor heroicus, heroical love, the malady of hereos, the lover's malady, erotomania,* and others. Sometimes apparently synonyms and sometimes clearly not, these different names have often been a source of confusion in themselves. But then what they referred to has also varied a great deal—from relatively unproblematic states of love to the sad, pining distress of unrequited love, to the agitated furor and derangement of an erotically aroused lover who finds no satisfaction, to the erotically insatiable conditions. At times some of these various conditions have been considered to be forms of melancholia or to be interwoven with melancholia in some way, but this has not been the case for all mental disturbances associated with love and has not always been the case for any particular type of such disturbances.

In his *Parallel Lives,* Plutarch (second half of first century) left us an account in which Erasistratus (first half of third century B.C.) was called in to examine a dejected young man, Prince Antiochus, the son of King Seleucus.[1] The physician carefully observed him over a number of days, noting his appearance and behavior in the presence of various visitors. Eventually he determined that Antiochus was in love with his young stepmother, Stratonice, on the basis of perceiving in her presence

> those signes in him, which Sappho wryteth to be in lovers (to wit, that his words and speech did faile him, his colour became red, his eyes still rowled to and fro,

and then a sodaine swet would take him, his pulse would beate fast and rise high, and in the end, that after the force and power of his hart had failed him, and shewed all these signes, he became like a man in an extasie and traunse, and white as a kearcher).

Plutarch specially noted that Erasistratus, in spite of Antiochus' efforts to hide the facts of the matter, "easely found his griefe, that love, not sicknes, was his infirmitie."

Aretaeus of Cappadocia (ca. 150) did not give separate attention to love-sickness, but in his chapter on melancholia he clearly distinguished between melancholia and a state of serious dejection due to unrequited love.[2] "A certain person" suffered from severe dejection and "appeared to the common people to be melancholic." Physicians undertook to treat him but "could bring him no relief." Aretaeus concluded that he was "in love, and that he was dejected and spiritless from being unsuccessful with the girl." The man "did not know that it was love; but when he imparted the love to the girl, he ceased from his dejection, and dispelled his passion and sorrow; and with joy he awoke from his lowness of spirits, and he became restored to understanding, love being his physician."

Galen of Pergamon (131–201) does not seem to have thought in terms of any form of distinct syndrome, but apparently he sometimes thought of love as an illness or as the cause of an illness. He indicated that lovers might become emaciated, pale, sleepless, and even feverish, and that this had been familiar to others before him.[3] In another context he outlined the case of a dejected and sleepless woman whose disturbance turned out to have been due to love.[4] He carefully examined her, questioned her while checking her pulse, and eventually determined that her distress was due to her being in love with Pylades the dancer. He clearly differentiated this dejected state due to a psychological disturbance from melancholia as a dejected state due to black bile. And in still another context, an extensive discussion of the passions as disorders of the soul, Galen stated that "excessive vehemence in loving . . . anything is also a passion," with the implication that it was a disorder of the soul and in need of treatment.[5] Also, in discussing the various excesses of appetite to which the concupiscible power of the soul might impel one, he referred to something akin to love-sickness as being among the loves "beyond all cure."[6] In this particular work Galen took the view that a lack of moderation in love was a disease of the soul, as was any disproportionate passion, but here he was more a moral philosopher employing a medical metaphor than a physician conceiving of an illness.

With Erasistratus, Aretaeus, and Galen, the cases cited involved a serious mental disturbance in the form of a dejected state as an outcome of unrequited love. For Erasistratus it was not a sickness, but it had to be carefully differentiated from a sickness. For Aretaeus and Galen it had to be differentiated from melancholia, a disease and a form of madness. Galen does seem to have entertained the idea of unrequited love causing an illness, but he apparently did not develop the idea of a distinct syndrome. Soranus of Ephesus (early second century) had not described such a syndrome either, but, in arguing against love as a cure for mania, he commented that "in many cases love is the very cause of madness" and added that one should not "disdain the views of those who have actually called love a form of insanity because of the similarity of the symptoms which the victims show."[7]

The earliest extant account of love-sickness as a distinct disease seems to be that found in the writings of Oribasius of Pergamon (325–403) under the heading "On Lovers," where he outlined the symptoms associated with distraught lovers.[8] The afflicted suffered from sadness and insomnia. Their eyes were hollow, although they were unable to cry; they appeared to be filled with voluptuousness; and their eyelids, the only part of the body not weakened, were continuously blinking. He noted that some physicians failed to recognize this illness and so prescribed misguidedly.

Much like Oribasius, Paul of Aegina (625–690) gave this condition a distinct status among the diseases of the head in a section entitled "On Love-sick Persons."[9] He began by stating, "It will not be out of place here to join love to the affections of the brain, since it consists of certain cares. For care is a passion of the soul occasioned by the reason's being in a state of laborious emotion." He then referred to such persons as being "desponding and sleepless" and proceeded to describe them in terms almost identical to those of Oribasius. He observed that thoughts of his beloved caused the lover's pulse to change from "its natural equability or order" due to the disorder of the soul, but he maintained that this pulse was "the same as that of persons labouring under care" rather than "peculiar to lovers."

Deriving their accounts of love-sickness from those of Oribasius and Paul and extending the tradition of pulse-lore stemming from Erasistratus and Galen, various Arabic medical authors—Rhazes, Haly Abbas, and Avicenna prominent among them—wrote of this disorder. Avicenna's (980–1037) description is representative of these Arabic accounts; he reflected these earlier traditions well, and in turn his version was particularly influential with later Western authors. In his *Canon of Medicine* he included a section on "Love" among the diseases of the head, along with the traditional forms of madness and other mental disturbances. He defined "this illness" as "a form of mental distress similar to melancholia in which a man's mind is excitedly and continuously preoccupied with beauty itself and with the forms and signs thereof." And he described the clinical picture as follows:

The signs are hollowness and dryness of the eyes, with no moisture except when crying, continuous blinking of the eyelids, smiling as though he had seen something quite delightful or heard something agreeable. And his breathing is disturbed; and he is either joyful and smiling, or despondent and in tears, murmuring of love; and specially when remembering his absent loved one; and all the bodily parts are dried up, except the eyes which are swollen due to much crying and wakefulness; and signs causing vapors to rise to the head; and restless movements. . . . The pulse itself is a pulse different from ordinary in every respect, just as is the pulse associated with dejection or lack of appetite or fear; and, further, this pulse and the disposition itself are altered when remembrance of the beloved occurs, and particularly when that happens suddenly; and it is possible from that to demonstrate who the beloved is, without him revealing it himself. . . . The beloved is one road to the cure itself; and the means whereby this is done is that many names are mentioned, and repeated, with the hand on the pulse itself. When it fluctuates considerably, this is repeated and tested many times, and then the name of the beloved becomes known. Then, similarly, mention her appearance and habits, and her skills, her family, where she lives, and connect each one with the name of the beloved, observing the pulse in the same way, so that when it is altered on the mention of one thing many times, one can determine from this the characteristics of the beloved from which she can be recognized. . . . Then if you cannot discover any other cure except that of uniting them in keeping with what is permitted by custom and law, you do this. We have seen those whose health and strength have been restored and flesh returned, after the person had been dried up and suffered from chronic diseases from depleted vigor due to an excess of love. When he was united with his beloved, in a short time his illness left him; and I viewed this as remarkable, and as demonstrating that our physical nature obeys our thoughts.[10]

Oribasius and Paul had implied that a state of dejection was consistently central to the clinical picture in love-sickness. For them, the sufferer was a desponding lover, pining from unrequited love. Avicenna stated that this disorder was similar to melancholia and indicated that the victim might be "despondent and in tears," but he also noted that such was not always the case. One way or another, though, love-sickness was closely associated with melancholia in the writings of many medieval medical authorities.

During the late medieval centuries and through the Renaissance, a large number of Western medical authorities drew on these Greek and Arabic sources to continue the traditional description of love-sickness. It remained common to present this condition as a separate disorder in which a state of dejection was central. As Avicenna had done, some explicitly likened it to melancholia while setting it apart as a distinct disease. Frequently the section or chapter dealing with it was grouped with the disorders of the head, usually just after or otherwise near the chapter on melancholia and often with some indication that it was thought to be melancholic in nature. And some authors included it within their chapter on melancholia as a variant type of melancholia.

By the end of the sixteenth century many medical authors had touched on this disorder in one or another of these ways, and their descriptive outlines were usually reminiscent of the earlier authorities already referred to above. Representative accounts toward the end of this century have been left us by Du Laurens and Platter. Prominent among the early seventeenth-century authors who included an account of love-sickness in a general medical text was Sennert. And two early seventeenth-century authors, Ferrand and Burton, devoted unusual attention to it, each drawing on much the same classical and medieval sources, each providing an overview of Renaissance thought on the subject, each indebted to Du Laurens, and each enriching their presentation with the fruits of extensive forays into the nonmedical literature on both love and love-sickness.

In what amounted to a review of medical thought on melancholia from Galen to the late sixteenth century, André Du Laurens (1560?–1609) alloted two chapters to "another kinde of melancholie, which commeth by the extremitie of love" and which reflected "how greatly a violent and extreame love may tyrannize in commanding both minde and bodie."[11] Setting it apart as a discrete subtype of melancholia, he referred to it as "amourous melancholie . . . which the Greeke Phisitions call *Erotike*, because it commeth of a furie and raging love; the Arabians call it Iliscus, and the common sort, the divine Passion" (*Discourse*, p. 117). Interweaving his views on pathogenesis with his clinical description, Du Laurens said:

> Love therefore having abused the eyes, as the proper spyes and porters of the mind, maketh a way for it selfe smoothly to glance along through the conducting guides, and passing without any perseverance in this sort through the veines unto the liver, doth suddenly imprint a burning desire to obtaine the thing, which is or seemeth worthie to bee beloved, setteth concupiscence on fire, and beginneth by this desire all the strife and contention: but fearing her selfe too weak to incounter with reason, the principal part of the minde, she posteth in haste to the heart, to surprise and winne the same: whereof when she is once sure, as of the strongest holde, she afterward assaileth and setteth upon reason, and all the other principall powers of the minde so fiercely, as that she subdueth them, and maketh them her vassals and slaves. Then is all spoyled, the man is quite undone and cast away, the sences are wandring to and fro, up and downe, reason is confounded, the imagination corrupted, the talke fond and sencelesse; the sillie loving worme cannot any more look upon any thing but his idol: al the functions of the bodie are likewise perverted, he becommeth pale, leane, souning, without any stomacke to his meate, hollow and sunke eyed, and cannot (as the Poet sayth) see the night either with his eyes or breast. You shall finde him weeping, sobbing, sighing, and redoubling his sighes, and in continuall restlesnes, avoyding company, loving solitarines, the better to feed & follow his foolish

imaginations; feare buffeteth him on the one side, & oftentimes dispayre on the other; he is (as *Plautus* sayth) there where indeede he is not; sometime he is as hot as fire, and upon the sudden he findeth himselfe as colde as ice: his heart doth alwaies quake, and his pulse keepeth no true course, it is little, unequall, and beating thicke, changing it selfe upon the sudden, not onely at the sight, but even at the very name of the object which he affecteth. (p. 118)

He then recounted the familiar tales of pulse lore and love-sickness associated with Erasistratus and Galen. He stated that this "miserable passion . . . hath brought many to such extremitie and dispayre, as that they have killed themselves" (p. 119). He thought that "love corrupteth the imagination" and in this way could "bee the cause of melancholie or of madnes." For in "thus busying both the body and minde, it so drieth the humours, as that the whole frame of temperature, especially that of the braine, is overthrowne and marred" (pp. 119–120). Finally, he took note of a more pleasant sort of "amorous melancholy" in which the lover's derangement involved happily imagining the presence of his absent beloved and imagining her to be "the most beautifull in the world" no matter what the reality (p. 120). In considering treatment, much as Avicenna had done, he remarked that "there are two waies to cure this amourous melancholie: the one is, the injoying of the thing beloved: the other resteth in the skill and paines of a good Phisition" (p. 121).

Among the forms of mental alienation or mental disorder, Felix Platter (1536–1614) included a "species of dementia by the name of HEROES," which he referred to as "the persistent fantasy of those who are oppressed by an ardent love . . . a fantasy originating in corrupted judgment and imagination."[12] He stated that it was so named "because it is customarily supposed to befall heroes or great personages which reason is rather ill considered since not even the poorest person on earth can dodge Cupid's darts."* Furthermore,

it so changes men that you would not know that the person was the same. It deranges women as well as men and young as well as old. . . . This disturbance of mind is a certain composite disorder from all the other passions of the mind, since disorders now of joy, now of sadness, now of wrath come to light in it and nothing is more inconstant than lovers, who, in order to be able to enjoy their love, become so wrapped in thought that they neglect corporal necessities like taking food, sleeping and other functions. They omit serious and important business or attend to it half-heartedly, and pay attention rather to personal neatness, music and other things by which they can please the one they love.

*Diethelm and Heffernan, "Platter." In his exhaustive and invaluable study of the emergence of such terms as *amor heros*, *amor heroycus*, *heroical love*, and *the loveres maladye of heros*, John Livingston Lowes clearly established their derivation from the Greek word transliterated as *eros*, and he demonstrated how misguided had been the tendency that associated them with *hero* and so led to the mistaken idea that love-melancholy was restricted to heroes, knights, and other noblemen. In the process Lowes provided a valuable study of the syndrome of love-sickness. John Livingston Lowes, "The Loveres Maladye of Hereos," *Modern Philology*, 1914, *11*, 491–546.

And when they are persuaded that they can have some success in love, they burst out in profuse joy, say and perform many foolish and often obscene things, and sometimes shamelessly perpetrate the basest crimes and are not afraid to expose themselves to grave dangers. Or if they give up hope of a mutually shared love and will, they continually afflict themselves with grief and woe and accept no consolations. They spurn useful advice and express their grief in a profusion of tears, frequent sighs, pallor (every lover grows pale) and heartache, by which they complain that they are especially tortured. Their pulse is irregular, depending on whether their mind is elated or depressed and is aroused and excited by the look or memory of the beloved (by which sign Erasistratus detected love) or is rendered dull and sluggish by despair. Oppressed by these symptoms they finally fall into serious illness, expose themselves to death or often, in the depths of despair, lay violent hands on themselves. (Diethelm and Heffernan, "Platter," p. 14)

In the early seventeenth century Daniel Sennert (1572–1637) included among his several chapters on melancholia one on *love-madness*. He stated:

> This Dilirium from Love may be referred to the Melancholy before mentioned, but because it hath something peculiar, and is more vehement than the rest, we shall speak of it in this Chapter. . . . It is a melancholy doting from too much love, for most Lovers by a blind sort of love, are carried from right Reason diversly, and sometimes it is so vehement that deprives a man of Reason, and causeth a Delirium.
>
> The first Cause is a strong impression of an amiable thing not good nor profitable, but lascivious by which men are mad with Reason; for if the species of a man or woman received by sight or discourse be strongly imprinted upon the memory, and presented often to the imagination and mind, there is such a desire of the thing loved, that it changeth the party much, so that he can neither eat nor sleep, but is much troubled.
>
> The remote causes are all things causeing love, as the knowledge of the object by sight or hearing: but the first cause is a fair Object, real, or appearing so, offered to the view, hence that saying. *The Eyes are leaders to love*, now idleness is a great cause why love taken by sight or hearing should insinuate it self into the mind, also solitariness, reading of love books, love discourse, and often converse with the Object. . . .
>
> The face is pale . . . they are watchful, their body pines, their eyes are hollow and heavy for want of Spirits, Lovers keep no decorum in their actions, speech and gesture; they speak and act many things without any gravity. Let the Physitian when he feels the pulse procure the party loved to be named, or letters brought, and at the mention of her, suddenly the pulse and the colour will be altered; not that there is a proper pulse in Lovers, but it so troubled, that it keeps neither natural evenness nor order.
>
> This is easily cured at first, but if it be rooted, it either turns to madness, or a consumption, or they kill themselves. [13]

Turning to the consideration of treatment, Sennert advised that "before the constitution of the brain be altered, it must be resisted, avoid solitariness and discourse and familiarity; keep the mind from sadness by all other delights, shake off the object, and let the patient have admirations from grave men." If the disturbance was beyond the help of such measures, he indicated that the same medical regimen was in order as was used for melancholia that primarily affected the brain. And, "if this disease be nourished by Venery and abundance of seed," he recommended a variety of remedies reputed "to quench the seed" (*Practical Physick*, p. 159).

The early seventeenth century also saw two authors give unusually detailed attention to love-melancholy; Ferrand devoted a whole book to this condition, and Burton gave as much attention to it, but as part of his *Anatomy of Melancholy*. Jacques Ferrand (fl. 1610) defined love itself as "a mixt disease, both of the body and the mind."[14] He then indicated that he would be drawing on the teachings of both Plato and Aesculapius in considering "amorous melancholy" or "erotique melancholy," on Plato for precepts "to cure the maladies of the mind" and on Aesculapius for medicines "for those of the body" (*Erotomania*, pp. 3–4). In defining this "Love Melancholy" he said that "*Love, or this Eroticall Passion is a kind of Dotage, proceeding from an Irregular desire of enjoying a lovely object; and is attended on by Feare and sadnesse*" (p. 31).

His clinical description was along by then well-established lines. The sufferer's eyes were hollow and dry, except if tearful; he was preoccupied, or smiling as if delighted by something he saw; he might be jocund and laughing, or weeping and extremely sad; he was pale, possessed of a languishing countenance, and troubled by "feeblenesse of the knees"; he was "perpetually sighing, and complaining without any cause"; and there was an "unequall and confused beating of the Pulse" (pp. 107–114). And he included in this chapter on "Signes Diagnosticke" references to the traditional pulse-lore accounts of Erasistratus, Galen, and others, along with just such an account from his own experience. In his chapter "The Symptoms of Love Melancholy" he added further clinical detail. After noting that "being not able to compasse our desires" led to "Griefe, and Despaire" (p. 9), he listed the following additional clinical possibilities: "heart-beating, swelling of the face, want of appetite, greife, sighing, causeles teares, insatiable hunger, extreame thirst, sownings, oppressions, suffocations, continuall watchings, Headach, Melancholy, Epilepsy, Ragings, *Furor uterinus*, Satyriasis; and diverse other desperate Symptomes." He also commented that "woemen are farre more subject to this passion, and more cruelly tormented with it, then men are," and added "the Green sicknesse" to the symptoms that might occur (p. 11).

In placing erotic melancholia or love-melancholy in context, Ferrand first accepted Galen's definition of melancholia as a "*Dotage without a Fever, accompanied with Feare, and Sadnesse*"; then took note of the three traditional types of melancholia, namely, that affecting the brain primarily, that affecting the general mass of the blood and the brain only secondarily, and that affecting the hypochondriacal region and the brain secondarily; and finally suggested that "Love Melancholy" was a form of "Hypochondriacall Melancholy" with the parts affected being "the Liver, and the parts adjoyning, from whence those black Fuliginous vapours doe arise, which ascending up to the braine, doe hinder and pervert the principall faculties thereof" (pp. 23–26). In one place he stated that these sufferers "have their imagination depraved, and their judgement corrupted" (p. 31); but in another he maintained that "sometimes the Imagination only is depraved" (p. 87). In contrast to melancholia that resulted from "Naturall Melancholy" (natural black bile), which was cold and dry, love-melancholy, like hypochondriacal melancholia, resulted from unnatural melancholy (unnatural or adust black bile), which was hot and dry as the result of "the Adustion of Choler, of the blood, or of the Naturall Melancholy" (pp. 63–66).

Finally, a note on the naming of this condition is in order here. From Ferrand's "la maladie d'amour ou mélancholie érotique" in the title of the French edition of 1623, the English translator drew the reasonable translation of "love, or erotique melancholy," but he added to his title the suggestion of "erotomania" as a synonym. Although Ferrand had not used this term in his title or in his text, on one occasion he had used the Greek term for which it was a transliteration, observing that some physicians referred to this condition by that name and that it meant love-madness.* He followed this by mentioning the view of those predecessors who thought that "Melancholy" (melancholia) and "Madnesse" (mania) differed only in degree, with the latter being severer; and he then implied that he accepted this view for his own study of the disorders stemming from love (*Erotomania*, p. 17). He also referred to the terms for this condition used by the Arabic medical writers; and he mentioned the late medieval use of the name "Heroicall Melancholy" (Fr.: *Amour heroïque*), apparently subscribing to its derivation from *heroes* rather than *eros* (ibid.).[15]

Then Robert Burton (1577–1640) addressed "Love-Melancholy" in exhaustive fashion in the third partition of his great collection of matters melancholic, which, although not strictly a medical work, included an impressive compilation of materials from classical, medieval, and Renaissance medical writings.[16] Some have suggested that Burton was significantly indebted to Ferrand for this part of his *Anatomy*, but, apart from his own disclaimer of such

---

*Jacques Ferrand, *De La Maladie D'Amour, ou Melancholie Erotique* . . . (Paris: Denis Moreau, 1623), p. 14 (see p. 16 in English translation). It may be that the use of the term *erotomania* in contexts dealing with love-melancholy stems from its introduction by Edmund Chilmead into the English translation of Ferrand's work. Certainly the use of it as a synonym for love-melancholy became much more common after the appearance of Chilmead's translation.

influence, it appears much likelier that whatever similarities exist stem from the many sources on which they both drew, prominent among which was Du Laurens.

After an extensive dissertation on love in general in which he suggested that love itself was "a species of melancholy" (p. 611), Burton came "at last to that Heroical Love, which is proper to men and women, is a frequent cause of melancholy, and deserves much rather to be called burning lust, than by such an honourable title" (pp. 653–654). This pathological love was beyond any usual bounds that we might think of for love. "It will not contain itself within the union of marriage, or apply to one object, but is a wandering, extravagant, a domineering, a boundless, an irrefragable, a destructive passion: sometimes this burning lust rageth after marriage, and then it is properly called Jealousy; sometimes before, and then it is called Heroical Melancholy. . . . It is confined within no terms of blood, years, sex, or whatsoever else" (p. 655). After briefly referring to various opinions on the nature of this "Heroical Love"— whether or not it was a disease, whether it was an illness of the body or of the mind, whether or not it was a form of madness—Burton made it clear that he viewed it as a disease and that he sided with the majority of physicians who "make it a species or kind of melancholy" and who dealt with it as a separate disorder (p. 658). And, in contrast to Ferrand, who viewed it as a form of hypochondriacal melancholia, and others, who maintained that the liver was the site affected, he thought of it as a form of "head melancholy" with both imagination and reason "misaffected" (pp. 154, 658–659). Parenthetically, it is of interest that Burton dealt with jealousy in a separate section as "a Species apart," as "a bastard-branch, or kind of Love-Melancholy," rather than following the many predecessors who viewed it as either a cause or a symptom of love-sickness (p. 821).

Turning to the clinical picture, he stated:

> Symptoms are either of Body or Mind; of body, Paleness, Leanness, dryness, etc. . . . Avicenna makes hollow eyes, dryness, symptoms of this disease, to go smiling to themselves, or acting as if they saw or heard some delectable object. Valleriola, Laurentius, Aelianus, Montaltus, Langius, deliver as much, the body lean, pale . . . hollow-ey'd, their eyes are hidden in their heads, they pine away, and look ill with waking, cares, sighs, eyes . . . lose their lustre, with groans, griefs, sadness, dulness, want of appetite, etc. . . . The Green-sickness . . . often happeneth to young women, a Cachexia, or an evil habit to men, besides their ordinary sighs, complaints and lamentations, which are too frequent. . . . All makes leanness, want of appetite, want of sleep ordinary Symptoms, and by that means they are brought often so low, so much altered and changed, that . . . one can scarce know them to be the same men. . . . Two of the most notable signs are observed by the Pulse and Countenance. (pp. 721–723)

Burton then recounted a number of the well-known pulse-lore tales, including those from Erasistratus, Galen, and Avicenna (p. 723). Further on he noted, "The Symptoms of the mind in Lovers are almost infinite, and so diverse, that no Art can comprehend them: though they be merry sometimes, and rapt beyond themselves for joy, yet most part, Love is a plague, a torture, an hell, a bitter-sweet passion at last" (p. 728). In the lists of mental symptoms

> fear and sorrow may justly challenge the chief place. . . . 'Tis full of fear, anxiety, doubt, care, peevishness, suspicion. . . . They are apt to mistake, amplify, too credulous sometimes, too full of hope and confidence, and then again very jealous, unapt to believe or entertain any good news. . . . These doubts, anxieties, suspicions, are the least part of their torments; they break many times from passions to actions, speak fair, and flatter, now most obsequious and willing, by and by they are averse, wrangle, fight, swear, quarrel, laugh, weep. . . . So their actions and passions are intermixt, but of all other passions, Sorrow hath the greatest share; Love to many is bitterness itself. (pp. 728–729)

Most of the rest of this section was devoted to the agonies, the glories, and the irrationalities of love.

As to the treatment of this disorder, Burton acknowledged the opinion of those who thought that it was incurable but then added that, "if it be taken in time, it may be helped, and by many good remedies amended" (p. 765). "As an idle sedentary life, liberal feeding, are great causes of it, so the opposite, labour, slender and sparing diet, with continual business, are the best and most ordinary means to prevent it" (p. 766). He cited various recommendations against foods "which cause venery, or provoke lust" and cautioned that wine must be used with considerable care or not at all (p. 767). He acknowledged the traditional prescription of coitus (p. 768). Some were said to be helped by music and various other entertainments or diversions (pp. 768–769). As to the possible use of "Physick, that the humours be altered," he indicated that the sufferers were to be treated with such measures as would be used for anyone suffering from melancholia, including bloodletting and various evacuative remedies (p. 769). He also referred to medicaments that were reputed to reduce sexual desire (pp. 769–770). He wrote of the gains to be had from the person's controlling himself, avoiding the company of someone who stimulated his desires, arranging a change of scene, being diverted by the experience of contrary passions, and confessing "his grief and passion to some judicious friend (the more he conceals, the greater is his pain) that by his good advice may happily ease him on a sudden" (pp. 770–777). On this latter he expanded later, stating that, among the many good remedies available, "good counsel and persuasion . . . are of great moment . . . especially if it shall proceed from a wise, fatherly, reverend, discreet person, a man of authority, whom the parties do respect, stand in awe of, or from a judicious friend, of itself alone, it is able to divert and suffice" (pp. 777–778). Finally, he followed another established tradition from the literature on love-sickness when he stated that "the last and best Cure of Love-Melancholy is, to let them have their desire" (p. 798).

Thus, from the late sixteenth to the mid-seventeenth century, the place of love-sickness or love-melancholy in medical writings had gradually grown from a circumscribed account in some association with melancholia to where Ferrand had devoted an extensive treatise to it alone and Burton's compilation from both medical and literary sources had the dimensions of a book within his larger work on melancholia. In addition, whereas the late medieval centuries had seen the emergence of love-sickness as a theme in the general literature of the Western world, during the sixteenth and early seventeenth centuries this literature increasingly featured examples of or allusions to such a disorder, and melancholic trends were increasingly a part of these literary accounts.

Although Avicenna had noted that sometimes it was not the case, for the most part the clinical picture was that of the desponding lover in the medical writings up to this time. But, in both the literary and the medical presentations of love-sickness during the Renaissance and later, it often seems that two contrasting conditions were being lumped together under this single rubric. At times it was a condition that involved unusually strong sexual desire, often associated with frustration of that desire and sometimes with excessive sexual activity. At other times it involved a pining, languishing, dejected lover, usually associated with unrequited love but occasionally with the loss of the beloved. Some authors seem to have been implying that these two symptom clusters were related to each other as two stages in the disorder of love-sickness, with the latter reflecting a worsening and a tendency to become chronic.[17] It is of special note that Ferrand alluded to the traditional relationship often suggested for melancholia and mania, namely, that melancholia was the less severe disorder, which might worsen and become mania, and he implied that just such a relationship existed between the desponding lover as the milder form or earlier stage and the excited, deranged lover as the severer form (*Erotomania*, p. 17). As Babb has pointed out, the relationship of these two forms as possible stages was the other way around for most authors. Also, although Ferrand indicated that nymphomania and satyriasis were versions of erotic melancholia as he conceived of it, most authors viewed these two conditions as quite distinct from love-melancholy. Love-sickness or love-melancholy was usually the outcome of frustrated sexual desires and entailed an obsessive preoccupation with the beloved.

A different perspective that is relevant here has been provided by Diethelm, who, in his valuable study of medical dissertations from this era, included a section on *sexual excitements* in his chapter on mania.[18] Considering these conditions in modern terms, he viewed the majority as probably having been either manic or schizophrenic excitements. Although he remarked that some appeared to have been depressive disorders and that transient depressive symptoms were not uncommon in these sexual excitements, he emphasized fear, suspiciousness, elation, and anger as having been more characteristic. In the cases Diethelm cited from the medical literature of this period the emphasis was on intense desire, frustration, and ensuing derangement; and there was little attention given to pining, dejected states, and unrequited love. In an interesting passage drawn from Peter van Foreest (1522–1597) the cases mentioned are clearly of the type that Diethelm emphasized, but the general outline in the accompanying explanatory note also from van Foreest is just as clearly the traditional condition so often referred to as love-melancholy. He stated:

> It is also a mental illness to be madly in love, and so doctors list love as one of the disorders of the brain which usually after a tragic struggle terminate in mania or melancholy. It is called EROS by the Greeks and AMOR by the Romans. . . . The part affected, therefore, is the brain itself as in melancholy or mania, into which diseases it (love) easily passes. The disorder, however, is a symptom of a corrupted imagination, because the mind conceives a beautiful image of a man, or woman, and the boy, or girl, gets such a desire for it, that the love is converted into insanity or furor. . . . For, as Paulus says, from a heavy solicitude of mind this furor arises and is contacted from a laborious movement of mind, or the cause of the disease is an image conceived in the mind and the corrupt imagination brought on by love, whence excessive solicitude often burns up the melancholic humor or brings on dry imbalance without the humor, and also brings on loss of weight and insanity. And so the first cause is excessive love, and afterwards the humors are burned up, and the conversion to melancholy and insanity takes place. These are the signs of that madness: The eyes are hollow, dry, tearless and blinking; the other parts of the body are uninjured; they are troubled only by this unworthy love. There is no variety of pulse which is particular to lovers but it is similar to that of the disturbed person. When the memory of the love comes back as the result of sight or touch, or the reading of a letter, the mind is struck at once, and so is the pulse, so that it manifests neither its natural evenness nor order.
>
> Lovers are also sad, downcast, sleepless, meditative, full of amorous sighs, pale, forgetful of food, and in danger of dying of the wasting away of desire.
>
> Their sighs are frequent; they mourn, weep, lament, wail, cry out and are overwrought. They are never at peace or repose. They speak foreign and incoherent things. They act silly, are delirious and are insane. They stab, strangle and kill each other. Indeed all these things grow out of black bile, which, we see, quite evidently rises in the course of this disorder. When they are thus excited they recite mournful tragedies, as the poets and tragedians have often shown by many examples. (*Medical Dissertations*, p. 64)

Once again we see that, when one turns to a sixteenth- or seventeenth-century medical source on this disorder, it is difficult to dissociate it from the melancholia of that era's medicine, and yet *both* manic and melancholic states were usually included when love-sickness was addressed.

With the seventeenth-century editions of Burton's work, attention to love-melancholy as a clinical disorder seems to have reached a high-water mark from which it gradually fell away and which was never reached again. But it continued to be mentioned in medical writings, usually among an author's sections on mental disorders and usually in some significant connection to melancholia. Later in the seventeenth century, Thomas Willis (1621–1675) took up the subject as he came toward the end of his chapter on melancholia. Earlier in the chapter he had differentiated two types of melancholia: the *universal* type, in which the afflicted were deranged on all or most subjects, and the *particular* type, in which the derangement was limited to one or two subjects, with essentially normal functioning in other spheres.[19] When he turned to the discussion of particular or special melancholia, he noted that such "sick respect a certain particular thing, or some kind of things, of which they think almost without ceasing; and by reason all the powers and affections of the soul being continually imployed about this one thing, they live still careful and sad." Among the many such pathological preoccupations that might lead to special forms of melancholia and thus "require the care of a Physician," he mentioned "*furious Love*," jealousy, religious melancholia, and lycanthropy, and he devoted a short section to each. Here he describes "Love-Madness":

> It is a most common observation, that if any one being taken with the aspect and conversation of any Woman, begins to desire her and to grow mad for her inwardly, and for his most devoted affection has nothing but loss and contempt allotted him, unless he be very much supported by a firm reason, or is averted as it were by other cross affections, there is a great danger lest he falls into Melancholy, Stupidity, or Love-Madness; with which passion, if by chance he be distemper'd, he forthwith seems transformed from himself, as it were into an animated statue, he thinks on, nor speaks of any thing but his Love; he endeavours to get into her favour, with the danger of both the loss of his Life and Fortune; in the mean time, he not only neglects the care of his household affairs, or of the publick, yea his own health, but becoming desperate of his desires, he oftentimes lays violent hands of himself: But if he be content to live, yet growing lean, or withering away both in Soul and Body, he almost puts off man; for the right use of reason being lost, omitting food and sleep, and the necessary offices of Nature, he sets himself wholly to sighing and groaning, and gets a mournful habit and carriage of body. (*Soul of Brutes*, p. 199)

As to the pathogenesis of "this Distemper," he wrote of "the Corporeal Soul of Man" not being able to "obtain and embrace" his beloved and so "grows wholly deaf to the Rational Soul, and hears not its dictates, but carrying only tragical notions to the Imagination, darkens the sight of the intellect." Willis continues:

> Forasmuch as the *Pracordia* (the more plentiful afflux of the Spirits being denied to them) do slacken of their motions, the blood heaped up in the bosoms of the heart, and apt to stand still, stirs up a great weight and oppression, and for that reason, sighs and groans; in the mean time the face, and the outward members grow pale and languish, for that the affluence of the Blood and Spirits is withdrawn: Hence in our *Idiom* or Speech, the Heart of despairing Lovers is said to be broken, to wit, because this Muscle is not lively enough actuated by the Animal Spirits, and so is shaken weakly and slowly, and doth not amply enough cast forward the blood with vigor, into all parts. (pp. 199–200)

Unconnected with his beloved, the afflicted person's "Animal Spirits" no longer serve him properly, and "from thence the vitiated Blood, and the Spirits, having gotten an acetous nature, an habitual *Melancholy* is introduced" (p. 200).

Although references to love-sickness were somewhat less prominent in the medical writings of the eighteenth century, and many of them were different in perspective from their seventeenth-century predecessors, the condition was far from ignored. Rather than describing a distinct syndrome, Friedrich Hoffmann (1660–1742) included love among the various factors which could cause the irregular motions of the circulation that he associated with melancholia.[20] Richard Mead (1673–1754) did not identify a syndrome of love-melancholy or erotomania, but he briefly mentioned madness brought on by love in his chapter on mania and melancholia. He stated that "nothing disorders the mind so much as love and religion. . . . Love is attended with hope, fear, jealousy, and sometimes with wrath, and hatred arising from the latter. . . . The Madness of persons in love is more generally of the maniacal, and that of superstitious people of the melancholick kind."[21] In his encyclopedic *Medicinal Dictionary* of the 1740s, Robert James (1705–1776) did not include an entry on either love-melancholy or erotomania, but, under the heading "amor (love)," he noted that love could lead to madness and numerous other disorders.[22] Without giving it any of the customary names, he then proceeded to outline the traditional clinical picture of love-sickness, citing Paul of Aegina and Oribasius.

Perhaps the clearest indication of the continuing recognition of love-sickness as a disease, and of its continuing relationship to melancholia is its place in the *Nosologia Methodica* of François Boissier de Sauvages (1706–1767).[23] Among his ten *Classes* of diseases, De Sauvages included as the eighth Class *Des Folies*, the forms of madness or insanity; and one of the four *Orders* within this class was *Les Délires*, the derangements or disturbances of intellectual function. Among the five main forms of deliria, in the spirit of Thomas

Willis he included *La Mélancholie* differentiated as a particular (or circum-scribed) derangement from *La Manie* as a universal (or generalized) derange-ment. Then, among his fourteen species of melancholia, he included *erot-omania*, noting *amorous melancholia* to be a synonymous term. In describing this disorder de Sauvages immediately dissociated it from satyriasis and nympho-mania, which he had already grouped among the species within another of his four Orders of madness. He said that erotomaniacs did not shamelessly desire to possess the object of their love, but, rather, regarded their beloved as a divinity whose every wish they strove to fulfill. Her presence rendered them joyful; her absence left them grieving. They neglected food, sleep, and their regular affairs. He alluded to its often hidden nature, and to the changes in countenance and pulse with the presence of or hearing the name of the beloved that revealed the nature of the disorder; and he cited Erasistratus and Galen in these regards. He mentioned the traditional "preferred remedy" of marriage with the beloved. But, if that was not possible, there were the familiar measures of prayers and fasting, the advice of wise men, a long voyage and the avoidance of reminders of the beloved, the avoidance of idleness, the dissua-sion from the regard for the beloved by playing up her faults, and the avoidance of foods that generated semen.

In his *De regimine mentis* of 1763, an essay on "the harmful and beneficial effects of the emotions on the body in health and disease," Jerome Gaub (1705–1780) addressed this disorder under the heading "Harmful Corporeal Effects of Unrequited Love."[24] He wrote:

> How the force and continuity of the functions slacken, how the condition of the body languishes and all the powers of the economy weaken and collapse when an ardent wish for some desired object is too long drawn out! Do not even the sturdiest races exhibit men who are troubled by peculiar ailments when assailed by a yearning, to which they do not yield soon enough, to return home after having tarried overlong in foreign parts, ailments that may end fatally when all hope of return is lost? How often do beautiful maidens and handsome youths, caught in the toils of love, grow ghastly pale and waste away, consumed by melancholy, green-sickness, or erotomania, when delays occur or the hope of possession is lost? (ibid., pp. 149–150)

After commenting that "recent instances might give offense," he cited several of the traditional cases in which an assiduous physician was able to discern that the afflicted person suffered from love-sickness, including the classical cases involving Erasistratus and Galen (p. 150). It is of special interest to note his allusion to those who suffered from "having tarried overlong in foreign parts," a reference to *nostalgia*, a condition that emerged as a disease entity in the seventeenth century and was considered a form of melancholia (see chap. 16).

Although he did not deal with any such disorder in his detailed attention to diseases in his *First Lines of the Practice of Physic*, William Cullen (1710–1790) had previously taken note of it in his *Nosology* as one of the variant forms of melancholia. "With vehement love, without satyriasis or nymphomania" was his brief description of this type of melancholia, and he indicated that this was what De Sauvages had called "amatorial melancholia" and Linnaeus "erotomania."[25]

Early in the nineteenth century, Jean-Etienne-Dominique Esquirol (1772–1840) wrote on a disorder that he termed *erotic monomania* in his title and *erotomania* throughout the text. He had introduced the term *monomania* to denote "that form of insanity, in which the delirium is partial, permanent, gay *or* sad."[26] He then subdivided monomania into two types: "monomania properly so called, which is indicated by a partial delirium, and a gay or exciting passion" and which "corresponds with maniacal melancholy, maniacal fury, or with melancholy complicated with mania"; and the monomania that "corresponds with the melancholy of the ancients, the *tristimania* of Rush, and the melancholy with delirium of Pinel." Although conceiving of monomania as the generic term, he proposed to reserve its usual use for the first of these two species, and he introduced the term *lypemania* for the second species, indicating that he would use *lypemania* and *melancholy* as synonyms (*Mental Maladies*, p. 202). It was in his chapter on the various types of monomania in the narrower sense of the first of these two species that he wrote about *erotomania*. He stated that it

> is a chronic cerebral affection, and is characterized by an excessive sexual passion; now, for a known object; now, for one unknown. In this disorder, there is a lesion of the imagination only. . . . It is a mental affection, in which the amorous sentiments are fixed and dominant, like religious ideas in theomania, or in religious lypemania. Erotomania differs essentially from nymphomania, and satyriasis. In the latter, the evil originates in the organs of reproduction, whose irritation reacts upon the brain. In erotomania, the sentiment which characterizes it, is in the head. The nymphomaniac, as well as the victim to satyriasis, is the subject of a physical disorder. The erotomaniac is, on the contrary, the sport of his imagination. . . . In erotomania, the eyes are lively and animated, the look passionate, the discourse tender, and the actions expansive; but the subjects of it never pass the limits of propriety. They, in some sort, forget themselves; vow a pure, and often secret devotion to the object of their love. . . . While contemplating its often imaginary perfections, they are thrown into ecstasies. Despairing in its absence, the look of this class of patients is dejected; their complexion becomes pale; their features change; sleep and appetite are lost. They are restless, thoughtful, greatly depressed in mind, agitated, irritable and passionate. The return of the object beloved, intoxicates them with joy. (pp. 335–336)

Esquirol described at length two cases in which the patient suffered deranged preoccupations regarding the beloved and imagined that the love was reciprocated, and yet was rational on other matters (pp. 336–338). He then noted that not all sufferers from this disorder fitted this same clinical picture, and went on to describe a pining, lovelorn condition in which the patients were "not irrational, but sad, melancholic, gloomy, taciturn" (pp. 338–339). In this context he alluded to the change in countenance and pulse that occurred with the sight or mention of the beloved, and proceeded to cite some of the traditional pulse-lore cases, along with the one that Ferrand had described from his own experience. He observed that "erotomania, like all forms of monomania, may degenerate" (p. 341). That is, rather than continuing as a circumscribed area of preoccupation and derangement, the disturbance might spread to more and more ideas and eventually to a generalized derangement. This disorder was more common in younger people, "especially those of a nervous temperament, a lively and ardent imagination"; and Esquirol cited "a life of indolence . . . masturbation . . . and continence" as predisposing factors. As to treatment, he mentioned "prolonged tepid baths, diluent drinks . . . together with a vegetable regimen," tonics, cold baths, diversions, and physical activity. In extreme cases, he suggested that "marriage is almost the only efficacious remedy," and, interestingly, drew a parallel here to the disorder called *nostalgia*, stating that "it is only the accomplishment of the desires of the patient, that can cure him" (p. 342).

In several important ways Esquirol's account of erotomania was a familiar one. He included the two subpatterns or subtypes that had become so familiar in the earlier literature on love-sickness or love-melancholy. Some were sexually stirred, excited, enlivened but frustrated and deranged, with delusional ideas about the object of their love. Others were troubled in the form of a pining, lovelorn state, suffered many of the symptoms that had been cited since classical times, were dejected, and seemed to suffer more from unrequited love than deranged love. The traditional pulse-lore found its way into his account. And he followed an established tradition in carefully distinguishing erotomania from nymphomania and satyriasis. On the other hand, his nosological scheme gave this disorder a rather different position than had been customary. His introduction of the notion of monomania provided a natural conceptual home for erotomania. Tending to involve a narrow sphere of preoccupation, and delusional ideas within a circumscribed realm, it fitted well in his scheme of monomanias. But it was no longer grouped with the melancholic or dejected conditions as it so often had been, and, instead, it was now found among the excited forms of monomania. Whether with agreement or disagreement, Esquirol's presentation was taken into account by many during the remainder of the nineteenth century.

A leading British author, Daniel H. Tuke (1827–1895), found much to agree with in Esquirol's account, but he was inclined to view Esquirol's "description of erotomania as but one of its forms—the sentimental—or as erotomania *proper;* and nymphomania . . . and satyriasis . . . as additional forms."[27] Although he paid his respects to Esquirol's notion of monomania, he did not employ it as a distinct nosological category as Esquirol had done. Among his five main categories of mental disorder, he included "Delusional Insanity" and "Emotional Insanity," noting that examples of monomania might occur under either heading (*Manual,* p. 100). Viewing erotomania as "rarely . . . , strictly speaking, monomaniacal," he categorized it under "Emotional Insanity" (p. 193).

Again giving careful attention to Esquirol's views on the subject, another British author, G. Fielding Blandford (1829–1911), questioned the very idea that erotomania was a form of insanity. As with several other disordered behavior patterns, he argued that erotomania was not "a special monomania" but, rather, a pattern of insane acts which might occur as symptoms in a case of insanity.[28] Such acts did not constitute insanity but were the results of the person's insanity; they were reflections of a disordered intellect, accompanied by delusions.

Many other nineteenth-century authors of texts on mental disorders took no note of erotomania at all. Still others merely made brief allusions to it.[29] And the occasional author followed Esquirol's lead and referred to it as "erotic monomania."[30] In our context it is of particular interest that there was a significant decrease in the tendency to associate erotomania with melancholic and depressive features, whether in describing or in naming the disorder.

In *A Dictionary of Psychological Medicine* Tuke touched on this disorder in several ways, providing some indication of its status toward the end of the century. He took note of *eromania, eroticomania,* and *erotomania* as synonyms, and then defined them as "terms used for those forms of insanity where there is an intensely morbid desire towards a person of the opposite sex, without sensual passion. Others define it as synonymous with Nymphomania and Satyriasis."[31] He referred the reader to *erotic insanity,* which he defined as "Insanity with symptoms tending towards special sexual excitement, as occurs in satyriasis. May be only sentimental" (2:696). This use of the term *sentimental* implied that it might be emotional in origin rather than physical, or stem from a lesion of the mental functions rather than from a disorder in the reproductive organs; such views were stated by Esquirol, as noted above. The tendency was clearly toward aberrant trends in sexual desire and sexual activity, with pining, dejected trends no longer being mentioned. Lingering traces of the connections with melancholia were reflected in his definition of *love-melancholy* as "a popular term for true erotomania" (2:752) and in his statement that *melancholia erotica* was a synonym for *erotic insanity* (2:796). A very similar view was provided in the *Dictionary of Philosophy and Psychology* at the beginning of the present century, where it was stated that erotomania was "a symptom of various mental troubles, characterized by a morbid and intense passion for the opposite sex; the sexual feeling is imaginative and emotional rather than carnal. The term is also used to express excessive sexual passion, and thus becomes synonymous with nymphomania in women, and satyriasis in men."[32]

An interestingly different perspective on erotomania was presented in a leading German textbook of the late nineteenth century. Richard von Krafft-Ebing (1840–1902) dealt with such clinical disorders among the paranoias in a section entitled *erotic paranoia*, where he gave *erotomania* as a synonym. This section was part of a large group of "Psychic Degenerations," or "disease-states affecting the abnormal, predisposed, or weakened brain," which were contrasted with the other large group of "Psychoneuroses," or "disease-states of the normal and robust brain." These two groups together constituted the category of "mental diseases of the adult brain" that he termed "functional psychoses," or "diseases without anatomico-pathologic lesions."[33]

Erotic paranoia was "another variety of paranoia, less studied and also relatively infrequent as compared with other varieties.

> In all cases of my observation the individuals have been peculiar, and their abnormal psychic characteristics could be referred to hereditary influences or to infantile diseases of the brain.
> The nucleus of the whole malady is the delusion of being distinguished and loved by a person of the opposite sex who regularly belongs to one of the higher classes of society. The love for this person is, as should be emphasized, romantic, enthusiastic, but absolutely platonic. . . .
> They early show a shy and awkward manner in society, which is especially noticeable in intercourse with persons of the opposite sex. Lively expressions of sexual instinct that finds relief in sensual satisfaction is sought in vain in these patients. In the male patients of my observation, who constitute the majority, there were indications of absence of sexual instinct, or perversity which led to onanism. (*Text-Book of Insanity*, p. 408)

The author then elaborated on the clinical history and description, cited two cases at length, and commented that he had "never seen a case recover" (pp. 408–413). Krafft-Ebing's delineation of what constituted erotomania is of particular interest to the modern psychiatrist in that it is remarkably similar to what later came to be termed *De Clérambault's Syndrome*. And his view that it was a form of paranoia is similar to that of various modern comments on erotomania.

In more recent years the term *erotomania* has become associated with a specific psychotic condition without apparent melancholic or depressive features. Carefully observed and described by Gaëtan G. De Clérambault (1872–1934), it has come to be referred to as *De Clérambault's Syndrome*, or *pure erotomania*.[34] This latter name had the implication of a primary or essential erotomania, as distinct from secondary or symptomatic erotomania, which occurred as an aspect of a psychosis of a paranoid type. The patient was usually a woman who had the delusional belief that a man was very much in love with her. The man was usually much older than the patient or her husband and of a much higher social status. The woman held the conviction of being in amorous communication with this man, who had been the first to fall in love and the first to make advances. De Clérambault emphasized that there was a sudden onset in contrast to the gradual development of paranoid states and secondary erotomanic conditions, that pride rather than love was crucial in the delusional process, that hallucinations were absent, and that the condition was chronic with the delusion persisting unchanged. He emphasized the importance of distinguishing this condition "from everyday infatuation, normal passion, and nymphomania on the one hand and from paranoid schizophrenia on the other."[35]

Other authors have tended to classify such erotomanic conditions as paranoid disorders of one sort or another, have argued against any status as a separate disorder, and have used the term *erotomania* descriptively to refer to a symptom cluster with erotic import as an aspect of the paranoid disorder.[36] It is of interest in our context to note that one of the recent studies, by Raskin and Sullivan, suggested that the erotomanic delusion "seemed to fill a vacuum in these patients' lives" and so masked a depression.[37]

CHAPTER SIXTEEN

Nostalgia

Emerging much more recently than either lycanthropy or love-melancholy, *nostalgia* was first described as a clinical syndrome in the late seventeenth century, eventually acquired the status of a variant of melancholia, and continued to be viewed as a distinct disorder until the beginning of the twentieth century.[1] In 1688 Johannes Hofer (1669–1752) authored the first description of this condition in the form of his medical dissertation, *De Nostalgia oder Heimwehe*. He acknowledged the German term *Heimweh*, used in Switzerland to denote "the grief for the lost charm of the Native Land," and the French term *maladie du pays*. Then he constructed the Latiniform term *nostalgia* for it, noting that it was "Greek in origin and indeed composed of two sounds, the one of which is *Nostos*, return to the native land; the other, *Algos*, signifies suffering or grief; . . . the sad mood originating from the desire for the return to one's native land."[2] He also allowed that others might prefer to refer to this condition as *nosomania* or *philopatridomania*, and some later authors mentioned these names.

Hofer described two cases at some length. (1) A man from Bern who was studying in Basel suffered "from sadness for a considerable time" and "finally fell victim to this disease." He developed a fever, anxiety, and palpitations, and his symptoms worsened to where he was thought to be dying and prayers were being said for him. The apothecary who attended him realized that he was suffering from homesickness (*Heimweh*) and recommended that he be sent home. As soon as the patient heard this and realized that the advice was being carried out, he felt better; and on the way home from Basel he improved considerably and had recovered by the time he reached Bern. (2) A young peasant girl from the Basel area, in a hospital after an accident, became homesick, and refused the food and medication that she needed. After constant complaints that she wanted to go home, her parents took her home and she rapidly recovered.[3]

From these cases and other evidence, Hofer concluded:

> "The persons most susceptible to this disease are young people living in foreign lands, and among them especially those who at home lead a very secluded life and have almost no social intercourse. When such individuals, even well-bred children, come among other peoples, they are unable to accustom themselves to any foreign manners and way of life, nor to forget the maternal care received. They are apprehensive and find pleasure only in sweet thoughts of the fatherland until the foreign country becomes repugnant to them, or suffering various inconveniences they think night and day of returning to their native land and when prevented from so doing, they fall ill." . . .
>
> As signs by which the imminence of the disease might be detected, Hofer lists a tendency to melancholy arising from the individual's nature, an aversion to foreign customs and social gatherings, intense annoyance and anger at any jokes aimed at the individual, as well as the slightest injustice or inconvenience, and constant expressions of praise for his native land coupled with disparagement of other regions. The actual occurrence of nostalgia is revealed by a continuing melancholy, incessant thinking of home, disturbed sleep or insomnia, weakness, loss of appetite, anxiety, cardiac palpitations, stupor, and fever.[4]

Hofer took note of such contributory factors as "preceding dangerous, chronic ailments, where the patient is not treated well or as he wishes, or atmospheric changes which act on the blood and the nervous spirits. Even greater . . . the impact of foreign usages and customs, as well as very different modes of life. . . . injustices and disagreeable situations experienced by the individual. All these influences . . . recalled to mind the better native land which had been left behind" (ibid.).

> As to its pathogenesis, the disease is due essentially to a disordered imagination, whereby the part of the brain chiefly affected is that in which the images of the desired persons and places are located. This is the inner part of the brain where the vital spirits constantly surge back and forth through the nerve fibres in which the impressions of the native land are stored. As a consequence of dwelling persistently upon them, these impressions become so profound that the vital spirits move in these channels of their own accord, continually evoking the impressions, just as things that impress us deeply reappear in our dreams. Once the vital spirits have made a path for themselves and widened it, they find it easier, as in sleep, to take the same path again and again. This is the reason for the indifference exhibited in this illness towards other persons, objects, and events, just as a person in a brown study does not notice things going on around him.
>   . . . Because the vital spirits are too occupied, they do not respond promptly to other impressions, and consequently do not flow in adequate quantity or potency to other parts of the brain to serve the natural functions. As a result, the appetite is not aroused, and the food is not properly digested because

the necessary nervous fluid is lacking. In turn, chyle of poorer quality enters the blood, thus the quantity of vital spirits produced is less than previously, and because of the continuous activity of the brain this lesser quantity is soon used up. For this reason, the patient's movements become increasingly feeble, the circulation of the blood slows down, thus producing a slower heartbeat and filling the patient with anxiety. A low grade fever develops, and after the bodily functions have been weakened because the vital spirits are exhausted, death ensues. "Experience shows that imagination alone can cause all this." (ibid., p. 342)

On prognosis, he stated that this condition was curable "if the yearning can be satisfied; incurable, mortal, or at least very grave when circumstances prevent its satisfaction." He thought that treatment should be "directed to correction of the disturbed imagination and amelioration of the symptoms." In its early stages he recommended

> a purgative, presumably to eliminate poorly digested food. If the patient were nauseated or if there were signs of viscid mucus in the stomach, an emetic was in order. Venesection was to be used if the patient was plethoric. Insomnia and restlessness were to be treated with narcotic mixtures. While these measures were being taken, the patient had to be given hope that he would return home as soon as his condition permitted; furthermore, he should have entertaining company to diminish his longing. However, if none of these measures is effective, the patient must be sent home, for experience shows that this action practically always produces a cure. On the other hand, most of those who cannot return finally die, or are driven mad. (ibid.)

Rosen has traced attention to a similar condition as "a state of deep despair" among soldiers in the wars of Western Europe in the early seventeenth century (p. 341). And, following Hofer's presentation, it had become established as a clinical entity in the medical literature by the beginning of the eighteenth century. For a long time there was a tendency to associate this disorder specially with Swiss nationals away from their native land or even merely away from their home region—to the extent that it was referred to by many as *Schweizerkrankheit*; and Swiss medical writers were particularly prominent among the contributors to the extensive "homesickness literature" (*Heimwehliteratur*) of the eighteenth century. But gradually it became accepted that this condition was no respecter of national origins, just as Hofer had originally maintained. It was noted in seamen away from home for long periods of time, in students studying in foreign countries, in serving girls working away from their home regions, and often in soldiers of other nationalities than Swiss serving abroad.

With the emergence of the extensive nosological schemes of the eighteenth century, the status of nostalgia as a distinct disease was further endorsed. François Boissier de Sauvages (1706–1767) included it among the numerous mental diseases grouped as *Des Folies*, the eighth of his ten Classes of diseases; but he placed it in Order II with *Les Bizarreries* or *Les Morosités*, the derangements of the desires, rather than grouping it with melancholia and the other traditional forms of madness.[5] He defined it as a species of fantasy that strongly influenced foreigners to return to their own country, with the result that, if prevented from doing so, they were tormented by sadness, sleeplessness, loss of appetite, and other serious symptoms. Particularly susceptible to this disorder were young people who left the bosom of their family to seek their fortune or as a result of falling ill. Separated from familiar things, they became preoccupied with memories of their homeland and yearned to return. De Sauvages mentioned three types: (1) *Simple nostalgia*, which he associated with students and soldiers away from home; (2) *Complicated nostalgia*, which accompanied various physical illnesses; (3) *Simulated nostalgia*, which occurred among members of the armed forces. Regarding treatment, he emphasized psychological measures, such as diverting entertainments and satisfying the sufferers' desires; but he remarked that, often, starting out on the journey home or even just the assurance that they will be returning home was enough to bring about an improvement.

In the latter half of the eighteenth century a large number of medical authors, De Meyserey, Van Swieten, and Auenbrugger among them, gave special attention to the incidence of nostalgia, both true and simulated, among soldiers in the armies of Western Europe. As the physician who developed the technique of percussion, Leopold Auenbrugger (1722–1809) in particular made some novel contributions to nostalgia. Although he described this syndrome in familiar terms, followed the emerging eighteenth-century trend of viewing the physical symptoms as stemming from emotional causes, and introduced nothing new in his considerations of treatment and prognosis, he took note of some significant new features such as a dull percussive sound on one side of the chest in such patients and the lungs adherent to the pleura in autopsies of those who died of the disease. In this early example of correlating clinical findings with autopsy findings, Auenbrugger may well have been dealing with instances of tuberculosis.[6]

In his *De regimine mentis* of 1763 Jerome Gaub (1705–1780) alluded to nostalgia or homesickness, along with love-sickness, as being among the "Harmful Corporeal Effects of Unrequited Love."[7] Then, in addressing the "Beneficial Corporeal Effects of Hope in Connection with Various Ailments," he referred to "the sufferers from homesickness who are revivified by hope alone when first they ready themselves to return to their native lands."[8]

In his *Essay on the Connection between the Animal and the Spiritual Nature of Man*, the dissertation with which he completed his medical studies in 1780, Friedrich Schiller (1759–1805) discussed the beneficial effects of mental pleasure on health and stated: "This is most obviously confirmed by the example of patients who have been cured by joy. Take someone back to his homeland who has been reduced to a skeleton by the most frightful nostalgia and he will become rejuvenated and return to blossoming health."[9] In their fine study of his medical and psychological writings Dewhurst and Reeves have persuasively presented Schiller's experience with Grammont, his severely melancholic friend and fellow medical student, as a very personal acquaintance with the problems of nostalgia (*Friedrich Schiller*, pp. 177–201). Among their references to the relevant medical literature of the era, these authors make particular mention of the influential work of Johan Georg Zimmermann (1728–1795), who had written about nostalgia in the 1760s, and of a medical dissertation in 1779 by another of Schiller's fellow students, Elwert, in which nostalgia received some attention (ibid., p. 293).

In the various nosological schemes that emerged under the influence of De Sauvages's contributions—such as those of Linné, Vogel, Cullen, and Sagar—nostalgia usually found its place. Although Vogel considered "*nostalgia* as a species of melancholy," and Cullen suggested that the "nostalgia of *Sauvage, Linnaeus* and *Sagar*" might be versions of the "partial insanity" that he defined melancholia to be, in his nosological system Cullen placed nostalgia in Class IV, *Locales*, instead of Class II, *Neuroses*, where melancholia and mania were included.[10] Within the *Locales* ("a disorder of part, and not of the whole body"), Order II was named *Dysorexiae* ("an erroneous or defective appetite") and included nostalgia, along with bulimia, polydypsia, pica, satyriasis, and nymphomania, in its first section, entitled "Erroneous Appetites" (*Nosology*, pp. 179–182). Cullen defined nostalgia in familiar terms as "an ardent desire, when absent from home, of returning thither"; and he followed De Sauvages closely in recognizing "its species" and "1. Nostalgia (*simplex*) without any other disease" and "2. Nostalgia (*complicata*) accompanied with other disorders" (p. 182). Interestingly, however, he added that "*Nostalgia* alone, if it can be called a disease, is not a local disorder; but I could not well separate an uncertain disorder, from the other *dysorexiae*" (p. 179). Thus, as we might well think today, he thought nostalgia to be in strange company among these "erroneous appetites."

Thomas Arnold (1742–1816) devoted a section to nostalgia in his *Observations on Insanity* in the 1780s. Arranging the various "species of insanity" into two "divisions"—(1) *ideal insanity*, what we might call hallucinatory conditions; (2) *notional insanity*, what we might call delusional conditions—Arnold included *pathetic insanity* in the second division and stated that it "exhibits a striking and melancholy picture, of the empire of the passions. In this species of insanity some one passion is in full, and complete possession of the mind."[11] *Nostalgic insanity* was one of the sixteen types of pathetic insanity.

The attachment to their kindred, to their friends, to their acquaintances, to the scenes in which they have passed the happy period of youthful innocence, and simplicity, in which whatever is dear to them is contained, and whatever has most nearly interested them has been transacted,—an attachment which all mankind, in some degree or other, experience,—is as amiable, when not immoderate and illiberal, as it is grateful and natural to the human heart. But like the other passions, and especially grief and love, both of which in some respects it much resembles,—the latter in its general nature, and the former in some of its effects,—when it becomes violent and unreasonable, not only leads to, but, under certain circumstances, actually is a variety of, pathetic insanity. (*Observations*, 1:207–208)

Melancholic and sorrowful conditions were included among the other forms of pathetic insanity, but there was much more besides. Thus, for Arnold, nostalgia had some classificatory affinity with melancholia, but by no means did he consider it a form of melancholia.

By the early nineteenth century, though, nostalgia had come to be more consistently viewed as a form of melancholia. In 1818 Johann Christian Heinroth (1773–1843) included homesickness or nostalgia among the "subspecies, variations, and modifications of melancholia" and said that "its entire character is that of pure melancholia, except that it is modified by a definite object."[12]

Well-known textbooks on mental disorders around the middle of the century make it clear that this view was, by then, well established. Ernst Von Feuchtersleben (1806–1849) stated that "the effects of melancholy on the body are most completely represented in what we call home-sickness (nostalgia); a disease which has been unnecessarily classed among the proper psychopathies, since it has no other specific pathognomonic signs except that of a heavily oppressed spirit, with the influence of this on the body, and exists without alienation of the personality." The implication here was that it was not a form of mental derangement or psychosis. He then went on to say that "it can only pass into insanity when in its higher degree, and after a long duration, and then it represents a 'melancholy with a fixed idea of domestic happiness' (that is, with a special cause)."[13] This idea of two levels of severity for nostalgia, one not insane and one insane, had been alluded to by Arnold and was used by others after Von Feuchtersleben. Further, this mode of thinking was already emerging as a way of conceiving of the melancholias more generally.

In his crucially important textbook Wilhelm Griesinger (1817–1868) conceived of nostalgia among "States of Mental Depression—Melancholia":

Another variety of melancholia is that form which is characterised by a longing for one's native land, and by the predominance of those ideas which refer to a return to one's home—HOME-SICKNESS. An analogous affection is sometimes developed in prisoners by want of employment, and frequently also by the cooperating influence of bad nourishment, damp cells, and onanism. . . .

Naturally, home-sickness is not always a mental disease. . . . In itself it is a mournful disposition of spirit suggested by external circumstances. It becomes insanity when this disposition so strongly impregnates all the faculties of the mind as utterly to exclude the entrance of any other sentiment, and when it is accompanied by delirious conceptions and hallucinations; a state in which physical derangements—e.g., loss of appetite, emaciation, etc.—are seldom absent. In short, home-sickness ought *in foro* to be regarded as a mental affection only when it presents the usual signs of insanity.[14]

In another important mid-century textbook John Charles Bucknill (1817–1897) and Daniel H. Tuke (1827–1895) gave considerable attention to nostalgia in their section on melancholia. They conceived of it as an instance of the "simple form" of melancholia, which meant that "there is here no disorder of the intellect, strictly speaking; no delusion or hallucination."[15] They stated: "Nostalgia . . . , homesickness, may sometimes be a variety of simple melancholia. Army surgeons see the most of it" (*Manual*, p. 161). Drawing heavily on "the celebrated Larrey," they proceeded to emphasize the incidence among soldiers and made the following observations:

> The mental faculties in nostalgic patients were the first to undergo a change . . . great exaltation of the imaginative faculty. The prospect of their native home presented itself to their mind's eye, . . . depicted in the most extravagant and delusive hues which a morbid fancy could suggest. . . . This state of cerebral excitement is accompanied, at the commencement of the disorder, by corresponding physical symptoms. The heat of the head is increased—the pulse accelerated; there is redness of the conjunctivae: and unusual movements of the patient may frequently be observed—perhaps occasioned by the uncertain pains in various parts of the body, of which he usually complains. The bowels are constipated; there is a general feeling of oppression and weariness, indicated by the patient frequently stretching himself and sighing. There is an inability to fix the attention, and the conversation is, in consequence, somewhat unconnected. (pp. 161–162)

These authors went on to note the possibility of worsening symptoms, both physical and mental. "The mental depression keeps pace with the decline of bodily strength, and is often manifested by weeping, sighing, or groaning. . . . A propensity to suicide is not unfrequently manifested when the debility becomes extreme" (p. 162). If unrelieved, such conditions might well lead to death, and they cited instances of serious intracranial findings on autopsy (pp. 162–163).

As Rosen has so effectively documented, nostalgia continued to be a critical concern to military authorities and military physicians. This concern had been prominent in the latter half of the eighteenth century, and this continued to be the case through much of the nineteenth century ("Nostalgia"). But, toward the end of the nineteenth century, with nostalgia already absorbed into the melancholias as a form or variant, this condition gradually faded from the nosological schemes. Nevertheless, it was still given respectful attention in the 1890s in Tuke's *A Dictionary of Psychological Medicine*, where it was stated that "there is a kind of melancholia which aetiologically has been called nostalgic melancholia, or nostalgia. . . . Nostalgia always represents a combination of psychical and bodily disturbances, and for this reason it must always be defined as disease, and may become the object of medical treatment."[16] The term *nostomania* was also mentioned and was defined as "the longing for home so morbidly intense that it has become a monomania" (*Dictionary*, 2:859). And the eleventh edition of the *Encyclopaedia Britannica* defined it as "home-sickness, the desire when away to return home, amounting sometimes to a form of melancholia."[17] Despite these lingering traces, the twentieth century essentially dealt with the distresses and disorders of members of the armed forces abroad, various refugees and displaced persons, and others suffering dislocation from their roots without returning to the concept of nostalgia, at least in any sense of a formal disease. A doctoral dissertation on nostalgia in 1940 stemmed from the study of American college students, led to an interesting review of the literature, but failed to revive nostalgia as a disease.[18]

V

Concluding Comments

CHAPTER SEVENTEEN

Overview and Afterthoughts

THE VICISSITUDES OF A CLINICAL DESCRIPTION

As we come to the end of a historical journey such as this, we may reasonably ask: Where have we been? What have we seen? And these questions might, just as reasonably, be answered in at least several different ways: how the clinical description has varied, how the explanatory schemes have varied, and how the treatment practices have varied.

To begin with, there is the clinical condition—call it disease, syndrome, or what you will—that has been at the heart of this study, that has been at the center of our observations throughout this journey. For the Hippocratics in the fifth and fourth centuries B.C., this clinical disorder was associated with "aversion to food, despondency, sleeplessness, irritability, restlessness" and was named *melancholia*. In another Hippocratic context, fear was added to sadness, and these two passions were given cardinal status as symptoms of melancholia; the idea of chronicity was introduced with the comment that when these emotional disturbances were "prolonged," the person suffered from melancholia. During the second century A.D., the clinical description acquired further details and took on a form that became more or less standard in Islamic and Western medical writings for nearly fifteen hundred years. Crucially contributed to by Rufus of Ephesus at the beginning of that century and then shaped by Galen later in the same century, the main features of this enlarged clinical description were the following: a chronic, nonfebrile form of madness in which the afflicted were usually fearful, sad, misanthropic, and tired of life, usually accompanied by the symptoms noted by the Hippocratics, often accompanied by a particular, circumscribed delusion, and sometimes accompanied by symptoms of gastrointestinal distress. Gradually, costiveness in particular became a gastrointestinal symptom mentioned in most cases. Suicidal thoughts and the danger of suicide were intermittently mentioned.

During the sixteenth and seventeenth centuries, several modifications were made in the clinical accounts of melancholia. First, the sadness, and often the fear as well, came to be described as being "without cause" or "without apparent cause." Although this element can be traced in occasional early descriptions, it gradually became a standard feature during the sixteenth century. Then, beginning in the sixteenth century, references to guilt, sometimes explicit, sometimes implicit, crept into descriptions of melancholia with increasing frequency. Although Bright in the late sixteenth century had taken considerable pains to differentiate the dejected state of melancholia from the similar state associated with "the conscience oppressed with sence of sinne," others were introducing such guilt-laden concerns into accounts of at least some cases of melancholia, and this became more common in the seventeenth century. Parenthetically, it is at least suggestive to find this feature emerging after the Reformation, and to note its increasing presence in accounts of melancholia in the post-Lutheran era of greater emphasis on individual responsibility and stern Protestant emphasis on guilt and punishment. The presence of a particular delusion had long been cited as a common symptom, and as early as Rufus it had been observed that the afflicted person seemed quite sane on topics other than that of his delusion. This latter point was not commonly mentioned for a long while, but in the sixteenth century it began to be referred to more often, and during the seventeenth century it became a frequent descriptive observation. During the eighteenth century this became a usual element in descriptions of melancholia to the point where it was being maintained that this *partial insanity* was the essential feature; but this view was already in question by the end of the century, and this feature was gradually abandoned during the first half of the nineteenth century.

In addition to such descriptive changes as those just noted, there were other shifts in descriptive content in which whole constellations of symptoms sometimes associated with melancholia were pruned away and given separate nosological status. First, there was the pattern of symptoms known as hypochondriacal—flatulence, digestive disturbances, various associated aches and pains—which were for many centuries grouped with sadness and fear to constitute one of the three classical subtypes of melancholia, a scheme suggested by Rufus and taken up by Galen. Variously known as flatuous melancholia, windy melancholia, and hypochondriacal melancholia, this condition continued to be recognized in this way until the latter half of the seventeenth century. Then, in a process crucially contributed to by Willis and Sydenham, this syndrome was separated out from melancholia as hypochondriasis, and the traditional notion of three types of melancholia was abandoned. Beginning with Boerhaave, hypochondriasis began a career as a milder disorder on a continuum of severity that could lead to melancholia, a distinct disorder, or even develop further into mania, another distinct disorder. Eighteenth-century authorities began to take pains to note that melancholia did not include symptoms of dyspepsia; such symptoms marked the disorder as that kindred disease, hypochondriasis.

Another constellation of symptoms with a long and intimate association with melancholia were those grouped under the diagnosis of mania—a state of derangement with excitement, at times grandiosity, and at times wild behavior—which constituted one of the three classical forms of madness, melancholia and phrenitis being the other two. Mania and melancholia were often likened to each other as chronic forms of madness without fever, and were just as often contrasted to each other as having opposite symptoms. Over the centuries, many authors observed that some cases of melancholia changed into mania, and vice versa; with Boerhaave came the continuum of severity, ranging from hypochondriasis to melancholia to mania; and in the nineteenth century Baillarger and Falret related a portion of these two disorders to each other as aspects of a single cyclical disorder. But from even classical times, rather than merely the irritability and restlessness often associated with melancholia, some cases were cited as being excited forms of melancholia, even involving grandiosity and related affects in some instances. For many centuries, a minority of the cases diagnosed as melancholia were of this sort, or had moments of this sort, and were often referred to as instances of adust melancholia. Early in the nineteenth century, melancholia underwent a significant reduction in its clinical content and a sharpening of its outlines as Esquirol separated out a minority group of monodelusional states with exalted mood, and thereafter its descriptive outline was usually restricted to severe depressive disturbances. And, after Esquirol, with melancholia no longer synonymous with partial insanity and with the very validity of partial insanity increasingly in question, melancholia gradually lost its status as even one form of partial insanity.

During the nineteenth century, although melancholia continued to be commonly associated with delusions, they gradually became less necessary to the accepted clinical description. *Simple melancholia* or melancholia without delusion emerged as a recognized subtype that might or might not worsen into *melancholia with delusion*. Increasingly, the emphasis was on affective disturbance as the essential element in the clinical picture rather than on delusional thinking. Although conceived of as secondary to the dejected state with its distressed preoccupation, the retardation of thought and physical activity was increasingly viewed as an aspect of the descriptive core. Although, often enough, the delusional type was described as monodelusional, with gradually greater frequency the person was described as delusional beyond such limits; and, when delusions were present, it was increasingly recognized that they were mood-syntonic, and thus tended to be delusions of guilt and sin, other forms of self-derogatory delusions, delusions of poverty, delusions of serious physical illness, or nihilistic delusions.

At the beginning of the twentieth century, Kraepelin brought mania and melancholia back into a more intimate connection than ever, collecting most such states together under the rubric *manic-depressive insanity* and using contrasting triads of symptoms to illustrate the cores of the respective clinical pictures: *mania* with its flight of ideas, exaltation, and overactivity; *depression* with its inhibition of thought, depression of feelings, and psychomotor inhibition. In the Kraepelinian tradition that dominated the first half of the twentieth century, the extended description of depression also provided a continuing home for many of the signs and symptoms from past extended descriptions of melancholia, clinical elements that had never really left melancholia's clinical picture and yet were not necessarily all present in any particular case: sleeplessness, loss of appetite, loss of weight, constipation, loss of sexual interest, restlessness, irritability, anxiety, self-derogatory concerns, suicidal inclinations, delusions. These descriptive trends have been argued about, removed and reinserted, added to and subtracted from, and refined in various ways; and yet this general constellation remains familiar and relevant to those who have known depressed patients well.

A PARADE OF THEORIES

Over a period of approximately two thousand years, from the Hippocratic writings to the late seventeenth century, the predominant scheme for explaining diseases in general, and mental disorders in particular, was the humoral theory. Of the four humors, the black bile, with its qualities of coldness and dryness, was the crucial one in the etiology and pathogenesis of melancholia. The substance of the brain was thought to be affected by an excess of black bile that caused this cold and dry disease. An important variation in the pathogenesis occurred in hypochondriacal melancholia, one of the three subtypes, in which a local excess of black bile in the primary site, the hypochondriacal region, was thought to give off smoky vapors that rose to the brain, affecting it secondarily to cause melancholia.

Shaped by Galen and various later Galenists, these explanations lasted well into the seventeenth century. By late in the century, however, the humoral theory was losing its preeminent place in medical explanations, and eventually these changes were reflected in the efforts to explain melancholia.

With his conceptual roots in the relatively new iatrochemical notions, Willis argued that melancholia was *not* caused by a melancholic humor, that is, the black bile. Instead of subscribing to the traditional elements, qualities, and humors, he held that all bodies were composed of the five principles of the chemists: spirit, sulphur, salt (the three active principles), water, and earth (the two passive principles). From their various motions and by their proportions in mixtures, these principles accounted for both normal phenomena and pathological conditions. Instead of citing humoral disequilibria, he turned to the doctrine of fermentation for his explanations of pathogenesis. He elaborated a chemical pathophysiology of the brain and animal spirits to explain the gloomy and disordered nature of the melancholic's thoughts. The nervous liquor, which was the vehicle for the animal spirits and was usually mild, benign, and subtle, was changed to an acetous and corrosive condition with functional and, at times, structural pathological changes in the brain; this nervous fluid had become vinegarish or sour as a result of fermentation. As to melancholia's sadness and fear, the blood tended to circulate less well and to stagnate in the praecordia, with reduced circulation to the head and extremities. The vital part of the soul became constricted in its function, and the animal part of the soul became less vigorous, resulting in sadness; and both parts of the soul were "suddenly repressed and compelled as it were to shake," with fear as a result. But these new explanations were short-lived in theories of melancholia, and mechanical explanations soon began to displace them. In fact, there were hydrodynamic notions interwoven with Willis's iatrochemical ideas.

The mechanical philosophy had gradually become a prominent feature of seventeenth-century science, and so the fundamental explanations of physical phenomena came to involve the motion and interaction of the various particles of matter. As an aspect of this trend, mechanical principles, corpuscular notions, and hydrodynamic theories changed the nature and language of physiology during the latter half of that century. And the far-reaching impact of Harvey's establishment of the circulation of the blood gave special encouragement to the use of hydrodynamic ideas. Then, by the 1690s, mechanical theories were being adapted to explanations of melancholia, and by the early eighteenth century such theories had become central to such explanations. Significant among the earlier efforts to so explain melancholia were those of Pitcairn, Hoffmann, and Boerhaave, each of whom developed medical theories based on hydrodynamic principles, dynamic microparticles, and forces of attraction. They each rooted their notions of pathogenesis in various forms of disordered flow in their system of circulations (blood, lymph, nerve fluid). Pitcairn's and Boerhaave's views were essentially vasocentric, with the basic disorder in fluid flow being in the blood. Although Hoffmann gave considerable attention to disordered blood flow in his explanations of disease, he veered toward a neurocentric view when he addressed mental disorders. For Pitcairn and Hoffmann the central theme in melancholia was a sluggishness or slowing of the circulation of the blood in the brain, resulting in a less lively nerve fluid and in the person's becoming slow and sad. Boerhaave, too, thought in terms of a slowing of the circulation of the blood, but he managed to retain a version of the black bile, reinterpreting its nature in mechanical terms.

By the mid-eighteenth century, the trend was away from the earlier corpuscularian notions and a vasocentric orientation, and toward a neurocentric system with an aetherial nerve fluid in which irregular motions could lead to melancholia. Influenced by Newton's speculations on nervous transmission and by recent electrical investigations, some thought that the nerve fluid might be electrical in nature. Increasingly, it was an aetherial nerve fluid that did not flow, but, instead, served as a medium for the transmission of oscillatory or vibratory motions. Melancholia was no longer the result of a slowing of flow in the nerve fluid, but, rather, a torpor or decreased mobility in a nerve fluid that did not flow. Cullen thought that the nerve fluid might be electrical in nature and constructed a theory of pathogenesis based on either too much or too little energy in the brain and mobility in the nervous fluid. Associating the anergic behavior of the melancholic person with the idea of a depleted state, he thought that melancholia was the result of a depleted amount of excitement. And his excited and depleted states are reminiscent of the charged and discharged electrical states of an emerging explanatory fashion.

Around the beginning of the nineteenth century, Rush returned to a vasocentric orientation for the explanation of disease in general, including melancholia. The basic cause was to be found in the blood vessels of the brain, especially the arteries, and led to morbid and irregular motions. Over the course of the nineteenth century, it was asserted, and reasserted, that mental disorders, including melancholia, were essentially diseases of the brain, with Griesinger's statement perhaps the most famous version of this credo. The vast majority of authorities emphasized hereditary factors as the primary causative influences; these factors were believed to lead to a "nervous constitution" or "irritable weakness" of the nervous system and so predispose the person to melancholia. Depressing emotions, long continued, might cause stagnation and slowing of the circulation; or circulatory slowing might lead to lowered nutrition of the brain, and so to a melancholic state. In more general terms, a vasocentric emphasis was often maintained, but it was reconciled with a neurocentric orientation by an emphasis on the circulation of the blood in the brain, with resultant cerebral pathology. But from the middle of the century onward there was increasingly a neurocentric emphasis with references to problematic states of the "nerve apparatus" and to irregularities or inadequate levels of the "nerve-force." Mental disorders, including melancholia, resulted from interruptions or disturbances of the processes of proper nutrition, stimulation, and repose of the brain. Cerebral hyperemia, or congestion of the cerebral vessels, was thought to lead to excited forms of insanity; and cerebral anemia, or a deficiency in the nutritive powers of the cerebral blood supply, and resultant nerve-cell decay, were thought to lead to depressed or melancholic forms of insanity. In another version, cerebral anemia led to psychic pain, thence to inhibition, and so to the symptom picture of melancholia. There were recurrent references to reduced nervous energy, lack of nervous energy, reduced nerve activity, lowering of the tension of the nerve energy, inefficiency or slackening in the mode of working of the nerve elements, undue feebleness of nerve action, fatigue or exhaustion of the nervous system, and a lack of nervous force. In summary, the century had emphasized hereditary predispositions, degeneracies, cerebral anemias, cerebral irritations, nutritional deficiencies of the brain, depleted nerve energies, defective nerve functions, and schemes of nerve cell deficiency.

In the twentieth century, efforts to explain melancholia and depression have brought into being their fair share of etiological hypotheses and hypothetical pathogenetic sequences. Often based on psychoanalytic and psychotherapeutic data, psychological explanations came to have a more important place than had usually been the case in the past. Against a background of inadequate or disturbed psychological nurturance in infancy and early childhood, with resultant personality developments entailing predispositions, themes of loss and of inadequate or diminished self-esteem have been thought particularly significant. Hostility and rage directed toward the self has waxed and waned as an explanation. Arguments have been put forward for various sociocultural factors as instrumental in the development of depression; they are often used in an effort to account for the same issues as the psychological explanations. But biologically based theories have continued to be prominent in twentieth-century efforts to explain depressive disorders. More sophisticated genetic investigations have strengthened the argument for a hereditary factor in many cases. Endocrine studies and data on electrolyte metabolism supported other theories. Especially prominent have been the themes and variations associated with the biogenic amine hypotheses. Earlier formulations of this sort suggested that depression was associated with a functional deficit of one or more neurotransmitter amines at critical synapses in the central nervous system. Although neuroscientists working in this realm have since argued that such a formulation is too simplistic, many of them seem convinced that some version of such a hypothesis will eventually prevail. As one group of authorities has put it, "The depressive disorders seem to be a group of interrelated neuroendocrinometabolic disorders."

A FEW THEMES AND MANY THERAPIES

Three basic principles and a small number of underlying themes have provided the underpinnings that supported a wide variety of treatment measures, both the giving of substances and the implementation of procedures. This was true in the medicine of ancient times, throughout the long reign of the humoral theory and Galenic medicine, and, to a surprising extent, during recent centuries as well. Over many centuries, no matter what medical theory or other scheme of reasoning was being used, it usually entailed the view that there was an optimal balance of factors that meant stability and health. An imbalance or a disequilibrium usually meant disease. And so, again and again, treatment measures were developed to return a state of disequilibrium to a state of equilibrium. This might be termed *the principle of equilibrium*, an ancestor of Bernard's homeostatic principle. Two other basic principles, secondary principles in relation to the primary principle of equilibrium, have been (1) *eliminating an excess*, or *supplementing a deficiency*, in order to reestablish a balance; (2) *the principle of contraries*, whereby a quality (or qualities) was thought to be in excess and therapeutic agents of the opposite quality (or qualities) were prescribed to neutralize the excess and restore a balance.

In the context of the humoral theory, with melancholia caused by an excess of black bile, a central theme was thus to eliminate this excess. Accordingly, one or another evacuative procedure was thought to be indicated, and a reputed capacity to evacuate black bile constituted an essential qualification for being prescribed. When the entire blood was affected, Rufus of Ephesus and Galen advised bloodletting for the purpose of evacuation, but otherwise they thought that this procedure was only very occasionally indicated. Their preferred mode of evacuation was through purgatives, with dodder of thyme, aloe, colocynth, and black hellebore variously mentioned. Some medicaments were suggested that were thought to cut or thin the thick humor and so facilitate the evacuant efforts of the purgatives. Evacuation by clysters was mentioned, as were medicaments that would serve evacuation as diuretics and sudorifics. Coitus was mentioned as both evacuative and calming. The reestablishment of the menstrual flow or the hemorrhoidal flow was thought to facilitate the evacuation of the pathogenic humor. This pattern of evacuative recommendations, with variations here and there, guided the therapeutics of melancholia over many centuries, even into the seventeenth century.

Much in the way of therapeutic advice was based on classical concerns with *the regimen—the six non-naturals:* air, sleep and wakefulness, food and drink, exercise and rest, evacuation and retention, and the passions—and was guided by the principle of contraries. The patient's diet should be planned so as to nourish him while avoiding foods that favored the production of black bile. Warming and moistening effects against the qualities of melancholia were sought through a careful choice of food and drink. Massages with warm and moist ointments were prescribed for this cold and dry disease. Warm baths were advised for the coldness and dryness. If possible, the air should be warm and moist. Melancholia's wakefulness was to be countered with remedies for sleep. Measures were recommended to divert the patient from his delusional preoccupations or to correct his thinking. Pleasant company was advised against his inclination to solitude, and diverting activities against his inclination to inactivity. The perturbations of sadness and fear were to be countered by a pleasant atmosphere, encouragement, and reassuring measures. Joy and gladness as warm and moist passions were sought in order to change the person's cold and dry sadness. Protection against suicidal inclinations was urged. As with most of the therapeutic measures outlined in this section, with only minor variations this regimen continued to be part of the treatment recommendations for melancholia over a period of fifteen hundred years or more.

Rufus urged the importance of early recognition and prompt treatment of melancholia; guided by this view, Galen emphasized treatment with frequent baths and a moist, nourishing diet as sufficient to cure melancholia when it was recognized in its early stages. This less drastic treatment program continued to be recommended over the centuries, being joined by Paul of Aegina's additional advice that "suitable exhilaration of mind" be provided.

For hypochondriacal melancholia in particular, with its various gastrointestinal symptoms, Rufus advised measures to relax the stomach, the promotion of good digestion, and mild cathartics. Such patients should be warmed by the application of heat to the hypochondriac regions. And Oribasius recommended fomentations and poultices with a decoction of various medicaments reputed to soothe intestinal pains and diminish flatulence.

In the still Galenic medicine of the seventeenth century, bloodletting, purgatives, and, to a lesser extent, emetics were recommended for melancholia with an eye to evacuating the black bile; often associated with these measures were traditional cautions that the purgatives should be gentle and that venesections should be undertaken with due respect for the patient's weakened state. Diet was to be light and easily digested, with appropriate attention to warm and moist foods in this cold and dry disease. Also emphasized were cheerful company and diverting activities, warm bathing, and moderate exercise. And it often seemed as though the prescriber had run down a checklist of the six non-naturals. Although he developed a somewhat different theory of melancholia in keeping with the chemical notions to which he subscribed, Willis changed very little in the way of therapeutic practices. He recommended venesection in moderate quantity, gentle purgatives, and emetics, with the aim of relieving the body of its burden of pathological materials. He wrote about stimulating and strengthening the animal spirits, an aim to be served by his evacuative remedies and by diverting the soul from its troubling passions and cheering up the person. Among other measures, he mentioned gentle hypnotics for sleeplessness, spa waters that contained iron and various remedies containing steel for the purpose of strengthening the nervous juice. Otherwise employing traditional remedies, Willis was innovative in advising the use of these metals, perhaps reflecting the Paracelsian trend toward the use of metals in therapeutics.

From Pitcairn in the late seventeenth century to Cullen in the late eighteenth century, we continue to find a remarkable consistency of therapeutic themes. Mechanical explanations for melancholia emerged and flourished, and yet they did little to change the treatment practices usually recommended. Bloodletting was usually advocated, but caution was urged in view of the melancholic patient's weakened state. Some authors thought that menstrual or hemorrhoidal flow should be promoted if they had been suppressed. Purgatives were consistently mentioned but always with the caveat that they should be mild. Some mentioned emetics, again with warnings that they not be too strong. There was the occasional mention of materials containing steel or iron for their tonic effect. Hypnotics were only rarely suggested. Dietary advice was frequently given, with the emphasis on a light yet nourishing diet for a weakened person in need of strengthening. Exercise was frequently recommended, and sometimes riding or travel, or both, with the goal of energizing a debilitated patient. Providing cheerful conversation, diverting the melancholic from his fixed line of thought, and stimulating other emotions were each commonly mentioned. The principle of contraries was often cited as the basis for a therapeutic regimen. Other central themes that supported treatment recommendations, sometimes made explicit but often implicit, were the evacuating of pathological materials, the dissolving or thinning of a thickening in the blood so that a slowed circulation might return to normal, the enlivening of a weakened nerve fluid, and the strengthening and bestirring of a weakened and slowed-down person.

Later, as mechanical explanations lost much of their preeminent position, patterns of treatment still changed relatively little. Cullen's neural pathogenesis, along with his aetherial nerve fluid, his hints of electrical explanation, and his view of melancholia as a state of depleted excitement, had only minor effects on his treatment of melancholia. As had various predecessors, he attempted to systematize new theories of physiology and pathogenesis without abandoning traditional therapeutic methods.

There was increasing attention to "management" and psychological interventions in eighteenth-century accounts of therapeutic advice for melancholia. Melancholia had long been approached in terms of a physiological psychology and thought to be rooted in a disordered physiology. Perhaps the influence of Stahl and Gaub on an emerging psychosomatic orientation during this century contributed to this increasing evidence that medical authorities thought that psychological measures might crucially change this condition. On the other hand, some of this advice seems to have derived from the older tradition of attention to the passions (as one of the non-naturals) on the basis of the principle of contraries.

At the beginning of the nineteenth century, Pinel demonstrated more of a tendency to break with the traditional therapeutics of melancholia than perhaps any single predecessor. In addition to his familiar questioning of the "rigorous system of coercion" that he found in his own institutions, he expressed serious reservations about treating melancholic patients "in the usual way, by copious and repeated blood-letting, water and shower baths, low diet"; and he developed grave reservations about medications in general, and evacuants in particular, although he considered tonic remedies appropriate. Instead, he advocated a program of moral treatment, that is, the development of a milieu and the implementation of attitudes designed to influence the troubled patient toward recovery. For melancholic patients he emphasized the importance "of forcibly agitating the system; of interrupting the chain of their gloomy ideas, and of engaging their interest by powerful and continuous impressions on their external senses." He advised pleasant surroundings and entertaining and diverting activities, although he was prepared to resort to "energetic measures of coercion" in the case of serious suicidal threat. He was also a strong advocate of the, by then, familiar art of counteracting debilitating passions by other passions of equal or superior force, a program usually guided by the principle of contraries. Of particular interest here is the fact that these significant changes were primarily based on clinical experience, both his own and that of influential colleagues in the institutional setting. Other contemporaries continued to follow a tradition of evacuative therapies.

Esquirol, Pinel's leading student, recommended much more a mixture of the traditional and the innovative. He advocated moral treatment in a way that marked him both as a student of his teacher and as a leader in his own right. He outlined much that was familiar, especially detailed advice as to regimen in the tradition of the non-naturals. For all the mildness of his use of such measures, however, he still found a basis for various evacuative remedies.

This mixture of approaches was reflected in the advice of contemporaries of Esquirol as well as many who came later. Then there were increasing references to milder approaches in early cases and less severe cases, with psychological measures emphasized more and medications and other procedures less. The severer the illness, the more the treatment measures resembled those of the past, although bloodletting was less and less frequently advocated. Opium was increasingly mentioned for sleeplessness and as a calming agent, only to be largely abandoned by the end of the century. In a change reflecting the growing availability of hospitals for mental disorders, hospitalization was usually recommended for severer cases, both as a protection against suicidal inclinations and as a means of removing the patient from the context in which his illness had developed. The principles of moral treatment were invoked for the care and management of both the milder and the severer cases, and for both those in and out of a hospital. Themes akin to the traditional attention to the non-naturals were often found embedded within the treatment advice, although usually expressed in much less explicit ways than previously.* By the end of the nineteenth century, ideas of nerve weakness and depleted nerve energy were often providing the rationale for more frequent recommendations of tonics and stimulants.

By the beginning of the twentieth century, Kraepelin's views on melancholia and depression were in the ascendancy. He built his therapeutic program with the "rest cure" as its foundation. He emphasized the removal of the patient from the context in which he had taken ill to an asylum in severer cases and "to a different boarding-place or into the associations of a happy family" in milder cases. The details of his program included bed rest, constant care, nutritious diet in small amounts at frequent intervals, warm baths rather than sedatives for insomnia, and precautions against suicidal inclinations. Hypnotics might be used if milder measures did not suffice. The "psychical influence" of those in attendance was emphasized, with a "gentle, friendly, and assuring" manner advocated for "alleviating distress, modifying the delusions, and relieving the anxiety." He advised against visits from relatives at the height of the disease. "Insight into the disease and the return of sleep and nutrition to the normal state" were thought to be indices of recovery.

Meyer recommended an approach with an even more central role for psychological measures. He advocated a search of the reactive picture for points of modifiability, for foci for intervention and change. He conceived of

---

*This continued to be the case on into the twentieth century. Further, Rippere's studies on modern "commonsense knowledge about depression" demonstrate that such knowledge is rooted essentially in the non-naturals. Vicky Rippere, "Some Historical Dimensions of Commonsense Knowledge about Depression and Antidepressive Behavior," *Behav. Res. & Therapy*, 1980, *18*, 373–385.

treatment as "service in behalf of the patient," but he underscored the importance of the patient as a collaborator in the treatment endeavor. Then he
outlined his own "common sense" version of psychotherapy, characterized by
kindly, humane overtones and a searching, practical use of the patient's life
history and current situation. He gave careful attention to the hospital milieu
and to how the patient might fit into the hospital regime and best be served by
it. In the process, he mentioned such matters as attention to sleep and nutrition, occupational therapy, hydrotherapy, and recreational activities. He
followed "a regime of work, rest, and play, socialization and discussion with
physicians."

Most writings on the treatment of melancholia and depression during
the first several decades of the twentieth century reflected the themes laid out
by Kraepelin and Meyer, until the emergence of the shock treatments in the
1930s, first with metrazol and then with electricity. Psychological treatment
measures—psychoanalysis and various psychotherapies—came to be used
increasingly, both in inpatient and outpatient settings. Then, more recently,
antidepressant medications—monoamine oxidase inhibitors and tricyclic antidepressants—have entered the scene as valuable therapeutic agents. And, for
bipolar affective disorders, lithium has come into frequent use.

METAPHORS FOR MELANCHOLIA

Threaded through the centuries of clinical descriptions and explanatory efforts are a number of figurative expressions aimed at conveying to the reader
what the experience of being melancholic was like or how someone came to be
melancholic. Several metaphors of particular interest and significance appeared and reappeared in these many accounts of melancholia.* Some of these
metaphors endeavored by their figurative mode of expression to enliven or

*In searching the literature on metaphor for clues as to how I might best express myself here,
I have been particularly influenced by the work of Max Black—by the richness of his views on the
subject, by his advocacy of a flexible yet disciplined use of the concept, and by the wisdom in his
extension of earlier, traditional uses of it. Of course, this does not make him responsible for how I
may have transmuted his views or for any lack of technical expertise in my comments: Max Black,
Models and Metaphors: Studies in Language and Philosophy (Ithaca: Cornell University Press, 1962), pp.
25–47; idem, "How Metaphors Work: A Reply to Donald Davidson," in Sheldon Sacks (ed.), *On
Metaphor* (Chicago: University of Chicago Press, 1979), pp. 181–192. From Black's own statements and his citations of others, I draw the following: metaphor is a figure of speech in which one
thing is thought of (or viewed) *as* another thing; metaphor entails the use of a word or phrase in
some new sense in order to remedy a gap in the vocabulary; a metaphorical expression has a
meaning that is some transform of its normal literal meaning; as a figure of speech, metaphor is
intended to serve the expressive and purpose functions of speech better than the plain or literal
statement; metaphors may evince feelings or predispose others to act and feel in various ways;
metaphor's effectiveness is in the evoking of an appreciative, understanding state in the reader/
listener; metaphors give insight, usually insight that literal expression would fail to give.

enrich the clinical description and thus enhance the reader's appreciation of what it was like to experience such symptoms. They endeavored to bring home something of the subjective world of the sufferer to the subjective world of the reader, so that the latter might better appreciate what it might be like to so suffer. Admittedly, some of the metaphorical expressions in the various accounts of melancholia were merely borrowed from previous authors and have a perfunctory ring to them; but numerous others, borrowed or not, conveyed something to the reader that he might well not have appreciated otherwise. In modern terms, I would be so bold as to suggest that there is no literal statement that would convey to a reader the distress of being in the throes of a severe depression. Without knowing from firsthand experience, or having at least learned with empathy directly from the distressed eloquence of a sufferer, it would require the enhancement of a metaphorical expression to bridge the gap of understanding, to draw the reader at least vicariously into the troubling subjective world of such a sufferer.

Although there are others to be taken into account, at least two metaphors stand out in the long history of melancholia: being in a state of darkness and being weighed down. Being in a state of darkness was a notion employed in a metaphorical sense by Galen in conveying to his readers something of what it was like to suffer from melancholia. He drew on this idea to illustrate the fear so regularly associated with melancholia. "As external darkness renders almost all persons fearful, with the exception of a few naturally audacious ones or those who were specially trained, thus the color of the black humor induces fear when its darkness throws a shadow over the area of thought [in the brain]."[1] It was as though darkening occurred as the result of a black substance, the black bile, throwing a shadow. In the same chapter on melancholia, Galen used another, quite different metaphor with an implication of darkening. In discussing hypochondriacal melancholia, he stated:

> For it seems that there is an inflammation in the stomach and that the blood contained in the inflamed part is thicker and more atrabilious. As some kind of sooty and smoke-like evaporation or some sort of heavy vapors are carried up from the stomach to the eyes, equally and for the same reason the symptoms of suffusion occur, when an atrabilious evaporation produces melancholic symptoms of the mind by ascending to the brain like a sooty substance or a smoky vapor. (*Affected Parts*, pp. 92–93)

Here it was as though a sooty vapor, derived from an atrabiliary mass, had arisen to the brain and there had the effect of a dark cloud of smoke.

In Alexander of Tralles and then in Ishaq ibn Imran, we find the second of Galen's two darkness metaphors: melancholia was a disease in which "a vapor rises from the black bile, and this presses forward to the seat of reason, dimming its light and confusing it, thus destroying the power of apprehension." Ishaq used this manner of speaking as though it had come to be accepted as a fact, as though the sense of employing a metaphorical expression had been lost by the user; and this became characteristic for many subsequent uses of the "rising vapor and darkening of the mind" figure of speech. Both the black bile directly darkening the mind and the hypochondriacal smoky vapors rising to darken the mind occurred again and again in later writings on melancholia, from Avicenna and Constantinus Africanus through various Renaissance authors down to Burton's encyclopedic account. At times they served to convey the notion of a darkness-induced fear, at other times a darkness-induced gloom or dejection, and still other times the darkness clouded the "vision" of the reason to account for poor judgment and delusional thinking. With increasing frequency, the spleen was the organ from which the melancholic vapors arose to trouble the mind; and the characteristic flatuousness or windiness came to be viewed as concrete evidence of vapors on the loose in the sufferer. Eventually, as hypochondriasis ("the Spleen" or "the Hyp") became separated out from melancholia as a distinct disease, the language of vapors went with it. Then, as hypochondriasis and hysteria came to be associated conditions, the metaphor of darkening vapors gradually disappeared, and yet the language survived as "the Spleen" became a colloquialism for hypochondriasis and "the Vapors" for hysteria.

The theme of feeling "weighed down" or being "weighted down" seems to have roots extending as far back as those of blackness and darkness. Simon has discussed the association of Ajax, memorialized in Homer's *Odyssey* and other writings, with images of both blackness and heaviness.[2] In his melancholia, Ajax was said to have "his mind weighted down." As with the darkness metaphors, in the process of being handed down, this notion gradually came to be used more and more and came into quite frequent use in the Renaissance. Alexander of Tralles urged the physician to be alert to the possibility that the melancholic person might feel as though his entire body was borne down by a sensation of heaviness. Ishaq wrote of "a feeling of heaviness in the head." By the ninth century in Old English, heaviness included among its meanings "oppressed condition of the body, members, or senses; torpor, drowsiness; dullness; want of animation." And, by the late medieval centuries, one of its meanings was as a synonym for "dejectedness of mind," sadness, sorrow, and grief. Cognates such as heavisome, heavity, and heavy had similar meanings. During the Renaissance, in writings on melancholia, "heavinesse without cause" began to be used as synonymous with "sadness without cause," just as "heavy-hearted" came to mean grieved, sad, or melancholy. It seems likely, indeed, that the drooping body posture of many a melancholic may have contributed to these images—the head and neck bent over, an impression of being "cast down," a "downcast" or melancholy look. Once again, sometimes there seemed to be a continuing awareness of using a metaphor, but gradually heaviness meant only sorrow. Then, with the first hints of a new trend in the seventeenth century and progressively more use in the eighteenth century, *depression* began to absorb the traditions of the weighed down and heaviness metaphor. With its own roots in "being pressed down," depression conveyed much the same impression, and, over the next two hundred years, its use slowly increased to where it achieved its familiar, twentieth-century status.

Another figurative language for melancholia revolved around the theme of "being slowed down." In this case, however, its roots seem to be no older than the seventeenth-century adaptations of mechanical theory to explain phenomena and processes of the animal economy (physiology). With a basic metaphorical source in water pipes, pumps, and hydrodynamics, a strong support for circulatory notions stemming from Harvey's circulation of the blood, and the enhanced prestige of mechanical explanations as a result of Newton's contributions, fluid-flow theories provided ideas of a circulation becoming slowed down or speeded up. Pitcairn, Hoffmann, and Boerhaave based their theories of the pathogenesis of melancholia on various forms of disordered flow in their system of circulations (blood, lymph, nerve fluid). Pitcairn's and Boerhaave's views were essentially vasocentric, whereas Hoffmann was inclined more to a neurocentric view, with nerve fluid flowing in supposedly hollow nerves. Pitcairn and Hoffmann wrote of a sluggishness or slowing of the circulation of the blood in the brain, resulting in a less lively nerve fluid and in the melancholic's becoming slow, timid, and sad. Boerhaave used the idea of a slowing of the circulation of the blood, but for him this mechanical process led to the accumulation of a "sludge" that then had the various melancholic effects; and he retained the traditional term *black bile* for this "sludge," though without the context of the humoral theory. These ideas of being slowed down nicely contrasted with a speeding up of the circulation to account for mania. And the readily observed diminished or inhibited physical activity of so many melancholic patients gave strong support for ideas of being slowed down. The sense of metaphor being used in these contexts was rapidly lost, what with the circulation of the blood having been demonstrated and a slowed fluid-flow thought to be a physiological fact. Then the trend was away from fluid-flow theories in the latter half of the eighteenth century. The language of being slowed down was used less and less, and became relatively uncommon in nineteenth-century accounts of melancholia. But the turn of the twentieth century saw a return of such notions, made explicit in phrases such as "slowing of thought," "mental sluggishness," and "retardation of the mental stream," and hidden in terms like "psychomotor retardation." Old metaphors may become dead, but they do not seem to fade away. For example, in his clinical accounts of melancholia Kraepelin not only wrote of "mental sluggishness" and "psychomotor retardation" but also reflected other old melancholic metaphors in phrases such as "the dark side of life" and "clouding of consciousness"; and, of course, his very use of the term *depression* was the outcome of the long history of another metaphor for melancholia.

A good number of other metaphors, usually of more recent vintage, might be traced in similar fashion in the history of melancholia and depression. Eighteenth-century theories of nerve weakness, inadequate tension in the nerves, and depleted nerve power or excitation contained important metaphors that came to serve explanations of melancholia. The late nineteenth century and the early twentieth century saw the active introduction of metaphors from the dynamics and energetics of physical science, often with a rapid loss of the sense of using a metaphor. Notions such as diminished nerve-force, depleted nerve-energy, diminished nerve tension, and nerve weakness abounded in explanations of melancholia. Studies in metabolism and nutrition seem to have been a source of many references to inadequate or disturbed nutrition of the brain in melancholia. "Feeling blue" and "the blues" gradually crept into common parlance, and later into clinical accounts, from eighteenth-century usages such as "the Blue Devils" for dejection and lowness of spirits, and candles burning blue smoke as an indication of the Devil's presence. And then there was Willis's wonderful metaphor of smoke and flame used to convey something of the nature of melancholia and mania, and the connection between them.

SOME AFTERTHOUGHTS

As we have seen, the boundaries of what has been diagnosed as melancholia have varied considerably over the centuries. In earlier centuries, clearly a wider range of conditions was included within those boundaries than has been the case since the early nineteenth century. By modern standards, a portion of those earlier cases would probably be diagnosed as schizophrenia, whether because depression within the experience of schizophrenia is now differentiated from major depressive disorders or whether as a reflection of efforts in more recent times to differentiate subdued and withdrawn states from subdued and depressed states. Certainly, the dilemmas of differentiation are sometimes so difficult that they have precipitated out the diagnosis of schizoaffective disorder. Sadness and fear (anxiety) have always been part of the syndrome of melancholia; depression and anxiety are commonly mentioned together as symptoms of modern major depressive disorders; and discouragement by whatever name along with anxiety in whatever form are surely common in the experience of suffering from schizophrenia.

An issue with some kinship to this one has kept recurring through much of the long history of melancholia. For many centuries, it took the form of whether the delusional thinking often present in melancholia reflected damage to the imagination or to the intellect. Perhaps to put it as a question as to whether or not melancholia entailed a thought disorder might stray into the realm of anachronism. But the actual questions were, was the damage to the imagination, with the reason or intellect correctly grasping the product of a deranged imagination? Or, was the damage to the intellect, with the deranged intellect misconceiving what was being accurately conveyed by the imagination? In terms of the classical theory of cerebral localization, the cell doctrine (see note * on p. 89), was the damage to the anterior cell of the brain or to the middle cell? Through the sixteenth century and into the seventeenth century, the balance of opinion favored the idea that the imagination was the faculty affected, with some suggesting that the faculty of reason might also become damaged, but only secondarily and depending on the extent and duration of the melancholic disorder. With the eighteenth century trend toward defining melancholia as partial insanity, there was an accompanying trend toward the view that the primary damage, albeit circumscribed, was to the intellect. With the triadic scheme of faculties shifting from imagination-intellect-memory to emotions-intellect-will, the emotional disturbance was thought of as secondary to the circumscribed damage to the intellect. But during the latter part of the eighteenth century, affects were increasingly given a central and fundamental place in considerations of mental life. This gradually led to assigning the emotions an importance that approximated that of the intellect—a far cry from the Stoic disapproval of affects! By the early nineteenth century, as opinion was shifting away from the conviction that melancholia was definable as partial insanity, the tendency was less and less to conceive of the emotional state being determined by primary damage to the intellect, and more and more to think of the primary damage being in the realm of the emotions with the intellect affected only secondarily under the influence of the emotions. As the nineteenth century progressed, this emerging notion of a primary affective disorder became central in considerations of melancholia, with delusional thinking not an essential feature, in fact occurring only if the melancholic disorder became severer or more protracted. Eventually this trend led to the influential Kraepelinian dichotomy at the end of the century: nondeteriorating conditions (affective disorders) grouped together as *manic-depressive disease*, and deteriorating conditions (thought disorders) grouped together as *dementia praecox*, later *schizophrenia*. In one form or another, a category of affective disorders has continued as a nosological home for melancholias and depressions, and a state of dejection has continued to constitute at least part of their essence. Although mood-syntonic delusions have continued to be common, delusions are not deemed essential to the diagnosis of an affective disorder. Affective disorders have continued to be differentiated from thought disorders, although this has not always been an easy task.

As we consider these various questions about where the boundaries of depressive disorders should be set and what should and should not be included within these boundaries, it becomes clear that depressive disorders have not achieved the status of *disease* in its more rigorous meanings. A set of ideal requirements would ask for a well-patterned group of signs and symptoms that varied within relatively narrow limits, a body of predictably recurring patho-anatomic and/or pathophysiologic findings, a specifiable and identifiable etiologic factor (or factors), a standard pathogenesis, and a predictable course and outcome. In the case of depressive disorders, for all the variations and for all the diagnostic difficulties that may occur, there have been a remarkable consistency of clinical content over the centuries and a significant coherence of symptoms and their relationships. Despite some shifts and changes, at any particular time this content has remained recognizably connected with its ancestors and its descendants. At the clinical level, the recurrence of relatively consistent patterns continues, most of the time, to allow the diagnosis of depressive disorder. But the lack of a consistent pathological anatomy or pathophysiology, and the variety of predisposing and precipitating factors, continue to mean that such a diagnosis—disease or not disease—is of the nature of a clinical syndrome. "Who was this sufferer before he became afflicted with a depressive disorder?" and "Who is he still?" continue to be crucial issues in understanding any specific instance of clinical depression. Much that prompted Meyer to argue for the status of *reaction type* rather than *disease* is still there to argue about. And much that supported the proponents of the endogenous-reactive dichotomy is still there to support them. Although the emergence of the germ theory of disease, of bacteriological and related fields, and of other important contributions to more rigorous standards for what is considered a disease has brought medicine to a different era, medicine in general shares more problems with the clinician dealing with someone's clinical depression than it often cares to admit.

From time immemorial, when someone has been dejected, sad, melancholic, or depressed, they have been open to a great range of reactions from other persons, all the way from rejecting and disapproving to accepting and concerned. In dealing with such matters, we must allow for the temperament, the character, the personality, or the circumstances of such other persons and recognize that they might, for their own reasons, have ranged from being impatient, harsh, or rejecting to being responsive, concerned, or solicitous. But, beyond such issues, at times dejected persons have elicited patterns of response that appear to have transcended the idiosyncrasies of the respondents. In my study of acedia, it became clear that there was a range of reactions from disapproval and harsh treatment to concern and compassionate treatment. Then, in my study of grief and mourning, a similar theme emerged. Such distressed states met a range of reactions from disapproval and vigorous admonitions to sympathy and comforting interventions. Surely this recurring tendency to dichotomous extremes and a continuum of response has had something to do with differences in the distressed persons. And in melancholia the disease, from the Hippocratic writings to the present, there have been definite indications that sadness or dejection was a crucial feature, and yet that irritability and a tendency to turn away from other people were also common features. The "others" in the immediate world of the severely dejected person, whether the latter was grief-stricken or severely melancholic, have found themselves faced with a range of expressions of distress, whether explicit or mute, from appealing solicitations for care and nurturance to irritating demands for attention and "supplies." And these others, in turn, have found themselves reacting across a range from sympathetic comfortings and concerned efforts to provide care to irritated, rejecting responses and harsh exhortations. Often enough, the troubled, distressed person has evoked a concerned response, up to a point; but, beyond that, many others have backed away or otherwise changed the nature of their response.

Whether the response has been instinctive or considered, tutored or untutored, respondents have often tried to understand, sometimes wittingly and sometimes unwittingly, what the sufferer was trying to "say." If the meaning of the distress was not made clear by the sufferer, what was being expressed? Might there have been a message in the distressed behavior? If so, what was the sufferer trying to communicate? During the twentieth century there have been repeated efforts to answer this sort of question, to a significant degree influenced by the orientations of Meyer and Freud. Freud addressed the undercurrent of irritability and complaint associated with the self-derogatory themes, and concluded that the irritability and anger derived from complaints that were really meant for the caregivers of the person's early childhood. In a manner of speaking, the anger and complaint indicated that the sufferer was strongly dissatisfied with his early care and sought better care from those around him. And legions of clinicians have experienced a depressive's undercurrent of complaint and anger almost as though it were aimed at them. In a penetrating study of the emotions, Shand maintained that sorrow was essentially a "cry for help or assistance." It is we humans' "means of calling others to our assistance," out of our sense of weakness or failure.[3] The manifestations of sorrow were intended "to obtain the strength and help of others" (*Foundations*, p. 315). In an interesting anticipation of ideas argued for in later times by clinicians, Shand stated that "the demand for sympathy is a development of the primitive cry for help. Unless others enter into and compassionate our afflictions they cannot or will not help us" (p. 316). He suggested that sorrow was always related to frustration, and he recognized the often intimate connections of sorrow with fear and anger. It is a short step from these views to those of the many clinicians who have known depressed patients and have thought that they discerned frustrated neediness, subtle (or not so subtle) complaint and hostility, or even frank complaint about loss, failure, or disappointment. Shand also identified as subtypes the vociferous distress of some sorrowing persons, the mute sadness of others, and the anergic discouragement and helplessness of still others (pp. 301–303). And he took note of melancholia as built on such sorrow, along with fear, suspicion, discontent, and delusions (p. 305). A few years after Shand, Rado referred to melancholia as "a great despairing cry for love"; and many years later, others found a "cry for help" in expressions of suicidal intent.

More recently, in a thoughtful review, Hill has argued in this tradition of finding a statement or a message in a patient's depressive state. After outlining the evidence for depression as a Kraepelinian disease entity, and then as a Meyerian reaction, he reasoned to the conclusion that "each depressed patient presents us with a complex posture of overt behavior and subjective experience." He saw this as "a total pattern of behavior which has the quality of a defensive posture, partly biologically determined."[4] He then went on to say,

> Symptoms, then, whether they be verbal expressions, deviant behavior, or simple motor postures or movements, are forms of communication. They are postures in the sense that they communicate the internal need state of the patient, his distress, his fear and anger, his remorse, his humble view of himself, his demands, and his dependency. The total postural pattern, conceptualized as having both a defensive and an adaptive function, can be broken down into elements which are physiological and behavioral, verbal and nonverbal, the latter involving facial mimetic expression, bodily attitudes, quality of vocalization, gestures, and movements. These convey emotional meaning, a complex form of communication, which is evocative of protective responses in the participant-observer when the latter's emotional sensitivity and empathy are sufficiently acute to receive the message. ("Depression," pp. 455–456)

One way or another, many have found their way to these sorts of answers to questions about the possible meanings in a depressed patient's symptoms. In a range from painful distress to insatiable neediness, from mute appeal to angry demand, they have thought that they discerned such inner meanings in the various clinical features of melancholia and depression. And, from the compelling effect of a needy distress to the repelling effect of an angry demand, their own responses have come to make better sense in these ways. But, if we think in terms of the endogenous-reactive dichotomy for a moment, some might be able to accept such ideas of communicative import much more readily for the reactive depressions than they would for endogenous depressions.

However objective we may become about *depression* or about a particular *depressed person*, however carefully we may manage to identify neurophysiological and neurochemical factors in clinical depressions, someone else's depression, defined as clinical or otherwise, is ultimately going to come home to us as a fellow human being who also has needs, who also knows something about personal losses, disappointments, and failures, who also knows something about being sad and dejected, and who has some capacity for distressed response to such a distressing state. With such distress, we are at the very heart of being human.

Notes

Page numbers in square brackets indicate direct quotations. Unless noted otherwise in a citation, translations throughout this work are my own.

CHAPTER 1 INTRODUCTION

1. [Hippocrates], *Works of Hippocrates*, trans. and ed. W. H. S. Jones and E. T. Withington, 4 vols. (Cambridge: Harvard University Press, 1923–1931), 1:lviii; W. H. S. Jones, *Malaria and Greek History* . . . (Manchester: The University Press, 1909), p. 100.

2. Richard Blackmore, *A Treatise of the Spleen and Vapours* . . . (London: J. Pemberton, 1725), p. 95.

3. [Robert Whytt], *The Works of Robert Whytt, M.D.* (Edinburgh: T. Becket, and P. A. Dehondt, and J. Balfour, 1768), p. 623.

4. Ph. Pinel, *A Treatise on Insanity* . . . , trans. by D. D. Davis (Sheffield: Cadell and Davies, 1806), pp. 143, 149. For the original text, see Ph. Pinel, *Traité Medico-Philosophique sur l'Aliénation Mentale, ou la Manie* (Paris: Richard, Caille et Ravier, 1801), pp. 143, 149.

5. John Haslam, *Observations on Madness and Melancholy* . . . , 2d ed. (London: J. Callow, 1809), p. 43.

6. Samuel Tuke, *Description of the Retreat* . . . (York: W. Alexander, 1813), p. 216.

7. Wilhelm Griesinger, *Die Pathologie und Therapie der psychischen Krankheiten* . . . (Stuttgart: Adolph Krabbe, 1845), pp. 152–208.

8. D. Hack Tuke (ed.), *A Dictionary of Psychological Medicine* . . . , 2 vols. (Philadelphia: P. Blakiston, Son & Co., 1892), 1:354.

9. Ibid., 2:787–798.

10. Emil Kraepelin, *Psychiatrie. Ein kurzes Lehrbuch für Studirende und Aerzte*, 2d ed. (Leipzig: Ambr. Abel, 1887), pp. 213–241, 281–287, 329–352.

11. Emil Kraepelin, *Psychiatrie. Ein Lehrbuch für Studirende und Aerzte*, 6th ed., 2 vols. (Leipzig: Johann Ambrosius Barth, 1899).

12. [Adolf Meyer], *The Collected Papers of Adolf Meyer*, ed. Eunice E. Winters, 4 vols. (Baltimore: The Johns Hopkins Press, 1951), 2:568.

13. Raymond Klibansky, Erwin Panofsky, and Fritz Saxl, *Saturn and Melancholy: Studies in the History of Natural Philosophy, Religion, and Art* (New York: Basic Books, 1964), p. 8.

14. Ibid., pp. 9–10.

15. [Hippocrates], *Works*, 4:11.

16. Klibansky et al., *Saturn and Melancholy*, p. 14.

17. [Hippocrates], *Works*, 1:1.

18. Henry E. Sigerist, *A History of Medicine*, 2 vols. (New York: Oxford University Press, 1951–1961), 2:320.

19. [Plato], *The Dialogues of Plato*, trans. B. Jowett, 2 vols. (New York: Random House, 1937), 2:59–60, 63.

20. G. E. R. Lloyd (ed.), *Hippocratic Writings*, trans. J. Chadwick, W. N. Mann, I. M. Lonie, and E. T. Withington (Harmondsworth: Penguin Books, 1978), p. 85.

21. Galen, *On the Usefulness of the Parts of the Body*, trans. and ed. Margaret T. May, 2 vols. (Ithaca: Cornell University Press, 1968), 1:232. See also, Galen, *On the Natural Faculties*, trans. Arthur John Brock (Cambridge: Harvard University Press, 1963), pp. 203–209.

22. Galen, *On the Affected Parts*, trans. and ed. Rudolph E. Siegel (Basel: S. Karger, 1976), p. 88.

23. Ibid., p. 90.

24. Galen, *Natural Faculties*, p. 213.

25. [Rufus], *Oeuvres de Rufus d'Ephèse*, trans. and ed. C. Daremberg and C. E. Ruelle (Paris: J. B. Baillière and Sons, 1879), pp. 356–357.

26. Klibansky et al., *Saturn and Melancholy*, p. 53.

27. Ibid., p. 52.

28. L. J. Rather, "The 'Six Things Non-Natural': A Note on the Origins and Fate of a Doctrine and a Phrase," *Clio Medica*, 1968, *3*, 337–347 [337]; I am indebted to Rather and to the following authors for both knowledge and perspective regarding the non-naturals: Saul Jarcho, "Galen's Six Non-Naturals: A Bibliographic Note and Translation," *Bull. Hist. Med.*, 1970, *44*, 372–377; Jerome J. Bylebyl, "Galen on the Non-Natural Causes of Variation in the Pulse," ibid., 1971, *45*, 482–485; Peter H. Niebyl, "The Non-Naturals," ibid., 1971, *45*, 486–492.

29. Rather, "'Six Things Non-Natural'", p. 341.

30. Bylebyl, "Non-Natural Causes."

31. Niebyl, "Non-Naturals."

32. Lester S. King, "What is Disease?" *Philos. Sci.*, 1954, *21*, 193–203 (quotation, p. 197).

33. Ibid.

34. Alvan R. Feinstein, *Clinical Judgment* (Baltimore: Williams & Wilkins, 1967), pp. 24–25.

35. H. Tristram Engelhardt, Jr., "Ideology and Etiology," *J. Med. and Philos.*, 1976, *1*, 256–268. p. 257.

36. Henry Cohen, "The Evolution of the Concept of Disease," in *Concepts of Medicine: A Collection of Essays on Aspects of Medicine*, ed. Brandon Lush (Oxford: Pergamon Press, 1961), pp. 159–169; Owsei Temkin, "The Scientific Approach to Disease: Specific Entity and Individual Sickness," in *Scientific Change*, ed. A. C. Crombie (New York: Basic Books, 1963), pp. 629–647; F. Kraüpl Taylor, *The Concepts of Illness, Disease and Morbus* (Cambridge: Cambridge University Press, 1979).

37. Cohen, "Concept of Disease," p. 160.

38. Peter H. Niebyl, "Sennert, Van Helmont, and Medical Ontology," *Bull. Hist. Med.*, 1971, *45*, 115–137.

39. Temkin, "Scientific Approach to Disease," p. 631.

40. H. M. Gardiner, Ruth Clark Metcalf, and John G. Beebe-Center, *Feelings and Emotion: A History of Theories* (New York: American Book Company, 1937), pp. 10–25. I am indebted to this valuable work throughout this overview of the history of theories of the emotions.

41. James R. Averill, *Patterns of Psychological Thought: Readings in Historical and Contemporary Texts* (Washington: Hemisphere Publishing Corp., 1976), pp. 271–301.

CHAPTER 2   MELANCHOLIA IN ANCIENT GREECE AND ROME

1. E. R. Dodds, *The Greeks and the Irrational* (Boston: Beacon Press, 1957); George Rosen, *Madness in Society: Chapters in the Historical Sociology of Mental Illness* (London: Routledge & Kegan Paul, 1968), chap. 3.

2. Hippocrates, [*Works of Hippocrates*], 4 vols., trans. and ed. W. H. S. Jones and E. T. Withington (Cambridge: Harvard University Press, 1923–1931), 1:127–131; 2:139–153.

3. In this introductory section I am indebted to the thoughtful overview by I. E. Drabkin, "Remarks on Ancient Psychopathology," *Isis*, 1955, *46*, 223–234.

4. Hippocrates, *Works*, 2:175.

5. Edwin Clarke and C. D. O'Malley, *The Human Brain and Spinal Cord: A Historical Study Illustrated by Writings from Antiquity to the Twentieth Century* (Berkeley and Los Angeles: University of California Press, 1968); Edwin Clarke and Kenneth Dewhurst, *An Illustrated History of Brain Function* (Oxford: Sandford Publications, 1972).

6. Hippocrates, *Works*, 1:263, 4:185.

7. [Hippocrates], *Oeuvres Complètes d'Hippocrate* . . . , trans. and ed. E. Littré, 10 vols. (Paris: J.-B. Baillière, 1839–1861), 5:354–357. The translation is by Owsei Temkin, *The Falling Sickness* . . . , 2d ed. (Baltimore: The Johns Hopkins Press, 1971), p. 55. Although never prominent in later accounts of melancholia, this view was occasionally taken note of. See, e.g., Galen, *On the Affected Parts*, trans. and ed. Rudolph E. Siegel (Basel: S. Karger, 1976), p. 89, and Andreas Laurentius, *A Discourse of the Preservation of the Sight* . . . , trans. Richard Surphlet (London: Ralph Iacson, 1599), p. 88.

8. [Aristotle], Problemata, in *The Works of Aristotle*, 11 vols., ed. J. A. Smith and W. D. Ross (Oxford: Clarendon Press, 1908–1931), 7:953ª–955ª.

9. Raymond Klibansky, Erwin Panofsky, and Fritz Saxl, *Saturn and Melancholy: Studies in the History of Natural Philosophy, Religion, and Art* (New York: Basic Books, 1964), pp. 17, 40–41.

10. Ibid., p. 40. See [Plato], *The Dialogues of Plato*, 2 vols., trans. B. Jowett (New York: Random House, 1937), 1:248–250 (*Phaedrus*, 244A-B, 245A).

11. Celsus, *De Medicina*, 3 vols., trans. W. G. Spencer (Cambridge: Harvard University Press, 1953–1961), 1:125.

12. Caelius Aurelianus, *On Acute Diseases and on Chronic Diseases*, ed. and trans. I. E. Drabkin (Chicago: University of Chicago Press, 1950), pp. 27, 561–563.

13. Klibansky et al., *Saturn and Melancholy*, p. 49.

14. [Rufus], *Oeuvres de Rufus d'Ephèse*, ed. and trans. C. Daremberg and C. E. Ruelle (Paris: J. B. Baillière and Sons, 1879), p. 358.

15. Klibansky et al., *Saturn and Melancholy*, p. 50.

16. [Aristotle], *Works*, 954ª.

17. [Aretaeus], *The Extant Works of Aretaeus, the Cappadocian*, ed. and trans. Francis Adams (London: Sydenham Society, 1856), pp. 298–299.

18. Wesley D. Smith, *The Hippocratic Tradition* (Ithaca: Cornell University Press, 1979), pp. 243–245.

19. Galen, *On the Affected Parts*, trans. and ed. Rudolph E. Siegel (Basel: S. Karger, 1976), pp. 89–94.

20. Rudolph E. Siegel, *Galen's System of Physiology and Medicine* (Basel: S. Karger, 1968), pp. 258–321.

21. For a summary of his physiology and pathology, written as a guide to a study of his medical psychology, see Stanley W. Jackson, "Galen—on Mental Disorders," *J. Hist. Behav. Sci.*, 1969, *5*, 365–384. Particularly valuable outlines of his physiology are to be found in Galen, *On the Usefulness of the Parts of the Body*, trans. and ed. Margaret T. May (Ithaca: Cornell University Press, 1968), 2 vols., 1:44–64; Max Neuburger, *History of Medicine*, trans. E. Playfair (London: Oxford University Press, 1910–1925), 2 vols., 1:240–273; and Siegel, *Galen's System*. I am also indebted to an excellent study by Owsei Temkin, *Galenism: Rise and Decline of a Medical Philosophy* (Ithaca: Cornell University Press, 1973).

22. Galen, *On the Natural Faculties*, trans. and ed. Arthur John Brock (Cambridge: Harvard University Press, 1963), pp. 203–215; Galen, *Usefulness of the Parts*, 1:232–235.

23. Siegel, *Galen's System*, p. 272.

24. Siegel, *Galen's System*, pp. 321–322.

CHAPTER 3   MELANCHOLIA IN MEDIEVAL TIMES

1. Owsei Temkin, "Greek Medicine as Science and Craft," *Isis*, 1953, *44*, 213–225 [213–214].

2. Owsei Temkin, "The Genesis of 'Scholastic' Medicine in Late Antiquity, Notably in Alexandria," in *Amer. Phil. Soc. Year Book*, 1957, pp. 448–450 [448].

3. H. E. Sigerist, "The Latin Medical Literature of the Early Middle Ages," *J. Hist. Med.*, 1958, *13*, 127–146.

4. Stephen D'Irsay, "Patristic Medicine," *Ann. Med. Hist.*, 1927, *9*, 364–378.

5. Ibid., p. 374.

6. W. D. Sharpe, "Isidore of Seville: The Medical Writings," an English translation with an introduction and commentary, *Trans. Amer. Phil. Soc.*, 1964, *n.s. 54*, pt. 2, 3–75 [7, 11, 19].

7. Ibid., p. 15; Sigerist, "Latin Medical Literature," pp. 137–138.

8. L. C. MacKinney, *Early Medieval Medicine* (Baltimore: Johns Hopkins University Press, 1937), pp. 106–151.

9. Ibid., pp. 148–149.

10. Ibid., pp. 49, 56; Owsei Temkin, "Medical Education in the Middle Ages," *J. Med. Educ.*, 1956, *31*, 383–391 [383].

11. Sharpe, "Isidore of Seville," pp. 11, 17; MacKinney, *Early Medieval Medicine*, pp. 47–50, 55–56, 64–73, 93.

12. P. O. Kristeller, "The School of Salerno," *Bull. Hist. Med.*, 1945, *17*, 138–194; C. H. Talbot, *Medicine in Medieval England* (London: Oldbourne, 1967), pp. 38–44.

13. This section on Arabic medicine is crucially indebted to Manfred Ullmann, *Islamic Medicine* (Edinburgh: Edinburgh University Press, 1978).

14. Henry E. Sigerist, *On the History of Medicine*, ed. Felix Marti-Ibañez (New York: MD Publications, 1960), pp. 124–125.

15. [Oribasius], *Oeuvres d'Oribase*, 6 vols., ed. U. C. Bussemaker and C. Daremberg (Paris: Imprimerie nationale, 1851–1876), 5:410.

16. [Alexander of Tralles], *Oeuvres médicales d'Alexandre de Tralles*, 4 vols., ed. F. Brunet (Paris: P. Geuthner, 1933–1937), 2:223–224.

17. [Alexander of Tralles], *Oeuvres*, 2:228.

18. [Paul of Aegina], *Seven Books*, 1:383.

19. [Paul of Aegina], *Paulus Aegineta*, 2 vols., ed. I. L. Heiberg (Lipsiae [Leipzig] and Berolini [Berlin]: B. G. Teubneri, 1921–1924), 1:156.

20. E.g., Pauli Aeginetae, *Opus de re medica* . . . , trans. Joannem Guinterium (Venetiis [Venice]: Andream Arrivabenum, 1542), p. 77.

21. E.g., Pauli Aeginetae, *Medicinae totius enchiridion, septem libris*, ed. Albano Torino (Basileae [Basel]: Joan. Oporini, 1551), p. 152.

22. E. R. Dodds, *Pagan and Christian in an Age of Anxiety* (Cambridge: Cambridge University Press, 1965), p. 53; R. A. Knox, *Enthusiasm. A Chapter in the History of Religion* (New York: Oxford University Press, 1950), pp. 29–31, 34–39; Origen, *Contra Celsum*, trans. and ed. Henry Chadwick (Cambridge: Cambridge University Press, 1965), pp. 395–398; Eusebius, *The Ecclesiastical History*, 2 vols., trans. and ed. Kirsopp Lake and J. E. L. Oulton (London: W. Heinemann, 1926–1932), 1:475–477.

23. Raymond Klibansky, Erwin Panofsky, and Fritz Saxl, *Saturn and Melancholy* (New York: Basic Books, 1964), pp. 84–85.

24. Ullmann, *Islamic Medicine*, p. 75.

25. Klibansky et al., *Saturn and Melancholy*, p. 85.

26. Ullmann, *Islamic Medicine*, pp. 37–38, 76. See chap. 2 above.

27. Constantini Africani, *Opera* . . . , 2 vols. (Basileae [Basel]: H. Petrus, 1536–1539), 1:280–281.

28. Avicennae, *Liber Canonis*, pp. 205–206.

29. [Bartholomaeus Anglicus], *Batman uppon Bartholome, His Booke De Proprietatibus Rerum* . . . (London: Thomas East, 1582), p. 89. This edition, "newly corrected, enlarged and amended" by Stephen Batman from the English translation by John of Trevisa in the late fourteenth century, did not involve any substantive change in the chapter on melancholia. As some indication of how widely known Bartholomew's work was, more than 70 editions had appeared by the late sixteenth century, including more than 20 incunabula, and many manuscript versions have survived, 18 in the Bibliothèque Nationale in Paris alone and 40 copies of the French translation. It had been translated into English, French, Spanish, and Dutch by the end of the fourteenth century.

30. As examples from the thirteenth and fourteenth centuries, see the writings of Arnaldus de Villanova, Gilbertus Anglicus, Bernard de Gordon, and John of Gaddesden. For further examples, see Nancy G. Siraisi, *Taddeo Alderotti and His Pupils* . . . (Princeton: Princeton University Press, 1981), chap. 7, regarding a number of Italian physicians from the same era.

CHAPTER 4   ACEDIA THE SIN AND ITS RELATIONSHIP TO SORROW AND MELANCHOLIA IN MEDIEVAL TIMES

1. John Cassian, *The Twelve Books* . . . *on the Institutes of the Coenobia* . . . , trans. and ed. Edgar C. S. Gibson, in Philip Schaff and Henry Wace, ed., *A Select Library of the Nicene and Post-Nicene Fathers of the Christian Church*, 2d ser., 14 vols. (Grand Rapids, Michigan: Wm. B. Eerdmans, 1955), 11:266–267.

2. Evagre le Pontique, *Traité Pratique ou le Moine*, intro. Antoine Guillaumont and Claire Guillaumont, 2 vols. (Paris: Les Editions du Cerf, 1971), 1:84–86; Siegfried Wenzel, *The Sin of Sloth: Acedia in Medieval Thought and Literature* (Chapel Hill: University of North Carolina Press, 1960), pp. 3–12.

3. Evagre le Pontique, *Traité Pratique*, 1:84–90, 2:520–527, 562–571; Evagrius Ponticus, *The Praktikos* and *Chapters on Prayer*, trans., with intro. and notes, by John Eudes Bamberger (Spencer, Mass.: Cistercian Publications, 1970), pp. 18–19, 23–24.

4. Cassian, *Twelve Books*, 11:266–267.

5. Evagre le Pontique, *Traité Pratique*, 1:57, 94–98; Wenzel, *Sin of Sloth*, pp. 12–14.

6. Wenzel, *Sin of Sloth*, p. 25.

7. Morton W. Bloomfield, *The Seven Deadly Sins: An Introduction to the History of a Religious Concept with Special Reference to Medieval English Literature* (East Lansing: Michigan State College Press, 1952), pp. 73, 84–86; Wenzel, *Sin of Sloth*, pp. 28–29.

8. Wenzel, *Sin of Sloth*, pp. 25–26.

9. Cassian, *Twelve Books*, 11:264–266.

10. Wenzel, *Sin of Sloth*, pp. 30–31.

11. Ibid., p. 32.

12. Bloomfield, *Seven Deadly Sins*, pp. 91–92, 97–99; Wenzel, *Sin of Sloth*, pp. 68–69.

13. John T. McNeill, "Medicine for sin as prescribed in the penitentials," *Church Hist.*, 1932, *1*: 14–26.

14. John T. McNeill and Helena M. Gamer, *Medieval Handbooks of Penance: A translation of the principal "libri poenitentiales" and selections from related documents* (New York: Columbia University Press, 1938), p. 44.

15. Ibid., pp. 45–46.

16. William A. Clebsch and Charles R. Jaekle, *Pastoral Care in Historical Perspective* (New York: Jason Aronson, 1975), pp. 102–112.

17. John T. McNeill, *A History of the Cure of Souls* (New York: Harper & Row, 1951).

18. Stephen D'Irsay, "Patristic Medicine," *Ann. Med. Hist.*, 1927, *9*: 364–378.

19. Geoffrey Chaucer, *The Canterbury Tales*, done into modern English verse by Frank Ernest Hill and newly revised for this edition (Avon, Conn.: Heritage Press, 1974), pp. 523–526.

20. [Petrarch], *Petrarch's Secret, or The Soul's Conflict with Passion*, trans. William H. Draper (London: Chatto & Windus, 1911), pp. 84–106; Siegfried Wenzel, "Petrarch's *Accidia*," *Stud. Renaissance*, 1961, *8*: 36–48.

21. Wenzel, *Sin of Sloth*, p. 160.

22. This might be an instance of the larger shifts in attitude outlined in Charles M. Radding, "Evolution of medieval mentalities: a cognitive-structural approach," *Amer. Hist. Rev.*, 1978, *83*: 577–597.

23. McNeill, "Medicine for sin"; McNeill and Gamer, *Medieval Handbooks*.

24. Raymond Klibansky, Erwin Panofsky, and Fritz Saxl, *Saturn and Melancholy: Studies in the History of Natural Philosophy, Religion, and Art* (New York: Basic Books, 1964), pp. 300–304.

25. Max Weber, *The Protestant Ethic and the Spirit of Capitalism*, trans. Talcott Parsons (New York: Charles Scribner's Sons, 1958), pp. 155–163.

26. Michel Foucault, *Madness and Civilization: A History of Insanity in the Age of Reason*, trans. Richard Howard (New York: Pantheon, 1965), chap. 2.

CHAPTER 5   MELANCHOLIA IN THE RENAISSANCE

1. Theophrastus Paracelsus, "The Diseases That Deprive Man of His Reason . . . ," trans. Gregory Zilboorg, in Henry E. Sigerist (ed.), *Four Treatises of Theophrastus von Hohenheim Called Paracelsus* (Baltimore: The Johns Hopkins Press, 1941), pp. 135–212 [152–153].

2. Theophrastus Von Hohenheim called Paracelsus, *Volumen Medicinae Paramirum*, trans. and preface by Kurt F. Leidecker (Baltimore: Johns Hopkins Press, 1949), pp. 43–44.

3. George Mora, "Paracelsus' Psychiatry: On the Occasion of the 400th Anniversary of His Book 'Diseases That Deprive Man of His Reason' (1567)," *Amer. J. Psychiat.*, 1967, *124*, 803–814.

4. Paracelsus, *Diseases*, p. 142.

5. Thomas Elyot, *The Castel of Helthe* (London: Thomas Berthelet, 1541), fol. 1–9. [facsimile reprint, intro. Samuel A. Tannenbaum (New York: Scholars' Facsimiles & Reprints, 1937)].

6. Andrewe Boord, *The Breviary of Helthe* . . . (London: William Middelton, 1547), book I, chap. 228 [facsimile reprint, Amsterdam: De Capo Press, 1971].

7. T. Bright, *A Treatise of Melancholie* . . . (London: Thomas Vautrollier, 1586), p. xii.

8. Richard Hunter and Ida Macalpine, *Three Hundred Years of Psychiatry: 1535–1860* . . . (London: Oxford University Press, 1963), p. 36.

9. Andreas Laurentius, *A Discourse of the Preservation of the Sight: of Melancholike Diseases; of Rheumes, and of Old Age*, trans. Richard Surphlet (London: Ralph Iacson, 1599), pp. 86–87.

10. See Stanley W. Jackson, "Melancholia and Partial Insanity," *J. Hist. Behav. Sci.*, 1983, *19*, 173–184.

11. Oskar Diethelm and Thomas F. Heffernan, "Felix Platter and Psychiatry," *J. Hist. Behav. Sci.*, 1965, *1*, 10–23.

12. Ibid., p. 15.

13. Ibid., p. 19.

14. Felix Plater, Abdiah Cole, and Nich. Culpeper, *A Golden Practice of Physick* . . . (London: Peter Cole, 1662), p. 29.

15. Ruth A. Fox, *The Tangled Chain: The Structure of Disorder in the Anatomy of Melancholy* (Berkeley: University of California Press, 1976), p. 1.

16. Robert Burton, *The Anatomy of Melancholy*, ed. Floyd Dell and Paul Jordan-Smith (New York: Tudor, 1948), pp. 148–149.

17. [John Dryden], "Absalom and Achitophel," [1681], in *The Poetical Works of Dryden*, 2d ed., ed. George R. Noyes (Boston: Houghton Mifflin, 1950), p. 111.

18. I am here indebted to the penetrating study of these themes by Klibansky, Panofsky, and Saxl and to the fine study of Ficino by Kristeller: Raymond Klibansky, Erwin Panofsky, and Fritz Saxl, *Saturn and Melancholy*, pp. 254–274; Paul Oskar Kristeller, *The Philosophy of Marsilio Ficino*, trans. Virginia Conant (Gloucester: Peter Smith, 1964). Babb, in his study of Elizabethan melancholy, has usefully epitomized Ficino's view of the melancholy character: Lawrence Babb, *Elizabethan Malady: A Study of Melancholia in English Literature from 1580 to 1642* (East Lansing: Michigan State University Press, 1951), pp. 60–61.

19. See chap. 15 for a detailed account of love-melancholy.

CHAPTER 6   MELANCHOLIA IN THE SEVENTEENTH CENTURY

1. Robert Burton, *The Anatomy of Melancholy*, ed. Floyd Dell and Paul Jordan-Smith (New York: Tudor, 1948).

2. Michael MacDonald, *Mystical Bedlam: Madness, Anxiety, and Healing in Seventeenth-century England* (Cambridge: Cambridge University Press, 1981), p. 117.

3. Thomas Willis, *Two Discourses Concerning the Soul of Brutes Which is that of the Vital and Sensitive of Man*, trans. S. Pordage (London: Thomas Dring, Ch. Harper, and John Leigh, 1683).

4. [Thomas Willis], *Willis's Oxford Casebook (1650–52)*, intro. and ed. Kenneth Dewhurst (Oxford: Sandford, 1981).

5. [Thomas Willis], *Thomas Willis's Oxford Lectures*, intro. and ed. Kenneth Dewhurst (Oxford: Sandford, 1980).

6. [Thomas Willis], *Dr. Willis's Practice of Physick, Being the Whole Works of that*

Renowned and Famous Physician, trans. S. Pordage (London: T. Dring, C. Harper, and J. Leigh, 1684), p. 2.

7. Lester S. King, *The Road to Medical Enlightenment, 1650–1695* (London: Mac-Donald, 1970), pp. 37–62.

8. [Thomas Sydenham], *The Works of Thomas Sydenham, M.D.*, 2 vols., trans. and ed. R. G. Latham (London: Sydenham Society, 1848), 2:84–117.

9. Kenneth Dewhurst, *Dr. Thomas Sydenham (1624–1689): His Life and Original Writings* (Berkeley and Los Angeles: University of California Press, 1966), pp. 61–62. This point was also made by Erwin H. Ackerknecht, *A Short History of Psychiatry*, trans. Sulammith Wolff (New York: Hafner, 1959), p. 29.

10. Hansruedi Isler, *Thomas Willis, 1621–1675: Doctor and Scientist* (New York: Hafner, 1968), pp. 57–63. It is appropriate here to acknowledge an indebtedness to Dr. Isler for his very useful study of Willis.

CHAPTER 7   MELANCHOLIA IN THE EIGHTEENTH CENTURY

1. Archibald Pitcairn, *The Philosophical and Mathematical Elements of Physick* (London: Andrew Bell and John Osborn, 1718), pp. xvii–xxviii, 19–35.

2. Friedrich Hoffmann, *Fundamenta Medicinae*, trans. and intro. Lester S. King (London: MacDonald, 1971), p. 13.

3. [Friedrich Hoffmann], *A System of the Practice of Medicine . . .* , trans. William Lewis and Andrew Duncan, 2 vols. (London: J. Murray and J. Johnson, 1783), 2: 298.

4. G. A. Lindeboom, *Herman Boerhaave: The Man and His Work* (London: Methuen & Co., 1968); Lester S. King, *The Philosophy of Medicine: The Early Eighteenth Century* (Cambridge: Harvard University Press, 1978), pp. 121–124.

5. [Herman Boerhaave], *Boerhaave's Aphorisms: Concerning the Knowledge and Cure of Diseases* (London: W. and J. Innys, 1735), p. 312.

6. Theodore M. Brown, "From Mechanism to Vitalism in Eighteenth-century English Physiology," *J. Hist. Biol.*, 1974, *7*, 179–216; Robert E. Schofield, *Mechanism and Materialism: British Natural Philosophy in an Age of Reason* (Princeton: Princeton University Press, 1970).

7. Philip C. Ritterbush, *Overtures to Biology: The Speculations of Eighteenth-Century Naturalists* (New Haven: Yale University Press, 1964), chap. 2.

8. Thomas S. Hall, *Ideas of Life and Matter: Studies in the History of General Physiology, 600 B.C.–1900 A.D.*, 2 vols. (Chicago: University of Chicago Press, 1969), 1: 391–408; Karl E. Rothschuh, *History of Physiology*, trans. and ed. Guenter B. Risse (Huntington, N.Y.: Robert E. Krieger, 1973), pp. 123–131.

9. Albrecht von Haller, *A Dissertation on the Sensible and Irritable Parts of Animals*, ed. Owsei Temkin (Baltimore: Johns Hopkins University Press, 1936).

10. Albertus Haller, *First Lines of Physiology*, intro. Lester S. King, 2 vols. in 1 (New York: Johnson Reprint, 1966), 1: 219–223.

11. Mary B. Hesse, *Forces and Fields: A Study of Action at a Distance in the History of Physics* (London: Thomas Nelson and Sons, 1961); Schofield, *Mechanism and Materialism*, chap. 8.

12. [Isaac Newton], *Isaac Newton's Papers and Letters on Natural Philosophy and Related Documents*, ed. I. Bernard Cohen (Cambridge: Harvard University Press, 1958), pp. 5–7.

13. [Isaac Newton], *Sir Isaac Newton's Mathematical Principles of Natural Philosophy and His System of the World*, ed. Florian Cajori (Berkeley: University of California Press, 1934), p. 547.

14. Isaac Newton, *Opticks, or a Treatise of the Reflections, Refractions, Inflections and Colours of Light*, 4th ed. corrected, foreword Albert Einstein, intro. Edmund Whittaker, preface I. Bernard Cohen, analytical contents Duane H. D. Roller (New York: Dover, 1952), pp. 353–354.

15. Richard Mead, *A Mechanical Account of Poisons in Several Essays* (London: R. South, 1702), p. A2.

16. [Richard Mead], *The Medical Works of Richard Mead, M.D.* (London: C. Hitch et al., 1762), p. 455.

17. Ibid., pp. iv–v, xix–xxvii, 176–177, 253.

18. Ibid., pp. xxiv, 252. In less explicit ways this shift is apparent in many passages throughout his *Works*.

19. Richard Mead, *Medical Precepts and Cautions*, trans. Thomas Stack (London: J. Brindley, 1751), pp. 12, 16.

20. William Cullen, *First Lines of the Practice of Physic*, new ed., 4 vols. (Edinburgh: Elliot and Cadell, 1786), 1:xvii.

21. Cullen, *First Lines*, 1:xix–lvi.

22. William Cullen, *Institutions of Medicine. Part I. Physiology*, 3d ed. (Edinburgh: Charles Elliot, 1785), pp. 29–32, 62–69, 73–74.

23. William Cullen, *The Works of William Cullen, M.D.* . . . , ed. John Thomson, 2 vols. (Edinburgh: William Blackwood, 1827), 1:17; idem, "Lectures upon the Institutions of Medicine," 5 vols. (unpublished manuscript of lectures delivered in Edinburgh, 1768/69, located in Yale University Medical Historical Library), 2:236–243, 245–254, 277–287.

24. "Lectures," 2: 2–5; Cullen, *Institutions*, pp. 97–101.

25. Hall, *Ideas of Life and Matter*, 2:91–95.

26. Stanley W. Jackson, "Force and Kindred Notions in Eighteenth-century Neurophysiology and Medical Psychology, Part II," *Bull. Hist. Med.*, 1970, *44*, 539–554.

27. Inci A. Bowman, "William Cullen (1710–1790) and the Primacy of the Nervous System" (Ph.D. thesis, Indiana University, 1975).

28. John Thomson, *An Account of the Life, Lectures, and Writings of William Cullen, M.D.*, 2 vols. (Edinburgh and London: William Blackwood and Sons, 1859), 1:397.

29. Cullen, "Lectures," 2:236–243, 245–254, 277–287.

30. Thomson, *An Account*, 1:317–318, 375.

31. William Cullen, *A Synopsis of Methodical Nosology* . . . , from 4th ed. corrected and much enlarged, trans. Henry Wilkins (Philadelphia: Parry Hall, 1793), p. 86.

32. Thomas Willis, *Two Discourses Concerning the Soul of Brutes Which is that of the Vital and Sensitive of Man*, trans. S. Pordage (London: Thomas Dring, Ch. Harper, and John Leigh, 1683), pp. 193–199.

33. Pitcairn, *Elements of Physick*, pp. 192–193; [Hoffmann], *Practice of Medicine*, 2:302–303; [Boerhaave], *Aphorisms*, pp. 314–318, 322–323; Mead, *Works*, pp. 490–494; Cullen, *First Lines*, 3:266–267, 269–272, and 4:184–186.

34. Guenter Risse, "Doctor William Cullen, Physician, Edinburgh: A Consultation Practice in the Eighteenth Century," *Bull. Hist. Med.*, 1974, *48*, 338–351.

35. Erwin H. Ackerknecht, *Therapeutics: From the Primitives to the 20th Century* . . . (New York: Hafner, 1973), p. 101.

36. L. J. Rather, "G. E. Stahl's Psychological Physiology," *Bull. Hist. Med.*, 1961, *35*, 37–49; idem, *Mind and Body in Eighteenth Century Medicine: A Study Based on Jerome Gaub's De Regimine Mentis* (Berkeley: University of California Press, 1965).

37. Timothy Rogers, *A Discourse Concerning Trouble of Mind, and the Disease of Melancholly* (London: Thomas Parkhurst and Thomas Cockerill, 1691), p. xxiii.

38. Burton, *Anatomy of Melancholy*, pp. 866–971.

39. Paul Delany, *British Autobiography in the Seventeenth Century* (London: Routledge & Kegan Paul, 1969).

40. Thomas Wright (ed.), *The Unpublished and Uncollected Letters of William Cowper* (London: C. J. Farncombe & Sons, 1925); Thomas Wright (ed.), *The Correspondence of William Cowper*, 4 vols. (New York: AMS Press, 1968); [William Cowper], *Memoir of the Early Life of William Cowper, Esq.*, 2d ed. (London: R. Edwards, 1816). Termed "my Narrative" by

Cowper, this work was written at Huntingdon, probably in 1766 shortly after he went to live with the Unwins. It was first published in 1816 by two different publishers in slightly varying texts, each with an anonymous editor: Maurice Quinlan, "Memoir of William Cowper: An Autobiography," *Proc. Amer. Philosophical Soc.*, 1953, *97*, 359–382. Although many literary authorities have discerned in some of his poems autobiographical data relevant to his melancholic episodes, I have restricted myself to Cowper's explicit statements in his letters and this *Memoir*.

41. Quinlan, *Memoir of William Cowper*, p. 363.

42. Wright, *Unpublished Letters*, p. 27.

43. Particularly relevant, and often referred to, examples from the extensive contemporary medical literature on the subject are works by Robinson and Cheyne: Nicholas Robinson, *A New System of the Spleen, Vapours, and Hypochondriack Melancholy* . . . (London: A. Bettesworth, W. Innys, and C. Rivington, 1729), and George Cheyne, *The English Malady* . . . (London: G. Strahan and J. Leake, 1733). Useful modern critical works examining the melancholic themes in the era's general literature are Amy Louise Reed, *The Background of Gray's Elegy: A Study in the Taste for Melancholy Poetry, 1700–1751* (New York: Columbia University Press, 1924); Oswald Doughty, "The English Malady of the Eighteenth Century," *Rev. English Studies*, 1926, *2*, 257–269; Eleanor M. Sickels, *The Gloomy Egoist: Moods and Themes of Melancholy from Gray to Keats* (New York: Columbia University Press, 1932); Cecil A. Moore, "The English Malady," in Cecil A. Moore, *Backgrounds of English Literature, 1700–1760* (Minneapolis: University of Minnesota Press, 1953), pp. 179–235, 245–247; John Frank Sena, "The English Malady: The Idea of Melancholy from 1700 to 1760" (Ph.D. diss., Princeton University, 1967); and Allan Ingram, *Boswell's Creative Gloom* . . . (Totowa, N.J.: Barnes & Noble, 1982).

44. [Thomas Willis], *Dr. Willis's Practice of Physick, Being the Whole Works of That Renowned and Famous Physician*, trans. S. Pordage (London: T. Dring, C. Harper, and J. Leigh, 1684), pp. 81–92; [Thomas Sydenham], *The Works of Thomas Sydenham, M.D.*, ed. R. G. Latham, 2 vols. (London: Sydenham Society, 1850), 2:84–118.

45. This point was made in a useful review of this condition by Fischer-Homberger: Esther Fischer-Homberger, "Hypochondriasis of the Eighteenth Century—Neurosis of the Present Century," *Bull. Hist. Med.*, 1972, *46*, 391–401.

46. [James Boswell], *Letters of James Boswell*, ed. C. B. Tinker, 2 vols. (Oxford: Clarendon Press, 1924); [James Boswell], *The Hypochondriack: Being the Seventy Essays . . . appearing in the* LONDON MAGAZINE *from November, 1777, to August, 1783 . . .* , ed. Margery Bailey, 2 vols. (Palo Alto: Stanford University Press, 1928); Ingram, *Boswell's Creative Gloom*.

47. W. Jackson Bate, *Samuel Johnson* (New York: Harcourt Brace Jovanovich, 1977), pp. 115–129, 371–389.

48. Ibid., pp. 115–116.

49. Ibid., p. 117.

50. [James Boswell], *Boswell's Life of Johnson* . . . , ed. George Birkbeck Hill, 6 vols. (Oxford: Clarendon Press, 1887), 1:144–145; Bate, *Johnson*, p. 121.

51. [James Boswell], *Boswell's Journal of a Tour to the Hebrides with Samuel Johnson, LL.D.*, ed. Frederick A. Pottle and Charles H. Bennett (New York: Literary Guild, 1936), p. 174; Bate, *Johnson*, p. 121.

52. Arthur Murphy, *An Essay on the Life and Genius of Samuel Johnson, LL.D.* (London: T. Longman et al., 1793), pp. 80–81; Bate, *Johnson*, pp. 121–122.

53. Ibid., pp. 381–382.

54. George Birkbeck Hill (ed.) *Johnsonian Miscellanies*, 2 vols. (Oxford: Clarendon Press, 1897), 1:26; Bate, *Johnson*, p. 371.

55. Bate, *Johnson*, pp. 372–380.

56. Katharine C. Balderston, "Johnson's Vile Melancholy," in *The Age of Johnson: Essays Presented to Chauncey Brewster Tinker* (New Haven: Yale University Press, 1949), pp. 3–14.

57. Hill, *Miscellanies*, 1:199.

58. [Samuel] Johnson, *History of Rasselas: Prince of Abyssinia*, ed. George Birkbeck Hill (Oxford: Clarendon Press, 1954), pp. 139–141, 149. Hunter and Macalpine have quoted these same passages, to which they have added their own interesting observations: Richard Hunter and Ida Macalpine, *Three Hundred Years of Psychiatry, 1535–1860 . . .* (London: Oxford University Press, 1963), pp. 417–418.

59. Samuel Johnson, *The Rambler*, in W. J. Bate and Albrecht B. Strauss (eds.), *The Yale Edition of the Works of Samuel Johnson*, vols. 3–5 (New Haven: Yale University Press, 1969), 5:298.

60. Hill, *Miscellanies*, 1:26.

61. Samuel Johnson, *Lives of the English Poets*, ed. George Birkbeck Hill, 3 vols. (Oxford: Clarendon Press, 1905), 3:338.

CHAPTER 8   MELANCHOLIA IN THE NINETEENTH CENTURY

1. Ph[ilippe] Pinel, *A Treatise on Insanity . . .* , trans. D. D. Davis (Sheffield: W. Todd, 1806), p. 136. For a history of the concept of partial insanity, including Cullen's and Pinel's places in it, see Stanley W. Jackson, "Melancholia and Partial Insanity," *J. Hist. Behav. Sci.*, 1983, *19*, 173–184.

2. Benjamin Rush, *Medical Inquiries and Observations upon the Diseases of the Mind*, 3d ed. (Philadelphia: J. Grigg, 1827), p. 72. Regarding partial insanity, see Jackson, "Melancholia and Partial Insanity."

3. Benjamin Rush, *Medical Inquiries and Observations*, 3d ed., 4 vols. (Philadelphia: Mathew Carey et al., 1809), 3:1–66. This and subsequent material on Rush's theory of disease are drawn mainly from his "Outlines of the Phenomena of Fever" on these pages.

4. E. Esquirol, *Mental Maladies. A Treatise on Insanity*, trans. E. K. Hunt (Philadelphia: Lea and Blanchard, 1845), pp. 199–233. This is essentially a slightly revised and expanded version of his lengthy entry on melancholia in 1819 in *Dictionaire des Sciences Médicales . . .* , 60 vols. (Paris: C. L. F. Panckoucke, 1812–1822), 32:147–183.

5. James Cowles Prichard, *A Treatise on Insanity . . .* (Philadelphia: Haswell, Barrington, and Haswell, 1837), pp. 30–36.

6. Johann Christian Heinroth, *Textbook of Disturbances of Mental Life: Or Disturbances of the Soul and Their Treatment*, trans. J. Schmorak and intro. George Mora, 2 vols. (Baltimore: Johns Hopkins University Press, 1975), 1:136, 214–215.

7. Ernest von Feuchtersleben, *The Principles of Medical Psychology*, trans. H. Evans Lloyd and B. G. Babington (London: Sydenham Society, 1847), pp. 276–277.

8. Jackson, "Melancholia and Partial Insanity."

9. John Charles Bucknill and Daniel H. Tuke, *A Manual of Psychological Medicine . . .* (Philadelphia: Blanchard and Lea, 1858), p. 152.

10. Ibid., pp. 155–156. This condition was later absorbed into Kahlbaum's *catatonia*.

11. Henry Maudsley, *The Physiology and Pathology of Mind*, 2d ed. (London: Macmillan, 1868), pp. xiii, 368.

12. R. von Krafft-Ebing, *Text-Book of Insanity . . .* , trans. Charles Gilbert Chaddock, intro. Frederick Peterson (Philadelphia: F. A. Davis, 1904), p. xiii.

13. George H. Savage, *Insanity and Allied Neuroses: Practical and Clinical* (London: Cassell & Co., 1884), pp. 151–152.

14. Charles Mercier, "Melancholia," in D. Hack Tuke (ed.), *A Dictionary of Psychological Medicine* . . . , 2 vols. (Philadelphia: P. Blakiston, Son & Co., 1892), 2:787.

15. George Beard, "Neurasthenia, or Nervous Exhaustion," *Boston Med. & Surg. J.*, 1869, *N.S. 3*, 217–221 [217].

16. Ibid., p. 218.

17. Henry Alden Bunker, "From Beard to Freud: A Brief History of the Concept of Neurasthenia," *Med. Review of Reviews*, 1930, *36*, 108–114. [109].

18. In addition to Bunker's study, see Charles E. Rosenberg, "The Place of George M. Beard in Nineteenth-Century Psychiatry," *Bull. Hist. Med.*, 1962, *36*, 245–259; John C. Chatel and Roger Peele, "A Centennial Review of Neurasthenia," *Amer. J. Psychiat.*, 1970, *126*, 1404–1411; and Eric T. Carlson, "George M. Beard and Neurasthenia," in Edwin R. Wallace and Lucius C. Pressley (eds.), *Essays in the History of Psychiatry* . . . (Columbia, S.C.: Wm. S. Hall Psychiatric Institute, 1980), pp. 50–57.

19. Maurice de Fleury, *Medicine and the Mind*, trans. Stacy B. Collins (London: Downey & Co., 1900), pp. 263–264.

20. Thomas Beddoes, *Hygëia* . . . , 3 vols. (Bristol: J. Mills, 1802–1803), 3: essay X, pp. 46–47.

CHAPTER 9   MELANCHOLIA AND DEPRESSION IN THE TWENTIETH CENTURY

1. Adolf Meyer, "A Review of Recent Problems of Psychiatry," in Eunice E. Winters (ed.), *The Collected Papers of Adolf Meyer*, 4 vols. (Baltimore: The Johns Hopkins Press, 1951), 2:331–385; originally appeared as a chapter in A. Church and F. Peterson, *Nervous and Mental Diseases*, 4th ed. (Philadelphia: W. B. Saunders, 1904).

2. Emil Kraepelin, *Compendium der Psychiatrie* (Leipzig: A. Abel, 1883).

3. Emil Kraepelin, *Psychiatrie. Ein kurzes Lehrbuch für Studirende und Aerzte*, 2d ed. (Leipzig: Ambr. Abel, 1887); idem, 3d ed. (Leipzig: Ambr. Abel, 1889); idem, 4th ed. (Leipzig: Ambr. Abel, 1893).

4. Emil Kraepelin, *Psychiatrie. Ein Lehrbuch für Studirende und Aerzte*, 5th ed. (Leipzig: Johann Ambrosius Barth, 1896), pp. 425–471.

5. Ibid., pp. 595–653.

6. Emil Kraepelin, *Psychiatrie. Ein Lehrbuch für Studirende und Aerzte*, 6th ed., 2 vols. (Leipzig: Johann Ambrosius Barth, 1899), 2:359–425.

7. Kraepelin, *Psychiatrie*, 2:359–361. Translation is by Adolf Meyer in Winters, *Collected Papers of Adolf Meyer*, 2:355–356.

8. Meyer, "Recent Problems," 2:360–361.

9. A. Ross Defendorf, *Clinical Psychiatry: A Text-Book for Students and Physicians*, from 6th German edition of Kraepelin's "Lehrbuch der Psychiatrie" (New York: Macmillan, 1902), pp. 282–283.

10. G.-L. Dreyfus, *Die Melancholie, ein Zustandsbild des manisch-depressiven Irreseins* (Jena: G. Fischer, 1907).

11. Emil Kraepelin, *Manic-Depressive Insanity and Paranoia*, trans. R. Mary Barclay, from 8th German edition of the "Text-Book of Psychiatry," ed. George M. Robertson (Edinburgh: E. & S. Livingstone, 1921), pp. 187, 190–191.

12. Theodore Lidz, "Adolf Meyer and the Development of American Psychiatry," *Amer. J. Psychiat.*, 1966, *123*, 320–332. In the following I am often indebted to this valuable study.

13. Winters, *Collected Papers of Adolf Meyer*, 2:142–143.

14. Adolf Meyer, *Psychobiology: A Science of Man*, foreword Nolan D. C. Lewis, ed. Eunice E. Winters and Anna Mae Bowers (Springfield, Ill.: Charles C Thomas, 1957), pp. 156–186.

15. Wendell Muncie, *Psychobiology and Psychiatry: A Textbook of Normal and Abnormal Behavior*, foreword Adolf Meyer (St. Louis: C. V. Mosby, 1939), pp. 242–295.

16. Oskar Diethelm, *Treatment in Psychiatry*, 2d ed. (Springfield, Ill.: Charles C Thomas, 1950), pp. 205–206.

17. Eugen Bleuler, *Textbook of Psychiatry*, trans. by A. A. Brill (New York: Macmillan, 1924), pp. 465–466.

18. D. K. Henderson and R. D. Gillespie, *A Text-Book of Psychiatry for Students and Practitioners* (London: Oxford University Press, 1927), p. 133.

19. D. K. Henderson and R. D. Gillespie, *A Text-Book of Psychiatry for Students and Practitioners*, 4th ed. (New York: Oxford University Press, 1936), p. 166.

20. Henderson and Gillespie, *A Text-Book of Psychiatry for Students and Practitioners*, 6th ed. (London: Oxford University Press, 1944), p. 239.

21. David Henderson and Ivor R. C. Batchelor, *Henderson and Gillespie's Textbook of Psychiatry for Students and Practitioners*, 9th ed. (London: Oxford University Press, 1962), p. 138.

22. Defendorf, *Clinical Psychiatry*, pp. 254–255.

23. Ibid., p. 258.

24. Dreyfus, *Die Melancholie;* Kraepelin, *Manic-Depressive Insanity*, pp. 187, 190–191.

25. George H. Kirby, "Review of Dreyfus' Die Melancholie . . . ," *State of New York State Hospitals Bulletin*, 1908–1909, N.S. *1*, 499–508.

26. Bleuler, *Textbook of Psychiatry*, p. 488.

27. August Hoch and John T. MacCurdy, "The Prognosis of Involution Melancholia," *Arch. Neurol. Psychiat.*, 1922, *7*, 1–17 [3].

28. Ibid., p. 16.

29. John T. MacCurdy, *The Psychology of Emotion: Morbid and Normal* (London: Kegan Paul, Trench, Trubner & Co., 1925), p. 140.

30. R. D. Gillespie, "The Clinical Differentiation of Types of Depression," *Guy's Hosp. Reports*, 1929, *79*, 306–344 (esp. pp. 313, 336–340, 342–344).

31. W. B. Titley, "Prepsychotic Personality of Patients with Involutional Melancholia," *Arch. Neurol. & Psychiat.*, 1936, *36*, 19–33 [32].

32. [Sigmund Freud], *The Standard Edition of the Complete Psychological Works of Sigmund Freud*, trans. and ed. James Strachey, Anna Freud, et al., 24 vols. (London: Hogarth Press, 1953–1974), 9:167–175; Karl Abraham, "Contributions to the Theory of the Anal Character," in [Karl Abraham], *Selected Papers of Karl Abraham M.D.*, intro. Ernest Jones, trans. Douglas Bryan and Alix Strachey (London: Hogarth Press, 1949), 370–392.

33. Saul H. Rosenthal, "The Involutional Depressive Syndrome," *Amer. J. Psychiat.*, 1968, *124*, supp. 21–35 (esp. pp. 26–29).

34. Smith Ely Jelliffe and William A. White, *Diseases of the Nervous System: A Text-Book of Neurology and Psychiatry*, 4th ed. (Philadelphia: Lea & Febiger, 1923), p. 921.

35. Ibid., pp. 1040–1046.

36. These issues are nicely traced in R. E. Kendell, *The Classification of Depressive Illnesses* (London: Oxford University Press, 1968), pp. 4–8; see also Aubrey Lewis, "States of Depression: Their Clinical and Aetiological Differentiation," *Brit. Med. J.*, 1938, *2*, 875–878.

37. Rosenthal, "Involutional Depressive Syndrome"; Kendell, *Classification*, pp. 9–13.

38. Rosenthal, "Involutional Depressive Syndrome," p. 32.

39. Kendell, *Classification*, p. 113.

40. Aubrey Lewis, "'Endogenous' and 'Exogenous': A Useful Dichotomy?" *Psychol. Med.*, 1971, *1*, 191–196.

41. Ibid., p. 193.

42. Gillespie, "Clinical Differentiation," pp. 308–311.

43. Lewis, "'Endogenous' and 'Exogenous,'" p. 194.
44. Edward Mapother, "Discussion on Manic-Depressive Psychosis," *Brit. Med. J.*, 1926, *2*, 872–879 [873].
45. Aubrey Lewis, "Melancholia: A Clinical Survey of Depressive States," *J. Ment. Sci.*, 1934, *80*, 277–378; idem, "States of Depression."
46. Joe Mendels and Carl Cochrane, "The Nosology of Depression: The Endogenous-Reactive Concept," *Amer. J. Psychiat.*, 1968, *124*, Suppl., 1–11 [10].
47. In addition to Mendels and Cochrane's study, further perspective on the various separatist versus unitarian arguments may be obtained from M. J. Heron, "A Note on the Concept Endogenous-Exogenous," *Brit. J. Med. Psychol.*, 1965, *38*, 241–245, and Lewis, "'Endogenous' and 'Exogenous.'" One might conclude that the differences between "splitters" and "lumpers" will always be with us.
48. Heron, "Endogenous-Exogenous," p. 245.
49. Eli Robins and Samuel B. Guze, "Classification of Affective Disorders: The Primary-Secondary, The Endogenous-Reactive, and the Neurotic-Psychotic Concepts," in Thomas A. Williams, Martin M. Katz, and James A. Shields (eds.), *Recent Advances in the Psychobiology of the Depressive Illnesses* (Washington: United States Government Printing Office, 1972), pp. 283–293 [284].
50. Robert A. Woodruff, Jr., George E. Murphy, and Marijan Herjanic, "The Natural History of Affective Disorders—I. Symptoms of 72 Patients at the Time of Index Hospital Admission," *J. Psychiat. Res.*, 1967, *5*, 255–263 [257].
51. Joseph Mendels, *Concepts of Depression* (New York: John Wiley & Sons, 1970), pp. 37–38.
52. Ibid., p. 38.
53. Ibid., pp. 38–40.
54. George Winokur, *Depression: The Facts* (Oxford: Oxford University Press, 1981), pp. 27–38.
55. Robert L. Spitzer et al. (eds.), *Diagnostic and Statistical Manual of Mental Disorders*, 3d ed. (Washington: American Psychiatric Association, 1980), pp. 205–224.
56. Robert L. Spitzer, Jean Endicott, Robert A. Woodruff, Jr., and Nancy Andreasen, "Classification of Mood Disorders," in Gene Usdin (ed.), *Depression: Clinical, Biological and Psychological Perspectives* (New York: Brunner/Mazel, 1977), pp. 73–103 [74–75].
57. Donald F. Klein, "Endogenomorphic Depression: A Conceptual and Terminological Revision," *Arch. Gen. Psychiat.*, 1974, *31*, 447–454.
58. J. Craig Nelson, Dennis S. Charney, and Donald M. Quinlan, "Evaluation of the *DSM-III* Criteria for Melancholia," *Arch. Gen. Psychiat.*, 1981, *38*, 555–559 [555].
59. Kendell, *Classification of Depressive Illnesses*; idem, "The Classification of Depressions: A Review of Contemporary Confusion," *Brit. J. Psychiat.*, 1976, *129*, 15–28; Gerald L. Klerman, "Affective Disorders," in Armand M. Nicholi, Jr. (ed.), *The Harvard Guide to Modern Psychiatry* (Cambridge: Harvard University Press, 1978), pp. 253–281; Mendels and Cochrane, "Nosology of Depression"; Mendels, *Concepts of Depression*.
60. [Freud], *Standard Edition*, 14:239.
61. Karl Abraham, "Notes on the Psycho-Analytical Investigation and Treatment of Manic-Depressive Insanity and Allied Conditions," in [Abraham], *Selected Papers*, pp. 137–156 [137].
62. Karl Abraham, "A Short Study of the Development of the Libido, Viewed in the Light of Mental Disorders," in [Abraham], *Selected Papers*, pp. 418–501 [457].
63. Ibid., pp. 457–459.
64. Ibid., p. 459.
65. Sandor Rado, *Psychoanalysis of Behavior: Collected Papers*, 2 vols. (New York: Grune & Stratton, 1956–1962), 1:46, 50.

66. Otto Fenichel, *The Psychoanalytic Theory of Neurosis* (New York: W. W. Norton, 1945), pp. 387–406.

67. Although the themes outlined in what follows recurred in many places in Klein's writings, I have drawn primarily on "A Contribution to the Psychogenesis of Manic-Depressive States" (1935) and "Mourning and Its Relation to Manic-Depressive States" (1940): Melanie Klein, *Contributions to Psycho-Analysis, 1921–1945*, intro. Ernest Jones (London: Hogarth Press, 1948), pp. 282–338 [312].

68. Edward Bibring, "The Mechanism of Depression," in Phyllis Greenacre (ed.), *Affective Disorders: Psychoanalytic Contributions to their Study* (New York: International Universities Press, 1953), pp. 13–48 [13–14].

69. Edith Jacobson, *Depression: Comparative Studies of Normal, Neurotic, and Psychotic Conditions* (New York: International Universities Press, 1971).

70. This section is indebted to the following reviews: Mendels, *Concepts of Depression*, pp. 71–93; Joseph J. Schildkraut, "The Biochemistry of Affective Disorders: A Brief Summary," in Nicholi (ed.), *Harvard Guide*, pp. 81–91; A. P. Zis and F. K. Goodwin, "The Amine Hypothesis," in E. S. Paykel (ed.), *Handbook of Affective Disorders* (New York: Guilford Press, 1982), pp. 175–190; and Joseph J. Schildkraut, Alan I. Green, and John J. Mooney, "Affective Disorders: Biochemical Aspects," in Harold I. Kaplan and Benjamin J. Sadock (eds.), *Comprehensive Textbook of Psychiatry/IV*, 4th ed., 2 vols. (Baltimore: Williams & Wilkins, 1985), 1:769–778.

71. Schildkraut et al., "Affective Disorders," p. 777.

72. Mendels, *Concepts of Depression*, pp. 77–78.

73. René A. Spitz, "Anaclitic Depression," *Psa. Study of the Child*, 1946, *2*, 313–342.

74. George L. Engel and Franz Reichsman, "Spontaneous and Experimentally Induced Depressions in an Infant with a Gastric Fistula: A Contribution to the Problem of Depression," *J. Amer. Psa. Assoc.*, 1956, *4*, 428–452.

75. I. Charles Kaufman and Leonard A. Rosenblum, "The Reaction to Separation in Infant Monkeys: Anaclitic Depression and Conservation-Withdrawal," *Psychosomatic Medicine*, 1967, *29*, 648–675.

76. Aaron T. Beck, *Depression: Causes and Treatment* (Philadelphia: University of Pennsylvania Press, 1967).

77. Aaron T. Beck, *Cognitive Therapy and the Emotional Disorders* (New York: International Universities Press, 1976).

78. Martin E. P. Seligman, *Helplessness: On Depression, Development, and Death* (San Francisco: W. H. Freeman, 1975).

79. Jules Bemporad, "Critical Review of the Major Concepts of Depression," in Silvano Arieti and Jules Bemporad, *Severe and Mild Depression: The Psychotherapeutic Approach* (New York: Basic Books, 1978), pp. 11–56 [40].

80. Mendels, *Concepts of Depression*, p. 64.

81. Ibid., pp. 64–70.

82. Anthony J. Marsella, "Depressive Experience and Disorder across Cultures," in Harry C. Triandis et al. (eds.), *Handbook of Cross-Cultural Psychology*, 6 vols. (Boston: Allyn and Bacon, 1980), 6:237–289.

83. See the valuable review of the evidence for such differences and their various explanations: Myrna M. Weissman and Gerald L. Klerman, "Sex Differences and the Epidemiology of Depression," *Arch. Gen. Psychiatry*, 1977, *34*, 98–111.

CHAPTER 10   THE VARIOUS RELATIONSHIPS OF MANIA AND MELANCHOLIA

1. Hippocrates, *[Works of Hippocrates]*, trans. and ed. W. H. S. Jones and E. T. Withington, 4 vols. (Cambridge: Harvard University Press, 1923–1931), 4:185.

2. Caelius Aurelianus, *On Acute Diseases and on Chronic Diseases*, ed. and trans. I. E. Drabkin (Chicago: University of Chicago Press, 1950), p. 563.

3. Ibid., p. 539.

4. Ibid., pp. 539–541.

5. Ibid., p. 561.

6. Aretaeus, *The Extant Works of Aretaeus, The Cappadocian*, ed. and trans. Francis Adams (London: Sydenham Society, 1856), p. 299.

7. Galen, *On the Affected Parts*, trans. and ed. Rudolph E. Siegel (Basel: S. Karger, 1976), pp. 89–94.

8. Ibid., p. 83.

9. Galen, *Opera Omnia*, ed. C. G. Kuhn, 20 vols. (Leipzig: Cnobloch, 1821–1833), 7:202, 14:740–741.

10. [Rufus], *Oeuvres de Rufus d'Ephèse*, ed. and trans. C. Daremberg and C. E. Ruelle (Paris: J. B. Baillière, 1879), pp. 356–357.

11. Galen, *On the Affected Parts*, p. 88.

12. [Alexander of Tralles], *Oeuvres Médicales d'Alexandre de Tralles*, ed. F. Brunet, 4 vols. (Paris: P. Geuthner, 1933–1937), 2:223–237.

13. Ibid., 2:226.

14. [Paul of Aegina], *The Seven Books of Paulus Aeginata*, trans. and ed. Francis Adams, 3 vols. (London: Sydenham Society, 1844–1847), 1:383–384.

15. Ibid., 1:383.

16. Robert Burton, *The Anatomy of Melancholy*, ed. Floyd Dell and Paul Jordan-Smith (New York: Tudor, 1948), pp. 121–122.

17. Thomas Willis, *Two Discourses Concerning the Soul of Brutes . . .*, trans. S. Pordage (London: Thomas Dring, Ch. Harper and John Leigh, 1683), p. 188. Willis's *desipientia* in the Latin was here Englished as "raving" but might also have been translated as "loss of reason."

18. Kenneth Dewhurst, *Thomas Willis's Oxford Lectures* (Oxford: Sandford, 1980), p. 131.

19. Kenneth Dewhurst (ed.), *Willis's Oxford Casebook (1650–52)* (Oxford: Sandford, 1981), p. 126.

20. Ibid., p. 127.

21. Kenneth Dewhurst, "A Seventeenth-century Symposium on Manic-depressive Psychosis," *Brit. J. Med. Psychol.*, 1962, *35*, 113–125.

22. Friedrich Hoffmann, *Fundamenta Mediciniae*, intro. and trans. Lester S. King (London: MacDonald, 1971), p. 71.

23. Ibid., p. 72.

24. [Herman Boerhaave], *Boerhaave's Aphorisms: Concerning the Knowledge and Cure of Diseases* (London: W. and J. Innys, 1735), p. 312.

25. G. A. Lindeboom, *Herman Boerhaave: The Man and his Work* (London: Methuen, 1968), pp. 3, 355–374.

26. Gerard Van Swieten, *The Commentaries upon the Aphorisms of Dr. Herman Boerhaave*, 11 vols. (London: John and Paul Knapton, 1754–1759), 11:2.

27. Robert James, *A Medicinal Dictionary . . .*, 3 vols. (London: T. Osborne, 1743–1745), 2: *mania*.

28. [Richard Mead], *The Medical Works of Richard Mead, M:D.* (London: C. Hitch et al., 1762), pp. 485–486.

29. John Baptist Morgagni, *The Seates and Causes of Diseases . . .*, trans. Benjamin Alexander and intro. Paul Klemperer, 3 vols. (New York: Hafner, 1960), 1:144.

30. R. Brookes, *The General Practice of Physic . . .*, 5th ed., 2 vols. (London: J. Newberry, 1765), 2:138.

31. [Editors], *Encyclopaedia Britannica* . . . , 3 vols. (Edinburgh: A. Bell and C. Macfarquhar, 1771), 3:149–151.

32. Stanley W. Jackson, "Melancholia and Partial Insanity," *J. Hist. Behav. Sci.*, 1983, *19*, 173–184.

33. William Cullen, *First Lines of the Practice of Physic*, 2 vols. in 1, ed. John Rotheram (New York: E. Duyckinck, 1806), p. 486.

34. Ibid., p. 497.

35. Joseph Townsend, *A Guide to Health* . . . *Designed Chiefly for the Use of Students*, 2 vols. (London: Cox, 1795–1796), 2:94.

36. Alexander Crichton, *An Inquiry into the Nature and Origin of Mental Derangement* . . . , 2 vols. (London: T. Cadell, Junior, and W. Davies, 1798), 2:220.

37. John Haslam, *Observations on Insanity* . . . (London: F. and C. Rivington, 1798), pp. 12–13.

38. Ibid., pp. 9–10.

39. Ph. Pinel, *A Treatise on Insanity* . . . , trans. D. D. Davis (Sheffield: Cadell and Davies, 1806), p. 145.

40. Ph. Pinel, *Traité Médico-Philosophique sur L'Aliénation Mentale, ou La Manie* (Paris: Richard, Caille et Ravier, 1801), pp. xxviii–xxix.

41. Heinroth, *Textbook* (preceding n. *), 1:64.

42. Ibid., 1:182, 186.

43. George Man Burrows, *Commentaries on the Causes, Forms, Symptoms, and Treatment, Moral and Medical, of Insanity* (London: Thomas and George Underwood, 1828), pp. 250–252.

44. E. Esquirol, *Mental Maladies. A Treatise on Insanity*, trans. E. K. Hunt (Philadelphia: Lea and Blanchard, 1845), pp. 202–203.

45. Jules Baillarger, "Note sur un genre de folie dont les accès sont caractérisés par deux périodes régulières, l'une de dépression et l'autre d'excitation," *Bulletin de l'Académie Impériale de Médecine*, 1853–1854, *19*, 340–352 (31 Jan. 1854).

46. Jean-Pierre Falret, "Mémoire sur la folie circulaire, forme de maladie mentale caractérisée par la reproduction successive et régulière de l'état maniaque, de l'état mélancolique, et d'un intervalle lucide plus ou moins prolongé," *Bulletin de l'Académie Impériale de Médecine*, 1853–1854, *19*, 382–400 (14 Feb. 1854). This is followed by a reply from Baillarger (pp. 401–414) and then some final comments from Falret (pp. 414–415), all from the same meeting of the Académie and published in the same issue of the *Bulletin*. Falret's earlier publication was "Marche de la folie," *Gazette des Hôpitaux*, 14 Jan. 1851; this lecture, and others by Falret from *La Gazette des Hôpitaux*, 1850–51, were reprinted together in J.-P. Falret, *Leçons Cliniques de Médecine Mentale* . . . (Paris: J.-B. Baillière, 1854). This publication of the *Leçons Cliniques* came out after the controversy had started.

47. Falret, "Marche de la folie," p. 19.

48. Baillarger, "Note sur un genre de folie," p. 352.

49. Falret, "Mémoire sur la folie circulaire," pp. 389, 397–399.

50. Baillarger, *Bull. Acad. Imp. Méd.*, 1853–1854, *19*, 401–414.

51. Otto M. Marx, "Wilhelm Griesinger and the History of Psychiatry: A Reassessment," *Bull. Hist. Med.*, 1972, *46*, 519–544.

52. W. Griesinger, *Mental Pathology and Therapeutics*, 2d ed., trans. C. Lockhart Robertson and James Rutherford (London: New Sydenham Society, 1867), p. 207.

53. Ibid., p. 234. In addition to the phrase of direct reference, he added a short paragraph paraphrasing their views.

54. Antoine Ritti, "Circular Insanity," in *A Dictionary of Psychological Medicine* . . . , ed. D. Hack Tuke, 2 vols. (Philadelphia: P. Blakiston, Son, 1892), 1:214–229 [215]. Ritti was already established as an authority on this subject on the basis of his *Traité clinique de la folie à double forme* (Paris: 1883).

55. These various views have been traced by Jelliffe: Smith Ely Jelliffe, "Cyclothemia—The Mild Forms of Manic-Depressive Psychoses and the Manic-Depressive Constitution," *Amer. J. Insanity*, 1911, *67*, 661–676.

56. Emil Kraepelin, *Psychiatrie: Ein Lehrbuch für Studirende und Aerzte*, 5th ed. (Leipzig: Johann Ambrosius Barth, 1896), pp. 425–471.

57. Emil Kraepelin, *Psychiatrie: Ein Lehrbuch für Studirende und Aerzte*, 6th ed., 2 vols. (Leipzig: Johann Ambrosius Barth, 1899), 2:359–425.

58. Ibid., 2:359–361. Translation is by Adolf Meyer, in Eunice E. Winters (ed.), *The Collected Papers of Adolf Meyer*, 4 vols. (Baltimore: The Johns Hopkins Press, 1951), 2:355–356.

59. G.-L. Dreyfus, *Die Melancholie, ein Zustandsbild des manisch-depressiven Irreseins* (Jena: G. Fischer, 1907).

60. Emil Kraepelin, *Manic-Depressive Insanity and Paranoia*, trans. R. Mary Barclay and ed. George M. Robertson (Edinburgh: E. & S. Livingstone, 1921), p. 1.

61. August Hoch and John T. MacCurdy, "The Prognosis of Involutional Melancholia," *Arch. Neurol. & Psychiat.*, 1922, *7*, 1–17.

62. Adolf Meyer, "The Problems of Mental Reaction Types, Mental Causes and Diseases," in Winters, *Collected Papers*, 2:591–603 (originally appeared in *Psychol. Bull.*, 1908, *5*, 245–261).

63. Adolf Meyer, "Constructive Formulation of Schizophrenia," in Winters, *Collected Papers*, 2:471–476 [476] (originally appeared in *Amer. J. Psychiat.*, 1921–1922, *78*, 355–362). Although this idea of manic-depressive illness as an "affective reaction-type" came to be very influential, Meyer's still later terms, *thymergasias* and the *thymergasic disorders*, for the manic-depressive group met relatively little acceptance.

64. Aubrey Lewis, "Melancholia: A Historical Review," *J. Ment. Sci.*, 1934, *80*, 1–42 [24].

65. Ibid., p. 25.

CHAPTER 11   HYPOCHONDRIASIS AND MELANCHOLIA

1. Gerard Chrzanowski, "Neurasthenia and Hypochondriasis," in *American Handbook of Psychiatry*, 2d ed., ed. Silvano Arieti, 6 vols. (New York: Basic Books, 1974–1975), 3:141–154 [144].

2. Galen, *On the Affected Parts*, trans. and ed. Rudolph E. Siegel (Basel: S. Karger, 1976), pp. 91–92.

3. Andreas Laurentius, *A Discourse of the Preservation of the Sight: of Melancholike Diseases; of Rheumes; and of Old Age*, trans. Richard Surphlet (London: R. Iacson, 1599), p. 125.

4. Felix Plater, Abdiah Cole, and Nich. Culpeper, *A Golden Practice of Physick . . .* (London: Peter Cole, 1662), p. 28. A modern translation of this passage is provided by Oskar Diethelm and Thomas F. Heffernan in a valuable paper: "Felix Platter and Psychiatry," *J. Hist. Behav. Sci.*, 1965, *1*, 10–23.

5. Oskar Diethelm, *Medical Dissertations of Psychiatric Interest: Printed before 1750* (Basel: S. Karger, 1971), pp. 92–93. This passage is taken from Platter's *Observationum Libri Tres* of 1614.

6. Plater et al., *Golden Practice*, p. 32.

7. Robert Burton, *The Anatomy of Melancholy*, ed. Floyd Dell and Paul Jordan-Smith (New York: Tudor, 1948), p. 350.

8. Thomas Willis, *Two Discourses Concerning the Soul of Brutes, Which is that of the Vital and Sensitive of Man*, trans. S. Pordage (London: Thomas Dring, Ch. Harper, and John Leigh, 1683), pp. 192–193.

9. [Thomas Willis], *Dr. Willis's Practice of Physick, Being the Whole Works of That Renowned and Famous Physician*, trans. S. Pordage (London: T. Dring, C. Harper, and J. Leigh, 1684), pp. 81–82.

10. [Thomas Sydenham], *The Entire Works of Dr. Thomas Sydenham . . .* , 3d ed., ed. John Swan (London: E. Cave, 1753), p. 408. He made special mention here of men "who lead a sedentary life, and study hard."

11. Kenneth Dewhurst, *Dr. Thomas Sydenham (1624–1689): His Life and Original Writings* (Berkeley and Los Angeles: University of California Press, 1966), p. 174.

12. [Friedrich Hoffmann], *A System of the Practice of Medicine . . .* , trans. William Lewis and Andrew Duncan, 2 vols. (London: J. Murray and J. Johnson, 1783), 2:45.

13. [Herman Boerhaave], *Boerhaave's Aphorisms: Concerning the Knowledge and Cure of Diseases* (London: A. Bettesworth and C. Hitch, W. Innys and R. Manby, 1735), p. 308.

14. Stanley W. Jackson, "Melancholia and Mechanical Explanation in Eighteenth-Century Medicine," *J. Hist. Med. & All. Sci.*, 1983, *38*, 298–319.

15. Gerard Van Swieten, *The Commentaries upon the Aphorisms of Dr. Herman Boerhaave*, 11 vols. (London: John and Paul Knapton, 1754–1759), 5:456–457.

16. B[ernard] De Mandeville, *A Treatise of the Hypochondriack and Hysterick Passions . . .* , 2d ed. (London: Dryden Leach, 1715), p. vii.

17. Richard Blackmore, *A Treatise of the Spleen and Vapours: or, Hypocondriacal and Hysterical Affections . . .* , (London: J. Pemberton, 1725), p. 1.

18. Nicholas Robinson, *A New System of the Spleen, Vapours, and Hypochondriack Melancholy . . .* (London: A. Bettesworth, W. Innys, and C. Rivington, 1729), pp. 196–197.

19. George Cheyne, *The English Malady: or, a Treatise of Nervous Diseases of all Kinds . . .* (London: G. Strahan and J. Leake, 1733), p. 194.

20. Robert Whytt, "Observations on the Nature, Causes, and Cure of those Disorders which are Commonly called Nervous, Hypochondriac, or Hysteric," in *The Works of Robert Whytt, M.D.* (Edinburgh: T. Becket, P. A. DeHondt, and J. Balfour, 1768), preface.

21. William Cullen, *First Lines of the Practice of Physic*, 2 vols. in 1, ed. John Rotheram (New York: E. Duyckinck, 1806), pp. 470–471.

22. William Cullen, *Institutions of Medicine. Part 1. Physiology*, 3d ed. (Edinburgh: Charles Elliot and T. Cadell, 1785), pp. 29–32, 62–69, 73–74.

23. William Cullen, *The Works of William Cullen, M.D. . . .* , ed. John Thomson, 2 vols. (Edinburgh: W. Blackwood, 1827), 1:17; idem, "Lectures upon the Institutions of Medicine," 5 vols. (unpublished manuscript of lectures delivered in Edinburgh, 1768–69, located in Yale University Medical Historical Library), 2:236–243, 245–254, 277–287.

24. Ibid., 2:2–5; Cullen, *Institutions*, pp. 97–101.

25. Thomas Arnold, *Observations on the Nature, Kinds, Causes, and Prevention, of Insanity*, 2 vols. in 1, 2d ed. (London: Richard Phillips, 1806), 1:174–175.

26. Stanley W. Jackson, "Melancholia and Partial Insanity," *J. Hist. Behav. Sci.*, 1983, *19*, 173–184.

27. Benjamin Rush, *Medical Inquiries and Observations upon the Diseases of the Mind*, 3d ed. (Philadelphia: J. Grigg, 1827), p. 72.

28. This and subsequent material on Rush's theory of disease are drawn from Benjamin Rush, *Medical Inquiries and Observations*, 3d ed., 4 vols. (Philadelphia: Mathew Carey et al., 1809), 3:1–66.

29. The nineteenth-century themes to be outlined in the following paragraphs can be traced in the following representative writings: E. Esquirol, *Mental Maladies. A Treatise on Insanity*, trans. E. K. Hunt (Philadelphia: Lea and Blanchard, 1845), p. 203; George Man Burrows, *Commentaries on the Causes, Forms, Symptoms, . . . of Insanity* (London: Thomas and George Underwood, 1828), pp. 258–259, 466–474; James Cowles Prichard, "Hypochon-

driasis," in *The Cyclopaedia of Practical Medicine* . . . , rev. ed., ed. John Forbes, Alexander Tweedie, John Conolly, and Robley Dunglison, 4 vols. (Philadelphia: Lea and Blanchard, 1845), 2:554–557; W. Griesinger, *Mental Pathology and Therapeutics*, 2d ed., trans. C. Lockhart Robertson and James Rutherford (London: New Sydenham Society, 1867), pp. 211–246; Daniel H. Tuke, "On the Various Forms of Mental Disorder," *Asylum J. Ment. Sci.*, 1857, *3*, 228–235; John Charles Bucknill and Daniel H. Tuke, *A Manual of Psychological Medicine* . . . (Philadelphia: Blanchard and Lea, 1858), pp. 164–169, 314–317; William Withey Gull and Edmund Anstey, "Hypochondriasis," in *A Collection of the Published Writings of William Withey Gull*, ed. Theodore Dyke Acland, 2 vols. (London: New Sydenham Society, 1894), 1:287–304 [orig. publ. 1868]; George H. Savage, *Insanity and Allied Neuroses: Practical and Clinical* (London: Cassell & Co., 1884), pp. 128–167; George H. Savage, "Hypochondriasis and Insanity," in *Dictionary of Psychological Medicine*, ed. D. Hack Tuke, 2 vols. (Philadelphia: P. Blakiston, Son, 1892), 1:610–618.

30. Fischer-Homberger has made some thoughtful observations along this line: Esther Fischer-Homberger, "Hypochondriasis of the Eighteenth Century—Neurosis of the Present Century," *Bull. Hist. Med.*, 1972, *46*, 391–401.

31. J.-P. Falret, *De L'Hypochondrie et Du Suicide* . . . (Paris: Croullebois, 1822), pp. 370–371.

32. Joseph Jastrow, "Hypochondria," in *Dictionary of Philosophy and Psychology* . . . , ed. James Mark Baldwin, 3 vols. (New York: Macmillan, 1901–1905), 1:491.

33. Ibid.

34. Chrzanowski, "Neurasthenia and Hypochondriasis"; F. E. Kenyon, "Hypochondriasis: A Survey of Some Historical, Clinical and Social Aspects," *Int. J. Psychiat.*, 1966, *2*, 308–326; G. A. Ladee, *Hypochondriacal Syndromes* (Amsterdam: Elsevier, 1966).

35. Stanley Lesse, "Hypochondriasis and Psychosomatic Disorders Masking Depression," in *Masked Depression*, ed. Stanley Lesse (New York: Jason Aronson, 1974), pp. 53–74.

36. D. K. Henderson and R. D. Gillespie, *A Text-Book of Psychiatry* . . . (London: Oxford University Press, 1927), p. 90. This summary statement remained unchanged in subsequent editions, up to and including the tenth edition in 1969.

37. Kenyon, "Hypochondriasis," pp. 311, 321.

38. Dean Schuyler, *The Depressive Spectrum* (New York: Jason Aronson, 1974), pp. 36–37.

39. Ladee, *Hypochondriacal Syndromes*, pp. 44–45.

40. Wayne Katon, Arthur Kleinman, and Gary Rosen, "Depression and Somatization: A Review," *Amer. J. Med.*, 1982, *72*, 127–135, 241–247.

41. Ibid., pp. 245–246.

CHAPTER 12　GRIEF, MOURNING, AND MELANCHOLIA

1. These and subsequent word meanings in this chapter are drawn from James A. H. Murray et al. (eds.), *A New English Dictionary* . . . , 13 vols. (Oxford: Clarendon Press, 1888–1933).

2. For one version of the use of these terms, see Beverley Raphael, *The Anatomy of Bereavement* (New York: Basic Books, 1983), p. 33.

3. N. G. L. Hammond and H. H. Scullard (eds.), *The Oxford Classical Dictionary*, 2d ed. (Oxford: Clarendon Press, 1970), p. 279.

4. Ibid.

5. For an account of "a stream of arguments and musings" on consolation in early Greek literature, plus an outline of Crantor's place in this tradition, see Robert C. Gregg, *Consolation Philosophy: Greek and Christian Paideia in Basil and the Two Gregories* (Cambridge, Mass.: Philadelphia Patristic Foundation, 1975), chap. 1.

6. Cicero, *Tusculan Disputations*, trans. J. E. King (Cambridge: Harvard University Press, 1966). Themes of the emerging tradition of consolation are particularly to be found in books I and III.

7. Seneca, *Ad Lucilium Epistulae Morales*, trans. Richard M. Gummere, 3 vols. (Cambridge: Harvard University Press, 1967–1971), 1: epistle 63, and 3: epistle 99; idem, *Moral Essays*, trans. John W. Basore, 3 vols. (Cambridge: Harvard University Press, 1965–1975), 2: bks. 6 and 11.

8. [Plutarch], *Plutarch's Moralia*, trans. Frank Cole Babbitt et al., 15 vols. (Cambridge: Harvard University Press, 1949–1976), 2:105–211; 7:575–605.

9. James Hastings (ed.), *Encyclopaedia of Religion and Ethics*, 13 vols. (New York: Charles Scribner's Sons, 1908–1927), 4:71–73.

10. [Aristotle], "Problemata," in *The Works of Aristotle*, ed. J. A. Smith and W. D. Ross, 11 vols. (Oxford: Clarendon Press, 1908–1931), 7:954b.

11. Celsus, *De Medicina*, trans. W. G. Spencer, 3 vols. (Cambridge: Harvard University Press, 1953–1961), 1:301.

12. [Alexander of Tralles], *Oeuvres Médicales d'Alexandre de Tralles*, ed. F. Brunet, 4 vols. (Paris: P. Geuthner, 1933–1937), 2:230, 233.

13. Andreas Laurentius, *A Discourse of the Preservation of the Sight: of Melancholike Diseases; of Rheumes, and of Old Age*, trans. Richard Surphlet (London: Ralph Iacson, 1599), pp. 86–87.

14. T. Bright, *A Treatise of Melancholie . . .* (London: Thomas Vautrollier, 1586), p. 90.

15. Robert Burton, *The Anatomy of Melancholy*, ed. Floyd Dell and Paul Jordan-Smith (New York: Tudor, 1948), pp. 148–149.

16. Friedrich Hoffmann, *Fundamenta Medicinae*, trans. and intro. Lester S. King (London: MacDonald, 1971), p. 71.

17. For a historical account of partial insanity, see Stanley W. Jackson, "Melancholia and Partial Insanity," *J. Hist. Behav. Sci.*, 1983, *19*, 173–184.

18. R. von Krafft-Ebing, *Text-Book of Insanity . . .*, trans. Charles Gilbert Chaddock, intro. Frederick Peterson (Philadelphia: F. A. Davis, 1904), p. 286.

19. Charles Mercier, "Melancholia," in D. Hack Tuke, *A Dictionary of Psychological Medicine*, 2 vols. (Philadelphia: P. Blakiston, 1892), 2:787.

20. A. Ross Defendorf, *Clinical Psychiatry . . .*, from 6th ed., Kraepelin's "*Lehrbuch der Psychiatrie*" (New York: Macmillan, 1902), p. 284.

21. Manfred Ullmann, *Islamic Medicine* (Edinburgh: Edinburgh University Press, 1978), pp. 73–74; Constantini Africani, *Opera . . .*, 2 vols. (Basileae [Basel]: H. Petrus, 1536–1539), 1:283–284.

22. Felix Plater, Abdiah Cole, and Nich. Culpeper, *A Golden Practice of Physick . . .* (London: Peter Cole, 1662), p. 31.

23. Oskar Diethelm and Thomas F. Heffernan, "Felix Platter and Psychiatry," *J. Hist. Behav. Sci.*, 1965, *1*, 10–23 [15].

24. Michael MacDonald, *Mystical Bedlam: Madness, Anxiety, and Healing in Seventeenth-century England* (Cambridge: Cambridge University Press, 1981), pp. 77–78, 103.

25. Ibid., pp. 158–159.

26. Ibid., p. 159.

27. Timothy Rogers, *A Discourse Concerning Trouble of Mind, and the Disease of Melancholly* (London: Thomas Parkhurst and Thomas Cockerill, 1691), p. v.

28. Eugene S. Paykel, Jerome K. Myers, Maria N. Dienelt, Gerald L. Klerman, Jacob J. Lindenthal, and Max P. Pepper, "Life Events and Depression: A Controlled Study," *Arch. Gen. Psychiat.*, 1969, *21*, 753–760.

29. [Sigmund Freud], *The Standard Edition of the Complete Psychological Works of Sigmund*

Freud, trans. and ed. James Strachey, Anna Freud, et al., 24 vols. (London: Hogarth Press, 1953–1974), 14:243. For a more detailed discussion of "Mourning and Melancholia," see 223–226.

30. Lorraine D. Siggins, "Mourning: A Critical Survey of the Literature," *Int. J. Psa.*, 1966, *47,* 14–25 [15].

31. E.g., Edward Bibring, "The Mechanism of Depression," in Phyllis Greenacre (ed.), *Affective Disorders: Psychoanalytic Contributions to their Study* (New York: International Universities Press, 1953), pp. 13–48.

32. For a more detailed discussion of Klein's views, see pp. 230–231.

33. Melanie Klein, "Mourning and Its Relation to Manic-Depressive States," in Melanie Klein, *Contributions to Psycho-Analysis: 1921–1945,* intro. Ernest Jones (London: Hogarth Press, 1948), pp. 311–338 [311].

34. Erich Lindemann, "Symptomatology and Management of Acute Grief," *Amer. J. Psychiat.,* 1944, *101,* 141–148; John Bowlby, *Attachment and Loss,* 3 vols. (New York: Basic Books, 1969–1980).

35. Colin Murray Parkes, *Bereavement: Studies of Grief in Adult Life,* foreword John Bowlby (New York: International Universities Press, 1972); Colin Murray Parkes and Robert S. Weiss, *Recovery from Bereavement* (New York: Basic Books, 1983); Raphael, *Anatomy of Bereavement.*

36. Edmund H. Volkart, with the collaboration of Stanley T. Michael, "Bereavement and Mental Health," in Alexander H. Leighton, John A. Clausen, and Robert N. Wilson (eds.), *Explorations in Social Psychiatry* (New York: Basic Books, 1957), pp. 281–307 [281].

37. George L. Engel, "Is Grief a Disease? A Challenge for Medical Research," *Psychosom. Med.,* 1961, *23,* 18–22.

CHAPTER 13   RELIGION, THE SUPERNATURAL, AND MELANCHOLIA

1. Penelope B. R. Doob, *Nebuchadnezzar's Children: Conventions of Madness in Middle English Literature* (New Haven: Yale University Press, 1974), pp. 7–10.

2. Raymond Klibansky, Erwin Panofsky, and Fritz Saxl, *Saturn and Melancholy: Studies in the History of Natural Philosophy, Religion, and Art* (New York: Basic Books, 1964), pp. 78–80.

3. Ibid., pp. 79–80.

4. Ibid., p. 80.

5. E. R. Dodds, *Pagan and Christian in an Age of Anxiety* (Cambridge: Cambridge University Press, 1965), p. 53; R. A. Knox, *Enthusiasm: A Chapter in the History of Religion* (New York: Oxford University Press, 1950), pp. 29–31, 34–39; Origen, *Contra Celsum,* trans. and ed. Henry Chadwick (Cambridge: Cambridge University Press, 1965), pp. 395–398; Eusebius, *The Ecclesiastical History,* trans. and ed. Kirsopp Lake and J. E. L. Oulton, 2 vols. (London: W. Heinemann, 1926–1932), 1:475–477.

6. Lawrence Babb, *Elizabethan Malady: A Study of Melancholia in English Literature from 1580 to 1642* (East Lansing: Michigan State University Press, 1951), pp. 49–50, 64–66.

7. I am indebted here to Knox, *Enthusiasm,* and to Michael Heyd, "Robert Burton's Sources on Enthusiasm and Melancholy: From a Medical Tradition to Religious Controversy," *Hist. European Ideas,* 1984, *5,* 17–44.

8. Jean Wier, *Histoires Disputes et Discours des Illusions et Impostures des Diables, des Magiciens, Infames, Sorcieres et Empoisonneurs . . . ,* 2 vols. (Paris: A. Delahaye and Lecrosnier, 1885), 1: bk. 3, chaps. 5–8, and bk. 4, chap. 25.

9. Reginald Scot, *The Discoverie of Witchcraft,* intro. Montague Summers (London: John Rodker, 1930), bk. 3, chaps. 9–11, 17.

10. Sydney Anglo, "Melancholia and Witchcraft: The Debate between Wier, Bodin, and Scot," in *Folie et Déraison à la Renaissance* (Brussels: Editions de l'Université de Bruxelles, 1976), pp. 209–228. Anglo effectively demonstrated how far Weyer really was from the unrealistic image of him advocated by Zilboorg and others. For this image, see Gregory Zilboorg and George W. Henry, *A History of Medical Psychology* (New York: W. W. Norton, 1941), pp. 207–235. Another account favoring a more realistic view of Weyer is Christopher Baxter, "Johann Weyer's *De Praestigiis Daemonum:* Unsystematic Psychopathology," in Sydney Anglo (ed.), *The Damned Art: Essays in the Literature of Witchcraft* (London: Routledge & Kegan Paul, 1977), pp. 53–75.

11. As on Weyer, Anglo provided valuable perspective on Scot: Anglo, "Melancholia and Witchcraft," and idem., "Reginald Scot's *Discoverie of Witchcraft:* Scepticism and Sadduceeism," in Anglo (ed.), *Damned Art*, pp. 106–139.

12. T. Bright, *A Treatise of Melancholie* (London: Thomas Vautrollier, 1586).

13. Important examples were Meric Casaubon, *A Treatise Concerning Enthusiasme . . .* , 2d ed. (London: Roger Daniel, 1656) [facsimile reproduction, intro. Paul J. Korshin, Gainesville: Scholars' Facsimiles & Reprints, 1970]; Henry More, *Enthusiasmus Triumphatus . . .* (London: J. Flesher, 1656); and Joseph Glanvill, *The Vanity of Dogmatizing* (London: H. Eversden, 1661).

14. I am here indebted to an excellent review by Michael Heyd, "The Reaction to Enthusiasm in the Seventeenth Century: Towards an Integrative Approach," *J. Mod. Hist.*, 1981, *53*, 258–280.

15. Thomas Willis, *Two Discourses Concerning the Soul of Brutes . . .* , trans. S. Pordage (London: Thomas Dring, Ch. Harper, and John Leigh, 1683), p. 199.

16. Richard Blackmore, *A Treatise of the Spleen and Vapours . . .* , (London: J. Pemberton, 1725), p. 158.

17. François Boissier de Sauvages, *Nosologie Methodique . . .* , 3 vols. (Paris: Hérissant, 1771), 2:730–731.

18. William Cullen, *A Synopsis of Methodical Nosology . . .* , from 4th ed. corrected and much enlarged, trans. Henry Wilkins (Philadelphia: Parry Hall, 1793), p. 121.

19. William Buchan, *Domestic Medicine . . .* , new, correct edition, enlarged—from the author's last revisal (Boston: Joseph Bumstead, 1813), p. 289. This passage appeared in the first edition, published in Edinburgh in 1769, and continued unchanged in later editions. This influential work enjoyed well over 100 separate editions in the next hundred years, including 19 editions in the author's lifetime. It was translated into numerous foreign languages and was widely read on the Continent and in the United States, as well as in Great Britain.

20. Although this section on religious melancholy was not in the first edition in 1769, it appeared beginning with editions of the early 1770s.

21. Thomas Arnold, *Observations on the Nature, Kinds, Causes, and Prevention, of Insanity*, 2d ed., 2 vols. (London: Richard Phillips, 1806), 1:217–218. All portions cited from Arnold's work were present in the same form in the first edition (1782–1786).

22. Johann Christian Heinroth, *Textbook of Disturbances of Mental Life . . .* , trans. J. Schmorak, intro. George Mora, 2 vols. (Baltimore: Johns Hopkins University Press, 1975), 1:195.

23. John Charles Bucknill and Daniel H. Tuke, *A Manual of Psychological Medicine . . .* (Philadelphia: Blanchard and Lea, 1858), pp. 172–173.

24. D. Hack Tuke, *A Dictionary of Psychological Medicine . . .* , 2 vols. (Philadelphia: T. Blakiston, Son, 1892), 2:797.

25. W. Griesinger, *Mental Pathology and Therapeutics*, 2d ed., trans. C. Lockhart Robertson and James Rutherford (London: New Sydenham Society, 1867), p. 240.

26. R. von Krafft-Ebing, *Text-Book of Insanity . . .* , trans. Charles Gilbert Chaddock, intro. Frederick Peterson (Philadelphia: F. A. Davis, 1904), p. 301.

CHAPTER 14   LYCANTHROPY

1. [Oribasius], *Oeuvres d'Oribase*, ed. U. C. Bussemaker and C. Daremberg, 6 vols. (Paris: J. B. Baillière, 1851–1876), 5:414–415.
2. Claudii Galeni, *Opera Omnia*, ed. C. G. Kühn, 20 vols. (Lipsiae [Leipzig]: Cnobloch, 1821–1833), 19:719–720.
3. [Paul of Aegina], *The Seven Books of Paulus Aeginata*, trans. and ed. Francis Adams, 3 vols. (London: Sydenham Society, 1844–1847), 1:389–390.
4. Manfred Ullmann, *Islamic Medicine* (Edinburgh: Edinburgh University Press, 1978), p. 78.
5. [Tommaso Garzoni], *The Hospital of Incurable Fooles . . .* (London: Edward Blount, 1600), p. 19. My attention was drawn to this passage by Babb, who cited it as representative: Lawrence Babb, *The Elizabethan Malady . . .* (East Lansing: Michigan State University Press, 1951), p. 44.
6. Robert Burton, *The Anatomy of Melancholy*, ed. Floyd Dell and Paul Jordan-Smith (New York: Tudor, 1948), pp. 122–123.
7. Kenneth Dewhurst, *Thomas Willis's Oxford Lectures* (Oxford: Sandford Publications, 1980), p. 129.
8. Thomas Willis, *Two Discourses Concerning The Soul of Brutes, Which is that of the Vital and Sensitive of Man . . .*, trans. S. Pordage (London: Thomas Dring, Ch. Harper, and John Leigh, 1683), preface.
9. Dewhurst, *Willis's Lectures*, pp. 125–129.
10. Stanley W. Jackson, "Melancholia and Partial Insanity," *J. Hist. Behav. Sci.*, 1983, *19*, 173–184.
11. Stephen Blancard, *A Physical Dictionary . . .* (London: Samuel Crouch and John Gellibrand, 1684), p. 182. Originally published in 1679, this translation from the Latin was the first medical dictionary in English.
12. Robert James, *A Medicinal Dictionary . . .*, 3 vols. (London: T. Osborne, 1743–1745), 2: *lycanthropia*.
13. [Herman Boerhaave], *Boerhaave's Aphorisms: Concerning the Knowledge and Cure of Diseases* (London: W. and J. Innys, 1735), p. 324.
14. Gerard Van Swieten, *The Commentaries upon the Aphorisms of Dr. Herman Boerhaave*, 11 vols. (London: John and Paul Knapton, 1754–1759), 11:137.
15. François Boissier de Sauvages, *Nosologie Methodique . . .*, 3 vols. (Paris: Hérissant, 1770–1771), 2:737–738.
16. William Cullen, *Synopsis of Methodical Nosology . . .*, from 4th ed. corrected and much enlarged, trans. Henry Wilkins (Philadelphia: Parry Hall, 1793), pp. 121–122.
17. Thomas Arnold, *Observations on the Nature, Kinds, Causes, and Prevention, of Insanity*, 2 vols. in 1, 2 ed. (London: Richard Phillips, 1806), 1:121–122.
18. Johann Christian Heinroth, *Textbook of Disturbances of Mental Life . . .*, trans. J. Schmorak, intro. George Mora, 2 vols. (Baltimore: Johns Hopkins University Press, 1975), 1:208.
19. J. E. D. Esquirol, *Mental Maladies: A Treatise on Insanity*, trans. E. K. Hunt (Philadelphia: Lea and Blanchard, 1845), pp. 250–251.
20. W. Griesinger, *Mental Pathology and Therapeutics*, 2d ed., trans. C. Lockhart Robertson and James Rutherford (London: New Sydenham Society, 1867), pp. 79–80.
21. E.g., Frida G. Surawicz and Richard Banta, "Lycanthropy Revisited," *Can. Psychiat. Assoc. J.*, 1975, *20*, 537–542; Harvey A. Rosenstock and Kenneth R. Vincent, "A Case of Lycanthropy," *Amer. J. Psychiat.*, 1977, *134*, 1147–1149.

CHAPTER 15   LOVE-MELANCHOLY

1. Plutarke, *The Lives of the Noble Grecians and Romanes* . . . , trans. from Greek into French by James Amyot; from French into English by Thomas North, 5 vols. (London: Nonesuch Press, 1929–1930), 4:274–275. The English of the Loeb Classical Library translation is a bit less colorful but provides essentially the same account: [Plutarch], *Plutarch's Lives*, trans. Bernadotte Perrin, 11 vols. (Cambridge: Harvard University Press, 1920), 9:93–97.

2. [Aretaeus], *The Extant Works of Aretaeus, The Cappadocian*, ed. and trans. Francis Adams (London: Sydenham Society, 1856), p. 300.

3. Claudii Galeni, *Opera Omnia*, ed. C. G. Kuhn, 20 vols. (Lipsiae [Leipzig]: Cnobloch, 1821–1833), 18B:18.

4. A. J. Brock, *Greek Medicine: Being Extracts Illustrative of Medical Writers from Hippocrates to Galen* (London: J. M. Dent, 1929), pp. 213–214.

5. Galen, *On the Passions and Errors of the Soul*, trans. Paul W. Harkins, intro. and interpret. Walther Riese (Columbus: Ohio State University Press, 1963), p. 32.

6. Ibid., p. 48.

7. Caelius Aurelianus, *On Acute Diseases and On Chronic Diseases*, ed. and trans. I. E. Drabkin (Chicago: University of Chicago Press, 1950), pp. 557–559.

8. [Oribasius], *Oeuvres d'Oribase*, ed. U. C. Bussemaker and C. Daremberg, 6 vols. (Paris: J. B. Baillière, 1851–1876), 5:413–414.

9. [Paul of Aegina], *The Seven Books of Paulus Aeginata*, trans. and ed. Francis Adams, 3 vols. (London: Sydenham Society, 1844–1847), 1:390–391.

10. Avicennae, *Liber Canonis De Medicinis* . . . , trans. Andreas Alpagus (Venetiis [Venice]: Junta, 1582), p. 206.

11. Andreas Laurentius, *A Discourse of the Preservation of the Sight: of Melancholike Diseases: of Rheumes: and of Old Age*, trans. Richard Surphlet (London: R. Iacson, 1599), pp. 117–118.

12. Oskar Diethelm and Thomas F. Heffernan, "Felix Platter and Psychiatry," *J. Hist. Behav. Sci.*, 1965, *1*, 10–23.

13. Daniel Sennertus, N. Culpeper, and Abdiah Cole, *Practical Physick* . . . , 2 vols. (London: Peter Cole, 1662–1664), 1:157–159. Despite this mode of presentation on the title page, Sennert was the author, and Culpeper and Cole were the translators.

14. James Ferrand, *Erotomania or A Treatise Discoursing of the Essence, Causes, Symptomes, Prognosticks, and Cure of Love, or Erotique Melancholy*, trans. Edmund Chilmead (Oxford: L. Lichfield and . . . Edward Forrest, 1640), p. 4.

15. For an authoritative discussion of the history of this mistaken notion, see Lowes, "Loveres Maladye" (n. * on p. 357).

16. Robert Burton, *The Anatomy of Melancholy*, ed. Floyd Dell and Paul Jordan-Smith (New York: Tudor, 1948). More than 200 pages are devoted to love-melancholy in this octavo edition, plus 45 pages on jealousy as a type of love-melancholy. In the smaller format Shilleto edition it is nearly 300 pages, plus 62 pages.

17. This observation has been made by Babb and has considerable wisdom in it: Lawrence Babb, *The Elizabethan Malady: A Study of Melancholia in English Literature from 1580 to 1642* (East Lansing: Michigan State University Press, 1951), pp. 128–174. A premier Burton scholar, Babb in this work has provided a valuable study of Renaissance materials on melancholia in general, including love-melancholy.

18. Oskar Diethelm, *Medical Dissertations of Psychiatric Interest: Printed before 1750* (Basel: S. Karger, 1971), pp. 61–70.

19. Thomas Willis, *Two Discourses Concerning the Soul of Brutes Which is that of the Vital*

and Sensitive of Man, trans. S. Pordage (London: Thomas Dring, Ch. Harper, and John Leigh, 1683), p. 188.

20. [Friedrich Hoffmann], *A System of the Practice of Medicine . . .* , trans. William Lewis and Andrew Duncan, 2 vols. (London: J. Murray and J. Johnson, 1783), 2:300.

21. [Richard Mead], *The Medical Works of Richard Mead, M.D.* (London: C. Hitch and L. Hawes, et al., 1762), pp. 484–485.

22. Robert James, *A Medicinal Dictionary . . .* , 3 vols. (London: T. Osborne, 1743–1745), 1: *amor*.

23. François Boissier de Sauvages, *Nosologie Methodique . . .* , 3 vols. (Paris: Hérissant, 1771), 2:728–730.

24. L. J. Rather, *Mind and Body in Eighteenth Century Medicine: A Study Based on Jerome Gaub's "De regimine mentis"* (Berkeley and Los Angeles: University of California Press, 1965), pp. ix, 149–152.

25. William Cullen, *A Synopsis of Methodical Nosology . . .* , from 4th ed. corrected and much enlarged, trans. Henry Wilkins (Philadelphia: Parry Hall, 1793), p. 121.

26. E. Esquirol, *Mental Maladies: A Treatise on Insanity*, trans. E. K. Hunt (Philadelphia: Lea and Blanchard, 1845), p. 200, emphasis added.

27. John Charles Bucknill and Daniel H. Tuke, *A Manual of Psychological Medicine . . .* (Philadelphia: Blanchard and Lea, 1858), p. 213.

28. G. Fielding Blandford, *Insanity and Its Treatment . . .* (Philadelphia: Henry C. Lea, 1871), pp. 189–190.

29. E.g., James Cowles Prichard, *A Treatise on Insanity . . .* (Philadelphia: Haswell, Barrington and Haswell, 1837), p. 28; Ernst von Feuchtersleben, *The Principles of Medical Psychology . . .* , trans. and ed. H. Evans Lloyd and B. G. Babington (London: Sydenham Society, 1847), p. 281; and T. S. Clouston, *Clinical Lectures on Mental Diseases* (London: J. & A. Churchill, 1883), p. 317.

30. Forbes Winslow, *On Obscure Diseases of the Brain, and Disorders of the Mind . . .* (Philadelphia: Blanchard & Lea, 1860), pp. 171–172.

31. D. Hack Tuke (ed.), *A Dictionary of Psychological Medicine . . .* , 2 vols. (Philadelphia: P. Blakiston, Son, 1892), 1:460.

32. James Mark Baldwin (ed.), *Dictionary of Philosophy and Psychology . . .* , 2 vols. (New York: Macmillan, 1901), 1:340.

33. R. von Krafft-Ebing, *Text-Book of Insanity . . .* , trans. Charles Gilbert Chaddock, intro. Frederick Peterson (Philadelphia: F. A. Davis, 1904), pp. 284–285.

34. The following discussion draws on the useful study of this order in M. David Enoch, W. H. Trethowan, and J. C. Barker, *Some Uncommon Psychiatric Syndromes* (Bristol: John Wright & Sons, 1967), pp. 13–24. See also Elisabeth Renard, *Le Docteur Gaëtan Gatian De Clérambault: Sa Vie et Son Oeuvre* (Paris: Librairie Le François, 1942), pp. 113–133. The basic source for De Clérambault's work is Gaëtan G. De Clérambault, *Oeuvre Psychiatrique . . .* , 2 vols. (Paris: Presses Universitaires de France, 1942).

35. Enoch et al., *Some Uncommon Psychiatric Syndromes*, p. 20.

36. Among the various recent articles that cite a case or several cases, Hollender and Callahan's is perhaps the most representative and judicious: Marc H. Hollender and Alfred S. Callahan III, "Erotomania or de Clérambault Syndrome," *Arch. Gen. Psychiat.*, 1975, *32*, 1574–1576.

37. David E. Raskin and Kathleen E. Sullivan, "Erotomania," *Amer. J. Psychiat.*, 1974, *131*, 1033–1035.

CHAPTER 16   NOSTALGIA

1. George Rosen, "Nostalgia: A 'Forgotten' Psychological Disorder," *Psychol. Med.*, 1975, *5*, 340–354. Throughout this chapter I am indebted to Rosen's valuable study.

2. Carolyn Kiser Anspach, "Medical Dissertation on Nostalgia by Johannes Hofer, 1688," *Bull. Hist. Med.*, 1934, *2*, 376–391 [380–381]. This article includes Anspach's translation of Hofer's dissertation, the first in English.

3. Ibid., pp. 382–383; Rosen, "Nostalgia," p. 341.

4. Rosen, "Nostalgia," pp. 341–342. I have here followed Rosen's translation rather than Anspach's.

5. François Boissier de Sauvages, *Nosologie Methodique* . . . , 3 vols. (Paris: Hérissant, 1771), 2:684–686.

6. George Rosen, "Percussion and Nostalgia," *J. Hist. Med. & Allied Sci.*, 1972, *27*, 448–450.

7. L. J. Rather, *Mind and Body in Eighteenth Century Medicine: A Study Based on Jerome Gaub's "De regimine mentis"* (Berkeley and Los Angeles: University of California Press, 1965), pp. 149–150.

8. Ibid., p. 174.

9. Kenneth Dewhurst and Nigel Reeves, *Friedrich Schiller: Medicine, Psychology and Literature* . . . (Berkeley and Los Angeles: University of California Press, 1978), p. 271.

10. William Cullen, *A Methodical System of Nosology*, trans. Eldad Lewis (Stockbridge: Cornelius Sturtevant, Jun., 1808), pp. 142, 182.

11. Thomas Arnold, *Observations on the Nature, Kinds, Causes, and Prevention of Insanity*, 2d ed., 2 vols. (London: Richard Phillips, 1806), 1:185.

12. Johann Christian Heinroth, *Textbook of Disturbances of Mental Life* . . . , trans. J. Schmorak and intro. George Mora, 2 vols. (Baltimore: Johns Hopkins University Press, 1975), 1:195.

13. Ernst Von Feuchtersleben, *The Principles of Medical Psychology* . . . , trans. H. Evans Lloyd and B. G. Babington (London: Sydenham Society, 1847), p. 187.

14. W. Griesinger, *Mental Pathology and Therapeutics*, 2d ed., trans. C. Lockhart Robertson and James Rutherford (London: New Sydenham Society, 1867), pp. 245–246.

15. John Charles Bucknill and Daniel H. Tuke, *A Manual of Psychological Medicine* . . . (Philadelphia: Blanchard and Lea, 1858), p. 158.

16. D. Hack Tuke (ed.), *A Dictionary of Psychological Medicine* . . . , 2 vols. (Philadelphia: P. Blakiston, Son, 1892), 2:858.

17. *The Encyclopaedia Britannica*, 11th ed., 29 vols. (New York: Encyclopaedia Britannica Company, 1910–1911), 19:822.

18. Willis H. McCann, "Nostalgia: A Review of the Literature," *Psychol. Bulletin*, 1941, *38*, 165–182.

CHAPTER 17   OVERVIEW AND AFTERTHOUGHTS

1. Galen, *On the Affected Parts*, trans. and ed. Rudolph E. Siegel (Basel: S. Karger, 1976), p. 93.

2. Bennett Simon, *Mind and Madness in Ancient Greece: The Classical Roots of Modern Psychiatry* (Ithaca: Cornell University Press, 1978), p. 231.

3. Alexander F. Shand, *The Foundations of Character: Being a Study of the Tendencies of the Emotions and Sentiments* (London: Macmillan, 1920), p. 314.

4. Denis Hill, "Depression: Disease, Reaction, or Posture?" *Amer. J. Psychiat.*, 1968, *125*, 445–457 [455].

Name Index

Index includes names cited in endnotes corresponding to the pages indicated.

Subject Index